Critics on Trial

Critics on Trial

AN INTRODUCTION TO
THE CATHOLIC MODERNIST CRISIS ,

Marvin R. O'Connell

THE CATHOLIC UNIVERSITY OF AMERICA PRESS
WASHINGTON, D.C.

The paper used in this publication meets the minimum requirements of American National Standards for Information Science—Permanence of Paper for Printed Library materials, ANSI Z39.48-1984.

∞

LIBRARY OF CONGRESS CATALOGING-IN-PUBLICATION DATA

O'Connell, Marvin Richard.
  Critics on trial : an introduction to the Catholic modernist
crisis / by Marvin R. O'Connell.
      p.   cm.
  Includes bibliographical references and index.
    1. Modernism—Catholic Church—History. 2. Catholic Church—
Doctrines—History—19th century. 3. Catholic Church—Doctrines—
History—20th century. I. Title.
BX1396.026   1994
273′9—dc20
93-41850
ISBN 0-8132-0799-1.—ISBN 0-8132-0800-9 (pbk.)

For Ralph and Connie McInerny

"I remember a house where all were good
To me, God knows, deserving no such thing:
Comforting smell breathed at very entering,
Fetched fresh, as I suppose, off some sweet wood."

You believe that reality is something objective, external, existing in its own right. . . . But I tell you, Winston, that reality is not external. Reality exists in the human mind and nowhere else.

—George Orwell, *1984*

Christianity is not based on a historical truth; rather it offers us a [historical] narrative, and says: now believe! But not, believe this narrative with the belief appropriate to historical narrative, rather : believe, through thick and thin, which you can do only as the result of a life. Here you can have a narrative, don't take the same attitude to it as you take to other historical narratives! Make a quite different place in your life for it. There is nothing paradoxical about that.

—Ludwig Wittgenstein, *Culture and Value*

Jesus preached the Kingdom, and, behold, it is the Church that has come.

—Alfred Loisy, *The Gospel and the Church*

Contents

Preface

IN ORDER TO MAKE CLEAR at the outset what this book is and what it is not, I can do no better than to quote myself when, twenty-five years ago, I presented to the reading public my history of the Oxford Movement. I was moved to take on this project, I wrote in 1968, "primarily because it seemed to me to be such a very interesting story. Yet it was a story hard to unravel, moving as it did through a social and intellectual milieu now gone. . . . Although I read hundreds of books of varying quality on the subject, I never found one that supplied a straight narrative account of the Movement intelligible to me and my generation. My modest object has been to fill that gap."

The same ambition has led me to examine the events and, even more, the personages associated with what has come to be called the Catholic Modernist crisis of a century ago. It too is a very interesting story, but a story much more difficult to unravel, and this for several reasons. The Modernist phenomenon first of all was not so neatly circumscribed as to time and place as was what Newman called "the religious movement of 1833." The Modernists moreover were by no means so homogeneous a group as those Oxford dons and students who allied themselves with Newman. And the issues related to Modernism were less clear-cut and much more abstruse than those assoicated with the Tractarian Movement. The very word "Modernism," in its Catholic context, defies precise definition. In 1930 Alfred Loisy observed that it was an "equivocal" term, and since Loisy's time the equivocation has become, if anything, more pronounced.

Yet, despite these and other serious differences, there were also some similarities. The Modernists as well as the Tractarians were deeply committed intellectuals who concluded that there was much amiss with the ecclesiastical establishments to which they belonged and for which they had an abiding affection. In both instances they offered unconventional solutions to the religious questions of the day, solutions they were convinced would reform and revivify their churches. And in both instances they fell afoul of authorities who refused to sanction their views and who, more than that, insisted on the right to impose upon the intellectual dissidents a measure of conformity. The sad result was in both instances, to quote Newman again, "the parting of friends."

My intent therefore is to tell the story of the Modernists rather than to analyse the phenomenon called Catholic Modernism. This latter task has been ably done, and continues to be done, by a great variety of historians, philosophers, theologians, and sociologists, whose work has illuminated the subject far beyond anything I have here to offer. The honor roll in this regard is very long and includes, among others, the names of Roger Aubert, Lawrence Barmann, Gabriel Daly, Ellen Leonard, Thomas Michael Loome, Émile Poulat, Bernard Reardon, David Schultenover, Xavier Tilliette, Paul Toinet, René Virgoulay, Mary Jo Weaver, and William Wernz, as well as the distinguished members of the Roman Catholic Modernist Working Group of the American Academy of Religion.

I have learned an immense amount from these scholars—as well as from those who preceded them in the field—and no doubt I have much more to learn. But I remain convinced that there is room also for a different kind of study, one that attempts to reconstruct the events in question by way of a chronological narrative which will supplement the venerable surveys by Jean Rivière (1929) and Alec Vidler (1935).

To do so I have employed the vast array of printed sources now available. These include first of all selected writings of the Modernists themselves, as well as the extensive correspondence published in recent years. I have also freely made use of letters and other documents accessible through biographical and autobiographical studies. I have been as scrupulous as I know how to be to try to avoid the biases unavoidably present in books in this latter genre. Thus, for example, I have utilized the letters quoted in Loisy's *Mémoires*, without, I hope, imbibing Loisy's own interpretation of them. Similarly, Albert Houtin's later hostility toward Loisy has seemed to me irrelevant to the fact that Houtin possessed contemporary documents—printed only after his death—of unique significance; the documents have mattered to me, not Houtin's judgment of them. Needless to say, my procedure has been far from exhaustive; the last word on the history of Catholic Modernism—if indeed it is ever spoken—must await the thorough examination of and the correlation among vast archival collections.

The passage of time has not divested the term "Modernist" of the equivocal character referred to above. For some Catholics today it is a badge of honor, for others one of opprobrium. I propose no solution to that debate. Indeed, I propose only to describe the progress of a human drama so rich and universal in meaning that continuing debate about it is only appropriate. In 1968 I subtitled my book "a History of the Oxford Movement." The present work I describe, less presumptuously, "an Introduction to the Catholic Modernist crisis." My hope is that it will serve this purpose.

I have incurred many debts during the years I have been engaged in this project. A particularly large one is that to the Lynde and Harry A. Bradley Foundation whose generous grant freed me for a significant period from my ordinary academic duties.

George Weigel, president of the Ethics and Public Policy Center in Washington, has been a good angel to me in this venture and in many others.

I am grateful to two of my former students, Barbara Turpin and Elizabeth McInerny, for the heroic bibliographical work they did for me.

Friends and colleagues, Philip Gleason and David Solomon read the entire typescript and, in doing so, steered me away from methodological and philosophical errors I am all too prone to commit. Professor Solomon also guided me to Malt Cottage in Storrington, West Sussex, and stood by my side, next to the holly tree, at George Tyrrell's grave.

My friend for nearly half a century, Father Richard Val Berg, gave the typescript his most minute attention. His comments and searching questions have been of incalculable value to me.

I have every reason to be appreciative of the patience and courtesy of David J. McGonagle, director of The Catholic University of America Press.

Finally, in the dedication, the lines of Gerard Manley Hopkins come *ex intimo corde meo*.

Notre Dame, Indiana   *Marvin R. O'Connell*
24 June 1993

Prologue

THE BROWN WATERS of the Marne wash the base of the gentle hill upon which lies Ambrières, in the ancient province of Champagne. The village is a jumble of colorless houses clustered along two or three streets which remain obscured from the flat fields and pasturage roundabout by thick groves of trees. At one edge of the village stands a large stone church, different sections of which were built at different times. Perhaps the oldest part of the structure is the facade with its small, triple-columned portal, from the wall above which protrudes a rather undistinguished rose window. The church, which has no steeple, is separated by a hundred yards of indifferently tended lawn from a medium-sized house where the curé once lived.

One afternoon in the late spring of 1940 a hearse approached Ambrières along the road from the south. It had passed through the rolling *champenois* countryside, between the Forêt du Val and the broad Lac du Der-Chantecoq, and then up the twisting narrow road that led into the center of the village. There, in the little walled cemetery, amid the garish decoration of their graves favored by the French peasantry, the coffin was lowered into a place already occupied by the corpse of a woman who had died seventy years before. Only three mourners, somber and wet-eyed, stood by: a young working-class couple and a maiden lady of late middle age, the deceased's niece. There was no religious ceremony.[1]

Thus it was, with no pomp and with hardly a nod from the great world outside, that Alfred Firmin Loisy was returned to the soil his fathers had tilled for countless generations. That world was, to be sure, much preoccupied at the moment with other concerns: Loisy had died of uremia on June 1, and only a few days after his burial the Germans launched a massive assault along a wide front from Sedan to Abbeville. They had already destroyed the Belgian army and had driven the British into the sea at Dunkirk, and now their mechanized

---

1. See Émile Poulat, "Les dernières années de Loisy," in *Critique et mystique* (Paris: 1984), 150–77.

units raced south and east toward Chalons-sur-Marne and Troyes. Verdun, where a million men had been killed and maimed in the first war, fell in a few hours. The Germans marched into Paris on June 13, and four days later Marshall Pétain—he who had proclaimed at Verdun in 1916 that "ils ne passeront pas"—begged them for an armistice.

The upright stone over Loisy's grave memorialized only Marie Maulandre, the woman who had preceded him there, until the next year when these words were inscribed beneath her name: "Alfred LOISY / PRETRE / Retiré du Ministère / et de l'Enseignement / Professeur au Collège de France / 1857–1940 / Tuam in Votis / tenuit Voluntatem." The epitaph had been of Loisy's own composition, and the duty of having it appropriately placed had been left to a trusted executor.[2] Ironic, subtle, carefully nuanced, even elusive, as Loisy had always shown himself to be in the millions of words he had published in his lifetime, so was he in this, his final verbal testament.

"Alfred LOISY, PRIEST." He had indeed been ordained a Catholic priest more than sixty years before, but he had set aside the soutane of office for more than half that time, apparently with little regret. "Retired from the ministry" was surely one way to express the dramatic shift in his career, but excommunicated *nominatim* by the pope as a heretic also fitted the facts of the case. "Retired from teaching" as well, most recently at the Collège de France, where he had assumed his professorial chair in 1909 and where he had delivered his final lecture—the subject that day was the Montanist heresy of the second century—on April 16, 1932, six weeks after the celebration of his seventy-fifth birthday.

Loisy gave up his Paris apartment readily enough—he never fancied life in the city—and settled year-round into his house at Ceffonds, about twenty miles from Ambrières. He engaged a young railway worker and his wife to see to his domestic needs. And although freed now from the duty of formal lecturing, he repaired daily to his writing desk with the same relentless self-discipline he had manifested throughout his life. Over the next seven years he published eight books.[3] He continued also to correspond with a wide variety of people, though, given his great age, most of his contemporaries had predeceased him, and, given his acerbic personality, he had alienated more than a few who had been his intimates.

During this last decade of Loisy's life Ceffonds became a place of pilgrimage for the handful of Catholic Modernists who had survived the struggles of thirty years before and for those who harbored some curiosity about them.[4] Loisy

2. See note 35, in chapter 19.

3. For a list, see Albert Houtin and Félix Sartiaux, *Alfred Loisy: Sa vie et son oeuvre* (Paris: 1960), 303–24. This work, published after its authors' deaths by Émile Poulat, is significant because of the documents entrusted by Loisy to Houtin, whom the former had chosen to be his biographer. They later became estranged. See also the updated list in Poulat, *Critique et mystique*, 322–27.

4. See, for example, M. D. Petre, *Alfred Loisy: His Religious Influence* (Cambridge: 1944), 1–3, 125–29, and Alec Vidler, *A Variety of Catholic Modernists* (Cambridge: 1970), 2–10.

himself had already mockingly dismissed those events as of only "antediluvian" interest,[5] but this judgment, even to the degree that it expressed its enigmatic author's real view, did not keep the votaries away. Nor did those stay away who hoped, for whatever reason, that Loisy would in the end repudiate his convictions and perhaps provide the drama of a deathbed conversion. These latter were doomed to disappointment, even as they endured the sharp hits of this sardonic master of dialectical thrust and parry. Do you believe in the immortality of the soul, one of them asked him in 1934. "I say," Loisy replied with a thin smile, "that that depends upon God."[6] And so the days, spent mostly in a room jammed with books, finally ran out for "le petit Loisy"— this frail, tidy, little man, always dressed in sober black or dark grey, his beard and the fringe of white hair round his head neatly trimmed, his sharp eyes behind rimless spectacles concentrated on the biblical documents that had been the subject of his study for six decades.

It seems peculiar on the face of it that Loisy did not choose a quotation from those capacious texts with which to adorn his tombstone. But perhaps he selected the line he did—"tuam in votis tenuit voluntatem"—because it is difficult to translate literally, or rather because it admits of different shades of meaning. If so, it would not have been out of character. The words at any rate came from the Catholic requiem liturgy, specifically from the oration the priest recited just before the body was interred.[7] An acceptable translation, in context, might be something like the following: "Grant, O Lord, this mercy to thy departed servant, that *he who held fast to thy will in his intentions*, may not receive punishment in return for his deeds." *Votum* in its plural form may indeed mean "intentions" or, more likely, "wishes," but its primary meaning is "vows," so that the clause could reasonably be rendered, "he who did thy will by keeping his solemn promises." The ambiguity, if that was what Loisy intended, was compounded by the concluding and hortatory part of the prayer: "As the true faith joined [the deceased] to the throngs of the faithful on earth, may thy mercy unite him to the choirs of angels in heaven." That faith was precisely what Loisy had formally and publicly long rejected, and that rejection lasted till the end. And it is difficult to imagine anyone who died more a recluse, more isolated, more un-united than he.

The self-description of the epitaph as "priest" is perhaps, upon reflection, less mysterious. Loisy had indeed repudiated the sacramental priesthood of Catholicism, and had done so with hardly a qualm. But he never ceased to consider himself and his scholarship as performing a mediating, and therefore a radically priestly, function. He no doubt subscribed to the definition of the

---

5. Alfred Loisy, *Mémoires pour servir à l'histoire religieuse de nôtre temps*, 3 vols. (Paris: 1930–31), 1:5.

6. Quoted in Poulat, *Critique et mystique*, 174.

7. "Fac, quaesumus Domine, hanc cum servo tuo defuncto misericordiam, ut factorum suorum in poenis non recipiat vicem, qui *tuam in votis tenuit voluntatem*: ut, sicut hic eum vera fides junxit fidelium turmis; ita illic eum tua miseratio societ angelicis choris. Per Christum Dominum nostrum."

sacerdotal role offered by his friend Henri Bremond, and, as a matter of fact, applied explicitly by Bremond to Loisy himself: "By the word 'priest,' I mean a man who, not content to live religiously, consistently preaches to those around him the duty of thinking and living religiously; a liaison officer, as it were, between humanity and the divine, whatever might be the invisible realities he includes in the category of the divine."[8] In this sense Loisy was content to see himself as a priest forever.

By the time the great German offensive of May 1940 began, Alfred Loisy, his feet showing signs of gangrene, had fallen into his final illness. Though he was only intermittently conscious, he reiterated his desire to be buried in the family plot in the cemetery of Ambrières. As one who had witnessed invasion of the Boche into his beloved *patrie champenoise* twice before, he was to be spared experiencing it a third time. But the prospect must surely have been on his mind when, on Easter Sunday, he remarked to a friend: "The world needs great leaders. . . . Never have I realized so clearly how little a weak man, whose pen is his only weapon, can do."[9]

8. Sylvain Leblanc [Henri Bremond], *Un clerc qui n'a pas trahi: Alfred Loisy d'après ses Mémoires*, ed. Émile Poulat (Rome: 1971 ed.), 118. The work was originally published in 1931. The translation and those that follow throughout this book are the author's.

9. Quoted in Petre, *Loisy*, 129.

CHAPTER I

Prodigy from Champagne

Neither our preachers nor our lecturers nor our catechists are at a level to speak competently to the questions that today preoccupy educated men and trouble their consciences. The major and minor seminaries only rarely can exhibit professors capable of seriously refuting those German errors that have become French.

—*Guillaume Meignan (1881)*[1]

THERE HAD BEEN Loisys living in the valley of the Marne for hundreds of years. By the late eighteenth century they had grown so numerous that different branches of the family peopled, it was said, whole villages. It did not seem particularly unusual therefore when, in 1851, Charles-Sebastien Loisy married a distant cousin, Justine Desnalis, with whom he shared a Loisy great-great-grandfather. The newlyweds settled on the Loisy farm on the outskirts of Ambrières, department of the Haute-Marne, in what old people still called the province of Champagne: he a hardworking man who knew how to command and how to make himself obeyed without ever lifting his voice; she a gay and talkative woman, given to kindly sarcasm, much devoted to her housekeeping, her garden, her poultry, her children.[2]

There were three children, of whom Alfred Firmin was the second, born on February 28, 1857, and baptized the next day. From the moment of his birth he had to endure the cross—the curse, Loisy himself might have said—of a frail constitution. He did not suffer unduly from any particular illness—he lived to a great age—but he lacked the physical size and stamina so important in a culture which necessarily put a premium upon manual labor. While his elder brother ran with the boys of the village, Alfred spent much of his childhood in the company of his younger sister and her friends. He became adept at sewing dolls' clothes, a skill with which he delighted his nieces many years later. He was not strong enough to perform the heavier tasks on the farm; he

1. Quoted in Roger Aubert, *Le pontificat de Pie IX* (Paris: 1952), 379.
2. For what follows, see Loisy, *Mémoires*, 1:10–23.

could feed the chickens, but work in the fields at planting and harvest time was quite beyond his capacity. This was a condition that greatly depressed him and eroded his self-esteem. It also led him in later years to sentimentalize the virtues of rural France in general and of his family in particular.

One forum remained, however, in which Alfred Loisy soon discovered he could compensate, to some degree at least, for his weak body. The schoolroom was a place where he shone as no one else did, where his remarkable intellectual talent could bring a sense of accomplishment denied to him in the rough masculine world of physical work and play. As a child and an adolescent he won all sorts of local and regional prizes for scholastic achievement. When he was an old man he used to thumb through a primary school report, dated March 7, 1868, which recorded that he had performed *très bien* in reading, writing, spelling, history, and geography, and *assez bien* in arithmetic. He did not cease to compete successfully in this arena for the rest of his life.

The religious atmosphere in which Loisy was reared was earnest without being ostentatiously pious. Most of the men in his family went regularly to church—except Charles-Sebastien who described himself as a skeptic—but only the women and children communicated (at Christmas and Easter) and assisted at all the offices of Sundays and feast days. The world of Ambrières, Alfred remembered, "took religion seriously as a wise and austere discipline." It was the old Gallican Catholicism, tinged with Jansenist reserve, that Loisy pointedly found more enduring than "the facile, sentimental, Ultramontane religion." The curé Loisy recalled best was a big man with a booming voice and a severe air, who had no time for newfangled devotions like that of our Lady of La Salette;[3] he frightened people a little, but his catechetical instruction was simple and solid. "He was a priest of the olden time," Loisy said with a nostalgia he reserved for his home country, "a strong man who still belonged to the Gallican church."

In 1869 Alfred matriculated at the secondary school in nearby Vitry-le-François. It was a small, lay establishment attended by farmers' sons who spent a few years there acquiring the rudiments of a general education. Loisy had no trouble winning all the laurels in the tiny classics department, but it pained him to be constantly in the company of boys more robust than he, who called him derisively "le petit Loisy." "The hapless 'petit Loisy' did not excel among his schoolmates except on the days of examinations." At the end of July 1870, as the Prussian war began, the pupils were taken to the railroad station to see Napoleon III, who was passing through Vitry on his way to the front. When the train slowed down and the emperor appeared at the door of his carriage, eveybody cheered lustily. "In the simplicity of my ignorance," Loisy remem-

---

3. La Salette was an alpine village near Grenoble where two peasant children in 1846 claimed to have had a vision of the Virgin Mary. A shrine-church was built on the site, and La Salette thereafter attracted thousands of pilgrims every year.

bered, "I cried 'Vive l'empereur' like all the others. It was, I believe, the only occasion in my life when I raised my voice in a political cause. The thought of it still sticks in my throat."

"Le petit Loisy" came home for the late summer holiday in time to witness the remnant of a French army straggling back toward Paris, German cavalry on its heels. On a hot day in mid-August three troopers rode into the Loisy farmyard and without dismounting, their hands on the butts of their pistols, civilly asked for a drink of water. On August 25 a corps of German infantry invested Ambrières and its environs, and its commander, a stiffly courteous old man, settled himself and his staff in the Loisy house. He took pains to reassure Charles-Sebastien that he would tolerate no looting or disorder: "It is not you who have wanted this war," he said, "it is your emperor." The general was good as his word; the only casualty Alfred Loisy remembered was a cow—"la plus belle vache"—which the soldiers slaughtered and roasted in the middle of the yard.

These troops departed after a few days to be replaced by others similarly well disciplined. The German occupation lasted well into 1871, and all the great events of the intervening months—Napoleon III's surrender at Sedan, the proclamation of the republic, Gambetta's frenzied efforts to carry on the war, the bloody rising of the Paris Commune and its no less bloody suppression—remained merely rumors in Ambrières, because the local newspapers published in nearby Saint-Dizier printed only what the Germans permitted them to print. Yet the foreign presence made little real difference in the day-to-day routine of the countryside; the average *paysan champenois* shrugged and observed that surely as the conquerors had come, so they would go away again. The unsettled times did affect Alfred Loisy to the extent that his formal schooling was interrupted for two years; he studied instead at home with borrowed books and under the eye of the curé. But he still clung to the hope that he might yet take his place shoulder to shoulder with the other men in his family. About this time he composed a little prayer to be said every night that God, through the intercession of our Lady of Lourdes,[4] would grant him enough physical vigor to be a good farmer. It was not to be.

The parish priest who monitored Alfred's lessons in 1871–72 was new to the village, and his arrival suggested to the fourteen-year-old boy another career option. He had never up till then considered the possibility of becoming a priest. Other people, remarking upon the combination of delicate health, precocity, studiousness, and gravity of manner, insisted that he was destined to be a curé, but not Alfred himself: "The priests I had known inspired more

4. In 1858 in Lourdes, in the department of Hautes-Pyrénées, a fourteen-year-old girl named Bernadette Soubirous claimed to have had several visions of the Virgin Mary, who called herself the "Immaculate Conception." The site, with its curative spring, soon attracted millions of pilgrims annually, as it does to this day. In 1854 Pope Pius IX had defined the Immaculate Conception—that Mary was conceived without Original Sin—as part of the deposit of Catholic faith.

respect in me than sympathy." But on the Sunday in September 1871 when the new pastor sang his first high mass in the parish church, he "felt a singular impression." All of Ambrières was aflutter, for the installation of a curé was still a matter of civic importance. The mayor and his council attended, wearing their sashes of office. The firemen, in uniform, gave a military salute at the elevation.

I was in my place in the family pew, to the right of my mother as usual. When the priest at the end of the liturgical procession, led by cross and banners, passed close to us, he appeared very moved, as no doubt he was. An instant later, when he turned to the altar, something said to me that one day I too would turn to that altar and that I too would say mass in this church.

Loisy afterward judged this experience "a sort of illumination" which, though it was ultimately realized, he never for a moment confused with "a sign from heaven."[5] Indeed, by the time he enrolled in the ecclesiastical secondary school in Saint-Dizier (in October 1872), he had pretty much put the "illumination" out of his mind. The school, operated by the secular clergy of the diocese of Langres, was a classics *collège* or *lycée* rather than a *petit séminaire*,[6] but religious and moral training played a large role in its program. Loisy, as usual, stood at the head of his class, and he also displayed a piety beyond the ordinary that his masters took due note of. His schoolfellows, at once awestruck at his scholastic achievements and contemptuous of him as timid, awkward, shabby, and "no good at games," assumed that he would be a priest, because, as the more malicious among them expressed it, he was clearly fitted for nothing else.

In October 1873 Alfred Loisy decided for himself. During the school's annual retreat he made up his mind that he could best serve God, humanity, and truth—a glittering prospect for a sixteen year old—by heeding an ecclesiastical vocation. Significantly (and, as succeeding years and crises would demonstrate, characteristically), young Loisy sought no counsel at this moment of profound personal commitment, consulted with no one, neither with the retreat master nor his confessor nor any other officer of the *collège*. His decision once arrived at was a fait accompli which needed only the formal endorsement of his parents. They gave their reluctant agreement, after some tears shed by Justine and some sleepless nights endured by Charles-Sebastien, because they also believed their second son was equipped for little else—at least so their second son chose to think they believed. And now that he had arrived at his

---

5. Alfred Loisy, *Choses passées* (Paris: 1913), 10.

6. The *petit séminaire* or minor or preparatory seminary served those teenagers who indicated some interest in becoming diocesan priests and who would otherwise have attended a *lycée* or *collège*. At about age twenty young men still intending an ecclesiastical career would move on to a *grand séminaire* or major seminary, where they would follow professional studies in philosophy and theology. The religious orders created similar institutions for their aspirants.

decision, he moved methodically to implement it. He left Saint-Dizier without the baccalaureate, and in October 1874 entered the *grand séminaire* of the diocese of Chalons-sur-Marne. Charles-Sebastien rode the train with Alfred to Chalons, walked with him from the station to the gloomy old seminary building next to the prefecture, and watched wordlessly as his son donned the soutane for the first time. "I put on the ecclesiastical garb," Loisy recalled, "with less joy than I had anticipated."[7] He wore it for the next thirty-four years.

THE BISHOP OF CHALONS-SUR-MARNE, fifty-seven-year-old Guillaume Meignan, enjoyed among his peers a reputation for scholarship. He had once been a professor of Sacred Scipture, and his mildly adventuresome publications on various biblical subjects had been numerous. When he came to Chalons in 1864, he found his major seminary staffed by members of a religious order, a not uncommon practice in Catholic dioceses around the world.[8] His first episcopal act was to replace the Vincentians with his own secular priests, over whom he had more direct control, in hopes that the seminary's academic quality might thereby be improved.[9] By the time Alfred Loisy arrived ten years later these hopes had gone aglimmering, and Meignan—who was destined for a greater see and a cardinal's red hat—contented himself with the cynical observation that his *grand séminaire* was hardly worse than any other in France.[10]

Between 1830 and 1870 the number of secular priests in France swelled to nearly 56,000, an increase of 39 percent during a period when the overall population grew by only 17 percent. With few exceptions each of the eighty-five dioceses maintained a major and a minor seminary to train aspirants to the priesthood; indeed, it was not unknown that even a diocese of middling size supported two minor seminaries.[11] The jewel in the crown of this system was the crowded *grand séminaire* of Saint-Suplice in Paris, divided into a philosophy faculty at suburban Issy-les-Moulineaux and a theologate in the city itself.

Nor was this numerical surge the only statistical evidence of Catholicism's remarkable rebound from the disasters it had experienced during the era of the French Revolution. In 1851 there were 34,000 nuns in France; twenty-five years later there were almost 128,000, even though by that time Alsace and

---

7. Loisy, *Mémoires*, 1:28–33.

8. In France at this date the Vincentians staffed twenty-four major seminaries, the Sulpicians twenty-two. The latter, though technically they did not form a religious order, nevertheless enjoyed a measure of independence from local bishops. See Adrien Dansette, *Histoire religieuse de la France contemporaine* (Paris: 1965), 376.

9. See Albert Houtin, *La question biblique chez les catholiques de France au XIX siècle* (Paris: 1902), 80.

10. Loisy, *Mémoires*, 1:40, stressed the cynicism. Meignan became archbishop of Tours in 1884 and cardinal in 1893, three years before his death.

11. Belley, for example. See Marvin R. O'Connell, *John Ireland and the American Catholic Church* (St. Paul, Minn.:1988), 43–44.

Lorraine—rich grounds for vocations to the religious life—had been lost to Germany. Over that same span of years the number of male religious multiplied by a factor of ten, to more than 30,000. Old orders and institutes suppressed after 1789—including the Dominicans, the Oratorians, the Daughters of Charity, the Trappists, and the Jesuits—were restored and exhibited a vigor reminiscent of the fervent days of their founders. In addition, dozens of new congregations of both men and women were established, providing the church with a host of nurses and missionaries and, above all, teachers. By the middle of the 1860s a fifth of French boys and more than half the girls received their primary and secondary education in church-related schools. Most of these pupils grew up to become practicing Catholics, as did many, though by no means all, of the children reared in those areas still linked to the traditional agricultural economy. And not a few of them participated actively in the works of charity and social amelioration sponsored by their parish or diocese.[12] Add to this high level of day-to-day Catholic activity an extraordinary outpouring of popular devotion to the Virgin and the saints, manifested by pilgrimages and shrines and a vast miracle literature connected to them, and it could be argued that the eldest daughter of the church was enjoying her healthiest condition since the Middle Ages.[13]

Yet these clear signs of vitality did not tell the whole story. In the first place, the church's quantitative expansion had reached its high tide by the early 1870s and indeed had begun by then to recede. The reasons for this were various, but not least among them was the sharp change in the political climate that occurred with the collapse of the Second Empire. The enigmatic emperor, Napoleon III, himself an unbeliever and a notorious philanderer, had sensed that public opinion, especially among the rural masses, still adhered more or less to the tenets of the old religion, and he therefore had courted ecclesiastical support by, among other things, increasing substantially that portion of the national budget devoted to religious purposes. But the disasters of 1870–71 put at serious risk this latest version of the union of throne and altar, and five years later, at the moment the long birth labors of the Third Republic were at last accomplished, a full-throated reaction was underway. "Clericalism, that is the enemy!" cried the republican politicians, echoing one of the dominant themes of 1789. They were to prove their point, but this time with the ballot box rather than the guillotine.

Was France a "Catholic nation," or was "the Catholic, Apostolic, and Roman religion," in the words of the concordat of 1801 which governed church–state relations, still "the religion of the great majority of French citizens"?[14]

12. Charles Pouthas, *Le pontificat de Pie IX* (Paris: n. d. [1968]), 115–17, and Aubert, *Pie IX*, 114–22.

13. See Thomas Kselman, *Miracles and Prophecies in Nineteenth Century France* (New Brunswick, N.J.: 1983).

14. English text in Colman J. Barry (ed.), *Readings in Church History*, 3 vols. (Westminster, Md.: 1965), 3:13–15.

Either proposition, despite the recent gains, was dubious at best. For one thing, the ordinary norms of Catholic regularity—attendance at mass on Sunday and reception of the Eucharist at Eastertime—revealed startlingly different incidences in different parts of the country. If most people, say, in Brittany and in the valley of the Garonne habitually performed their religious duties, hardly 15 percent of the 350,000 or so nominal Catholics in the diocese of Orléans bothered to make their Easter duty in 1875. Rapid urbanization— the population of Paris quadrupled between 1801 and 1881—led more often than not to alienation from the church and its ministrations, almost universally so after a generation or two. A contemporary estimate indicated that one in twelve Parisian women went to mass weekly, and one in fifty men. And those city-dwellers who did take religion seriously were almost exclusively middle class; by contrast, in the blue collar district of Belleville about 1,500 persons out of a possible 60,000 belonged to the local parish.

Profound demographic changes in the countryside, moreover, were eroding the traditional base of Catholic loyalty. Rural France was not only shrinking in the face of industrialization, it was also being transformed internally. The same new roads and railways that made it feasible for throngs to go on pilgrimage to Lourdes and La Salette also opened the formerly static peasant culture to a multitude of novel influences and opportunities, not all of them in accord with the venerable customs with which religion had been for centuries so closely intertwined. The gradual spread of technical schools into formerly remote districts entailed not only instruction about up-to-date agricultural methods but also the promotion of patterns of life far removed from those that the village culture had so long preserved. Young farmers who, after passage of the conscription law of 1874, had to go off into the larger world for military training came home less ready to accept the straitened conventions revered by their ancestors, less ready to take off their caps when they met the curé in the village square. Since at least 80 percent of French diocesan priests had been recruited from peasant homes like Alfred Loisy's, the modification in the tone and values of peasant life was bound to have a long-lasting effect upon the whole Catholic community.

So, in a different way, was the fact that the French religious orders had become virtually the preserve of the bourgeoisie. The age-old tension between seculars and regulars was thus intensified by class distinction, and resentment by fellow Catholics that the orders controlled upward of one-third of the ecclesiastical property in France made it easier for the anticlericals to win public support by concentrating their attacks on the monks and friars. This combination of internal disarray and external threat was confronted meanwhile by a generally unreflective Catholic leadership, clerical and lay, who watched with dismay as the church's prestige and political influence declined precipitously year by year and election by election. Most of the bishops and practically all the gentlemen called for the restoration of the monarchy, but hopelessly split among legitimists, Orleanists, and Bonapartists,[15] they could not agree as to what kind of monarchy it ought to be. Nor could they grasp the increasingly obvious truth that the solid majority of their Catholic constituents no more wanted a king than did the radicals or the socialists.[16]

BISHOP MEIGNAN OF CHALONS-SUR-MARNE was something of an exception in that, if not a republican at heart, he at least believed that accommodation with the republican reality was the only sensible course for the church to follow. There were those—Alfred Loisy included—who thought Meignan the kind of man for whom accommodation with the powers that be was the single ruling principle of an ambitious life. He had, after all, opposed the definition of papal infallibility at the First Vatican Council—a last gasp for Gallicanism—and yet as time passed and circumstances changed he proved himself enough an Ultramontane to receive from Rome one promotion after another, until finally he was elevated to the College of Cardinals. But to bow to the inevitable does not necessarily make one a trimmer. In fact, all the bishops were Ultramontanes now: the Revolution and its aftermath had destroyed the old Gallican church, so that now French Catholics needed the pope to defend them against the inroads of the state rather than the other way around. As for Meignan's last honor, it simply demonstrated that he was shrewder than most of his colleagues. The red hat was conferred upon him only when the pope himself became convinced that the best way for French Catholics to defend themselves and their spiritual heritage was to adjust to the legitimacy of the Third Republic.[17]

Meignan also had better insight than the other bishops, and was more forthright than they, about another serious problem facing the church in France. "If our religion were not divine," he observed on one occasion, "it would long since have been smothered under the weight of our ignorance."[18] He was referring primarily to his own seminary at Chalons and to the French seminary system generally, but his caveat might have had a broader application. Indeed, it might have been applied to Meignan himself. As for the great Catholic names of the recent past—Montalembert, Lacordaire, Pie, Maret, Dupanloup—all of them had been prolific writers of passionate eloquence, but they had been preachers and poets, not scholars. They had persuaded by the fire of their sincerity and the beauty of their imagery, not by the cogency of their arguments. They represented the rush of a post-Enlightenment romanticism now exhausted and incapable of confronting the relentless march of the natural sciences, positivist philosophy, and critical history which had been issuing

---

15. The pretenders to the throne represented respectively the old Bourbon line (expelled in 1830), the descendants of Louis Philippe and the house of Orleans (1848), and the Napoleonic regime (1870).

16. See Dansette, *Histoire religieuse*, 371–91.

17. See chapter 8.

18. Quoted in Dansette, *Histoire religieuse*, 378.

from the German universities for a generation.[19] Luckily for French Catholics, the absence of a recognizable university tradition in their own country gave them a breathing space; but the luck would not last forever.

The seminaries were ill-equipped to address the problem. As Meignan discovered at Chalons, sweeping away one staff and replacing it with another could not dislodge entrenched custom, even when the bishop took a direct interest in the matter. Nor was such custom to be altogether despised: seminaries were above all schools of virtue, and in attaining this objective they succeeded admirably. The French secular clergy were high-minded, hardworking, and personally austere, and the ten or twelve years spent in a preparatory and then a major seminary helped make them so. Even Ernest Renan—the most famous apostate of his time and himself once a seminarian—paid them tribute: "I spent thirteen years in the intimate company of priests, and I never discerned a shadow of a scandal." Moreover, seminaries were places of professional preparation, not research centers. Once ordained, the young priest would serve in a parish where he would be called upon to say mass, administer the other sacraments, preach simple sermons to simple people, and catechize the children. His most intellectually challenging task was probably the work of the confessional, and even that demanded very little sophistication.

But, despite their undoubted merits, the seminaries allowed and indeed fostered an intellectual program that was little short of scandalous. Training the mind had been reduced to an afterthought, so much so that serious study was almost held in contempt. Liturgical and private prayer, some manual labor, some organized games, attention to minute observance of the rule as a means of harnessing the will and the passions, and a good deal of idleness: this was the stuff of the seminarian's day. In the classroom, professors worked from a curriculum featuring dull lectures about the wickedness of Voltaire and about the abominations that had arisen out of the Revolution. On his own the student was expected merely to read textbooks written in inelegant Latin, manuals that amounted to little more than lists of propositions to memorize. His intellect was seldom stimulated and never challenged. He never heard of Kant or Comte or, for that matter, of Thomas Aquinas or the other great Scholastic doctors. The sciences, mathematical and physical, were simply ignored, as was any consideration of Christian art. Sacred Scripture and the works of the ancient church fathers were capsulated for the student into a series of proof-texts whose only purpose was to bolster the arid propositions found in the awful manuals. This was what passed for the higher education of the diocesan clergy. And, since from the students of today came the teachers of tomorrow, no means of correction appeared ready at hand: for, as Bishop Meignan discovered at Chalons, where could a faculty trained in some other, better way be found?

19. See Aubert, *Pie IX*, 211–16.

DURING THE FIVE YEARS HE SPENT THERE, Alfred Loisy enjoyed a tenuous kind of happiness in the seminary of Chalons. He got along better with his schoolfellows and they with him than had been the case at Saint-Dizier: these older, more mature students—about fifty of them altogether[20]—preparing themselves for a profession put less value than boys did upon physical strength and proficiency in athletics. Loisy liked "the regular life, in which the employment of every hour was fixed and in which one had fully half of each day to oneself." The relatively sumptuous celebration of the liturgy and the round of other pious practices provided him with much emotional satisfaction.[21]

But what passed for cultivation of the mind in the *grand séminaire* was quite another matter. The members of the faculty, with one impermanent exception, were incapable, in Loisy's harsh judgment, of offering any intellectual training worthy of the name. The vulgar and pretentious professor of moral theology had appointed himself the watchdog of orthodoxy, which was defined for him in the strident pages of *L'Univers*, the national organ of extreme Ultramontanism. The professor of dogma and canon law boasted of his two years in Rome, during which brief interval he had earned doctorates in both those subjects. "He was a Lorrainer by birth," Loisy observed acidly, "but he might as well have been an Italian, being at once clever and lazy." A typical lecture by the professor of Scripture and church history—"a holy man as innocent as it was possible to be of critical judgment"—explained that Saint John in the Apocalypse had explicitly prophesied the convening of the Vatican Council. Over this little melange presided the rector, one Abbé Roussel, a veteran parish priest with no scholarly attainments or interests, whose sole concern appeared to be the maintenance of firm discipline.

Loisy was put off by Roussel's stern and unbending demeanor, though in the long run the rector proved to be a good friend. In the meantime Loisy discovered in the young professor of philosophy, Abbé Ludot, a helpful mentor. Ludot had no particular philosophical training beyond his own seminary course, but he read widely and had an inquiring mind. He gave Loisy a supplemental reading list which included standard Catholic liberals like Montalembert and Lacordaire—not, it should be noted, Kant or the German critics or the positivists of whom Loisy remained entirely ignorant. He was strongly moved by Montalembert's rhapsodic *Monks of the West*, and Lacordaire so impressed him that he contemplated for a while becoming a Dominican. None of these authors was "critical," and so none of them contributed to the development of Loisy's scientific methodology—indeed, as early as 1884 he recorded that "this liberalism was a far cry from my own." Yet, lively and provocative, Montalembert and the others furnished him with a taste for history as well as

20. Houtin and Sartiaux, *Loisy*, 15.
21. Loisy, *Choses passées*, 25–27.

some relief from the humdrum philosophy manuals that comprised most of his required reading. The higher reaches of philosophical investigation, as the seminary defined them, certainly did not humble him: "I doubted, in spite of myself, the objective reality of metaphysical conclusions."[22]

Ludot, who was known to speak disparagingly of the editors of *L'Univers* and to be less than enthusiastic about the conciliar definition of papal infallibility, rapidly became a persona non grata to his colleagues. At the end of Loisy's first year at Chalons he was dismissed from the faculty and assigned as curé to a large country parish. He went off to his new post cheerfully enough, but his favorite pupil saw the transfer as an instance of his bishop's "cunning" cynicism. In order to placate a few reactionaries, Meignan, himself an anti-infallibilist at the Vatican Council, "had lightheartedly sacrificed a man whom he admired and whose faith, as he knew very well, was sounder than his own."[23] Ludot's departure in any case removed whatever intellectual excitement Loisy had experienced in his seminary curriculum; the new professor of philosophy was a much more conventional specimen.

As he moved from 1875 into the formal study of theology, Loisy, as he remembered it, underwent constant tedium mixed with large doses of inner distress. It was one thing to let the emotions loose in prayerful reflection upon the Christian mysteries; it was quite another to subject those same mysteries to rational analysis. He did not yet regard the dogmatic superstructure as resting upon the air; Renan many years before had had this intuition when a seminarian at Saint-Sulpice, but Loisy was not so precocious.[24] He suffered rather from doubts about specific doctrines: the Trinity, grace, the divinity of Christ. "Now that I had to think about these things and not just feel them, I was in a state of perpetual agony. My intelligence was unsatisfied, and my timid, childlike consciousness made me tremble before the question that pressed itself upon me, in spite of myself, every moment of the day: is there reality that corresponds to these theories?" And the moral tracts were equally disturbing. The casuistry he studied was "less the general science of ethics, the reasoned conception of duty, than the specific spiritual direction suited to the confessional. That manner of specifying duty confused me as much as the Catholic manner of understanding truth. Could I justify myself in the face of such complicated rules?"

Conscientiously Loisy revealed his problem to his confessor, for whom it was no problem at all. Merely excessive scruples, the good priest said, the best cure for which was to think about something else. This simple, well-intended advice did not help much, for though Loisy continued fervent in prayer and felt no desire to return to the secular state, the intellectual misgivings lingered

22. Houtin and Sartiaux, *Loisy*, 15–19, 377.

23. For this and what follows, see Loisy, *Choses passées*, 27–47.

24. See, for example, Ernest Renan, *Souvenirs d'enfance et de jeunesse* (Paris: 1959 ed.), 164–84. *Souvenirs* was originally published in 1883.

on. At one point he "plunged boldly," on his own and with no direction, into the study of the *Summa theologiae* of Saint Thomas Aquinas. He went through the tract on the Trinity article by article, an exercise he described later with ill-concealed contempt: "The speculations of Saint Thomas on the Trinity . . . had upon me the effect of a huge logomachy . . . [and] left, as it were, a void."

Another extracurricular activity brought more solace. Loisy began to study Hebrew under the tutelage of an upperclassman who knew a smattering of the sacred language. "Immediately I felt as though I were accomplishing something." Once his amateur tutor's knowledge was exhausted, Loisy continued the work alone. He compared Greek and Latin versions of Genesis to the Hebrew text and reveled in the insights his extraordinary gift for languages afforded him, but "[h]aving no critical commentary to deal with, I could make no troubling discoveries."

At the end of June 1878, his intellect still uneasy but his will firm, Alfred Loisy was ordained a subdeacon and so assumed the obligations of celibacy and the daily recitation of the breviary. He had taken a step he understood to be irrevocable. The following September, at the instance of Abbé Roussel, who intended him to return to the seminary as a professor, Bishop Meignan sent him for higher study to the theological school at the Catholic University of Paris.

TWENTY-TWO UNIVERSITIES, the glory of the medieval past, had existed in France before 1789.[25] The Revolution had swept them all away, to the regret of only a few vested interests, since they were even more decayed and moribund, if that were possible, than the Oxford and Cambridge of the same period.[26] Over the next century the very idea of institutions devoted to an inquiry into the whole of human knowledge was abandoned; not until 1896 did France have genuine universities again. Substituted for them during the revolutionary period were the so-called *écoles speciales*, all of them located in Paris and each of them designed to meet some specialized vocational need. The École Polytechnique, which trained civil and military engineers for the state, was the most highly esteemed among them, but there were several others. The École Normale Supérieure, for example, provided teachers and administrators for the secondary schools, and the École Centrale des Arts et Manufactures technical experts to serve in industry.

To this pragmatic and statist system—even the celebrated École des Chartes was chiefly concerned with training civil servants who would be archivists in the communes and departments—Napoleon I added the *facultés*, which he set

25. For much of what follows, see Marvin R. O'Connell, "Duchesne and Loisy on the Rue de Vaugirard," in Nelson H. Minnich et al. (eds.), *Studies in Catholic History in Honor of John Tracy Ellis* (Wilmington, Del.: 1985), 589–616.

26. See Marvin R. O'Connell, *The Oxford Conspirators: A History of the Oxford Movement, 1833–1845* (Lanham, Md.: 1991 ed.), 50–63. This work was originally published in 1969.

up in Paris and in sixteen provincial towns. The emperor dubbed the whole centrally controlled educational system *l'université*, but in fact neither the specialty schools nor the faculties belonged to a university in the older (or newer) sense. They had no legal or moral connection to one another. Each *faculté* enjoyed instead an independent status as an examining board for entry into the various professions. The faculties of law and medicine performed this function adequately enough, but professors of the humanities and the sciences did little more than award degrees to teachers trained elsewhere and deliver popular lectures to local elites. They were miserably paid and often took another job on the staff of a *lycée* or a *collège*, thus blurring whatever distinction there may have been between higher and secondary education. The most prestigious professors had been the likes of François Guizot—much more a politician than an educator—and Victor Cousin, literary figures and men of the world, but not by any measure serious scholars. Research was unknown. Laboratories and libraries went virtually unsupported; in 1869–70 the law faculty at Paris spent less than Fr 1,000 on its library holdings, and the *facultés* at Marseilles spent nothing at all. The accomplishments of Pasteur and, later, of Charcot were the fruits of individual genius and owed nothing to the *université*. Reformers, especially those who admired the booming German universities, deplored this anomalous and inefficient structure, but they could do little to change it. They did manage, however, on the eve of the war with Prussia, to establish another *école speciale* which was unique in that it neither catered to specific career preparation nor acted merely as a degree-dispensing—a licensing—agency. The École Pratique des Hautes Études, small and underfunded as it was, did have nevertheless the distinction of being the first French graduate school and center for advanced and disinterested research.[27]

There remained one curious survival from all this wreckage and experimentation. The Collège de France, established in Paris during the sixteenth century, continued to function in its own building on the Left Bank, independent, as it had always been, of the ordinary institutions of higher learning. It was a kind of populist academy whose courses were free and open to the public. It neither held examinations nor conferred degrees. Ernest Renan, its brightest luminary in the 1880s, described the Collège de France as a center in which were taught not so much the sciences as the disciplines struggling to become sciences.[28]

The state's educational monopoly had indeed been breached, first at the primary level and then, in 1850, at the secondary. "Free" schools meant in practice Catholic schools, and *lycées* and *collèges* operated under clerical auspices multiplied. But not until after the shock and humiliation of the war of 1870

27. See Theodore Zeldin, "Higher Education in France," *Journal of Contemporary History* 2 (July 1967): 53–60.
28. See Anon., *Le IVe centenaire de Collège de France* (Paris: 1932).

did the Catholics succeed in carrying this principle of confessional independence to the university level as well. This they did while the National Assembly elected in 1871, with its Catholic and monarchist majority, still had life.
By virtue of legislation passed on July 12, 1875, private institutions of higher
learning received official sanction. Regional groups of bishops scrambled to
take advantage of the act of July 12. Catholic universities were founded within
the year at Paris, Angers, Lyon, and Lille, and, a little later, at Toulouse. It
was a bold venture to move so quickly, without teachers or students or facili-
ties of any kind. But the bishops knew, as everyone knew, that the National
Assembly was soon to give way to a new Chamber of Deputies in which a
republican and anticlerical majority might very well come into control of all
the coercive organs of the state, and they wanted their new *universités* to be in
place before that dire day arrived.[29]

Their decisiveness served them only up to a point. By 1879 the anticlerical
parties were firmly in the saddle. They expended a good deal of energy in re-
forming to their taste the primary and secondary levels of education and, above
all, in getting the religious orders out of the schools, and in some cases out of
the country. They did little, however, to address the problems inherent in the
cumbersome apparatus of *écoles spéciales* and *facultés*, aside from adding modest
amounts of money to their budgets. But they did strike down the fledgling
Catholic universities which, in 1880, were deprived of the use of that title,
deprived also of the right to grant degrees. In a small gesture of vindictiveness,
this latter provision was made retroactive to 1875; all degree students had to
pass examinations administered exclusively by state-appointed boards.[30]

As if official hostility were not trouble enough, the bishops quickly learned
that in founding virtually at once five universities—now to be called "institutes"—they had seriously overreached their resources. Endowments were
nonexistent, and fee-paying students were reluctant to attend schools that
could not offer recognized degrees. Poverty brooded over the *instituts* as relentlessly as did the enmity of anticlerical politicians; only the Institut Catholique
of Lille gave any evidence of adequate funding.[31]

BUT, AS ALWAYS IN MATTERS FRENCH, Paris was the place that mattered, and the establishment set up there was the most visible and the most
important. Under the leadership of Cardinal Guibert, twenty-five bishops
whose dioceses were relatively near the capital participated in the founding of
the *institut* and sat on its governing board.[32] The real driving force behind the

29. Édouard Lecanuet, *L'Église de France sous la troisième république. Les dernières années de Pie IX,
1870–1878* (Paris: 1931), 251–63.

30. René Aigrain, *Les universités catholiques* (Paris: 1935), 39–41.

31. See John J. Keane, "The Catholic Universities of France," *Catholic World* 47 (1888): 293, and
J. Calvert, "Catholic University Education in France," *Catholic University Bulletin* 13 (1907): 191–210.

32. Alfred Baudrillart, *L'Institut catholique* (Paris: 1930), 16–18.

project, however, was Maurice le Sage d'Hauteroche d'Hulst. Born in Paris in 1841, educated at Saint-Sulpice and in Rome, where he earned doctorates in theology and canon law, d'Hulst was ordained priest in 1865 and ministered to a working-class Parisian parish until the war with Prussia, during which he served as an army chaplain. Guibert appointed him his secretary in 1872 and a year later a vicar-general especially charged with planning for the new university. He became its vice-rector in November 1875, with control of most of the day-to-day operations in his hands; in 1881 he was named rector of the Insititut Catholique of Paris and domestic prelate.[33]

Mgr. d'Hulst belonged to the school of Montalembert and Bishop Dupanloup, a liberal to be sure, but no republican. A lifelong monarchist and an intimate of the Orleanist pretender, he comported himself like the aristocrat he was. His long narrow face with its aquiline nose over a severely wide mouth testified to the cultivation and to the self-confidence which only inherited position could give. He sat for a time in the Chamber of Deputies where, amid the democratic rough and tumble, he was not a notable success. A *litterateur* rather than a scholar, he made his mark in the pulpit of Notre Dame, though some worshippers there claimed he could not be heard, so weak was his voice. His sermons were at any rate published in accord with the convention of the day, and upon them rested much of his reputation.[34] Alfred Loisy recalled him mockingly as a great improvisor, "who came now to improvise a university."[35] Not so much profoundly reflective nor even very well educated, d'Hulst was dedicated and industrious, and he possessed the proper social connections. He gave the best that was in him to the cause of Catholic higher education in France. The times were not propitious for that task, and it may have been just as well that he brought to it something of the spirit of *noblesse oblige*.

The law of 1875 had specified that the private universities it permitted had to be composed of at least three faculties. At Paris this injunction was carried out with the establishment by March 1876 of the faculties of arts, sciences, and law. Plans were also drawn up for a faculty of medicine, though in the end obstacles proved too daunting to achieve that ambition. A faculty of theology had not been contemplated at first; the objective of the universities was the advanced education of laymen, not of clerics who alone, it was supposed, had any business studying divinity or any interest in doing so. But Rome intervened forcefully, and as a result an École Supérieure de Théologie was created in 1878 and became a full-fledged *faculté* of the *institut* in 1889.

This development caused some awkwardness for Mgr. d'Hulst. Rome's insistence on the point probably stemmed from a desire to erect a counterpoise to the six theology *facultés* that Napoleon I had included in his structure of

33. The standard biography is Alfred Baudrillart, *Vie de Mgr. d'Hulst*, 2 vols. (Paris: 1921).

34. See also d'Hulst's *Mélanges philosophiques* (Paris: 1892), "a collection of essays dedicated to the defense of spirituality by the return to the tradition of Catholic education."

35. Loisy, *Mémoires*, 1:73.

higher education. These bodies—Bishop Meignan as a young man had taught in one of them— had in fact never flourished, but the Roman authorities continued to regard them with deep suspicion, more perhaps because they remained bastions of Gallicanism than because of their indifferent intellectual quality. The French bishops, for their part, had sent few students to the Napoleonic faculties and had instead concentrated their energies and resources into building up their own seminary system. The papal initiative therefore tended to bring forward a competition, not so much between the Institut Catholique and the state faculties—which were anyhow suppressed by the Chamber of Deputies in 1886, with their function, such as it was, absorbed into a new *sciences religieuses* section of the École Pratique des Hautes Études—as between the Institut Catholique and the diocesan seminaries.

So d'Hulst had another problem to wrestle with, alongside a chronic shortage of money and a hostile political climate. He pressed on like a good soldier nonetheless, and a theological school was duly set up within the framework of the *institut*. It was necessary also to incorporate a *séminaire universitaire* to see to the discipline and spiritual formation of the talented clerical students who, it was hoped, would come to Paris in droves from their dioceses to study philosophy and theology. D'Hulst entrusted this task to a staff of three Sulpicians, an obvious choice indeed, but a shrewd stroke as well, in that it established a cordial link between the divinity school and the Society of Saint-Sulpice which operated the great Parisian seminary and which, besides, enjoyed a wide influence across the country.

SULPICIAN PATRONAGE was deemed crucial, because the bishops outside Paris hesitated to send very many of their seminarians to the divinity school, and Alfred Loisy, who was a member of the tiny first class that matriculated in the autumn of 1878, did not think they had sent their brightest ones either.[36] As for Loisy himself, he was from the first desperately unhappy. He disliked Paris and disliked the school even more. He missed the Marne Valley and all its associations. The only attractive person he met at the Institut Catholique was the professor of ecclesiastical history, Louis Duchesne[37]—"I succumbed at this first encounter with genuine science"—but even he could not relieve young Loisy's homesickness or prop up his always precarious health. At the new year, his nerves in tatters, Loisy went home to Ambrières where his physician prescribed a month's complete rest and forbade a return to Paris. By the end of January 1879 he had gone back to the seminary at Chalons.

Bishop Meignan was not amused. The young man had thwarted the episcopal will, and the young man had to pay the price, as Loisy found out upon his ordination as priest on the following June 29. Meignan assigned him as pastor

36. "Mes condisciples n'étaient pas très intelligents." See Houtin and Sartiaux, *Loisy*, 22.
37. See chapter 4.

to the worst parish in the diocese, to a village where hardly a glimmer of Christian practice survived. Loisy stayed there six months, contemplating his fate in the cold and empty church, until Abbé Roussel interceded for him and arranged a transfer to another, rather better pastorate near Ambrières.

Altogether Alfred Loisy spent about a year and a half as a country priest, and during that time his health improved markedly. He had plenty of leisure to pursue his studies; he even began to plot out in his mind a large book "in which I would prove, from history and philosophy, the truth of Catholicism." But whatever abstract devotion he held for the *champenois* countryside, Loisy did not intend to remain there, banished forever from the academic life. He therefore initiated the "diplomacy" by which he hoped to regain the bishop's favor and to secure for himself, at worst, a professorship at Chalons. Roussel had meanwhile died in 1880 and could no longer help him, but d'Hulst and Duchesne could, by recommending to Meignan that this exceptionally brilliant subject of his be allowed to resume his formal studies and earn the appropriate theological degrees. In the spring of 1881 Loisy went to see the bishop and asked permission to return to Paris. Meignan received him kindly, called him "mon bon petit Loisy," and, no doubt satisfied that the young man had learned his lesson, acceded to his request. On May 12 Abbé Alfred Loisy, having shaken the proverbial dust from his feet, took up residence at the Institut Catholique.[38]

Nothing much had changed from his earlier experience there, except of course the name of the institution which by law could no longer call itself a university.

38. Loisy, *Mémoires*, 1:77–80.

CHAPTER 2

Aeterni Patris

The Thomist philosophy and theology, quite fairly compared with other philosophies like the Buddhist or the Monist, with other theologies like the Calvinist or
the Christian Scientist, is quite obviously a working and even a fighting system;
full of common sense and constructive confidence; and therefore normally full of
hope and promise. Nor is this hope vain or this promise unfulfilled. In this not
very hopeful modern moment, there are no men so hopeful as those who are today
looking to St. Thomas as a leader.

—*G. K. Chesterton (1933)*[1]

ROMAN NIGHTS during the high summer tend to be clear and still and
hot. The dust of centuries hangs like a shroud over the domes and ancient monuments. On the left bank of the Tiber, where the Janiculum Hill
looms over the Vatican, the umbrella pines, their limbs drooping as though
weary and disheartened, look like black etchings pasted against the starry sky.
Over the space of the three hundred yards or so that separates the river from
the towering obelisk in the middle of the Piazza di San Pietro an almost eerie
silence prevails, broken only by the occasional caw of a night bird swooping
from one balustrade to another or, perhaps, by the banter of a party of late
revelers, their voices sharpened by the wine they have drunk and by the need
they feel to contest somehow the thick, uncertain darkness through which they
make their way.

It was nearly midnight on July 13, 1881—two months and a day after Abbé
Alfred Loisy had returned from Champagne to the Institut Catholique of
Paris—when a small group of people huddled together at the inner end of the
piazza, at the foot of the steps leading up to the great bronze doors of the
basilica. Persons of quality, clerical and lay, garbed to match the gloom of the
witching hour, they waited patiently until there emerged from a side entrance
of the papal palace, almost hidden from their view by one of the immense

---

1. G. K. Chesterton, *Saint Thomas Aquinas* (New York: 1956 ed.), 189–90.

pillars of Bernini's colonnade, six men who bore upon their sholders a wooden coffin. The little assembly fell in behind them to form a somber cortege that moved cautiously out of the piazza and into the jumble of crooked streets and alleys of the Borgo. Off to their right rose the shadowy outlines of the hospital of Santo Spirito, built upon the site once occupied, in the eighth century, by a pious British prince who, with his retainers, had settled in that quarter of the city and given it its original name, the burgh—the borgo—of the Saxons.

The procession proceeded straight east, along the Via dei Corridori, silent save for the murmured invocations and responses of the rosary: "Pater noster qui es in coelis; Ave Maria gratia plena." When they reached the vast pile of the Castel Sant' Angelo, the mourners turned sharply to the right and began to cross the river on the bridge likewise named for the holy angels. As Bernini's sculpted images of Saints Gabriel and Michael looked down impassively, out of the darkness at the farther end of the bridge a crowd suddenly appeared brandishing torches and raising raucous yells that echoed over the water: "Death to the pope! Death to the priests! Throw that filthy carcass into the river!" A few stones rattled down among them, and a few more obscenities were shouted, but the pallbearers and their companions pressed grimly forward. Though they were jostled a little as they stepped off the bridge and onto the right bank—where a squad of policemen stood nervously off to the side— and though the noise and commotion followed them for a few blocks, no further attempt was made to impede the procession's progress.[2]

THE CAREER OF A PUBLIC PERSON has much to do with symbols and gestures, and that scuffle at the Ponte Sant' Angelo, minor in itself, possessed a wealth of symbolism. In the coffin lay the remains of Pope Pius IX—né Giovanni Maria Mastai-Ferretti—who had died three years earlier. Three years before that, in 1875, the pope, then eighty-three, had drawn up a will in which he expressed his desire to be buried in the basilica of San Lorenzo fuori le Mura. This venerable edifice, just off the Via Tiburtina, a couple of miles across the *centro* of the city from the Vatican, traced its origins back to the third century when Lawrence the Deacon, a martyr much revered by the Roman populace, had been buried nearby in a cemetery situated outside the protective walls built by the Emperor Aurelian. A symbolic association had sprung readily to Pius IX's mind: according to tradition Saint Lawrence had been slowly roasted to death on a gridiron by the emperor's soldiers, while he, Pio Nono, no doubt believed that, though his people loved him, the powerful of this world had treated him with an analogous cruelty.

The parallel was perhaps not so outlandish as it first sounds. When he died

2. See Pierre Fernesolle, *Pie IX, pape (1792–1878)*, 2 vols. (Paris: 1963), 2:398–400, and Eduardo Soderini, *Il Pontificato di Leone XIII*, 3 vols. (Rome: 1933), 2:47–56. For the text of Leo XIII's formal protest (4 August, 1881), see Hubert Bastgen, *Die Römische Frage: Dokumente und Stimmen*, 3 vols. (Freiburg-im-Breisgau, 1919), 3:106–8.

in February 1878, and his corpse lay in state in Saint Peter's, the people of Rome filed past it in reverent homage for three solid days. Yet so strained were the relations between church and state in Italy, and particularly in Rome—which until a scant eight years earlier had been papal territory—that the new pope deemed it imprudent to carry out fully the terms of his predecessor's last will. The body therefore was interred in a temporary grave inside the walls of the Vatican, where Pius IX in 1870 had chosen to "imprison" himself—a powerful and poignant symbol—rather than to accede to the loss of the civil jurisdiction the popes had exercised for a thousand years. Then, when his remains were making passage to their final resting place, the people of Rome, or at least some of them, hurled taunts and blasphemies and insults at them.

So it appeared that paradox which, no less than symbol, had marked the thirty-two-year-long pontificate of Pius IX was to continue even after his death. He was a man who inspired extravagant devotion and intense hatred. Corpulent and genial, strikingly handsome even into old age, Pio Nono was impressionable, utterly fearless, a careless, even an inept, administrator who liked to call himself "the captain of the ship."[3] He was given to extreme swings of mood, traceable, perhaps, to the epilepsy from which he suffered in his youth.[4] He was as fascinated as a small boy by mechanical gadgets of all kinds. Conscious of his dignity, to be sure, he nevertheless preserved a warmth and affability which delighted the crowds that came from all over the world to see him. He was in fact an uncalculating populist at heart, who never considered himself above a quip or a pinch of snuff or a hug for a small child. He practiced a piety as unaffected as it was emotional, and he remained all his life impatient of subtlety and indeed of any intellectual nuance—the mind of a grasshopper, a bemused adversary had observed, and the soul of an angel; "a good priest," Prince Metternich had concluded, "warm of heart but weak of intellect."[5]

Pius IX's inability to differentiate among the diverse currents of thought that swirled through the nineteenth century was his greatest weakness. He never grasped, for example, the import of the profound changes European society underwent during his lifetime, when the old agricultural economy gave way to an industrialized system dominated by an aggressive middle class and a vast urban proletariat, and when monarchies had to surrender their immemorial powers to more or less liberal and representative regimes. Similarly, his flirtation with political reform at the beginning of his pontificate, which had ended in bitter disillusionment when the revolutionaries of 1848 drove him temporarily into exile, left him incapable of finding merit in any form of progressivism. The famous aphorism "A free church in a free state" was an abomina-

---

3. Quoted in Wilfrid Ward, *The Life of John Henry Cardinal Newman*, 2 vols. (London: 1912), 2:211.

4. Aubert, *Pie IX* (Paris: 1952), 14.

5. Quoted in D. A. Binchy, *Church and State in Fascist Italy* (Oxford: 1970 ed.), 18.

tion to him whether enunciated by the loyal Catholic, Count Montalembert, or by the inveterate foe of the papacy, Count Cavour.[6]

But this intellectual incapacity was coupled with a formidable moral strength. Pio Nono dedicated himself with all his warm heart to defend what he conceived to be the interests of the church he had been divinely chosen to lead. Not one jot or tittle of traditional law or custom would he compromise away. Nothing would be given up without a struggle. No defeat, no personal humiliation could turn him aside, and no challenge went unaccepted. The unblinking courage with which he confronted his enemies was one source of the immense and unprecedented popularity he enjoyed with the masses of ordinary Catholics. But what they admired as dutiful steadfastness seemed to the political and intellectual elites a malevolent intransigence provoking them to ridicule and rage. The pope's very candor was an offense to them, and at the same time a harbinger of a consummation they devoutly wished for. When in 1864 he solemnly declared it erroneous to say that "the Roman pontiff can and ought to reconcile and harmonize himself with progress, with liberalism, and with modern civilization,"[7] the editors of one Paris newspaper retorted, with a mixture of horror and delight, that the statement represented "the supreme act of defiance hurled at the modern world by an expiring papacy."[8] Eleven years later, Ernest Renan entertained his companions at a fashionable dinner party by explaining how the stubborn foolishness of Pius IX would lead inevitably to the swift demise of the papacy and of the Catholic church itself.[9]

Those Parisians who listened to Renan that evening in 1875 did not need to look far for confirmation of this prophecy. The barque of Peter under the captaincy of Pius IX appeared adrift upon a sea of troubles. The kingdom of Italy was by no means unique in its fierce hostility to the institutional church. In France itself the impending general elections guaranteed that a new spasm of anticlericalism lay just over the horizon. The constitution recently adopted in Spain had severed the ancient link between church and state and had sparked a series of violent antipapal demonstrations. The Austrian government, in 1874, had unilaterally repudiated its concordat with the Holy See, selectively suppressed the religious orders, and proclaimed the equality of all sects. In neighboring Germany there raged at the same time the so-called *Kulturkampf*, in the course of which nuns and priests were expelled from the country and many bishops went to jail. A succession of Russian tsars pursued an increasingly brutal program designed to separate their Catholic subjects in Poland

---

6. Both counts claimed to have originated the maxim. See Marvin R. O'Connell, "Montalembert at Mechlin: A Reprise of 1830," *Journal of Church and State* 26 (Autumn 1984): 516.

7. This is the eightieth of the eighty propositions forming the celebrated *Syllabus of Errors*. For an English text, see Barry (ed.), *Readings in Church History*, 3:70–74.

8. For this and other reactions, see Marvin R. O'Connell, "Ultramontanism and Dupanloup: The Compromise of 1865," *Church History* 53 (June 1984): 211–17.

9. Humphrey Johnson, *The Papacy and the Kingdom of Italy* (London: 1926), 41.

and the Ukraine from their Roman allegiance. Switzerland launched its own version of the *Kulturkampf*, and even in Belgium, where liberals and Catholics had for decades enjoyed harmonious relations, a quarrel over educational policy led to unprecedented confessional tensions the year Pio Nono died. Nor did the situation in traditionally Catholic countries over the seas appear much different: in Mexico, Argentina, and Chile anticlerical regimes made no secret of their designs upon first the property and then, in some instances, upon the very existence of the Catholic church.[10]

Yet, in the midst of these tumults, other kinds of evidence suggested that Renan's prediction might have been, at the very least, premature. During Pius IX's pontificate 216 new dioceses had been erected, bringing the worldwide total to 1145. National hierarchies had been established in England, Denmark, Holland, and Greece, countries where for centuries the practice of Catholicism had been proscribed. Heightened missionary activity in Asia and Africa—spearheaded by the French and the Irish but by no means restricted to them—created hundreds of new Catholic communities on those continents. Immigrants brought about virtually the same result in Canada and the United States and even, to a degree, in Britain.[11] Meanwhile, as if to thicken the paradox, the old European churches in Belgium, in the German-speaking lands, and particularly in France made peace with the middle classes and flourished materially as though the disasters of the Enlightenment and the Revolution had never occurred.[12]

Pius IX, moreover, in putting together a well-oiled machine in the departments and bureaus of the Roman curia, had dramatically transformed the practical relations between the ecclesiastical center and the multitude of local Catholic communities. The papacy during his time assumed a preponderant direction over the day-to-day fortunes of the universal church. This administrative achievement—analogous to the process of centralization in function going on at the same time within secular states—may perhaps have been due less to calculation than to a simple reaction to unforeseen circumstances. The immense personal popularity of Pio Nono, in the new age of the penny press and cheap fares to Rome, played an important part in this development, but so did other, rather more abstruse factors. Revolutions had destroyed the powers of the old prince-bishops and the aristocratic class from which they had sprung. The Vatican's unexpectedly successful policy of engaging in direct diplomatic negotiations with the governments of nominally Catholic countries in Europe and Latin America, and of entering into formal treaties or concordats

---

10. Charles Pouthas, *Le pontificat de Pie IX* (Paris, n. d. [1968]), 330–33, and Roger Aubert, "L'église catholique de la crise de 1848 à la première guerre mondiale," and F. B. Pike, "L'église et la societé civile en Amérique latine jusqu'a la fin du XIXe siècle," in Roger Aubert et al. (eds.), *Nouvelle histoire de l'église*, 5 vols. (Paris: 1975), 5:98–120, 363–69.

11. Pouthas, *Pie IX*, 329–30.

12. See chapter 1.

with them, had strongly eroded centers of local ecclesiastical authority. In some places—in the United States and in Austria, for example[13]—tensions dividing the bishops from the lower clergy became severe enough to necessitate the interposition of a referee or an arbiter, a role the pope and his Roman administrators were more than happy to fill. Old fashioned Gallicanism, rendered more or less obsolete by liberal governments that professed sectarian neutrality, received its coup de grâce at the First Vatican Council in 1870; the definition of papal infallibility, while it was much more moderate than the most zealous Ultramontanes—and, no doubt, Pius IX himself—had wanted, nevertheless brought with it a large measure of prestige. In short, the long-admitted theoretical authority of the pope—a fullness of jurisdiction granting him the right to intervene in any Catholic community, any where, at any time—had acquired a capacity for practical implementation to a degree without precedent over the previous nineteen centuries. It was richly ironic that just at the moment the papacy lost its ancient temporal power in central Italy its control over ecclesiastical decision making should have been so much enhanced.[14]

ON THE INTELLECTUAL FRONT, however, the area most meaningful to people like Ernest Renan, the Roman church appeared even more poverty-stricken and vulnerable than its French daughter. In the spring of 1846—the year Pius IX was elected—Guillaume Meignan, then a young priest resident in Rome, reported to a friend back in France: "Roman theology is altogether too careless of all that happens around it. Generally speaking, rationalism is badly understood and is opposed with futility. History has not a single celebrated representative. Linguistics are neglected. The study of medicine is backward and of law is [stagnant]."[15] Some months later John Henry Newman, recently converted to Catholicism and preparing himself in Rome for ordination, shared with one of his Oxford-trained disciples his impressions of sacred studies in the Eternal City. He had been told

that we should find very little theology here, and a talk we had yesterday with one of the Jesuit fathers here shows we shall find little philosophy. It arose from our talking of the Greek studies of the Propaganda[16] and asking whether the youths learned Aristotle. "O no—he said—Aristotle is in no favor here—no, not in Rome:—not St. Thomas. I have read Aristotle and St. Thos, and owe a great deal to them, but they are out of favor here and throughout Italy. St. Thomas is a great saint—people don't

13. See O'Connell, *John Ireland*, 166–73, and John W. Boyer, *Political Radicalism in Late Imperial Vienna: Origins of the Christian Social Movement, 1848–1897* (Chicago: 1981), 343–46.

14. Roger Aubert, "L'Église catholique de la crise de 1848 à la première guerre mondiale," in Aubert et al. (eds.), *Nouvelle histoire*, 5:65–79, and Aubert, *Pie IX*, 262–310. For the workings of an all-important curial office, see Carlo Falconi, *Il Cardinale Antonelli* (Milan: 1983), 257–75.

15. Quoted in Aubert, *Pie IX*, 184.

16. The Congregation of the Propaganda was the curial bureau in charge of Catholic activities in mission lands, of which, in 1846, England was one. Attached to it was a seminary in which Newman was attending lectures.

dare to speak against him—they profess to reverence him, but put him aside." I asked what philosophy they *did* adopt. He said *none.* "Odds and ends—whatever seems to them best. . . . *Facts* are the great things, and nothing else."[17]

From these testimonies it would appear that Pio Nono had been handed an intellectual legacy that paid as little attention to the treasures of the past as to the dangers of the present. The trouble was that during his long pontificat hardly anything happened to reverse this sorry state of affairs. With some notable exceptions in archaeology and in the publication of primitive Christian manuscripts—much of the latter edited by resident Frenchmen and Germans—the caliber of scholarly activity in Rome remained as slipshod as Meignan and Newman had found it to be. The notoriously ineffectual pontifical universities routinely awarded doctorates to clerical students who did little more than fulfill a year's residency requirement. Except for a handful of Jesuits at the Gregorian, hardly any of the professors in these institutions engaged in serious research. And what made the situation worse, and very difficult to correct, was the arrogant self-satisfaction indulged in by most of the insular Roman academics. Enemies of the papacy delighted in stressing these deficiencies, but friends found them no less trying. Even so pious and loyal an Ultramontane as the German historian Johannes Janssen was scandalized by the neglect of the incomparably rich Roman archives, by the shoddy organization of the libraries, and by the indifference of the authorities to scientific work of any kind. He sadly quoted a young Italian acquaintance: "Here studies are dead. The only thing that counts here is getting ahead."[18]

Neither Pius IX nor his immediate entourage was equipped to appreciate the long-term peril involved in such attitudes. Their own very bad education tended to make them not only obtuse but suspicious, worrying that some clever tricks might be played on them. Not that the pope, embattled as he was, could have been blamed for harboring misgivings about the world of secular scholarship, which appeared in its own way as hostile to the church as the politicians did. Renan was by no means the only member of the European intelligentsia who predicted, and hoped for, the eradication of Catholicism. The seeds of tragedy, however, were sown by the clumsy manner in which Pius IX's Vatican dealt with Catholic scholars, an evil fruit bred in the intellectual wasteland that papal Rome had allowed itself to become. Indeed, the officials of the Roman curia were habitually skeptical and wary of any learned initiative, however well intentioned and whatever its source, and their style of reponse was all too often heedless administrative fiat. A spectacular example of this occurred in 1863, with the issuance of the so-called Munich Brief, which chided the participants in a conference of university historians and theologians

17. Newman to Dalgairns, 22 November, 1846, in Stephen Dessain et al. (eds.), *The Letters and Diaries of John Henry Newman*, 31 vols. (London and Oxford: 1961–), 11:279.
    18. See Aubert, *Pie IX*, 185–88.

convened in that city, and which laid down the principle that all scientific research carried on by Catholics had to be authenticated by the decisions of the Roman congregations.[19]

It may well have been that this particular intervention had been sparked at least partly by the Teutonic insensitivity of the conference's organizer, the distinguished historian Ignaz von Döllinger, who pompously compared the "German school," which defended Catholicism "with artillery," to the "Roman school," armed only "with bows and arrows." But, as was so often the case in matters of this kind, the subtle Newman discerned beyond rivalries of the moment the crux of the problem. Confrontation had replaced the process of mature deliberation. "Why was it," he asked rhetorically, "that the Medieval Schools were so vigorous?" Because, he replied, the process then had been one of creative interplay between the magisterium and individual researchers who, "when they went wrong, a stronger and truer intellect set them down—and as time went on, and the dispute got perilous, and a controversialist obstinate, then at length Rome interfered—at length, not at first. Truth is wrought out of many minds, working freely." But the very *scholae* that gave scope to the disputatious give-and-take so essential to the maturation of Thomas Aquinas and his contemporaries had gone whistling down the wind. "As far as I can make out this [freedom] has ever been the rule of the Church till now, when the . . . French Revolution having destroyed the Schools of Europe, a sort of centralization has been established at headquarters—and the individual thinker in France, England, or Germany is brought into immediate collision with the most sacred authorities of the Divine Polity."[20]

THE CONCLAVE THAT FOLLOWED the death of Pius IX was brief, reaching only into the third scrutiny when, on February 20, 1878, the cardinal-camerlengo, Gioacchino Pecci, secured forty-four out of a possible sixty-one votes, accepted the homage of his former colleagues, and declared that henceforth he would be called Leo, the thirteenth pontiff to bear that name.[21] Pecci, descended from the petty nobility of the old Papal States, had as a youth joined the papal civil service and had thrived there so much that in 1843 he had been consecrated an archbishop and sent as nuncio to Belgium. This first venture in diplomacy had not been particularly successful, though no doubt the young prelate—he was only thirty-three—learned important lessons for the future.[22]

19. Aubert, *Pie IX*, 205–9, and J. Friedrich, *Ignaz von Döllinger: Sein Leben auf seines schriftlichen Nachlasses*, 3 vols. (Munich: 1901), 3:159–70.

20. Newman to Ornsby, 26 March, 1863, *Letters and Diaries*, 20:424–26.

21. The standard account is Soderini, *Leone XIII*. See also the second volume of Josef Schmidlin, *Papstgeschichte der neuesten Zeit*, 4 vols. (Munich: 1939). For a brief summary, see Raymond H. Schmandt, "The Life and Work of Leo XIII," in Edward T. Gargan (ed.), *Leo XIII and the Modern World* (New York: 1961), 15–48. See also the bibliography in Aubert et al. (eds.), *Nouvelle histoire*, 5:764–66.

22. On this point, see Soderini, *Leone XIII*, 1:106–55, who, better informed, corrects the rosier

He had been until lately the archbishop-bishop of Perugia,[23] having come to Rome and taken up residence in the Palazzo Falconieri as camerlengo only in 1877. Indeed, some cynics suggested that the dying Pius had named Pecci to that once powerful but now largely ceremonial post because of a tradition that the camerlengo—whose only remaining significant function was to preside over the conclave—could not himself be elected. If so, the old pope's intent to exclude Pecci, no less than the alleged tradition itself, came to naught, as did the speculation of those electors who found Pecci an attractive candidate on the grounds that his uncertain health at age sixty-eight would likely mean a short pontificate: Leo XIII reigned for more than a quarter of a century, and did not breathe his last until he was well into his ninety-fourth year.

There is no proof, to be sure, that Pio Nono—a notoriously affable man who, even when vexed, had a good word to say about almost everybody—had wished to keep Pecci off the papal throne, nor that the cardinals who voted for him had done so with implicit aspiration that he enjoy a happy but limited term in office. Yet Pecci, appointed to Perugia in 1846, a few months before Pius IX's own election, had spent virtually the whole of that tumultuous pontificate up the Tiber from Rome amid the rolling hills and purple landscapes of Umbria, thus reduced to a peripheral position in which clearly the pope and his advisers were determined, for whatever reasons, to keep him. As for the cardinal-electors, they were a group of sober-minded men who, given the record at hand, might well have decided that at least some of the misfortune that had befallen Pius IX had happened precisely because he had lived and reigned, humanly speaking, too long. So the conclave, as it has so often done in the history of the papacy—as it was to do again when Leo XIII himself passed from the scene—turned to a nominee strikingly different from the incumbent who had just died.

One must not, however, read too much into that decision. Papal continuity was a lodestar for whoever sat upon the throne of Saint Peter, and, though a pope might quietly set aside this or that initiative undertaken by a predecessor, he never explicitly repudiated it. Nor is there the slightest reason to suppose that the views of Leo XIII differed substantially from those of Pius IX. But style was something else, as were personality, emphasis, and method. In this instance even the sharp physical contrast between the two men pointed toward much deeper and more significant disparities in disposition and temperament: the stout, ruddy, affable, narrowly zealous Pius IX; and Leo XIII, seemingly tall because he was thin almost to the point of emaciation, physically ugly except for his graceful and expressive hands, cerebral, austere, subsisting on a few lire worth of food a day, courteous but reserved, punctilious, a man of scholarly habits who valued his privacy and disliked crowds, sophisticated and

picture drawn in Édouard Lecanuet, *L'Église de France sous la troisième république. Les premières années du pontificat de Léon XIII* (Paris: 1931), 5.

23. He held the personal rank of archbishop, though Perugia was not an archdiocese.

cosmopolitan, a bureaucrat who savored above all else the arts of governance and who, for their sake, restrained a propensity toward impatience and bad temper.[24]

A SIGNAL OF THE NEW PAPAL MOOD came on Leo XIII's very first day in office, when he cabled Kaiser Wilhelm in Berlin his pledge to do all in his power to bring to an amicable settlement the church–state conflict in Prussia and other parts of Germany. And indeed what chief minister Otto von Bismarck and his aides had dubbed the *Kulturkampf* did, after much haggling, come to an end, but not without some sacrifice of local Catholic prestige and influence; the barons of the German Center party despised Bismarck and his policies with a passion the more remote Leo XIII could never have mustered.[25] The pope's German initiative was followed by similar undertakings in other troubled areas, like Spain, where Leo urged the Catholic populace to give up their fantasies of a Carlist monarchy and to adjust themselves to the unobjectionable features of liberal institutions, lest worse befall them;[26] and, in a more renowned case, France, where eventually the pope urged reluctant Catholics to rally to the support of the Third Republic—the policy of *ralliement*, as it came to be called—a plea to accept the real world as it was and not as they might have liked it to be.[27]

Leo XIII has been called, rightly, a "universalist" pontiff, to distinguish him from his more narrowly focused predecessor and successor.[28] But the legitimate accommodation to changing events that he urged upon his spiritual children in other lands he proved himself less willing to apply at home. The fall of the Papal States and their incorporation into the Kingdom of Italy, inevitable in the wisdom of hindsight, did not necessarily seem so at the time. In fact, Italian foreign policy over the next generation was obsessed with preventing the recrudescence of the popes' temporal power: the Triple Alliance of the 1880s with Austria and Germany contained guarantees to Italy in this regard, and as late as 1915 the Treaty of London, whereby Italy agreed to enter World War I on the side of the Allies, included a clause prohibiting the Holy See from any participation in a peace conference, lest its territorial claims receive international notice.[29] The "prisoner of the Vatican," similarly obsessed, scornfully rejected in advance any proposal of rapprochement from a government guilty, he maintained, of unprovoked invasion and pillage. Over the twenty-five years of his pontificate he formally protested Italian aggression to

---

24. See the comparison in Aubert, "L'Église catholique," 9–14.

25. See Edward Crankshaw, *Bismarck* (New York: 1981), 344–45, and Margaret Lavinia Anderson, *Windhorst: A Political Biography* (Oxford: 1981), 273–86, 344–52.

26. Aubert, "L'Église catholique," 110–12.

27. See Xavier de Montclos (ed.), *Le toast d'Alger. Documents, 1890–1891* (Paris: 1966), 4–43.

28. Binchy, *Church and State*, 55–56.

29. Carlton J. H. Hayes, *A Generation of Materialism, 1871–1900* (New York: 1941), 49–51, and Binchy, *Church and State*, 58, 296.

the European powers no less than sixty times. The observances of the pope's golden jubilees of ordination (1887) and of episcopal consecration (1893), carefully orchestrated by himself, were occasions upon which the Catholic world was encouraged—indeed instructed—to express outrage at the treatment inflicted upon its venerable head.[30] As long as Leo XIII lived, no one who sought an audience of the king at the Quirinal Palace would be received within the precincts of the Vatican. Two exclusive and competing court nobilities grew up, the "whites" around the king, the "blacks" around the pope. The grandiose liturgical celebrations that had formerly brightened papal Rome were no longer celebrated.

"We looked upon the king [of Italy] as simply a victorious brigand," loyally observed one English Catholic visitor to Rome during these years.[31] But, in fact, forced annexation of the Papal States was not the only or even the most destructive aspect of the political campaign against the church. Suppression of "useless" religious orders and confiscation of their property, seizure of collegiate foundations and their funds, elimination of the distinct jurisdiction of ecclesiastical courts, the control of seminaries, and the secularization of marriage, education, and charitable trusts: this standard anticlerical legislation, put on the books first in Piedmont and then, when unification was complete, in Italy at large, posed the threat, as Catholics saw it, of gradual strangulation.

Latin anticlericalism was (and is) a phenomenon difficult for northerners to understand. It included elements of Enlightenment skepticism, age-old resentment at the economic and legal advantages enjoyed by the clergy, and a certain familiarity with clerical mores—not surprising given the relatively large number of priests and religious—that inevitably bred a measure of contempt. In Italy Catholicism's hold had been so firm and so pervasive for so long that critics of it, since the days of Machiavelli, had had to adopt, at least rhetorically, a strongly militant opposition. This inclination had if anything increased during the nineteenth century when resistance to an otherwise triumphant liberalism had been spearheaded by the popes and their minions. By Leo XIII's time there was added to ordinary liberal hostility the virulent anti-Catholicism of Freemasonry, which purported to supply for its votaries a substitute ritual as well as a substitute dogma.[32] Intricately interwoven with these various interests and values was the emerging nationalism, new to Italy—for so long, in Metternich's words, merely "a geographical expression"—and apparently at odds with the international pretensions of the church.

Yet in some respects Italian anticlericalism seemed almost frivolous when

30. See the documents assembled in the Archivio Segreto Vaticano, Segreteria di Stato (1878–1914), rubric 1.

31. Maisie Ward, *The Wilfrid Wards and the Transition*. 1. *The Nineteenth Century* (New York: 1934), 56.

32. See Albert Lantoine, *Histoire de la franc-maçonnerie française* (Paris: 1925), and José Sánchez, *Anticlericalism: A Brief History* (Notre Dame, Ind.: 1972), esp. 143–60.

compared to the harshly rationalist variety practiced in France or the violence-prone kind in Spain. Perhaps that was because in Italy the strategy of those who harassed the church was never really clear, not even to themselves. Were the anticlericals moved by simple dislike of the androgynous sacerdotal caste, by a desire to keep priests from meddling in matters that did not concern them, by a reluctance to be ruled by priests, as had been the case in the old Papal States? Or were they, in imitation of Renan, convinced of the superstitious wickedness of Catholicism and therefore dedicated to its destruction root and branch? For Leo XIII this may have been a distinction without a difference, but in fact the oppression he publicly deplored was softened by countless implicit understandings, *combinazioni*, deals worked out at the local level, laws passed and never enforced, even secret lines of communication maintained between the Quirinal and the Vatican, in short, by the Italian genius for practical compromise. Thus the pope might forbid Italian Catholics to vote in general elections, but not in local ones.

This is not to say that there was no persecution or that periods of acute tension did not give rise to nasty incidents. The peasant masses may have gone for the time being virtually untouched by the quarrel, but it was very different for the educated urban Catholic who found a career in the civil service or the professions blocked by Masonic influence, often heard his religion mocked and blasphemed in the most sophisticated circles, and sometimes had to put up with abuse (mostly verbal) from shiftless toughs. "You go to Mass too often" was the warning such a person frequently heard.[33]

Here was the school in which Leo XIII and his curia learned to define the word *modern*. It had small attraction for them. It meant, among other things, the derision of the sacred, the theft of age-old endowments, the imposition by an elite of a positivist and agnostic mind-set upon formerly Christian peoples. The pope determined to encounter the challenge of modernity, not with the simplistic reaction of his predecessor, but with a *combinazione* of his own: a reluctant acceptance of those aspects of the phenomenon he judged morally neutral; a fierce opposition to the parts of it—like Freemasonry and socialism and the general drift of unbelief—most objectionable to him; a resolve to keep control of events in his own hands by maintaining and even strengthening the structure of centralized decision making he had inherited from his predecessor; and, finally, a determination to demonstrate that the old church, far from being passé, could, out of the wealth of its tradition, contribute positively to the earthly as well as to the eternal well-being of contemporary men and women.

The pope and his advisers, deeply marked by their Italian experience, were no less suspicious than their predecessors of any initiative or movement that appeared to imperil what was left of the institutional equilibrium. Diplomacy was their strong suit. They were astute and hard-working, and, for the most

33. Binchy, *Church and State*, 46–51.

part, sure-handed—even smugly so, some of them—but they were administrators and rulers, not thinkers. Nor did the concerns of thinkers take precedence with them. "The Roman Church governs itself by the views of the masses," one shrewd observer wrote, "whether represented by the direct manifestations of their likes and dislikes, or, indirectly, by the attitude of governments. But neither princes nor people are interested in the conciliation of intelligence and religion."[34] Perhaps the situation might have been less provocatively described by saying that pastoral concern for the overwhelming majority of Catholics who had no intellectual pretensions always weighed most heavily on the papal scales.

Even so, given Leo XIII's reflective temperament, it is not surprising that his program revealed early on an intellectual component which was both speculative and pragmatic and through which he hoped to provide an intellectual context for his diplomatic and social policies. The surprise was that *Aeterni Patris*, the pope's third encyclical, dated August 4, 1879, laid out a set of principles that seemed to many—friends and enemies alike—so boldly anachronistic and irrelevant. Yet the passage of time was to show that of the many memorable statements issued over the years from this pope's energetic pen— encyclicals on the nature of liberty, on Christian marriage, on historical studies, on the relationship between capital and labor, "on the condition of the working classes,"[35] and on a host of other subjects—*Aeterni Patris* possessed special significance by reason not only of its content but of its timing. It was promulgated at the beginning of Leo's pontificate and thus provided a kind of guidepost for things to come. More than that, the call for a restoration of a "Christian philosophy" and specifically for the revival of the teaching of Thomas Aquinas was a tacit admission that the church's house of intellect stood in grave need of repair. In committing himself to this long-term reform, the wily Gioacchino Pecci was not forgetting the more immediate crises that faced him. Until his powers began to fail toward the end of his long life, he proved himself an extraordinarily subtle, sophisticated, and well-informed man, but even he thought he discerned behind, say, the biblical scholar who questioned the Mosaic authorship of the Pentateuch, an anticlerical politician anxious to close the Catholic schools, suppress the religious orders, and enshrine, once more, the Goddess of Reason upon the high altar of Notre Dame.

LEO XIII began the argument of *Aeterni Patris* by insisting that the fulfillment of Christ's commission to the apostles, to teach all nations what had been revealed to them, had been "the constant aim" of the church through the centuries, had evoked the "incessant labors of individual bishops, . . . the

---

34. Duchesne to von Hügel, 2 March, 1894, quoted in Michael De la Bedoyere, *The Life of Baron von Hügel* (London: 1951), 7.

35. This was the justly renowned *Rerum novarum* of 15 May, 1891. For the English text, see Claudia Carlen (ed.), *The Papal Encyclicals, 1878–1903* (Raleigh, N.C.: 1981), 241–61.

published laws and decrees of councils, and especially the constant watchfulness of the Roman pontiffs, to whom, as successors of the blessed Peter in the primacy of the apostles, belong the right and office of teaching and confirming their brethren in the faith." But human reason, led astray by bad science and shallow philosophy, has consistently thrown up obstacles to the propagation of divine truth and thereby brought confusion and unhappiness down upon humankind: witness "the bitter strifes of these days . . . that vex public and private life." Sound intellectual principles, on the other hand, though they cannot by themselves discern the data reserved to revelation, can be, when properly applied, of inestimable assistance.

The natural helps with which the grace of the divine wisdom, strongly and sweetly disposing all things, has supplied the human race are neither to be despised nor neglected, chief among which is evidently the right use of philosophy. For not in vain did God set the light of reason in the human mind; and so far is the superadded light of faith from extinguishing or lessening the power of the intelligence that it completes it rather, and by adding to its strength renders it capable of greater things.

To this Christian philosophy, to this handmaiden of a robust theology, Pope Leo gave a broad historical dimension. The doctors and Fathers of the early church, he argued, had themselves been philosophers, had themselves "well understood that, according to the divine plan, the restorer of human science is Christ, who is the power and the wisdom of God, and in whom are hid all the treasures of wisdom and knowledge." From Justin Martyr to Augustine of Hippo they had all appreciated that "in the case of such doctrines that the human intelligence may perceive, it is . . . just that philosophy makes use of its own method, principles, and arguments." This tradition was brilliantly continued by the Scholastic masters who flourished in the medieval universities and who "addressed themselves to a great work—that of diligently collecting, and sifting, and storing up, as it were, for the use and convenience of posterity the rich and fertile harvests of Chrisitian learning scattered abroad in the voluminous works of the holy Fathers."

But no one accomplished this and related tasks with as much acuity as the "angelic doctor," Thomas Aquinas:

With his spirit at once humble and swift, his memory ready and tenacious, his life spotless throughout, a lover of truth for its own sake, richly endowed with human and divine science, like the sun he heated the world with the warmth of his virtues and filled it with the splendor of his teaching. Philosophy has no part which he did not touch finely at once and thoroughly; on the law of reasoning, on God and incorporeal substances, on man and other sensible beings, on human actions and their principles, he reasoned in such a manner that in him there is wanting neither a full array of questions, nor an apt disposal of the various parts, nor the best method of proceeding, nor soundness of principles or strength of argument, nor clearness and elegance of style, nor a facility for explaining what is abstruse.

Such enthusiasm for "this remarkable man"—even to the rather startling extent of praising Saint Thomas's "elegance of style"—Pope Leo maintained was in accord with the approbation of the faculties of the great universities of Europe, with the endorsement of a score of religious orders, and with the blessings of earlier pontiffs and ecumenical councils—most recently that of the Vatican, in which the Thomistic dictum that the human mind is capable of grasping metaphysical reality was powerfully proclaimed.[36]

But besides such authoritative pronouncements, the discipline itself exhibits a preeminent intellectual value. Leo XIII professed himself convinced that the revival of the philosophy of the schools—Scholasticism, particularly that variety of it proposed explicitly by Thomas Aquinas—would contribute to the "advancement" of all the arts and sciences, would, "if judiciously taught," lend them "force and light and aid." And he brushed aside vigorously any charge of anachronism: "If anything is taken up with too great subtlety by the Scholastic doctors, or too carelessly stated—if there be anything that ill agrees with the discoveries of a later age, or, in a word, improbable in whatever way—it does not enter our mind to propose that for imitation for our age." To avoid such an aberration the pope offered one sure technique and, in doing so, drew a perhaps crucial distinction between Scholasticism and Thomism:

Let carefully selected teachers endeavor to implant the doctrine of Thomas Aquinas in the minds of students, and set forth clearly his solidity and excellence over others. . . . But, lest the false for the true or the corrupt for the pure be drunk in, be . . . watchful that the doctrine of Thomas be drawn from his own fountains, or at least from those rivulets which, derived from the very fount, have thus far flowed, according to the established agreement of learned men, pure and clear. Be careful to guard the minds of youth from those which are said to flow thence, but in reality are gathered from strange and unwholesome streams.[37]

So the pope made his proposal to restore intellectual respectability to the Catholic community rest practically upon the humdrum recommendation of texts composed in the thirteenth century. *Tolle, lege*, he said in effect, take up and read what Saint Thomas himself has written, and the first giant step will have been taken. Beware, he added in the same breath, many of Thomas's interpreters and strictly avoid most of them. To give flesh to the bare bones of his words, the pope commissioned a critical edition of the *Opera* of Aquinas, resulting in the celebrated Leonine Edition.

36. Most of the attention given to the First Vatican Council (1870–71) has understandably focused upon the dramatic struggle over papal infallibility, which resulted in the constitution "Pastor aeternus" of 18 July, 1870. More important, however, in the present inquiry was the constitution on faith, "Dei Filius," promulgated the previous 24 April, in which the capacity of the unaided human intelligence to demonstrate the existence of God and related matters was solemnly decreed. For the documents, see Henricus Denziger et al. (eds.), *Enchiridion symbolorum, definitionum, et declarationum de rebus fidei et morum*, 28th ed. (Freiburg-im-Bresgau, 1952), 491–500. For useful commentary on "Dei Filius," see Roger Aubert, *Le problème de l'acte de foi* (Louvain, 1969 ed.), 131–222.

37. Carlen (ed.), *Encyclicals, 1878–1903*, 17–27.

IF LEO XIII'S APPEAL was not quite a voice crying in the wilderness, his call for a restoration of Thomism as the norm for Catholic intellectuals echoed emptily, at first, in most places. Not untypical was the reaction of one American bishop, who prudently named the new seminary he founded after Saint Thomas Aquinas, but who confided to his intimates that he "fail[ed] to see the good in Leo XIII['s] letter on Philosophy." To this prelate and his subjects Thomism was hardly more than an antique curiosity easily picked up by a few months of casual examination.[38] Professors in seminaries, where one might have expected the pope's writ to have enjoyed the heaviest weight, smilingly paid formal obeissance to *Aeterni Patris*, and continued to ignore the Thomistic texts and to teach out of the same psuedo-Scholastic manuals as before.[39] Indeed, the same unsystematic accumulation of "facts," about which the Roman Jesuit had commented to Newman in 1846,[40] seemed as securely the methodological norm as ever.

And yet, by that time, a quiet revolution had already begun in Italy. Eighteen-forty-six, the very year Pius IX was elected and Gioacchino Pecci went to Perugia, Canon Gaetano Sansevirino founded in Naples an academy of Thomistic studies. On the original faculty of that institution was a thirty-five-year-old Jesuit, Matteo Liberatore, who in 1850 left Naples for Rome where he assumed direction of a new Jesuit journal, the *Civiltà Cattolica*. By then an eccentric German confrere of Liberatore named Josef Kleutgen was well established there, zealously introducing Thomist principles to the seminarians at the German College and applying those same principles to the consulting work he was frequently called upon to perform for various Roman congregations.[41] Meanwhile Pecci, who remembered how impressed he had been by a maverick Thomist professor he had had during his student days, opened a center for the study of Aquinas in Perugia, to which his brother Giuseppe came as a teacher and a young Dominican friar named Tommaso Zigliara as a student. For all these budding Thomists—who no doubt shared the wonderful exhilaration that accompanies singeing the beard of accepted convention—the election of Pecci to the chair of Peter must have seemed an intervention of Providence almost too good to be true.

38. O'Connell, *John Ireland*, 568.

39. For an example, see David G. Schultenover, *George Tyrrell: In Search of Catholicism* (Shepherdstown; W.V.: 1981), 29–32. Such manuals were still commonly used when I was a seminarian in the 1950s. They were written, their authors noted near the title page, "ad mentem sancti Thomae." I was as mystified by this phrase as were observers of seminary education in the late nineteenth century: see, for example, Lecanuet, *Les dernières années . . . de Pie IX*, 293.

40. See note 17, this chapter.

41. See, for example, the long and detailed analysis provided by Kleutgen in 1857 for the Congregation of the Index of the work of his fellow Jesuit, the Austrian Anton Günther, printed in Konrad Deufel, *Kirche und Tradition* (Munich: 1976), 437–87. Günther's books were placed on the Index, a quasi-judicial sentence to which he submitted. For Kleutgen, who "linked Germany to Rome," see also Thomas Franklin O'Meara, *Romantic Idealism and Roman Catholicism: Schelling and the Theologians* (Notre Dame, Ind.: 1982), 189–91.

Aeterni Patris—early drafts of which were written by Kleutgen and Libera-tore[42]—was immediately followed by the pope's determined efforts to fashion, at least in Rome, an institutional setting in which the ideals of the encyclical might be pursued. The long moribund Academy of Saint Thomas Aquinas was activated. Faculties of the pontifical universities—the Propaganda, the Angelicum, the Appolinare, and most notably the uniquely influential Gre-gorian—were purged of those professors like Newman's informant of thirty years before.[43] These papal initiatives, however, bore little fruit at the start: the pool of competent neo-Thomists was too small and shallow to provide ef-fective replacements for those dismissed, one of whom was banished to far-off Holland. But time and relentless exertion on the part of the pope and his auxil-iaries gradually altered this circumstance, so that after a generation of neo-Scholastic predominance in Rome—affecting directly the church students from all corners of the world who matriculated there—the papal reforms had clearly taken hold; and not only in the Eternal City but in places as far away as Fribourg in Switzerland and Louvain in Belgium, where distinguished cen-ters of Thomistic studies had also been established.[44]

Quality too had improved, so much so that one cautious English Catholic commentator, no Thomist himself, was moved to observe: "The Encyclical was for a time applied in a somewhat restricted sense. By degrees, however, the largeness of the doctrine of Aquinas has also had, inevitably, its effect in broadening a method of philosophy which in many modern scholastic manuals had lost its original elasticity."[45] And the distinguished Harvard philosopher Josiah Royce exulted particularly in the restoration of the classical texts. In Royce's view contemporary Protestantism had pretty much given up on the intellectual dimensions of Christian dogma; not so Catholicism, with the re-sult that its philosophical concerns ranged far beyond mere "technicalities," and tried to engage—so Royce thought—the modern world. "Pope Leo, after all, let loose a thinker amongst his people—a thinker, to be sure, of unques-tioned orthodoxy, but after all a genuine thinker whom the textbooks had long tried, as it were, to keep lifeless, and who, when once revived, proves to be full of suggestion of new problems and of an effort toward new solutions."[46]

But these statements of qualified approval came at the end, not at the begin-ning, of Leo XIII's pontificate. The struggle for the mind of the Catholic church meantime was joined, and that struggle was by no means over when Pope Leo

---

42. See Gerald A. McCool, *From Unity to Pluralism: The Internal Evolution of Thomism* (New York: 1989), 6–13.

43. See Luciano Malusa, *Neotomismo e Intransigentismo Cattolico* (Milan: 1986), 278–80, and Pierre Thibault, *Savoir et pouvoir* (Quebec: 1972), 151–55.

44. Roger Aubert, *Aspects divers du neo-thomism sous le pontificat de Léon XIII* (Rome: 1961), 40.

45. Wilfrid Ward, in the *Fortnightly Review* (1903), quoted in J. Derek Holmes, "Some English Reactions to the Publication of *Aeterni Patris*," *Downside Review* 93 (October 1975): 279.

46. Josiah Royce, "Pope Leo's Philosophical Movement: Its Relation to Modern Thought," *Tablet* (London) 102 (15 August, 1903): 260–62, excerpted from the *Boston Evening Transcript*, 29 July, 1903.

died in the summer of 1903. The Leonine revival of Thomism had, however, defined dramatically the terms that, willy-nilly, contestants on both sides would employ. The first of these was the Scholastic rejection of the "modern" philosophical tradition that began with Descartes and was confirmed most persuasively by Kant, that one's knowledge of reality—one's "philosophy," taking the word in its broadest sense—must be essentially a reflection on one's own mental states; and the adoption of "commonsense" realism, rooted in the sensualism of Aristotle and in the epistemology based upon it as taught by Saint Thomas.[47] It was not accidental that Liberatore, as early as 1857, had attacked Kant's ethical doctrine on the basis of the latter's allegedly skewed theory of knowledge.[48] Nor had Kleutgen chosen idly when he titled his two most important books *Die Theologie der Vorzeit* (5 volumes, 1853–74) and *Der Philosophie der Vorzeit* (2 volumes, 1860–63): *Vorzeit* meant for him the Scholastic golden age, the time before Descartes and systematic doubt and all the evils that flowed therefrom, when Saint Thomas had reigned supreme among the doctors.

This rather naïve view of history had its counterpart in *Aeterni Patris* itself. Thus one found there a perplexing tendency to mix together indiscriminately the development of the theological and philosophical disciplines. And one would never gather from the content of the encyclical that Scholastics had over the centuries quarreled incessantly among themselves, that in fact public acceptance of the teachings of Aquinas had experienced many ups and downs, that even "common sense realism" had for long periods been obscured by scholastic nominalism. But then an intellectual movement rooted in the central importance of texts six centuries old appeared distressingly static to those contemporaries of Leo XIII for whom history had become a vital and relentless process of deveopment.

IN HIS LAST WILL Pius IX had directed that his tomb in Saint Lawrence-Outside-the-Walls should be austere and simple in the extreme. Instead, some time after the perilous journey of July 13, 1881, was completed, his remains were laid to rest within an extravagant funerary chapel that cost a quarter-million lire. The artistically sophisticated may have judged the monument in dubious taste, but even they had to admit that its medieval motif was appropriate. More significant, it was paid for by the pennies of ordinary people from all over the world, people who wanted to express their veneration for Pio Nono. Here was one among many signs of contradiction.

47. See, for instance, Gerald A. McCool, "The Centenary of *Aeterni Patris*," *Homiletic and Pastoral Review* 79 (January 1979): 8–15.

48. Matteo Liberatore, *Institutiones philosophicae: Ethica et Jus Naturae* (Rome: 1857), 3–9.

CHAPTER 3

"Land-travel or Seafaring"

I am a convert only in the sense of having, owing to a variety of circumstances, had to regain and to conquer for myself, morally, spiritually, and intellectually, a positive faith in the Catholic religion.

—*Friedrich von Hügel (1906)*[1]

LEO XIII'S FIRST PROMOTIONS to the College of Cardinals were announced in the late winter of 1879, about six months before the issuance of *Aeterni Patris*. Even the keenest Vatican observers probably missed the significance of two of the appointments. The red hat bestowed upon Giuseppe Pecci, the new pope's older brother, could be explained as simply an instance of good-natured nepotism. And the promotion of the Corsican Tommaso Zigliara was similarly attributed to Leo XIII's cordial, almost paternal relationship with the forty-five-year-old Dominican, whom he had ordained to the priesthood more than twenty years before. But the fact was quite otherwise. Both the elder Pecci and Zigliara had been for years closely involved in the Thomistic revival in Italy; for them and for it the pope had large plans.[2]

Among the foreigners elevated at the same consistory, Leo appeared anxious to strike an ideological balance. Thus he honored Louis-Édouard-Desiré Pie, bishop of Poitiers, who unabashedly claimed a high rank among the toughest, most unbending conservatives, among the most ultra of the Ultramontanes in the whole universal hierarchy. Over against Pie stood the most celebrated designee of all, the Englishman John Henry Newman, priest of the Oratory. "Il mio cardinale," the pope said of Newman, "my very own cardinal." Resistance to his appointment had been formidable. "It was not easy," Leo insisted, "it was not easy: they said he was too liberal." Such opinions had been common within the Roman curia for twenty years, and Newman took quiet satisfaction

---

1. Von Hügel to Bishop, 23 May, 1906, quoted in *Dublin Review* 227 (July 1953): 289.
2. See chapter 2.

that they could no longer enjoy official sanction: "The cloud is lifted from me forever."

Though he suffered from a heavy cold and a cough during his stay in Rome, Newman was pleased that the festivities connected with his elevation went off splendidly. Leo XIII received him with special marks of honor and affection. Italian ladies who saw him at the various functions squealed with delight at the frail and venerable figure. "Che bel vecchio!," they exclaimed. "Che figura! Pallido si, ma belissimo." Newman was indeed an old man now. Seventy-eight years had stooped him, had turned his hair all white, had left his narrow face with its great hooked nose pale, as the ladies said, as alabaster. But not a whit of his natural dignity had deserted him, nor his shy warmth. The eyes were as brilliant as ever, the hands as expressive, and the high-pitched voice was as musical as it had been a half-century before when, from the pulpit of the Church of Saint Mary the Virgin, he had spent Sunday afternoons bewitching a generation of Oxford undergraduates.[3]

One particularly moving moment in the round of celebrations came on May 14 when Newman, now cardinal deacon of the Holy Roman church under the title of San Giorgio in Valabro, paid a ceremonial visit to the English College on the Via di Monserrato. Once the old man was settled in the common room, the crowd of dignitaries gave way for a strikingly handsome woman of late middle age. "My lord cardinal," she said, reading from a single sheet of paper,

we, your devoted English, Scotch [*sic*], Irish and American children at present residing in Rome, earnestly wishing to testify our deep and affectionate veneration of your Eminence's person and character, together with our hearty joy at your elevation to the Sacred Purple, . . . feel that in making you a Cardinal the Holy Father has not only given public testimony of his appreciation of your great merits . . . but has also conferred the greatest possible honour on all English-speaking Catholics who have long looked up to you as their spiritual father.[4]

The noble spokeswoman was Lady Herbert of Lea. Back in England her son-in-law likewise rejoiced in the honor bestowed upon one to whom he remained "deeply, profoundly indebted."[5]

BARON FRIEDRICH VON HÜGEL was an intensely serious man, serious even about his amusements. It was not enough for him to listen to Gilbert and Sullivan; he had to learn all the tunes and lyrics from *Pinafore* and *Iolanthe* by heart. He read philosophical treatises in four modern languages as well as Homer and the Old Testament in the original. But he also read *The Woman in*

---

3. See Marvin R. O'Connell, "Newman: The Victorian Intellectual as Pastor," *Theological Studies* 46 (June 1985): 329–33.

4. Full text in Ward, *Newman*, 2:464.

5. See Lawrence F. Barmann, *Baron Friedrich von Hügel and the Modernist Crisis in England* (Cambridge: 1972), 5.

White and *Lorna Doone* and Thackeray, Trollope, and Scott. Browning he treasured most of all. "We . . . read some Browning last night," he reported to his young wife, absent because of her delicate health. "How I'd like to read you . . . *Any Wife to Any Husband*: it is such a noble poem. And *Waring* which has such an exquisite bit about springtime. Don't I just like Browning—I think the way never to get tired of him, is to read a little of him at a time, but that *thoroughly*, and never to stop, if possible, in the middle of a piece. It all hangs so much together that fragmentary reading ruins it all."[6]

He was only twenty-two at the time, and he already had a solemn and analytical theory of poetry reading. And he already prized the rollicking lines of *Waring*, the first stanza of which afforded a clue—though of course the baron did not recognize it as such—to the part he was destined to play in the tragedy that lay ahead.

> What's become of Waring
> Since he gave us all the slip,
> Chose land-travel or seafaring
> Boots and chest or staff and scrip,
> Rather than pace up and down
> Any longer London-town.

From Rome to Paris to London-town: the multilingual and peripatetic Friedrich von Hügel would provide, whether by land or by sea, whatever fragile unity or coherence possessed by the movement to be labeled Catholic Modernism.

So fateful a role fell to his lot more out of the accidents of his background and education than out of any design. His father, Baron Carl, of an old Rhineland family, had ably served the Austrian Empire as soldier and diplomat. He had entertained as well an abiding, even a consuming, interest in scientific subjects, particularly horticulture. Still unmarried in his late thirties, Baron von Hügel indulged his taste for travel in exotic lands, and spent six uninterrupted years tramping across the Orient and gathering plant samples which he had transported back to his estate near Vienna. While in India he met a Scottish engineer and military officer named Farquharson, a widower with an infant daughter. In 1851 Carl von Hügel and Elizabeth Farquharson contracted a December–May marriage: he was fifty-six, she but nineteen.

Three years earlier he had reentered the imperial service, just in time to experience the upheavals of 1848. When in March of that year the Viennese mob drove Prince Metternich from power, Carl von Hügel had been given the ironic duty of conducting to safe exile the aged and now discredited arbiter of Europe, whose wife had once been his own brother's lover.[7] The revolutionary

---

6. Quoted in De la Bedoyere, *Hügel*, 4.

7. See Guillaume de Bertier de Sauvigny, *Metternich* (n. p. [Paris]: 1986), 473–75. De la Bedoyere, *Hügel*, 15–16, makes the story better than it was by confusing Baron Carl with his brother Clemens.

turmoil had subsided by the year of his wedding, and von Hügel, appointed minister to the court of the grand duke of Tuscany, took his bride to Florence. There, on May 5, 1852, their son Friedrich was born.

The little baron spent the first seven years of his life in the most beautiful city in Europe. Among the first sights he saw were the bronze doors of the Duomo, the Ponte Vecchio, the watchtower soaring gracefully over the Piazza della Signoria, and, across the amber waters of the Arno, toward Castelfiorentina, the vine-covered Tuscan hills. Long afterward he was to describe himself as a pre-Reformation Christian, in the sense of one dedicated to a Catholicsm untroubled by the Protestant challenge and therefore broader, freer, never touchy or defensive. He took some comfort in having as his birthplace the city where such a Catholicism, he believed, had achieved its finest artistic and intellectual flower.[8]

The child spoke German to his father, English to his mother. He learned Italian as a matter of course, and French, still the language of the diplomat and the gentleman, as a duty. He never went to school, then or later. A succession of tutors trained him in the classics and in mathematics, and the rest of the time he read on his own, voraciously and with a markedly Teutonic self-discipline. He did not recall at the end of his life that his father had had much influence on him—"neither my brother nor I ever directly knew him well except as a worn man of 70–75."[9] Yet the cast of Friedrich von Hügel's mind was German, much of what he read was written in German, and, if the convoluted English prose style he acquired is any indication, he thought in German as well. He mirrored his father too in his deep fascination with science, though horticulture was not his passion: "As a boy I grew up with a keen interest in entomology and geology; they helped to develop in me, I think, a double consciousness, of cumulative evidence as an instrument of knowledge [and] of successive stages of development as a subject matter of knowledge."[10]

This urbane and somewhat haphazard educational regimen continued in Brussels to which Carl von Hügel was posted as minister when Friedrich was eight, and seven years after that in England where the old baron, perhaps at the instance of his wife, settled his family upon his retirement from the diplomatic corps. Friedrich brought his books in a half-dozen languages and his collection of rocks and insects to Torquay, and prepared to cultivate in himself the style of an English gentleman of scholarly tastes and independent means. He never quite managed it, for, though he lived in England for the rest of his life, he always remained a thoroughly cosmopolitan man, innocent of national feeling, essentially rootless, with no old school tie or shared memories to rec-

8. See his remarks of October 1918 to a meeting of the nondenominational Christian Student Movement, quoted in Bernard Holland (ed.), *Baron Friedrich von Hügel: Selected Letters, 1896–1924* (London: 1927), 40–41.

9. Quoted in Barmann, *Hügel*, 1. There was a third child, Pauline, who died unmarried in 1901.

10. Quoted in De la Bedoyere, *Hügel*, 17.

ommend him to his peers. His foreign habits and mannerisms routinely startled his neighbors, some of whom supposed him to be, in 1914, a spy. Only
then did he bother to become formally a British subject.

In 1870, when he was eighteen, Freidrich von Hügel came of age in more
than the ordinary meaning of that phrase. His father died, and he himself underwent a prolonged crisis which was at once physical, emotional, and spiritual. He was struck down by a severe attack of typhus which permanantly
impaired his health. For many years he suffered from ill-defined nervous disor-
ders, and even after these had ceased to trouble him he was never robust. His
correspondence was filled with references to the state of his health about which
he worried incessantly. Only months after his wedding he had to flee his bride
and go off with his mother to a health spa in the Midlands—where a chief
diversion was the reading of Browning's poetry—while his wife, herself also
sickly, went with her mother to another watering place. Their houses at
Hampstead, and later at Kensington, resembled infirmaries, crowded as they
were with medicines and nostrums, and with one or the other of them confined
to bed for days at a time.

The typhus also laid upon von Hügel his heaviest physical cross, the deafness that increased with the years and that inevitably introverted him and
made him seem more eccentric than he was. "Deafness," he wrote bitterly,
"means crippledness and a handsome crop of little humiliations." It also meant
a limiting of social communication and a preference for monologue over conversation. The deaf von Hügel was driven to an ever-stronger dependence upon
the members of his family and a small coterie of friends, about whom he was
not as discerning as he might otherwise have been.

Illness and bereavement provided the occasion for what the young baron
called his "first" conversion. At a moment when " 'the world,' which till then
had looked so brilliant to me, turned out so distant, cold and shallow," he
encountered a Dominican friar who helped him to pull away from the muddle
of late-adolescent insecurities, many of them sexual in origin, and to start
down a mystical road from which he never swerved. The details of this experience remain obscure, but, given its results, it must have been extremely intense. Certainly, nothing in his childhood had prepared him for it. His father
had been a conventional Catholic, for whom religion was hardly less a matter
of class loyalty than of conviction. The baroness, raised a Presbyterian, had
become a Catholic while Friedrich was still a small child, but, though she
practiced rather more fervently than her husband, there is no evidence that she
exerted much influence in this regard over her son. His religious education
had been minimal, and if his own reminiscences can be trusted, his instincts
were anything but pious. All the more remarkable, then, that this boy of eighteen should have become that great rarity, a man of mystical prayer. At seventy
he tried to explain how it happened.

When I began to try to be good—to serve God—I already, alas, found myself involved in gravely bad habits and inclinations. But this, once I was, by God's grace, awakened to long to be straight and true—to go direct to God and Christ—had one great advantage. I saw young fellows around me fretting to be *free*, to be their own sole, full masters. They fretted against this or that thing; against this or that person. They thought if only they could get away from these, they would indeed be free. But I myself *could not feel that to be nearly enough*; I was too little happy in myself to fiddle-faddle at such little things. I wanted, *I had to*, get rid of—not those other people and their orders, etc.: but I had somehow to become free from *self*, from my poor, shabby, bad, all-spoiling *self*! *There* lay freedom, *there* lay happiness![11]

Daily meditation, much reflective reading of the Bible, mass and communion twice during the week and sacramental confession almost as often: these were the staples of the baron's interior life from this time onward, and no controversy or crisis, no intellectual unsettlement, could cause him to deviate from them. Over a long period he made an annual retreat with the Jesuits, and even after he had quarreled with them and stopped that pious practice he could tell a young friend, "Under God I owe my salvation to the Jesuits. But," he added in his deaf man's shout, "don't *you* ever become a Jesuit!"[12] Later on his apparent ease in divorcing devotional from scholarly pursuits assumed a legendary character among associates who could not, as the baron manifestly could, call into question the articles of the creed and then repair to the parish church to spend an hour in adoration of the Eucharistic Sacrament.

THE ANTECEDENTS of Friedrich von Hügel were not at all mean or pedestrian, but in England they appeared pale in comparison to those of the frail young spouse with whom he yearned to share the charms of Browning. Indeed, it was through his marriage in 1873 that the Austrian baron gained entrée to the charmed circle of Catholic aristocrats and intellectuals—most of them, unlike himself, converts—who weaved their way through the upper reaches of late Victorian society.[13] Lady Mary (Molly) Herbert was the daughter of the Liberal party statesman Sidney Herbert, who, just before his premature death from Bright's disease in 1861, had been elevated to the peerage as first Baron Herbert of Lea. Herbert, the intimate of Peel, Gladstone, and Palmerston— Herbert, as Gladstone remembered him, of "the beautiful and sunny spirit," "that singular harmony and singular variety of gifts"[14]—had been a younger son of the earl of Pembroke and had served as a cabinet minister off and on for

11. Von Hügel to "a Girl," 27 February, 1922, in Holland (ed.), *Selected Letters*, 352.

12. Quoted in De la Bedoyere, *Hügel*, 61.

13. On this and related personal matters, see the perceptive remarks of Lawrence Barmann, "Friedrich von Hügel as Modernist and as More than Modernist," *Catholic Historical Review* 75 (April 1989): 213–16.

14. Philip Magnus, *Gladstone, a Biography* (London: 1963), 156, and John Morley, *The Life of William Ewart Gladstone*, 3 vols. (London: 1903), 2:88.

fifteen years before his death. Monckton Milnes, never one to caress verbally without leaving a small trail of blood, said of him, "[Herbert] was just the man to rule England: birth, wealth, grace, tact, and not too much principle."[15] But principle in plenty Herbert displayed in his relationship with Florence Nightingale, who, in her struggle to bring decent health care to the British soldiers fighting in the Crimea, found in him a patron and a protector, and found in Herbert's wife, coincidentally, one of her closest friends.[16]

In 1846 Herbert had married Elizabeth A'Court Repington, a general's daughter, a remarkably beautiful woman with great dark eyes and a "glowing olive skin." She bore him seven children who, however, gave her small pleasure once he died. "You will say the children ought to be a comfort to me, but I suppose I am not naturally fond of children—at any rate I have never been used to be much with them. He was *my all*. He is gone."[17] Among their intimates when first married had been an Anglican clergyman of their own age named Henry Edward Manning, "dear Archdeacon Manning," who had been a school-fellow of Sidney Herbert at Harrow, and then had gone on to Balliol College, Oxford, as Herbert had to Oriel, when the two of them as undergraduates had competed with each other in stirring debates in the Union. In 1851, following in the wake of so many upper-class intellectuals identified in one way or another with the Oxford Movement, Manning had joined the Roman Catholic church, and fourteen years later—to the surprise and somewhat to the chagrin of distinguished Catholics and Anglicans alike—Pius IX appointed him archbishop of Westminster, and later cardinal, the preeminent Roman ecclesiastic in all of Britain, as he was to remain until his death in 1892.[18]

Lady Herbert of Lea, once her husband was dead, looked to Catholicism as an increasingly attractive ideological haven; so, at one moment in her troubled life, had Florence Nightingale who likewise knew the energetic Manning and prized him because of his support for her philanthropic activities. "Why cannot I enter the Catholic Church at once," exclaimed the imperious Miss Nightingale testily, "as the best form of truth I have ever known, and as cutting the Gordian knot I cannot untie." Not now, replied Manning, and probably not ever. His judgment proved correct in that, despite her superficial feelings, she had no genuine calling to Rome.[19] Elizabeth Herbert, on the other hand—who after her conversion styled herself Mary Elizabeth—he guided into the Catholic church in 1865, and ever afterward addressed her as "my child."[20]

She paid a stern price for her apostasy: her powerful Herbert kin caused her

15. *Dictionary of National Biography* (London: 1938 ed.), 9:663–65.

16. Cecil Woodham-Smith, *Florence Nightingale* (New York: 1983 ed.), esp. 219–20 and 248–51.

17. Quoted in Woodham-Smith, *Nightingale*, 47, 250.

18. See O'Connell, *The Oxford Conspirators*, 424.

19. Woodham-Smith, *Nightingale*, 64–65.

20. See Manning's letters to her at the time of her conversion, in Edmund Sheridan Purcell, *Life of Cardinal Manning, Archbishop of Westminster*, 2 vols. (London: 1896), 2:237–43. For Lady Herbert's

younger children to be removed from her care and to be raised as wards-in-chancery. "I fear you must look for no other sympathy in your family," Manning warned her, "for the English people on this subject have lost their own nature." Nor did she receive any such sympathy except from her eldest daughter, Lady Mary, who after eight years of tortuous contention followed her into the church—a decision that brought them both into direct contact with the other great convert, Cardinal John Henry Newman.

Friedrich von Hügel's younger brother, Anatole, a clever naturalist who ultimately became curator of the Cambridge University Museum of Archaeology and Ethnology, married Eliza ("Isy") Froude, who had introduced her good friend, Lady Mary Herbert, to Friedrich. Isy—so brimming over with charm and egalitarian good spirits that she called the rather formidable young baron "Freddy"[21]—was the daughter of the celebrated naval engineer William Froude, and thus the niece of Newman's intimate during the early stages of the Oxford Movement, Richard Hurrell Froude (and, incidentally, of the historian, James Antony Froude). Her father, though an incurable agnostic, remained until his death in 1879 among Newman's most cherished friends. Indeed, it could be said that Newman had had William primarily in mind when he crafted the arguments in the *Grammar of Assent* (1870), arguments designed to show how one could achieve certainty in one's religious belief.[22] They did not persuade Froude, but his friendship with Newman was not disturbed when his wife and children became Catholics. Among the latter, Newman especially doted on Isy who, he said, reminded him strikingly of her uncle Hurrell. "My Molly," Friedrich von Hügel replied when Lady Mary told him of her conversion, "next to almighty God and Our Lady, . . . you certainly owe most to Eliza Froude."[23] Newman agreed. "I congratulate you on your good work," he wrote Isy on May 25, 1873, "He who has 'begun it, will (I trust and pray) perfect it unto the day of Christ.' " "No one," he added drily, "can say that she has been hasty."[24] The wedding took place six months later.

The newlyweds, even before they set out on their continental honeymoon, had "begun a joint letter to [Newman] in London to thank you for your kind renewal of your promise to say mass for us on the day of our marriage—but our letter never got finished. . . . We felt your great kindness very much, and will not, assuredly, be quick to forget it."[25] Lady Mary had done the actual

change of name, see her introduction to her translation of F. Lagrange, *Life of Monseigneur Dupanloup*, 2 vols. (London: 1885), 1:v–vi.

21. See, for example, Maisie Ward, *The Wilfrid Wards and the Transition*. 2 (New York: 1937), 502.

22. Ian Ker, *John Henry Newman: A Biography* (Oxford: 1989), 519.

23. Quoted in De la Bedoyere, *Hügel*, 8.

24. Dessain et al., eds., *Letters and Diaries*, 26:316. Newman wrote to Lady Mary the same day: "Thank you for your most welcome letter. God reward you for your straightforward obedience to His voice; and He will. I mean, with his blessing, to say Mass on Tuesday morning for you."

25. Quoted in Dessain, et al., eds., *Letters and Diaries*, 26:388.

composition of this pious screed. That the original had remained unfinished stood as a tribute, one might have reasonably hoped, to the preoccupations of young love. However that may have been, Friedrich von Hügel himself had probably first met Newman in 1869, when he was seventeen. That year at any rate he first read one of Newman's books, the novel *Loss and Gain*, which, he said, "made me realize the intellectual might and grandeur of the Catholic position." He wrote his first letter to Newman five years later, after his marriage, and told the older man, with a dash of the redundancy that was unhappily a permanent component of his literary style, "how deeply, profoundly indebted I am to you for what you have been to me by means of your books."[26] Correspondence between the two continued over the next decade regularly, though not frequently by Victorian standards. In 1876 the baron came with his young wife on pilgrimage to Birmingham where he had several interviews with Newman.

If Lady Herbert of Lea admired Manning, she, like most other upper-class English Catholics, loved Newman.[27] Her son-in-law, who scarcely knew Manning, certainly revered Newman, but love was something else, and positive influence was too. Von Hügel in his youth consulted Newman on various theological topics—the problem of evil, for example, and biblical inspiration—and when the cardinal died in 1890 the baron testified again to the intellectual debt he owed, "above all" to the *Grammar of Assent*. But in fact his mental world had little in common with that of Newman, whom he found in retrospect "much too tentative and cautious," a "sad and somber character," "a great cedar under which very few can shelter." "I used to wonder, in my intercourse with John Henry Newman, how one so good, and who had made so many sacrifices to God, could be so depressing."[28]

THE FERVOR OF THE RELIGION practiced by the baron and his baroness did not turn their home at 1 Heathfield Gardens, Hampstead, into a depressing place. The neighborhood had a cheerfully genteel look to it. The von Hügels' large house stood at the top of the street, two-and-a-half storys high, with room for gardens on one side and in the back. Banks of tall windows along the front opened the interior to cool breezes and warm sunshine. Von Hügel determined to be a better husband and father than Baron Carl had been, and he succeeded. Lady Mary and the three daughters she bore—Gertrud, Hildegard, and Thekla—received from him a full measure of warmth and love. If his wife could not enter readily into his passion for study, there was still much to be shared with her bearded young husband once his sexual inhibi-

26. For the quotations, see Barmann, *Hügel*, 5.
27. For Lady Herbert's comments after Manning's death about his "Protestant hardness" and his "fear" of "any affectionate intimacy with a woman," see Purcell, *Manning*, 2:80.
28. For the quotations, see De la Bedoyere, *Hügel*, 31–33, and Barmann, *Hügel*, 5–6.

tions—"my scruples as to . . . touches, kisses, etc."[29]—were resolved. Their income of £1,200 a year was more than adequate for a leisured, genteel life. They read novels aloud together, and of course poetry. The baron closely supervised his children's education and religious formation, but he could be light and frolicsome with them too; they remembered him carrying one or another of them on his shoulders and singing to them in his hoarse, tuneless way snatches from the operettas they had enjoyed together.

They traveled regularly to the Continent. When at home, and not ailing, they entertained guests—ecclesiastics and savants for the most part—whom the baron, likely as not, would have accompany him on rambling afternoon walks across Hampstead Heath. One such visitor was the shy and diffident young Oxford convert and now a Jesuit, Gerard Manley Hopkins, whose family lived nearby.[30] Another frequent walking companion till his death in 1882—for whom shyness and diffidence were almost moral faults—was William George Ward, enfant terrible of the Oxford Movement, as he was stormy petrel of the English Catholic Revival. It would be hard to conceive of anyone more different from von Hügel in taste and temperament and scholarly commitment than Ward—"Of the two views proposed," he liked to say, "I, as usual, adopt the more bigoted"—and yet the baron felt for him an appreciation and an affection he could never offer to Newman: "[Ward was] one to whom I owe so much, one so penetrating and swift of mind, so massive and large in sympathy and will, a man every inch of him, a friend of friends, a father and a playfellow to one so all but utterly unlike himself."[31]

Von Hügel paid some attention to local civic affairs and considerably less to national politics; given his lack of citizenship he could not even vote in a British general election until 1918. His natural inclinations led him to sympathize with Tory policies—a stance confirmed for him later by his admiration for Arthur Balfour and George Wyndham—particularly with regard to Ireland and Home Rule.[32]

BUT SUCH MATTERS were only of peripheral interest. His thoughts were consistently elsewhere. The bulk of Friedrich von Hügel's waking day was spent at his desk where he pored over massive tomes written in various langauges, studied the New Testament in Greek and the Old in Hebrew, filled heaps of notebooks with jottings and précis, wrote long, abstruse letters in his spidery hand. He might have devoted himself in any case to a life of amateur

29. De la Bedoyere, *Hügel*, 4.

30. See Humphry House and Graham Storey (eds.), *The Journals and Papers of Gerard Manley Hopkins* (London: 1959), 234, 423. Hopkins was acquainted with both Anatole and Friedrich. The latter observed that when Hopkins said mass for the nuns at Roehampton "he impressed them all so much, they all felt he must be a saint."

31. For von Hügel's lengthy and perceptive tribute to W. G. Ward, see Wilfrid Ward, *William George Ward and the Catholic Revival* (London: 1893), 364–75.

32. See Ward, *The Wilfrd Wards*, 2:81–87, 390–98.

scholarship simply because it was in accord with his tastes and because he had the financial independence to do so. But in fact his religious conversion dictated the direction of his studies and defined their seriousness. He attacked them with a profound sense of vocation. He addressed himself in particular to those intellectual problems posed for religion by the scientific and historical disciplines, most radically posed in Germany whose culture he shared and understood. Indeed, his later position as liaison had a strong Germanic flavor: within his own circle of English, French, and Italian progressive Catholics he alone had traveled extensively in Germany, was familiar with German savants and their works, and applauded with enthusiasm their achievements in post-Kantian philosophy and biblical criticism.[33] He urged his friends—to little effect for the most part—to learn German so that they could discover for themselves the high level of scholarship practiced routinely and uniquely within the German university system. It did not seem to bother him that the Germans, preoccupied with intellectual quarrels of their own, appeared little inclined to involve themselves in the broils of less-sophisticated foreigners.[34]

The baron at any rate possessed an inherited predeliction for science and its method, so that he could approach with empathy the dominant systems of thought of the time. His linguistic skills, virtually unheard of in England and rare enough elsewhere, opened for him all the information relevant to his interests, and made of him ultimately a kind of bibliographical clearinghouse for putative scholarly colleagues all over Europe.

Von Hügel eagerly communicated with such people; his correspondence with the aging Newman was far from unique. Whenever he read a book or article which favorably impressed him, the baron sought to acquaint himself with the author either in person or by letter. One result of this practice was that he gradually became the single known quantity, the human point of reference, among different scholars in different lands, who were working on comparable historico-scientific questions. He increasingly saw it as his duty to bring such thinkers together, if not in the flesh, then by way of his own mediation. It was a role he was remarkably suited to play, because, despite his intense personal religiosity (or perhaps in some degree due to it), he adopted in intellectual matters a very broad attitude that carried him comfortably across confessional and partisan lines. Among his German contacts he became equally devoted to the professional and personal virtues of "dear Professor [Rudolf] Eucken," a Catholic, and to the *"astonishing"* knowledge and probity of Ernst Troeltsch, a Protestant.[35] His sympathy indeed sometimes amounted to naïveté, and his constant straining for consensus and accommodation led some crit-

33. See, for example, von Hügel to Petre, 26 September, 1900, in Holland (ed.), *Selected Letters*, 88–95.

34. See Thomas Franklin O'Meara, *Church and Culture: German Catholic Theology, 1860–1914* (Notre Dame, Ind.: 1990), 165–71. But also see Thomas Michael Loome, *Liberal Catholicism, Reform Catholicism, Modernism* (Mainz: 1979), 110–20.

35. See Barmann, *Hügel*, 73, 167.

ics to discern in him more of the genes of his diplomat-father than they liked.[36]

It may have been the conditions imposed by this task of honest brokerage that kept von Hügel from becoming a first-class scholar himself. Or it may have been that the lack of university training deprived him of a steady focus, left him prey to passing enthusiasms, and produced in him the same sort of insecurity that afflicted that other self-educated Catholic polymath, Lord Acton (for whose views he had little sympathy).[37] One admiring contemporary[38] called von Hügel "the most learned man living," and there was a sense in which the compliment rang true. No one had read as much or remembered as much as the baron had about a greater variety of theological subjects. No one was more industrious or conscientious. Yet there clung to him an aura of amateurism at least until 1908 when appeared his magnum opus, the scarcely readable *The Mystic Element in Religion*. By that date von Hügel was fifty-six years old, and his publications before then had been trifling.[39] He had risked nothing professionally in the scholarly wars, because he had no profession to risk. And anyway by 1908 the scholarly wars were practically over. Von Hügel was, in short, a well-fixed private layman, free to indulge his interests in a private manner and free also to encourage, cajole, and admonish others less advantageously positioned than himself.

ON MAY 5, 1884, Friedrich von Hügel, in the company of Lady Mary and their two little daughters, celebrated his thirty-second birthday in Paris. That happy event occurred early in the family's two-month-long French holiday. Ten days later the baron began a spiritual process which culminated in what he considered his second and definitive conversion and which put the seal upon his mission in life. The setting was the presbytery of the parish of Saint-Augustin—a relatively recent foundation, up the Boulevard Malsherbes from the Madeleine—and the agent was a secular priest named Henri Huvelin,[40] whom the baron described later as "the greatest manifestation of sheer holiness which I have been privileged to watch and to be moved by at close quarters. . . . I owe more to this Frenchman than to any man I have ever known in the flesh."[41] When they met—and it is uncertain as to exactly how they met[42]—Abbé Hu-

36. See, for example, Loisy, *Mémoires*, 3:471.

37. See, for example, L. V. Lester-Garland, *The Religious Philosophy of Baron F. von Hügel* (New York: 1933), 60–62

38. Charles Gore, successively Anglican bishop of Worcester, Birmingham, and Oxford, whose High Churchmanship mingled with social activism and an increasingly critical theology.

39. See the list printed in Barmann, *Hügel*, 254–56.

40. Actually christened Marie-Joseph-Philippe, but called Henri. See F. Ferrier, "Huvelin," in M. Prevost et al. (eds.), *Dictionnaire de biographie française* (Paris: 1989), 18:103–4.

41. Friedrich von Hügel, *The Mystical Element of Religion as Studied in Saint Catherine of Genoa and Her Friends*, 2 vols. (London: 1923 ed.; orig. ed. 1908), 1:vii, and *Essays and Addresses on the Philosophy of Religion* (London: 1921), 286.

42. See Peter Williams, "Abbé Huvelin, Mediator of a Tradition," *Bijdragen Tijdschrift voor Filosofie en Theologie* 42 (1981):247.

velin, at forty-six, had had a brief career as a teacher in a *petit séminaire*, but for sixteen years had been engaged in parochial ministry, and since 1875 had been vicar of Saint-Augustin. There, "suffering from gout in the eyes and brain, and usually lying prone in a darkened room, he served souls with the supreme authority of self-oblivious love, and brought light and purity and heart to countless troubled, sorrowing or sinful souls."[43] Huvelin in these implausible circumstances proved to be an extraordinarily effective confessor and spiritual guide to the famous intellectuals, ladies of high society, and nameless poor who crowded his anteroom. His most sensational achievement had been to effect the deathbed conversion, in 1881, of Émile Littré, an especially virulent anticlerical politician. Perhaps in the long run an even more significant feat of Huvelin, which occurred three years after von Hügel first met him, was to bring back to the Catholic faith Charles de Foucauld, destined for fame and martyrdom as "the Hermit of the Sahara."[44]

For von Hügel the relationship lasted until Huvelin's death in 1910. Each time the baron traveled to Paris—perhaps on a dozen occasions after 1884—he paid several visits to Saint-Augustin. For instance, in the spring of 1886 he went to see Huvelin for lengthy conferences, one of which included sacramental confession, every day from May 26 through May 29, and for another one on May 31. When back in England the baron kept in touch with his director by post.[45]

Huvelin's dicta on prayer, self-abnegation, gentleness, devotion to the truth came to form the center of von Hügel's spiritual ideals. He helped von Hügel to accept his deafness and his indifferent health, and to avoid falling into self-pity or undue depression. He disdained the miraculous—"I have a *strong* antipathy for miracles," he told the baron[46]—and urged his client to seek salvation through the fulfillment of his scholarly calling. But, he warned, "only a very deep, very true, very vibrant interior life will be a sufficient safeguard against the spirit of purely negative criticism [*critique*]." A scholar's lot is to be lonely, "and isolation, you will always return to it, because it is your vocation." Still, for this very reason, Huvelin urged the baron to recite a decade of the rosary every day, "to prevent [his] interior life from losing touch with the devotion of the people."[47]

---

43. Friedrich von Hügel, *Eternal Life: A Study of Its Implications and Applications* (Edinburgh: 1912), 374–75.

44. See Lucienne Portier, *Un précurseur: l'abbé Huvelin* (Paris: 1979), 49–57, 93–108.

45. There was only one meeting after 1900, in 1907. See Williams, "Abbé Huvelin," 249–51. Von Hügel sharply reduced his travels abroad after 1903 when he moved his family from Hampstead to a house near the Kensington Gardens.

46. For this and most of the quotations that follow, see the notes von Hügel kept of interviews with Huvelin in 1886 and 1893, partially printed in Holland (ed.), *Selected Letters*, 58–63, and published in full in James J. Kelly, "The Abbé Huvelin's Counsel to Baron Friedrich von Hügel," *Bijdragen Tijdschrift voor Filosofie en Theologie* 39 (1978): 63–69.

47. Friedrich von Hügel, *Essays and Addresses on the Philosophy of Religion*, 2d ser. (London: 1926), 234.

What this director said never flew in the face of an inquirer's predispositions or prior experience. Huvelin built on what was already there. His genius as a director was as much his ability to confirm a penitent's strengths as his sense of a penitent's specific needs. Much of his advice to von Hügel was prefaced by phrases like "pour vous," "c'est votre état," "il faut que vous." "For you prayer should be more a permanent condition than a precise and deliberate act." "It is your state in life to find more sorrow in the church than elsewhere." "To achieve genuine contrition it is necessary for you to have self-hatred indeed, but of a variety calm and peaceful, which brings you to prayer; not God's detailed view of your faults, but a general one."

Von Hügel came away from these sessions not so much chastened as strengthened. They were for him experiences specially sacred and precious, because they fulfilled the conditions of the splendid motto Newman had chosen for his cardinal's coat of arms, "cor ad cor loquitur": indeed, heart spoke to heart in the dark, stuffy, upper room of the presbytery of Saint-Augustin. As far as the character of his scholarly mission was concerned, von Hügel heard nothing from Huvelin that did not set sparks dancing through his mind. Take apologetics, Huvelin said, not in the conventional way, but "as it is found in life, as it presents itself to the spirit which is candid and solitary in the face of the real. Ordinary apologetics is worth nothing. It is often ingenious, but quite fraudulent." Do not seek orthodoxy, seek the truth, which "for you is a luminous point losing itself little by little into obscurity."

And what about the conventional Catholic philosophers and theologians, the Scholastics with their neat syllogistic arguments and brash certitudes? "What are certainties for others for you are merely hints, indications, outlines. Scholasticism, even Saint Thomas, the greatest of the Scholastics, cannot explain everything. The living truth flees definitions from whatever direction. The Scholastics think they can put the moon in a bottle; perhaps they could, if the moon were a cheese." "Scholasticism clarifies things by impoverishing them. It cuts great roads in all directions through a virgin forest. It succeeds in seeing the forest more clearly, but how many beautiful trees have been sacrificed." "The Scholastics do not understand that life, all life, escapes analysis. What they dissect is the dead body. . . . Pass them by," Abbé Huvelin advised von Hügel, "with a gentle, very gentle, smile; pass them by."

CHAPTER 4

The Rue de Vaugirard

The first law of history is not to dare to utter falsehood; the second not to fear to
speak the truth; and moreover, no room must be left for suspicion of partiality or
prejudice.

—*Leo XIII (1883)*[1]

EARLY IN 1884, just as Baron von Hügel and Lady Mary were laying
plans for their little family's springtime trip to Paris, the aged Cardinal
Newman, in his austere rooms at the Oratory in Birmingham, was reading the
proofs of what was to be his last publication. "I am indeed desirous," he wrote,
"of investigating for its own sake the limit of free thought consistently [*sic*]
with the claims upon us of Holy Scripture; still, my especial interest in the
inquiry is from my desire to assist those religious sons of the Church who are
engaged in Biblical criticism and its attendant studies, and have a conscientious fear of transgressing the rule of faith." The article drew the basic distinction between biblical inspiration as it applied to faith and morals on the one
hand, and to temporal facts on the other.[2] "It seems unworthy of Divine Great-
ness," said Newman, "that the Almighty should, in his revelation of himself
to us, undertake mere secular duties and assume the office of a narrator . . .
or historian or geographer, except so far as the secular matters bear directly
upon divine truth."[3]

This paper on inspiration was a slight and tentative piece—the effort of a
very old man—yet, because of the eminence of its author it attracted a good
deal of attention. A professor in the Irish seminary at Maynooth complained

1. Pope Leo XIII, "Letter" on historical studies, 18 August, 1883. For the English text, see Barry
(ed.), *Documents*, 3:86–93.
2. John H. Cardinal Newman, "An Essay on the Inspiration of Scripture," *Nineteenth Century* 15
(February 1884): 185–99. See J. Derek Holmes and Robert Murray (eds.), *On the Inspiration of Scripture*
(Washington, D.C.: 1967), 101–31. See also the perceptive remarks of James T. Burtchaell, *Catholic
Theories of Biblical Inspiration since 1810* (Cambridge: 1969), 74–78.
3. For a brief summary, see O'Connell, "Newman as Pastor," 342–44.

54

that, even if historical data in the Scriptures were not objects of faith, they nevertheless had to be accepted as true, since all of Scripture was inspired.[4] But from the vacation spa at Saint-Valery-sur-Somme issued a response of quite a different kind. On July 1 Friedrich von Hügel wrote the cardinal ecstatically and described how "the repeated reading of your article" elicited in him "profound interest" and gave him "subtle help" in his own scriptural research. "I was much interested the other day in Paris," he continued in his fractured English, "to hear myself (at a soirée given by the Rector of the Institut Catholique as such) the Rector (Mgr. d'Hulst), the Professor of Apologetics (the Abbé de Broglie), and the Professor of Ecclesiastical History (the Abbé L. Duchesne), all these, while discussing your papers, agree to their conclusions and maintain that their subject was the burning religious question of the hour."[5]

Clearly von Hügel during this sojourn in Paris, besides his decisive spiritual encounters at Saint-Augustin with Henri Huvelin—"that truly masculine saint"[6]—had come into contact as well with other forward-looking French Catholics, alert as he was rapidly becoming to the intellectual challenges the church had to face in the modern world. Concerning how fateful this meeting was to prove to be, the baron at the time had no more inkling than did the old cardinal in Birmingham. "My dear Baron," Newman replied cautiously, "it pleased me to think that my Article in the xixth century [*sic*] was acceptable to you. Of course it is an anxious subject. It is easy to begin a controversy— and difficult to end it."[7]

THE RUE DE VAUGIRARD, which stretches south and west from the Luxembourg to the Porte de Versailles, is the longest street in Paris. In 1881, the year Alfred Loisy returned to the Institut Catholique, it ran between a gauntlet of elegant four- and five-storied houses, fronted in beige stucco, which on the lower floors boasted tall windows and ornamental black iron balustrades, smartly polished, and on the roofs a festoon of chimneys. At the northeast extremity of the Vaugirard the hill of Sainte-Genevieve rose gently toward the Pantheon and the massive buff-colored pile of the Sorbonne, site of the medieval university that Napoleon I had replaced with his *facultés* and *écoles speciales*. Here, on the Left Bank of the Seine, beat the intellectual heart of France.

The compound of the Institut Catholique was established at the corner where the Vaugirard intersected with the rue d'Assas—a hallowed spot for Catholic Frenchmen, because here, in the old Carmelite convent, had died

4. See Ker, *Newman*, 735–36. This challenge prompted Newman to write a short rejoinder in explanation. See Holmes and Murray (eds.), *Inspiration*, 132–53.

5. Von Hügel to Newman, 1 July 1884, quoted in Dessain et al., eds., *Letters and Diaries*, 30:383.

6. Von Hügel's judgment in 1922, quoted in De la Bedoyere, *Hügel*, 47.

7. Von Hügel to Newman, 1 July, and Newman to von Hügel, 21 July, 1884, in Dessain et al., eds., *Letters and Diaries*, 30:382–84.

many of the martyrs of the September massacres of 1792. The Carmelites had returned to their former ministry, and their church—Saint-Joseph des Carmes, a medium-sized building, domed and somewhat squat and dark inside, decorated with undistinguished frescoes and paintings—served also as the chapel for the *institut.*

Alfred Loisy found that little had changed during the thirty-month interval of his absence from the school of theology.[8] The small band of students was still taught dogmatics by the same corpulent Italian Jesuit, Scripture by the same shy Parisian, Scholastic philosophy by the same Dominican. To be sure, there had been one notable addition to the faculty: the Italian, Pietro Gasparri, destined for great fame as a papal diplomat, now filled the newly created chair of canon law.[9] But dominant as before—like a colossus among pygmies—stood the burly figure of the thirty-five-year-old professor of ecclesiastical history, Louis Duchesne.

Born at Saint-Servan on the Breton coast, he was a child of six when his father, a commercial fisherman, was lost at sea. Madame Duchesne raised Louis and his five siblings in that stern dedication to religious faith that was a byword in Brittany—so much so that as a grown man her famous son described his holidays as "a two month retreat under the direction of my mother." At thirteen he entered the Collège Saint-Charles, which served as the *petit séminaire* for the diocese of Saint-Brieuc, where he studied the classics and won all the prizes. The bishop of Saint-Brieuc was impressed enough by young Duchesne's talents to send him to Rome for his theology—there he was a schoolfellow of Maurice d'Hulst—and, after ordination, to assign him to the faculty of Saint-Charles. He taught there for four years, and long afterward, during a sentimental reunion, he was moved to say, "My roots have always been here."[10]

There was a sense in which this trite remark was profoundly true, if not of the little backwater clerical *lycée,* then at least of Brittany as a whole. Duchesne ultimately became the consummate cosmopolitan, at home in salons in Paris, Rome, and Alexandria. Life among a provincial intelligentsia could never have satisfied him. Yet part of him remained a Breton peasant—this bald, stocky, thick-fingered man, given to hard work, broad humor, and town-pump gossip, whose eyes never lost their cast of wariness. The faith he had imbibed from his mother perdured too, though many on both sides of later quarrels judged him more shrewd and self-serving than sincere in asserting it. He came back home at any event at the end: when he died in Rome in the spring of 1922, after the solemn obsequies at San Luigi dei Francesi, attended by a throng of

8. See chapter 1.

9. Gasparri (1852–1934), as Pius XI's secretary of state, signed the Lateran Treaties of 1929, establishing the Vatican State and putting an end to the Roman Question.

10. Claude d'Habloville, *Grandes figures de l'église contemporaine* (Paris: 1925), 3–5.

prelates and diplomats, his remains were brought back to Saint-Servan and buried within sight of the sea.[11]

Louis Duchesne, at least at the beginning of his career, displayed considerable difficulty in keeping his opinions to himself. He returned from his studies in Rome an ardent and outspoken Ultramontane, much to the annoyance of his bishop, who adopted a much less exuberant view of the prerogatives of the pope and who had stood with the inopportunist minority at the First Vatican Council.[12] The bishop perhaps foresaw that such youthful enthusiasm would pass away in time, as indeed it did; in the meanwhile, he decided to temper that enthusiasm by dispatching the young priest to the fountainhead of Gallicanism in Paris for an advanced degree.[13]

He arrived there in the spring of 1871, just in time to witness the horrors of the rising of the Commune. It was not a healthy moment for a cleric to be abroad in the streets of the City of Lights—the communards shot, among many others, the archbishop of Paris—but Duchesne quietly went about his business, always with a stout walking stick in his fist, and nobody bothered him. He duly enrolled in the Sorbonne—now the state theological faculty in Paris which, like all the Napoleonic faculties, was essentially an examining entity—and, at the same time, in the École Pratique des Hautes Études.[14] The latter institution, devoted exclusively to research, offered no degree, but it gave Duchesne his vocation as historian. Under the direction of the finest masters available in France, he plunged into the technical details of philology and paleography and thereby began to unravel some of the mysteries of Christian antiquity that had first intrigued him during his student days in Rome. He determined to prepare a thesis for the Sorbonne on the *Liber pontificalis*, a critical edition, in effect, of a sixth-century document indispensable for the history of the early popes as well as for Roman archaeology and topography. It was a mammoth task, but Duchesne proved equal to it. Over a two-year period he relentlessly pursued the hundred and more extant manuscripts across France, Italy, and the Levant, and in the process carved out for himself a permanent place in the scholarly community. His edition of the *Liber*, when it appeared, was hailed as a triumph of scientific skill and *critique*.[15]

Here was the important word. Duchesne had shown himself to be a "criti-

11. P. d'Espezel, "Duchesne," in *Dictionnaire d'histoire et de géographie ecclésiastiques* (Paris: 1960), 14:965–69.

12. Most of the hundred or so bishops who at the council opposed the definition of papal infallibility maintained that they did not deny the substance of the doctrine but considered promulgating it "inopportune," given the circumstances of the time. They left Rome, and thus abstained, before the final vote.

13. Jean-Marie Mayeur, "Mgr. Duchesne et l'université," in École française de Rome (eds.), *Monseigneur Duchesne et son temps* (Rome: 1975), 318.

14. See chapter 1.

15. H. Leclerq, "Monsignor [*sic*] Duchesne," in *Dictionnaire d'archéologie chrétienne et de liturgie* (Paris: 1925) 6:2681–85.

cal" historian, applying the techniques of modern scholarship to the data of Christian origins. He had moreover demonstrated the capacity to be a "higher critic," because he was concerned with the authenticity of the document at hand: had it in fact been written by the authors to whom it was attributed, and did it in fact issue from the era it purported to represent? Such procedures, which seem commonplace now, were relatively new in 1875, and they were virtually unknown in Catholic circles. One reason for this was that the assault launched by critical method upon the texts of the New Testament, first in Germany and then spreading elsewhere, made people with a Christian commitment extremely uneasy. David Strauss's *Leben Jesu*, which argued that all the supernatural elements in the Gospels were based upon "myth," had appeared as early as 1836. A generation later, in 1863, Ernest Renan, the seminarist of Saint-Sulpice turned agnostic, published his *Vie de Jésus*, an immensely popular and influential book based on the assumption that the truth of the Scriptures depended solely upon reading them in the light of the literary methods and sources of their authors and which thus reduced the person of Jesus to that of an amiable Galilean social reformer with no moral or supernatural significance.[16] It mattered little that Renan's scholarship was judged by German critics as superficial and indeed spectacularly wrong in many matters of fact; the impact of the book was heady and liberating for, among many others, the feminist George Sand, who proclaimed exultantly, "Behold, Jesus demolished forever."[17] At the same time such conclusions caused, understandably, fear and dismay in pious Catholic hearts, to say nothing of diocesan chanceries or the Roman curia.

Some of Duchesne's later opponents maintained that it was a kind of peasant guile—a *prudentia carnis*—that prompted him to refrain from applying his criticism to the Bible and therefore to elude the censures leveled against the Modernists by the ecclesiastical authorities. Alfred Loisy—who to his cost did immerse himself in the biblical controversies and whose relationship, incidentally, to Duchesne was always ambivalent—contended rather that Duchesne had never been a Modernist, not because of the way in which he did historical inquiry, but because he had been too cynical ever to share in "the hopes of Modernism."[18] To be sure, a deeply sardonic strain did run through Duchesne's temperament, though Loisy's judgment of him may well have been simply an instance of one cynic recognizing another. Duchesne, at any rate, found himself under the shadow of magisterial suspicion often enough to cause one to wonder at his alleged craftiness. During the storms and tumults to come, his field of research—the history of the ancient Christian church— proved to be only a little less risky than that of the Scriptures themselves.

16. For a summary, see Marvin R. O'Connell, "Modernism in Retrospect," *Center Journal* 1 (Summer 1982): 97–99.

17. See Dansette, *Histoire religieuse*, 328, and Aubert, *Pie IX*, 212.

18. See Émile Poulat, "Mgr. Duchesne et la crise moderniste," in *Modernistica* (Paris: 1982), 140.

For it appeared nearly as ominous to the undiscriminating to challenge certain hallowed historical legends as it did to call into question the revelation of the New Testament, on the grounds that giving up one cherished tradition inevitably involved a threat to all the others. No generation is immune from the notion of the seamless garment or the domino effect. Duchesne's edition of the *Liber pontificalis* seemed to many a case in point. The document had undergone in the course of the Middle Ages constant editorial tampering so that it had become virtually useless as a source for the history of the centuries it purported to treat. Duchesne remorselessly stripped away the legendary and apochryphal incrustations and let the treatise, as it were, speak for itself. The performance was on its own terms impressive and gained favorable notice even from German scholars, which was the ultimate accolade.

Among others impressed were the consultants at the Ministry of Public Instruction. Since 1859 the French government had supported a research center in Athens which included in its curriculum a three-month period of study in Italy. In 1873 it was proposed to detach this feature from the École Française d'Athènes and expand it into a full-fledged program of its own. Thus was born the École Française de Rome, and Duchesne was a member of its original staff. He taught paleography and earned thereby a stipend of Fr 2000 as well as rich public praise from his superiors for his "lively intelligence, the sureness of his critical science, his paleographical skill, his profound knowledge of original sources."[19] Nor did the republican political victories of the late 1870s materially affect the auspicious reputation he had thus earned; Father Duchesne was assured by a succession of anticlerical governments that his connection with the official *université* might continue as long as he liked, and several years later, at the height of the crisis over religion and education, he did return to it.[20]

But in the meantime he threw in his lot with the new Catholic universities. D'Hulst recruited him for the Paris faculty of arts, and—of special note to those attuned to symbolic links—the aged Bishop Dupanloup of Orléans, leader of the liberal faction at the recently prorogued Vatican Council, became his formal sponsor with the governing board of bishops, which, in January 1877, gave unanimous assent to his appointment as professor. The trouble had started, however, even before that. Stories spread out of his home diocese about Duchesne's habitual impertinence, his neglect of certain "venerable devotions," his lack of a genuine "ecclesiastical spirit." Had he in fact dismissed Pius IX's authority and contemptuously referred to the pope simply as "Giovanni Mastai?" Had he in fact refused publicly to pray the litany of the Virgin because he could not abide the sentimentality of Marian piety? Duchesne denied all—his retreat from extreme Ultramontanism, he said, left his ideas

19. A. Geoffroy, "La nouvelle École française de Rome," *Revue des deux mondes* 16 (1876): 818–19. Geoffroy was the first director of the school.

20. Mayeur, "Mgr. Duchesne et l'université," 324.

about the papacy no more radical than those of Dupanloup, who had of course accepted the council's decree on papal infallibility—and he pointed, with good reason, at the nasty anonymity of his accusers as a prima facie reason to disallow their testimony. "I am deeply hurt," he wrote, "that any of my confreres could believe me capable of saying such foolish and irreverent things."[21] Hurt perhaps, but hardly surprised that his nameless detractors came from among his "confreres," his fellow priests, schoolmates, and Breton curés who had nothing to gain from Duchesne's fall save the sweet satisfaction of leveling the talented; envy has always been the peculiarly clerical sin.

Not that Duchesne was without defenders. D'Hulst stood by him through thick and thin. The vicar-general back in Saint-Brieuc, while admitting that the young historian had a weakness for "imprudent language" and for drawing unflattering word portraits of important people—his characterization of the members of the French hierarchy as "mitred sacristans" would become celebrated—nevertheless argued strongly that "these eccentricities" were not the true measure of the man. Similarly, the bishop of Saint-Brieuc intervened in Duchesne's behalf when, late in 1877, the edition of the *Liber pontificalis* was delated to the Congregation of the Index in Rome. The bishop—no mitred sacristan he—wrote testily to the cardinal-prefect of the congregation and warned him not to meddle in what was an issue internal to the French church.[22] This was bold conduct for a provincial bishop, who had been on the losing side at the council, so to confront a powerful curial cardinal, but the prefect responded mildly, once Duchesne announced his willingness to abide by a Roman decision. A routine commission was set up, and it recommended merely some minor cosmetic changes should the critical edition of the *Liber* be published.

But Duchesne could not stay out of trouble for long. In 1881, three years after he had transferred from the arts faculty of the *institut* to the theological school, a disgruntled colleague made public a copy of lecture notes in which Duchesne argued that the traditional doctrine of the Trinity had not been clearly taught in the church before the definitions of the Council of Nicea in 325. This opinion was harshly attacked in a journal published by the Institut Catholique of Lille, and Duchesne replied in kind, as did d'Hulst.[23] The controversy increased in acrimony until November 1882, when the superior-general of the Sulpicians suddenly decreed that henceforth no Parisian seminarians would be allowed to follow Duchesne's course. Crusty old Henri Picard was not a man to trifle with; the archetype of the austere and unbending Gallican priest, he wielded enormous influence with the French bishops, many of whom, as young men, had been under his charge—he was, for instance, con-

---

21. Paul Poupard, "Mgr. Duchesne à l'Institut catholique de Paris," in *Monseigneur Duchesne*, 305–7.

22. A partial text appears in d'Habloville, *Grandes figures*, 28.

23. Leclerq, "Monsignor Duchesne," 2689–91.

fessor to Archbishop Richard, the coadjutor of Paris. His prohibition meant in effect that Duchesne no longer had any students to teach. The theological school hastily arranged a leave of absence for its ecclesiastical historian.[24]

Once again the Vatican was called upon to provide a referee. The noted Jesuit theologian Cardinal Franzelin asked Duchesne, through d'Hulst, to clarify his position. This Duchesne did—his point, he said, had been that the trinitarian doctrine of the ante-Nicene fathers showed development, not from error to truth, but from the less clear and precise to the more—and there, Franzelin apparently satisfied, the matter rested. Yet d'Hulst felt constrained to assure the cardinal, in a letter of February 1883, that it was not Duchesne "who set the tone" in the theological school and that the *institut* planned to appoint soon a second professor of ecclesiastical history whose "inclinations will be different from those of M. Duchesne."[25]

But two years later the rector ran out of room to maneuver. A pious legend cherished by the church in France was that several of its dioceses—Sens, Troyes, and Chartres, among others—had been founded by one or another of the seventy-two disciples mentioned in the Gospels. In an article in the *Bulletin critique*—a journal he had begun to publish in 1880—Duchesne put this old canard under close historical scrutiny and found it, needless to say, wanting. His tone was tart and scornful.[26] The fury provoked in some quarters by this exposé was white hot. The archbishop of Sens was particularly exercised at the challenge to the apostolic origins of his see; he wrote to d'Hulst complaining bitterly of this assault upon approved tradition and of "the most offensive mockery displayed in various passages of this most regrettable article." The bishops, he said, cannot tolerate anyone demolishing "the origins of the most respectable churches at the head of which God has placed said bishops in order to defend them."[27]

The fuss proved to be the last straw. Duchesne offered to resign and go back to Brittany where his bishop would give him "a little rural parish by the seaside. I shall not be in the least embarrassed, once my scientific career is finished, to become the pastor of fishermen and peasants."[28] It is to be doubted that Duchesne intended this conventional protestation to be taken seriously. D'Hulst at any rate, with the help of Archbishop Richard, worked out a facesaving device whereby Duchesne went on leave of absence again, this time, it was said, in order to prepare his edition of the *Liber pontificalis* for the press. And the rector also protested publicly the loss of his star colleague, this

24. Baudrillart, *Vie de d'Hulst*, 1:459–61.

25. Quoted in Poupard, "Duchesne à l'Institut catholique," 309.

26. See Albert Houtin, *La controverse de l'apostolicité des églises de France au XIXe siècle* (Paris: 1903), 159–62.

27. Leclerq, "Monsignor Duchesne," 2693–95, and Poulat, "Duchesne et la crise moderniste," 141–42.

28. Quoted in Poupard, "Duchesne à l'Institut catholique," 310–12.

learned, powerful, and "priestly" man, "without a scintilla of doubt the most distinguished, the most brilliant member of our university [*sic*], one of the very few professors that the state system holds in high esteem, the only one it envies us."[29] The envy was no figment of d'Hulst's imagination, for the prestigious École Pratique des Hautes Études quickly offered an appointment to Duchesne, who never returned to the Institut Catholique (though his name remained technically on the books till 1895, when he went to Rome as director of the École Française) and who, accepting it, wore his soutane in those rarefied and anticlerical precincts as jauntily as ever. But a thorn of bitterness had been pressed into him. "These absurd attacks," he wrote his new friend, Friedrich von Hügel, "have quite worn me out and filled me with disgust."[30]

LOUIS DUCHESNE was not a sparkling lecturer, at least not at the beginning of his ill-starred career at the Institut Catholique of Paris. The cutting wit that so enlivened his private conversation did not reveal itself at the podium. His voice was faint and toneless, and some students complained about the tediousness of his presentations.[31] In an era when eloquence and literary flair were so valued that Renan was the great academic figure, Duchesne's dry, somewhat pedantic approach to his material was not calculated to win widespread favor. "The course in ecclesiastical history," Alfred Loisy noted, "was very substantial if a little confused." "Father Duchesne," he added, "did not express himself with the clarity and facility one would have liked."[32]

Loisy was not then or ever a man free with compliments, so that this half-praise of Duchesne might be deemed something of a tribute. The older man in any event took the younger in hand when the latter returned to the *institut* in 1881. Duchesne arranged first that Loisy be awarded the baccalaureate within weeks of his arrival. He then persuaded d'Hulst to permit Loisy to count his two-months' residence in 1878 and in May and June of 1881 as equivalent to a full academic year, which meant that Loisy could qualify for the licentiate after two terms, instead of the normal four, of course work.[33] When Abbé Paulin Martin, the professor of Scripture and Hebrew fell ill in December 1881, Duchesne saw to it that his protégé was named instructor in Hebrew. All this haste and cutting of corners—which says as much about the parlous state of the infant *institut* as it does about Duchesne's influence or

29. Quoted in D'Espezel," "Duchesne," 971. For Duchesne's extensive scholarly productivity, see the final columns (2711–35) of Leclerq, "Monsignor Duchesne," where 429 published items are listed, 185 of them written by the end of 1885.

30. Quoted in Poulat, "Duchesne et la crise moderniste," 142.

31. Poupard, "Duchesne à l'Institut catholique," 308. Apparently Duchesne's performance in this regard improved with the passage of time; see d'Espezel, "Duchesne," 970.

32. Quoted in Houtin and Sartiaux, *Loisy*, 22.

33. For the sake of convenience, the terminology employed here is the conventional one. In fact, the government forbade its use outside state faculties, so that for bachelor, licentiate, and doctor were substituted auditor, lector, and master. See Houtin and Sartiaux, *Loisy*, 29.

Loisy's brilliance—appeared justified when Loisy passed his licentiate's examination magna cum laude in June 1882. D'Hulst in any event was persuaded enough to request the bishop of Chalons to assign Loisy to the *institut* permanently. Meignan readily agreed and wrote Loisy a cordial letter with a small sting of mockery at the end: "When you visit Chalons do not forget that the bishop's palace will be your hotel. We shall talk about exegesis."[34]

Armed with his license, Loisy from 1882 no longer had to attend classes in the theological school. D'Hulst suggested that he enroll at the École Pratique des Hautes Études and take courses in Assyriology and Egyptology. This he did, and he also at this time began to follow Renan's lectures at the Collège de France. (Duchesne went with him the first time, lest the formidable hammer of orthodoxy should overawe le petit Loisy.) He regularly attended these lectures for three years, though he never in all that time attempted to speak to the great man personally—an opportunity he later regretted having failed to take.[35] But as he listened admiringly to this most moving of pedagogues, Loisy was quietly pondering the elements of a vast intellectual project whereby the rationalism of Renan could be overturned by the proper application of the very *critique* which Renan championed.

EVEN BEFORE HE HEARD RENAN, however, Loisy had been set upon the path of critical history by a curious combination of opposites. For his study during the vacation of 1881 Duchesne loaned him the volume of the Gospels in Tischendorf's celebrated edition of the Greek New Testament.[36] Thus was the young priest introduced to that German scholarship which over previous generations had revolutionized research into ancient literature, including the Bible. Tischendorf himself was a "lower" or "textual" critic, concerned, that is, to reconstruct the document as it was when it left its author's hand. Such work provided the raw material with which the "higher critic" could proceed to analyse the text for its authenticity and meaning in accord with the circumstances of its production—the sort of evaluation Duchesne had made of the *Liber pontificalis*. Years afterward Loisy recorded the strong impression reading Tischendorf had left on him.

I was astonished as I continued to read at not having noticed before the contradictions [in the Gospels]. It appeared to me very clearly, as it must to any man who does not close his eyes to it, that these books needed to be interpreted as freely as they had been composed. One cannot treat as rigorously historical texts that are not historical. My temerity, if temerity it was, did not yet go so far as to contest the substantial reality

---

34. Loisy, *Choses passées*, 383.

35. Houtin and Sartiaux, *Loisy*, 34.

36. Konstantin Tischendorf (1815–74) was a professor of theology at Leipzig, and the discoverer and editor of biblical manuscripts, including the Codex Sinaiticus. Between 1841 and 1869 eight editions of his Greek New Testament were published with a full critical apparatus of the variant readings.

of the recorded facts, particularly those that figure in the creeds of the church. For example, I saw well enough that the accounts of the birth of Christ, in Matthew and in Luke, proceeded from different traditions and were mutually exclusive, . . . but I did not yet deny what, in these accounts, was of Catholic faith, like the virginal birth of the Savior.[37]

Almost immediately after this exhilarating if unsettling experience, Loisy went through a kind of antithesis which served to confirm his newfound dedication to *critique*. Abbé Martin taught Scripture as well as Hebrew in the Institut Catholique. His illness in December 1881 provided Loisy with the chance to teach Hebrew, but it also meant that he and his confreres had to continue their Scripture course at the *grand séminaire* of Saint-Sulpice, a ten-minute walk away. Martin had been, in Loisy's judgment, bad enough: "A good and simple man, not without erudition and good intentions, but totally lacking in critical spirit and perhaps, toward the end of his life, lacking as well in good sense."[38] Far worse was the Sulpician Fulcran Vigouroux, at whose feet Loisy now had to sit, and who fit, he said, "into the category of the great bores of all time, very far beneath Bossuet, it goes without saying, who always accompanied his most villainous exploits to the sound of splendid rhetorical music. M. Vigouroux, by contrast, was as dull in his style as in his misdeeds. . . . I must say that the teaching and books of this grand Catholic apologist of the Bible did more to turn me away from orthodox opinions than all the rationalists combined, including Renan."[39] As he emerged from the classroom at Saint-Sulpice, coldly angry and frustrated, Loisy reflected ruefully on the warning he had received shortly before from one of his fellow priests in Chalons: do not be led astray by the bold speculations of M. Vigouroux![40]

Loisy retreated into his teaching and studying, ever more remote from his colleagues. "I live in a solitude more or less complete," he wrote in the notebook in which he kept track of his mass intentions.[41] In the early summer of 1884—just weeks after the soirée at which von Hügel had met d'Hulst and Duchesne—Loisy made his annual retreat during which he came to what seemed at the time a settled conclusion about his future.

37. Loisy, *Choses passées*, 56–57.

38. Loisy, *Mémoires*, 1:181. Commented the other great French Catholic scripturist of the time, Marie-Joseph Lagrange (in *M. Loisy et le modernisme* [Paris: n. d. (1932)], 18), "M. Paulin Martin, . . . a distinguished Syriac scholar, countenanced the most hackneyed opinions, even in the matter of textual criticism of the New Testament, in which the Vulgate rather supported the critical approach."

39. Loisy, *Mémoires*, 1:189, and *Choses passées*, 58. Once more Lagrange's comment (*Loisy et modernisme*, 14) is pertinent: "The erudition of M. Vigouroux was prodigious and impeccable from the point of view of the fullness of his citations. One was nevertheless astonished at the self-assurance of his criticism. Was his approach simply candor? . . . Or was it the imperturbability of a person determined not to desert his principles? In any case, he who feels the need perpetually to defend the Bible does not do justice to its dignity."

40. Loisy, *Mémoires*, 1:80.

41. February 11, 1883. This *carnet* was among the private papers Loisy in 1907 entrusted to his collaborator and disciple, Albert Houtin, with whom he later fell out. Large extracts from it are printed in Houtin and Sartiaux, *Loisy*. The specific reference here is p. 35.

Every being in existence has a special end determined by God himself; this particular end is subordinated to the general end of the universe, which is the revelation and glorification of God. . . . Each person has his vocation. . . . Most vocations amount principally to personal sanctification. But some have for their object the sanctification of others. Indeed, in such cases one can sanctify oneself only by sanctifying others. The building up of the body of Jesus Christ requires several kinds of workers: some are pastors, others doctors. Now it is necessary that the pastor have some of the same qualifications as the doctor, and vice versa; but it is also necessary that individuals be committed principally to the one or to the other.

My vocation appears to be a vocation of doctor.[42]

It was a noble aspiration, nobly expressed, but it did not itself calm the intellectual turmoil within him. Nor did his relentless and ever more engrossing study of ancient texts. The more he learned about and practiced critical methods the more out of the mainstream of ecclesiastical life he found himself. His resolution to write a doctoral thesis on biblical inspiration was at first heartily approved by Mgr. d'Hulst, but then, after considering the likelihood of "clamors from the theologians," the rector reversed himself, explaining that the ecclesiastical power structure remained deeply suspicious of anything that smacked of critical history, and he urged his young colleague to choose a less-dangerous topic.[43]

As he pondered his situation he sought to find "the causes of my discouragement: ennui, bodily weakness, disappointments of all kinds." Reflecting upon his reception of the subdiaconate—"the worst mistake of my life," he called it much later[44]—he felt a deep ambivalence about the irrevocable commitment it had involved. "It came much too soon," he wrote, "I was only twenty-one years old. Three years later I would no doubt have drawn back. Had I seen and felt then what has been given me since to know and experience, I would not have had the courage to give myself to God. . . . But now [1884] I am persuaded I did the right thing to accept ordination; if the choice were given me today, I would actively pursue it." He felt the sting of loneliness that his temperament no less than his priestly promises had imposed on him: "My heart is ailing, because I cannot love, and because I am nevertheless capable of it, and because I have such a need for it. And yet I have achieved serenity of spirit and of conscience." Amid these restless and often contradictory ruminations, he often turned his mind's eye back toward the *champenois* countryside and the scenes of an idyllic boyhood when affection had abounded: "I am now more than ever attached to my family. For my sister I offer nothing less than a kind of worship, and her future is at this moment my only real concern."

Personal reflections for Alfred Loisy, however, could not be separated from professional ones, and he gradually came to terms—ambiguous terms, to be

42. Houtin and Sartiaux, *Loisy*, 40–41.
43. Loisy, *Mémoires*, 1:131.
44. Loisy, *Choses passées*, 46.

sure—with "the interior struggle" that had been his lot since his days at the seminary in Chalons.

I have decided to toil for and serve the church, which has demonstrated by its acts that it is the educator of humanity. Without forsaking its tradition, but always intent on returning to that tradition's spirit rather than its letter, it remains an essential institution and the most divine thing present upon the earth. True, it has compounded the subtleties of the theologians; but it has also collected under its aegis the principles of order, of devotion, of virtue which guarantee happiness to the family and peace to society. To wish to establish something in the moral order leaving Christ and the church out of account would be today to indulge in a utopian gesture. It goes without saying that much of the church's discipline is obsolete, that its liturgy does not entirely conform to the needs of the times, that the literal sense of its theological formularies becomes each day less supportable. That at any rate is what I believe will become clearer to me as I study the past of the church, as well as its present and that of humanity.

Yet as he mused over these ideals and labored in his own way to realize them, gloom and uncertainty were never far away. It often seemed to him as though he had prematurely aged. "Logic wearies me unto death. It is not necessary that life proceed along a straight line. Indeed, for most people life forms a circle. They see early on what they are capable of seeing; . . . their existence turns on a single orbit. They are the happiest of all." "Life is very sweet when it is lived by a person who is young, healthy, intelligent, generous. He smiles at existence, and existence smiles at him. Sickness, on the other hand, and anxiety and strictures of the heart remind us of inevitable death and so of unhappiness."[45]

LOISY WROTE THESE LAST LINES at the end of 1886, when he was twenty-nine, and when, never robust, he had fallen ill again. He struggled through the early part of the new year until finally he consulted a physician, who diagnosed his condition as the early stages of pulmonary tuberculosis. Mgr. d'Hulst hurriedly arranged that the young luminary of the Institut Catholique should spend a period of recuperation in the salubrious environs of the Riviera. A solicitous Louis Duchesne accompanied "le petit Loisy" to the railroad station, settled him in the proper carriage, and tucked blankets around him, all the more affectionately because, as he confessed later, he never expected to see his sometime protégé alive again. But four months at Cannes, under the perpetually blue sky, and with the mild breezes blowing off the gently rolling sea, brought Loisy back to the state of delicate health that would be his into old age. He stayed at a hostel for priests similarly afflicted—the house, given its function, bore the hopeful name Villa of Roses—where he was soon well enough to indulge his taste for sardonic commentary. "The place was not very

45. Quoted in Houtin and Sartiaux, *Loisy*, 46–47.

gay," he remarked. He remembered visits by two bishops passing through the city: one a Frenchman "who spoke little and who probably had not much to say even had he had a penchant for conversation"; and the other an Italian, a nobleman proud of his lineage and given to a combination of grand airs and trivial chitchat. "These prelates displayed a marked reserve when I was introduced to them as a professor of Hebrew and Assyriology."[46]

In the late spring of 1888 Alfred Loisy, his ordinary vigor restored, returned to Paris. He took a modest flat in the rue d'Assas, just off the rue de Vaugirard, but in doing so he by no means committed himself to remain simply a professor of antique languages at the Institut Catholique. The following year presented an opportunity to improve his prospects considerably. The death of the incumbent left vacant the chair of Assyriology at the École Pratique des Hautes Études. Loisy, who had been the star pupil of the instructor just dead—in fact he was the only person who had to date earned a certificate in that subject at the école—coveted the post, which would have added significantly to his income of Fr 5,000 annually and which, attaching him to the state *université*, could not but have furthered his career. His application for the chair did not require him to resign from the Institut Catholique, nor did he intend to do so. Holding simultaneously two positions in roughly the same academic field was not unusual among the professorial class, as demonstrated by Duchesne who since 1885 had been technically on the staffs of both the *institut* and the école.

Duchesne indeed was Loisy's trump card. The combination of the younger man's undoubted qualifications, together with his mentor's support within the faculty of the école, seemed certain to assure a favorable recommendation to the cabinet minister who actually made the selection. But Duchesne did nothing to persuade his colleagues to endorse Loisy's cause, a failure that the latter, highly sensitive to an affront, real or imagined, never completely forgave. Duchesne later denied that had ever promised any intercession, and Loisy grudgingly admitted that no formal commitment had been made. Nevertheless, he was bitterly disappointed at what he conceived to be a dereliction of friendship, and Duchesne's subsequent explanations did nothing to heal the breach:

Duchesne told me several times that he did not want other ecclesiastics with him or near him along the path he had laid out for himself. They might possibly be competitors in some future endeavors of his, and even when they could not possibly be considered rivals, he still disliked having them nearby. Public opinion was little favorable to the clergy; it could easily take offense at seeing a number of priests in official positions. For Duchesne, who was interested only in the advancement of his own career, every priest who did work similar to his was a rival. He saw himself as the sole representative of the clergy in accumulating the honors of official science.[47]

---

46. Houtin and Sartiaux, *Loisy*, 47–48.
47. Quoted in Houtin and Sartiaux, *Loisy*, 49–50.

Loisy seldom forgave and never forgot. "Between Duchesne and me," he wrote in 1913, "there has been no exchange of ideas since June 11, 1889."[48] And forty years after the event its effect still rankled: "[With Duchesne] I was dealing with a frightened man who feared that by his trust he might have furnished me with weapons I could have used against him and who therefore begged me not to take advantage of the situation."[49]

Some months later Loisy received another check to his aspirations, this time, as things turned out, with portentous results. It had long been assumed by all parties that the young linguist, busily winding up his doctoral dissertation, was the heir-apparent to the chair of Scripture in the theology school of the Institut Catholique. But when Paulin Martin died in January 1890, the appointment went to, of all people, Fulcran Vigouroux. It was a patently political tactic, an attempt on d'Hulst's part to appease Icard, the powerful Sulpician superior, and through him Cardinal Richard (since 1886 archbishop of Paris in his own right). The rector fobbed off a surprised and bitterly disappointed Loisy with the smooth assurance that a professorship would be his as soon as his doctoral degree was in hand. He even suggested, perhaps facetiously, that Loisy go to Rome during the Easter holiday and bring back a doctorate of divinity which could be secured simply by paying the costs of a meaningless examination. Loisy's ambition, however, did not go to such scandalous lengths, and he insisted that he proceed to the degree of doctor of theology in accord with the standard norms of the Institut Catholique.[50]

On March 7, 1890, the feast of Saint Thomas Aquinas, Alfred Loisy submitted and formally defended his dissertation—on the canon of the Old Testament—at a solemn convocation of his colleagues, presided over by the bishop of Chartres. At the conclusion of the academic ceremony the company repaired to the Carmelite church nearby, where, in the presence of the Blessed Sacrament, the new doctor solemnly recited the profession of faith of Pius IV, which included the lines: "I receive the Holy Scriptures in the sense in which our holy mother the church has held them and does hold them now, the church to which belongs the right to judge the genuine meaning and the interpretation of the Scriptures; I will not receive nor will I ever interpret the Scriptures except in accord with the unanimous judgment of the Fathers of the church." Loisy, of course, was thoroughly familiar with this wording, but when he read it aloud, the echo reverberating through the sanctuary, he "felt the need to catch his breath," and he paused. The hard eye of Mgr. d'Hulst brought his mind back to the demands of the ritual, and he completed the recitation without further hesitation. The rector said to him afterward, smiling, "I wish I could have shortened it for you."[51]

48. Loisy, *Choses passées*, 100.
49. Loisy, *Mémoires*, 1:167.
50. Loisy, *Choses passées*, 102.
51. Houtin and Sartiaux, *Loisy*, 50–51.

So Alfred Loisy was duly named professor of sacred Scripture in the Institut Catholique of Paris. But the prior appointment of Vigouroux threw a long shadow over his new dignity. It meant that he had for a senior colleague— a supervisor almost—an intransigent traditionalist who was, besides, highly influential within the closed clerical world. The situation presented a daunting challenge to one who had by now dedicated himself to disengaging "our holy mother the church" from the conventional interpretation of the Bible. As for solemnly swearing to do what he had no intention of doing, Loisy shrugged the deed off as a semantic triviality: "I could profess the faith of Pius IV, because in doing so I promised nothing; the terms of the oath were contradictory."[52]

52. Loisy, *Mémoires*, 1:187. Pius IV (1499–1565) presided over the final and definitive session of the Council of Trent. From his time all those engaged in ecclesiastical teaching had to take publicly the so-called Professio fidei Tridentina.

CHAPTER 5

The Ghost of Descartes

What then is this Cartesian spirit that is supposed to be so bad? What ought one think about it? How should one come to understand it? Is its substitution for the Scholastic spirit in itself such a terrible thing? The Cartesian spirit is good sense applied to scientific research, it is human reason exerting itself to be liberated from the prejudices of pride and ignorance. . . . The grand Cartesian principle, which exists in every man taken individually, is the faculty of learning and understanding the truth to the degree that the truth is knowable for the human spirit.

Lucien Laberthonnière (1884)[1]

AIX-EN-PROVENCE is an ancient town, lying on the right bank of the River Arc, a little northwest of Marseilles and northeast of Toulon, at the crossroads of the principal trade routes to Italy and the Alps. The Roman dictator Marius annihilated a large barbarian host on this site a hundred years before the birth of Christ. The ruins of the Roman city—called *Aquae sextae* in Latin—still remain, as do traces of the succeeding dominance of Visigoths, Franks, and Lombards. Muslim invaders from Spain sacked the town in the eighth century. During the Middle Ages Aix was a famous center of art and learning, a home of the troubadours who spun out their romances in the lilting Provençal tongue. The cathedral of Saint-Sauveur was built at the end of the twelfth century, the university founded early in the fifteenth. During the centuries that followed a new town grew up south of these venerable remains, rows of handsome public and private buildings interspersed with fountains and little plazas and caressed, most of the time, by bright sunshine and breezes from the nearby Mediterranean. The Industrial Revolution had largely passed Aix by, but it continued into the late nineteenth century to provide a market for the farmers round about. The gently rolling hinterland, with its groves of olive and almond trees, was a favorite subject of the Postimpressionist Paul

---

1. Lucien Laberthonnière, "L'esprit cartésienne et l'esprit scholastique," in Louis Canet (ed.), *Oeuvres de Laberthonnière*, 8 vols. (Paris: 1935–55), 3:313–14.

Cézanne, who was born and who died at Aix. Émile Zola spent part of his schooldays there.

Henri Bremond, born July 31, 1865,[2] was a generation younger than Cézanne and Zola, whom he never knew. But he was almost the exact contemporary of another *Aixois* destined for even more fame and more trouble than he was to endure himself: Charles Maurras, the founder of Action française. Though Bremond left Provence at the age of seventeen and, save for one brief but significant period, never lived there again, the region did not cease to work its charm upon him. Even that subtlety which came to be such a marked characteristic of his own Bremond could relate to the genius of the land of his birth. "Despite the apparent spontaneity of its effusions," he wrote many years later,

Provence allows others to see only as much of itself as it chooses. It is necessary to lie in wait for it, to catch it by surprise, in order to get a glimpse, even for a moment, of the dark flame of its passions. More than that, one must always reckon, in matters Provençal, with the unexpected: the sudden about-face, the impulses of the imagination, the surprises wrought by the spirit and by the heart. Mobile, restless, impatient—it seems at times as though an ancient Saracen fever were burning once more, so much so that Provence at first disconcerts those who have not experienced over a long period the deep-seated steadiness of its intentions, of its loves, of its intelligence.[3]

Pierre Bremond came from a long line of notaries and himself practiced that profession successfully enough to provide comfortable circumstances for his wife, Thomasine Pons, and his family. It was a very pious household—three of the Bremond brothers became priests and one of their sisters a nun[4]—and a fairly contentious one. This latter condition stemmed from Pierre's obsession with politics. He was a passionate legitimist, dedicated to the cause of the Bourbon pretender, the Comte de Chambord or, as his partisans called him, "Henri V." "Those who were not raised in this atmosphere," Henri Bremond recalled, "can scarcely appreciate the impact the Comte de Chambord had on our families. . . . We literally lived on his thought, on his words, on his picture displayed all over the house." Soon enough, however, the boy adopted a certain detachment about the fortunes of the monarchy, especially as he listened to the incessant wrangles on the subject between his father and his mother's uncles, who were liberal republicans and even, Pierre suspected gloomily, unbelievers. Perhaps Henri Bremond's later distaste for what he called "rigid" positions, fanatically adhered to—what his opponents, however, labeled his studied and self-interested imprecision—can be traced back to these quarrels

2. He was baptized Henri Marie Joseph François-Regis Ignace. The last name was in honor of Saint Ignatius Loyola, founder of the Jesuits, whose feast is celebrated on 31 July.

3. Henri Bremond, *La Provence mystique au XVIIe siècle. Antoine Yvan et Madaleine Martin* (Paris: 1908), 6.

4. Jean Dagens, "Introduction à Henri Bremond," in Maurice Nédoncelle and Jean Dagens (eds.), *Entretiens sur Henri Bremond* (Paris: 1967), 1–3.

in the drawing room of the house on the Place des Prêcheurs.[5] The addled Chambord had at any rate thrown away any chance for the throne when his Bremond namesake was six years old by outlandishly demanding that the tricolor be replaced by the lily flag of the Bourbons.[6] Even this absurd gesture Pierre Bremond heartily endorsed, and when he died in 1884 it was sadly noted that he had outlived his prince by less than a year.

Thomasine Pons had died five years before that, when her son Henri was fourteen. This was a severe blow for the boy, for he was particularly attached to his mother, whom he remembered all his life for her "gentle irony," her "extraordinary capacity to fascinate." She favored English novels and introduced Henri to Walter Scott, "all of whose books I read with passion. . . . My Anglomania dates from tender years." His brother André recorded later that when their mother died Henri experienced a prolonged period of depression, one result of which was his failure, in 1880, to pass the first stage of the examinations for the baccalaureate.[7] Up to that time his perfomance at the Collège du Sacré-Coeur of Aix had been outstanding, especially in literary subjects. The double shock of bereavement and scholastic disgrace brought about what André called his brother's "definitive conversion," a "new level of fervor," which led in turn to his decision to embrace the religious life.[8]

Henri Bremond's experience with the Society of Jesus was less tempestuous than that of his great friend of later years, George Tyrrell, but it was no more satisfying. From the moment he left the society in 1904—two years before Tyrrell was expelled from it—Bremond hinted strongly that his had been a "forced vocation."[9] There is reason to accept this conclusion, though the evidence is necessarily circumstantial and much after-the-fact. Henri may have been moved to his resolution first of all by simple filial affection; his bereaved father had been educated by the Jesuits and remained always deeply devoted to them. Several Jesuits held faculty positions at the Sacré-Coeur, and the director of the school at the time recalled many years afterward that one of them—"a respectable man surely, but of a cast of mind too absolute and rather narrow"—had been particularly solicitous about the motherless Bremonds, turning himself virtually into their tutor. "Henri Bremond," wrote the director, himself a secular priest and later a bishop, "was not made for the inflexible and highly programmed life to which an imprudent zeal dispatched him."[10] Charles Maurras recollected being regaled by Henri and his brothers who disdained marbles and stamp collecting in favor of a game of "comparative criti-

5. André Blanchet, *Henri Bremond, 1865–1904* (Paris: 1975), 17–8.

6. See Denis Brogan, *The Development of Modern France (1870–1939)* (London: 1953), 82–87.

7. The baccalaureate was the certificate granted by a secondary school—a *lycée* or a *collège*—and required before a student could apply for admission to a *faculté* or *école speciale*. See chapter 1.

8. Obituary notice by André Bremond, *Études* 217 (5 October, 1933): 29–53.

9. The evidence is summarized by Blanchet, *Bremond*, 19–27.

10. Guillibert to Merry del Val, 24 June, 1921, printed in André Blanchet (ed.), *Histoire d'une mise à l'index. La "Sainte Chantal" de l'abbé Bremond d'après documents inedits* (Paris: 1967), 242–47.

cism," in which "they allotted equitably blame and praise upon our various professors." No doubt the influential Jesuit father was one of the teachers who received favorable notice, since two of Henri's three brothers also eventually joined the society.

But possibly the most intriguing clue to Bremond's attitude in 1882 appears in an autobiogrphical note of 1923. "I took from my father," he wrote, "what I would call my *Jacobitism*, my attachment to lost causes and individuals." Certainly, he demonstrated this characteristic more than once, in his persisting friendship for Tyrrell and Loisy, for example, and in his forlorn defense of the Sillon.[11] In 1882, when the Third Republic was passing through one of its periodic anticlerical spasms, no cause in France appeared more lost than that of the Jesuits. The Left, abetted not a little by the pious foolishness of the Comte de Chambord and his followers, had swept into power with the slogan "Clericalism, that is the enemy!"[12] The government's first target was, as usual, the Society of Jesus, whose four French provinces were dissolved and their members dispersed by the decree of March 29, 1880.[13] Enforcing the order resulted in minor disturbances in some places, including Aix, where two hundred people gathered at four in the morning outside the Jesuits' residence in the rue Lacépède in hopes of turning away the police.[14] These efforts were to no avail, however, and so the Jesuits got to wear once again—as they have so often in so many places—the badge of official disapproval. To a young and impressionable Jacobite it must have seemed a badge of honor.

This latest suppression of the society was the reason why there were Jesuits teaching at Sacré-Coeur, which ordinarily was a *collège* staffed exclusively by the secular clergy. And it was the reason why Henri Bremond ultimately became a man of two cultures.[15] On November 24, 1882, he departed Aix for Sidmouth, on the Devonshire coast, where the noviciate of the Jesuit province of Lyon, expelled from its residence in Montciel, had taken refuge. The United Kingdom served throughout the nineteenth century as a haven for persons exiled from the Continent for ideological reasons; it made little difference what the ideology was, whether that of Marx or of Louis Napoleon or of a bedraggled band of French Jesuits—a mark of noble generosity, no doubt, but a mark also of John Bull's serene, imperial self-confidence.

PEAK HOUSE, SIDMOUTH —"an old mansion located in the middle of a park, surrounded by beautiful trees and by rich green lawns that stretched

11. See chapters 9 and 19.

12. See chapter 1.

13. See Édouard Lecanuet, *L'Église de France sous la troisième république. Les premières années du pontificat de Léon XIII*, 61–65, and Martin R. Harney, *The Jesuits in History* (New York: 1941), 382–84.

14. Maurras to Vallat, 10 September, 1952, in Charles Maurras, *Lettres de prison* (Paris: 1958), 355–57.

15. Dagens, "Introduction à Henri Bremond," 3–4.

down toward the sea," as the novice-master described it[16]—was the scene of Bremond's first real experience of the kind of spirituality he had committed himself to by entering the Society of Jesus. It may seem incongruous that a group of young Frenchmen should undertake the classic "grand retreat" of thirty days, conducted according to the norms laid down in Saint Ignatius's *Spiritual Exercises*, in a little port in Devon, where nannies still extorted good behavior from the children under their charge by threatening to produce otherwise a wicked Jesuit to punish them, and where the derived adjective "jesuitical" still retained its pejorative connotation. Yet so it was in a world that had changed drastically since the sixteenth century, when Ignatius had written his celebrated book and when the Spanish Armada had sailed within cannon shot of Sidmouth harbor.

But in one limited sector of human activity the world had not changed so much after all. Just as the society founded by Ignatius—despite all its powerful enemies and well-publicized ups and downs—had dominated the intellectual and political life of the Catholic church since the Reformation, so also had its spiritual ideals dominated the church's devotional life.[17] The Jesuits may have been with some justice castigated and lampooned as advisers to corrupt monarchs and directors to frivolous ladies of high fashion, but they were also confessors to untold millions of ordinary people, preachers of undoubted skill and persuasiveness, authors of the most influential spiritual books, heads or key resource persons of authoritative Vatican congregations, editors of widely read journals and newspapers—like the the *Civiltà Cattolica*[18]—directors of a system of secondary schools arguably the best in Europe or, for that matter, anywhere in the world, professors in the seminaries training the parish priests who would carry their version of what the Catholic life should be to the countless men and women in the pews. And whatever apostolate they engaged in, all the Jesuits shared a training rooted in the *Spiritual Exercises*.

During the twenty-two years he was a Jesuit, Henri Bremond underwent the Ignatian thirty-day retreat on two or possibly three occasions.[19] He no doubt also experienced the shorter three- and seven-day retreats numerous times, and, once ordained himself, directed such shortened versions of the original discipline. For the method of spiritual formation found in the *Exercises* was perceived by its devotees to be of almost unlimited variety, adaptable to people from all walks of life and in all stages of ascetical development. Indeed, the *Exercises* was not a book to be read but a manual to be used by a skilled

16. Quoted in Blanchet, *Bremond*, 29.

17. See the uniquely perceptive treatment in H. Outram Evennett, *The Spirit of the Counter Reformation* (Cambridge: 1968), 43–67.

18. See chapter 2.

19. The experts differ. Compare Blanchet, *Bremond*, 30–32, with Henri Bernard-Maître, "Les *Exercices spirituels* de Saint Ignace de Loyola intérpretés par l'abbé Henri Bremond," in Nédoncelle and Dagens (eds.), *Entretiens*, 169.

director so that its full impact would issue in the "spiritual exercise" of the retreatant, as the title implied. But supple and widely applicable as the technique may have been, for the Jesuit aspirant himself the crucial encounter with the *Exercises* came at the beginning of the noviciate. Then he received the full treatment, as it were: thirty silent days of meditations and ascetical practices designed to concentrate all his powers—cognitive, volitional, affective—upon a consideration, first, of his own sinfulness and the consequent need for purification, then on the Passion, Resurrection, and ultimate triumph of Christ, and finally of the need to implement these lessons by ranging himself behind the standard of Jesus, whose disciplined, self-denying, even remorseless soldier he would henceforward be. Four centuries of history have demonstrated the spectacular success this kind of holy indoctrination could achieve.[20]

But not for everybody. Bremond did not comment publicly upon his initial retreat at Sidmouth until the end of his life, by which time he had long repudiated the ascetic ideals of the *Exercises* and, having established himself as the brilliant but not unbiased chronicler of French Catholic spirituality,[21] had demonstrated deep distrust of any systematic and inflexible approach to the interior life, which is what he judged the Ignatian method to be. Bremond had decided that the Christian vocation had to be a mystical and individualist experience, not a lock-step conformity to a set of abstract rules. At Sidmouth

I confronted the text [of the *Spiritual Exercises*] but without much enthusiasm. A first experience which, I hasten to say, proved absolutely nothing. Saint Ignatius intended the *Exercises* only for very select men already trained. I was only eighteen [actually seventeen] years old. . . . Between me and the text loomed at the door the amiable person of the master of novices. I found his explanations very long indeed. And besides that, nothing but an immense ennui. For enrichment of spirit during those thirty days, I turned to botany. In the garden, though it was winter, the first red shoots of a rhubarb peeked out, a plant new to me.[22]

"Ennui," an untranslatable word that includes in its meaning melancholy, listlessness, and boredom, seems to have been an occupational hazard for nineteenth-century French intellectuals.[23] And the muted mockery—rhubarb in a wintry garden—had become by 1928 an integral element of Bremond's style. But reminiscence in any event remains suspect, and there is no contemporary evidence that Bremond found his Jesuit experience a burden so early on. A

20. See the remarks in Marvin R. O'Connell, *The Counter Reformation, 1559–1610* (New York: 1974), 108–11.

21. Bremond's magnum opus in eleven volumes, *Histoire littéraire du sentiment religieux en France,* was published between 1915 and 1932.

22. A note written by Bremond, about 1928 and published posthumously by Jean-Claude Guy, "Henri Bremond et son commentaire des *Exercises* de saint Ignace," *Revue d'ascétique et de mystique* 45 (1969): 191–223.

23. For other examples, see Marvin R. O'Connell, "Montalembert at Mechlin: A Reprise of 1830," *Journal of Church and State* 26 (Autumn 1984):517–18, 523. For Loisy's confession to the phenomenon, see chapter 4.

year after that first retreat, in December 1883, he and his confreres moved from Sidmouth to Hastings, where they spent two years. From 1885 till 1888—while that other Jesuit aspirant, George Tyrrell, was serving his second tour in Malta—Bremond studied philosophy at Mold, just over the Welsh border from Chester. The French called the institution St. David's College, a rather pretentious name for a converted prison, a vast, gloomy building that accommodated 120 or so students, its ambience perhaps best expressed by "the very narrow windows, high up on the walls, covered by iron bars and frosted glass, and impossible to see out of without standing on a stepladder."[24]

Meanwhile, the anticlerical tide in France rolled to and fro. By 1888 the Jesuits were back in place, their legal expulsion for the moment a dead letter. The province of Lyon functioned again more or less normally, so that Bremond was able to do his apprentice teaching of the humanities at *collèges* first at Mongré and then at Dôle. But the provincial theologate, out of prudence, was maintained at Mold, and so at the end of 1890 Bremond returned to Wales. "Great God!" he exclaimed in 1902, "I have nightmares over those dreadful classes in theology I suffered through for four years—yes, four years!"[25] In fact, the theology course lasted only three years, but, looking back, they seemed, as had the similar length of time endured studying Scholastic philosophy, interminable to him, like a tunnel with no light at the end of it. But they did finish at last, and Bremond—a slender, handsome youth of twenty-seven, with close-cropped black hair, a cleft chin, and slightly hooded eyes—was ordained priest on September 8, 1892, slightly less than a year after George Tyrrell had received the same sacrament.

In their various comings and goings the two young Jesuits never met. But the long and tedious years Bremond spent in England and Wales left a deep imprint on him. Though he remained always Gallic to his fingertips, he nevertheless considered that his time of formation had provided him with a second home. He learned the subtleties of the English language, not only from books—he was especially fond of the novels of George Eliot and Dickens[26]—but also in the idiom of the common people to whose children he taught their catechism and whose cottages he visited, consistent with ordinary Jesuit pastoral practice, in the neighborhood around Mold. So enchanted did he become by the British scene that, years later, when he contemplated writing about mystics and mysticism, his original intention had been to concentrate his researches in England.[27] He read the works of the Tractarian John Keble and, more surprisingly, of W. G. Ward—no mystic he—but he was especially enthralled by Newman, whose subtlety and sensitivity, he liked to think, matched his own. "Have you ever read the *Apologia* of Newman," he wrote to

24. Quoted in Blanchet, *Bremond*, 34.
25. Quoted in Alfred Loisy, *George Tyrrell et Henri Bremond* (Paris: 1935), 5.
26. Henry Hogarth, *Henri Bremond: The Life and Work of a Devout Humanist* (London: 1950), 3.
27. Dagens, "Introduction," 3.

Charles Maurras at the beginning of 1892. "There is an expression in it that I never think of without also thinking of you: 'I have not sinned against light.' I heartily wish that you could understand what is meant by a sin against the light."[28] Maurras had lost his faith while a pupil at the Collège de Sacré-Coeur of Aix; his schoolfellow there, though he scarcely realized it, had now embarked upon a long journey during which the light would be often enfolded in shadow.

"HAVE I YET RESPONDED to the threats and sarcasms in your last letter?" Henri Bremond wrote at the end of March 1909.

Always you the wolf and I the lamb. I traveled twenty kilometers to see you before you left, and this despite the symptoms of the 'flu. I found you haggard and pale, like a man suddenly aroused from sleep, and I learned the reason for it was that you were arguing philosophy with a workman! You told me to wait a moment. The moment passed in the chill of a dark corridor. The moment got longer. Everything I could hear indicated that the two disputants were haggling over the nature of eternity, and all the while I am shivering more and more. Then out of respect for this philosophical debate—which you would not expect me to adhere to even after seven years of scholastic argumentation—I made for the door at a gallop in hopes of getting rid of my 'flu in time, not eternity.[29]

Philosophical debate was never Bremond's strong suit or pressing interest, yet he recognized quality wherever he saw it and was willing to pay playful salute to his correspondent's passion for mental exercise of that sort. Circumstances had at any rate put the two of them in the same distressful boat by 1909 and had bonded them in an unlikely friendship. And not them only: Lucien Laberthonnière, a deeply introspective man who chose his friends sparingly, nevertheless never turned away from those who had run up against foul weather. "I have loved him from the first time I met him, and always since," said George Tyrrell, who died that summer.[30]

Marie Paul Lucien Laberthonnière was born on October 5, 1860, in a modest, one-story house in the village of Chazelet, in the valley of the River Indre, south of Tours and west of Bourges. He was the sixth and youngest child—and fifth son—of Sylvain Laberthonnière, a shoemaker, and Marie Gallien, a seamstress. Chazelet, with a population of about six hundred, looked like countless other French villages of the time: a single street lined on either side by low houses, with a church surrounded by a grove of trees at one end, and the towers of the nearby chateau looming up inside the now dried-up medieval moat. Marie Laberthonnière did most of her business with the great folk who

28. Quoted in Blanchet, *Bremond*, 41.

29. Quoted in Marie-Thérèse Perrin, *La jeunesse de Laberthonnière* (Paris: 1980), 20.

30. Quoted in von Hügel to Laberthonnière, 17 July, 1909, in Jean Steinmann, *Friedrich von Hügel: Sa vie, son oeuvre, ses amitiés* (Paris: 1962), 338–39. See also Marie-Thérèse Perrin (ed.), *Laberthonnière et ses amis* (Paris: 1975), 193.

still resided occasionally in the castle. Beyond lay the meadows and tilled fields, marked off by rows of elms and clumps of blackberry bushes.

Besides his ordinary work, Sylvain Laberthonnière doubled as sacristan, trimming the candles in the church and ringing the angelus bell three times a day, among other routine duties. In Chazelet this office was considered a signal honor: here, in this region of the old province of Berry, the immense majority of country people still practiced the old faith with something of the old fervor. The rhythm of the seasons meshed with liturgical observances and with the values of hardworking, simple peasants about whom it was easy—as Alfred Loisy did[31]—to romanticize. In the autumn of 1907, long after he had left Chazelet, when he was living in Paris as a controversial savant with sophisticated friends like Henri Bremond—indeed, within weeks of having read the condemnations of a papal encyclical directed against, among others, himself— Lucien Laberthonnière scribbled down this remark in the margin of a theological treatise he was writing: "Everyone has known simple souls for whom Jesus Christ was an altogether different thing from the historical personage lost in the darkness of time; who truly have listened to his voice and lived by his teachings! They attained a science of Christ, a science of life." "An altogether different thing"—*tout autre chose*—the untutored recognition of which leads to "a science of Christ": here was the *crise moderniste* in a nutshell.

Lucien grew up in the normal way of village boys, going to school and playing games and sharing in household chores. As the baby of a large family, he received perhaps more attention than his siblings with whom, however, he appears to have been then and always on affectionate terms. To his only sister Ursula, married and a mother while Lucien was still quite a child, he offered, in his early twenties, a remarkable tribute: she was one who "in my moments of discouragement gives my spirit a 'sursum corda,' one who prays for me and loves me. . . . O my sister, you will be my consolation and support upon the earth." His brother Ernest, whose health was delicate, was given specific charge over little Lucien by two hardworking and often preoccupied parents, and the tie between the brothers became extremely close. When Ernest died of tuberculosis in 1878, Lucien remembered him as "this young man of ardent and profound thought, who was my guide and most loving and devoted friend." For his father, who died a few months after Ernest, Lucien invoked the image of a peasant-poet in the romantic style of George Sand, without however succumbing to the saccharine extreme of her literary image. "The peasant," he observed with commendable realism, "had to have now and then a sort of ecstatic revelation to beguile him in his chronic fatigue and to benumb his cares, but the real consciousness of these sentiments was beyond him." As for his mother, he wrote for her poetry—rather remarkably bad poetry—of his own: "Pleure, pleure, ô ma pauvre mère—Weep, weep, o my poor mother. /

31. See chapter 1.

Your son is unhappy, unhappy at the age of twenty. / Tell me, what is there left for me to hope for?"[32]

At the moment these lines of doggerel were composed, in January 1883, Marie Laberthonnière indeed had cause to weep, having recently buried both a son and a husband. And now her youngest child had also been diagnosed as tuberculous. Lucien, singled out by the local curé for his piety and good nature, had left home at thirteen and enrolled in the *petit séminaire* of Saint-Gaultier, which served the diocese of Bourges. Here, on the banks of the Creuse, where an eleventh-century priory had once stood, he spent seven years, happy ones for the most part. He liked his schoolmates—lads like himself from villages like Chazelet—and they him. His professors were sturdy priests of the diocese upon whom he bestowed a full measure of adolescent devotion. He found the study of the classics and the humanities congenial and easily won all sorts of scholastic prizes.[33] But he was most captivated by the romantic poets he now encountered, Chateaubriand first—"his dreaminess, his rapture at the world of nature, . . . his imagination, his need to flee from reality, even the intimate griefs that he grasped to himself and caressed, I savored all this"—then Lamartine, and, most of all, Musset. "I reveled in the poets of the nineteenth century, because they so well understood the human heart."

Whether due to savoring the primordial gloom of the romantic poets, or to the death of his brother and father, or to the simple process of maturation—most likely a combination of all of these—Lucien's last year at Saint-Gaultier was darkened by depression and by doubts about his vocation to the priesthood. He passed nevertheless, in 1880, to the *grand séminaire* at Bourges, the operation of which the bishop had entrusted to the Sulpicians. These pioneers in conducting priestly training made no bones about their priorities: a seminary was to be before all else a school of virtue, a place where young men should learn discipline, self-control, and obedience. The tasks they would take on in the future were those of pastors of souls, for which a decent preparation in philosophy and theology was also necessary, yet clearly of secondary importance. Young Laberthonnière did not kick against this goad, but the rigor of the Sulpician regimen did nothing to resolve his doubts; indeed, they became more painful and he began to wonder whether he was losing his faith. "O my God," he wrote in the journal he now began to keep, "seeing that my heart has such a need for love, make it turn to you, make it rest in you, make it live for you." One priest to whom he turned for advice—significantly, not a Sulpician—urged him to substitute detached analysis for "these illusions," for "these troubles of the heart and imagination which are common enough for all men on the grim passage from childhood to an adult's estate." In time Laber-

32. For the quotations and for much of what follows, see Perrin, *La jeunesse de Laberthonnière*, 15–67. In this admirable reconstruction Madame Perrin uses a journal kept by Laberthonnière in the major seminary and a few letters, all preserved in the Biblioteque Nationale.

33. For a similar expereince at a slightly earlier date, see O'Connell, *John Ireland*, 44–54.

thonnière would follow this counsel, or rather he would modify it by trying to mesh the affective and the analytical with, to be sure, debatable results. But first he had to endure another crisis, the fear that he too might be carried off by consumption: "What can my fickle dreams now impart to me? [he concluded in the poem to his mother] / After having donned the raiment of the Levite / Now must I take it off, / Now must I fling myself into the world!"

It proved not to be so bad as that. The disease in his lungs gradually abated, and after an eighteen-month leave Lucien returned to Bourges to resume his professional preparation. The unsettlement of his spirit seems also to have dissolved during this interval. "Drive far from me, Lord," he prayed in October, 1883, "this melancholy, this discouragement, this distressing sadness which up till now has paralyzed my energies. I want at all cost to live the life of a Christian and to make myself worthy to be a priest. To live by the will and not by fancies, that is the necessity." The prayer was apparently answered to Laberthonnière's satisfaction, for the uncertainties of the preceding years tormented him no more. Not that his earlier poetic aspirations were abandoned; they were rather rechanneled as he applied himself to the required philosophical and theological studies. In these he took a strongly independent line, confirming perhaps what one of his professors later remarked ruefully to him: "You were never undocile at the time I knew you, but you were in your docility more ready to yield to feeling or to the voice of the heart than to arguments from reason. You chose yourself the kind of work you would do, and it often sufficed that one directive had come from higher up for you to follow another."

Had Laberthonnière asserted himself thus in matters of piety the Sulpicians would never have indulged him. But his religious fervor was above question, and indeed he linked that fervor directly to his intellectual endeavors, which, in the judgment of the seminary staff, was to his credit. "I have dreamed and I have suffered," he noted in his journal. "In my solitude my thought has progressed. . . . Above all I have remained a Christian. Indeed I have become a more convinced Christian, a Christian philosopher." And later he wrote to a friend: "I will not conceal from you that in studying philosophy I have made it a matter of the [whole] spirit. . . . In the hubbub (*tohu-bohu*) that the theologians have made of their discipline, it seems to me that I distinguish clearly what is properly and essentially Christian from the explanations of a childish philosophy." He was referring to the manual Scholasticism taught him in the seminary, but he had no more regard for the Thomism recommended by Leo XIII in *Aeterni Patris*, the issuance of which encyclical led him to compose, in 1884, an extraordinarily precocious and presumptuous essay, "The Cartesian Spirit and the Scholastic Spirit."

O modern Scholastic philosophers [he wrote with youthful passion], you who dream foolishly of entrapping in your formulas a human soul which has come to a consciousness of itself by genuine reflection! This soul which has felt the flame of life, which has understood, which has experienced the thirst for infinity, which loves science, a true and positive science, not an imaginary one, a science that is also poetry—you would like to force that soul to fit into your categories. Try instead to capture the passing wind and force it into a circle or a square. Your attempts will be just as vain as that.[34]

Lucien Laberthonnière—physically robust now with burly good looks and stout peasant shoulders—was ordained a subdeacon on February 28, 1885. "My God, it is finished. Now I am yours forever more. My life can have no legitimacy except in service of the church." He also wrote down that day resolutions for the future, imposing on himself a half-hour of private prayer a day, a careful recitation of the breviary, a daily practice of "corporeal penance beyond the ordinary," and an habitual austerity with regard to food and dress. "My vocation seems to be one of study. I must therefore hold myself ready to sacrifice all temporal advantages in order to pursue it. I must keep lit in my heart the sacred fire, the love of science and of truth, and never indulge in vulgarity."

THIS LAST ENTRY suggests that Laberthonnière had already decided—as Alfred Loisy had done a few years earlier—that his future was not to be that of a country curé, but the precise direction he had chosen did not become clear until after his ordination to the priesthood a year later. Then he acted with an unwonted dispatch. In October 1886 he sought and received the permission of his bishop to join the Oratory, and at the end of that month he left Berry forever. It proved to be a fateful decision.

The institution Laberthonnière joined—l'Oratoire de Jésus-Christ et de Marie Immaculée—followed in its general lines the model established in the sixteenth century by Saint Philip Neri.[35] An "oratory" was a congregation of secular priests who lived together but who took no vows and who supported themselves out of their own private means. The rule they followed was extremely adaptable, designed to give the fullest possible scope to individual aspirations, an attractive feature to Laberthonnière. The Oratorian tradition gave emphasis to priestly service by way of preaching and the confessional, and there followed from those obligations a certain, admittedly ill-defined, commitment to scholarship. Baronius and Mansi had been Oratorians, and so had the great Cartesian philosopher Nicolas Malebranche (d. 1715). These circumstances were not lost upon Laberthonnière, as they had not been upon Newman who, when he became a Catholic and was searching for an appro-

34. Laberthonnière, "L'esprit cartésienne," 327 (also see note 1, above).
35. See Antonio Cistellini, *San Filippo Neri: L'Oratorio e la Congregazione oratoriana, Storia e Spiritualità* (Brescia: 1989), and Anon., "L'Oratoire de France: Centenaire de sa restauration, 1851–1953" (Issoudin, n. d. [1932]).

priate ministry within his new communion, one that would best satisfy himself and his fellow Oxford converts, concluded that the Oratorian ideal was particularly suitable.[36]

In 1852—a few years after Newman had introduced the Oratory into England for the first time—it was restored in France, where it had been suppressed since the Revolution. Among the second founders of the institute was Auguste J. A. Gratry, a distinguished if somewhat eccentric theologian—he employed calculus to prove the existence of God—celebrated as much for his personal sanctity as for his peculiar views. He and his colleagues in their work of restoration followed the traditional Oratorian genius, with one, typically Gallican, difference: they insisted upon a measure of administrative centralization, unknown in Italy or England, which placed ultimate authority in the hands of a superior-general.

Laberthonnière left no record of the year of noviciate he spent at Sceaux. In October 1887 he began his teaching career at the Oratorian *collège* at Juilly, northeast of Paris. In his very first class he challenged his pupils with a series of rhetorical questions. "What is a philosopher? A philosopher is one who loves and who personally seeks out *the Truth*. I exist, and within me there is a whole world which is called thought. What is all this about? Who am I? Where do I come from? What is the purpose of my life? What is this world that surrounds me?"[37] The new professor thus exhibited admirable fervor—to say nothing of dedication to the grand Cartesian principle of a "whole world of thought within"—but he was in fact raw and untrained, with no formal academic credentials. He therefore began this same year to follow courses at the Sorbonne on a part-time basis, a practice he continued till 1894, by which time he had accumulated—not without some temporary setbacks—the conventional degrees.[38]

These were, for the most part, busy and fulfilling years. In his personal life, Laberthonnière, though never troubled as he had been during his seminary days, continued to fidget over his internal states and his external relationships. There were times when he regretted having given up the relatively independent life of a country curé, for he found the regime of a religious community in many respects irksome. "I return from holiday," he wrote, "and a painful period begins. I miss the countryside and my friends." Obedience was not a virtue he practiced easily; he admitted a tendency to judge his superiors harshly and to rebuff any approaches from them. He wondered if he were not leading a double life, a "hail-fellow" on the outside and yet radically and secretly "egotistical," "a life of appearances," in short, "a deceitful life." He recognized the source of the dichotomy:

36. See Placid Murray (ed.), *Newman the Oratorian* (Dublin: 1969), for Newman's unpublished papers on the Oratorian vocation.

37. Quoted in Perrin, *La jeunesse de Laberthonnière*, 79.

38. Paul Beillevert (ed.), *Laberthonnière: L'homme et l'oeuvre* (Paris: 1972), 16–7.

Like every one else, I feel the need of sympathy, and with me it is an immense need. It has been the source of my energy up till now. I love solitude, and yet at the same time I find isolation intolerable. I have found some sympathy, and I thank God for it. But I am convinced that as one grows older, human sympathy means less and less. Having left my home and those to whom I was attached, I am increasingly alone.[39]

Such gloomy ruminations—and these musings were hardly more than that—appeared to have had no adverse professional effects, though Laberthonnière's intensely introspective temperament must never be left out of account. He proved in any event to be a gifted teacher, and his scholarly exertions began to bear fruit as well. In 1890 he published his first book review in Duchesne's *Bulletin critique*. If the appearance of his prose in those pages provided a sign of future preoccupations, so did the title he gave, a year later, to his first article: "Philosophy Is an Art."[40] Descartes remained the center of his studies and, more than that, their inspiration. "There is a grandeur in Descartes," he wrote. "Too bad for those who do not realize this." "What I admire most in Descartes, even more than his ideas, is his method of philosophizing. In following it I have staked out my own interior independence." Only one quality was lacking to his hero, and, in supplying that, Laberthonnière hoped to contribute something of his own to the meaning of the philosopher's vocation: "What Descartes lacks is religious sentiment. . . . One never feels that thought with him is prayer. . . . He has a great soul, certainly. But the attitude he assumes is that of a stoic gentleman, . . . a mathematician rather than a philosopher. He fails to elicit the feeling of mystery. Infinity is for him too simply an idea."[41]

Even so venerable a master as Descartes could not quite satisfy Laberthonnière's need for an intellectual soul mate, for a friend "whose heart would completely understand my heart. I dream of him very often, this friend." In the spring of 1894 the dream at last came true. "I shall never forget the emotion I felt, in the midst of my restless solitude, when I read the opening pages of *L'action*. I found there finally a living echo of all those conflicting currents swirling around inside me." He took up his pen and wrote a letter to the author, a man named Maurice Blondel whom he had never met: "Monsieur, I have just finished reading your book for the third time; and I shall return to it, or rather I shall hold fast to it, because it ranks among those treatises that are never exhausted."[42]

NOT EVERYONE REACTED as positively as Laberthonnière did to reading the book with the curious title, *Action: An Attempt at a Critique of Life and a*

---

39. Quoted in Perrin, *La jeunesse de Laberthonnière*, 82–85.

40. "La philosophie est un art," *L'enseignement chrétien* 10 (16 Nov., 1891): 321–25.

41. See Perrin, *La jeunesse de Laberthonnière*, 86–96, and Joseph Beaude, "Laberthonnière et Descartes," in Beillevert (ed.), *Laberthonnière*, 113–29.

42. Laberthonnière to Archambault, autumn 1928, and Laberthonnière to Blondel, 18 April, 1894, in Claude Tresmontant (ed.), *Correspondance philosophique* (Paris: 1961), 65–68.

Science of Practice. Actually it was a dissertation presented to the Sorbonne for a doctoral degree, defended orally in June 1893, and published the following November. When a schoolfellow heard the topic Blondel had chosen, he exclaimed, "A thesis on action, great God, what could that be?"[43] Similar puzzlement was not lacking among the final examiners. "Your thought is obscure," one of them complained to the candidate, "and your manner of writing obscures it still more. I would struggle a whole hour over one of your pages without managing to understand it. I calculate it took me a month and a half to read your thesis."[44] Worse than the obscurity, charged another, was the thesis's "totally conservative spirit, its orthodox preoccupations, its fidelity to the dogmas and precepts of a certain church."[45] The degree was granted, reluctantly, and Maurice Blondel walked out of those hallowed academic halls to spend a long life trying to be understood and trying to demonstrate his fidelity to the teachings of "a certain church."

Blondel,[46] like Henri Bremond, came from a distinguished line of provincial solicitors, though his family was by far the more prosperous. He was a Burgundian, born November 2, 1861, at Dijon, a road and rail hub noted for its mustard and its black currant liqueur, *cassis de Dijon*. The town traced its origins back to Roman times, but its best days—it was a commercial and educational center of some note toward the end of the eighteenth century—had passed when Maurice was growing up there. His was a placid childhood, and he harbored none of the sharp memories Loisy did of the presence of the German armies in 1870. During the summer holidays, spent at a country house at Saint-Seine-sur-Vingeanne, near Dijon, Maurice rambled across the uplands, taking note, with fascination, of all the sights and sounds around him and of the beauty of a vibrant nature, teeming mysteriously with life. His collection of insects must have rivaled that of the young Friedrich von Hügel. At Saint-Seine he made another discovery, similarly destined to affect him all his life, that of the spiritual riches of the Roman liturgy, celebrated in the local church with much more splendor and reverence than in his home parish.[47]

Maurice attended the municipal *collège* in Dijon and then the *faculté* of law there, intending at first to follow the profession traditional among the men in his family. But casual exposure to the writings of certain philosophers, partic-

43. Quoted in René Virgoulay, *Blondel et le modernisme* (Paris: 1980), 20.
44. Quoted in Houtin, *Modernisme*, 12.
45. See Bernard Reardon, *Liberalism and Tradition: Aspects of Catholic Thought in Nineteenth-Century France* (Cambridge: 1975), 224–26.
46. Due perhaps to his extreme diffidence and his piety no less than to his total preoccupation with matters intellectual, materials have been lacking for an adequate biography of Blondel, who died in 1949. Snippets of information can be gleaned from various short notices and in collections of correspondence. See also Jean Lacroix, *Maurice Blondel* (New York: 1968) and Dominique Folscheid (ed.), *Maurice Blondel: Une dramatique de la modernité* (Paris: 1990). Of particular value are his spiritual diaries dating from 1883, published posthumously in two volumes under the title *Carnets intimes* (Paris, 1961–66).
47. Lacroix, *Blondel*, 11–13.

ularly Leibnitz, so enthralled him that the prospect of further legal studies paled and ultimately was abandoned. He determined to enroll in the École Normale Supérieure and become a professor of philosophy. This was more easily decided than done: it was only on the third try that Blondel managed to pass the qualifying examinations and, in 1881, set off for Paris.

He was by then an intensely, almost terrifyingly, religious young man. During his tenure as a student at the École Normale, and for years afterward, he constantly worried that he might be selfishly turning his back upon God's call to the priesthood. "I want to want with God," he wrote in the very first entry of his intimate diary, dated Novemeber 24, 1883. "I want what God wants, in the manner in which God wants it of me. I do not know what this is, but with him I can do all the things I cannot do by myself."[48] The irreligious, not to say antireligious, atmosphere of academic Paris did not dampen Blondel's ardor. He read a chapter of the *Imitation of Christ* each morning, and then tried during the day to implement its lessons. He cultivated a set of likeminded friends and schoolmates who, despite all, remained practicing Catholics, though it may be assumed that few of them could match Blondel, for example, in his eucharistic piety. He made it a regular practice to drop in every day at a little chapel on the rue d'Ulm where the Blessed Sacrament was exposed for devotion. "My God," he wrote in March 1884, "I want to bring to you here as often as possible a short moment of adoration, to offer myself to you here for the sake of those souls who, even in this school I attend, outrage you and bring mankind's curses upon you. I ask you on my knees to accept the offering of my heart and make it less unworthy of yourself." "The Eucharist," he added, "captures the whole of the Christian spirit." And, a few months earlier, after reflecting on his own shortcomings, he observed poignantly: "My God, I wish I were the good bread of the altar, over which you would pronounce the words of transubstantiation!"[49] The comparison with von Hügel, whom he was not to meet until many years later, hardly needs to be stated.

Yet Blondel, for all the discrimination he endured for the sake of "a certain church," was not without support within the confines of the École Normale. Among his professors Elme Caro, whatever his intellectual idiosyncrasies, was at any rate a theist—"much too grand a rhetorician perhaps," Blondel shrewdly observed, "weak though very intelligent, more broad-minded than precise."[50] Émile Boutroux, under whom Laberthonnière was to study a decade later,[51] acted as Blondel's academic adviser, and did so with constancy and wholeheartedness. But no one was so important for the furtherance of Blondel's

---

48. Blondel, *Carnets intimes*, 1:17.
49. Blondel, *Carnets intimes*, 1:41, 19.
50. Blondel, *Carnets intimes*, 1:21.
51. Beillevert (ed.), *Laberthonnière*, 16.

career, and no one had so profound and lasting an influence upon him, as did Professor Léon Ollé-Laprune.

Ollé-Laprune, in his early forties when Blondel met him, was Parisian-born and Parisian-educated. He had proceeded through the ranks of the *université* until, in 1875, he was appointed *maître de conférences* in the École Normale. He was a fervent Catholic and even an unabashed Ultramontane who, later, deeply impressed by Leo XIII, proclaimed that "on all sides Rome is turned to, Rome is listened to, and what the pope does, what the pope says, echoes throughout the world." This was hardly a position calculated to gain the sympathy of his colleagues at the École, nor the tolerance of the anticlerical politicians in control of the state after 1878. So when, in 1880, he added his name to a formal protest after the suppression of the religious orders, the minister of education suspended him for a year from his academic duties. Shock and disgust were universal among Ollé-Laprune's professional associates, who admired him as much for his character and his affability as for his demonstrated scholarship, and the students published a letter of support for him. (The letter, incidentally, was drafted by Jean Jaurès, the future socialist leader, whose anti-Catholic credentials were, even as a youth, of the highest order.[52])

Little wonder, then, that the shy and pious Maurice Blondel found in Ollé-Laprune a hero and a model. "He was a man," Blondel said, "of modesty and precision and fine discernment, whose sympathy, whose charity perhaps I should say, was universal. Truly, we who knew him, we who received his smile, his kindly words, the grip of his hand, can do no more than say: You should have known him too; there is nothing I can teach you about such a man. He was unique, and he revealed himself completely in the sincerity and the shining unity of his character." But Blondel, a man of the intellect if ever there was one, admired more than his mentor's moral qualities. "What Léon Ollé-Laprune wanted was, by a reciprocal intussusception of the practical with the speculative, to make philosophy a growth or development of the being who thinks while he acts and acts while he thinks; that is to say, by a profound and histological assimilation of all elements—sensible, intellectual, moral, historical, social, ascetic, religious—thus to promote a Christian philosophy, genuinely philosophical and genuinely Christian."[53] Here was a goal Blondel took unto himself.

The formidable shade of Descartes brooded heavily over these *normaliens*. "I think, therefore I am" was certainly not the last word in modern French philosophical circles, but it was the first. If philosophy in its broadest sense means knowledge of causes, then it is crucial to determine immediately the subject who knows and the object that is known. Ever since Descartes's time, in the early seventeenth century, it had been the fashion to seek knowledge by

52. Harvey Goldberg, *The Life of Jean Jaurès* (Madison, Wis.: 1968), 20.
53. Maurice Blondel, *Léon Ollé-Laprune: L'achèvement et l'avenir de son oeuvre* (Paris: 1923), 32, 177.

examining one's own thoughts and inner states. The individual thinker was, so to speak, cabined up within himself, able to come to terms with other reality only by reflecting on his own judgment about it. There had been, to be sure, many deviations from various aspects of the Cartesian intuition—Ollé-Laprune himself, for example, had written a book about Malebranche who had differed from Descartes in several important respects—but the core tenet remained intact. "Philosophy," Ollé-Laprune once observed, "is essentially . . . an examination of the ideas one has in one's mind, and an effort to see clearly." As for ethics, Ollé-Laprune's special subject: "To have a real and living idea of [a moral act] one must have it within oneself, through intimate experience of the reality itself."[54] This was not just a lesson that Blondel learned from Ollé-Laprune—or that Ollé-Laprune had learned from his own *maître*, the Oratorian Gratry—it was the heart of the intellectual culture they lived in, it was, almost, the air they breathed. If to philosophize was to make "an effort to see clearly," and if the answers to all human questions lay ultimately within oneself, then the philosopher's task was plain. Maurice Blondel looked within and saw what seemed to be the philosopher's stone. He called it *action*. "I am going to set myself the task of studying action, because it seems to me that the Gospel attributes to action alone the power to show forth love and to seize upon God."[55]

LATE IN 1884, his course work finished, Blondel traveled on holiday to Italy. He came back to Dijon for a while, and then took up a series of temporary teaching positions in several secondary schools, including the fashionable Collège Stanislas in Paris. He was small and slim, with delicate features, and looked younger than his years despite a receding hairline and a scraggly beard. He practiced his faith as fervently as ever, and he still wondered whether he should be a priest. But he had no doubt about another vocation, and in 1889 he applied for and received licence from the Sorbonne to prepare a doctoral thesis in philosophy. To compose it he retired to that scene of his boyhood delight, the Blondel country house at Saint-Seine-sur-Vingeanne. He stayed there for two years, with hardly an interruption, thinking and writing and listening to the myriad of sounds of the natural world outside his window.

By *action* Blondel meant a great deal more than the ordinary connotation of the word in French or English. It was not "action" as activity that he sought to seek out but rather that primal source of human energy, that dynamic principle, that *élan*—another word that eludes definition—which lay deeply beyond faculties like consciousness and imagination and which produced human activity of every kind. Like Ollé-Laprune, Blondel was adamant in his conviction that philosophy was not a matter of intellect alone, a kind of mental game

54. Quoted in Reardon, *Liberalism*, 212, 216.
55. Blondel, *Carnets intimes*, 1:85. The date of the notation was 10 October, 1886.

one played for the pleasure it afforded; such an attitude—of which, he said, both Aristotle and Descartes, in their different ways, were guilty—he dismissed as dilettantism. Philosophy was a matter of life and death. "Yes or no," Blondel threw down the challenge in his introduction, "does human life make any sense, and do human beings have a destiny? I act, to be sure, but without knowing what action is, without having wished to live, without knowing exactly who I am or even if I am. . . . If one consults the immediate evidence, action is a fact in my life, the most general and the most constant of all, the expression in me of a universal determinism. It is produced even without me."[56]

The drive of this "universal determinism" reverberated throughout every phase and compartment of human existence. It could be understood only if the total texture of life were put to the test.

Reflective consciousness would grasp only roughly, by the projection of an infinity of detail, the genuine motor power at work; it is the repercussion of interrelated repercussions. The imagination could never have a distinct representation of it; nor can we attribute this drive of ours simply to the power of custom, until, by repeated practice and by the verification of all elementary actions, we have adjusted the subordinate powers, traced out all the alternative paths, established all the habitual connections, and succeeded in proportioning energy to resistance.

It is entirely inappropriate to proceed by way of a dissection into parts abstractly isolated. It is necessary rather to study living complexity and concrete psychology. For in the movement of life there runs a circuit which perpetually shuts itself down, only in order to reopen itself and function again. Every point of arrival is only a point of departure.[57]

But this flux of human endeavor, this flood of human *action*, with all its arrivals and departures, was neither, Blondel argued, chaotic nor incomprehensible. Behind it all—indeed, around, above, beneath, within it all—worked the power of the will, the "universal determinism," pushing, thrusting, inspiring the human person toward fulfillment of himself. It was as though Blondel had turned the basic Cartesian dictum round to read, "I will, therefore I am." And what a thorough examination of the whole texture of the seamless garment of human experience revealed to Blondel—and to anybody else who made the effort—was that this *natural* aspiration—rooted in the very center of human existence, driven by the most powerful human force—could

---

56. Maurice Blondel, *L'action: Essai d'un critique de la vie et d'une science de la pratique* (Paris: 1893), vi–vii. The first edition went out of print within eighteen months. Blondel never ceased fussing with the original text, and subsequent editions contained many changes and additions. In 1950, the year after Blondel's death, the Presses Universitaires de France reprinted the original edition. It need hardly be said that the description in the narrative does scant justice to the book's depth and subtlety. Helpful summaries, among many, are Reardon, *Liberalism*, 227–37, Peter Henrici, "Les structures de *L'action* et la pensée française," in Folscheid (ed.), *Blondel*, 32–43, and Henri Bouillard, *Blondel and Christianity* (Washington, D.C.: 1969), 4–16.

57. Blondel, *L'action*, 157.

not be realized by *natural* means. Therefore, since all native objects fell short of satisfying the deepest of human needs, the inescapable *philosophical* conclusion was that human beings were compelled by their own nature, by the complex vitality and vigor of their *action*, to submit to something beyond nature. Not that philosophy could determine what that something was, for if it could, then that something would itself lie within the scope of nature. Nevertheless, Blondel's argument might well call to mind a famous line from one of his favorite authorities, Augustine of Hippo: "O Lord, thou madest us for thyself alone, and our heart is restless until it repose in thee."[58] Here at any rate was an opportunity to have a real and modern philosophy in harmony with Christian revelation. Here was Blondel's plan for escape from dreary positivism and scientism, and no less from the pedantic and mechanical intellectualism of the Scholastics. And here—to employ the technical terms that later on would cause much consternation—was a method of *immanence* to reach out to, and even capture, *transcendence*. *Action* has revealed itself the mediator between the natural and the supernatural.[59]

DIFFIDENT and even self-effacing out of religious conviction Maurice Blondel may have been in his style of life, but there was a core of iron running through him. He never flinched from the consequences of the intellectual positions he held. His degree in hand and his controversial thesis published at the end of 1893, he nevertheless did not receive a position on the staff of a university that he might have routinely expected, because French academe was reluctant to accept a colleague whose views it despised—to the degree that it understood them. So Blondel spent much of 1894 traveling through the Low Countries, Scandinavia, and Germany, and at the end of the year he married Mademoiselle Rose Royer, thus putting to an end the irresolution that had troubled him since his childhood. A year later his wife bore him a son.

Instrumental in helping Blondel arrive at the decision to remain in the lay state[60] was Henri Huvelin, who was recommended to him by a friend. Sometime in the late summer of 1893 Blondel duly went to Saint-Augustin and, though unimpressed by Huvelin's preaching, sought a private conference with the priest, who apparently succeeded in bringing spiritual solace to the young philosopher. When Blondel sent notice to him of his forthcoming marriage, Huvelin replied: "Thank you for your letter, my dear friend. . . . Oh, I know very well how these excessive incertitudes can suddenly vanish. . . . I pray very much for you, for your happiness. Think of me as very close to you and accept my religious affection."[61]

So the lines had begun to converge. Blondel had now taken on Freidrich

58. See Maurice Blondel, *Dialogues avec les philosophes* (Paris: 1966), 172–73.
59. See, e. g., *L'action*, 400–404.
60. See Blondel, *Carnets intimes*, 1:491.
61. The evidence for the relationship, adequate but thin, is in Portier, *Huvelin*, 82–84.

von Hügel's spiritual mentor, as presently Henri Bremond was to do: for him the vicar of Saint-Augustin always remained simply "ce saint abbé Huvelin."[62] The warmhearted Lucien Laberthonnière, bedazzled as admittedly few others were by *L'action*, first wrote to and then met Blondel, thus initiating a friendship and a collaboration that would last till the corrosion of a quarrel over principle tragically separated them. And one can even conceive of the lines as forming a kind of rough circle. At the end of 1896 Blondel finally received a permanent university appointment, at Aix-en-Provence, where he was to stay for the rest of his long and productive life. Some months later Bremond, who had been teaching at a Jesuit college at Saint-Étienne, returned to his native city to spend his tertiary year, during which time he followed Blondel's courses and found himself captivated by the gentle demeanor and the fiercely combative mind of the author of *L'action*.[63]

Meanwhile, Alfred Loisy had been dismissed from the faculty of the Institut Catholique of Paris.

---

62. Portier, *Huvelin*, 88–93.

63. After the two years spent in the noviciate, the Jesuit aspirant studied philosophy and theology, was ordained, and assigned for several years to do some work of the order. Then he was withdrawn for another noviciate-like year of prayer, reflection, and study—what the French called "le Troisième." It is unknown why Bremond was assigned to Aix for this purpose. See Blanchet, *Bremond*, 68–70.

CHAPTER 6

Victorian Twilight

Cardinal Manning was a great champion of the scholastic philosophy, but I do not think he had time to read much of it. He championed it mainly as an inspiring idea. It became one of his watchwords, like the "pastor of his flock" and the "priest according to the order of Melchisedech" and the "rock of Peter." It was the divinely given weapon to smite the infidel philosopher hip and thigh.

—*Wilfrid Ward (1913)*[1]

WHEN IN THE HIGH SUMMER of 1884 Friedrich von Hügel returned to Hampstead from his French holiday, he was in a mood of optimism and good humor. The times seemed particularly propitious for the kind of religious scholarship to which he wanted to contribute. Since the fractious disputes among Gallican and Ultramontane Catholics had reached a climax at the First Vatican Council in 1870, a measure of serenity seemed to hold the field. Virtually all the inopportunist bishops had accepted the conciliar decree on infallibility, which itself had proved much more moderate than the extreme Ultramontanes had hoped and their opponents had feared. In France the fervidly doctrinaire anticlericalism of the late 1870s had given place to a more subdued policy of accommodation. In Germany the prolonged church–state crisis known as the *Kulturkampf* had withered away, while most Germans ignored the schismatic Old Catholic movement which had raised a quixotic banner of opposition to the council. The pope's civil princedom in Italy was indeed gone, but the sky had not fallen as a result, and even the staunchest defenders of the temporal power, like Cardinal Manning, while they continued to deplore the clumsy aggressiveness of the Italian government, were prepared to adjust their position to the new realities and to soften their rhetoric. And, particularly heartening to the likes of von Hügel, there was a different pope, one who appeared anxious to adapt the church's eternal verities to the aspirations of the nineteenth century, one who, if he had promoted the study of

1. Quoted in Ward, *The Wilfrid Wards*, 1:209.

Scholasticism, had also, in 1883, thrown open the Vatican archives to scholarly research and had proclaimed that the Catholic church had nothing to fear from genuine historical inquiry.[2]

To be sure, the baron's new friend, Abbé Duchesne, was not so optimistic. The difficulties he had undergone in the name of untrammeled research, which led to his departure from the Institut Catholique, contributed also to the souring of a temper which was anyhow naturally sardonic. His abundant correspondence with von Hügel, which began in 1885,[3] is sprinkled with dour predictions and especially with warnings about the baron's enthusiasm for biblical criticism. "When I risk my neck for having denied the apostolic foundation of the diocese of Sens, it hardly seems a good idea to introduce novel opinions about the authenticity of the Penteteuch." Duchesne indeed wondered whether "science was not destined to disappear from the church." The theologians were the culprits, he said in the spring of 1885, "these powerful inducers of sleepy neglect," who "provide the Catholic people with whatever intellectual nourishment they imbibe." So dead is theological thought, so far removed from the modern and positive conception of knowledge, that contemporary Catholics "scarcely realize that there even is a Bible or that the accepted exegesis has been thoroughly discredited. They feel no need for a reformed exegesis. Such is particularly the case in France and Italy where for centuries the clergy have read the Bible with about as much attention as they have the Koran."

That these harsh judgments and dire premonitions were delivered in a strictly private fashion—and, incidentally, that they issued from one who for prudential reasons was to abstain scrupulously from engaging in the approaching public battle of the Bible—does not deprive them of their cogency or, as it turned out, of their prophetic character. The shrewd *Breton* accurately read the signs of the times. Beneath the relatively calm outer flow of events a new crisis was developing, a crisis that would affect the educated Catholic elites first and then the masses at large. The institutional church had fended off the challenges involved in the higher criticism, which had so ravaged mainstream Protestantism, largely by ignoring them. But the questions would not go away, and the restlessness was growing.[4] Duchesne, dedicated intellectual that he was, nevertheless worried about the consequences to the faith of ordinary people:

Upon reflection I must say that to the degree that they run up against our conventional exegesis, the more the masses of the ordinary Catholics are slipping away from us. Soon

2. See Owen Chadwick, *Catholicism and History: The Opening of the Vatican Archives* (Cambridge: 1978).

3. For a summary of the circumstances, see Bruno Neveu, "Lettres de Monseigneur Duchesne, directeur de l'école française de Rome, à Alfred Loisy et à Friedrich von Hügel," *Mélanges de l'École française de Rome* 84 (1972): 561–62.

4. See Rivière, *Modernisme*, 72–93, and O'Connell, "Modernism," 97–99.

only those will be faithful who know nothing about the matter. Shall I "have compassion on the multitude?" The "multitude" now stand outside our boundaries. If we want them to come back, we cannot impose upon them critical and exegetical fantasies drawn from a culture entirely different from their own. We have let go of Ptolemy, so let us also let go of those interpretations the maintenance of which brings dishonor to the Bible and to our consciences as serious and educated men.[5]

BUT ENGLAND was not France or Italy, as the chauvinistic English were the first to insist. And that sophisticated polymath Friedrich von Hügel had, despite his foreign ancestry, adapted himself fully to the life of an English gentleman. These were the twilight years of the Victorian era, with plenty of threats and alarums of their own, but for the leisured upper class to which von Hügel belonged they were a time of serene acceptance of the bounty that liberalism and empire had brought in their train. The baron, like most of his peers, took for granted his privileged status which allowed him, during what one of his biographers calls these "placid years,"[6] to pursue happily his intellectual hobbies: he supplied little reviews for Duchesne's *Bulletin critique*;[7] he intensified his study of Hebrew with a Jewish teacher; he wrote a pamphlet or two which reflected his now all-consuming interest in biblical subjects. He spent much time with his daughters, the third and last of whom was born in 1886, taking direct charge of their education, but playing with them too. Indeed he proved himself adept at combining play with instruction, nor was he too fastidious to share with them outings of apparently small cultural value, like attendance at Buffalo Bill Cody's Wild West Show. His health continued delicate, and he was easily fatigued and often ill—taking the children to see Queen Victoria's Golden Jubilee celebration in 1887 quite "knocked him up." But such spells did not spoil the baron's frolicsome disposition, as his middle daughter, Hildegard, recalled it. As a grown woman she could see in her mind's eye her father carrying her round the room on his shoulders and bellowing out the tunes from *H.M.S. Pinafore*. Presumably she and her sisters heard him sing more than once:

> Oh, he might have been a Russian,
> A French or Turk or Prussian,
> Or perhaps Italian!
> But in spite of all temptations
> To belong to other nations,
> He remains an Englishman!

The lyric must have seemed particularly pertinent to the baron.

His overriding interest remained religious. His pious practices if anything

5. Quoted in Poulat, "Mgr. Duchesne et la crise moderniste," 142–43.
6. De la Bedoyere, *Hügel*, 51–64.
7. For a list of the pieces written between 1885 and 1891, see Barmann, *Hügel*, 254.

deepened under Abbé Huvelin's direction. Most of his friends and acquaintances had some ecclesiastical connection or other. Of all the lessons he taught his daughters, those from the catechism he deemed most important. Scholarship and religion became inseparably linked in his mind, a circumstance that dominated his conversation, determined his companionships, and dictated the kind of books he read. If his marriage into the English Catholic aristocracy had served to sharpen his youthful conversion, his tutelage to Huvelin had sealed his sense of vocation.

The local Catholicism of which he found himself a part was a peculiar institution which had no parallel on the Continent. In this regard England surely was not France or Italy. In those two countries, one with a small Protestant minority and the other with no Protestants at all, the Roman church still professed to preach the religion of the nation. That claim became daily more difficult to sustain, for in fact French and Italian Catholicism had been pretty much reduced to the status of the religion of the village, at the moment when the village as a social phenomenon was fading away. And even there it did not go unchallenged: curés and *pastori* watched with dismay as the enfranchised peasant masses, or what was left of them, tended increasingly to vote for shrill, anticlerical politicians. The studied indifference to the church on the part of most of the elites, the relentless paganization of the new urban proletariats, the withering scorn of the intelligentsia, the undisguised hostility of Freemasons and positivists and socialists: all this was familiar coin to continental churchmen. It was primarily circumstances such as these that prompted Leo XIII to put forward his various educational and social initiatives, and later to try to come to terms with the political reality represented by republican regimes in the New World as well as in the Old.

The situation of Catholics in England was far different. There the established church was Protestant, and whatever wrath soi-disant enlightened men and women felt toward religion was usually directed toward Canterbury rather than toward Rome. The wrath itself was in any case muted when compared to the Continent. The United Kingdom of Great Britain and Ireland had been spared the revolutionary furor that had afflicted almost every European country for three or four generations beginning in 1789 and that had everywhere exhibited a strong anticlerical, and often antitheistic, component. In Britain, on the contrary, a revival of religious feeling, especially among the lower classes, influenced first by Methodism and then by the Evangelical wing of the Church of England, was itself an antidote to revolution.[8] Religious indifferentism had no doubt increased dramatically by von Hügel's day, but hostility had not. This circumstance was due in large measure to the genius for accommodation manifested for three centuries by the Church of England, within whose ample

8. I refer to the venerable theory expounded by Elie Halévy in the first volume of *The History of the English People in the Nineteenth Century*.

embrace could be found Christians with diametrically opposed views and, indeed, Christians with no doctrinal views at all.[9] Nor can one leave out of account that related—and admirable—achievement of English culture, a robust commitment to toleration along with a constitutionally protected regard for individual freedom.

Such broad-mindedness, to be sure, had not traditionally been extended to Roman Catholics. Animosity toward Rome, rooted in a perception of historical events which, by the late nineteenth century, had degenerated into vapid myths about Good Queen Bess and the Gunpowder Plot, had been bred into English bones and English psyches. Catholicism for most Englishmen remained beneath contempt, representing for them as it did mummery and priestcraft indulged in by inferior Latins and Celts. Such an attitude received confirmation by the continuing difficulties Westminster had in governing Ireland, and even more by the flood of poor Irish Catholic immigrants who poured into the slums of the large British cities during the nineteenth century. Popular disdain, however, had the advantage of rescuing the Catholics from the overt persecution that had been their lot in earlier times when they had been considered dangerous; the Penal Laws proscribing them and their religion had been repealed, and except for an occasional spasm of local violence they were left alone.

Daniel O'Connell, leader of the movement that had won civil rights for Catholics in the late 1820s, had expressed the common Irish opinion when he said his only regret was that Emancipation had also benefited his English coreligionists, who had done nothing themselves to attain it. He was referring to those who came to be called the Old Catholics,[10] that handful of noble and gentry families—Howards, Talbots, Petres, Vaughans, and Cliffords—which, together with their tenants and retainers, had stubbornly held to the old faith through all the vicissitudes of the penal times.[11] They had paid dearly for their steadfastness and courage, symbolized best perhaps by the priest-holes still to be found in more than a few great houses in the Midlands and the North. Even after the worst of the oppression had passed away—the bloody executions first and then the routine harassment, the ruinous fines, the perpetual fear of a knock on the door in the middle of the night—the English Catholics still remained "in Coventry," still were ostracized from the public life of the nation, until O'Connell and his Irishmen inadvertently delivered them. Little wonder that centuries of such treatment had left the English Old Catho-

9. For a fuller statement, see Marvin R. O'Connell, "The Beginning of the End, the End of the Beginning: Newman and Tract XC, " *Renascence* 43 (Fall 1990–Winter 1991):6–8.

10. Not to be confused with the "Old Catholics" on the Continent who had seceded from the Roman church in protest over the decree of papal infallibility passed by the First Vatican Council.

11. See Bernard Ward's volumes (1909–15) on the history of the English Catholics before Emancipation. For a different view, see John Bossy, *The English Catholic Community, 1570–1850* (New York: 1976).

lics wary of religious enthusiasm which, the lessons of the past had taught them, could only lead to trouble. Little wonder that they were deeply suspicious of, and indeed embarrassed by, exuberant Irish piety and continental Ultramontanism.

To this curious mix of Irish immigrants and native gentry was added, from the 1840s, a third element: the converts to Catholicism from that uniquely English phenomenon, the Oxford Movement. [12] The secession from the Church of England of a considerable portion, but by no means the majority, of the so-called High Church party and its adhesion to Rome brought into English Catholicism an intellectual component that neither the hod carrier nor the country gentleman was quite prepared to deal with.

Nor were the Oxford converts themselves of one mind as to what contribution they were to make to their new communion. The two most prominent among them, John Henry Newman and Henry Edward Manning, both of whom ultimately became Roman cardinals, were permanently at odds with one another, not only by reason of their conflicting personalities but also because of their profoundly different principles. [13] Newman remained after his conversion what he had always been, a scholar, a writer of incomparable prose, a subtle and sensitive thinker who combined intellectual boldness with practical caution. Manning too displayed a striking consistency: the crusading Anglican archdeacon, who lambasted callous landlords on behalf of the rural poor during the 1840s, became the crusading Catholic archbishop who, after 1865, made himself champion of those exploited urban masses who had to live, as his friend and ally, General William Booth of the Salvation Army, expressed it, "in darkest England." Manning despised the values and manners of the upper middle class from which he had sprung, a circumstance that contributed to making him an ardent Ultramontane. Newman, by contrast, always remained to his fingertips an English gentleman with whom other gentlemen, Anglican or Catholic, could identify. He and his colleagues at Birmingham had a natural affinity with the Old Catholics, who, socially and temperamentally, were so much like themselves. Here was one more source of contention between the cardinals, for Manning routinely excoriated the Old Catholics for their alleged "worldliness" and indifference to the plight of the Irish poor. [14]

By the time Friedrich von Hügel and Lady Mary were starting their family, and the young baron was forming those scholarly habits which would be his for a lifetime, the domination of the two aged princes of the church over the

12. The literature on the movement is immense. For the best contemporary accounts of it, see John Henry Newman, *Apologia pro vita sua*, ed. by Martin J. Svaglic (Oxford: 1967), and R. W. Church, *The Oxford Movement: Twelve Years, 1833–1845* (London: 1891). For a narrative account, see O'Connell, *Oxford Conspirators*, passim.

13. See Marvin R. O'Connell, "Newman: The Limits of Certitude," *Review of Politics* 35 (April 1973): 147–60.

14. See, e. g., Vincent Alan McClelland, *Cardinal Manning: His Public Life and Influence* (London: 1962), 3–25.

little English Catholic community they had sacrificed so much to join was beginning to wane. Their imprint upon that community, however, in all its contentiousness, was to continue. A double strain of Manningite isolationism and suspicion toward modern English society, versus a Newmanite spirit of accommodation, persisted, and there was no doubt to which party von Hügel belonged, however ambivalent his personal feelings toward Newman may have been. The baron would therefore have taken Louis Duchesne's judgment with more than a grain of salt: "Every year is for me a lamentable spectacle of [the French] episcopate composed of imbeciles. Our present archbishop [of Paris, Richard] is a mitred sacristan. What a distance between him and Newman or Manning! . . . You are lucky, you English, in having cardinals who are great men." But when Manning died in 1892—two years after Newman—von Hügel wrote to Wilfrid Ward, "How utterly that good Cardinal Manning has left us without ideas for real, detailed guidance through the problems of our times, hasn't he."[15]

IF EVER THERE WERE A CHILD of the Oxford Movement, it was Wilfrid Ward. His father was William George Ward, "Ideal" Ward as his Oxford contemporaries always called him, from the title of the controversial book he had published in 1844, *The Ideal of a Christian Church*, in which he advanced the extraordinary argument that an Anglican could hold in good faith "the full cycle" of Roman Catholic doctrine and practice. An ordained clergyman, he had been fellow and mathematics tutor at Balliol at the time, a disciple of Newman and Pusey in religious matters, but much more radical in his catholicizing views than they. He was a man immense in physical girth and immense too in charm and affability, so that even if his extreme opinions outraged his associates, he never lost their affection. When, early in 1845, the University of Oxford censured his book and, as punishment, formally deprived him of his degrees, he laughingly took to signing his correspondence, "W. G. Ward, Undergraduate."[16] Manning, then a crusty and diligent Anglican archdeacon, dismissed Ward as "a light-minded man, . . . less censurable for his opinions than for the moral habits which appear to govern him. . . . His manner of asserting has in it the restlessness and wilfulness of a schoolboy."[17] There is an arresting irony in the fact that these two men were destined to become such stout allies, but even so the personal relationship between them was never easy.

Six weeks after the censure Ward married Frances Wingfield, a parson's daughter and a hot-eyed Tractarian like himself. This act confirmed in some circles Ward's reputation for levity, since he had been a fervent champion of clerical celibacy. But, as he cheerfully pointed out, he was simply applying

15. Quoted in De la Bedoyere, *Hügel*, 49, 62.
16. See O'Connell, *Oxford Conspirators*, 404–8.
17. Manning to Pusey, 5 March, 1845, Pusey Papers, Pusey House, Oxford.

the rigorous logic he had used in describing himself, once stripped of his degrees, as an undergraduate: only the Roman church, he said, could boast of a genuine priesthood, one condition of which was the exercise of celibacy; but since he clearly was not cut out to lead a celibate life, he could not expect to be a real priest. This was an example—perhaps a trivial one—of the relentless way Ward drove every principle to its logical conclusion, his habitual method of argumentation. As for being "light-minded," Ward, despite his geniality and his penchant for Italian opera and frivolous French plays, was deadly earnest about those matters he cared about, which were almost exclusively religious. "You will find me narrow and strong," he told his subordinates when he was appointed editor of the *Dublin Review*[18] in 1863, "*very* narrow and *very* strong."[19]

William George and Frances Ward became Roman Catholics in September 1845—a month before Newman took the same step—and settled near Ware, in Hertfordshire, in the vicinity of Saint Edmund's College, a direct descendant of the fabled institution at Douai, in Belgium, where English Catholics-in-exile had received an education throughout penal times. Four years later Ward received an unexpected windfall when he inherited large property holdings in Hampshire and on the Isle of Wight. From then on he was by any accounting a rich man, a status, however, that meant little to him. He had no professional interests except theology and philosophy, and the notion that he should adopt the style of a country gentleman merely aroused his mirth. "If anyone can bear [the temptations of] wealth, it is you," Newman told him. But wealth did guarantee Ward leisure to do what he liked, and so he accepted it gratefully. As did his long-suffering wife, who bore him nine children and who had to manage all the burdens of the household with no help from her husband.

They continued to live at Ware (but they also took a townhouse in London, especially for the opera and theater season), and for many years Ward taught the seminarians at Saint Edmund's. He worked his students hard, and he was not shy about complaining at the generally low quality of education they received. "The whole philosophical fabric which occupies our colleges," he charged, "is rotten from the floor to the roof. Nay; no one who has not been mixed up practically in a seminary would imagine to how great an extent it *intellectually debauches* the students' minds." His candor caused annoyance among some prominent English ecclesiastics, and when quiet inquiries were made at Rome about the propriety of a married layman teaching divinity students, Pius IX is said to have observed to one of his clerical entourage, "It is a novel objection to anyone who is engaged in the work of God that he has

---

18. Founded in 1836 by an Irish Catholic practicing law in London, the *Dublin Review*, despite its name, was always an English journal. Since 1961 it has been called the *Wiseman Review*.
19. Ward, *The Wilfrid Wards*, 1:7.

received one sacrament of Holy Church which neither you nor I can possibly receive."[20]

Wilfrid was the sixth of the Ward children, born at Ware on January 2, 1856 (and so a little less than four years junior to von Hügel). His childhood and that of his siblings was dominated by the gargantuan personality of his father, who imposed upon all around him his own set of values—"*very* narrow and *very* strong."

The Catholic Church [Wilfrid recalled] was our one serious interest; our dreams and our day-dreams were of its Offices and its hierarchy. It was assumed, as a matter of course, that when we grew up the boys of the family would be priests and the girls nuns. This consummation, moreover, was not to be unduly delayed, as a dialogue in one of our stories—we were prolific writers—shows. One interlocutor, evidently tainted by the world, maintains that a girl should wait until she is twenty before becoming a nun. The other, filled with the zeal of the Lord, rebukes him. "What! Would you give your best years to the world, and only the poor remainder to Almighty God?"[21]

Three of Wilfrid's sisters did indeed become nuns and one brother became a priest (and ultimately a bishop).[22] Wilfrid himself strove mightily to satisfy his father's wishes in this respect, but to no avail. Private tutoring, then a spell at the school operated by the monks of Downside Abbey, and then a couple of years at Saint Edmund's provided Wilfrid with the basics in the classics and mathematics, though he was never an outstanding student. He much preferred cricket and football to parsing Greek verbs. He was most enthralled by a first exposure to the stage and to music, and in this at least he proved himself his father's son. Indeed, Wilfrid became in time an accomplished, if always an amateur, musician, one who delighted his friends with his virtuoso performances at the keyboard and with his splendid singing voice.

In 1874 Wilfrid was enrolled in Manning's ill-fated Catholic University College at Kensington.[23] This institution, which collapsed amid ridicule and minor scandal after scarcely four years, had been designed to substitute for the Oxford and Cambridge young Catholics were still forbidden by their bishops to to attend. The all-powerful Manning, vigorously supported by W. G. Ward, remained unalterably opposed to the "mixed education" provided by the Protestant universities, and hardly less opposed to the class-exclusiveness Oxbridge then represented. In his reminiscences Wilfrid Ward often lamented the ban that had prevented him from experiencing Oxford and which was not

20. Quoted in Ward, *The Wilfrid Wards,* 1:67–68 and 12.

21. Unpublished reminiscences quoted in Ward, *The Wilfrid Wards,* 1:27.

22. Bernard Ward was also the historian of the process of Catholic Emancipation in Britain. His distinguished seven volumes, the last of them published in 1915, are still standard. He died (1920) as bishop of Brentwood. See above, note 11.

23. See Purcell, *Manning,* 2:497–505, and Robert Gray, *Cardinal Manning: A Biography* (New York: 1985), 257–58.

lifted until after Manning's death. Yet at the time he seems to have appreciated the high quality of the faculty Manning had secured for Kensington without, however, committing himself to really serious study. He was in fact drifting, unable to decide what he should do with his life. ""My father, seeing that I did not intend to be a priest—the only career which aroused any enthusiasm in him—was wholly without interest in my plans." His plans, always vague and unfocused, became increasingly desperate attempts to gain his father's attention and approval. He dabbled through a philosophy course in London University, but not with the fierce dedication the elder Ward demanded. Wilfrid turned then for advice to Herbert Vaughan.[24]

Vaughan was that rarity, a scion of the Old Catholic gentry who was an ardent disciple of Manning.[25] His family displayed an almost incredible relish for the religious life: five of his seven brothers became priests and all six of sisters nuns. As a young man he had been for several years W. G. Ward's colleague at Saint Edmund's, during which time he had become friend and spiritual guide to the whole Ward family. It may have been his utter lack of intellectual sophistication that recommended him to the elder Ward, who often worried that his own highly cerebral approach to religion might lead him to forget the fundamental simplicity of the Sermon on the Mount; Vaughan used often to observe, ruefully, that as a country gentleman he was more at home with saddle and gun than he was with books. It may have been this squirelike quality—so different from the rigid Manning and the cerebral Newman—that recommended him to Lady Herbert of Lea, von Hügel's mother-in-law, with whom he was on the friendliest terms.[26] Vaughan at any rate, by the time Wilfrid Ward brought his troubles to him, was bishop of Salford (Manchester), and his counsel was refreshingly direct and unascetic: "Go to America. There are plenty of nice Catholic girls over there. Find one with plenty of wool [i. e., money] on her back. They like to marry Englishmen. Sing to her and she will marry you soon enough. Then you can come back here and go into Parliament or do anything else that you like. The first thing is to have enough money to make you independent."[27]

But such worldly wisdom could not satisfy Wilfrid, whose elemental desire, though he could not clearly discern it, was to please the father whom he admired so much. He fretted that "those who carried out the unworldly maxims of the Oxford Movement to such logical extremes seemed . . . to be pitting logic against the experience of life." Yet those unworldly ideals still shone

---

24. Standard biographies are J. G. Snead-Cox, *Life of Herbert Vaughan*, 2 vols. (London: 1910), and Arthur McCormack, *Cardinal Vaughan* (London: n. d. [1966]). Snead-Cox also wrote the entry in the *Dictionary of National Biography*, 2d supplement (1901–11): 550–54.

25. For an example of the alliance, and hence his antagonism toward Newman, see Vaughan to Manning, 29 March, 1867, printed in Dessain et al., eds., *Letters and Diaries*, 23: 92–93.

26. See Shane Leslie (ed.), *Letters of Herbert Cardinal Vaughan to Lady Herbert of Lea, 1867–1903* (London: 1942).

27. Quoted in Ward, *The Wilfrid Wards*, 1:51.

brilliantly for him, still provided him with the only measure of value he possessed. And so, with increasing intensity, he began to ask himself, why should I not be a priest? "The joy with which this [proposal] was received by my family and friends can hardly be exaggerated. It was almost as though the Prodigal Son had returned and the fatted calf had to be killed." From the moment the proposal was made Wilfrid's father's "whole face used to light up when he saw me." Manning took pains to congratulate him, and Vaughan, ever ready to adjust the claims of ambition to the circumstances, predicted that one day Wilfrid would be a cardinal. In October 1877—perhaps at the very moment Alfred Loisy, student in the *grand séminaire* at Chalons-sur-Marne, was contemptuously thumbing through the pages of the *Summa theologiae*—Wilfrid Philip Ward had his name entered upon the roll of the English College in Rome, and began following the lectures in the Gregorian University.[28]

He spent only eight months in Rome, but that brief stay left a deep impression on him. It was an exciting time in public affairs: the new kingdom of Italy was still deeply at odds with the papacy, violently deprived only a few years before of the last vestiges of its temporal power. The relatively youthful King Victor Emmanuel II died while Wilfrid was in residence at the English College, and so did the aged Pius IX. Wilfrid years later recalled the audience he and his fellow students had with Leo XIII shortly after the latter's election: introduced to the pontiff as the son of a distinguished convert, who had joined the church with Dr. Newman, Wilfrid found himself chatting amiably with the pope who clearly had misunderstood the interpreter and thought Newman was his father.[29]

La città itself, as well as its inhabitants, left him nothing but happy memories. Unlike some of his countrymen who purported to be shocked by it, he liked the rather casual piety of the Italians, and in the same spirit, commenting on the pomp and liturgical splendor of the Vatican—much curtailed, to be sure, since the fall of papal Rome in 1870—he pooh-poohed the notion that the pope should "live in a small house dressed like a dissenting minister." But it was the history of the place that most fired his mind and imagination, and no doubt contributed to the kind of intellectual work he would do later on. To walk along the streets from the English College on the Via di Monserrato out·through the Forum to the Colosseum, and, on a fine day, farther out to San Giovanni di Laterano, and back again across the Campodoglio was to tread upon stones that almost cried out the dramatic account of a half-dozen civilizations, and especially the rich, varied, and more often than not edifying story of the Roman church.

Such intellectual excitement, however, Wilfrid Ward did not find in the

28. Ward, *The Wilfrid Wards*, 1:77, and 51–53.
29. Ward, *The Wilfrid Wards*, 1:60.

formal schooling to which he was subjected. Indeed, he pronounced that aspect of his Roman episode "very trying." The lessons were tedious, jejune, and superficial. "We were taught the various philosophical positions as the 'right view,' and if any of us did not find those positions convincing, we were accounted heterodox. Thus philosophy which professed to prove the rational duty of accepting Theism and revelation was not really enforced by reason but by authority." So it was that more than a full year before Leo XIII issued *Aeterni Patris* and initiated his attempts to reform, along Thomistic lines, the faculty of the Gregorian University,[30] Wilfrid Ward had arrived experientially at the pejorative definition of "Scholasticism" which he would, understandably, maintain all his life.

For young Ward, as for many northerners, the Roman climate proved unhealthy, and in May 1878 Bishop Vaughan arranged his transfer to the seminary at Ushaw, near Durham. This institution was, like Saint Edmund's in Ware, a lineal descendant of the old English college at Douai. "My life at Ushaw was very happy," but "the habits of idleness I had . . . contracted at school still clung to me. Neither Kensington nor Rome had effected a radical cure." He read much, "in a desultory way," and enjoyed the companionship of his schoolfellows. "I had a great affection and admiration for the manly religion of the place." Much of his time was spent in conducting the sixty-voice choir and in overseeing other, extraliturgical musical performances, including his own weekly recital of Beethoven's piano sonatas. But by the early months of 1881 he recognized that he had in fact no priestly vocation, a judgment "I think proved by the fact that up to very recent years [he was writing about 1912] I have occasionally had dreams, accompanied by all the painful sensations of a nightmare, in which I had become a priest with no true calling and with the most unfortunate consequences."[31]

And so Wilfrid Ward came home again—home being by this time divided between an estate built at Freshwater, on the Isle of Wight, and Hampstead, where W. G. Ward after 1873 regularly leased a house for part of the year, the occasion of his acquaintance with and growing affection for Friedrich von Hügel. "My father was bitterly disappointed," but "he did not blame me," Wilfrid noted, because he too had desired to be a priest but had found the requirement of personal austerity and celibacy a barrier he conceived to be beyond his capacity to surmount. Wilfrid, now twenty-five, faced again the familiar problem of finding a life's work and, at a deeper psychic level, of coming to terms with his father. "But . . . in 1881, as in 1876, he failed to help me." There followed a dispirited few weeks at the Inner Temple, with the thought, swiftly dissipated by fifty or so boring pages in a law book, of a career at the bar. Then, reflecting on his enjoyment of opera and the theater, Wilfrid im-

30. See chapter 2.
31. Quoted in Ward, *The Wilfrid Wards*, 1:64–69.

pulsively decided to become an actor, until, having confided this news to one of his sisters, she told him "with freezing contempt, 'You had better not tell Papa, he would heartily despise the development.' " He did not tell Papa, but after six months of distressful idleness he confided once again in Bishop Vaughan, who urged him to make a spiritual retreat after which, the bishop predicted with the confidence of a genuinely pious man, young Ward would be in a mental state to arrive at some definite conclusions about the future.

Then came a turning point in this poignant domestic drama. Wilfrid shyly showed his father some "fugitive essays and notes" he had written at Ushaw. They dealt with the interplay between the act of faith and the wishes of a believer, the kind of subject dear to W. G. Ward's heart (and indeed dear to the hearts of all the Oxford converts). The old man—now within a year of his death—responded excitedly that the papers contained a very significant argument, and he immediately put his son in contact with friends from his Oxford days who were prominent in the editorial rooms of the learned journals published in London. The upshot was that the first installment of what evolved eventually into Wilfrid Ward's first book, *The Wish to Believe*, appeared in the *Nineteenth Century* for February 1882. Thus at a stroke were swept away the hesitations and antagonisms that had marred the relationship between father and son, and at the same time was launched a career in which the son, while always paying reverential heed to the father's views and the father's aspirations, forged a distinct intellectual position of his own. This happy turn of events occurred just in the nick of time, for a few months after Wilfrid's article appeared W. G. Ward died. In his last hours his mind wandered incoherently for the most part. Once, opening his eyes and seeing Wilfrid at his bedside, he smiled and said, "I had a pleasant interlude yesterday. Who do you think came to see me? Our old friend 'Figaro.' "[32]

Astonishing was the speed with which Wilfrid Ward—who out of desperation had aspired to the stage only a brief time before—assumed a comfortable place in the upper reaches of English social and literary life. Part of his success was due to doors opening to him out of affectionate memory of his father. He breakfasted with Prime Minister Gladstone at 10 Downing Street, and was a frequent guest of Benjamin Jowett at the Master's Lodge at Balliol College, Oxford. He went for long walks with Lord Tennyson, a neighbor of the Wards on the Isle of Wight. The poet laureate had greeted W. G. Ward's death with a moving tribute:

> Farewell, whose living like I shall not find,
> Whose faith and work were bells of full accord,
> My friend, the most unworldly of mankind,
> Most generous of all Ultramontanes, Ward.

32. Ward, *Wilfrid Wards*, 1, 74–85.

But had Wilfrid not used his newfound confidence and connections to produce genuinely good work of his own, his privileged status would not have lasted.

His first project was a work of filial piety which brought him into an important new relationship. He compiled into two volumes a collection of his father's articles, published in various journals over the years, and titled it *Essays on the Philosophy of Theism*. In July 1884 Friedrich von Hügel told Newman that "some months ago" he was "flattered but somewhat surprised and embarrassed" when the younger Ward had asked permission to dedicate the book to him.[33] But he accepted the compliment, and so the friendship he had once shared with the father passed on to the son. "My dear Baron von Hügel," Wilfrid Ward wrote, "in offering these volumes of my father's philosophical essays for your acceptance, I am doing what I believe he would himself have done had he lived to republish them. They treat for the most part of subjects which you frequently discussed with him, and on which I know he valued your opinion. . . . May I add that it gives me great pleasure on personal grounds to be the means of offering the book to you."[34]

The publication occasioned another, even more significant connection. Ward sent a copy of the book to his godmother, the dowager duchess of Norfolk, who responded by expressing her thanks while wondering whether such cerebral material might not be somewhat beyond her. Then, in an obviously more congenial vein, she invited her godson to join her and her charges for Holy Week services, to which he could lend his "magnificent voice to the rescue of our feeble attempts here in the wilderness." The "wilderness" was Uckfield, in Sussex, where the duchess had retired with various children and grandchildren. Ward accepted the invitation, and so he met Josephine Hope, to whom before the end of 1884 he proposed marriage. Josephine was the daughter of James Hope-Scott, an Oxford convert received into the Catholic church with Manning at the Jesuit church, Farm Street, London, in 1851. He had been a distinguished lawyer and a close friend of Newman. His second wife[35] and Josephine's mother had been Victoria Howard, elder sister of the duke of Norfolk, hereditary earl-marshall of England, first noble of the realm, and, so to speak, as the oldest of the Old Catholic aristocracy, the titular lay head of Catholic England. By the time Josephine was thirteen she and her three siblings were orphans, taken into the care of their grandmother, the dowager duchess. Josephine was bright, pretty, intimidatingly intelligent and creative, a young woman fluent in French and Italian, self-taught in theology and the

33. Von Hügel to Newman, 21 July, 1884, quoted in Dessain et al., eds., *Letters and Diaries*, 30:383.

34. W. G. Ward, *Essays in Theism*, 2 vols. (London: 1884), 1:dedicatory page (dated March, 1884).

35. Hope's first wife had been a granddaughter of Sir Walter Scott, through whom he inherited Abbotsford, at which time he had added "Scott" to his original surname. The children of his second marriage did not use the hyphenated form.

philosophy of religion, blessed with "the terrible earnestness of the Oxford Movement" of which she too was an heir. And when Wilfrid Ward first proposed to her, she refused him.

But he was persistent, and she gradually came round to a happier view of him. They were married on November 24, 1887, to a chorus of congratulations from the small, tight circle of English Catholic high society.[36] Even Manning and Newman could agree to rejoice at the occasion. Ward's older brother settled on him a permanent income from the family estate which, together with Josephine's inheritance, assured them a life of leisure and comfort. But there had been a silent guest at the wedding too, the shade of William George Ward, at whose monumental biography his now tranquil and self-confident son was busily at work.[37]

ON THE DAY WILFRID WARD and Josephine Hope were married, a young Jesuit scholastic was lecturing to a roomful of indifferent students enrolled in the college his order operated on the island of Malta. George Tyrrell, whose fate was to be so closely intertwined with that of von Hügel and Ward, never opened his infant's eyes upon the splendor of a Tuscan sunset, never mingled familiarly with dukes and cardinals. The mean back streets of Dublin, and that city's even meaner suburbs, provided Tyrrell with his boyhood home— to the extent that he ever had a home. Nine years younger than von Hugel, Tyrrell was born on February 6, 1861, a month and a week after the death of his father. His family belonged to the Protestant ascendancy class, but to the social periphery of it; there were few clear connections between Dorset Street and Dublin Castle or the vice-regal lodge. William Henry Tyrrell had been a talented but impecunious Tory journalist who left his widow and children little more than the memory of his integrity and his bad temper. Mrs. Mary Tyrrell had to make do for herself, her crippled son Willie, her daughter Louisa ("Louy"), and baby George on £30 a year.

The result was a poverty that often dipped below the level of even minimum respectability. They led a vagrant life, sometimes together, sometimes separated, always moving or on the verge of moving. During the eighteen years George Tyrrell lived in Ireland he resided in eighteen different places.[38] He thought afterward that his mother—gentle, loving, yet incurably feckless— enjoyed a peculiar kind of solace in relocating with this relative or that or in farming out her children even to strangers. George and Louy, in any case, sibling rivals, usually stayed together, while Willie, older than they and decidedly clever, was much of the time at boarding schools as a scholarship stu-

36. Ward, *The Wilfrid Wards,* 1:130–58.

37. *William George Ward and the Oxford Movement* was published in 1889 and *William George Ward and the Catholic Revival* in 1893.

38. David G. Schultenover, *George Tyrrell: In Search of Catholicism* (Shepherdstown, W. Va.: 1981), 5.

dent. Willie Tyrrell, the only father figure his brother ever had, had been maimed in a childhood accident, and his shrunken body was racked by more or less continuous pain. George remembered him, when at home, as "the director and inspirer of our games from his throne on the sofa, our oracle on a thousand matters not reached by formal instructions, and also our assiduous tormentor and tease," an embittered dwarf who knitted as a relaxation from his otherwise constant reading.[39]

George Tyrrell's reminiscences of his youthful religiosity have a gloomy naturalistic ring to them. "Of sin, in the religious sense, I had . . . no thought whatever. Had I died with my wits about me it would have been as an animal, without a touch of fear or hope. The sense of *right* and *wrong* I think I always had, but its implications I did not understand, and I explained it away. . . . There only remained with me the non-moral restraint of a certain refinement, or perhaps prudery, of taste, that made me shrink from what was inherently disgusting or coarse, or at least unredeemed by some sparkle of wit or humor." He delighted in the Gospel stories and songs his vaguely Evangelical mother would recite of a winter's evening, but when her widowed sister, a stern and overbearing Calvinist, came to live with them, he discovered that the Christian religion had another side which was distinctly uncongenial to him. "I first remember being taken to church—an old Huguenot refugee chapel—and wondering what on earth it was all about. . . . The prayers and the litany and the sermon, and, above all, the sitting still and keeping silent and general repression, made church-going an agony all the years of my early childhood."[40]

The instability of that childhood was reflected in Tyrrell's experiences in school. He learned quickly, was bored easily, and chronic idleness was the natural consequence. Formal study and memorization were dead bones to him. He despised routine. He needed to have his imagination engaged, or his aptitude for mechanical tinkering; otherwise he resisted the efforts of teachers to cram his mind full of set formulas or to get him to seek answers to questions he did not care about. So often the "new boy" in school, George readily assumed the role of outsider, in the classroom or on the playing field. Organized games interested him only until he had mastered their intricacies. "It was the improvised novelty that ever appealed to me," not cricket or football with their arbitrary rules and their insistence on discipline and team play. He resented "being ordered about by my equals," and so he preferred more individualist forms of exercise, "like gymnastics and fighting and tearing about, and climbing and courting danger, provided it was informal, and not obligatory or according to rule." Another reason to eschew conventional sports was that "I always disliked competition, partly from an absurd sensitiveness which made me dislike being worsted, partly from an absurd sympathy which made me

39. M. D. Petre, *Autobiography and Life of George Tyrrell*, 2 vols. (London: 1914), 1:25.
40. Petre, *Autobiography of Tyrrell*, 1:92, 20.

dislike worsting others." Here was a quality, however commendable in itself, little calculated to win the hearts of schoolboys. "Yet I was the most universally liked boy in the school from my ninth year onwards."[41] A poignant memory for a man of forty, beset by rejections on all sides, but hardly a credible one.

One of the schools George Tyrrell attended had as headmaster a kindly Church of Ireland clergyman who combined Evangelical theology with a taste for ritualist liturgy. Before classes each day he presided at a choral morning prayer and then preached briefly to the pupils on a passage from Scripture. Young George was charmed and apparently moved by these services, so far a cry from what went on in the Huguenot chapel, and as he advanced into his teens he grew more curious about religious matters. He listened attentively—more attentively than either of them realized—to the arguments between his mother and Willie, who by now professed to be an agnostic and who scoffed at Mary Tyrrell's earnest, nondoctrinaire Protestant piety. When Willie was away, George took up the quarrel, with so much vigor indeed that the long-suffering woman was driven almost to distraction.[42] But if George imitated his brother's surly manner, the intellectual path he chose to follow was very different. George Tyrrell, at fourteen, began to dabble in Romanism.

Though brought up in the midst, as it were, of a papist sea, his acquaintance with Catholicism had been slight. Religious and racial bigotry was essential to Tyrrell's heritage, and interaction between the Catholic masses of Dublin and a Protestant in his position must have been as superficial as that between a lower-class white and the blacks all around him in the Atlanta of the same date—a Catholic housemaid here, a shopkeeper there. Popery was the religion of an inferior people; the humblest member of the ascendancy took that as the first article of his creed and recognized that his own survival depended on maintaining it. And yet—who knows?—the very outrageousness of the idea of becoming a Catholic may have made it powerfully attractive to Tyrrell, as it had to Edward Gibbon a century before.

Precocious as he was, Tyrrell did not plunge all at once. He began by attending services in one of the two High Church parishes in Dublin—dizzily advanced by the Orange standards of the Church of Ireland, but really, Tyrrell observed later, "of the Laudian type or early tractarian school," its sacramental emphasis symbolized by a communion table designed to look like an altar, and yet unequivocally committed to "a good solid dislike of popery." "At first there was not a scrap of religious motive" in George's participating in this, for him, heady ritual and in his pressing it upon his hapless mother. "I believed as little as ever; it was simply that I had taken a side in an argument for trivial reasons enough, and I fought for it as I fight for all my opinions and choices, tooth

41. Petre, *Autobiography of Tyrrell*, 1:53–55.
42. Petre, *Autobiography of Tyrrell*, 1:60–76.

and nail." Besides, along with the singing and the vestments came an adolescent thrill at the wickedness of it all: "The birettas and cassocks [worn by the clergy] made the fibers of one's Protestantism quiver." But the experiment also had an effect that went beyond what young Tyrrell had anticipated: "I felt instinctively what I, long afterwards, understood clearly, namely, that the difference between an altar and a communion table was infinite; that it meant a totally different religion, another order of things altogether, of which I had no experience."[43]

A warfare had been let loose within George Tyrrell's spirit. When his mother refused to accompany him any longer to the ritualist parish, he sneaked off to it alone. He communicated there, and at least once went to confession. He secreted crucifixes and holy pictures in his room, slept on boards, wore a penitential girdle beneath his clothing—"antics," as he later labeled these activities, inspired by "the same instinct which, at an earlier age, made me buy a gun and sword and dress up as a soldier." He wrestled with prayer as fiercely as Jacob wrestled with the angel, but as yet without faith or even much hope, driven by an undefined longing to cry, "Oh God, if there be a God, save my soul, if I have a soul," after which often "I would start up from my knees and say, 'Oh, this is all humbug and sham!' " He pored over manuals of piety in search of systems of self-mastery and moral reform, not out of a sense of sin but out of a need for some order and coherence in his life. This wretched boy, fatherless, rootless, belonging to nothing and to no one, picked his way through the externals of religion toward Huvelin's "luminous center" which he could not see and could not be sure was there, toward something firm and planted and unchanging that might give meaning to them, and to himself.

By the beginning of 1876, scarcely fifteen years old, he had determined to become a clergyman, though he told nobody and had no clear idea what such a vocation entailed. Then, that summer, Willie suddenly died, and George was brought "rudely face to face with the problem of life's meaning and value; and [Willie's death] made me *feel* what my rationalism had taught me for so many years, that what most men lived and fought for was mere vapor and illusion; that there was no logical or defensible resting place between the ark of God and the carrion that floated on the surrounding waters—between divinity and piggery." He remembered having asked Willie, "shortly before [he died], where he thought the soul went after death, and he had said: 'Where the flame goes when the candle is burnt out.' "[44]

During this time, 1876–77, Tyrrell was supposed to be studying for a competitive scholarship in Hebrew at Trinity College, Dublin, but his habitual indolence combined with his religious obsession—especially compulsive after Willie's faint flame had burned out—led him to leave the mysteries of the

43. Petre, *Autobiography of Tyrrell*, 1:97–101.
44. Petre, *Autobiography of Tyrrell*, 1:107–16.

most sacred of languages pretty much unplumbed. He preferred to go off by himself and read Montalembert's massive and highly romanticized *Monks of the West*—Loisy was reading that book at about the same time—whose "concrete presentment of the reality and force of religion in action made me first wish to be, not merely respectably moral, but like these men, who were enthusiasts and wholly God-possessed." Montalembert's account of Saint Benedict so stirred him that "straight in the teeth of my Protestant conscience I prayed to the saint, if perchance he might hear or help." Then he picked up the psalter, and his eye fell upon the Ninety-first Psalm: "Because he has hoped in me, I shall deliver him; I shall protect him, because he has known my name; he will call to me, and I shall hear him." The "coincidence" (as he called it afterward) flooded through the boy's heart like the balm of Gilead.[45]

But it proved little help for the task at hand. During the summer of 1877 Tyrrell failed the Trinity examination, and a year later he failed it again. He did not care. By that time he was frequenting Roman churches for mass, benediction, confession (but not communion), "and though my taste was revolted and my reverence shocked by the tawdriness and falsity of the decorations, and the perfunctoriness of the priests in their graceless ministrations, yet there was a certain sense of rest and reality about it, inasmuch as I felt it was the bottom towards which I was graviating." By then too he had fallen in with Robert Dolling, destined for fame as an Anglo-Catholic social reformer.[46] Dolling tried to give Tyrrell a more refined and intellectualized appreciation of High Anglican thought and thus stop his headlong rush to Rome. But it was medicine applied too late. Tyrrell was already fantasizing about being a Roman priest, "graceless ministrations" and all, and even—the ultimate repudiation of his culture and class—a Jesuit.

Dolling realized early on that the game was lost, that Tyrrell had convinced himself that his anguished mind would find no relief in second-generation Tractarianism. But the parson in him did not give up. Early in 1879, when he left Dublin to organize a religious club for workers in London, Dolling invited Tyrrell to go with him. Tyrrell accepted, but he did so knowing full well that escape from Ireland would mean shaking off what little hold Dolling's ideals still had upon him. With a heartlessness he bitterly reproached himself for later, Tyrrell simply walked out on his impoverished mother and sister and arrived in London, as he sardonically put it, "on the feast of All Fools, 1879."[47] He never saw Ireland again, but something of Ireland lived on in him—in his wit, his lyricism, his deep melancholy.

Two weeks later George Tyrrell knocked on the door of the presbytery of the Jesuit church, Farm Street, in fashionable Mayfair. He told the priest who

45. Petre, *Autobiography of Tyrrell*, 1:118–24.

46. See Schultenover, *Tyrrell*, 16–20. For Dolling, see C. E. Osborne, *The Life of Father Dolling* (London: 1903).

47. Petre, *Autobiography of Tyrrell*, 1:135–49.

met him in the parlor that he wished to become a Catholic. In the person of that priest the long shadow of John Henry Newman fell, lightly to be sure, upon Tyrrell for the first time. Albany James Christie had been an undergraduate at Oriel from 1835 and a fellow of the same college from 1840. Through his time in Oxford he had been a stout Tractarian, more under Pusey's influence than Newman's, but it was Newman who had persuaded him that in his state of mind he could not honestly accept Anglican ordination. Christie had resigned his fellowship and had come to live with Newman at the latter's retreat at Littlemore during the portentous summer of 1845. He was received into the Catholic church on October 18 of that year, nine days after Newman himself. Until 1847, when he joined the Society of Jesus, he had remained more or less in Newman's entourage. He had resided at Farm Street for many years.[48]

Tyrrell testified that Christie was very kind to him at their first meeting and over the succeeding months, "but I learned nothing from him that I did not know before, and got no light on any point that was previously obscure." He particularly resented the priest giving him a copy of the Penny Catechism to read, as though doing so had been a calculated insult to him and to other prospective converts. Such at any rate was the way an embittered Tyrrell remembered the incident more than twenty years later. Yet here might be one of many instances when Tyrrell's mood in 1901 played tricks on his memory. Christie, himself a convert as well as a person of some experience (he was sixty-two) and cultivation, would hardly have adopted a procedure insulting to converts. And anyway the penny catechism must have appeared to him a perfectly appropriate book to offer to this agitated Irish man-child who had suddenly been dropped on his doorstep.[49]

The events that followed fell over one another with a speed and heedlessness—by all parties concerned—which were truly astonishing. On May 18, scarcely a month after his first appearance at Farm Street, George Tyrrell was formally received into the Roman Catholic church and baptized *sub conditione*. The simple ceremony over, Father Christie asked him about his plans for the future and seemed not at all surprised when Tyrrell haltingly confessed his desire to enter the exalted Society of Jesus. Christie saw no reason to delay his admission, but the Jesuit provincial, to whom he referred Tyrrell, proposed that the eighteen-year-old neophyte serve for a trial period on the staff of a Jesuit institution so that he might attain some sense of the ethos of the society. So Tyrrell went off for a year to colleges in Cyprus and Malta[50]—both British possessions at the time—before he entered the noviciate in September 1880.

Tyrrell said later that this period of probation, most of it spent in Malta,

48. See Ward, *Newman*, 1:21, 84, and Meriol Trevor, *Newman: The Pillar of the Cloud* (London: 1962), 354.

49. Petre, *Autobiography of Tyrrell*, 1:156–60.

50. See Francis Edwards, *The Jesuits in England* (London: 1985), 213.

had totally disillusioned him, had stripped away all the romantic notions he had nurtured about the spiritual soldiers of Saint Ignatius. The real Jesuits he met and lived with were all too human. They were with hardly an exception constricted, trivial men who used up their lives in trivial tasks. Yet, though he felt this way (if his later account is to be believed), he subjected himself to the austerities of the novitiate anyway, hoping against hope that the Jesuit calling would ultimately prove to be what he was looking for. "I did not, after my Maltese experience, either love or reverence the society—I never did at any time; but gradually I got interested in it as a system, as a life; I wanted to comprehend it and put it together, rather than question it." With only these dubious motives to support him it is small wonder that Tyrrell found the noviciate an uninterrupted trial; that he despised his classmates, prattling boys who cared for little besides athletics; and that he engaged in a series of petty quarrels with the novice master, "a narrow intense man with an unwavering belief in the opinions and the cause he had embraced, and an absolute incapacity of seeing the other side." The only positive experience he recalled from these two years was the reading of a book by Lacordaire.

Nevertheless, at the end of them, when his superiors recommended he terminate his association with the Society of Jesus, Tyrrell, astoundingly, pleaded that he be allowed to take vows, and at the last moment they, just as astoundingly or perhaps more so, consented. So Tyrrell, now a fledgling Jesuit, moved up to the next rung of the the the training ladder, to philosophical studies in the seminary at Stonyhurst in Lancashire. Here too, amid the stark and rainy north-of-England landscape,[51] he could not but kick against the goad, for if the horarium was not so wearisome as in the novitiate, and the superiors somewhat more agreeable, the Scholastic philosophy he was expected to devote himself to seemed to him as juvenile as his fellow students. There was, however, a weapon at hand, now that Pope Leo XIII, in *Aeterni Patris*, had called for the reform of Scholasticism by insisting that the writings of Saint Thomas Aquinas supply the fundamental texts in all ecclesiastical faculties. The English Jesuits, who were accustomed to filtering Aquinas through what Tyrrell called, with justice, "his third rate commentators and imitators," were busy trying to evade the papal directive. Predictably, Tyrrell decided to "throw myself wholly into the task of mastering [*sic*] and defending . . . the Thomistic system of philosophy and theology." Instead of studying Aquinas-according-to-Suarez and other manualists, Tyrrell studied the texts of Saint Thomas himself. Though he was generous in his praise—"Whatever order or method there is in my thought, whatever real faculty of reasoning and distinguishing I have acquired, I owe it to St. Thomas"—he left no record of precisely what texts he read, in what order he read them, and how they formed

---

51. A good description of Stonyhurst and its environs a few years before Tyrrell's arrival is in Paddy Kitchen, *Gerard Manley Hopkins* (New York: 1979), 129–30.

his philosophical outlook. One cannot help but conclude that he was guilty of the same sort of presumption as Loisy, at Chalons-sur-Marne, a few years earlier. Indeed, in the light of what happened later, one gets the queasy feeling that Tyrrell, always a careless student, carried away with him from the backwater of Stonyhurst the dangerous illusion that by a desultory, undirected perusal of the *Summa theologiae* he had "mastered" the immensely difficult Thomistic system.

In 1885, still intellectually ill at ease, he finished his formal study of philosophy, and, in accord with the Jesuit regimen, he was assigned to teach in a college for the three years preceding theological studies and ordination to the priesthood. Coincidentally enough, he was posted back to Malta. He recalled that by then he "had begun to feel the limits of scholasticism rather painfully."[52] George Tyrrell had apparently forgotten any distinction he had earlier drawn between Scholasticism and pure Thomism. In his baggage lying at Thames-side at any rate was a copy of Newman's *Grammar of Assent*. Perhaps that book appealed to him—as it had to Friedrich von Hügel[53]—precisely because it was so far removed from the dry-as-dust syllogisms imposed on him in the philosophical course at Stonyhurst. "I had a great dislike of paper logic," Newman once observed, and so did the young Irishman who now, for a time, became Newman's disciple. As the ship made its tedious way across the Mediterranean, he had plenty of leisure to reflect on the master's words:

The concrete matter of propositions is a constant source of trouble to syllogistic reasoning, as marring the simplicity and perfection of its process. Words, which denote things, have innumerable implications; but in [syllogisms] it is the very triumph of that clearness and hardness of head . . . to have stripped them of all . . . conatural senses, to have drained them of that depth and breadth of associations which constitute their poetry, their rhetoric, and their historical life, to have starved each term down till it has become the ghost of itself, and everywhere one and the same ghost, . . . so that it may stand for just one unreal aspect of the concrete thing to which it properly belongs, for a relation, a generalization, or other abstraction, for a notion neatly turned out of the laboratory of the mind, and sufficiently tame and subdued, because existing only in a definition.[54]

Tyrrell during these years had plenty of leisure also to ponder the fate of his mother and his sister, and to let his guilt wrap itself round him like a mantle. Mrs. Tyrrell and Louy stayed in Dublin till 1880. By then the older woman had contracted cancer of the breast, had undergone painful and only partially successful surgery, and, out of a bewildered sense of loyalty to her son, had become a Catholic. "I do not think it made much difference in her spiritual

---

52. Petre, *Autobiography of Tyrrell*, 1:198–278, treats the matter in detail.
53. See chapter 3.
54. J. H. Newman, *An Essay in Aid of a Grammar of Assent* (London: 1906), 267. The best summary is Charles Stephen Dessain, *John Henry Newman* (London: 1966), 147–59.

life, for better or for worse," George said. "She was too old to change her habits of thought, and carried her Bible-reading and extempore prayer to the end." She and Louy, hoping to see something of George, moved in with a relative living in London—the same old nomadic pattern repeated for the last time— and there, in the spring of 1884, Mary Chamney Tyrrell died. "Perhaps had I lived at home," her son reflected with that familiar self-loathing of his, "I might have broken those hearts whose love was everything to me, and to which my love was everything. That is my faint hope, and the salve of my conscience, when I think, with bitterness, how I abandoned the life of affection for the service of as barren a mistress as truth, and let the substance of life escape me in the pursuit of shadows."[55]

Tyrrell's "pursuit of shadows" on his second tour of duty in Malta lasted till 1888. He left no formal memoir of that interval, but later, when harsher times had befallen him, he looked back upon it with some nostalgia. "The companionship and care of children," he said wistfully, "is of all educations the best and most humanizing. My three years at Malta with such were, I am sure, the three purest and best years in some ways since I entered the hardening school of religious life."[56] The next stage in "the hardening school" also occupied him for three years, in the prescribed theology course taught at Saint Bueno's College in North Wales. On September 21, 1891—feast of Saint Matthew the Apostle—George Tyrrell was ordained priest by the bishop of Shrewsbury. He left no record of the day of his first mass.[57]

55. Petre, *Autobiography of Tyrrell*, 1:227–29.

56. Quoted in Petre, *Autobiography of Tyrrell*, 2:30.

57. Petre, *Autobiography of Tyrrell*, 2:33. Miss Petre, who knew him better than anyone, observed that Tyrrell was not "the man of 'first Masses,' 'first Communions,' or first celebrations of any kind. But what his Mass was to him no one who ever attended his altar could doubt."

CHAPTER 7

École Large

I recognize with all urbane persons that M. Loisy writes much better than I do. If he has proclaimed publicly "that Père Lagrange has a peculiar gift for misinterpretation and distracting fancies," he has done so no doubt to invite me to read this book of his with sharper attention. Yet once or twice he has called into question my sincerity. This is always disagreeable to a writer.

—*M.-J. Lagrange (1932)*[1]

IN THE SUMMER OF 1888, six months after their wedding, Wilfrid and Josephine Ward went to Paris to attend the first International Catholic Scientific Congress. This event, which was initiated by Maurice d'Hulst and several of his colleagues at the Institut Catholique and which was to be duplicated several times over the next decade, took its inspiration from a small gathering of progressive savants held in Normandy a few years earlier. D'Hulst explained that his object in convening the meeting was to "stimulate the preparation of papers or reports the object of which would be primarily to determine the actual state of science relative to various questions which, because of their relationship to the Christian faith, have special interest for Catholics."

The rector realized, however, that this project would arouse deep suspicion within the breasts of his more-conservative coreligionists, who were already uneasy at the course ecclesiastical scholarship—particularly biblical scholarship—appeared to be following. He therefore took great pains to prepare for the congress carefully and secretly, and he even traveled to Rome beforehand to present his plans in person and thus, he hoped, head off any objection the curia, ever-vigilant and wary at the prospect of intellectuals in assembly, might raise. D'Hulst secured Roman agreement, however reluctant, for his idea, but not without a sharp reminder that a stern papal eye would be fixed upon the meeting he proposed: at the end of December 1887 three critical

---

1. M.-J. Lagrange, *M. Loisy et le modernisme: À propos des "Mémoires"* (Paris: 1932), 5. Loisy's *Mémoires* had been published in 1930–31.

studies of the Old Testament, written by prominent French scholars were inscribed, with much publicity, on the Index of forbidden books.

Wilfrid Ward participated in the congress in a semiofficial capacity as one of its twelve honorary chairmen. He and Josephine found the whole affair "most interesting," but "by far the most remarkable address we heard was the inaugural speech of Monsignor d'Hulst himself. It reflected the general feeling among learned Catholics which prompted these congresses."

Faith is changeless [d'Hulst said among other things], science is not. It is the glory of the word of God to be always one with itself. It is the virtue of human thought that it is never content with itself, but must always be forcing wider the boundaries of its knowledge. But given two things in relation, one at rest, the other in motion, it is inevitable that the points of contact between them should be constantly shifting. . . . [Thus] you [often] have one party saying, "There is obvious contradiction, science is wrong"; and the other retorting, "The hypothesis is sufficiently certain; therefore you have misinterpreted the doctrine." . . . Of course if the supreme authority intervenes with a precise definition of the dogma in question, believers are once more at one. But authority rarely treats of the movement of scientific hypotheses. . . . Meanwhile Catholics generally take one of two lines: there are the bold, and these are sometimes rash; and the cautious, who are sometimes reactionary.[2]

The Wards returned to England and their new home near Freshwater, on the Isle of Wight, with Wilfrid both enthused and sobered by his Parisian experience. D'Hulst's speech, he wrote in his characteristically restrained manner, gave "the keynote to the anxious movement of thought in the Catholic Church which our time has witnessed."[3]

Another, much less heralded lecture was delivered at the congress by the *maître de conférences* of the Institut Catholique, Abbé Alfred Loisy. His subject was highly esoteric, a learned commentary on a Babylonian hymn to the sun god and the magical formula attached to it. The performance, impressive as it may have been to the few equipped to appreciate it, would hardly have been memorable save for the fact that among Loisy's audience was the vicar-general of the diocese of Soissons, Eudoxe-Irénée Mignot.[4] This forty-six-year-old priest, a schoolmaster's son who had risen rapidly through the clerical ranks, would become two years later bishop of Fréjus and ten years after that archbishop of Albi. A reflective and generous man, Mignot maintained all his life an unbounded admiration for the scholar's vocation which, because of the administrative tasks assigned him, he was unable to pursue himself. His meeting with Loisy was fateful for both of them: no one was to support the exegete and his work more loyally than Mignot and no one was to suffer more when separa-

2. Quoted in Houtin, *Question biblique . . . au XIXe siècle*, 129–34.
3. Wilfrid Ward, "Unchanging Dogma and Changeful Man," in *Problems and Persons* (London: 1903), 109–10.
4. Émile Poulat, *Histoire, dogme et critique dans la crise moderniste* (Paris: 1979), 448–64. See also the article in *Dictionnaire de théologie catholique* (Paris: 1929), 10:1743–52.

tion inevitably occurred. As for Loisy, seldom willing or able to cultivate intimacy with anybody, he confessed toward the end of life to only "two great friendships"—one with Mignot, and the other with Friedrich von Hügel. "[Mignot]," Loisy wrote, "was one of those who patiently anticipate the eventual triumph of the truth. . . . He was loving and admirably devout, [one] in whom the modern spirit harmonized perfectly with the traditional virtues."[5]

It is doubtful, however, that the casual acquaintance with the vicar-general of Soissons did much in the short run to soothe Loisy's troubled spirit. The immediately preceding years had been difficult ones, and those that followed had granted him little solace. He had finally attained his professorship within the Institut Catholique of Paris, but only at the cost of swearing to a formulary in which he did not believe.[6]

DURING THE VERY AFTERNOON Abbé Loisy was performing that exercise in mental reservation, March 7, 1890, Albert Lagrange, a slender, bearded, balding man with great dark eyes, quietly observed his thirty-fifth birthday. He did so aboard a small packet plying its way out of Marseilles east across the Mediterranean. Two days later, on March 9, 1890, amid a driving rain and heavy seas, he disembarked at Jaffa on the coast of Palestine. He made his way from there thirty miles or so inland to Jerusalem, or rather to a small, dilapidated building which, shaded by one drooping tree, stood forlorn just outside the Damascus Gate, along the road to Nablus. Here he was greeted by four French Dominican friars who the year before, thanks to the largesse of the French consul in Jerusalem, had secured the property and opened a little chapel and—characteristically Dominican—a house of studies. They called their mission Saint-Étienne, because it supposedly stood upon the site of the stoning of the protomartyr Saint Stephen. Lagrange was a Dominican too, and no longer Albert but Marie-Joseph, the name he had assumed with his religious vows. He came armed with a mandate from the heads of the three French Dominican provinces to begin a school dedicated to the study of the Bible, and eight months later, on November 15, Père Lagrange delivered his inaugural lecture in the new institution's single room, "longer than it was wide," that had once been a slaughterhouse. This enterprise begins, he said, "humbly and especially in poverty. Our scholastic equipment consists of a single table, a blackboard, and a map. It also begins with the help of our Lady Mary, of our good Saint Stephen, and in the confident belief that God also wants this school."[7]

Palestine in those days still belonged within the crumbling Ottoman Empire, but that "sick man of Europe" was rapidly approaching his demise, and the chanceries of Britain, France, and Russia exerted more power in the area

5. Loisy, Mémoires, 3:354.

6. See chapter 4.

7. F.-M. Braun, L'oeuvre du père Lagrange (Fribourg, Switzerland, 1943), 14ff. The text of the inaugural lecture appears in Marie-Joseph Lagrange, L'écriture en église (Paris: 1990), 103–14.

than did the faltering writ of the sultan. Indeed, a rough and informal kind of troika had been in force for half a century, whereby the interests of the various Christian denominations in the Holy Land were traditionally guaranteed by three of the Great Powers: Orthodox depended on the Russians, Protestants on the British, Catholics on the French. In that heyday of European colonialism even virulently anticlerical governments in Paris recognized the utility of a religious presence—so long as it was French—in places as far removed from each other as Algiers and Saigon and Dakar. So it was not surprising that the representative of the Third Republic in Jerusalem should have played a leading role in the founding of Lagrange's celebrated École Pratique d'Études Bibliques.

Lagrange came originally from that slice of eastern France which had nurtured, from north to south, Loisy, Blondel, and Bremond. Son of a highly esteemed director of a firm of notaries, Albert was born in Bourg-en-Bresse on the feast of Saint Thomas Aquinas, March 7, 1855, and was thus a little less than two years Loisy's senior. His Burgundian heritage seemed to mean less to him than it did to Blondel, or perhaps it was the mystique of the Holy Land, once he had settled there, that lent him the aura of a cosmopolitanism not unlike that cultivated by Louis Duchesne. Or it may have been that he never quite related emotionally to his native town, in which his parents had settled only after their marriage. His father, Claude-Pierre Lagrange, sprang from peasant stock out of the Charolais region, while his mother, Elisa Falsan, belonged to the upper stratum of bourgeois society in Lyon. Their famous son, conscious as were all his contemporaries of the severity of class distinctions in those days, later marveled that his parents, given their different backgrounds, achieved so harmonious a union. He recalled—and not in jest—that Elisa's father had expressed a willingness to entrust his daughter to Claude-Pierre, because that sturdy young man, a peasant who had made of himself a lawyer, might be the best safeguard for her at a time, just after the revolutions of 1848, when the "red menace" appeared a serious and perhaps a permanent peril.[8]

Certainly their intense religiosity was one source of their conjugal compatibility. Monsieur Lagrange had been a seminarian before he went to Lyon and won acceptance at the bar, and Mademoiselle Falsan, to whom he had been introduced by a mutual priest friend, had hesitated to accept his proposal only because she wondered whether she had a vocation to the convent. Fidelity to the church and undisguised piety they took for granted: Albert recalled that his father communicated four times a year, an unusual frequency for a layman at the time. Domestic cohesion was also secured by the dominating personality of M. Lagrange, who proved to be a benign autocrat of the breakfast table and

8. M.-J. Lagrange, "Notes sur ma vie," in P. Benoit (ed.), *Père Lagrange: Au sevice de la Bible. Souvenirs personnels* (Paris: 1967), 225–33. The autobiographical account printed here was written and amended during the 1930s.

indeed of all familial affairs. His wife, in contrast, often ill and often away taking the healing waters at Plombières or some other health spa, remained for her children a relatively shadowy if revered figure.

Albert was, like Alfred Loisy, a precocious but delicate lad, so much so that his anxious mother took him, when he was only three, on pilgrimage to Ars in hopes that the blessing of the saintly curé might effect in her son more robust health.[9] No discernible miracle occurred, but Lagrange, again like Loisy, lived far beyond the biblical allowance of three score years and ten, and often under starkly austere conditions. In 1864, after private tuition in Bourg, Albert enrolled at the *petit séminaire* at Autun, a decision that occasioned one of the few quarrels he remembered his parents engaging in. Madame Lagrange preferred that her frail child go to school with the Dominicans in Lyon, whom she knew and loved, but her husband insisted upon Autun, where he himself had been a student twenty years earlier.

It was a remarkable institution for its time and place. Its clerical founders were determined that it should be a secondary school of a quality equal or superior to any *lycée* or *collège* in France, and, if Lagrange himself is to be believed, they largely succeeded. The classics were well taught as would have been expected, but so were the living languages, German and English, and so were sciences like physics, chemistry, botany, and entomology. The least satisfactory courses in the curriculum, curiously enough, were those in religion, which both professors and students treated with scant interest.[10] But in fact French minor seminaries like Autun did not cater exclusively to those intending a career in the church, nor did most of their students pass on to the *grand séminaire*. Albert Lagrange, though regular in his religious duties and boyishly devout, felt no call to the priesthood while he was at Autun.

He confessed in later life to having been an undisciplined student, given habitually to reveries and fantasies—"boldly idle (*franchement paresseux*)," as he ruefully put it. Instead of systematic study he indulged himself with romantic excursions of the imagination by reading, in defiance of the rule, novels like Bulwer Lytton's *The Last Days of Pompeii* and Scott's *Ivanhoe*. He worked by fits and starts, and only because he knew his father expected it of him did he strive enough to win an academic prize or two. There was, however, one exception to this undistinguished record of achievement: thanks to the persistent proddings of a particularly gifted teacher, Albert discovered within himself an aptitude for and a growing love of Greek language and literature. Though of

9. L.-H. Vincent, "Le père Lagrange," *Revue biblique* 47 (1938): 323. Jean-Marie Vianney (1786–1859), the curé d'Ars, near Lyon, was visited by upwards of 20,000 penitents a year during the last years of his life. He was considered a saint long before his canonization in 1925.

10. "Curiously" perhaps, but consistently. From 1944 till 1950 I attended an American minor seminary, very much designed according to the French model. The level of instruction in the academic subjects was very high, while the courses in religion, taught only half the time, were almost an afterthought.

course he could not have known it at the time, by applying himself as vigorously as he did to this subject he had embarked upon his life's work.

His father could not have known it either, and, although gratified by this lonely sign of Albert's diligence, he began to worry about his son's future. Did the boy want to be a notary, or perhaps an engineer? Was he preparing to make himself fit for any honorable profession? The father determined to expose the son to the real world and its prospects. Albert recalled accompanying his father during a school holiday on a tour of the mines near Morceau. "I was astonished at the power of the machines, . . . but I felt more bewildered than attracted. . . . Clearly I was not cut out to be an engineer."

Shortly afterward he traveled with Monsieur Lagrange to Dijon—Blondel, a boy of five, was somewhere in the vicinity—and witnessed with fascination the skill his father and the other attorneys displayed arguing a legal brief in a courtroom there. But once more the fifteen-year-old devotee of Greek mythology could not discern a path he wanted to follow himself. "I observed the contending juridical arguments without understanding them, yet with the desire that one day I might be able to speak with such eloquence."

Aboard the train returning them to Bourg—it was the late summer of 1870—there was a contingent of soldiers, one of whom kept crying out, "On to Berlin!" For the benefit of father and son an officer cheerfully traced out on a map of the prospective theater of military operations how the armies of Napoleon III would shortly demolish the upstart Prussians. Monsieur Lagrange, however, was not so sanguine. Like Henri Bremond's father, he had always been staunch, if not so fanatical, in the legitimist cause. He claimed his as one of only two votes cast in Bourg against the plebiscite of 1851 which had created the Second Bonapartist Empire. Now, in 1870, he supported that regime, only because he feared that its demise would open the door to disorder and red socialism. His reservations about the ability of the empire to sustain itself when confronted by Bismarck's policy of blood and iron were more than justified by the disasters at Metz and Sedan.[11]

Albert Lagrange described himself, when a youngster, as "a precocious liberal." Once at Autun he had got into trouble with his masters by proposing to convert into verse Fénelon's *Télémaque*, a venerable treatise still regarded with deep suspicion by clerical conservatives.[12] Confronted with the wickedness of such a project, this boy—"*ce gamin*"—retorted that "he renounced

11. See Denis Brogan, *The Development of Modern France* (London: 1953), 20–34.

12. François de Salignac de la Mothe Fénelon (1651–1715), archbishop of Cambrai, wrote *Télémaque* (1693) for a grandson of Louis XIV to whom he had been tutor. It was a cautionary tale about the duties monarchs owed to their peoples, and was therefore considered subversive by those who advocated the theory of the divine right of kings. The latter position was most strongly advocated by Jacques Bossuet (1627–1704), bishop of Meaux, who also quarreled bitterly with Fénelon over the issues of mysticism and the literal interpretation of the Bible. French Modernists often invoked Fénelon as a hero, and castigated Bossuet as a villain (see, e. g., Loisy's remark, chapter 4, note 39). For this information I warmly thank my friend and colleague, Thomas A. Kselman.

liberalism no more than had Father Lacordaire."[13] But the defeat of 1870, promptly succeeded by the horrors involved in the rising of the Paris Commune, sobered and hardened him and shifted him toward the Right. Along with other young Catholics of "the vanquished generation"—"Vanquished by whom?," he asked rhetorically and bitterly—he watched with growing apprehension the successes of the anticlerical parties of the Left, which, he feared, would lead inevitably to socialism and disorder. In the end "I became a convinced royalist, but never a militant, never enrolled in those proper political circles that would have have given me a place in high society." Perhaps this reserve resulted in part at least from the conviction that even Gambetta, the tribune of the Left, had acknowledged an inclusive and nonpartisan view of French national purpose when he cried, "Do not talk about Alsace-Lorraine, but never stop thinking about Alsace-Lorraine."[14]

The Prussian war and the Commune had a more immediate effect also upon Albert Lagrange. His formal education was several times interrupted, once with high drama: a band of heavily armed Spaniards, self-described members of Garibaldi's legion on their way to aid the communards in Paris, actually occupied the *séminaire* and closed it down for a brief time. With the gradual return of normalcy Albert finally completed his course and left Autun but without his baccalaureate, a deficiency redressed by way of an independent examination administered at Bourg. Now, at seventeen, he possessed the ticket of entry to *l'université*, but still without a settled idea as to his future. He spent a not altogether comfortable year within the bosom of his increasingly impatient family; his mother, normally pliable and indulgent toward him, chided him for his "indolence of character." Her son considered for a while imitating an admired elder brother and becoming a professional soldier. He even took the entrance examination for the military academy at Saint-Cyr, but, to his own relief and that of his parents, he failed it. Finally, he decided to emulate his father and prepare himself for a career in the law which, Monsieur Lagrange maintained, would be of use to him whatever occupation he ultimately chose. Interrupted only by a year of compulsory service in the army— which did his health no discernible harm and from which, he said later, he gained valuable experience and lasting friendships—Albert Lagrange's scholastic preparation continued in Paris, where he matriculated at the École de Droit of the Université Catholique, as the institution was called in 1875.[15]

13. Henri Dominique Lacordaire (1802–61) was a celebrated preacher and spiritual director, and restorer to France of the Dominican Order (which had been suppressed in 1790). A youthful disciple of Lamennais, he maintained an uneasy balance between Ultramontane theology and political liberalism, and was elected to the Assembly of the Second Republic in 1848. He is alleged to have said at the end of his life, "I die a penitent Catholic and an impenitent liberal." For a brief but moving endorsement, see John Henry Newman, *Apologia pro Vita Sua*, ed. by Martin J. Svaglic (Oxford: 1967), 254–55.

14. Lagrange, "Notes," 230–51.

15. L.-H. Vincent, "Le Père Lagrange," *Revue biblique* 47 (1938):321–24.

A student again, Lagrange once more applied himself by whim rather than by whole-hearted dedication. The Roman legal tradition interested him, as did certain aspects of international law, but he was bored by torts and precedence and the tedious repetitions of the penal code. He committed himself with much greater enthusiasm to lectures in the humanities which he simultaneously followed at the Sorbonne as, he maintained, a kind of diversion. Nor did he neglect the charms to be found uniquely in Paris of theater and museum and musical performance. Nothing could have been more enchanting than to be young and to find oneself discussing with amiable companions all the lively political and social questions of the day within the gorgeous confines of the Luxembourg Gardens. Intellectually he became more and more enamored of ancient Greek literature, and, his imagination fired, he sensed even at this tender age the relationship between a culture and the physical locale in which that culture has flourished. "Once a man has seen Athens," he observed later, signaling the character his biblical studies would display, "he is in a better position to understand Greek history." In July 1878 he received his doctorate without particular distinction, defending a thesis on the origin and applications of Roman law. Three months later he was admitted as a student to the philosophical faculty of the *grand séminaire* of Saint-Sulpice at Issy.[16]

When, half a century afterward, he wrote down the memories of his youth, Lagrange was tantalizingly vague about the details of this apparently abrupt change of direction. He seemed suddenly ashamed—at least in retrospect—of the drift and lack of focus he had so far displayed in his life. He had reduced himself to the status of a Parisian *bouvalardier*, a "*flâneur*," a lounger and loafer. The pieties imbibed at the family hearth and nourished at Autun still exerted a strong influence upon him, enhanced, if anything, by the threat to them he discerned in the programs of the anticlerical government. "My faith at that moment was absolute," he recollected, "rendered all the more combative by the dangers to it that were accumulating on the political horizon." But there were problems of personal morality he did not specify but which, he feared, threatened the integrity of his system of beliefs. "I was sick at heart." One day he was at the race track at Longchamp where a friend informed him that a telegram from Bourg had arrived at his lodgings in the city. Lagrange did not reveal what its contents were—perhaps another maternal admonition—but the remarkable result of it was that he made his way immediately to Issy. "I went to the front of the church, to the shrine of the Virgin. I prayed with

---

16. The *grand séminaire* of the diocese of Paris, Saint-Sulpice, "was composed of two houses," Ernest Renan explained (*Souvenirs d'enfance et de jeunesse* [Paris: 1983 (1883)], 117 and 153), the theologate in "the vast barracks-like quadrangle" on the Place de Saint-Sulpice and near the church of the same name, located in the city on the Left Bank of the Seine; and the other "its junior branch (*succursale*)" in the suburb of Issy, where aspirants spent two years studying philosophy. The normal progression called for passage from Issy to Saint-Sulpice properly so-called, and then ordination. Renan himself attended both institutions during the 1840s, and testified to the great influence the Sulpicians had upon his life.

unwonted ardor, and when I finished I was a different person. I went out and bought a rosary to replace the one I had lost." He hurried then off to Bourg and told his parents—"whom I loved with a unique tenderness"—that he intended to be a priest. So it was that Lagrange, like so many of the personae in this drama, experienced a sudden, almost Augustine-like, conversion.

He stayed at Saint-Sulpice for only a year, because, in the midst of his formal philosophical studies, a new set of doubts followed hard on the heels of the earlier ones. This time, however, a solution came quickly and easily. Lagrange's admiration for the Order of Preachers was by no means restricted to legendary figures like Lacordaire; from his boyhood he had been familiar with those Dominicans who were close friends of his father and particularly of his mother. And from the day he arrived at Issy to stay, his Sulpician directors encouraged him to weigh seriously the prospect of exercising the priesthood under the vows of a friar rather than in the parochial ministry subject to the direct rule of a bishop. "The liturgical celebration of every Dominican feast day," he recalled, "added to the attraction I felt." On October 6, 1879, within the venerable walls of the thirteenth-century convent of Saint-Maximin in Toulouse, Lagrange was invested with the white habit of the Order of Preachers, and surrendered the Christian name Albert in favor of Marie-Joseph.[17]

The months spent by Lagrange at Issy were especially significant because of a lifelong friendship and professional association he formed there. Pierre Batiffol,[18] born in Toulouse in 1861 (and thus Lagrange's junior by six years), was the son of an instructor in a local *lycée*. He had matriculated at Issy a year before Lagrange, and he was to go on to establish a distinguished record of academic achievement, which included stints, under the benign direction of Louis Duchesne, at both the Institut Catholique and the École des Hautes Études. Later, after his ordination as a secular priest, he served for two years on the staff of San Luigi dei Francesi, the French church in Rome, during which time he was closely involved in the researches of Giovanni Battista de Rossi, probably the most distinguished Christian archaeologist of his day.[19] Blunt and often caustic, Batiffol provided a marked temperamental contrast to the gentler, more introspective Lagrange, but, odd couple as they may have seemed, their scholarly partnership, begun in earnest conversations as seminarists at Issy, was to endure through the tumultuous years that lay ahead.

Those tumults were to turn largely upon the relationship, as Batiffol put it, "between questions of history and questions of theology: should the domain of facts discovered by history be entirely independent of the interpretations

17. Lagrange, "Notes," 269–77.

18. The standard biography is Jean Rivière, *Monseigneur Batiffol* (Paris: 1929). Rivière also wrote the notice in *Dictionnaire d'histoire et de géographie ecclésiastiques* (Paris: 1932), 6:1327–30. See also the bibliographical notice in *Dictionnaire de théologie catholique*, "Tables générales," 385–86. See also Poulat, *Histoire, dogme*, esp. 364–92, and *Modernistica*, esp. 150–57.

19. Aubert, *Pie IX*, 186–87.

and deductions to which these facts give rise and which belong to the competence of the theologians?"[20] The mature Batiffol did not think so, nor did Lagrange, whose Dominican training played a crucial role in the development of
his attitude on this thorny issue. Almost from the beginning of his membership in the order his superiors, conscious of his linguistic abilities, had destined him for advanced scriptural studies. But first he had to pass through a
rigorous theological schooling which, in accord with Dominican tradition,
was based upon the texts of Thomas Aquinas. For Lagrange the four years dedicated to this strict regimen acted as a kind of intellectual catharsis, a completion of his spiritual conversion, wherein the carelessness and whimsicality that
marked his student days at Autun and at Paris were eliminated forever.

The ideal Leo XIII wanted to impose upon the universal church through
Aeterni Patris had been honored in Aquinas's own order consistently, if not
always with distinction. "The basis of the teaching we received," Lagrange
remembered, "was the *Summa theologiae* of Saint Thomas, studied directly from
the text, question after question, article by article. Nothing could have
equaled this daily contact with the letter of the greatest of theologians. . . . I
had no taste for the debates among modern theologians. . . . In a word, I
considered Saint Thomas the harmonious conclusion of all Catholic doctrine,
and not the point of departure for quibbles and evasions."[21] It hardly needs
saying how far removed Lagrange's experience was in this regard from that of
Loisy and Tyrrell, who read the *Summa* on the sly, so to speak, and who, deprived of the direction as well as of the intense and methodical application
such a difficult study requires, ended up contemptuous or hostile toward it.

Lagrange had his adventure in Thomism not at the provincial motherhouse
in Toulouse but at Salamanca. The same governmental decree expelling the
religious orders that sent the stripling Jesuit Henri Bremond to England sent
Lagrange and his brethren to Spain. The revered friary of San Esteban, long
deserted, was reopened and offered refuge to the exiled French Dominicans
until 1886. Their life was harsh, but not without its consolations, one of
which was the realization that they trod on the same stones as had the great
Dominican Schoolmen of the sixteenth century, among them Vittoria and Me-
dina and Domingo Bañez, the latter of whom had on these very premises regularly dispensed counsel and sacramental absolution to "the incomparable" (as
Lagrange called her) Saint Teresa of Avila. Perhaps it was this hallowed setting
along with his devotion to the eminent Carmelite mystic—who was buried
only a few kilometers away—that nurtured the sense of spiritual discernment
which Lagrange cultivated during his years in Spain and which never left him
afterward. He passed through the conventional phases of ascetical development, the ups and downs, as it were, of *la vie dévote*—from "this profound joy,

20. Quoted in Poulat, *Histoire, dogme,* 367.
21. Lagrange, "Notes," 283–87.

this elation with things divine" to "the inability to pray, the painful dryness, the dismaying realization that one might be an alien in God's house"—until, in the end, he convinced himself that "I could find Jesus Christ in my prayer, Jesus Christ in my brethren, Jesus Christ everywhere." He exhibited the species, and indeed the degree, of explicit piety that would have embarrassed a Loisy or a Bremond, but maybe not a George Tyrrell and certainly not a Friedrich von Hügel. At the close of 1883, in any case, a few months after the death of his redoubtable father, Marie-Joseph Lagrange was ordained priest, *ad titulum paupertatis* in the Order of Preachers.[22]

During the two admittedly confused years that followed—a confusion engendered by a regime so unsure of its ultimate legitimacy as the French Third Republic—Père Lagrange, as he now was, taught ancient church history, with five lectures a week, to his younger brethren in Salamanca. He carried this work forward from August 1886, when the community was allowed to return to Toulouse, where he also enrolled in the courses in scriptural criticism taught at the local Institut Catholique. These latter classes, Lagrange wrote, "made me realize painfully how ill-prepared I was" technically for serious biblical research. His superiors realized it too, and in the autumn of 1888 they sent him off to the University of Vienna, which could introduce him to the latest findings of German scholarship. Here Lagrange studied, not Scripture itself, but Scripture's "philological bases," in which he felt particularly deficient. He pursued with zest "these purely technical subjects"—ancient Egyptian language, Assyrian, Arabic, the standard rabbinical writings—"until I learned about the projected biblical foundation in Jerusalem."[23]

"SINCE I NEVER HAD A GIFT for describing landscapes," Lagrange once observed, "even when their beauty impressed me profoundly, I have for the most part refrained from trying to do so. I must say, however, that I was ravished, truly moved by my first sight of the Holy Land; I felt myself abandoned with delight to an historical perspective of times long ago. I had so loved the Book, and now I stood on the very ground where the Book had assumed its form." His rapture was not diminished by the magnitude of the task before him. The École Biblique began with four professors and three students, all Dominicans. Lagrange's professional colleagues included an Arabist, a geographer, and—inevitably in a Dominican house—a systematic theologian. Largely without apparatus and or even books, the program of studies was similarly modest. Not so the aspirations of the director, who from the first planned initiatives for the École across the whole range of orientalist research. He was confident that eventually a great library would be established, that archaeological digs would be opened, that scholars would flock to Saint-Étienne from all

22. Lagrange, "Notes," 274–86.
23. Lagrange, "Notes," 279–90.

over the world. In the spring of 1891 Lagrange launched his grandiose design by putting up a little classroom building.

And a year later he founded the *Revue biblique internationale*. That such an enterprise succeeded so quickly outdistanced even the headiest of the director's ambitions. Back in Paris to drum up support for the École, he found the idea of linking the publication of a learned journal to the foundation in Jerusalem pressed upon him by several experts in the field, not least by Loisy's Sulpician colleague at the Institut Catholique, Fulcran Vigouroux. An intrigued Lagrange applied for permission to his Dominican superiors, who cheerfully agreed, on the condition that enough advance subscriptions be sold to assure the venture's solvency. So typically prudent a ruling appeared to scuttle the idea, until a friendly Parisian publisher came forward and guaranteed that his firm would absorb any losses incurred by the review.

This happy turn of events left Lagrange the congenial task of assembling a corps of editorial collaborators. He found them, priests all, among the ranks of Dominicans, Jesuits, and seculars. Pierre Batiffol, back now in Paris and chaplain of the Collège Sainte-Barbe, was one of the first recruits, and a few years later he was given overall charge of the Parisian side of the operation. In 1926, looking over the list of scholars who had joined him in founding the *Revue biblique*, Lagrange wrote:

Perhaps none of these names attracted as much attention as the absence of the name of Monsieur Loisy. With his two books on the [scriptural] canon . . . he had attained first rank among biblicists. His penetration, his critical spirit, the clear and incisive manner in which he expressed his views, his extensive knowledge: all this combined to make me want to associate with us this proficiency which could only grow greater. There were, however, differing opinions about him. Some people attributed to him reckless views. I did not want to decide anything without talking to him heart to heart. I called on him, but he was not at home, . . . and, once gone from Paris, I could not make up my mind to put a proposition to him in writing.[24]

One wonders why not.

Lagrange for his part wondered whether Loisy would have accepted the invitation had it been extended. He rather doubted it, because, he said, Loisy always preferred to be *"chez lui,"* and indeed he soon founded a journal of his own which appeared a few months after the first issue of the *Revue biblique*. Lagrange was certainly correct in surmising that Loisy, the quintessential individualist, would have had no interest in forming part of a team. As for the alleged "reckless views," Lagrange's worries in this regard may well have been prompted by Batiffol, who had known Loisy as a fellow student at the Institut Catholique and who disliked him intensely. Loisy was destined, Batiffol used to say, "to turn out bad," and it was important neither "to compromise with

---

24. M.-J. Lagrange, "Fondation et développement de l'École biblique," in Benoit (ed.), *Lagrange,* 31–41.

him nor to be compromised by him."[25] Loisy himself, as always coldly courteous, merely remarked that his own efforts in the field of biblical studies were probably too simple for association with the Dominicans' prestigious board of editors.

Loisy at any rate had now embarked upon his spectacularly prolific career. His first book—his doctoral dissertaion on the history of the canon of the Old Testament—had been, as Lagrange observed, well received in scholarly circles. He followed up on this success with a similar study of the New Testament. Before he died in 1940 he published sixty books, all of them serious and many of them very long, as well as nearly three hundred articles in learned journals.[26] Not Duchesne[27] nor even Lagrange himself—whose personal bibliography totalled 1,786 items[28]—could match the lifelong productivity of "le petit Loisy."

He worked prodigiously, and with a sophisticated economy of effort. Thus every course of lectures he delivered was forthwith put in press, often in the journals he founded and edited for that purpose. And he worked according to a plan that he had nurtured since the period, during the mid-1880s, when he had wrestled interiorly with doubts about his vocation as a "doctor" in the church. His mission, "imposed by a combination of signs and circumstances," was to create a new apologetic consistent with the insights of modern critical history, "to rescue Catholicism from the leaden sheath into which it had been thrust by the philosophy of the Middle Ages and the false science of the Jesuits. . . . There is movement. The mountain is shaking. The glacier is melting."[29]

He proceeded with great circumspection. He never made a statement, whether viva voce or in print, without protesting his unswerving loyalty to the teaching authority of the church, or without claiming sanction for his views from some patristic source or conciliar decision. When a reviewer praised one of his early books for its "originality," he explicitly repudiated that judgment. So cautious was he in this regard—"so intent to pledge his respect for tradition, his blind submission to all required opinions, . . . in order to reassure orthodox pieties"—that he became something of a comic figure to discriminating skeptics. Even so, Loisy knew what he was about; the audience he catered to was the younger clergy, like those who sat in his classroom at the Institut Catholique and their brethren, already staffing parishes and institutions across France, who read his books and articles. These men, he said publicly and piously, simply wanted to know more about the Bible, "desired to

---

25. Quoted in Albert Houtin, *Mon experience, vol. 2, Ma vie laique* (Paris: 1928), 152–53. See also Poulat, *Histoire, dogme,* 364–65.

26. The complete list appears in Houtin and Saritaux, *Loisy,* 304–24.

27. See chapter 4.

28. The complete list appears in Braun, *Lagrange,* 193–286. Lagrange wrote many monographs and other larger works, but the overwhelming majority of the 1,786 items were short book reviews.

29. Houtin and Saritaux, *Loisy,* 57–58.

complete the excellent yet necessarily imperfect initiation they had received in their seminaries." But in his private notebook he added: "After several years of teaching, when I shall have pupils in every corner of France, my ideas will be more easily accepted; the way will have been prepared, and I shall find plenty of people to support me."[30]

Subtle and discreet Loisy assuredly was, and not altogether candid about his ultimate objectives; but he never sacrificed his essential convictions nor the courage that went with them. *Suaviter in modo,* to be sure, but also *fortiter in re.* When Abbé de Broglie, a very senior colleague at the Institut, mildly questioned one of his positions, Loisy replied: "It is necessary to inquire into the documents before one uses them. I realize that M. de Broglie can consider the authenticity of the Pentateuch as demonstrated. He is within his rights. But would not his position be much enhanced if it were based upon critical grounds rather than on a mere hypothesis?" During the winter of 1892 Loisy wrote a prospectus for the journal he was about to found—*L'eseignement biblique*—and here, amid a prudently crafted set of orthodox platitudes, he revealed the real thrust of his program:

Certainly, no one should be surprised to see us applying the historical and critical method to scriptural science. This is not to say that we should ever lose sight of the supernatural character of the sacred books, nor the dogmatic principles which are the infallible rule of exegesis; but we do have to conform ourselves to the necessities of the present time. "A historian," M. Renan has written [in *Vie de Jésus*], "is precisely what a theologian can never be. History is essentially disinterested. . . . The theologian has an interest, his dogma. Reduce that dogma as much as you like, it still bears . . . for the critic an unsustainable weight." This passage . . . contains many errors, but they are errors very widely diffused, and they cannot be refuted by syllogisms. So we are confronted with the assertion that a theologian cannot be a historian in the full sense of the word, even when he deals with biblical history. It is up to us, the theologians, to prove the contrary by the fact that we show ourselves as capable as anyone else to perform critical work—real and sincere critique—and even, in a very true sense, free criticism, because, on the terrain of biblical history, as in every other subject, faith directs rather than obstructs the investigations of science, and because the certain conclusions of criticism cannot be in opposition to the certainties of faith.[31]

There is a mendacious irony in Loisy including himself among the theologians, for his whole purpose was to drive a wedge between theology and history. Or rather—a better image—to plumb the fault line which in fact, he was convinced, separated the two disciplines and which had been papered over by "the philosophy of the Middle Ages and the false science of the Jesuits." The performance was as smooth as the prose was elegant. Alluding to one of the most hotly controverted subjects of the day, Loisy, with disarming candor,

---

30. Houtin and Saritaux, *Loisy,* 54–56, 38. See also Loisy, *Mémoires,* 1:136.
31. Quoted in Houtin and Saritaux, *Loisy,* 54–55.

addressed his students at the beginning of the academic term, in the autumn of 1892:

The church can of course promulgate a definitive statement about the origin of the Pentateuch; but at the present time one cannot find a single Catholic theologian, genuinely informed about this subject, who would support the notion that Moses's authorship of the first five books of the Bible should be presented to Catholics as a matter of faith or as a truth in accord with the principles of faith. By the same token, it would be unthinkable to deprive Moses, by solemn definition, of such authorship either in whole or in part. Whence it follows that an authoritative definition upon a subject of this kind has small chance of happening, and so the historical critic remains free to examine the question with appropriate prudence and maturity.[32]

By such a rule all questions remained open, and the rhetorical tactic Loisy adopted involved, as he admitted later, "an enormous equivocation."[33]

The balancing act succeeded at least for a while and at least to the degree that authoritative displeasure was muted—though d'Hulst worried and was heard to murmur on occasion that Loisy was making of himself "a little Renan."[34] But in public the rector defended Loisy, as he had Duchesne; he might have done so less eagerly had he known his young colleague's real state of mind. Loisy for his part was not unaware that he walked upon ecclesiastical thin ice, and he looked round for powerful allies. One possibility was Mgr. Meignan, formerly his own bishop of Chalons-sur-Marne,[35] now archbishop of Tours and cardinal-elect. On October 24, 1892, this grand personage gave audience to his former diocesan in a Paris hotel room. "Believe me, mon petit Loisy," said the archbishop, as he chain-smoked cigarettes, "believe me, it is necessary to be prudent. I helped enlist you into the ranks of science, so I have the right to speak. Take care! This is the advice of a father. If you expose yourself to danger, those who think as you do will not come to your support. . . . You will destroy yourself for nothing."[36]

But the counsel came too late, even assuming that Loisy would or could have followed it. Almost at the moment it was tendered Henri Icard had decided to intervene against Loisy as he had against Duchesne exactly a decade earlier.[37] The superior of the Sulpicians decreed that none of the seminarians under his charge should attend Abbé Loisy's scriptural lectures any more. "I have heard one of the better students attest," Icard wrote d'Hulst, "that the more they followed M. Loisy's lectures, the less love and regard they felt for the Holy Bible."[38] The rector was incensed by what seemed to him one more

32. Alfred Loisy, "La Critique biblique," in Études bibliques (Paris: 1903), 109–10 (reprinted from L'eseignement biblique [November–December, 1892]).

33. Loisy, Choses passées, 90.

34. Baudrillart, Vie de d'Hulst, 1:476.

35. See chapter 1.

36. See Loisy, Choses passées, 116–23, for the whole interview.

37. See chapter 4.

38. Baudrillart, Vie d'Hulst, 1:483.

unwarranted intrusion into the affairs of the academy he administered under such difficult circumstances, but, as Loisy later observed in his best sarcastic mode, "M. Icard was a man whom even a rector of the Institut Catholique, a gentleman, a grand-nephew of popes and archbishops, did not dare challenge." D'Hulst determined instead to grapple by indirection with the problem posed by his brilliant but unconventional professor of Scripture. He "believed the moment had come to try to act upon Catholic opinion broadly considered. His desultory readings and conversations had convinced him, at least vaguely, that theology was obstructing the legitimate development of the human sciences, especially history, by raising a barrier of prejudice disguised under the claims of religion."[39]

Ernest Renan died that same fateful October 1892. Almost every French intellectual interested in religious matters used the occasion to comment not so much upon the career of the author of the *Vie de Jésus* as upon the future prospects of the biblical criticism of which Renan had been the popularizer. D'Hulst chose for his literary vehicle the venerable Catholic journal the *Correspondant*, which traced its lineage back to the heyday of liberal Catholicism associated with the likes of Montalembert and Lacordaire.[40] The rector of the Institut Catholique suggested in an article, published on October 25, that perhaps Renan had been seduced into unbelief by the very naïve manner in which the biblical exegesis had been presented to him at the Saint-Sulpice of the 1840s. When the sky did not fall upon him after this modest sally against the Icards and the Vigourouxs, d'Hulst decided to press forward.

On January 20, 1893, Alfred Loisy received a copy of a printer's proof, and with it a covering note:

Dear Friend, Before sending this corrected proof to the printer I want you to see it. You will note that it is primarily an act of policy, designed to secure for us little by little some tolerance, and then liberty, and to show the inquisitors that they are ignoring some salient facts.

This is (1) why I play the role of reporter; (2) why I give prominence to the median position; and (3) why I have not named you, though you have filled my thoughts. Sincerely yours, M. d'Hulst.[41]

The article was titled "La question biblique," and it appeared in the January 25 issue of the *Correspondant*. It recounted the impasse currently troubling Catholics with regard to biblical studies. It identified two schools of apologetic thought: "That which accepts as genuine history, infallible by reason of divine inspiration, every narrative which does not clearly manifest the character of a parable; and that which, after having set aside dogmatic and moral teaching, believes it can make a choice among the scriptural texts according to the proce-

39. Loisy, *Choses passées*, 112–14.
40. See Édouard Lecanuet, *Montalembert*, 3 vols. (Paris: 1902), 3:111–29.
41. Quoted in Loisy, *Choses passées*, 125–26.

dures of historical criticism." D'Hulst did indeed adopt the mode of a reporter, but it was not difficult to discern that his sympathies lay with the second of the two positions, which he called the *école large*, and that his espousal of some kind of *école moyenne* between the two was a ruse. For how, it was reasonably asked, can there be mediation between extremes when one of the poles does not exist? "These words," wrote a moderate reviewer, "are a trumpet blast. Are they the signal of an assault upon the traditional apologetic? Many people think so."[42]

The predicament the rector, too clever by half, had got himself and his young colleague into was grounded in the fact that his *école large*, a hodgepodge of half-digested opinions from various disconnected sources, was a figment of his own imagination. Or of his own "incompetence," Loisy derisively observed. The position he sketched out may have possessed a certain logic and coherence, but no Catholic theologian, committed to the teachings of the Councils of Trent and the Vatican, could have possibly adhered to it.[43] Nor, ironically, did it describe Loisy's views, which were far more radical and which d'Hulst could have easily ascertained had he not been too lazy and too arrogant to search them out.

It had been perfectly evident all along [Loisy wrote] that my fashion of explaining errors in the Bible was entirely different from that of the *école large*. I continued to think that the Bible, being a book written by human beings, did not escape the conditions of every human book, and could not be in accord with the truth of any other epoch, even in matters of faith and morals, except the epoch of its composition. The *école large* infuriated the theologians by speaking of errors in the Bible, and it defied the evidence by pretending that the doctrinal teaching of Scripture was the same as that of the church.[44]

Mgr. d'Hulst's article produced a firestorm of published recriminations and responses, and instead of gaining a measure of "tolerance" for Loisy, it brought that heretofore obscure young scholar precisely the notoriety that most threatened his cherished program. D'Hulst himself hurried to Rome to head off any possible intervention by the Holy See. From there, on April 15, he wrote a friend: "I do not think it possible to restrain Loisy. His is a spirit too vigorous, too original, too self-willed to admit of modification. I think it will be necessary to change his role, to restrict him to oriental languages and retire him from exegesis." This ploy the rector put into effect a month later, but it only prolonged the agony temporarily. Loisy meanwhile, fulfilling d'Hulst's de-

42. See Houtin, *La question biblique*, 149–51.

43. E. g., see the decrees of session 4 at Trent and session 3 at the First Vatcian Council, printed in Henry Denzinger, Clement Bannwart, and Karl Rahner (eds.), *Enchiridion Symbolorum, Definitionum, et Declarationum de Rebus Fidei et Morum* (Freiburg-im-Breisgau: 1952), 279–81, 493.

44. Loisy, *Choses passées*, 128–29. For an excellent treatment of the difference between Loisy's views in 1893 and those of the so-called *école large*, see William J. Wernz, "The 'Modernist' Writings of Alfred Loisy: An Analysis" (unpublished doctoral dissertation, University of Iowa, 1971), 14–16.

scription of his character, promptly gave a lecture in which he scoffed at those who, he said, "wish to restrict orthodox science within the circle of what they call traditional opinions. . . . Neither their fears nor their clamor seem justified."[45] The publication of these remarks only days before the annual meeting of the episcopal board governing the *institut* proved to be the last straw; the bishops voted on November 15 to disallow the erstwhile professor of Hebrew from serving on the staff in any capacity. So, on November 18, 1893, Alfred Loisy wrote d'Hulst a bitter letter of resignation: "Your object has been achieved, Monseigneur. The instruction given in your faculty of theology can no longer disquiet anybody. . . . You want students, always more students, and to get them you are willing to sacrifice your personal views, to sacrifice men you love and esteem. And to what good? Do you think you can avoid the future by turning your back on it?"

Two days later, on November 20, the tough old Sulpician Henri Icard died. Louis Duchesne heard the news while he was vesting for mass in the sacristy of the Carmelite church. Placing the biretta on his broad head and grasping the base of the chalice, he strode toward the door of the sanctuary, saying, "Old Icard! He must have died of joy."[46]

45. Alfred Loisy, "La question biblique et l'inspiration des Écritures," *Enseignement biblique* (Novenber–December 1893), reprinted in *Études bibliques* (Paris: 1903), 152–53.
46. Houtin and Saritaux, *Loisy*, 62–72.

CHAPTER 8

"The God of All Providence"

The idea of God as author of a book is more contradictory, more absurd in itself, than the notion of a toad-man or a snake-woman. It is an infantile myth.

—*Alfred Loisy* (1930)[1]

AT THE MOMENT of Alfred Loisy's dismissal from the Institut Catholique of Paris—"the catastrophe," to use his own word[2]—Marie-Joseph Lagrange was far away in Jerusalem, tending to the affairs of his new little school. "It was imprudent of me," he admitted later, but he resolved nevertheless "to ask M. Loisy to become a collaborator of the *Revue biblique*. . . . It appeared simply perverse to me that the most competent of French Catholic biblicists should be removed from a struggle for which we would have need of all our forces." Yet the misgivings of eighteen months earlier about Loisy's "reckless views"[3] had not gone away: "Of course it had to be clearly understood that, if M. Loisy agreed to join us, it would have to be in accord with our line, not his." An important negotiation of this sort, Lagrange thought, was too delicate and complicated to be handled through a correspondence passing over a long distance, so he asked Pierre Batiffol to make the proposal viva voce, and the latter, setting aside at least for once his personal dislike of Loisy, complied.

The obsequies of Henri Icard provided him with an opportunity. "When I left the church after the funeral," he wrote Lagrange on November 23, 1893, "I paid a visit of condolence to poor Loisy. As to collaborating with the *Revue biblique*, he seemed little inclined. 'I would only compromise you and nothing more,' he said to me sadly. And of course he is right." Some months afterward Loisy sent his definitive refusal direct to Jerusalem: "I have been very touched by the testimony of sympathy Father Batiffol brought me in your name and also by the offer to collaborate in the work of your journal. For the time being I think it inopportune for me to publish anything."[4]

1. Loisy, *Mémoires*, 1:306, commenting on *Providentissimus Deus*.
2. See Houtin and Saritaux, *Loisy*, 70.   3. See chapter 7.
4. Quoted in Lagrange, *Loisy et modernisme*, 79–81.

Alfred Loisy was not a man given to sentimentality or indeed a man easily "touched" by any human gesture. But he may have been in this case genuinely moved by Lagrange's offer, because it confirmed that, contrary to rumor, the professionals associated with the *Revue* and the *École biblique* had not been the ones who had complained in Rome about his teachings. Yet complaints had been made there, as Maurice d'Hulst had discovered the preceding spring when the curial officials had warned him that he must offer "the most solid guarantees" of the Institut's orthodoxy in its biblical teaching if he wished to avoid a condemnation with names explicitly named.[5] The rector had learned, moreover, that the pope intended shortly to address in an encyclical the questions raised by the higher criticism and to speak authoritatively about its practice among Catholic exegetes. The rector concluded that the price demanded of his beloved institut was the partial sacrifice of Loisy, which the French bishops, the smell of blood strong in their nostrils, consummated by demanding the exegete's removal even from the chair of oriental languages. To use d'Hulst's own metaphor, Loisy had committed the fatal error of "throwing himself in the path of a moving locomotive."[6]

The image was not altogether inappropriate, though Loisy wryly observed that in reality it had been the rector who had pushed him in front of the speeding train. There was justice in this qualification of the figure of speech, because Leo XIII's encyclical "on the study of Sacred Scripture"—issued coincidentally the very day of Loisy's forced resignation, November 18, 1893—explicitly rejected the tenets of that *école large* of biblical interpretation which d'Hulst had invented out of his own fancy and into which, without the exegete's permission or knowledge, he had situated Loisy: "The system of those who . . . concede that divine inspiration regards the things of faith and morals, and nothing beyond, . . . cannot be tolerated."

In accord with the usual papal formalities, the encyclical received its title from the opening words of the original Latin, *Providentissimus Deus*.[7] "The God of all Providence" had bestowed upon humankind the inestimable gift of grace, and accompanying it a capacity to plumb even divine mysteries through "unwritten Tradition and in written Books, which are therefore called sacred, . . . because, 'being written under the inspiration of the Holy Ghost, they have God for their author.' " In this last clause the pope was quoting directly the decrees of the Vatican Council, and indeed throughout the document he insisted, characteristically, that norms of judgment in scriptural matters must

---

5. Baudrillart, *Vie d'Hulst*, 1:481.

6. See chapter 6 and Loisy, *Mémoires*, 1:274.

7. See *Acta Sanctae Sedis* 26 (1893): 269–92. Quotations are from Carlen (ed.), *Encyclicals, 1878–1903*, 325–38, which reproduces the translation in the (London) *Tablet* 83 (6 January, 1894): 5–11. "The God of All Providence" has a pleasant literary ring to it, but is a fairly free translation of *providentissimus Deus*, which might be better, if more awkwardly, rendered, "the most provident God" or "the most foreseeing Deity."

rest upon conciliar and patristic precedents. Nor should it ever be forgotten that the sacred books "have been delivered to the Church," which has been designated their ultimate guardian and protector. From the time of the apostles to our own day, "the Church has never failed in taking due measures to bring the Scriptures within reach of her children, and . . . she has ever held fast and exercised that guardianship conferred upon her by Almighty God for the protection and glory of His Holy Word."

Upon the proper study and appreciation of the Bible, the pope argued, rest not only holiness of life and sacred oratory, but also doctrinal integrity. Scripture cannot be separated from theology; indeed, the two are so dovetailed and intertwined that they present two aspects of a single intellectual reality. Like an echo from *Aeterni Patris*, the pope more than once in this encyclical asserted that in the elucidation of biblical materials the methodology of Thomas Aquinas was to be the model. Of course "it is [not] forbidden, when just cause exists, to push inquiry and exposition beyond what the Fathers have done, provided one carefully observes the rule so wisely laid down by St. Augustine: not to depart from the literal and obvious sense [of the text], except only where reason makes it untenable or necessity requires: . . . 'If in these books I meet anything which seems contrary to truth, I shall not hesitate to conclude either that the text is faulty, or that the translator has not expressed the meaning of the passage, or that I myself do not understand.' "

"I myself do not understand": this Augustinian motto highlighted the chasm that separated the papal from the critical mentality. A critic such as Loisy was convinced that modern philology and scientific history had provided the keys to a thorough understanding of the biblical texts, so long as they were treated comparatively with other ancient writings. Leo XIII, on the contrary, cheerfully accepted the prevalence within the Bible of "obscurities," passages whose genuine meaning—an inextricable mix of the human and divine—would remain mysterious despite the efforts of clever men. Those efforts are by no means wasted—indeed, they are highly laudable—but they must remain always consistent with the abiding principle that "the Holy Fathers are of supreme authority, whenever they all interpret in one and the same manner any text of the Bible." And what of textual analysis and "internal evidence," so prized by the critics? The pope showed the back of his hand:

There has arisen, to the great detriment of religion, an inept method, dignified by the name of the "higher criticism," which pretends to judge of the origin, integrity and authority of each Book from internal indications alone. It is clear, on the other hand, that in historical questions, such as the origin and handing down of writings, the witness of history is of primary importance, and that historical investigation should be made with the utmost care; and that in this matter internal evidence is seldom of great value, except as confirmation. To look upon it in any other light will be to open the door to many evil consequences. It will make the enemies of religion much more bold and confident in attacking and mangling the Sacred Books; and this vaunted "higher criticism" will resolve itself into the reflection of the bias and the prejudice of the critics.

Leo XIII had kept his bargain with d'Hulst, in that no person or institution was censured by name in *Providentissimus Deus*. But among French Catholic intellectuals there was little uncertainty as to which targets the pope was aiming at. Lagrange and his associates in Jerusalem determined to keep their heads firmly down: "We were absorbed by the discovery of the oriental and Palestinian milieu; under the charm of these new horizons, which illuminated so many matters, . . . we were far removed from the controversies of schools and books."[8] Paris was not so conveniently remote, and Duchesne, quipping that papal vanity needed to be constantly assuaged, insisted that the Institut Catholique send a message of formal adhesion to Rome. This was done, despite the feisty Pierre Batiffol's dismissal of the gesture as "a sign of cowardice."[9] Loisy too found it prudent "to prostrate myself humbly at the feet of Your Holiness" and to assure the pontiff, in a letter written on December 7, "of my fidelity to the teachings of the church and particularly to those contained in the encyclical on sacred Scripture. . . . It seemed necessary to me to apply with prudence the critical methodology, . . . in order to combat the adversaries of the Bible with their own weapons." But any novelty in such a procedure was only "apparent." "It is sad in the extreme for a priest . . . dedicated to biblical studies to be accused of fostering dangerous opinions. . . . But I take deep consolation in coming today, in the simplicity of my heart, to swear to the vicar of Jesus Christ my most complete submission to the doctrine promulgated in the encyclical."[10]

Loisy enclosed with the letter a memorandum in which he proposed how, in pursuing his research, "I might conform myself . . . in perfect submission . . . to all the instructions of the magnanimous pontiff, Leo XIII." With an acquaintance attached to the École Française de Rome acting as intermediary, these documents were placed directly into the hands of no less a personage than Mariano Rampolla del Tindaro, the Vatican secretary of state. "Very Illustrious Sir," Cardinal Rampolla replied on December 31, "the Holy Father has received your letter with particular pleasure, . . . and he has read your memorandum with close attention. . . . He remains very content and very satisfied at your full submission to the instructions of the Holy See in a matter so important and so delicate. . . . However, in considering all the facts, His Holiness deems it more opportune and expedient for you, that in following your generous inclination to devote your talents to the glory of God and the well-being of your neighbor, you do so in some other branch of science." "Excellent ad-

8. Lagrange, *Souvenirs personnels*, 53.
9. Houtin and Saritaux, *Loisy*, 74.
10. Loisy, *Choses passées*, 388–90.

vice," Loisy recalled sarcastically years later, "but since it was merely advice and since I was the only judge of my own interest, . . . I decided to continue my work as before."[11]

ON THE AFTERNOON of October 18, 1893—a month to the day before the issuance of *Providentissimus Deus*—Friedrich von Hügel called on Alfred Loisy in his apartment on the rue d'Assas. The baron had asked for the appointment in a letter sent a week earlier, in which he explained that he, together with Lady Mary and their three daughters, planned a stopover in Paris for a few weeks on their way to the south of France where they would spend the winter. No record survives of the conversation on that occasion, nor those at the meetings held between the two on October 20 and 24, but, given Loisy's habitual caution and rigid self-possession, it seems unlikely that he would have confided to this stranger any details of the personal and professional crisis he was passing through. The baron at any rate, once he had settled his family at Saint-Raphaël on the Riviera, wrote warmly to Loisy and assured him that their encounters had "deepened and expanded [his] sympathy."[12]

Loisy's name, to be sure, had been known to von Hügel for some time before the two actually met. During the summer of 1890 a learned orientalist had, at the baron's request, initiated him into the study of Hebrew, a pursuit von Hügel was to carry forward with his wonted dogged determination—under a variety of mentors but for the most part on his own—over the next six or seven years. That same savant had also recommended Loisy's research to the baron who, by the autumn, was busy scrutinizing Loisy's dissertation, the *Histoire* of the canon of the Old Testament, published in Paris earlier in the year.[13] He was very favorably impressed, as he wrote to Wilfrid Ward on October 21: "In these 250 pp. you have an extraordinary production, the very thing we want, . . . containing every date and composite authorship demanded by Wellhausen and Kuenen; you don't get that every day!" Invoking the names, as he did, of two of the most prominent and progressive Protestant scripturists was no irrelevance on von Hügel's part: along with his studies of the Hebrew language he was also reading closely the latest scholarship on matters related to the Old Testament and seeking out, especially at Oxford and Cambridge, those specialists most in tune with the academic trends in the continental universities.[14] The result of these inquiries was the conviction that the Roman Catholic position on exegetical questions was hopelessly out of date.

11. Houtin and Saritaux, *Loisy*, 74–75, and Loisy; *Choses passées*, 155–56, where the author describes his "memorandum" having been "as audacious as it was candid."

12. Barmann, *Hügel*, 38.

13. See chapter 7.

14. De la Bedoyere, *Hügel*, 67–70, and Barmann, *Hügel*, 11–14, 31–37. Abraham Keunen (1828–91), who taught at Leyden, was the most prominent Dutch exponent of the higher criticism, especially with regard to the Pentateuch. Some of his works were translated into English by J. W. Colenso, bishop of Natal and, because of his views on the inerrancy of the Bible, a highly controversial figure

It would be wrong, however, to conclude from this particular judgment that von Hügel for a moment considered his loyalty to Catholicism in any sense at stake. Indeed, he was always alert to find in those Protestant scholars whose works he studied so assiduously evidence for traditional Catholic positions. For example, a few weeks before his fateful initial meeting with Alfred Loisy he composed for private circulation a short treatise that he called, modestly, "Some Notes on the Petrine Claims." The arguments he advanced there were neither novel nor spectacular, but they did invoke Protestant authorities to shore up those scriptural sources—like the Gospel of Matthew, 16: 18[15]— that had been conventionally used to justify the pope's primacy.[16]

Not until the end of April 1893 did von Hügel directly contact Alfred Loisy. He wrote the embattled exegete to convey his esteem and to request a photograph which he wanted to place on his desk, he said, next to that of Duchesne. He also wrote Mgr. d'Hulst, congratulating him on the publication of the controversial "La question biblique" and offering to translate it and have it published in the *Dublin Review*. D'Hulst's notion of an *école large* evidently found more favor with the baron than it did with Loisy.[17] But inconsistencies of this sort seldom bothered von Hügel once his enthusiasm had been engaged, and in this case he decided to forego simple translation and instead write an article encompassing and endorsing the views of both d'Hulst and Loisy, even though these were hardly in harmony with each other. He could expect that the *Dublin Review* would print such an essay, because that journal belonged to the cardinal archbishop of Westminster, who now, since Manning's death, was the old family friend Herbert Vaughan.[18] "Cardinal Vaughan . . . kindly came up on Friday," von Hügel told Ward on May 8, "and was really *great* in his utter non-inflation and perfect approachableness. I hope and believe he will continue to keep an open eye and ear for us and our work and principles." The cardinal apparently agreed that the article should be published in the *Dublin Review*, but, like so many of the baron's literary projects, this one was never completed.[19]

ALFRED LOISY, meantime, was now without employment. And, worse than that in the long term, he had acquired an even more implacable opponent than Henri Icard had been, in the person of Cardinal Richard, the archbishop

within the Anglican communion. Julius Wellhausen (1844–1918), the leading exponent within German university circles (Halle, Marburg, Göttingen) of the higher criticism, made his reputation particularly in his analysis of the multiple sources of the Book of Genesis.

15. "And I say to thee that thou art Peter, and upon this rock I will build my church, and the gates of hell shall not prevail against it."

16. See Friedrich von Hügel, *Some Notes on the Petrine Claims* (London: 1930), esp. 17–30. This work, published posthumously, bears the date 2–7 September, 1893 (v).

17. See chapter 7.

18. See chapter 6.

19. Barmann, *Hügel*, 36–37.

of Paris, once Icard's student and later the Sulpician's penitent. François Richard de la Vergne, scion of a well-to-do landowning family, came originally from Nantes. After serving five years as bishop of Belley, he was appointed coadjutor of Paris in 1875, and succeeded to that see in 1886. A robust seventy-three at the time his long duel with Loisy began, he was tall and round-shouldered, with a great beak of a nose that dominated a narrow face. In manner he was habitually affable, and he unfailingly displayed the effortless courtesy of the aristocrat he was. Though titular head of the French hierarchy, he did not possess a personality strong enough to dominate his fellow bishops. Yet he was steadfast—stubborn even—in his loyalty to the principles he believed himself committed to as a churchman.[20] Some of his priests made fun of Richard behind his back, and called him "the holy mule." Loisy's friend, Bishop Mignot, dismissed him as "a worn-out royalist."[21] But Loisy himself provided, understandably, a sharper, more self-interested perspective:

Among the moments in my life that have imposed upon me the most severe moral strain, I can think of nothing more agonizing than the conversations I had the honor to have with the late archbishop of Paris. He was a man from another age; the language he spoke was entirely unintelligible to me, nor did he understand anything I said. He was not very cultivated, but he was far from being as limited as his clergy sometimes maintained. He had brought with him from Brittany a faith of granite that no doubt had ever touched. He wanted to be just; he was good; I have heard intimates say of him that he was full of charity. But he was very ill-prepared to understand the biblical question or, for that matter, any contemporary questions. . . . He conformed himself with docility to the traditions of the church, and never left room for an idea of his own. . . . Absolute submission of the intelligence was for him a sacred mystery, a mystery however that in fact disguised a sickness of the soul. To have entertained a thought of his own . . . would have seemed to him simply the fruit of a prideful spirit that had delivered itself to Satan.[22]

Nor did the passage of years soften Loisy's judgment. "This intellectual corpse, this holy fossil, this stupefying spiritual emptiness that was Cardinal Richard," he declared in his *Mémoires*. The archbishop offered the young scholar his "paternal counsel" and assured him of his "benevolence," which only served as a source of further exasperation: "Yes, the very sincere benevolence of Torquemada for Victor Hugo, in which people are burned to death out of mercy."[23]

On December 1, 1893, Cardinal Richard wrote to "mon cher Monsieur Loisy" a short note in which he demanded that the publication of *L'enseignement biblique* be suspended until further notice. Loisy replied, with chilly formality, that he had already taken that step and quoted a few lines that he had dis-

20. Dansette, *Histoire religieuse*, 455.
21. Houtin and Saritaux, *Loisy*, 272.
22. Loisy, *Choses passées*, 148–49.
23. See Loisy, *Mémoires*, 2:73, 14–19.

patched to the subscribers to his little journal: "In accord with his filial submission to the recent directives of the Sovereign Pontiff, Leo XIII, the director of the *Review* feels the need to devote himself for some time to silent reflection."[24] So, no longer a professor or an editor, the young peasant-priest from Ambrières—he was just thirty-five—had to find some way to make a living. Though he could not bring himself to solicit openly an appropriate clerical post—*"une situation honorable"*—he was not above enlisting the intercessory aid of his ever-amiable former colleague at the Institut Catholique, Abbé de Broglie, whose aristocratic credentials gave him easy and frequent access to the cardinal. On three separate occasions, when he and Richard had dined together, de Broglie had tried to insinuate into the conversation Loisy's name as a suitable candidate for the sinecure of a canonry at the cathedral of Notre Dame, but each time the cardinal had reacted so negatively and so vehemently that de Broglie gave up the undertaking in despair. Loisy meantime had been informed by the archdiocesan vicar-general that he would be assigned to a chaplaincy as soon as one became available. Loisy responded by saying that he would be content to accept such an office in one of the Catholic *lycées*. When he heard this proposition Richard growled, "No. If he goes to a place like that, filled with impressionable youths, all he will do is spread his pestilential ideas."[25]

The abortive intervention of de Broglie in Loisy's behalf represented an uneasiness edging into guilt felt by various people as a result of the turn events had taken. Two or three bishops to whom Loisy sent word of his distress responded cordially enough, though none of them offered to provide him with a *position convenable*. Maurice d'Hulst, de Broglie's close friend and associate, was keenly affected by the deprivation of the young exegete, with whom he, d'Hulst, had erroneously associated the opinions of *l'école large*. At the end of January 1894 the rector wrote to Loisy: "I do not forget for a single moment the obligation of justice and friendship I owe to you." When sufficient time has passed, and when Cardinal Richard has gone to his eternal reward, as that prelate shortly must, there can be no reason, the rector said, why Loisy should not assume again the professorship of oriental languages in the Institut. The response was frigid: "I do not wish you, Monseigneur, to be unaware that I consider it neither possible nor desirable that I should return to the faculty of the Institut Catholique in any capacity whatsoever." There followed a desultory and, on Loisy's side, a bitter correspondence, and then, in November 1896, Mgr. Maurice d'Hulst died, a full dozen years before the tough old archbishop of Paris.[26]

24. Loisy, *Choses passées*, 387–88.
25. See Houtin and Sariaux, *Loisy*, 75–76.
26. Loisy, *Choses passées*, 157–61. In retrospect Loisy was less bitter toward D'Hulst who, he said, was not intrinsically a bad man: "The fault lay rather with the institution he served so devotedly, with the political spirit of Rome and of the French bishops, with the reign of terror which from this time on descended upon Catholic intellectual life."

Meanwhile, and more remarkably, Henri Icard's successor as superior of the French Sulpicians, who unguardedly described himself as a "liberal," felt constrained to offer Loisy amends for the "harshness" with which Icard had treated him. Arthur Captier, confident as d'Hulst had been of Richard's imminent demise, proposed that Loisy accept a post at the church of San Luigi dei Francesi in Rome—where both Duchesne and Batiffol had served a term in earlier days—and there at his scholarly leisure await the cardinal's happy death.[27] But to a man of Alfred Loisy's tastes and habits this suggestion, however well intentioned, verged into fantasy. So it was that not until September 1894 did the former professor receive a definitive appointment: chaplain to the Dominican nuns and their pupils at a convent school in Neulliy-sur-Seine, one of Paris's more fashionable suburbs.

SAINT-RAPHAEL on the Riviera, where Friedrich von Hügel and his family spent most of the winter of 1893–94, lay only a few miles from the ancient port of Fréjus. Before the baron left Paris for the South, Loisy had urged him to call on the bishop of Fréjus and Toulon in whom he would find, the exegete promised, a kindred spirit. The prelate thus recommended was that Eudoxe-Irénée Mignot, formerly of Soissons, with whom Loisy had been on increasingly intimate terms since their first encounter in 1888.[28] One day toward the end of November the baron walked the few miles that separated the health spa where he was staying and Fréjus, a "little, sleepy, sun-baked, profoundly southern town," which enjoyed at least one romantic association: to its now "dried-up Roman harbor" Octavian had sent some of the Egyptian galleys captured at the battle of Actium.

Bishop Mignot was fifty-one, a tall, erect, handsome man, tending toward chubbiness, with dark eyes and "a finely modulated voice." He displayed immediately a candid, spontaneous disposition, which von Hügel came to think in later years was perhaps too sensitive and a little naïve, but which betrayed not a sign of affectation or hubris. He entertained his guest "in his rambling old palace, in his study—a high up turret-chamber looking out on to the sea." The room was filled with books, among which the most notable were various editions of the Bible in Hebrew, Greek, Latin, French, and English. The bishop could read all these languages, but he spoke only French, a circumstance that von Hügel—that linguist par excellence—considered a serious handicap. Predictably their conversation turned on the biblical controversies then brewing, about which, valuing as they both did "the inductive, analytic, experimental trend," they found themselves of one mind. Indeed, they remained so until Mignot died a quarter-century later, when the baron paid tribute to a friendship that had helped see both of them through many a crisis.[29]

27. Houtin and Saritaux, *Loisy*, 76–77.
28. See chapter 7.
29. Friedrich von Hügel, "Eudoxe-Irénée Mignot," *Contemporary Review* 113 (May 1918): 519–26.

Loisy—not without bias, to be sure—used to say that Mignot was more intelligent than the rest of the French hierarchy combined. This sentiment was doubtless an exaggeration, as was the assertion, from the same source, that the initial meeting between von Hügel and Mignot may have signaled the beginning of the movement later called Catholic Modernism.[30] Yet Mignot was in truth a formidable figure, thoughtful, strong, and persistent in his views, loyal to his friends almost to a fault, singularly free of the cant that disfigured the deportment of too many of his mitered colleagues. And there is no question that he, like von Hügel, played a pivotal role in the tragedy that was about to unfold.

His assignment to Fréjus and Toulon, in 1890, was itself evidence of factors at work that profoundly complicated the intellectual issues that were of primary interest to Loisy and von Hügel, and indeed to Mignot himself. Since 1801, after the tumults of the French Revolution, church–state relations in France had been governed by the provisions of the concordat entered into between the Consulate of Napoleon Bonaparte and the Holy See, a formal agreement that had survived through all the monarchist and republican regimes that had followed. The treaty had been battered by incessant conflict, and its terms had been often mutually misrepresented, but by the 1890s it still functioned and still incorporated the procedures designed to promote harmony—or at least to avoid confrontation—between the government of the day and, in the words of the concordat itself, "the Catholic, Apostolic, and Roman religion, [which] is the religion of the great majority of French citizens." A key article calculated to secure a measure of balance between Gallican and Ultramontane interests stated that "nominations to bishoprics . . . shall be made by the First Consul [and his duly constituted successors], and canonical institution shall be given by the Holy See."[31]

What had in fact developed over nearly a century of contention was a process of negotiation over each episcopal appointment. The bargainers were, for the Vatican, the nuncio to Paris, and, for the government, the minister of cults, sometimes prompted by self-serving cabinet members, and even on occasion by the prime minister himself.[32] During the year 1890 five vacancies had to be filled, into two of which the ministry, backed by the president of the Republic, insisted on placing its own candidates. One of these "candidati officiali alle sedi vacanti" was Mignot. Indeed, so anxious was the government to settle the matter that on June 1 the minister requested "l'assenso del Santo Padre" to the selection be dispatched to Paris "per telegrafo."

The testimonial documents the nuncio accordingly hurried off to Rome for the most part portrayed Mignot very flatteringly. One bishop praised his

---

30. Loisy, *Mémoires*, 1:293.
31. Barry (ed.), *Readings*, 3:13–15.
32. See, e. g., Marvin R. O'Connell, "The Bishopric of Monaco, 1902: A Revision," *Catholic Historical Review* 71 (January 1985): 28 (n. 13).

"great tact," his skills as an administrator, and his "firmness." Another described him as "probably the most intelligent priest in the diocese of Soissons. He speaks well, he writes beautifully, and with precision and force." Even those chronic antagonists, Henri Icard and Maurice d'Hulst, who had been respectively Mignot's teacher and his schoolfellow, could agree in this instance upon a positive assessment. The archbishop of Cambrai observed that Mignot's "piety was not something readily discerned from the outside," but he remained confident that the candidate had "a genuine, even a tender, devotion" to the person of Jesus and to the Eucharist. And though Mignot had attributed to him "certain rationalist tendencies," the archbishop ascribed "this supposition to his natural curiosity and to the freedom he sometimes takes in debating with naïve persons and pressing the force of objections, not indeed to the truths of the faith but to . . . certain commonly held opinions." The archbishop, finally, drew a distinction more significant than he perhaps realized: Mignot's "theological learning (*science ecclésiastique*)" was adequate, while his knowledge of the Scriptures "was quite extraordinary."[33]

The pope formally assented to Mignot's appointment to Fréjus and Toulon on June 4, 1890, and five months later he initiated a startling shift in his diplomatic policy toward France. It is hard not to assume that the two events were related, at least to the extent that swift accommodation had been given to the government's nominee—a man once suspected of "rationalist tendencies"—as a sign of the Vatican's desire for a new era of cooperation. Leo XIII at any rate, as the hostility of the Third Republic toward the church intensified, had watched with growing apprehension the apparent inability of French Catholics to mount any meaningful resistance. One cabinet after another, dominated not simply by oldfashioned anticlericals but by Freemasons and positivists who were virulently opposed to Catholicism on ideological grounds,[34] left an enduring stamp upon the public life of the nation. The Catholics—or rather what passed for their visible and articulate leadership—seemed able to offer as an alternative only the repudiation of the Republic itself. Nor did it matter whether such spokesmen were clerical or lay, liberal or conservative in other respects. Thus the theological progressive Maurice d'Hulst remained as staunchly dedicated to a restoration of the monarchy as did the traditionalist Cardinal Richard who, when confronted once by a young priest describing himself as a republican, exclaimed in shocked tones, "Ah,

---

33. See Domenico Ferrata [nuncio to Paris] to Rampolla, 1 June, 1890, Archivio segreto Vaticano, Segretario di stato (1878–1914), rubric 248 (1890), fascicle 6, wherein are enclosed the testimonial letters cited in the text. The five dioceses were Bordeaux, Bayonne, Évreux, Dijon, and Fréjus and Toulon. The other "official candidate" was the vicar-general of Orléans, François Flautin, who went to Évreux. The archbishop of Cambrai had been previously bishop of Soissons and hence Mignot's superior.

34. See chapter 1, and, among many other works, Dansette, *Histoire religieuse*, 402–30, and Lecanuet, *Les Premières années du pontificat de Léon XIII* 46–100, 119–44, 181–220.

you will be an abysmal failure in the sacerdotal office. The Republic is impossible in France!"[35] For people like Richard *la République* did not mean simply a form of political organization; it stood rather for the guillotine and the September massacres and the laic laws, for the red terror, for a malevolent power bent upon robbing France of its Catholic heritage. Compromise with it was impossible.

The practical difficulty with this judgment, however sincerely held, was that it conflicted with the facts registered at most general and local elections: royalist sympathy was restricted to a hard-line, largely upper-class minority that was fast ebbing away. Even those Catholics who still went to mass—and their numbers remained considerable in many parts of the country—stubbornly refused to vote for the monarchist candidates their priests recommended. Leo XIII, who could count as readily as the next man, decided to intervene—as he had already done in Germany[36]—in defiance of the deep-seated convictions of the local elites: from the supreme Roman authority came the directive that tactical compromise, unpalatable as it might prove for many, was an absolute necessity if the church were to survive in France. Catholics must no longer bind themselves to the dying cause of the monarchy, and no longer stand aloof from the real political world for the sake of a fantasy; instead, they must "rally" to the Republic, because clearly the Republic was not going to pass away.[37]

At first glance it would seem that neither the dramatic circumstances in which the policy of *ralliement* was unveiled in November 1890—with the cardinal of Algiers proposing a toast "à la République" at a banquet attended by royalist naval officers[38]—nor the failure of that policy in the long run to preserve the concordat,[39] certainly Leo XIII's major intention, should have had a direct bearing upon abstruse arguments over biblical criticism and immanentist philosophy. Yet the initiation of the *ralliement* at the very moment when these controversies were heating up did involve the pope in certain unintended risks and inconsistencies. Embittered royalists understandably asked some awkward questions: Why is it permissible to collude with positivist politicians but not with positivist historians, when all of them, brothers under the skin, aim at the destruction of traditional Catholicism? Why is it that episcopal candidates with "rationalist tendencies" now find acceptance with the successor of Saint Peter?

35. Dansette, *Histoire religieuse*, 390.

36. See chapter 2.

37. For a good summary, see Alexander Sedgwick, *The Ralliement in French Politics* (Cambridge, Mass., 1965).

38. See Montclos (ed.), *Le toast d'Alger*, passim, and James E. Ward, "The Algiers Toast: Lavigerie's Work or Leo XIII's?," *Catholic Historical Review* 51 (1965): 173–91.

39. See John McManners, *Church and State in France, 1870–1914* (New York: 1972). The concordat was unilaterally repudiated by the French government in 1905.

YET EUDOXE-IRÉNÉE MIGNOT knew full well to what forces he owed his elevation. He had dutifully sent an acknowledgment to the papal secretary of state, and pledged his "absolute fidelity to the Holy See," but he had done so briefly and laconically, and with none of the rhetorical excess so unhappily common among his Ultramontane colleagues.[40] He understood that, stemming as they did from political neccessity, his credentials at the Vatican were problematic at best, and during the early weeks of 1894, he shared with his new friend Friedrich von Hügel his doubts that the pope would ever be shown a letter he, Mignot, had written urging as large a measure of freedom as possible for Catholic biblical scholars.[41]

This plea had been occasioned by the issuance of *Providentissimus Deus,* which the baron too had studied carefully and which had left him with mixed emotions. He was ill through much of January, but as spring approached he had recovered sufficiently to hold several conversations about the encyclical with Mignot. Late April found him back in Paris trying to persuade Loisy and Duchesne that the papal pronouncement might well turn out to be a positive development. Perhaps he was remembering 1870 and the definition of papal infallibility: "I have never been anything but an Ultramontane. . . . I have ever been glad of the Definition of 1870."[42] At least, the baron pointed out, the pope had not closed discussion on two most explosive issues, the historicity of the Old Testament and the Mosaic authorship of the Pentateuch. The Frenchmen were less sanguine.[43]

The family was settled again into the house in Hampstead when von Hügel, on May 21, told Wilfrid Ward that he "came home, after seeing so much of my best friends abroad and getting to know much more, I think, than anyone in England . . . about what is going on under the surface and is brewing for the future." He was determined, he added, not to comment publicly on the encyclical unless it were attacked, and then only "for the purpose of utilizing the only opportunity we insiders [shall] have, perhaps for many a long day, for respectfully widening out our bases and getting breathing space."[44]

The attack upon *Providentissimus Deus* duly came from the English intellectual establishment, temperate enough and courteous as might have been expected in the pages of semilearned journals like the *Guardian,* the *Spectator,*

---

40. Mignot to Rampolla, Soissons, 28 June, 1890 (see note 33, above). Contrast Mignot's restraint with the sycophancy of his predecessor, now translated to Dijon. Frederic-Henri Oury to Leo XIII, Fréjus, 27 June, 1890 (see note 31, above): "In confiding to me the diocese of Dijon, your Holiness has given new proof of your paternal goodness. My first duty, in learning of this, is to hurl myself at your feet, in order to thank you, in order to proclaim once and for all my attachment to the common Father, and my perfect submission to the infallible Doctor. . . . I prostrate myself at your feet, very Holy Father, imploring the apostolic benediction, and I declare myself the most devoted, the most obedient, and the most loving of sons."

41. Eudoxe-Irénée Mignot, Letters of 4 and 19, January, quoted in De la Bedoyere, *Hügel,* 77.

42. Von Hügel to Ward, n.d. [about 1902], quoted in Ward, *The Wilfrid Wards,* 1:301.

43. See, e.g., Loisy, *Mémoires,* 1:297.

44. Quoted in Barmann, *Hügel,* 43.

and the *Contemporary Review*, but sufficient for the baron to follow through on his resolution to speak out. Cardinal Vaughan, puzzled by the mild fuss, nevertheless welcomed von Hügel's offer to write an essay on the subject for the *Dublin Review*. On June 14 the baron outlined his intentions to Ward, with whose views, as he knew, he was not in full accord. "I am [not] going to make [the article]—formally—. . . a defense of the Encyclical. . . . With all my heart I hold its central doctrine, and with all my heart I believe that its own commentary, if one works up one part with and into another, defends and leaves the doctrine thoroughly defendible. . . . [But] the real question to my mind is whether there is or is not such a thing as a science of the Bible (as distinguished from its dogmatic and devotional use)."

That indeed was the question, and von Hügel remained convinced that the papal instruction admitted an interpretation consistent with the aims of moderate biblical critics, among whom he decidedly included Loisy. "As to his work upsetting people's minds"—Ward's persistent worry—"anyone who would really mend our present position must do so." Yet genuine *critique* "is not directly intended" for the majority of the faithful. "I . . . have long ago found out that hardly any women and but a minority of men . . . are ripe for these discussions." Must the work of specialists therefore be restricted? "Are we going to have no manuals of obstetrics or gynecology till these can be safely put into the hands of the average young man or woman?"[45]

Surely "average" persons, of whatever sex or rank, would have found von Hügel's contribution to the *Dublin Review* hard sledding. He not only finished the essay originally proposed, but he tripled it in size: three related articles appeared between October 1894 and October 1895, eighty-eight pages of print altogether.[46] They displayed their author's immense erudition and industry, as well as his almost entire incapacity to express himself clearly in his adopted tongue or indeed to lend rational organization to a narrative.[47] Long quotations from German, French, and English sources were stitched together without any sense of rhetorical cohesion.[48] Obiter dicta mingled abruptly with metaphysical speculation and pious professions. Material was divided into so many numerical headings and subheadings, linked by no apparent transition, that confusion compounded itself. Verbs were invented, including barbarisms

45. Quoted in Ward, *The Wilfrid Wards*, 1:311–12.
46. Friedrich von Hügel, "The Church and the Bible: The Two Stages of Their Interrelation," *Dublin Review* 115 (October 1894): 313–41; 116 (April 1895): 306–37; and 117 (October 1895): 275–304.
47. The following two sentences—von Hügel, "Church and Bible," *Dublin Review*, 115:320—are far from untypical of the baron's prose: "And there is always some danger of our losing the greater by too eagerly seeking after the lesser, because of the strain and cost of keeping intellectual self-control and, with it, that 'Faith which comes' in part 'from self-control.' And this will be so specially in times of change in the direction of men's observation and in the furniture of their imagination."
48. This was the case with all three essays, but particularly so with the second, in which the baron was intent upon establishing the scholarly community's view on the Mosaic authorship of the Pentateuch; see von Hügel, "Church and Bible," *Dublin Review* 116 (April 1815): 312–21.

such as "precisionize." The anecdotes were too labored and obscure to serve any useful purpose.[49] Nor did the baron's editors preserve him completely from incorrect grammar and error of fact.[50]

And yet, despite these faults, the articles did make their author's point, and rather tellingly at that. It may have been that von Hügel's warmth and sincerity could not be concealed even by his deaf-man's insensitivity to words. It may have been that the intuition with which he began his argument came so clearly from a genuinely devoted heart: the very majesty of the God who has deigned to reveal himself to us, with all our limitations, must determine our method of seeking him and of finding in him the way to moral probity. "I would point out that it is . . . this absolute incomprehensibility which gives room for continuous apprehension [by human beings] on and on, ever fresh and ever new, of the one inexhaustible God; and this, not only here but even, indeed, still more hereafter."

So when the Bible and the church confront one another, the baron maintained, there are "two stages in their interrrelation." The first one does not "necessarily involve the Bible as such, but only as containing certain documents of human authority. Now this human authority has to be established by human, historical means and methods." Once such documents have been authenticated by scholarly procedures, the church intervenes to teach "conclusively . . . the existence, nature, and range of the divine authority of the Bible: . . . our second stage." "Revelation and a Church are practically identical, but . . . Revelation and Scripture are not; the former are [sic] necessary, the latter but contingent consequences of man's creation. . . . Relations between the necessary Church and contingent Scripture are necessarily twofold, and must ever be kept carefully distinct: Scripture qua human document, and, as such, one of the several proofs of the Church's authority; [and] Scripture qua Divine Library, re-given to us as such by that authority."[51]

Whether Moses wrote down the words contained in the first five books of the Bible was for the historians to decide; how those words unerringly described God, his attributes, and his dealings with humankind was for the church to proclaim. Here was the crucial distinction that seemed to von Hügel capable of safeguarding the rights of both the higher critics and the ecclesiastical magisterium. From it followed all the rest of his meandering argument. Certainly, for instance, when *Providentissimus Deus* identified the "vaunted 'Higher Criticism' " with rationalist "bias and prejudice," what the pope meant to reprove, said von Hügel, was "accepting the too hurried and too subjective conclusions of individual scholars as though they were the calm and final word of science." And anyway "such studies cannot reach, do not claim

49. See, e.g., von Hügel, "Church and Bible," *Dublin Review* 116: 336–37.
50. See, e.g., von Hügel, "Church and Bible," *Dublin Review* 115:319, 116: 311.
51. Von Hügel, "Church and Bible," *Dublin Review* 115: 314–16, 116:306.

to attain the spiritual truth of Scripture, reserved for humble purity of heart, and the true teacher of us all."[52]

THE FIRST OF THE THREE *Dublin Review* articles was published in October 1894, just as von Hügel and his family were leaving England to spend another winter on the Continent, this time in Rome. The baron, taking the seventeen-year-old Gertrud with him, departed some weeks ahead of Lady Mary. As usual he arranged to pass through Paris, calling on Loisy at Neuilly on October 25, and holding conference with Duchesne on several occasions. The latter had fervently taken up the cause of reunion between the churches of England and Rome, a will-o'-the-wisp enterprise which, during the mid-1890s, concentrated on attempting to get the pope to accept the validity of Anglican orders. The advocacy of Duchesne—whose antennae never failed to detect a trend—in behalf of a venture that lay far outside his area of expertise gave off more than a hint of calculation. For it was widely known that Leo XIII, anxious to be remembered as "the pope of reconciliation," looked with cautious favor on initiatives that might lead to corporate union, in which possibility he was strongly encouraged by his most influential aide, Cardinal Rampolla. Leo's record settling the *Kulturkampf* in Germany and foisting the *ralliement* on French Catholics, without much reference in either case to local sensitivites, intimated that, if convinced of the Anglican position, he would not hesitate to set aside the strong objections of the English Catholic hierarchy.[53] The trouble was that pope knew even less about the true state of the Church of England than did Duchesne.[54]

Von Hügel never could summon up much enthusiasm over the question of Anglican orders. Outsider though he was himself, yet he had many and cordial contacts within the Church of England, and he understood far better than naïvely hopeful French and Italian clerics how small a minority the High Church party represented—a sixth of the clergy, some said, or maybe a tenth. As to the specific issue, he thought it "possible" but not "certain"—and not provable—that the sacrament of holy orders had continued to be administered within the Anglican communion in a manner consistent with Catholic doctrine, despite the repudiation of Rome during the era of the Protestant Reformation. He was eager, as always, that civility be maintained, "that English Catholics, on their part, should try and generate just a little more light and a little less heat," and predictably he wanted the matter considered on its historical merits. But these did not necessarily lend comfort to those Anglicans

52. Von Hügel, "Church and Bible," *Dublin Review* 117: 278, 303.

53. See Vaughan to Miecislaus Ledochowski [prefect of the Congregation of Propaganda], 18 September, 1894, in Archivio di Propaganda Fide, Inghliterra, 48:72–75, which attempts to explain the complexities of Anglicanism, wherein the High Church votaries abandon "la severa simplicità delle funzioni protestanti" and are instead "attrati dallo splendore della nostra liturgia."

54. Barmann, *Hügel*, 54–66, and De la Bedoyere, *Hügel*, 78–92.

pressing their suit at the Vatican. As the baron ruefully observed, in reference to the Protestant iconoclasts of the sixteenth century, "To throw down altars and break altar stones was a strange way" to profess the sacrificial, and hence priestly, character of the reformed Eucharist and its ministers.[55] But out of friendship for Duchesne and a general disposition to promote the progressive agenda whenever he could, von Hügel fell in willingly enough with Duchesne's suggestion that while in Rome he lobby the curia on Anglican orders as well as on the biblical question.[56]

The baron and his daughter traveled in a leisurely fashion across southern France, and then to Basel, Milan, and Genoa, where the shrine of Saint Catherine—the fifteenth-century mystic, Caterinetta Fieschi, who was to figure so prominently in von Hügel's most significant literary achievement[57]—was specially opened for them. They arrived in Rome on November 9, 1894, and stayed there until the following May. It proved to be a time somewhat out of joint for the baron. He could not get a formal audience with the pope, though his wife and daughters assisted at a papal low mass and were shocked by the eighty-six-year-old Leo's appearance: "They had never seen a man more clearly ravaged by old age. The mass took almost an hour, and the pope had to hold on to the altar lest he fall."[58] Cardinal Rampolla, the secretary of state, received von Hügel three or four times and was cordial if noncommittal when the baron pleaded for maximum liberty for biblical scholars, explained why *Providentissimus Deus* had created a poor impression at Oxford and Cambridge, and—almost as an afterthought—asked for serious consideration of the Anglican claims.

This last request was hardly necessary: Rome was all agog over the prospect of the imminent conversion of England. Von Hügel met a young Barnabite priest, Giovanni Semeria—destined to figure prominently in his future endeavors[59]—who harbored the most romantic notions of the British Empire's benign religious influence.[60] Leo XIII himself was busy preparing a special and complimentary letter *Ad Anglos*. Cardinal Vaughan came to Rome to pour cold water on this heedless enthusiasm, and to explain to uncomprehending Latins the mysteries of High, Low, and Broad Church politics in England. His reward for imparting such realities was that everybody, from the pope on down, was cross with him.

55. Quoted in Ward, *The Wifrid Wards* 1:288, 295.

56. The definitive treatment of the subject of the negotiations over Anglican orders is John Jay Hughes, *Absolutely Null and Utterly Void* (Washington, D.C.: 1968); see esp. 59–62, 160–62, 223–27, 295–306.

57. Von Hügel, *The Mystical Element of Religion as Studied in Saint Catherine of Genoa and Her Friends*, 2 vols. (London: 1908).

58. Quoted in Loisy, *Mémoires*, 2:157.

59. For brief biographical notes of Semeria, see Houtin and Saritaux, *Loisy*, 402, and Barmann, *Hügel*, 55–56.

60. Ward, *The Wilfrid Wards*, 1:283.

Some Vatican functionaries were cross also with von Hügel, but on different grounds. Curial officials less courteous than Rampolla dismissed the baron's efforts as an impertinence and hinted that his entrée to high Vatican offices had more to do with his social rank than with any professional competence. Though it stemmed largely from resentment at a layman's intrusion into areas that clerics regarded jealously as their own, there was some justice in this insinuation: von Hügel must have often appeared to harassed bureaucrats to be merely an upper-class busybody and nuisance. But not even a casual acquaintance, to say nothing of one who knew him well, could fail for long to appreciate the baron's noble intentions and disinterestedness, whatever causes he was espousing. Vaughan and von Hügel went riding or walking almost every Tuesday afternoon that winter, and though their conversation often went at cross purposes, there resulted no lessening of their mutual affection.

Yet the intensity with which the baron threw himself into his intellectual activities possessed its darker side. It spilled over into a picky and obsessive desire to regulate every detail of the lives of his wife and daughters. More than that, his preoccupation with scholars and religious affairs led Lady Mary to feel shut out of the most important concerns of her husband's life. The baron, after all, had long concluded that "hardly any women" had the capacity to discuss the biblical studies that so engrossed him. In May 1895 an unhappy Molly returned directly to Hampstead, while Friedrich went back by way of Paris. From there, after making his usual rounds, he wrote her a long letter in which he recounted his concerns for Gertrud, who was with him—"I am going to have a good tête-à-tête talk with that dear little thing"—and his anxiety that his "unrest, over-intensity and absorption, . . . [my] getting into *everything* . . . makes you suffer, my good truest friend and wife. . . . Now I see quite clearly how unlovely, how unchristlike, how unsaintly this is, and how it always tends to limit or undo the good I might otherwise achieve. . . . It is not, as Abbé Huvelin made clear to me, a matter of sex; it applies to everything and everybody that I get really occupied with." He pledged to her, in his sweetly disingenuous way, "that full loyalty of thought and judgment and affection which I am so proud to owe to you in a way and degree in which I can owe it to no one else."[61] Though he did his best, he found the promise hard to keep.

WILFRID WARD did not share his friend von Hügel's opinion that women lacked the ability to enter fully into scholarly activities; at least he did not think so about the woman he had married. From the beginning of their life together Ward and Josephine Hope pursued common intellectual interests and exchanged ideas with refreshing directness.[62] This is not to suggest any confu-

---

61. Quoted in De la Bedoyere, *Hügel*, 84–86.
62. See, e. g., the extracts of letters written during April 1890, in Ward, *The Wilfrid Wards*, 1:188–96.

sion of masculine and feminine roles within the conventional family setting, or indeed that any woman in those days felt as free as her spouse to move easily through academic salons and lecture halls. Nor did Josephine show the slightest reluctance to assume the obligations imposed upon her by the laws of domesticity: she considered herself first and last a helpmeet and mother. But in assuming these happy burdens she had not thereby forfeited her substantial powers to analyze and create, and her husband seldom published an article or delivered a lecture without first submitting it to his wife for her evaluation. The Wards were fortunate, as were the von Hügels, in enjoying economic security and therefore the leisure that opened so many vistas for them; they were more fortunate in sharing a commitment to the life of the mind, which saved their marriage from one source of strain experienced by the baron and the baroness.

The Wards' daughter, in her memoir of her parents, titled one chapter, "A Biographer and a Novelist in a Houseful of Children."[63] Five children were born between 1888 and 1896,[64] during which interval the young family left the Isle of Wight to settle briefly in Hampstead and then, until 1900, in Eastbourne on the Sussex coast. Molescroft House, standing on the edge of the South Downs, was large and comfortable and, though the grounds were confining for so many energetic people, there were frequent outings to Beachy Head and Pevensey Castle, and the seaside was only minutes away. Like Friedrich von Hügel, Wilfrid Ward was anxious to be closer to his growing children than his own father had been to him, and, albeit sometimes awkwardly, he joined in their games and indulged their fancies. He also—again like von Hügel—acted the part of pedagogue, but within healthier and more realistic limits. "My father was only a good teacher," one of his daughters recalled, "to a very good learner. He lacked a teacher's patience, and decided that a thing one could not do quickly was 'out of one's line.' "

Until he enthusiastically took up golf in later years, Wilfrid's own recreation consisted in a daily walk, weather permitting, across the Downs, often at first in the company of his renowned Eastbourne neighbor, the aged Thomas Huxley. They shared a deep interest in music and in the philosophy of religion, but their conversations on these rambles covered a wide range of subjects, including now and then the politics of the day. Once, when Huxley challenged a statement issued by Prime Minister Gladstone, Wilfrid asked, "Do you mean that he is untruthful?" "No," answered Huxley, "he is not clearheaded enough to tell a lie." The brief period of this friendship—Huxley died in 1895—was reminiscent of the earlier one between the Wards and Lord Tennyson,[65] and it demonstrated again Wilfrid Ward's extraordinary fund of em-

63. Ward, *The Wilfrid Wards*, 1:228–46.
64. Maisie (1888), Wilfrid Edward Hope (1890), Theresa Victoria (1891), Herbert Joseph (1894), and Leo Paul (1896).
65. See chapter 6.

pathy for persons of distinction, whatever their age or however much their values differed from his own. There could have been little natural affinity between the dedicated young Catholic intellectual and the old Darwinian warrior, who had been, incidentally, a harsh opponent of Wilfrid's father.[66]

At Molescroft a certain ordered and cheerful chaos prevailed, understandable in a household in which, as a friend of Josephine remarked, each offspring was treated as though it were an only child. Wilfrid, the biographer, proved largely impervious to the inevitable noise and interruptions. He wrote steadily every day in his book-lined study, quickly producing a first draft and then painstakingly reworking the text until he was satisfied enough with the result to read it aloud to his wife. Only after her insights had been incorporated did he send the material off to the publisher. The second volume of the life of W. G. Ward appeared in 1893 and the biography of Nicholas Wiseman four years later, both of which received highly laudatory reviews.[67] These major works, however, by no means exhausted Wilfrid Ward's energies. There were essays and commentary to compose for journals, lectures to deliver, a vast correspondence to keep pace with. And there were great issues within the Catholic church to ponder and worry over.

Of course Josephine, the novelist, had a harder time avoiding domestic distraction. The major burden in managing the lively household fell upon her. Several benighted priests—but not Cardinal Vaughan, godfather to her fourth child—plainly told her that her aspirations to be a writer had to be sacrificed on the altar of hearth and home. She ignored them. Most days she found two or three hours to toil, paragraph by painful paragraph—no easy first draft for her—on a piece of fiction, or later on the literary criticism that appeared in prestigious periodicals. While at her desk she could not bear any intrusion, and so she took her manuscript away from the domestic hubbub and literally hid from the family in some remote upstairs room. The fruit of this dedicated labor ripened slowly: it took seven years to finish her first novel. But before she died Josephine Hope Ward published ten more books.[68]

THE ART of the biographer has many similarities to the art of the novelist. Each unfolds for an inquirer the development of character through a series of interconnected events, and to do so successfully each must constantly engage the faculty of literary judgment. "A biography," Wilfrid Ward insisted, "is *not* primarily an accumulation of evidence. It is a picture."[69] This circumstance

66. Wilfrid Ward, "Thomas Henry Huxley," in *Problems and Persons* (London: 1903), 226–59.

67. Wilfrid Ward, *William George Ward and the Catholic Revival* (London: 1893) and *The Life and Times of Cardinal Wiseman* (London: 1897).

68. Her *One Poor Scruple* (London: 1899) drew this comparison, from a reviewer in *Punch*, to a more famous female novelist with the same surname: "[It is] far and away better work than anything which the authoress of *Robert Elsmere* has given to the world. Mrs. Wilfrid's is to Mrs. Humphry's, as fine Lafite to small beer." For a list of Josephine Ward's books, see Ward, *The Wilfrid Wards*, 2:577.

69. Wilfrid Ward, "Candour in Biography," in *Problems and Persons*, 187.

helps explain why the Wards, husband and wife, depended so much upon one another for technical assistance in their writing. It may also account for their uncommon intellectual compatibility, but only to a degree. The genuine source of their union went much deeper. "Between my wife and myself," Wilfrid once said, "there was complete unity of interests so far as all serious things were concerned."[70] And the most serious thing of all was their shared vision of what a thoughtful Catholicism at the beginning of the twentieth century could and ought to be. Nor did they differ as to the guide best suited to lead to the fulfillment of that vision. Though Josephine kept the photographs of two beloved heathens, Tennyson and Huxley, on her writing desk, the only real icon venerated in the house of Ward was John Henry Newman.

During the mid-1890s this Newmanesque ideal seemed to the Wards threatened from two directions. On the Right stood the remains of the old "siege mentality" that had predominated within the Catholic church since the Reformation. In the train of the reformers had marched the absolutist kings and the Jansenists, the Josephists, and the Voltaireans. Confronted by these mortal challenges to her survival "[the church] decided that rigid definition, and the concentration of her own forces, were the only course, if vital principles were to be effectively defended. Her work became primarily militant. Organized zeal and skilful debate were at a premium. The intellectual element, properly so-called, was necessarily for a time sacrificed for the controversial and devotional. Acute polemic, intense and united esprit de corps, the spirit of the martyr, and, above all, absolute military obedience, became essential to the preservation of the organism."

Sacrificed "for a time." The booming Catholic revival of the nineteenth century demonstrated that the validity of the siege model had passed away. The signals included not just the missionary triumphs of the French in Asia and Africa, not just the crowded churches in the United States, not just the success of the German Catholics, through the Center party, in establishing themselves as a potent political force—indeed, in strictly political terms the church had experienced as many recent defeats as victories. For Wilfrid and Josephine Ward what mattered most had been the sea change in "the intellectual element, properly so-called." The mechanistic aplomb of the Enlightenment lay in tatters, the forces of cold unbelief had gone into sullen retreat. After three hundred years of erosion Protestantism itself, as a coherent system of thought, teetered on the brink of dissolution. Through the trenches and barbed wire behind which the old church narrowly preserved its essential character had trooped, hats in hand, refugee-savants of the caliber of Brownson, Frederick Schlegel, Montalembert, Möhler of Tübingen, and Newman himself. The opportunity was not to be missed: "If Cardinal Newman is right in maintaining that assimilation with the thought surrounding it is a normal process in the

---

70. Quoted in Ward, *The Wilfrid Wards*, 1:158.

Catholic and Roman Church, and if the proverb 'History repeats itself' is true, there may be . . . hope for a very far-reaching change both within the Church and without; of a far wider assimilation of contemporary thought within, of the consequent diminution of prejudices . . . without." The "state of siege" was an abnormal condition, an aberration, which, however, was imperative and understandable under the circumstances. "The Index [of forbidden books] may now be in its present form an anachronism; but at an earlier date, in the unsettled state of public thought, to read heresy in any shape was for fickle and weak minds a snare." But at a still earlier date, "in the Middle Ages, when the authority of the Church was acknowledged, a large measure of free debate and free assimilation among individuals was the habit of the hour; . . . in Cardinal Newman's words, the intellect then 'enjoyed a licentious revel.' " So it could, and should, be again.

"Assimilation" was the key concept in the Wards' argument. And assimilation itself, as Newman always maintained, takes its own time, assumes its own rhythm. If the danger from the Right was to resist the process, the danger from the Left, no less perilous, was to attempt to hurry it beyond the pace of its own genius.

If a Papal Encyclical, even in our own day, reaffirms the time-honoured and technical doctrine that there is no "error" in Scripture—preferring to indicate in general terms that this does not involve its accuracy in things not pertaining to salvation, rather than to give the weight of an official approbation to some special adjustment of theology to an incomplete science—can we not see in such a procedure the habitual prudence of a Church surrounded by intellectual enemies? Is there no value in the sense of sacredness which refuses to break with the patristic formula that the Scriptures "do not err," leaving its reconciliation with modern criticism to be worked out gradually, as far as possible by the old theological principles, instead of uniting with those who, in their alarm, throw the whole cargo overboard, and invent brand-new terminology and doctrines? Such revolutions do not come natural [*sic*] to the Church of the ages.[71]

Here was why Wilfrid Ward at this juncture remained suspicious of—but not hostile toward—the speculations of Alfred Loisy, and why he began to grow fretful too that von Hügel—"for whose character I have ever had a profound admiration, . . . a saint and a mystic as well as a scholar and a thinker"—did not take proper account of the severe danger looming on the Left. Not that Ward pretended to any expertise in the field of biblical criticism. But he noted that with the promulgation of *Providentissimus Deus*, "I think my divergence from von Hügel . . . began. . . . He was . . . disposed to identify complete toleration of hypotheses, which would revolutionize the received opinions, with the freedom necessary to the very existence of biblical science." Such a claim "included (as I thought) an exaggerated estimate of the

71. Wilfrid Ward, "The Rigidity of Rome," in *Problems and Persons*, 75–76, 82, 84–85. The essay was originally written in 1894.

scientific character of biblical criticism. It was very plausible to say that all the conclusions of any science must be true; but to call all the conjectures which [a scholar] formed in the course of his studies the conclusions of science was less plausible." Ward believed that von Hügel, whose enthusiasms tended quickly to wax and wane—"his geese were apt to be swans"—failed to appreciate two crucial points: "that revolutionary speculations might destroy faith for many before they were corrected and modified," and that if those who strove "to secure freedom for clearly ascertained or highly probable conclusions" brought forward "even tentatively speculations which seemed to the authorities wild and revolutionary, the whole movement would be discredited as dangerous and fanciful and impracticable."[72]

So indeed it turned out.

As to the other matter preoccupying Catholic intellectuals at the moment, the Wards took a similarly moderate position. "It is tolerably evident," wrote Wilfrid in 1894, "that at the present hour there can be no approach to corporate reunion between Rome and any considerable section of Englishmen. The divergences are too deep and extensive. . . . But does this mean that a state of war is to continue? Surely not. . . . Present reunion and war are not exclusive alternatives. A sense of brotherhood with our fellow-Christians, a determination to work with them where we can, to be absolutely just where discussion of differences is necessary, . . . a programme not indeed of reunion but of *rapprochement*."[73]

When, two years later, a disappointed Pope Leo XIII accepted the recommendation of a commission he had appointed, and declared, in the bull *Apostolicae Curae*, that Anglican orders were "absolutely null and utterly void," there was neither consternation nor surprise at Molescroft House, Eastbourne.[74]

72. Quoted in Ward, *The Wilfrid Wards* 1:300, 308, 310, 318.
73. Wilfrid Ward, "Rigidity," in *Problems and Persons*, 90–92.
74. See Hughes, *Absolutely Null*, 236.

CHAPTER 9

A French Connection

I have read several times Blondel's little brochure, and am much impressed with it, though I do not pretend to enter into all his ideas owing to my unclearness as to much of his meaning. Wherever I understand him I agree with him; especially, e. g., in his criticism of the insufficiency of current forms of apologetic; and also in his wider view of saving faith. It has driven me back to reconsider views of my own which I have always felt were censurable theologically as rash, but which would not always be rash.

—*George Tyrrell (1897)*[1]

IN MARCH, 1895, while he was in Rome lobbying Cardinal Rampolla in behalf of the higher biblical criticism, and with rather less fervor in behalf also of Anglican orders,[2] Friedrich von Hügel met Maurice Blondel for the first time. Later that spring they held several more conversations amid the splendors of Florence, the baron's birthplace and his favorite city.[3] Blondel's name was already familiar to von Hügel: he had read *L'action* when it appeared in 1893 and had recommended it enthusiastically to friends and associates. He spoke of its "astonishingly living pages," and, in the third of his essays on the church and the Bible, quoted approvingly Blondel's description "of the noble folly of living, and, if need be, dying, to save one's soul."[4] Despite the marked temperamental differences between the two—von Hügel was warmly emotional and expansive, while Blondel was reserved and introspective—they had much in common: both were extremely devout laymen of independent means, both tireless workers in their chosen fields of research, both alert to contemporary developments in history and science, and both dedicated to bringing tra-

1. Tyrrell to von Hügel, 6 December, 1897, quoted in Petre, *Autobiography of Tyrrell*, 2:90–91. Blondel's "brochure" was his "Lettre" on apologetics, for which see below.
2. See chapter 8.
3. De la Bedoyere, *Hügel*, 84, and René Virgoulay, *Blondel et modernisme* (Paris: 1980), 105–6. See also the brief notation in Blondel, *Carnets intimes*, 2:32.
4. Von Hügel, "Church and Bible," *Dublin Review* 115:322, 117:303.

ditional Catholic thought into line with the insights provided by modern scholarship. Both were unabashed elitists, who found it hard to function effectively outside a small circle of intimates. They even shared a finicky concern for their physical health that sometimes bordered on hypochondria. There was besides the baron's penchant for identifying wholly with those he admired, so that their ideas became his ideas or rather *our* ideas. Thus had he, whether consciously or not, entered into compacts with Duchesne, Loisy, and Bishop Mignot. And as he waged his little campaign for progressivism along the corridors of the Vatican, he grew convinced that solidarity among right-thinking intellectuals, in their various fields of study, was an absolute necessity to combat successfully the immense power of the common enemy, Scholasticism, "that mountain of ice," as he said to Blondel, "floating in the middle of the southern sea."[5]

But Blondel had more immediate problems to contend with first. At the time of these opening dialogues with von Hügel he was still without employment. His degree from the Sorbonne in hand had not opened to him the doors of the state system of higher education as it should have done. The published version of *L'action* had drawn the fire of the officially entrenched rationalists and positivists. Despite "his sincerity, his boldness of vision, his dialectical subtlety," wrote one prestigious reviewer, Blondel had tried in his book to dethrone genuine philosophy for the sake of a fanciful "immanence" that "sees a transcendent quality in every human act. . . . He will find among the defenders of Reason adversaries who are courteous but resolute." The resolution, if not the courtesy, was made plain when the chief academic inspector for the Department of the Seine recommended that the aspiring young philosopher be refused a university position, a decision sustained by the inspector's immediate superiors. The result was that professionally Blondel wandered through the wilderness for two years, until one of his former professors interceded in his behalf with the minister of education, Raymond Poincaré, to whom the professor was related. Finally, at the end of April 1895, Blondel was appointed to the faculty of the University of Lille, and eighteen months later to that of Aix-en-Provence, where he was destined to serve for more than three decades.[6]

In fact, contrasted with that of the rationalists, the commentary on *L'action* by Catholic savants, who could arguably be lumped together and labeled Scholastics in some sense or other, had been favorable, though cautious. The ever-genial Paul de Broglie, for instance, praised the book's challenge to positivism: "[Blondel displays] a wholly personal methodology which does not lack a certain power and which opens numerous brilliant vistas," but, he added with a swipe at the philosophical establishment, that methodology will remain diffi-

5. See Poulat, *Dogme, critique*, 534–35.
6. See chapter 5, and Virgoulay, *Blondel*, 23–26. Poincaré, a literary man in his own right, later served five times as prime minister and, during World War I, as president of the Republic.

cult to understand for those unacquainted with "the obscure and enigmatic theories prevalent over the past quarter-century at the École Normale." Another Catholic writer, less restrained than most of his fellows, proclaimed *L'action* a "great book," which signaled the end of the reign of positivism and evolutionism and which contributed to a reawakening of a human reason capable of "courageously setting out on its final march" and arriving "at the metaphysical, at God, at the doorstep of Christianity."[7]

But it was a more or less off-hand remark that most caught Blondel's own attention. The author of *L'action*, observed Charles Denis,[8] director of the *Annales de philosophie chrétienne*, has attempted "to bring back Christian apologetics to a psychological terrain." When he read this "interesting article" in October 1895, Blondel wrote immediately to "Monsieur le Directeur" to "protest against certain fashions of interpreting my thought, and even against certain manners of praising it." Far from intending to reduce apologetics to a *terrain psychologique*, he insisted that his was an exclusively philosophical enterprise, one which particularly concerned itself with methodology: "In the order of rational certitudes this is of capital importance." He requested space in the journal to state his position more fully, and Denis agreed.[9]

The upshot was a series of six articles which appeared in the *Annales* each month (except April) from January through July of 1896.[10] They bore the awkward and forbidding title, "A Letter on the Demands of Contemporary Thought in the Area of Apologetics and on the Philosophical Method in the Study of the Religious Problem."[11] Apologetics had been traditionally considered that branch of theology that attempted to establish, usually by way of philosophical or historical arguments, the rational grounds of belief. Strictly speaking, it was not part of theological science at all—at least not for the Scholastics—since its demonstrations did not proceed from principles provided by divine revelation. The apologist, by this reckoning, was a kind of precursor to the theologian; his job was to show dispassionately the fittingness, the historical probability, the accomplishments, and hence the attractiveness of revealed religion. Invoking a distinction far from trivial, apologetics set out not to prove that an act of supernatural faith was reasonable—an assignment impossible by definition—but to contend that a person who made the leap of faith was not acting unreasonably.

7. Quoted in Virgoulay, *Blondel*, 35–36.

8. For a short bio-bibliographical notice of this eccentric priest, see Houtin and Saritaux, *Loisy*, 345–46. For a fuller (and unfriendly) treatment, see Albert Houtin, *Ma vie laique* (Paris: 1928), 127–39. Von Hügel dismissed Denis as "a quick-witted Philistine." In 1905 Blondel himself became proprietor of the *Annales de philosophie chrétienne*. See chapter 17.

9. Felix Alcan (ed.), *Les premiers écrits de Maurice Blondel* (Paris: 1956), 3–4.

10. See Blondel, *Carnets intimes*, 2:58–59.

11. Maurice Blondel, "Lettre sur les exigences de la pensée contemporaine en matière d'Apologétique et sur la méthode de la Philosophie dans l'étude du problème religieux," *Premiers écrits*, 5–95, from which quotations in the text are taken.

Blondel began his "Lettre" with a withering dismissal of the conventional apologetical models. "Science is incompetent and metaphysics, at least in its traditional form, is powerless when it is a question of attracting the spirits of today to Christianity." Some arguments customarily employed by apologists are bogus, others stem from scientific confusion, still others from an inadequate understanding of true philosophy. "It is not sufficient to establish separately the *possibility* and *reality* of the supernatural; it still has to be shown that to adhere to it is *neccessary for us*." Here sounded loud and clear the sustained echo from *L'action*, behind which reverberated that Cartesian axiom restricting knowledge, and hence judgment and choice that follow upon knowledge, to phenomena of the mind's own intuition. [12] Blondel returned to the same point again and again. "Nothing can enter into a man which does not come out of him and not correspond to his need for development." "Philosophy limits its range (*portée*) to internal determinism of thought and action without encroaching upon or supplying for the real order. It comprises therefore a specifically defined and strictly encompassed kind of knowledge and of life." And he applied the principle remorselessly, as, for instance, in the case of "miracles," which apologists in the past had routinely brought forward as a motive of credibility: "For philosophy no contingency is impossible; since the idea of fixed general laws in nature and indeed of nature itself is a mere idol, and since each phenomenon is singular and unique, there is without doubt, if one thinks about it, nothing more in a miracle than in any ordinary activity. But, by the same token, there is nothing less in an ordinary activity than in a miracle." [13]

Blondel cheerfully admitted that "Thomism offers us . . . an inventory as complete, an exposition as well ordered . . . of every natural and supernatural *object* of knowledge and of faith [as possible and is] capable of exercising an irrepressible force of conviction for anyone who can grasp this powerful synthesis." But what good, in the modern world, is this "powerful synthesis?" "Thomism appears to many as an exact description of things, but it is really . . . a static account. . . . Once a man has entered this system he finds assurance. . . . But first he must gain entrance. And since he starts from principles which, for the most part, are disputed in our time, since he does not offer any way of substantiating them by his method, [and] since he presupposes a host of assertions that are precisely those today called into doubt, . . . one must not treat this triumphant exposition as the last word."

There has never been yet, strictly speaking, a Christian philosophy; what bears that name does not deserve it, neither from a philosophical or a Christian point of view. . . . Scholastic philosophy . . . is first and foremost an adaptation of the thought of the ancient world, [which] . . . tended to . . . proclaim absolute judgments about the truth on every . . . subject, so as to put theory above practice. . . . The philosophic

12. See chapter 5.
13. Blondel, "Lettre," *Premiers écrits*, 5–6, 13–14, 34, 70.

spirit that gave birth to Scholasticism is the same spirit that attacked it, indeed destroyed it, and will, as it works itself out, contribute to the progress of a Christian philosophy. It is this progression, with all its irregular ups and downs, that we must seize upon, if we are to understand both the marvelous fruitfulness and the incurable sterility of "Neo-Scholasticism."[14]

And that same progression led Blondel to his solution. The natural and the supernatural move along parallel lines that never meet, never can meet. But, he argued with breathtaking self-assurance, there remains a way to bring them into conjunction: "The happy boldness that it now seems indispensable to arm ourselves with leads us to resort to the method of immanence, and to apply it fully and with unbending rigor to the examination of human destiny. This method alone is capable of defining the problem and resolving it." That primeval drive, that "universal determinism" which lay behind and around and within every human *action*,[15] provides "the immanent affirmation of the transcendent. . . . If the method of immanence is confined to determining the dynamism of our inner states, without first worrying about their objectivity or subjectivity, it then becomes simply a matter of analyzing this inescapable idea of dependence of the intellect and will, with all the consequences that implies. Then there would be no longer a problem of the supernatural." Here, then, was the breakthrough, here was the way in which the parallel lines could converge. Not that even "true philosophy" could discern the data of revealed religion, but it could, by employing the method of immanence, legitimately—nay, apodictically—comprehend the supernatural "not just as a historical reality, not just as a hypothetical possibility, not just as an optional gift." To be sure, the Christian order does involve all these things, and much more. But they all remain impervious to the mind of modern man, which can, however—and must—grasp the supernatural "as something indispensable and at the same time inaccessible to unaided human effort." Here was a "genuinely philosophical apologetics." And here, finally, was a bold challenge:

To those who try to suppress the march of mind, or who are as irritated at it as they are ignorant of it, or who follow it always a little to the rear, as though dragged along by their adversaries, or who try to restore antique reason and antique philosophy upon their original foundations, or who, judging the new ways of philosophizing as enigmatic or needlessly complex, do not try to understand them and then call them unintelligible, because they hope to attain their ends by simpler means: to all these I cannot refrain from saying with all possible force, "No, your task will prove impracticable, your ambition disappointed, your intervention arrested."[16]

FRIEDRICH VON HÜGEL was so impressed by Blondel's "Lettre" that he bought fifty copies of it and distributed them to his friends. But—in a classic

14. Blondel, "Lettre," *Premiers écrits*, 27–28, 54–57.
15. See chapter 5.
16. Blondel, "Lettre," *Premiers écrits*, 38–41, 52.

instance of the pot calling the kettle black—he could not refrain from protesting about the obscurity of its prose. "Alas, I have to admit," Blondel replied, "that what I write is difficult to understand; if you only knew the pains
I take to express my poor thought clearly." Yet a labored and abstruse style,
with all its paradoxes and unfamiliar imagery and wearisome repetitions, was
perhaps not without its uses: "I am continually struck by how necessary it is
to avoid being provocative, to respect official declarations, in order to assure
the renewal of the church from top to bottom, the revivification of the whole
organism. More and more I see the importance and also the difficulty in such
an enterprise."

But the "Lettre" did provoke a chorus of disapproval from the Scholastic
community, and not because its thesis was misunderstood. Typical was a
writer in the *Revue thomiste* who pointed out that Blondel's whole argument—
his "method of immanence"—rested upon an objectionable theory of knowledge. Blondel reacted with some bitterness. "For [these people]," he told von
Hügel, "it is an article of faith that cognition is the adequate substitute or the
transparency (*décalque*) pure and simple even of material things. All that has
happened since Saint Thomas that is not Thomist is Kantian, that is to say,
heretical. . . . This is the dogmatism that is imposed on us as the only authentic form of orthodoxy." Philosophical realism may not have been quite an article of faith, but it lay at the heart of the official notion of what a Christian
epistemology ought to be. Little wonder, then, that in the Vatican of *Aeterni
Patris* Blondel's views should have been received with more than a little suspicion. When von Hügel, spending the winter of 1897 in Rome, heard rumors
that Blondel's work might be censured because of its "subjectivism," the
baron, quite out of character, played a political card: "I told Cardinal Rampolla
that any condemnation would sadden and irritate many people, especially the
youth and precisely those Frenchmen who supported the *ralliement* policy of
the cardinal and the Holy Father."[17]

It may be doubted that this threat proved worrisome to the artful Rampolla,
who knew full well how small an impact the tortuous speculations of a young
and unknown provincial academic had upon the French body politic. Blondel
at any rate remained uncensured, though he had earlier heard some of the same
rumors. "I am told that certain Thomists," he wrote a friend at the end of
September 1896, "want to denounce me to the Index. Pray for me, my dear
Reverend Father, first that I do not desert my legitimate liberty of thought,
and then that the reprisals of the unhappy Scholastics do not go too far. What
do you advise me to do: speak out, keep silent, or call for a meeting?"[18]

The question was probably asked in jest. The reply in any event does not

---

17. Correspondence between Blondel and von Hügel quoted in Poulat, *Histoire, dogme*, 534–36.
18. Blondel to Laberthonnière, 1 October, 1896, in Claude Tresmontant (ed.), *Maurice Blondel,
Lucien Laberthonnière: Correspondance philosophique* (Paris: 1961), 102.

survive, but if it did it would no doubt give off a pugnacious sound, because the friend to whom the request for prayer was addressed was Lucien Laberthonnière, who never shirked a fight. Since the spring of 1894, when the flush of excitement over *L'action* had led Laberthonnière to initiate contact,[19] the relationship between him and Blondel had ripened to the point that the salutations of their letters—they met rarely, only when Blondel traveled to Paris—gradually changed from "Monsieur" and "Reverend Père" to "Mon bien cher ami." And the Oratorian, though a year older than Blondel, had already defined in terms of warfare the junior status that was his in this budding partnership: "I can only assume the attitude of a soldier who fights under the orders of his chief."[20]

Military metaphors fell readily from Laberthonnière's lips at the time, because these middle years of the decade brought much struggle into his life. This stocky bantam of a man, with his taut facial features and flashing eyes, with his compulsive neatness and passionate impatience with what he considered humbug, was always to a degree at war with himself. But now he had also to contend with the difficulties of combining his duties as a teacher and administrator at the *collège* at Juilly—he had been appointed prefect of studies there in October 1895—with the demands of a graduate student pursuing an exacting academic course at the Sorbonne. He dreamed of putting together a vast doctoral thesis, a philosophical "Critique du christianisme," but this project proved beyond him. Indeed, distracted and ill, he failed to secure his *agrégation*, the formal admission to a doctoral field.[21]

Most trying of all, however, was the internal situation that had developed at Juilly. Never altogether comfortable with his religious superiors, Laberthonnière finally came into open conflict with the director of the *collège*, whom he accused of financial mismanagement and tyrannical behavior. When his repeated protests fell on deaf ears, he appealed his case to the superior-general of the French Oratorians, who, dedicated to peace at any price, removed Laberthonnière and reassigned him to the École Massillon in Paris. The weak wrongheadedness of this decision become clear a couple of years later when the director at Juilly had to be dismissed and Laberthonnière, of all people, sent to replace him.[22]

Meanwhile, in the midst of all these commotions Blondel's self-styled "soldier" was in no mood to welcome complacently attacks upon his general. His hopes for an advanced university degree might go aglimmering, and his position within his religious community might remain unsettled. But his aggressive disposition could abide neither the verdict nor the tone of the commentary

19. See chapter 5.

20. Laberthonnière to Blondel, 30 July, 1896, in Marie-Thérèse Perrin (ed.), *Laberthonnière et ses amis* (Paris: 1975), 20.

21. Beillevert (ed.), *Laberthonnière*, 17.

22. Perrin, *La jeunesse de Laberthonnière*, 100–107.

on Blondel's "Lettre" on apologetics that appeared in the *Revue thomiste*: "This lad," wrote a prominent Dominican disdainfully, "has put together propositions that are heretical, erroneous, or recklessly rash."[23] Laberthonnière countered with an article of his own, his first notable publication, which appeared in two successive issues of a competing learned journal and which he called "Le Problème religieux."[24]

If Laberthonnière in this piece placed his belligerent nature on display, he also expressed his warm and deeply felt spirituality. The latter succeeded better than the former. Indeed, his description of the traditional apologetics was at best a caricature, a straw man easy to throw down, and yet his very mode of controversy, superficial as it may have been, taught a lesson worth remembering through the controversies that lay ahead. Laberthonnière and those trained as he had been did not draw—in 1896 could not have drawn—a distinction between good and bad Scholasticism, between the shallow manuals then commonly used in Catholic seminaries and religious houses and the kind of nuanced Thomism recommended by Leo XIII in *Aeterni Patris*. So the low level of the Oratorian's attack should come as no surprise. "To admit," he wrote, "that a rational apologetics has by itself the power to produce not just the science of the object of faith, but faith itself in souls, would be to admit that dialectics is a means sufficient for salvation. And once that is admitted, one would have to admit further that it is the sole and indispensable means of salvation; for if it brings faith into reality, it would mean that faith could not be made real in any other way." What the Scholastics do, Laberthonnière maintained, however strongly they deny it, is to render the adhesion to revelation the necessary and logical consequence of their accumulated syllogisms. This *scholastique rationaliste* seems hardly to be preferred to rationalist positivism.

To reduce genuinely human response to revelation to an intellectual exercise, and thus to ignore the total complexus of thought and will and aspiration signified by the word *action*, is to impoverish it beyond recognition. "To tell the truth, every speculative solution is in reality a practical solution expressed abstractly." Without employing the method of immanence, Blondel's two parallel lines of nature and supernature must remain ever sadly distinct. Faith comes from the gratuitous gift of God's grace, to be sure, but there must be at work within each of us—for an act of faith is intensely personal and individual—a receptive faculty, a medium of collaboration, if that divine work is to be efficacious. Faith fills a void in us, answers an acute need, which reaches through the mere intellect to the deepest recesses of our being. "Faith," argued Laber-

23. M. B. Schwalm, "Les illusions de l'idéalisme et leur dangers pour la foi," *Revue thomiste* 4 (September 1896):413–41. For a good summary of this particular controversy, see Roger Aubert, *Le problème de l'acte de foi* (Paris: 1969), 296–302.

24. Laberthonnière, "Le problème religieux à propos de la question apologétique," *Annales de philosophie chrétienne* 133 (1896–97): 497–511, 615–32. Reprinted in *Le réalisme chrétien, précédé de essais de philosophie religieuse* (Paris: 1966), 135–67.

thonnière, "appears as the encounter of two loves, not just as a linkage of two ideas. It is not an abstract conclusion, it is a living action." Saint Paul said that "faith comes from hearing," but surely that adage means more than a simply external proclamation. "How will anyone understand God when he addresses the ears or the eyes, unless from the first he has spoken also to the heart?"[25]

Traditionalist Catholic philosophers and apologists predictably—and understandably—growled about the subjectivism manifested by "Le Problème religieux," along with its Kantian overtones and, they believed, its dangerously fideist tendencies. But Blondel, just as predictably, was delighted with the articles. "My very dear friend," he wrote after the second of them had appeared, in February 1897, "I find in your essays so much light, such force and innovation. Nothing of this has been said before, even approximately, so far as I know. And you have said it with such precision, you have such control over yourself and your thought, a mastery which cannot fail to impress upon the reader that what you say is *essential* to the religious problem. After my tumultuous 'Lettre,' confused and passionate, where I march back and forth at random, you have brought down from on high a clarity in the face of which few eyes can remain closed. How I thank God for the good these pages will do."[26]

Laberthonnière meanwhile had settled into his new assignment at the École Massillon, the Oratorian *lycée* on the quai des Célestins. He served for a year as professor and department chairman, and then was named director of the institution. In addition to these professional burdens he also took up again a course of graduate studies at the Sorbonne. None of these activities precluded him from continuing to ponder and write about the matters that had occupied him in composing "Le Problème religieux."

Nor did they prevent Laberthonnière—this furiously energetic man—from forming a new set of relationships which proved to be casual and yet not insignificant. About this time he began to frequent meetings held, first at the Collège Stanislas and later in the crypt of the basilica of Sacré Coeur on Montmartre, of a group that called itself Le Sillon ("the Furrow"). This organization was made up of young Catholic activists, mostly middle class and, in the beginning at least, mostly alumni of the fashionable Stanislas. Many of the charter members of Le Sillon had been pupils of Blondel, who had taught at the Collège Stanislas for a year or two before he received his degree. They remembered their former teacher with warmth and gratitude—from faraway Aix-en-Provence he continued to encourage them—and any friend of his, Laberthonnière discovered, was a friend of theirs. Inspired by the policies of Leo XIII, particularly by the social encyclical *Rerum Novarum* and by the *ralliement*, they aimed at a grassroots renewal of Catholicism in France. They were blessed with a remarkably charismatic leader, Marc Sangnier, himself a product of the Stan-

25. Laberthonnière, "Le problème religieux," in *Réalisme*, 136, 144, 147, 153, 158.
26. Blondel to Laberthonnière, 18 February, 1897, in Tresmontant (ed.), *Correspondance*, 107–8.

islas, and were unencumbered by much theory, save the commitment to a Christian democracy that meant merely, in Sangnier's words, "the social organization that tends to develop to the highest degree the conscience and responsibility of the individual."[27]

Le Sillon published a journal, supported reading rooms and study clubs, organized groups of young workers and students, even engaged in some political activity—all in the name of a fervent and uncomplicated Catholicism that was held in as much suspicion by a portion of the ecclesiastical establishment as by the jaded barons of the Third Republic. Eventually it set up chapters in every corner of France, and its 20,000 or so members exerted an influence far beyond their numbers.[28] But the movement, for all its efforts to bring a moral and spiritual leaven to fin-de-siècle French life, remained largely indifferent to the kind of intellectual questions that fascinated Laberthonnière. In later years, when he had got to know the Oratorian rather well, Étienne Gilson shrewdly observed that though "there was no real rapport between Father Laberthonnière's philosophy and the social and political ideas of Le Sillon, yet they did share the same [Catholic] enemies, and these in turn shared two characteristics: they all called themselves 'Thomists,' and they were all, if memory serves, politically allied to Charles Maurras."[29] Maurras's Action française did indeed compete with Le Sillon and at one point appeared to vanquish it, though it might be said with some confidence that Sangnier and his colleagues, as precursors to the various cadres of Catholic Action of the 1930s and to the Christian Democratic party—the Mouvement républicain populaire—of the 1950s, triumphed in the end.[30]

However that may be, Laberthonnière's sympathetic contacts with the young idealists of Le Sillon, and Blondel's too, help authenticate an aspect of their work too easily overlooked. Running through their recondite treatises about theories of knowledge and grace was a strong ethical current. They wanted, in Blondel's words, "to revivify the whole organism" of the church, to bring to bear upon Catholicism philosophical principles that would not only reconcile it with modern thought but would also enhance the moral conduct of all believers. They intended to accomplish on the intellectual level something analogous to what Le Sillon proposed to do through its various good works on the practical, day-to-day level: to liberate Catholicism from the dead hand of an arid and valueless bourgeois culture. Similarly, to grasp the meaning of *action* and to appreciate the unique benefit provided by the method of immanence could free believers from a sterile intellectualism that lacked the capacity

27. Quoted in Dansette, *Histoire religieuse*, 652. For more details, see Michael Sutton, *Nationalism, Positivism and Catholicism* (Cambridge: 1982), esp. 151–52, 168–71.

28. See Jeanne Caron, *Le Sillon et la démocratie chrétienne, 1894–1910* (Paris: 1967), and Jean de Fabrègues, *Le Sillon de Marc Sangnier* (Paris: 1964), esp. 35–61.

29. Quoted in Madeleine Barthélemy-Madaule, *Marc Sangnier, 1873–1950* (Paris: 1973), 50.

30. See Dansette, *Histoire religieuse*, 744–46 and chapter 19.

to inspire them to seek the highest ethical norms or, perhaps, even a mystical vocation. "Philosophy," proclaimed Blondel, "has the function of removing the basis of morality away from human judgment and from the always insufficient clarity of human thought."[31] "In every soul that progresses," agreed Laberthonnière, who, in a less formal mode, described what he called "moral dogmatism," "something of God reveals itself every day. And a soul that progresses is a soul that opens itself, clarifies itself, and becomes goodness (*bonté*). . . . It is in the living God that the soul learns to understand itself and that it affirms its belief in him. . . . One believes in understanding, and one understands in believing. And the result is a complete transformation of the soul."[32]

BLONDEL SENT A COPY of his "Lettre" on apologetics to Alfred Loisy, whom he had never met. The exiled exegete[33] received it with unwonted warmth, not because he was in the least attracted to involved philosophical argument but because the "Lettre" sounded a corollary that was music to his ears. "Theologians," Blondel had written, "do not allow philosophers to encroach upon their area of expertise, [and] they are right to act this way. . . . But it follows that philosophers, if they would be true to themselves, must not and cannot allow theologians to enter their field. Each science thus remains inviolable."[34] What was true of philosophy's autonomous rights ought to be true also of biblical criticism. "You and I are innovators," Loisy wrote in response. "Your philosophy can act in concert with my exegesis. They can even be said to share the common traits of having been accused of heterodoxy and of having escaped (let us hope) the censures that some people would like to attach to them. . . . What you say about the autonomy of philosophy seems incontestable to me. I believe that critical history enjoys the same independence. But . . . we preach in the wilderness, I am very much afraid, between the fanatics of science and the rationalists of the faith."[35]

Neuilly-sur-Seine, the "wilderness" in which Loisy was now confined, was a serene and prosperous suburb just to the north of Paris. It lay on the edge of the Bois de Boulogne, once a royal hunting preserve long since converted into a vast park, where children on summer excursions from the city played along the winding paths and marveled at the exotic animals penned up in the little menagerie. The gardens, nurturing countless species of plants and trees, were carefully planned and carefully tended, but not formal in any elaborate sense. Here, among the tall pines that loomed out of the mist of morning like ghostly sentries, "le petit Loisy" took his daily constitutional.

31. Blondel, "Lettre," in *Premiers écrits*, 82.

32. Lucien Laberthonnière, "Le dogmatisme moral," *Annales de philosophie chrétienne* 38–39 (August–November 1898), 531–62, 27–45, 146–71; reprinted in *Réalisme*, 84.

33. See chapter 7.

34. Blondel, "Lettre," in *Premiers écrits*, 49.

35. Loisy to Blondel, 25 February, 1897, in René Marlé (ed.), *Au coeur de la crise moderniste* (Paris: 1960), 34–35.

He resided in modest, book-crammed rooms at the Dominican convent school nearby. The demands placed upon him as chaplain were not heavy, but he carried them out with the utmost punctiliousness. He said daily mass for the sisters, and gave regular catechism lessons to the pupils. These girls sometimes found his forms of expression elusive, as when he described creation as "the relationship between the universe and its principle," yet they considered him a sympathetic counselor both in and out of the confessional. The more perceptive among them, and the nuns as well, noticed that he often appeared haggard and withdrawn, which perhaps led them to appreciate him the more. When Marie-Joseph Lagrange called on him at Neuilly in 1895—only the second and, as it turned out, the last time the two met—the mother-prioress confided to her fellow Dominican how highly she prized her chaplain; she worried that the convent might lose his services, since he often expressed a desire to be located closer to Paris and its libraries. "Of course," observed Lagrange, "religious superiors are always satisfied with chaplains who do not interfere in the affairs of the convent, and M. Loisy had other things on his mind."[36]

What Loisy had on his mind were the same concerns with biblical criticism as before. He did not publish anything during his first two years at Neuilly, but he kept up with recent specialized literature that interested him, thanks to the largesse of various editors of learned journals, who sent him copies of new and relevant publications. The reclusive life suited him. With one or two exceptions he avoided the local clergy, though occasionally he was visited by young priests, former students, who found him amiable, if guarded. His one month's holiday a year he spent, as he had always done, at the family farm in Ambrières, where he reacquainted himself with the beloved countryside of Champagne. When on these occasions Alfred said the Sunday mass and preached in the village church, his father sat in the Loisy pew, for Charles-Sebastien, during his last years, had returned to the practice of his religion, and had even, at the persuasion of his wife, gone to confession. In the late spring of 1895 his son presided at the old man's funeral.[37]

At the beginning of the next year there appeared, for the first time since 1893, a publication signed by Alfred Loisy. It was a relatively inconsequential piece in a new and obscure journal,[38] but it was a harbinger of things to come, a sign that the exegete had decided to end his self-imposed scholarly silence. Over the following three years Loisy put in press, not counting book reviews, twenty-five articles on a great variety of biblical subjects, totalling about 600 pages of print. Establishing a precedent that would become commonplace during the Modernist controversies, no less than seven of these essays were written

---

36. Lagrange, *Loisy et modernisme*, 91.

37. Houtin and Saritaux, *Loisy*, 82–87.

38. Alfred Loisy, "La confession de Pierre et la promesse de Jésus," *Revue anglo-romaine* 2 (December 1895): 49–58. This journal, as its name suggests, was dedicated to the cause of Anglican-Catholic reunion (see chapter 7). It survived for only a year.

under a pseudonym.[39] They adhered to their author's previous mode of composition, in that they combined with technical competence and adventuresome critical speculation an explicitly stated reverence for the conventions. Thus, for example, "There is no truly critical commentary outside the tradition, nor any truly traditional outside the critical. Criticism is in fact deformed if it tries to proceed without the tradition which protects and interprets it."[40]

Several journals solicited Loisy's contributions,[41] but he hankered after a permanent and more reliable organ for his views. Accordingly, in 1896, he founded a new periodical of his own, the *Revue d'histoire et de littérature religieuses*. Mindful, however, of Cardinal Richard's animosity and of that prelate's insistence that his earlier journal, *L'enseignement biblique*, be suppressed,[42] Loisy took great care to disguise his involvement in this project behind a board of editors, of whom he was only one in seven.[43] But there was no doubt of Loisy's dominant position, nor of his use of the journal as a personal platform: of the twenty-five articles mentioned above, Loisy wrote sixteen of them for this *Revue*, most of them under noms de plume. His intentions he shared with Maurice Blondel:

> Have you heard about our new *Revue*, directed by a consortium of clerics and laypeople, which is devoted to subjects in which a discussion of the philosophy of religion would be most appropriate. We cannot be very generous to contributors, for we are as poor as Job. We write exclusively out of our devotion to the truth, and so we can only offer thanks to those who help us. Let me send you a copy of the *Revue*, and in case there is some philisophico-historical subject you might find worthy of your attention, we would accept it with pleasure.[44]

BLONDEL DID NOT IN FACT write anything for Loisy's journal, but it survived even so, through many threats and alarums, for more than twenty-five years. If the subscription list was never large, printing and distribution costs in those halcyon days were minimal, and the original capital outlay sufficed to launch the *Revue* and see it over the first precarious year or two. Each member of the editorial board contributed Fr 100, and Friedrich von Hügel Fr 500.[45]

Loisy's return to the scholarly lists provided for the baron a bright moment

39. E. g., Étienne Sharp, Pierre Molandre, François Jacobé. For a list, see Houtin and Saritaux, *Loisy*, 312–14. For a discussion of the pseudonymous literature that abounded during the crisis of Catholic Modernism, see Poulat, *Dogme, histoire*, 621–78.

40. Quoted in Houtin and Saritaux, *Loisy*, 85.

41. E. g., *Revue des religions*, *Journal asiatique*, and even Lagrange's and Batiffol's *Revue biblique* (July 1896).

42. See chapter 7 and Loisy, *Choses passées*, 171–73.

43. The other six were Paul LeJay of the Institut Catholique de Paris; Henri Margival of the same institution; the art historian Pierre de Nolhac; the paleographer Georges Digard; Édouard Jordan of the École Normale Supériure; and the young orientalist, Loisy's former student at the Institut Catholique, François Thureau-Dangin. See Loisy, *Mémoires*, 1:392–94.

44. See note 35.

45. Loisy, *Mémoires*, 1:393.

in what was otherwise a season of gloom. He sensed that the Vatican in the winter of 1897 was not so friendly a place as it had been the year before. Cardinal Rampolla appeared affable as ever, but von Hügel gradually came to the conclusion that the secretary of state was merely indulging his diplomatic habits and had no real interest in promoting the intellectual concerns close to the baron's heart. Other Roman acquaintances, like the young nobleman and seminarist Eugenio Pacelli,[46] also seemed more distant: "[I] thought I noticed a change in his mind." The sudden death of Maurice d'Hulst the preceding November heightened his despondency, as did the sad letters Bishop Mignot wrote him from Fréjus about the deterioration of biblical studies since the issuance of *Providentissimus Deus*. "I see myself," the baron confided to Loisy, "that the situation has grown worse, narrowed, darkened."

Louis Duchesne—now Monseigneur Duchesne and permanent resident in Rome as head of the École Française—offered sardonic jests, but only in prudent privacy. Meanwhile, a commission of cardinals quite publicly promulgated the authenticity of the so-called Johannine Comma, despite the virtually unanimous view of Scripture scholars to the contrary.[47] On his way through Paris in the spring the baron complained bitterly to Loisy about this arrogant attempt to shore up a dogmatic teaching—that of the Trinity—by twisting the clear historical evidence. Loisy of course listened with sympathy, as did Lucien Laberthonnière, whom von Hügel met on this occasion for the first time. Another new acquaintance, however, Abbé Marcel Hébert—a friend of Loisy—appeared to accept the outrage with equanimity. The baron could not have known at this date that Hébert—a kindly, modest, obliging man who had already exchanged belief in a personal God for a vague philosophical symbolism—had small interest in the stratagems of the ecclesiatical bureaucracy.[48]

Back in England during the summer, von Hügel was further disheartened by the relish with which most of his coreligionists had welcomed the pope's refusal to recognize the validity of Anglican orders.[49] But most of all he was troubled by the psychological affliction being endured by his favorite daughter. Gertrud, now twenty, had been for several years her father's closest confidante. He had even introduced her into the charmed penitential circle presided over by Abbé Huvelin.[50] With her he shared not only his scholarly aspirations but also his concerns and worries over the state of the church. His impatience with obtuse prelates and narrow-minded Scholastics became hers, in a manner

---

46. Pope Pius XII (1939–58).

47. An interpolation in the text of 1 John, 5:7–8, the words in italics: "For there are three that bear record *in heaven, the Father, the Word, and the Holy Ghost, and these Three are One. And there are three that bear witness in earth,* the Spirit, and the Water, and the Blood, and these three agree in one." The interpolation appears only in very late manuscripts and is not included in Jerome's original text of the Vulgate. See F. L. Cross, (ed.), *Oxford Dictionary of the Christian Church* (London: 1963), 729.

48. See Rivière, *Modernisme*, 140–53.

49. De la Bedoyere, *Hügel*, 94–96.

50. Portier, *Huvelin*, 76.

and to a degree that disquieted the other women in his family, Lady Mary and her strong-willed mother, Lady Herbert of Lea. The baron's personal piety was such that revelation of alleged warts on the body ecclesiastic did not disturb his inner serenity. Not so Gertrud. Her physical health was as frail as that of her parents, and by the summer of 1897 her nerves were unraveling as well. She had entered into a genuine crisis of faith. On September 20, her father, in his alarm, picked up his pen and addressed a letter to Father George Tyrrell, of the Society of Jesus.

The baron had been acquainted with some of the young Jesuit's articles, published over the immediately preceding years in his order's journal, the *Month*, and in other periodicals. But what had impressed him most had been Tyrrell's first book, which had appeared earlier in 1897 and which von Hügel, in his customary fashion, had not only bought and read but had strongly recommended to his friends among the intelligentsia. *Nova et Vetera*—"new things and old"—the book was called, and a perusal of this collection of "informal meditations" brought prompt solace to the anxious father—books always had a soothing effect on the baron—if not to the tormented daughter. "Doubtless [the book] contains little or nothing that has not been said before, and said better," its author observed with conventional modesty. "Yet in many cases the truths are said in the writer's own way; and so far he can claim to bring forth from his treasury old things and new: old, because truth is eternal; new, because its expression is infinitely variable." The "treasury" contained 330 little essays, most scarcely a page long, unconnected, each headed by a Latin motto of spiritual uplift which Tyrrell translated and commented upon, each a small jewel of style and pious sentiment. Perhaps Von Hügel's eye first fell upon number 223, "Steadfast Peace."

Funda nos in pace. " 'Stablish us in peace." Peace of soul may be founded on the sands or on the rock; nor can one tell which while calm endures. It was when the windy tempest of affliction blew and the rain descended and the floods came and the storm beat against her on Calvary that Mary stood . . . like Mount Sion, the City of Peace. . . . What trifles upset us and cast us into the blues; what trifles elate and excite us! . . . What is it 'stablishes the rocks and mountains, but their weight? Levity . . . is the symbol of unsteadiness. And what is weight, but a strong draw to the centre? *Funda nos in pace*, i. e., enlarge our heart, that it may be drawn more forcibly, more irresistibly to God, our Centre.[51]

There may have been nothing here to have stirred the baron's scholarly juices, but it savored of the calm spiritual direction that might prove helpful to Gertrud. "She and I work entirely together," he explained rather pointlessly.[52]

During the brief interval since his ordination to the priesthood in the late

51. George Tyrrell, *Nova et Vetera* (London: 1897), 270.
52. Von Hügel to Tyrrell, 29 September, 1897, quoted in De la Bedoyere, *Hügel*, 100.

summer of 1891,[53] and the completion of his prescribed spiritual and theological preparation, George Tyrrell had served in a variety of capacities. In 1893 he had been assigned for a few months to the Jesuit mission in Oxford, Saint Aloysius, where he was as restless and unhappy as Gerard Manley Hopkins had been fifteen years earlier.[54] From there Tyrrell was sent to a working-class parish in Saint Helen's, near Liverpool, to spend a year in the parochial ministry, an experience he never repeated nor desired to repeat. A tendency developed later for some of his Catholic friends to romanticize this fleeting episode: "He never should have left Saint Helen's," they would say when hearing of his latest quarrel with the ecclesiastical authorities. Tyrrell himself never fell into this fanciful conceit, this bogus gesture to democracy; he never thought that the humdrum service of a blue-collar congregation in a dirty industrial town was intrinsically worthier and purer for a priest—and especially for a Jesuit—than other, more cerebral apostolates. Indeed, a few years later, when his troubles had begun and the bluff Cardinal Vaughan had suggested he go back to the parish "and save souls," Tyrrell had rejected the advice as an invitation to "a sort of moral suicide."[55] He went in 1894 from Saint Helen's to a more remote corner of Lancashire, the seminary at Stonyhurst, as professor of philosophy, not a suicidal assignment, perhaps, but one guaranteed to renew the struggle of his student days, in that same dreary place, between Tyrrell's notion of unadulterated Thomism and the more standard, for Jesuits at any rate, Suarezian variety. He survived for two years, and his dismissal, which he felt keenly, marked a long early step toward his ultimate alienation from the Society of Jesus. "I was turning the young men into Dominicans," he explained sarcastically after transfer to the Jesuit church in Mayfair, where he went into residence in 1896. In this assignment he had come, so to speak, full circle, back to London and back to the house where Albany Christie had greeted him in 1879.[56]

That house was a handsome four-story brick structure, 114 Mount Street, alongside of which was a little park that circled around behind the church which itself fronted on Farm Street, halfway between Berkeley Square and Park Lane. The neogothic church building boasted a facade which was a reproduction of the west front of Beauvais cathedral and a magnificent high altar, designed by Pugin. Here, at the heart of the de facto capital of the world, the Jesuits of the English province maintained an informal intellectual headquarters, a scriptorium as it were, of gifted individuals encouraged to write and to speculate, occasionally called to the pulpit or the confessional in the church next door, but never obliged to the regimen of an ordinary presbytery or of a classroom. George Tyrrell thus joined some of the cleverest among his confreres in an enterprise that, for the first time really, gave him the leisure to

53. See chapter 6.
54. See Eleanor Ruggles, *Gerard Manley Hopkins: A Life* (New York: 1944), 184–85.
55. Petre, *Autobiography of Tyrrell*, 2:34–39.
56. See chapter 6.

put his considerable literary talents to use. Nor did he waste the opportunity, as the productivity of the years after 1896 amply demonstrated.

Tyrrell, however—even leaving aside serious ideological differences—did not always prove an easy colleague or companion. He was a jumble of paradoxes and contradictions. At once self-doubting and self-righteous, continuously examining his own motives and those of others, introspective and intense, sad in the peculiarly self-absorbed way a Celt is sad, he was wistful around animals and often intolerant of human beings. Yet he could be, even so, warm and funny and outgoing, not just affectionate and indulgent, but capable of identifying himself with others and winning their abiding loyalty to a remarkable degree. But even this apparently endearing quality upset his tender conscience, made him feel guilty of what he called himself his "duplicity," his "chameleon-like" temperament, because such accommodation seemed to fly in the face of his uncompromising and oft-proclaimed dedication to abstract truth. "Of course," he once defended himself lamely, "[So-and-so] speaks of 'Tyrrell and I'; and so do twenty people who have little in common with one another. . . . It only means that when I agree with people I say so; and when I don't, I hold my tongue unless something is to be gained by a wrangle."

And wrangles there were, aplenty, but quick Irish quarrels, Tyrrell's friends used to say, brought to a boil by a hot Irish temper that doused itself almost before it was ignited. They loved him, not just because he was charming, and most of the time thoughtful, but because they discerned in him a ruthless honesty about himself and his relation to the religion that at once attracted and repelled him. Such tension was by no means remote from the experience of many of Tyrrell's intimates, and so when he cried out they thought they heard Everyman speaking through him: "My real unhappiness is the [opposition] between my life and my ideals; which is accentuated as the latter grow more clear and imperative. I am morally tired of the conflict, and seem to have lost all faith in myself. If I could live up to the best that I know, I should be absolutely happy."

Unprepossessing in appearance—small and so strikingly thin that his clothes shrouded rather than covered him; his close-cropped hair, and wide, heavily lipped mouth, and eyes sunk deep into darkened sockets, lent him a gauntly simian look—George Tyrrell suffered more or less constantly from a sharp sting in the flesh. Severe migraine headaches and their accompanying nausea left him often prostrate days on end, only "half-alive," as he put it, unable to abide any human contact. Sick to his stomach so much, he ate carelessly and seldom, reducing himself to a virtual state of malnutrition and thus further aggravating his illness. The doctors solemnly warned him that mental fatigue from overwork brought about the pain and the bilious attacks, and yet it was only work that afforded him any lasting relief.[57]

57. Petre, *Autobiography of Tyrrell*, 2:3–24.

On October 10, 1897, Father Tyrrell called upon the von Hügels at Hampstead. He spoke at length to Gertrud, who quickly fell under his shrewd and kindly spell. Within a month she seemed to have weathered the worst of her inner storm, and Tyrrell was able to confirm, gently but candidly, what the family physician had already recommended, that Gertrud would soon mend if she and her father were separated for some little time. Von Hügel, overwhelmed by remorse, readily agreed. "I see so increasingly," he told Tyrrell, "the . . . fault . . . of my influence, the dwelling so constantly and freely on the detailed humanities in the Church; the drawing out and giving full edge to religious difficulties; the making too much of little intellectual and temperamental differences between myself and most Catholics," including poor Gertrud's mother, sisters, and doting grandmothers. "I have dropped my own child, my first-born, whom God gave me to carry and to guard." When the baron departed in the late autumn to spend his customary winter in Rome, Gertrud stayed behind in England, where she continued to receive the ministrations of her new director.[58]

Tyrrell's *Nova et Vetera* was followed the next year by another "selection of meditations and studies," to which he gave the title *Hard Sayings*. These essays, however, were longer than the earlier ones, more sustained, more argumentative, though they too displayed their author's wonderful lyricism and his profoundly personal religiosity, qualities that never deserted him, despite all the troubles to come, and never failed to captivate Gertrud von Hügel and all the other distressed souls to whom he gave solace. "Let us once look upon the love-worn face of the Man of Sorrows," he wrote in a piece called "The Gospel of Pain," "and read in its lines, its tear-stains and blood-stains, the record of the ravages of Divine love, pent up and compressed within the narrow walls of a finite heart." What gave special immediacy to Tyrrell's words was their strong sense that he himself had piercingly experienced what pain was, what despondency was. "Because we would be angels and not men, because we expect more of ourselves than God expects of us, because our pride revolts against the necessary limitations of humanity, we fall into sullen discouragement, and since we cannot be all, and do all, and have all, we will be nothing, and do nothing, and have nothing, but will sit with knees relaxed and idly hanging hands."[59] There was a sense in which everything Tyrrell published in the course of his life had a devotional object, and indeed reflected his own devotion. But *Hard Sayings*, with its frankly didactic tone, also represented not so much a new departure, as a new element laid on top of what had been present before.

ANOTHER NEW ELEMENT—more directly speculative—was also emerging in Tyrrell's mind and work. Before von Hügel left for Italy that

58. De la Bedoyere, *Hügel*, 100–102.
59. George Tyrrell, *Hard Sayings* (London: 1898), 151, 381.

autumn of 1897 he offered the Jesuit his seal of social as well as spiritual approval by inviting him for long rambles across Hampstead Heath. The baron was much impressed. Tyrrell is "such a capital man, just the sort we want," he told Wilfrid Ward, who, for his part, recalled with satisfaction the laudatory reviews of his books Tyrrell had written some years earlier.[60] There can be no doubt that for Tyrrell this new friendship was the most important turning point in his life, a moment when a host of new vistas opened to him. Up till the beginning of his intimacy with von Hügel, he had expended much of his energy arguing with his fellow Jesuits, which was, in a way, carrying on a constant argument with himself. In 1891, for example, he had written a piece he called "Aquinas Resuscitatus," in which he rehearsed all the historical reasons to justify Leo XIII's *Aeterni Patris*,[61] and then had asserted, approvingly, that the Neo-Scholastics "aim at nothing less that making the 'Summa' of Saint Thomas the text book of Christendom, . . . a universal standard" with "differences . . . more or less eliminated, and all schools of opinion merged, as far as possible, into one great Catholic school."[62]

Here, of course, was an expression of Tyrrell's ongoing disagreement with his fellow Jesuits, who wanted to adapt the teaching of Aquinas in a manner that would accord with their own classical commentators. But Tyrrell, almost by second nature, had to quarrel, and, once he had met von Hügel, once he had listened to those seductive deaf-man shouts that were part and parcel of all conversations carried on during walks across the heath, he wondered about the earlier positions he had so stoutly defended; his perspective began to change, his inner confidence to wane, the gallery of his opponents to alter. "Philosophy . . . is very dispensable for most individual [Catholics]," he wrote during the months immediately after he had first encountered von Hügel, "but not so for society as a whole. There must be those who frame laws, who search out truths, who correct errors and abuses, else the corruptive tendency of tradition would be unchecked." Thomism, he argued now, provides the legitimate "word-language" to achieve this end. "To suppose, however, that in using Aristotle for this purpose the Church thereby commits herself to his philosophy as the only possible, or the best possible, would be almost as foolish as to suppose that she regarded ecclesiastical Latin as the best possible language." And here, surely, was a lesson learned at Hampstead: the Chinese might express the reality of the Virgin's Immaculate Conception without employing a language consistent with that of the schools. "Similarly, if the facts which [the church] expresses as 'transubstantiation' or 'hypostatic union' or 'trinity' can

60. See Tyrrell to Ward, 12 December, 1893, in Mary Jo Weaver (ed.), *Letters from a "Modernist"* (London: 1981), 3–4. These are the expertly annotated letters of Tyrrell to Ward, 1893–1908. Tyrrell, following his unfortunate custom, destroyed the letters he received from Ward.

61. See chapter 2.

62. [George Tyrrell], "Aquinas Resuscitatus," *American Catholic Quarterly Review* 16 (October 1891): 673–90.

be faithfully conveyed in the philosophy of [George] Berkeley, well and good. But [the church] does not guarantee the translation." Scholasticism, Tyrrell granted at this relatively late and crucial date, may lend to Catholic thought "clearness, order [and] stability," the "gain" from which is "immense." But— and this assertion signaled a significant shift in his thinking—"When [the church] condemns certain formulae and verbal expressions, she takes them only according to the sense they bear in the philosophy which she has adopted, and takes no account of the sense other philosophies may attach to them."[63]

This rather baffling statement may have issued from an initiative taken by von Hügel, for the baron had been quick to introduce Tyrrell to his latest enthusiasm, Blondel's philosophy of *action*. "I have read several times Blondel's little brochure," Tyrrell wrote in December 1897, referring to the "Lettre" on apologetics, "and am much impressed with it, though I do not pretend to enter into all his ideas owing to my unclearness as to much of his meaning." The fascination combined with puzzlement continued through the next year, and "without much profit, for [Blondel's] style is most obscure, especially for me, whose language is scholastic, though my thought is mystic." But the work of Blondel's most ardent disciple was another matter. "[Laberthonnière's] 'Le Dogmatisme moral,' " Tyrrell told the baron on the last day of 1898, "was a great joy to me, as giving a clearer insight into the 'Philosophy of Action,' or rather the Philosophy of the heart and of concrete human nature. I felt at home there in nearly everything, and doubt not but I shall be able to fit it all into my own mind without any violent revolution."[64]

The French connection, thus established, was solidified from another, unexpected quarter. In the early summer of 1898 Tyrrell received a letter, postmarked Aix-en-Provence, congratulating him for an essay recently published in the *Month*, titled "Liberal Catholicism." Given the currency of that particular phrase over many decades—and the controversies that had surrounded it— it was at first blush curious that this short article made no reference to the debates that had raged within the Catholic intellectual community since the days of Lamennais.[65] Perhaps by describing liberalism in the crudest possible way, and by stoutly disassociating all right-thinking Catholics from it, Tyrrell intended, by a calculated effort, to deliver himself from any such label. "If to be 'Liberal,' " he wrote, "is to be a utilitarian of the vulgarest type; if it is to have a secret contempt for anything that savours of mysticism, or that cannot be rationalized or made 'common-sense,' . . . then be my soul with the nar-

63. George Tyrrell, "The Church and Scholasticism," *American Catholic Quarterly Review*, 23 (July 1898): 550–61.

64. Quoted in Petre, *Autobiography of Tyrrell*, 2:90–91. A confusion in the dates of these letters is corrected in Schultenover, *Tyrrell*, 83. Also, for Laberthonnière, see note 32, above.

65. See, e. g., Marvin R. O'Connell, "Montalembert at Mechlin: A Reprise of 1830," *Journal of Church and State*, 26 (Autumn 1984): 515–36, and "Ultramontanism and Dupanloup: The Compromise of 1865," *Church History* 53 (June 1984): 200–217.

row-minded and let my last end be like his."[66] It is not impossible that his correspondent from Aix interpreted, and applauded, this remark as a coded hit against Scholastic rationalism. Tyrrell at any rate replied warmly and in terms that suggested his treatment of "liberal Catholicism" had not been altogether candid: "My dear Father Bremond, Thank you very much for your kind and encouraging letter. I suppose we have neither of us any right to expect to find a majority in agreement with our hopes and aspirations after a wider spirit. Indeed, I feel it would be bad for me, and I should only move too fast and speak too hastily, were it not that I have to retard my pace so as to keep more or less in line with the very conservative body to which I belong."[67] So began an association that was to end with such poignancy at Tyrrell's deathbed eleven years later.

Henri Bremond[68] had left England nearly ten years earlier, but the place and its people had lost none of their fascination for him. He continued to read journals like the *Month*, and to ponder the English scene, and on occasion to offer his countrymen modest analyses of the intellectual and religious life across the Channel.[69] When he first wrote Tyrrell, he was just finishing his tertiary year in his hometown of Aix-en-Provence, during which time he had attended the lectures and cultivated the friendship of Maurice Blondel. As a matter of fact, the work of continuing religious formation—the objective of the tertiary—was guided more by the young lay-professor than by any of Bremond's Jesuit directors. "There is no spiritual reading," Henri wrote his brother Jean, "that does me as much good as my intimate and intense conversations with B[londel]. They have given me the ideas I need to orientate myself for this Lent [of 1898]. I'm going to begin by preaching on *religious anguish*."

Abstract speculation was never Bremond's strong suit, but, amid his teaching and counseling duties in various Jesuit *lycées* in the south of France, he had found an excitement in the bold methodology of the philosophy of *action*, at

66. George Tyrrell, "Liberal Catholicism," *Month* 91 (May 1898): 457. If the sentiment quoted in the text would have pleased Bremond, the following (456), with its elitist overtones, would have similarly pleased von Hügel: "True liberalism is really for the very few who are capable of thinking widely, deeply, and temperately; whereas for the great majority, who . . . have neither leisure, ability, nor education, they must take their thought ready-made from others. . . . It is only one here and there—a Dante or a Newman—who can be trusted to 'liberalize.' "

67. Tyrrell to Bremond, 6 July, 1898, quoted partially in Petre, *Autobiography of Tyrrell*, 2:72. For the full text, see Anne Louis-David (ed.), *Lettres de George Tyrrell à Henri Bremond* (Paris: 1971), 39–40. These letters of Tyrrell, of which I make great use in succeeding chapters, are now in the Biblioteque Nationale. For this edition they were translated into French by Mlle. Louis-David. Therefore my quotations of them are retranslations, my English prose, that is to say, not George Tyrrell's. Bremond's side of the correspondence of course does not survive.

68. See chapter 5.

69. In *Études*, the monthly of the French Jesuits, Bremond published lengthy reviews of Wilfrid Ward's two books about his father: 62 (1894): 5–24, 279–303 (signed "H. Mauvoisin [see Blanchette, *Bremond*, 84]); of Liddon's *Life* of Pusey: 67 (1896): 77–94, 449–60; and of Purcell's *Life* of Manning: 69 (1896): 250–71. The full title of the Jesuit journal is *Études religieuses philosophiques, historiques et littéraires*.

least to the degree that he understood it. "I am not fully sure of the tenor of your thought," he had breathlessly confided to Blondel before the two met, "[but] I have read and reread *L'action* which is a world in itself." The philosopher responded with the great deference he always exhibited when dealing with priests, and asked if Bremond were a professional theologian. "I am merely a poor victim of whimsy," the latter answered, "affected by an incurable *superficiality*" and by a philosophical background limited to a little Ollé-Laprune, a little Newman, and "a few scraps of Scholasticism." He then asked shyly for permission to send Blondel an offprint of a recently published article on the relationship between religious conversion and what Bremond called the "psychology of faith."[70] Blondel was delighted with the essay, praised its "concreteness," its "grasp of the nature of the interior life," and then he indulged in what would prove to have been a brilliant feat of prophecy: "You ought and you can accomplish much good in the construction of a 'psychological apostolate,' an apostolate founded upon a consciousness close to the intimate experience and the asceticism of the mystics."[71] Bremond, after much stumbling and many false starts, had finally had his life's work pointed out to him.

After his tertiary at Aix Bremond, in September 1898, was sent to a *collège* in Lyon. From there he wrote Blondel and asked him to send a copy of "Le Dogmatisme moral" to "the Reverend G. Tyrrell, a friend of Baron von Hügel and, consequently, a friend of yours and of Father Laberthonnière." Blondel obliged, and Tyrrell, thanking Bremond, asked suspiciously, "What are you doing at Lyon? Have you fallen into the hands of the Philistines?" So he had, or so it must have seemed to the fledgling chronicler of mysticism, who had been assigned—at the height of the passions associated with *l'affaire Dreyfus*—as chaplain to those pupils planning to attend the military academy at Saint-Cyr! Such a bizarre misappointment lent substance to Tyrrell's further reflections, one more-or-less disillusioned Jesuit speaking to another: "It is exactly the elasticity of the Spirit of [our founder, Saint Ignatius Loyola] which is needed now to mediate between the old and the new. . . . As far as the S[ociety of] J[esus] is true to the spirit of elasticity which gave birth to her, she will be able for the work. It is a curious crisis in her history. Von Hügel and many others despair of us."[72]

70. Henri Bremond, "M. Brunetière et la psychologie de la foi," *Études* 70 (1897): 647–69, 748–63.

71. Blanchet, *Bremond*, 86–90.

72. Tyrrell to Bremond, 2 October 1898, in Louis-David (ed.), *Lettres*, 41–42.

CHAPTER 10

The Ghost of Newman

We must take Newman just as he is, with his sceptical intelligence and profoundly believing soul, on the pain of misunderstanding the originality, and of sacrificing the opportunities, of his "message."

—*Henri Bremond (1906)*[1]

EVEN BEFORE SHE MARRIED Wilfrid Ward, Josephine Hope kept one or another of Cardinal Newman's books on her dressing table and every day read a short passage. She tended to favor the novels—*Loss and Gain* and especially *Callista*—as well as the poetry and the poignant self-revelation found in the *Apologia*. Not that she shied away from the more intricate material presented in the sermons or in the philosophical treatises; an artist herself, she grasped early on how Newman's style and thought intertwined. But it was the personality of "our great teacher," as she always described him, that attracted her most and that led her gently to cherish his doctrine. If Newman had lived and labored in relative obscurity and had endured much misunderstanding, this too had had a purpose. "If he had not been set apart in a desert place," she wrote, invoking the image of John the Baptist, "should we of this generation go out to learn from his voice? Indeed he was one of the few great men who are alone while they live that they may leave immortal thoughts to be the companions of those that come after them."

Josephine's husband, of course, was no less captivated than she. As early as 1890, the year the cardinal died, there had been talk that he might be asked to prepare the definitive biography—the well-received first volume of the life of his father had appeared the year before. Wilfrid Ward did eventually write Newman's biography, his magnum opus indeed, but the project for a variety of reasons was put off for two decades. Meanwhile, awesome memories of Newman brooded over the lively household in Eastbourne, often intruding, it seemed, into conversations during meal times or during outings along the

---

1. Henri Bremond, *Newman: Essai de biographie psychologique* (Paris: 1906), viii.

downs. That awesome presence, at least in retrospect, proved occasionally oppressive. "Don't try to pretend," one of the Ward daughters said to her sister, long after they were both grown and gone, "don't try to pretend that you didn't get dreadfully bored with Cardinal Newman."[2]

The Wards' dear friend, Friedrich von Hügel, had come to share a measure of that young girl's disenchantment rather than her mother's feelings of personal devotion.[3] He did not, however, fail to appreciate the cardinal's intellectual achievements, and as always he was eager to share his enthusiasm. A beneficiary in this case was Alfred Loisy, to whom the baron had presented as a gift Newman's *omnia opera*.[4] Early in his scholarly career, Loisy recalled, "my author of predilection had been Renan," but "from 1894 to 1900 it was Newman, tolerably broadened *(passablement elargi)*, whom I thought to employ against the Protestant theologians."[5] The book-crammed little rooms in the Dominican convent of Neuilly-sur Seine provided the setting in which there took definitive shape in Loisy's mind a project he had long contemplated: a lengthy apologetical treatise that would render a defense for Catholicism against modern critics like Renan and liberal Protestants like Auguste Sabatier and Adolf von Harnack.[6] And in the works of Newman, "tolerably broadened," he discerned the mechanism whereby the enterprise could be initiated.

Or rather in a specific work, *An Essay on the Development of Christian Doctrine*, in which Newman argued that the Catholicism of the ancient church and the Catholicism preached by Rome in the nineteenth century were, despite apparent differences, essentially the same. This was the book Newman completed in 1845, on the eve of his reception into the Roman church, and it served as an explanation, so to speak, of its author's painful change of allegiance. But, far more than a personal testament, *Development* also showed how, in Loisy's words, "a perfect Anglican became a perfect Catholic, by discovering that Catholic development was rooted in the genuine logic of Christianity, indispensable for its preservation, as divinely legitimate as Christianity itself, from which it is not possible, in essence, to distinguish it." Perhaps Harnack has displayed "more erudition" than Newman, but has he a better "understanding of Christianity in the rich diversity of its life," or does he grasp as clearly "the intimate relation that exists among all the forms and varieties of that life?" As for those "impressed by certain insights advanced" by "the learned dean of the faculty of Protestant theology [of Paris]," they will find in Newman's *Development* a "better documented" argument and a witness to "a more complete reli-

---

2. Ward, *The Wilfrid Wards*, 1:151, 240.

3. See chapter 3.

4. Loisy, *Mémoires*, 1:415.

5. Quoted in Houtin and Sartiaux, *Loisy*, 86.

6. Loisy, *Choses passées*, 174–75, and Poulat, *Histoire, dogme*, 74–88. Auguste Sabatier (1839–1901), professor of reformed theology at Strasbourg, then dean (1895) of the Protestant faculty of theology of Paris; and Adolf von Harnack (1851–1930), professor of theology in and rector (1900) of the University of Berlin, were both celebrated theoreticians of liberal Protestantism.

gious experience"—presented besides in a "more open and impartial spirit"—than in any of the writings of Sabatier.[7]

Loisy recognized that the intelligibility of Newman's theory of development of Christian doctrine—and its persuasiveness—depended upon acceptance of "the principle that a living idea, real and not abstract, which takes possession of the human spirit, follows in its development a line altogether different from that of a geometric axiom, from which conclusions are mathematically deduced, one from the other." Given the nature of Christianity as history has revealed it, one can assume—it is "antecedently probable," Newman himself might have said—that Christianity

had to undergo a development, because it was a living fact made up of various components, and a doctrine susceptible of different applications; because it was a universal religion that could not help but be transformed, enriched, and enlarged by the effect of its relations with the world in which it had been called to live; because it was impossible, even for the most important matters of belief, to bind itself to the letter of Scripture without decaying into a vain cult of formularies; because Scripture proposes, indeed provokes, numerous questions to which it has no answers; because even scriptural revelation reveals progressive development, so that it is vain to argue that development should stop short with the death of the last apostle; and finally because the idea of a doctrine absolutely perfect from its origins and incapable of profiting from later researches, applications, and experiences is inconceivable and absurd.[8]

It may be wondered whether the subtle but ever-cautious Newman would have entirely subscribed to these rather sweeeping and exuberant justifications of his theory. This is not to say that Loisy in any measure falsified or distorted Newman's views or failed to distinguish them clearly from his own. And it was no small thing in itself to have straightforwardly accepted the challenge that had been virtually ignored by Catholic intellectuals over the previous fifty years:

[The theory of development] is undoubtedly an hypothesis to account for a difficulty; but such too are the various explanations given by motions of the heavenly bodies, and it is as unphilosophical on that account to object to the one as to object to the other. . . . [I]nfidelity has its views and conjectures, on which it arranges the facts of ecclesiastical history; and it is sure to consider the absence of any antagonist theory as evidence of the reality of its own. . . . An argument is needed, unless Chsristianity is to abandon the province of argument; and those who find fault with the explanation here offered of its historical phenomena will find it their duty to provide one for themselves.[9]

Loisy aimed instead to add to Newman's original thesis by applying its principles to areas of inquiry the cardinal, for whatever reason, had neglected. The

---

7. "A. Firmin," "Le développement chrétien d'après le cardinal Newman," *Revue du clergé français* 17 (1 December, 1898): 5, 20.

8. "Firmin," "Développement," 6.

9. J. H. Newman, *An Essay on the Development of Christian Doctrine* (London: 1878 ed.), 30–31.

theory ought for instance to deal with more than mere Christianity, which, after all, "in a very true sense" is a development of the various phases of Judaic history leading back to the Patriarchs, who themselves "have their point of departure in the religion of prehistoric humanity." Also, Loisy argued that the very origins of Christianity need fuller elaboration, particularly "the manner in which revelation itself entered into the development and linked itself to it," a question made imperative by the biblical research carried on since Newman's time.[10] And finally, "one could rightly reproach Newman for often having appeared to reduce Christian development to the movement of ideas, to the progress of belief, to the fixing of dogmas," as indeed the title of his book suggested.

It is necessary rather to distinguish in every complete development a threefold moment. There is first the fact itself or the act of development, the vital and almost unconscious phenomenon, which results in a belief affirmed and extended by large and more fruitful moral principles, by an authority that increases its influence and transforms its mode of action, and by a worship that assumes responsibility for new devotions. This is the *real* moment of development. After that the development becomes more reflective, due in part to the resistance it encounters and has to explain away. This is the *theological* moment of a development, and, in matters of consequence, it gives way in turn to the *dogmatic* moment, that is to say, to the formal consecration of the development by a decision of the church.[11]

Here surely was a development of development, and in later years controversy would rage over the degree to which it could be said to have Newman as its progenitor. Loisy for his part maintained that if the theory had not found an honored place in the offical theological manuals Catholicism itself was the loser. "What has Christian theology been since the end of the first century if not a constant and always renewed effort to establish some sort of equation or permanent correspondence between the interpretation of revealed dogmas and the intellectual progress of humanity?" Newman's evolutionary thesis—published fourteen years before Darwin's *Origin of Species*—provided Catholics with a warrant for dismissing the static abstractions of the Scholastics as inconsistent with the plain evidence of history. "Catholic theology has had in our days the great doctor of whom it stood in need. Nor has that doctor failed to promote devotion to the church and traditional orthodoxy and, simultaneoulsy, the scientific spirit. He has failed only to attract disciples."[12]

LOISY DID NOT CONSIDER himself a disciple of Newman—or anybody else's for that matter—but neither did he, as one of his severest critics charged, cynically employ the cardinal's reputation as "a cover" for an attack upon Cath-

10. Loisy's praise for Newman's work did not include the cardinal's article on inspiration (see chapter 4), which he parenthetically dismissed as "an incorrect opinion"; see "Firmin," "Développement," 20.

11. "Firmin," "Développement," 13–14.

12. "Firmin," "Développement," 19–20.

olic orthodoxy.[13] Nevertheless, recognizing that the radical character of the article on *développement* might well arouse an already hostile establishment, he prudently followed a now familiar course and published it under a pseudonym. Five more articles written by "A. Firmin"—his second name preceded by the initial of his first—were to appear over the next two years, not in his own little *Revue* but—a further dictate of prudence—in the *Revue du clergé français*, a liberal journal edited by one of Loisy's former students at the Institut Catholique.[14]

The Firmin articles were intended to introduce "a philosophical and historical interpretation of Catholicism which would at the same time provide an apologia for the church and effect in it the reforms necessary if it were to accomplish its mission in the contemporary world."[15] But even so weighty and ambitious an undertaking did not consume all the energies of the reclusive scholar of Neuilly. He continued to publish learned pieces in various journals on various biblical subjects, twenty or thirty pages each most of them, some under his own name and some pseudonymously. And, it need hardly be said, he continued as well to perform the chaplain's duties to the nuns and pupils of the school down to the last jot and tittle.

As before, he did not invite camaraderie with the local clergy. One fairly frequent visitor during this time, however, was Abbé Marcel Hébert, director of a Parisian *lycée*, the École Fénelon, and to him Loisy offered only a guarded welcome. Six years Loisy's senior, Hébert had been trained at Saint-Sulpice and had served for a while as a country curé in the diocese of Orléans. He had come to Paris and begun his career as an educator in 1879. He soon became an intimate of d'Hulst and particularly of Duchesne, who introduced him to Loisy. A man of singular charm, affectionate, generous, and self-effacing—"the most perfect person I ever met," was a widely held judgment of him[16]—Hébert was almost universally beloved, even by Loisy who admitted very few into his circle of friendships.

Yet the appearance of Hébert at Neuilly could not but have made the prudent exegete somewhat uneasy. Though not a scholar in any serious sense, Hébert was passionately interested in post-Kantian philosophy, the study of which had led him gradually to give up the central doctrines of Catholicism and indeed of theism. He loved the church and its people too much to leave them, and so he rationalized his priestly ministry into a larger service of that "Humanity" which, he maintained, benefited from the moral and cultic "symbols" Catholicism provided it. Loisy was not prepared to go so far—at least not yet—and anyway Hébert's vague symbolism possessed little appeal to his positivist mind. He may have read with more exasperation than sympathy the

13. Albert Houtin, in Houtin and Sartiaux, *Loisy*, 86.
14. Summaries of the articles appear in Poulat, *Histoire, dogme*, 74–88.
15. Loisy, *Choses passées*, 170.
16. Albert Houtin, *Mon experiénce*, 2:161.

pamphlet that Hébert printed in 1899 and circulated to a few friends and which he called *Souvenirs d'Assise*.

> I am not an agnostic, since I affirm the Divine. But what is the Divine? The conception I have formed of it is imperfect. . . . Consequently I do not know how to find the absolute and the definitive in Christ himself or in the church that stands in his place. . . . The truth is in Christ and in the church, . . . but it resides there only in the general orientation given to thought and activity.[17]

But Alfred Loisy, at the end of the summer that year, was preoccupied by concerns other than this and other similarly obscure sentiments. On September 8, 1899, Leo XIII directed an encyclical to the bishops of France "on the education of the clergy." *Depuis le jour* the document was called,[18] and, in reasserting the traditional norms of seminary training as distinguished from "innovations inspired by utilitarian motives and working to the detriment of the solid formation of the mind," it issued a warning against "the disturbing tendencies [in] . . . the interpretation of the Bible which would shortly, were they to prevail, bring about the ruin of its inspiration and supernatural character." "Some Catholic writers have thought it a clever idea" to adopt the "strange and perilous tactics" of the higher critics as a way of rebutting attacks on the Bible. In *Providentissimus Deus* "we have spoken our mind on this rash, dangerous policy. While encouraging our exegetists to keep abreast with the progress of criticism, we have firmly maintained the principles which have been sanctioned in this matter by the traditional authority of the Fathers and Councils, and renewed in our own time by the Council of the Vatican."

The encyclical was promulgated while Loisy was on his annual month's holiday in Ambrières. He had probably not yet read it when, on September 20, at about four in the afternoon,

> my mother . . . heard the noise of a body falling on the floor of my room. She hurried there and found me lying in a pool of blood. During that day I had experienced some slight vomiting of blood, but I had not told her so, for fear of alarming her. But then a sharper stomach hemorrhage had occurred, causing me to faint and indicating the seriousness of the illness. I took to my bed. Three days later another hemorrhage brought me to the verge of death. During the days that followed it became clear that, if I survived, a long period of convalescence would be necessary.

And so he dictated a letter to Cardinal Richard in which he resigned the chaplaincy at Neuilly-sur-Seine. Neither the cardinal nor any of his functionaries did Loisy the courtesy of acknowledging this communication, but he learned shortly from the Dominican prioress that no time had been wasted in supplying the convent with a successor.[19]

---

17. Quoted in Rivière, *Modernisme*, 147.
18. For the English text, see Carlen (ed.), *Encyclicals, 1878–1903*, 454–64.
19. Loisy, *Choses passées*, 207–8.

Had Alfred Loisy possessed a rather more pious mind-set, he might have attributed his illness to an intervention of Divine Providence. He had long fretted at his exile in Neuilly, and now he had ample excuse to escape from it. Indeed, the arrangements he swiftly made, once he had sufficiently recovered, suggest more than a little forethought. "By the beginning of November [1899] I was installed at Bellevue." Not only installed there, but comfortably ensconced under the patronage of a wealthy family, the head of which was a distinguished member of the Académie française. Paul Thureau-Dangin enjoyed a high reputation in political as well as in literary circles, and, as a self-described liberal Catholic, he was much in sympathy with what he understood to be the program of M. l'Abbé Loisy. Thureau-Dangin's attitude in this regard had been largely influenced by Loisy's article on *Développement*, for he was a devotee of Newman and had just finished a large book on the history of Catholicism in England in the nineteenth century.[20]

Though canonically he was still a priest of Chalons-sur-Marne, the archdiocese of Paris awarded Loisy sick leave and a pension of Fr 800. This sum, together with mass stipends, a small income from his father's estate, and modest but regular payment for his publications assured him the means of living in comfortable independence. He took a first-floor apartment in a large and handsome house fronted by a garden and a pretty courtyard on the Boulevard Verd-de-Saint-Julien in Bellevue, a quiet street in that working-class suburb on the southwest edge of greater Paris. In the largest of the three rooms striking prints of Newman and Fénelon, along with a large photograph of Bishop Mignot, decorated the walls. An altar was the most prominent piece of furnishing. Thanks to the intervention of Mignot, the Holy See had granted Loisy, because of his uncertain health, an indult allowing him to offer mass daily in his apartment rather than repairing to the local parish church. The bedroom-study and the small dining room, where he received his infrequent visitors, also displayed conspicuous signs of priestly austerity and demeanor: the breviary carefully set out here, the crucifix hanging there. And though Loisy did not hide his satisfaction that his new lodgings lay in the diocese of Versailles, and therefore outside the jurisdiction of Cardinal Richard, neither did he keep it a secret that he went dutifully into Paris every other week in order to make his confession to one of the Sulpician fathers.[21]

ALMOST AT THE VERY TIME Alfred Loisy was struck down by his bleeding ulcer, mid-September 1899, Henri Bremond was settling into the Jesuit residence at 15 rue Monsieur in Paris. Here he joined the dozen or so of his confreres who edited and published *Études*, a fortnightly journal which treated

20. Paul Thureau-Dangin, *La renaissance catholique in Angleterre*, 3 vols. (Paris: 1899). His son was François Thureau-Dangin who had been Loisy's pupil at the Institut Catholique. See chapter 9, note 43, and chapter 16.
21. Loisy, *Choses passées*, 208–9, and Houtin and Sartiaux, *Loisy*, 89, 94.

religious topics in a more or less learned fashion and which catered primarily
to a clerical audience. Bremond accepted this new appointment with a sense
of deliverance. Several tours of tedious secondary-school teaching, and a seemingly interminable year at Lyon spent counseling future military cadets,[22] had
helped to weary and disillusion him. At thirty-four he had been a member of
the Society of Jesus for half his life, and he had come to realize that some of
the activities Jesuits commonly performed as a matter of course were beyond
him. He had no gift for the kind of improvisation necessary for a teacher in a
classroom filled with clever boys, nor was he suited for the style of pulpit oratory then in vogue: "I was absolutely incapable," he recalled, "of learning by
heart and then delivering a prepared text."[23] But he had already demonstrated
in his published articles that he could write brilliantly and movingly, and so
it was in accord with the traditional genius and practice of the Society of Jesus—to employ its men in ways that took advantage of their strengths—to
have assigned Bremond to the staff of journalists located in the rue Monsieur.

Shortly before his removal there, in February, he had met Friedrich von
Hügel for the first time. The baron, wintering on the French Riviera, traveled
through the districts nearby renewing and solidifying his scholarly relationships. He passed a week with Maurice Blondel. He paid a visit to Bishop Mignot, with whom he discussed the gloomy prospects of Catholic biblical studies; but that prelate, shortly to be promoted to the archdiocese of Albi, was
not without his frivolous side, and he delighted in disclosing to von Hügel
the mysteries of a new-fangled invention, the gramaphone. A similarly light
moment came when, in the company of Padre Giovanni Semeria—the young
Barnabite friar, whose eloquence and progressive views had already earned him
notoriety in Italy—he wasted a few francs at the gaming tables of the famed
casino in Monte Carlo. As to Bremond, who went from Lyon to the resort town
of Aix-les-Bains to see him, the baron could hardly contain his enthusiasm:
"His is a delightfully, astonishingly fresh and open, unartificialized, swiftly
sympathetic mind. With less of a mental, specifically philosophical, training
and fixity of intellectual purpose about him than Fr. Tyrrell, he is perhaps his
equal in his ready, quite spontaneous understanding of all that is great and
hopeful, earnest and Christian, in modern thought and trouble."[24]

No doubt this meeting had been inspired, and perhaps arranged, by George
Tyrrell. Bremond's assignment to the rue Monsieur in any event placed him
in a situation not unlike that of Tyrrell at Farm Street, London,[25] a coincidence
that drew them closer to each other. Both men found themselves in an intellectual enclave where they were given scope to do what they did best. But they
also both carried maverick reputations into houses that put a premium on con-

22. See chapter 9.
23. Quoted in Blanchet, *Bremond*, 102.
24. See De la Bedoyere, *Hügel*, 121–22.
25. See chapter 9.

ventionality. Neither the *Month* nor *Études* may have been as conservative and Ultramontane as their sister Jesuit publication in Rome, the *Civiltà Cattolica*, but they could hardly have been called bold by Bremond's and Tyrrell's rapidly evolving standards.

"Do they realize whom they have brought into their fortress?," Bremond wondered. "My hope is at any rate that I shall be able to *blondelize* them at my leisure."[26] He soon discovered that each of his new colleagues had reserved to himself his own "flower bed" into which others were forbidden to tread: one saw to the articles dealing with scriptural questions, another dealt with moral theology, and so on. Bremond was instructed to concentrate his efforts exclusively upon literary criticism and to refrain from involving himself in other matters. The directive moved him to invoke again playful military imagery in a dispatch to von Hügel.

Here I am in the venerable and holy citadel. I've crossed the draw-bridge . . . and begun to ferret out all the secrets of the place. Artillery is trained from all angles upon any biblical critics who might approach our walls and, if they come too close, buckets of burning oil are positioned to repel any assault upon the tradition. Are you not going to rescue me from such horror? But no, you understand that now you have a friend inside the place; you see me here, like Rahab, hanging a red cord from the walls of Jericho.

The baron was disturbed to think that restriction to literature meant forsaking the "psychological portraits," especially of English Catholics, that Bremond had already proved himself so adept at drawing, but the latter reassured him: "Literature will be my Leah, but Newman will be my Rachel."[27]

Such proved to be the case: Newman in all his complexity continued to fascinate Bremond. Indeed, translations of the cardinal's books and studies of the master himself—particularly the psychological ones favored by von Hügel—constituted a significant portion of his life's work.[28] His fervor, however, sometimes led to exaggeration, as when, later, he maintained that "if Newman did not dictate *L'action*, he surely sent his disciples to the school of Father Laberthonnière and Monsieur Blondel." Maurice Blondel, in fact, was little acquainted with Newman's works and not much interested in them until Bremond pressed the *Grammar of Assent* upon his attention, and that came too late to influence seriously his already developed thought. Blondel showed similar reserve with regard to the increasingly bitter controversies over the

26. Bremond to Blondel, 13 and 21 August, 1899, in André Blanchet (ed.), *Henri Bremond, Maurice Blondel: Correspondance*, 3 vols. (Paris: 1970–71), 1:224, 228.

27. Letters of 30 September, 26 October, and 4 November, 1899, quoted in Blanchet, *Bremond*, 106–7. The harlot Rahab acted as the Israelites' informant inside Jericho; see Joshua, 2. The patriarch Jacob labored seven years for the hand of the beloved Rachel, only to be deceived into wedding her ugly sister Leah instead. After another seven years—"and they seemed unto him but a few days, for the love he had to her"—he finally gained Rachel, his preferred wife. See Genesis, 29.

28. See the list in Schultenover, *Tyrrell*, 373.

biblical question.[29] But such circumspection did not in the least bother Bremond or lessen his devotion. Neither a historian nor a philospher himself, and always something of a gadfly, he felt no uneasiness at serving two masters, or even three or four.

The two years Bremond spent on the rue Monsieur were difficult. He did his duty to his assignment well enough, but what he conceived to be the cramped and intolerant attitudes of his colleagues made daily life for him less than pleasant. Moreover, in all the great Catholic issues of the day—whether modern apologetics or Americanism[30] or *l'affaire Dreyfus*—it seemed to him that editorially *Études* always assumed the most reactionary position. Bremond found some relief in, so to speak, extracurricular activities, like preaching retreats. "Do not scold me for these dissipations," he begged von Hügel. "Without doubt during [these exercises] I neither read nor write anything. But it is truly beneficial to immerse myself again from time to time in the real world. Otherwise the only reality I encounter comes from hearing confessions."

Yet the reality itself could bring with it its own measure of pain. In mid-December 1899 Bremond participated in a pontifical mass at Lyon. "The church was full, and the cardinal was gorgeous in scarlet and gold. From the pulpit a Dominican proclaimed that the church has solved the social question, and the gross Lyonnaise bourgeosie drank in his eloquence, because it did not threaten their purses. I was exasperated. The scarlet and gold seemed to me a derision. The whole Catholic system appears admirably organized to quiet the consciences of the rich and powerful by consigning all troubles to the evil passions of the masses." A few days later, in the midst of a retreat for women—"very great ladies indeed"—Bremond proposed a serious reading of the Gospel without much hope, however, that his hearers would take its imperatives seriously. "What I said to those women could not be said at Rome or wherever the church has become simply a vehicle of temporal power, of worldly honors, of riches. . . . Is this where we have come after so many centuries? Where are the saints?"[31]

Bremond's discontent touched a great variety of issues and indicated that the approaching crisis within the Catholic church would not be limited to quarrels over philosophy and scientific history. But what worried him personally at this moment was whether or not he should take final vows as a Jesuit. This milestone was scheduled for the late winter of 1900. "My cross right now," he confided to Blondel, "is analogous to that of Newman before his conversion. 'The [Anglican] bishops are suspicious of me,' he said, 'and I realize they have reason.' In one sense, does not the church have reason to be suspicious of me?" If so, the suspicion was mutual: "Does not intellectual and even

29. Virgoulay, *Blondel*, 261–63, 109–10.
30. See chapter 11.
31. Quoted in Blanchet, *Bremond*, 109.

moral development (*epanouissement*), at least for the time being, absolutely have to separate from the church?" Such was Henri Bremond's frame of mind on the eve of committing himself permanently to the organization most militantly dedicated to preserving an ecclesiastical system he thought in many respects "atrocious."[32]

Once in Paris in the autumn of this "very bad year" of uncertainty, Bremond, at Blondel's urging, sought out Lucien Laberthonnière and the confessor *sans pareil*, "the saintly Father Huvelin."[33] Not surprisingly, he also turned for advice to his kindred spirit in England. Tyrrell's comments were more pragmatic than pious. Most people, he wrote with weary resignation, have their fate settled for them by "inexorable circumstances, without much reference to their aptitudes and tastes, . . . and often in contradiction to them. The result is that if my destiny is more or less painful, I do not differ from the great majority." If one at the age of forty "looks back and sees that he should have done something other than what he actually did," one can console himself that "it is usually wiser to muddle through to the end rather than to fritter life away on alternatives that would perhaps be just as erroneous." A man in Bremond's position inevitably and understandably worries about erring in a choice that involves irrevocable commitments. But such decisions have to be made, even at the risk of "disagreeable elements"; otherwise "human society would become impossible."

It is in virtue of principles such as these that I pronounced my final vows, recognizing them as contained in the contract I had already made when, a young boy in my credulity, I believed that the Society was such as Paul Féval painted it;[34] . . . The deception was no greater than normal, no matter what the vocation. . . . The principles [of the Society], for too long forgotten, are forward-looking and devoted to progress. And it is to them that I bind myself, not to the views of this or that Jesuit. Then I can live not only *in* the Society but in a certain sense *for* the Society, . . . in order to make it a little less narrow, a little more human and open.

These were the thoughts, Tyrrell concluded, that "I have felt vaguely for a long time justify my own position. I believe that in most respects your difficulty is the same as mine."[35]

On February 2, 1900, the Feast of the Purification of the Virgin, Henri Bremond swore final vows in the Society of Jesus.

BY THEN, HOWEVER, Tyrrell's own difficulties with the Society had reached a new and ominous stage. An article of his, published at the very time of his letter of advice to Bremond, had been delated to the Jesuit general in

32. Bremond to Blondel, 19 December, 1899, in Blanchet (ed.), *Correspondance*, 1:249.
33. Portier, *Huvelin*, 89.
34. Féval was the author of *Jésuites!* (Paris: 1877), a highly romanticized account of the Society.
35. Tyrrell to Bremond, 22 December, 1899, in Louis-David (ed.), *Lettres de Tyrrell*, 59–60.

Rome. That worthy was allegedly so upset by the piece that he had fallen ill and taken to his bed. "The theologians to whom our provincial [in England] referred it," Tyrrell bitterly reported early in the new year, "can find in it no proposition worthy of theological censure; though His Paternity [the general] finds it 'offensive to pious ears.' I wish Rome would either define pious ears, or give a list of them so that one might know." Two long Latin letters of censure had been dispatched from the Roman headquarters, along with the directive that Tyrrell submit a formal retraction and that he write from now on only for Jesuit publications. "We have little hope . . . of standing against this stark-mad fanaticism; and the whole incident reduces this Roman centralization to an absurdity. We are not even allowed to know England and English as well as Italians and Spaniards do."[36]

The brief essay thus rendered notorious was called "A Perverted Devotion."[37] It was rather playful in tone, but deadly serious in content. The devotion Tyrrell thought "perverted" was that which honored God's justice in consigning sinners to perpetual torment. The fault he laid explicitly at the feet of the Scholastic theologians, whose "pert rationalism" changed a bleak and appalling mystery into "an obvious truth of common sense." It is outrageous for one to maintain that "such a doctrine as that of hell [contains] no perplexity for his reason, no shock to his affections, no violation of his sentiments." The theologians arrogantly pretend to answer everything, and they answer nothing. They fail to grasp the fundamental truth that "we are in the region of faith and mystery, and must wait the answer to these riddles in patience and humility."[38]

"A Perverted Devotion" was written toward the end of a busy and productive year for Tyrrell. Besides publishing a dozen articles of varying lengths— one of them a review of Josephine Ward's first novel—he saw through the press his third book, *External Religion: Its Use and Abuse*, drawn from a series of lectures he had delivered to the Catholic undergraduates at Oxford. The opportunity to read and reflect and then to offer the educated Catholic public informed commentary was the whole point of an assignment to Farm Street, and Tyrrell took full advantage of it. He continued to puzzle over the obscure texts of Blondel. If he ran out of scholarly studies to peruse, he could count upon von Hügel to supply him with the latest new ones, including the baron's own thirty-five dense pages on the methodology of the first six books of the

36. Tyrrell to Bremond, 18 January, 1900, and Tyrrell to von Hügel, 10 March, 1900, in Petre, *Autobiography of Tyrrell*, 2:118–20. For a detailed account, based on Roman archives, see David G. Schultenover, *A View from Rome on the Eve of the Modernist Crisis* (New York: 1992), 83–92. Thanks to the kindness of my friend Professor Mary Jo Weaver of Indiana University, I have been able to peruse the rough proofs of this important study.

37. *Weekly Register* 100 (16 December, 1899): 797–800, reprinted in M. D. Petre (ed.), *Essays on Faith and Immortality* (London: 1914), 158–71.

38. See Petre, *Autobiography of Tyrrell*, 2:112–30.

Bible,[39] "a most interesting pamphlet . . . which has made me almost regret the resolve that I made some years ago to turn away from a question so far beyond my ability and leisure."[40]

Tyrrell's sharp mind poked restlessly at the exciting new ideas that littered the mental landscape in this last year of the nineteenth century. His self-taught, pugnacious Thomism, more a youthful assertion of autonomy than a mature intellectual commitment, had been swept away by a few gibes from von Hügel. Into this vacuum, such as it was, rushed a hodgepodge of half-digested lore. "[My] language is scholastic, though my thought is mystic," he concluded.[41] The quest for holiness—his own and that of those with whom he dealt and for whom he wrote—always enjoyed primacy of place with Tyrrell. Increasingly he saw his role as a ministry to Christian men and women who found the traditional modes of religious expression incompatible with modern culture. What science had wrought for such people was a crisis of faith to which, Tyrrell was coming to believe, the institutional church responded too often with barren abstractions or even out-and-out humbug. The number of his immediate disciples may never have been large, but their unyielding devotion to him was a better measure of his worth and his influence than any mere counting of heads. Through the blinding headaches and the nausea, through the moods of self-loathing, through all the doubts that had afflicted him from Dublin to Malta to Stonyhurst, George Tyrrell never ceased striving after the blessed vision of peace, for himself and for all God's wayward children. The love he inspired stands as a permanent tribute to him as a man and a priest.

Just at this time Tyrrell was passing through a phase his friend Maude Petre later called "mediating liberalism."[42] This position had for its chief spokesman Wilfrid Ward, whose constantly repeated theme—that the Catholic church had outgrown the "siege mentality" imposed upon it since the Reformation and therefore could now adopt, within prudent limits, "a far wider assimilation of contemporary thought"[43]—struck a responsive chord in Tyrrell, at least for the moment. His spiritual intimacy with Ward's friend, von Hügel—he now occasionally heard the baron's sacramental confession[44]—helped promote this new relationship. By 1899 Ward and Tyrrell were in frequent and cordial correspondence, with the former rejoicing in the latter's assurance, "I have been always a devout disciple of Newman."[45]

Early in the year Ward offered Tyrrell a clear seal of approval by inviting him to join the Synthetic Society. This prestigious discussion club, whose

---

39. Friedrich von Hügel, "The Historical Method and the Documents of the Hexateuch," *Catholic University Bulletin* 4 (1898):198–226, 1–7.
40. Quoted in Petre, *Autobiography of Tyrrell*, 2:92.
41. See chapter 9.
42. Petre, *Autobiography of Tyrrell*, 2:98–111.
43. See chapter 8.
44. De la Bedoyere, *Hügel*, 106.
45. Tyrrell to Ward, 22 September, 1898, in Weaver (ed.), *Letters from a "Modernist,"* 5.

membership over the twelve years of its existence included a prime minister, several Anglican bishops, and the much-beloved dean of English Unitarians, James Martineau, was founded in 1896. It met regularly at the Westminster Palace Hotel, near the Houses of Parliament, and, after dinner, a member read a paper in accordance with the society's objective "to consider existing Agnostic tendencies and to contribute towards a working philosophy of religious belief."[46] Besides Ward, a founding member, von Hügel was among the small number of Catholics who belonged to the Synthetic, as was the brilliant if eccentric "Willie" Williams, an Eastbourne neighbor of the Wards.[47] Tyrrell was unsure about "represent[ing] the Jesuits among the sort of men whom you have gathered together. . . . I am not a man of all round education owing chiefly to my wilful perversity in youth; nor am I easy and expansive in society; nor am I ready of tongue in debate and discussion." But he finally agreed "to join by way of experiment, . . . if you think my wit sufficient to atone for my ignorance."[48] No one ever called into question George Tyrrell's wit.

Nor his industry. Along with all his other activities Tyrrell decided "after long hesitation" to confront his growing uneasiness as a Jesuit by writing an analysis of the Society's basic document, the *Spiritual Exercises* of Saint Ignatius. It was a labor of love and, to a degree, of desperation. He was anxious, as he told Bremond early in October, not to "blind people to the real character of the Society and [so to] nourish a pernicious illusion about it. But, on the other hand, were my book to succeed in reviving the large and liberal spirit of St. Ignatius, it would act like new wine poured into old bottles; they would either stretch or break. . . . Frankly I'm afraid the Society is too old to stretch. . . . But if it still possesses youth enough it might, even while representing the conservative principle, play a great role in the coming transformation of the Catholic Church."[49] Perhaps Tyrrell's understanding of Saint Ignatius's "large and liberal spirit" was itself an illusion. However that may be, after working steadily on this project for some months, he suddenly destroyed the almost completed manuscript. "[I] do not regret it," he said. And then, a little later, he revealed a reason why: he had decided that a religious order should function as "a band of fellow-spirits as long as [the founder is] alive to keep up the first fervour. After his death they should die out ruthlessly. All the misery comes from a mistaken loyalty to the letter of the founder's rule, which at last slays the spirit. Where more than with us [Jesuits]?"[50]

46. See Ward, *The Wilfrid Wards*, 1:344–79, 417–20. The wide-ranging discussions occasioned by Arthur Balfour's *Foundations of Belief* (1895) led indirectly to the founding of the Synthetic. Professional politician and amateur philosopher, Balfour at that time was leader of the House of Commons in the ministry of his uncle, Lord Salisbury. Later he was prime minister (1902–5), and still later he served in various coalition cabinets (1915–22).

47. See William J. Williams, *Newman, Pascal, Loisy and the Catholic Church* (London: 1906).

48. Tyrrell to Ward, 3 February, 1899, in Weaver (ed.), *Letters from a "Modernist,"* 7.

49. Tyrrell to Bremond, 2 October, 1899, in Louis-David (ed.), *Lettres de Tyrrell*, 56.

50. Letters of September and November 1900, quoted in Petre, *Autobiography of Tyrrell*, 2:77–80.

But even before he arrived at that conclusion Tyrrell had taken a significant turn, or rather completed a turn that he had begun several years before. In November 1899 there appeared "The Relation of Theology to Devotion," which, despite its brevity, must rank among his most important publications.[51] By "theology" he meant Scholastic theology, the attempt "to translate the teachings of Catholic revelation into the terms and forms of Aristotelian philosophy, and thereby give them a scientific unity." It is "abstract, orderly, and artificial," while "devotion," the direct result of one's confrontation with what God has revealed, is "concrete, disorderly, and natural." Each may be "lamentably imperfect" in itself, but surely—an echo from Blondel and Laberthonnière—"it is less misleading to take a confused, general view of an object than to view one of its parts or elements violently divorced from the rest." Devotion needs theology to preserve it from anthropomorphic "puerilities and superstitions"; but theology stands in even greater need, because it "tends to . . . excessive abstraction and vague unreality."

The Christian revelation is not merely a symbol or creed, but it is a concrete religion left by Christ to His Church; it is perhaps in some sense more directly a *lex orandi* than a *lex credendi*;[52] the creed is involved in the prayer and has to be disentangled from it. . . . What does [the church] care about the metaphysics of transubstantiation, except so far as metaphysicians have to be answered in their own language, and on their own assumptions. . . . "This is My Body" is nearer the mark than metaphysics can ever hope to come; and of the two superstitions, that of the peasant who is too literally anthropomorphic is less than that of the philosopher who should imagine his part of the truth to be the whole.[53]

Saints, not savants, are the real teachers of the church, for they preserve in concrete action the pristine revelation which, far from developing, exercises its power precisely by way of its original bluntness. While Loisy for his own purposes tinkered with Newman's theory of development, Tyrrell appeared ready to abandon it altogether.

Tyrrell sent the proofs of the article to von Hügel. The baron was ecstatic: "[It] strike[s] me as the finest thing you have yet done. . . . It is really splendid. I thank God for it. It is of course a deep encouragement to me in my own work." Following his usual practice, von Hügel sent off copies to Blondel, Laberthonnère, Loisy, and Semeria, rejoicing all the while "that you are let say these things, in your Order and by your Order."[54]

The fuss caused by "A Perverted Devotion" only weeks later put an ironic edge to the baron's optimism. Tyrrell, after a lengthy exchange with the Latin

51. *The Month* 94 (November 1899): 461–73. Tyrrell republished it three times, including in *The Faith of Millions*, 2 vols. (London: 1902), 1:228–52. See the analysis by Schultenover, *Tyrrell*, 92–96.

52. When reprinted in *Through Scylla and Charybdis* (London: 1907) the essay was retitled "Lex Orandi, Lex Credendi."

53. Tyrrell, *Faith of Millions*, 1:228, 231, 250, 239–40, 245.

54. Von Hügel to Tyrrell, 8 October, 1899, in Holland (ed.), *Letters of von Hügel*, 77.

censors, was forced to publish a retraction: "An absolutely fatuous and un-
meaning letter to the Editor of the *Weekly Register* . . . is the mouse of which
the labouring mountain has at last been delivered." One line from the censured
article he no doubt bitterly reflected upon: "Though God and Reason demand
that I should often believe to be white that which seems black to me, yet never
am I asked to believe that what seems black to me yet *seems* white."[55]

A consolation through the affair had been the support of his English confreres, but that was not enough to save him from a period of severe depression.
He stopped saying mass for a while, and he told Wilfrid Ward that he might
leave the church altogether.[56] This mood, however, quickly passed, and in the
summer of 1900 Tyrrell agreed with his superiors that prudence called for his
removal from Farm Street. He was assigned to the Jesuit mission in Richmond, Yorkshire. "I feel horribly selfish," he wrote from there on August 8,
"in running away from my responsibilities to this haven of absolute quiet, but
can only justify it by the thought that my leisure may eventually be more
profitable to others than my fussiness."[57]

IN JULY, 1900, a month before he went off to his northern exile, George
Tyrrell preached what proved to be his last Ignatian retreat. In attendance was
a thirty-seven-year-old woman named Maude Domenica Petre. Dressed simply
and severely, her dark hair piled untidily atop her head, her rather plain face,
with its deep-set eyes and slightly protruding teeth, offered small testimony
to the intelligence and sensitivity that burned within. She was a nun, indeed,
she was the English provincial of the small and unusual religious order she
belonged to. The Daughters of the Heart of Mary, founded during the French
Revolution, took the traditional vows, but they neither lived in community
nor wore a habit nor adopted new names. To all outward appearances they
were merely pious spinsters. Petre had joined the congregation in 1890, the
year it received final approval from Leo XIII.[58]

She was the daughter of a younger son of the thirteenth Baron Petre, a renowned name among the English Old Catholics.[59] For three centuries, ever
since the Reformation, the Petres had stood by their faith despite persecution
and all the vicissitudes imposed by the Penal Laws. By contrast her mother, a
daughter of the earl of Wicklow, was a convert to Catholicism, for whom her
religion became "the golden thread that twined itself in and out of all other
interests." Maude recognized a double inheritance in the religious characteris-

55. Petre, *Autobiography of Tyrrell*, 2:116–29.
56. Ward to von Hügel, 27 February, 1900, quoted in Ward, *The Wilfrid Wards*, 1:326.
57. Quoted in Petre, *Autobiography of Tyrrell*, 2:131.
58. Ellen Leonard, *Unresting Transformation: The Theology and Spirituality of Maude Petre* (Lanham, Md.: 1991), 16–17.
59. See chapter 6.

tics of her father and mother: "ardour and imagination, fervour and devotion, in the latter; . . . firmness, tenacity, and independence in the former."[60]

Both her parents died when Maude Petre was nineteen. "My first home was . . . my last one, for I never had a home, in its full and perfect meaning, again." She maintained affectionate attachments to her numerous siblings and their children, but she did not hanker after marriage herself. In an era when career women were a rarity, a Catholic (and indeed at this date an Anglican) at least had open to her an alternative to conventional domesticity. The intense religiosity of her upbringing no doubt contributed to the decision she ultimately made to remain single and to become a nun. She never regretted it. "I am glad I did not marry when I was young. . . . I do not doubt that I could have been happy as wife and mother, and I should have had an anchorage in life which is lacking to the single. But, on the whole, I am glad I have lived my own life, and shared the life of others in a measure which I could not have done as a married woman. And my true love affair was to come later, in a form which could never be crowned with fulfillment."[61]

In 1885, still unsure of her ultimate vocation, Maude Petre "went to Rome . . . to study scholastic philosophy, to the great amusement of the ecclesiastics there to whom I had introductions." She did so on the advice of her confessor, with whom she had shared her "difficulties and doubts." The good priest considered her doctrinal uncertainties simply "temptations" which could be best treated by a good dose of Scholasticism. And where better than in the Rome of *Aeterni Patris*? Petre, at twenty-two financially independent and with "no duties or ties to impede me," adopted this "fairly crazy idea" as her own. There was no question of a woman enrolling in any of the pontifical universities; so, under the direction of a tutor—and accompanied by a chaperone—she settled down every evening to read "a textbook by that terrible dry-as-dust [Matteo] Liberatore,"[62] as well as selected parts of Aquinas's *Summa theologiae*.

Her overall reaction to the Roman scene—so different from that of the young Wilfrid Ward a few years earlier[63]—was less than enthusiastic. "How well I remember my visits to the different shrines, . . . and how I endeavored to find devotion [there]. . . . I fought down my distaste." But the impression left upon her by the superficial introduction to Thomism was far more positive and lasting. In this she differed significantly from those with whom she was destined to be most closely associated in the future. To them the "scholastic process appeared dry, cold, purely rational, if not merely logical. . . . I found that same process spiritually exhilarating, and full of the possibilities of prayer. Like physical exercise to the body it seemed to expand one's soul, to

---

60. M. D. Petre, *My Way of Faith* (London: 1937), 3–14.
61. Petre, *My Way*, 141, 129.
62. See chapter 2.
63. See chapter 6.

open the lungs to the winds of eternity." Indeed, had the times been less fretful, Maude Petre might have served as a mediating angel, for, after she read and was enthralled in 1898 by Laberthonnière's "Le dogmatisme moral,"[64] no one grasped better than she the essential differences between the two parties in conflict.

It is . . . a question of the contrast between faith and certainty. Laberthonnière and his school make their appeal to faith, and maintain that faith is of the whole soul, whereas certainty is of the intellect and reason alone. And they regard Thomism as a system of compelling demonstration, a subjugation of the soul to the rational faculty, so that it seems to them as though St. Thomas had equipped the Church with a means of coercion; man was to be made to believe first in God, and then in the whole theological system, and this because he could not rationally do otherwise and not because, spiritually, he would not wish to do otherwise.

And what further rouses their passionate indignation is that they find that Thomism has possessed itself of theology, and has propped itself on the authority of the Church. Almost it seems to them a plot.[65]

Back in England Petre turned her hand to writing. Several of her articles in the *Month* were well received. Friedrich von Hügel, who had been a close friend of her mother, became an informal mentor, recommending plans of reading and specific books to her. He "was a great liberator; he opened the door to many imprisoned souls. . . . His was a wonderful friendship and a golden gift." This was the judgment of Petre's last years, after estrangement between her and the baron no longer weighed heavily upon her.[66] Meantime, in 1896, she published her first book, a study of religious philanthropy in the life of Saint Peter Claver.[67] None of these activities, however, nor the entry into the religious life, gave permanent rest to what she described as her innately skeptical mind. The doubts she had brought with her to Rome were with her still. She met George Tyrrell once or twice during these years and published a review of one of his books. But the crucial encounter between them took place at the retreat of July 1900, with Tyrrell still smarting from recent reprimands and Petre, "overwhelmingly shy, especially with men near my own age," still "suffering from a tired and tortured faith." She crossed now into a new dispensation: "From the hour in which George Tyrrell entered my life something happened for good."[68]

DURING THAT SUMMER of discontent, Alfred Loisy lived the quiet scholar's life in his rooms in Bellevue. Back at his desk every day, and working with

64. See chapter 9.

65. Petre, *My Way*, 171–84.

66. Petre, *My Way*, 254–56.

67. Peter Claver (1581–1654) was a Jesuit missionary in South America, where he championed black slaves and attempted to alleviate their misery. He was canonized in 1888. See Leonard, *Transformation*, 19.

68. Petre, *My Way*, 129, 162, 272.

the relentless regularity that made him so prolific, he resumed the series of articles on biblical subjects begun before his illness of the preceding year. And as before some of them appeared under his own name, some under pseudonyms. A favorite among the latter at this date was "Isidore Després," who earlier had sarcastically taken to task "the Dominican savant," Marie-Joseph Lagrange, for allegedly equivocating on the hot issue of the authorship of the opening books of the Old Testament.[69]

"Després" surfaced again in June 1900, this time with a similarly ironic commentary on Leo XIII's reassertion of official resistance to the higher criticism in *Depuis le jour*.[70] "It is clear," wrote "Després," "that the Holy Father does not appreciate, either for itself or for its scientific value, the work of Catholic critics." Wedded to outmoded Scholasticism, the "traditional view" is that the study of Scripture "has no other raison d'être save to support dogmatic theses [and] to furnish arguments against heresy and incredulity." It never occurs to the pope or his advisers that "the science of the Bible could enjoy a relatively independent existence, like all the other human sciences, with its own object and method, both of them purely historical. This for Catholic theology is a notion absolutely novel and almost revolutionary," however much for granted it is taken in learned circles all over the world. Such a benighted attitude explains why "the very severe words of the Sovereign Pontiff have no need of explanation" and why "it would be almost impertinent to want to justify them."[71]

"The irony of M Després," Loisy recalled, "was not without a certain bitterness" and imprudence. These qualities greatly disturbed Friedrich von Hügel, and out of deference to "such an excellent friend, who is the definition of benevolence," Loisy refrained from republishing the article as he had originally planned to do. Nor did the piece arouse any official indignation.[72] The same could not be said for what proved to be the last of the essays published in the same journal by "A. Firmin."

The series that had begun with an elaboration of Newman's theory of doctrinal development had moved through four more separate pieces that criticized from various angles the liberal Protestantism espoused by Harnack and Sabatier.[73] The sixth article, treating the origins of the Hebraic religion, was written about the time Maude Petre was making her retreat under the direction of George Tyrrell. "Firmin" turned now from the previous theoretical considerations to the hard ground of history, and the fireworks exploded on the

69. "Isidore Després," "Opinions catholiques sur l'origine du Pentateuque," *Revue du clergé français* 17 (15 February, 1899):526–57.

70. See p. 182, above.

71. "Isidore Després," "La lettre de Léon XIII au clergé de France et les études d'Écriture sainte," *Revue du clergé français* 23 (1 June, 1900): 14–15.

72. Loisy, *Choses passées*, 215, 211.

73. See notes 6 and 15, above.

very first pages. Historical science has demonstrated that the term "biblical tradition" cannot be understood as it was among Catholics in the eighteenth century. Not even the most conservative exegetes or apologists would maintain, as Bossuet did then, that Creation occurred exactly 4,004 years before the birth of Christ. Yet that kind of presumptuousness is still the dominating attitude, and it has to be replaced by a realization of vast areas of ignorance.

The chronological data in the Bible now resembles for us a flimsy netting (*filet*) flung like a bridge over an abyss the limits of which cannot be seen. For us to represent scientifically the primitive history of humanity at the same time as the ancient history of Israel, we have to recognize stretches of darkness. We can say immediately that the history of Israel is relatively clear since Samuel and Saul. Before that, going back to Moses, one can discern out of the void patches of dim twilight and no more. And before Moses, back to Abraham, all is night. The first chapters of Genesis do not teach us and are not intended to teach us in what circumstances man and religion made their appearance in the world and how they behaved in the course of prehistoric times.

What appears at the dawn of history is not a religion but "a veritable chaos of bizarre, fluctuating, changing opinions, of gross and puerile superstitions, of weird, cruel and often immoral practices." Reforms, like those of Confucius and Buddha, are attempted and fail, or, at best, only half succeed. "Only one essential reform, comprising a whole series of secondary reforms and of progress dearly purchased, ends in a result as perfect, it seems, as the human condition will allow: This is what began with Moses, found its term in Jesus, and is perpetuated by the church."[74] Here was an outline of a development never dreamed of by Newman.

In the next issue of the *Revue du clergé français*, that dated Octber 23, a notice, signed by Cardinal Richard, appeared directly after the title page: "['La religion d'Israel'] is in contradiction with the constitution *Dei Filius* promulgated by the Vatican Council. It also contradicts the rules given by the Sovereign Pontiff, Leo XIII, in the encyclical *Providentissimus Deus* for the interpretation of Scripture. We forbid further publication of this material in the *Revue*."[75]

Years later Loisy claimed to have been puzzled by this particular intervention. The cardinal had not submitted the article for examination to "a committee of theologians," as would have been the ordinary procedure. And the real identity of "Firmin," if that had been the issue, had long been known in the little world of the French Catholic intelligentsia.[76] "The whole business ap-

74. "A. Firmin," "La religion d'Israel, les origines," *Revue du clergé français* 24 (15 October, 1900): 338–39.

75. Printed in Loisy, *Choses passées*, 392. The note "À suivre" ("to be continued") appeared on the last page of the article (363), and this is the "further publication" the cardinal forebade. Loisy ultimately added two more essays to this one and published them together in a small book, *La religion d'Israel* (Paris: 1901).

76. See Poulat, *Histoire, dogme*, 637–38.

peared to have happened precipitately as if [Richard] had acted under orders," and Loisy remained convinced that those orders had come from Rome. In any event he reacted promptly and with spirit. "I am not prepared," he wrote on October 26 to one of Richard's aides, "to discuss the judgment of His Eminence with regard to a certain pseudonym, nor do I wish, at least for the present, to increase by way of public explanation the emotional response this judgment could produce. . . . But I do not think that I can profit any longer from the liberality of His Eminence, and therefore I return to you the whole [Fr 800] of the pension I received this year from the archdiocese of Paris."[77]

77. Loisy, *Choses passées*, 216–20.

CHAPTER II

Roma Vigilans

As far as intellectual weaknesses are concerned, there are none recognized here [in Rome], and people here resent it deeply that others should find any such. You think there are advantages in the generous eloquence of Semeria, in the fine exegesis of Loisy, in the philosophical designs of Blondel; you realize to what needs this kind of work responds and what good it could do. Here everything of that sort is judged as a manifestation of an indiscreet curiosity about the future, as an indirect criticism of things as they are. . . . Your little exercises will be tolerated or else ignored as long as you don't raise an uproar, . . . as long as you don't find an enemy to denounce them.

—*Louis Duchesne (1899)*[1]

"IT IS NOT NECESSARY, is it, to cry 'Dreyfus, Dreyfus,' all the time," the old pope said irritably. And then he added: "Could you not occasionally say something pleasant about Monsieur Loubet?" The object of this papal scolding, at an audience granted in September 1899, was Père Vincent de Paul Bailly, editor of the mass circulation paper *La Croix*, operated by the little religious order he belonged to, the Assumptionists.[2] A few months earlier, in an interview with a rather more prestigious Parisian newspaper, *Le Figaro*, Leo XIII had spoken indirectly but clearly enough on the same subject: "Our religion has already consecrated the just cause of thousands of martyrs. . . . We learn our lesson in such matters with our Master on Calvary. Happy the victim whom God recognizes as just, so as to identify his cause with that of God's own Son who died for us."[3]

Émile Loubet,[4] to whom the pope referred, was at the time president of the French Third Republic. His prime minister was René Waldeck-Rousseau, a

1. Duchesne to von Hügel, 2 March, 1899, in Neveu (ed.), "Lettres . . . de Duchesne," *Mélanges*, 84:589.
2. See *Dictionnaire de biographie française* (1941): 19:1359–61.
3. Quoted in Dansette, *Histoire religieuse*, 554–56.
4. See Soderini, *Leone XIII*, 2:516–18.

pragmatic lawyer considered a moderate with no strong ideological commitments. But the furious politics that had erupted in the general election of 1898 left little room for moderatation. Captain Alfred Dreyfus,[5] convicted of treason on the basis of forged documents, had been stripped of his military rank and imprisoned on Devil's Island. A series of kangaroo courts martial declined to void the verdict, and most conservatives, Catholics prominent among them, continued to insist upon his guilt, despite the gradual revelation of overwhelming evidence to the contrary. As a Jew and a loyal though rather laconic republican—he was by all accounts a humdrum, colorless sort of man—Dreyfus rapidly became a symbol that reached far beyond himself; indeed, his ultimate exoneration and reinstatement went hardly noticed. But his case sparked a renewal of the quarrel that had been raging in France since 1789. The cry went up that the Republic, along with all the secular ideals of the great French Revolution, stood once more in danger from the same old forces of reaction, led by the army and the church. The majority in the Chamber of Deputies, echoing the sentiments of the electorate, demanded action. The artful Waldeck-Rousseau determined to give them a victim, without, however, upsetting the delicate balance of political interests, without encouraging the red socialists, without, above all, disturbing civil order. He gave them the Assumptionists.[6]

L'Affaire Dreyfus convulsed French public life for a generation. It also occasioned the final stage in the century-long struggle between church and state and with it the collapse of Leo XIII's policy of *ralliement*.[7] Occasioned, not caused: for in fact the struggle had only taken a respite during the early and mid-1890s; no minds had been changed then, no diminution of mutual antipathy had occurred. And in fact the *ralliement* had not really been accepted by the French Catholic leadership, clerical or lay. The bishops, with only a few exceptions, had scarcely even given it lip service. For the most part, they maintained a sullen silence, out of regard for the pope's office and revered person, but in their hearts they clung to their monarchist hopes and shared the view of their candid colleague, Monseigneur Freppel of Angers: Leo XIII, he said, was plainly wrong to think "the Republic, *in France*, is simply a form of government as in Switzerland or in the United States for instance, and not a doctrine, a doctrine fundamentally and radically contrary to Christian doctrine."[8] The irony was that *La Croix* had vigorously supported the papal initiative, only to jettison its commitment to reconciliation over its obsession with Dreyfus. That obsession was by no means confined to the Assumptionists, but the campaign they mounted was remarkable for its virulence and for its pandering

5. The literature on the subject is enormous. For a useful survey, see Jean-Denis Bredin, *The Affair: The Case of Alfred Dreyfus* (New York: 1986).

6. Brogan, *Development of France*, 358–60.

7. See chapter 8.

8. Quoted in Brogan, *Development of France*, 264.

to that strain of anti-Semitism always so close to the surface of French society.

So the Dreyfus case moved the hostilities onto center stage once more. New laws were passed in the Chamber of Deputies, or old ones revived, banning the "unauthorized" religious orders. But even before they took effect, the prime minister moved against the Assumptionists. On Monday, January 22, 1900, the police closed and sealed the offices of *La Croix*, and arrested Bailly and one of his associates. The following Thursday Cardinal Richard, in a gesture of solidarity, paid a highly visible call at the mother-house of the Assumptionists on the rue François Ier. But Waldeck-Rousseau, his finger always on the pulse of public opinion, had chosen his target well. Père Bailly—with his wild, unkempt beard and glittering eyes reminiscent of the American abolitionist John Brown, on the eve of his execution—had by his literary excesses opened himself and his colleagues to retribution. When the prime minister issued a formal reprimand of the cardinal and suspended the salaries of six other bishops who had sent messages of sympathy to the Assumptionists, hardly a word of dissent was heard.[9]

So the first year of the new century began badly for the cardinal of Paris, so much so that one might have expected him to classify the scribblings of an obscure bookworm like Alfred Loisy as a minor annoyance. Yet deep down he and others in his position judged the threats and alarums to be all of a piece. Dreyfus and Waldeck-Rousseau and Loisy: enemies of the church without and enemies within. Meanwhile, at the Vatican Leo XIII—who had likened the sufferings of Dreyfus to those of Christ and who feared, with reason, that worse than Waldeck-Rousseau was to come—brooded over the ruins of the most cherished ambition of his pontificate.

A CERTAIN SADNESS attaches to the realization that a distinct season is coming to an end. The end of a life, of a romance, even of a holiday, inevitable as it may be, possesses its measure of poignancy. The approaching termination of a political regime also displays some aspects of melancholy, but mixed with them are elements of hope and wonder about the future, about the changes that are doubtless to occur, about ambitions perhaps soon to be achieved. The anticipation in such circumstances can be keen: "Round him waiting hungry sons" is the poet's way of evoking the situation of a medieval king.[10] The bishop of Rome had no sons in the flesh, but, as the beginning of the twentieth century coincided with his ninetieth year, the expectation of his imminent demise stirred more than a little interest.

"The pope is ill, and it seems unlikely that he will recover."[11] So Louis

9. Dansette, *Histoire religieuse*, 569–70. See also Elisabeth Hausser, *Paris au jour de jour. Les événements vus par la presse, 1900–1919* (Paris: 1968), 16.

10. T. S. Eliot, *Murder in the Cathedral*, part 1.

11. Duchesne to von Hügel, 2 March, 1899, in Neveu (ed.), "Lettres . . . de Duchesne," *Mélanges*, 84:589.

Duchesne reported on Leo XIII's eighty-ninth birthday. This prediction, like so many similar ones, proved to be mistaken. The pope was destined to live another four years, frail, to be sure, his skin like brittle parchment and his slender figure wispy and halting in its movements, but still alert enough when the occasion demanded it. But to Duchesne, now director of the École Française de Rome, the dismal reality did not hinge upon the fate of the little old man behind the Vatican walls. "The pope lives now only with his physicians and his servants," he wrote from the splendor of the Palazzo Farnese where he worked and resided. Each of the major curial officers "is now master in his own house: Rampolla for politics, Ledochowski in his immense empire, Mazzella in theology and the inquisition."[12]

But even if the pope should reassert himself or be replaced, the situation here would not be materially different. The problem here is a systemic and permanent one. The church would shatter to pieces were it not for politics, the governments, the press, etc. This [curial] world does not hold the view that the faith should be reasonable. It is satisfied with survival and, on the practical level, with concerted action with its representatives. This can go on for a long time yet.[13]

Monseigneur Duchesne was always given to exaggeration, and he was notorious for tailoring his opinions to the dispositions of those with whom he shared them. The likes of von Hügel and Loisy expected just such bitter observations from him. Besides, he was still smarting over the failure of his quixotic campaign to get the papacy to recognize the validity of Anglican orders.[14] But Duchesne, his personal foibles aside, was raising a complaint to be heard often in coming years, a complaint much more radical than that an aged pontiff had had to delegate much of his authority to trusted aides. Nothing, he charged, would ever change; nothing would alter "the Roman temperament [*le naturel romain*]." "The curia will always be a nest of intrigues, with only a trifling change in the personnel of the intruguers. Oh, how happy I am not to be a part of it, and how much I would regret becoming involved in it."[15]

Fresh in Duchesne's mind as he wrote these words was the curious phenomenon of Americanism—dubbed "the phantom heresy," by one of those deeply affected by it.[16] Only weeks before Leo XIII had issued an apostolic letter,

---

12. Mariano Cardinal Rampolla was secretary of state; Miecislaus Cardinal Ledochowski prefect of propaganda (and hence in charge of mission lands, including the United States—see below); and Camillo Cardinal Mazzella, S. J., at various times prefect of the congregations of studies and of the Index.

13. Duchesne to Loisy, 16 March, 1899, in Neveu (ed.), "Lettres de . . . Duchesne," *Mélanges*, 84: 294–5.

14. See chapter 8.

15. Duchesne to von Hügel, 2 March, 1899, in Neveu (ed.), "Lettres . . . de Duchesne," *Mélanges*, 84:589.

16. See Félix Klein, *Americanism: A Phantom Heresy* (n. p.: 1951). In a considerable literature the basic treatment remains Thomas T. McAvoy, *The Great Crisis in American Catholic History* (Chicago, 1957). For a perceptive analysis of the historiography, see Philip Gelason, " 'Americanism' in American Catholic Discourse," in *Speaking of Diversity: Language and Ethnicity in Twentieth-Century America* (Baltimore: 1992), 272–300.

Testem Benevolentiae,[17] in which he declared it wrong to assert that the Holy Ghost bestows more charisms in the present day than in earlier ages; that direct inspiration obviates the need for spiritual direction; that natural virtues are preferable to supernatural, because the former prepare the Christian better for action in the world; that therefore active virtues are to be preferred to passive ones like humility, meekness, and obedience; that the vows taken by members of religious orders inhibit liberty and hence are out of step with the imperatives of the present age; that new methods, more in harmony with contemporary reality, should be employed to convert non-Catholic Christians.[18] Such views constitute a great danger "to Catholic doctrine and discipline, inasmuch as the followers of these novelties judge that a certain liberty ought to be introduced into the Church," analogous to that liberty "now the law and foundation of almost every civil community" and particularly associated with the polity of the United States. Because of this latter fact some people have lumped these opinions together and labeled the bundle "Americanism," notably, the pope was careful to say, people not themselves Americans. Therefore—in a stunning non sequitur—he called upon the bishops of the United States to repudiate such ideas.

The archbishop of Baltimore, to whom the letter was addressed, did so in no uncertain terms: "This doctrine," Cardinal Gibbons told the pontiff, "which [is] . . . extravagant and absurd, this Americanism as it has been called, has nothing in common with the views, aspirations, doctrine and conduct of Americans."[19] If so, where could the villains described in *Testem Benevolentiae* be found? In France, it seemed, Leo XIII's special obsession. The translation into French of a biography of a progressive American priest had led to a heightening of the quarrel among Catholics already bitterly divided over the *ralliement.* The publication had been edited by Abbé Félix Klein, a professor of literature at the Institut Catholique of Paris. A mild, courteous, somewhat timid man—and a neighbor of Alfred Loisy in Bellevue—Klein had written a somewhat exuberant and argumentative preface to the book, in which he maintained that the church in the United States had pioneered a spirituality appropriate to an age of scientific discovery and growing personal independence, a spirituality more supple, more interior—though by no means inactive in addressing the needs of the modern world—and more sensitive to the promptings of the Holy Ghost in a manner and degree that promised to enrich the traditional ecclesiastical structures.[20] The book had gone into seven printings and had made Klein, for a while, a minor celebrity.

17. English text in McAvoy, *Crisis,* 379–91.

18. This summary is taken from David Killen, "Americanism Revisited: John Spalding and *Testem Benevolentiae,*" *Harvard Theological Review* 66 (1973): 420–21.

19. Quoted in John Tracy Ellis, *The Life of James Cardinal Gibbons,* 2 vols. (Milwaukee: 1952), 2:71.

20. Summary in McAvoy, *Crisis,* 166–68. See also O'Connell, *John Ireland,* 439–40, 462–63.

Alfred Loisy later testified to the obvious, that Americanism, phantom or not, had nothing to do with the philosophical and critical issues now pressing for attention among European Catholic intellectuals. As for Klein, he was merely "an amiable fellow," a "most inoffensive liberal."[21] This want of connection may not, however, have been so obvious at the time. Loisy indeed, busy with his books in Neuilly and Bellevue, remained aloof from the Americans, who, he decided, had "no precise or fixed ideas, save in political and social matters,"[22] but not so some of his friends. In January 1899, the most visible Americanist prelate, John Ireland of Saint Paul, had hastened to Rome in a vain attempt to avert the promulgation of *Testem Benevolentiae*. A month later he published a letter in the *Osservatore Romano* in which he accepted the pope's judgment while seconding Gibbons's denial that the proscribed opinions had any currency in the United States.[23] In composing this statement, Ireland had had the help of that candid foe of intrigue, Louis Duchesne. "The stylistic awkwardness of the letter, written in French, does not disprove the collaboration. It was left there, or put there, in order that no one would suspect the assistance given the archbishop of St. Paul by Duchesne."[24] Friedrich von Hügel too was in close contact with the leading Americanists, whom he described as "excellent," "warm-hearted," and "open on biblical matters." He grieved at the "Roman humiliation" experienced by Archbishop Ireland.[25]

That humiliation was worse than the baron knew. Before he departed Rome in the spring of 1899 Ireland was asked by some functionary in the curia whether he believed in the divinity of Christ.[26] The archbishop of Saint Paul understandably found the question impertinent and insulting, and yet, from another perspective, it was not without a certain logic. Here was a man who gloried in his modernity—"Let all things be new," he had declared approvingly in a famous speech, "is the watchword of humanity today, and to make all things new is humanity's strong resolve."[27] Ireland, always a conventionally orthodox Catholic, would never have dreamed of demanding a "new" doctrine of the Trinity. But other men, similarly committed to the modern, seemed ready to do so. The archbishop of Saint Paul had once hoped to recruit Alfred Loisy for the faculty of his seminary.[28] Perhaps the question asked of him was not altogether presumptuous.

21. Loisy, *Mémoires*, 2:252–53.

22. Loisy *Mémoires*, 1:547.

23. O'Connell, *John Ireland*, 461–63.

24. Loisy, *Mémoires*, 1:523–24. Ireland, who had been educated in France, spoke and wrote the language fluently, though in a very simple style.

25. Von Hügel to Semeria, 15 January, 1897 and 21 September, 1899, in Giuseppe Zorzi (ed.), *Auf der Suche nach der verlorenen Katholizität. Die Briefe Friedrich von Hügels an Giovanni Semeria*, 2 vols. (Mainz: 1991), 1:351, 389.

26. O'Connell, *John Ireland*, 1–3.

27. John Ireland, "The Church and the Age," *The Church and Modern Society. Lectures and Addresses*, 2 vols. (New York: 1903), 1:107.

28. See O'Connell, *John Ireland*, 575, 585, and Houtin and Sartiaux, *Loisy*, 57, 64–65.

A genuine concern at any rate was developing within Leo XIII's entourage about dangerous alliances forming under the catchall banner of modern progress and adaptation to the contemporary world. And for those officers of the curia with a conspiratorial turn of mind, evidence close to home suggested possibly ominous connections. For example, an American priest, closely associated with Gibbons and Ireland, lived in a flat at number 61 Via Tritone. As early as 1897 soirées were held there each Tuesday attended by persons of various nationalities, whether residents of Rome like the host or visitors from abroad. They playfully dubbed their meeting-place "Liberty Hall" and their association "the Lodge."[29] Rumor had it that they excelled in witty and scathing criticism of the established order. Their provocative use of the terminology of Freemasonry may have been intended merely as an irritant to Vatican officialdom; more troubling was the attendance of certain ecclesiastics—perhaps even a cardinal now and then—who favored the reversal of the papacy's policy of nonrecognition of the Italian government. Louis Duchesne was a frequent guest on Tuesday evenings and Friedrich von Hügel an occasional one.

John Ireland believed that Leo XIII had intervened personally to soften the tone of *Testem Benevolentiae* and to distinguish Americanism in the positive sense of the word from a few bizarre ideas "set afloat in France."[30] If so, it indicated that Duchesne was mistaken in thinking the aged pope was no longer master in his own house. But it also meant that to the degree Cardinals Ledochowski and Mazzella, among others, succeeded in pressing forward a conservative agenda—in discerning and then exposing a conspiracy against the church on behalf of the forces of modernity—they did so with at least tacit approval from Leo. For the incurably naïve, like Ireland and von Hügel, the easy and natural way to explain this unhappy turn of events was to excuse the sovereign and blame the wicked ministers: Ledochowski, the tough old Prussian-Pole, who during the *Kulturkampf*, had been imprisoned by Bismarck, from whom he had learned all the arts of tyranny; and Mazzella, the characteristically cunning Italian Jesuit, ever on the lookout to suppress independence of thought. For the incurably cynical, like Duchesne, any interpretation was irrelevant. "The pope can change, or one or another of his advisers can disappear or be neutralized by somebody else; it will make no difference in the long run. . . . The whole point is to pass religion along in accord with traditional methods."[31]

ROMOLO MURRI had no quarrel—at least not yet—with traditional methods in passing religion along. What concerned him and other fervent young Italian Catholics was the social and political condition of their country. Intel-

29. Gerald P. Fogarty, *The Vatican and the Americanist Crisis: Denis J. O'Connell, American Agent in Rome, 1885–1903* (Rome: 1974), 257.

30. McAvoy, *Crisis*, 285.

31. Duchesne to von Hügel, 2 March, 1899, in Neveu (ed.), "Lettres . . . de Duchesne," *Mélanges*, 84: 589.

lectual elitists like Duchesne might fret at what appeared to them to be a hardening attitude of hostility within the Roman curia toward their endeavors. Murri by contrast found there encouragement and hope that a new day was about to dawn for *il pópulo Italiano*. In particular, he venerated and gloried in the leadership of Leo XIII, "that youthful nonagenarian."[32]

The bitter antagonism between church and state in Italy had continued unabated throughout the pontificate, however much informal arrangements between the two sides may have softened practical situations.[33] The pope still forbade the faithful to participate in national politics. As late as 1895 he reiterated his *non expedit*, insisting that it was still not expedient for Italian Catholics to vote in general elections. And woe betide any ecclesiastic who strayed from that policy. The founder and long-time editor of the *Civiltà Cattolica* was expelled from the Society of Jesus when he advocated reconciliation between the Vatican and the Quirinal. Likewise, a pamphlet with a similar recommendation written by the widely admired bishop of Cremona, Geremia Bonomelli, was immediately placed on the Index of forbidden books, and the bishop was obliged to retract its contents from the pulpit of his cathedral.[34] The same fate might have befallen any of the ordained "conciliationists" chattering away on a Tuesday evening at Liberty Hall, had they made their views public.

The pope continued to indulge his fondness for diplomatic solutions by attempting to inveigle the European powers into restoring to him at the very least civil jurisdiction over the city of Rome. Earlier successes had perhaps beguiled him too much; royalist Italy, like republican France, remained impervious to papal diplomacy.[35] Balancing this failure, however, was a record of remarkable domestic success. Under the leadership mostly of laymen and the lower clergy, Italian Catholics put together an organizational structure that to a degree negated their exclusion from the public life of the nation. Diocesan and parochial associations multiplied into the thousands, offering Catholics mutual support and social cohesion. Cooperatives and rural banks were founded, workingmen's clubs and trade unions organized, journals and newspapers established. Ultimately these institutions and activities coalesced into a national movement, the Opera dei Congressi e dei Comitati Cattolici.[36] This loose organiztion experienced many ups and downs, many internal squabbles and rivalries, but on the whole it prospered. After 1887 and an especially fierce outbreak of government-supported anticlericalism, it enjoyed the wholehearted support of Leo XIII.

32. Quoted in Binchy, *Church and State*, 62–63.

33. See chapter 2.

34. G. Mollat, *La question romaine de Pie Vi à Pie XI* (Paris: 1932), 394–95. See also L. Jadin, "Bonomelli (Geremia)," *Dictionnaire d'histoire et de géographie ecclesiastiques* (Paris: 1937), 9:1087–88.

35. For Leo XIII's mixed record, see the analysis of James E. Ward, "Leo XIII: The Diplomat Pope," *Review of Politics* 28 (1966): 47–61.

36. Aubert, "Pastorale et action catholique," in Aubert et al. (eds.), *Nouvelle histoire*, 5:151–54.

The leaders of the Catholic Congress reciprocated by manifesting an enmity and contempt for the liberal state which, if anything, outdid the pope's own. "The Christian transformation of society," said one of them, will "be brought about with the support of the people, under the church's guidance, against all forms of liberalism." Here was a direct challenge to those classically liberal politicians and capitalist entrepreneurs who had ruled Italy since the seizure of Rome, and it aroused much sympathy in a country enduring the curses, as well as the blessings, of rapid industrialization and urbanization. Even the members of the traditional ruling class began to sense, as the century was drawing to a close, that they had more to fear from the socialist agitators than from the priests. They were, some of them, prepared for a rapprochement with their erstwhile clericalist opponents, on the grounds that the political spectrum in Italy had shifted into the standard European pattern of the propertied versus the proletariat, of Right versus Left.[37] But the Catholic Congress was having none of it. "Let us approach the working man, who is escaping us," urged the same spokesman. Let us above all shun "the bourgeois liberals who call upon the priest's help to hold back the passion of the masses."[38] And Pope Leo encouraged that attitude in his celebrated encyclical *Rerum Novarum* (1891), which argued for a more equitable distribution of wealth and property, as well as for the rights of workers to organize and protect themselves against capitalist excess.

Meanwhile, in the inevitable course of things, a new generation of Italian Catholics had come to the fore, a generation that knew neither Cavour nor Garibaldi. Though to them the old church–state quarrels were hardly relevant any more, these *giovani cattolici* were just as contemptuous of liberalism as their predecessors in the Congress had been. They had the organizational achievements of those predecessors to build upon, and, as they assumed as their ideological mandate the sophisticated social teaching of *Rerum Novarum*, so also did the most aggressive of them endorse the pope's *non expedit*. This was because—a fact perhaps obscured by the uses of later terminology—the liberalism they had grown up despising was an elitist politics, a cabal of oligarchs, far removed, they maintained, from the interests of the masses of the people. The *non expedit* served a double purpose: it prevented those faithful Catholics who feared the rise of socialism from succumbing to the temptation of allying themselves with the liberals; and it provided time for the formation of a grand, popular movement which would bring about a genuinely Christian democracy.[39] In promoting this apparently contradictory position—to foster democracy by spurning the franchise—Romolo Murri found his mission in life. "Catholics ought to refrain [from voting]," he wrote, "not only out of obedi-

37. Denis Mack Smith, *Modern Italy* (London: 1962), 191–97.
38. Quoted in Richard Webster, *Christian Democracy in Italy* (London: 1961), 5.
39. Webster, *Christian Democracy*, 3–12.

ence to the Supreme Pontiff, but also with the conscious determination to render the most useful and, in the present circumstances, the best possible service to their own cause."[40]

Murri, born near Ascoli Piceno in 1870, came from the Marches, that part of central Italy bordering the Adriatic Sea. At fourteen he entered a regional minor seminary, and four years later moved on to the Capranica College in Rome, where he earned honors in philosophy, theology, and law. Padre Murri—he was ordained for the diocese of Fermo in 1893—emerged from his studies a patriot and an ardent Ultramontane, more interested, however, in practice than in theory. He was not untypical of a class of idealistic young Italian clerics whom his later associate, Ernesto Buonaiuti, remembered:

What a beautiful time it was for those young priests who followed their vocation and gave flight to their hopes, under the auspices of a pontificate so favorable to bold endeavors and courageous initiatives. It seemed, between 1890 and 1900, that the clergy . . . was going to attract and indeed absorb all the souls who felt beating and vibrating within themselves the dream of a great spiritual renewal. . . . So many youthful spirits, inside the austere cloister of the seminary, stayed on watch during the first nights of the new century, waiting, with anxious and prayerful attention, for the dawn of the kingdom of God.[41]

Murri from the beginning of his priesthood was a dynamo of action. Not for him the sedentary life of parish or classroom. He determined that he should be apostle to all of Italy, and the best way to accomplish that in modern times was to devote himself to organization and to journalism. In 1895 he established a union of students, the Federazione degli universitari Cattolici Italiani, the first of many leagues and associations that would owe their origin to him. As for the written and spoken word, his flair was immediately evident. His natural gift for platform oratory quickly made him a star at the rallies held by the Catholic Congress in various parts of the country, just as his fiery tirades against the corrupt liberal regime and in behalf of the pope's temporal power were stirring the readers of the confessional press.[42]

A contemporary described Murri as "a small man, very thin, with a swarthy complexion, bursting with energy, very outgoing, very lively, above all very headstrong. . . . Will-power wrapped in intelligence, that is the best way to characterize this active little man."[43] By the beginning of 1898 he had started a journal of his own, the *Cultura Sociale*, in which he wrote the essays later published under the appropriate title *Days of Battle*. Thus, for example, in August of that year he expressed in trenchant prose the essence of his message: "The pope sees himself in opposition to a fictitious Italy, the immense liberal

40. Quoted in Giampiero Cappelli, *Romolo Murri: Contributo per una Biografia* (Rome: 1965), 39.
41. Quoted in Rivière, *Modernisme*, 90. See also Cappelli, *Murri*, 2–3.
42. Houtin, *Modernisme*, 109.
43. Quoted in Rivière, *Modernisme*, 280–81.

state with all its hangers-on, dressed up as though it were the real Italy. The Italian clergy, backing up the pope, sees itself as the only force capable from now on of making headway against, of mounting even a gesture of resistance to, the terrible invasion of the official bourgeoisie that threatens to deluge us and to suppress all liberty."[44]

The events of May 3–8, 1898—the "fatti di Maggio"—proved a turning point in Murri's career. Bread riots in several Italian cities brought a violent response from the government. Troops were employed to restore order, and there was a bloody confrontation in Milan. Alleging collusion between Catholics and revolutionary socialists, the cabinet ordered the suppression of thousands of local Catholic organizations and the arrest of several leaders of the Catholic Congress.[45] These bogus charges merely heightened the tension. Murri, too young and raw to merit special attention from the police, seized the opportunity to press for an ever more radical program. In the wake of the May riots, and the consequent vacuum in the Catholic leadership, he founded the Lega Democratica Nazionale, an association explicitly independent of the ecclesiastical hierarchy. The idealism that this association stimulated and represented had nothing directly to do with people like Loisy and Blondel and Tyrrell, of whom at this date Murri had scarcely heard—except in its dedication to progress and liberty and an ill-defined modern spirit. Yet the day was not far off when the political activists and the scientific researchers would arrive at a meeting of minds.[46]

For the time being, however, the formation of such an alliance was held in check by the veneration Murri and his closest associates felt for Leo XIII.[47] Their trust in the old pontiff appeared vindicated with the appearance, in January 1901, of the encyclical *Graves de communi Re*.[48] "Christian Democracy," wrote Leo, "by the fact that it is Christian, is built, and necessarily so, on the basic principles of divine faith, and it must provide better conditions for the masses." But "it would be a crime to distort this name of Christian Democracy to politics, for, although democracy, both in its philological and philosophical significations, implies popular government, yet in its present application it must be employed without any political significance, so as to mean nothing else than this beneficent Christian action in behalf of the people." Romolo Murri received the encyclical with enthusiasm,[49] even though doubts were by then beginning to form in his mind whether, in Italy at the beginning of the twentieth century, "beneficent Christian action" could in fact "be employed without any political significance."

44. Quoted in Pietro Scoppola, *Crisi Modernista e Rinnovamento cattolico in Italia* (Bologna: 1961), 142.

45. Aubert, "Pastorale et action," 706–7.

46. See Rivière, *Modernisme*, 90–91.

47. See Rivière, *Modernisme*, 90–93.

48. English text in Carlen (ed.), *Encyclicals, . . . 1878–1903*, 480–86.

49. See Giorgio Candeloro, *Il Movimento cattolico in Italia* (Rome: 1974), 292–94.

VON HÜGEL MAINTAINED that Murri was too much a Scholastic in his thought patterns ever to have been a Modernist,[50] and certainly his preoccupations always remained social and political. But other young clerics, with whom he became more or less intimate, followed closely the critical and philosophical debates going on outside Italy. Among these was Salvatore Minocchi, Murri's schoolfellow at the Capranica. Student and later professor of Hebrew in Florence, his interest in biblical studies was genuine enough, though he was himself more a facilitator than a scholar. In 1901—following the familiar pattern made possible by the modest publishing costs of the time—Minocchi founded a journal, the *Studi Religiosi*, which provided a platform for bright and adventuresome young Italian Catholics who committed themselves to a spiritual renewal as eagerly as himself and Murri.[51] Two years later, when he was forty-three, Minocchi made a much-publicized pilgrimage to Tolstoy's place of retirement in Jasnaïa Poliana. "I would hope," said the great novelist and self-styled mystic, "that the clergy would abandon the church. The church, Catholic and Orthodox alike, has falsified the gospel and corrupted the true conception of the Christian life." Tolstoy had been excommunicated from the Orthodox church a few years earlier.

Minocchi was accompanied on this romantic journey by the Barnabite friar Giovanni Semeria. In their respectful response to the Russian sage the two Italian priests testified to their conviction that, "despite everything," the Christian life "continues to be nourished within the bosom of the church and the living Gospel is still preached there." Their duty, they said, was to avoid giving scandal by "useless apostasy" and, instead, "to raise the Church to the level of their own religious ideals."[52] Semeria by that time had been for several years a friend and indeed a disciple of Friedrich von Hügel,[53] and he had also made the acquaintance of Loisy and the liberal Protestant theologian Paul Sabatier.[54] His sympathies, largely framed by these foreign influences, were reflected in the splendid oratory that had earned him his reputation across the length and breadth of Italy. But he was no more a serious scholar than Minocchi or Murri, and his romanticism sometimes verged into delusion; he entertained the fancy, for example, that, thanks to the kinship of Anglicanism and Catholicism, the British Tommy had carried devotion to the Virgin Mary to the far outposts of the British Empire.[55]

Cut from very different cloth was Giovanni Genocchi. Nearly a decade older than Murri, Minocchi, and Semeria—who were often guests at his table—

50. See Loisy, *Mémoires*, 2:561.

51. Rivière, *Modernisme*, 91.

52. Quoted in Houtin, *Modernism*, 111–12.

53. See chapter 10. For an example of the baron's role as absentee teacher, see von Hügel to Semeria, 5 June, 1903, in Zorzi (ed.), *Briefe . . . von Hügels an . . . Semeria*, 2:476–81.

54. See chapter 10.

55. Ward, *The Wilfrid Wards*, 1:283.

Genocchi belonged to a small and obscure religious order. He was a man of broad experience in the ecclesiastical world, having served in the Vatican diplomatic corps in Damascus and Constantinople and as a missionary in New Guinea before returning to Italy in 1897 as local superior of his congregation. He was also genuinely learned in a way his younger colleagues were not: even Loisy thought him an astute critic, and von Hügel, who regularly wintered in Rome during the late 1890s, discovered in him a soul mate almost from the moment the two met.[56] To such persons it was no small recommendation that Genocchi early on gained the enmity of Cardinal Mazzella, who instigated his dismissal from the biblical lectureship he had briefly held in one of the pontifical universities. This "sudden, absolute, forced discharge of my good and brave Father Genocchi," as von Hügel complained to Maurice Blondel, was one more unhappy sign of the Roman times as far as "our poor biblical critics" were concerned.[57] Genocchi, for his part, reacted to his embarrassment rather less heatedly: "[It was] painful," he observed in an awkward English syntax the baron must have appreciated, "not certainly for my case which is to me perfectly indifferent, but for the consequences that may follow: to the evil of our Church."[58] Genocchi at any rate, whatever his scholarly opinions, had the instincts of a *politique*, and he took care that the animosity of even so powerful a bureaucrat as Mazzella did not break his lines of communication with Leo XIII. In this he succeeded: he remained securely a *persona grata* with the pope.

Finally, in the spring of 1900, there was added to this small circle of talented but as yet little-known Italians, all clerics, a figure of national and even world renown. Antonio Fogazzaro was a true literary lion, a novelist, critic, and poet whose works were read and applauded all over Europe.[59] In April 1900 he was inducted into the Italian Senate, a body of parliamentary grandees not elected but appointed by the king. The post was largely honorific, in Fogazarro's case a recognition of his artistic achievements. Nevertheless, the new senator took seriously the committees and commissions he served on, with the result that now he came frequently to Rome from his ordinary residence in Vicenza. During these sojourns he often visited a friend's house on the Piazza Rondanini, a place also frequented by Genocchi and like-minded intellectuals.

Fogazzaro brought an entirely different perspective to the little group of zealots. At fifty-eight he was a generation older than Genocchi and—with his thick grey hair and moustache, his pince-nez, his frock coat and high collar— must have appeared grandfatherly to the others. He was a layman. His whole life had been devoted to the lonely craft of literary creation, and yet he prided himself upon being a man in full contact with the currents of his time. The

56. See the notice in Houtin and Sartiaux, *Loisy*, 356, and De la Bedoyere, *Hügel*, 105–6.

57. Von Hügel to Blondel, 29 July, 1898, in Marlé (ed.), *Au cœur*, 26.

58. Genocchi to von Hügel, 24 July, 1898, in Zorzi (ed.), *Briefe . . . von Hügels an . . . Semeria*, 2:377.

59. For a bibliographical list, see Robert A. Hall, Jr., *Antonio Fogazzaro* (New York: 1978), 147.

fact that he had been honored by the House of Savoy provided a clue to his orientation: he was a liberal Catholic of the old school, one who had admired Cavour and the Risorgimento and who deplored papal intransigence over the Roman question. His closest clerical friend was Bishop Bonomelli of Cremona. Nor did he see the quarrel between the Vatican and the Quirinal as a political matter. "My convictions . . . are entirely religious," he wrote in 1896. The intentions and deeds of those who seized Rome in 1870 may have been unworthy, "but I am convinced, profoundly convinced, that [those] events . . . were most salutary for the Church, that they mark the beginning of her purification and regeneration and of the ascension of the Roman Pontificate towards sublime heights."[60]

Such sentiments may have received, at first, short shrift from the likes of Romolo Murri, but they were consistent with the pattern of Fogazzaro's life. The religion that suffused his thought and action had to contain above all a capacity for vibrant purification, personal and institutional. And that purification was for him a by-product of growth. Fogazzaro testified to this conviction not only in the emotions displayed in his fiction and poetry, but also in his solemn if amateurish critique of modern science. He was fascinated, for example, by Darwininan evolution, and he liked to say that both the scientists and their opponents had put the cart before the horse; it was not a question of man *descending* but rather of *ascending* from a lower state. He had lost his faith as a young man and had regained it after an experience at once religious and intellectual, brought on by reading a little treatise by the French Oratorian A.J.A. Gratry, the same Gratry who had inspired Ollé-Laprune, and through him Blondel and Lucien Laberthonnière.[61] Indeed, when in 1898 he was given a copy of Laberthonnière's "Le dogmatisme moral," Fogazzaro discovered in it—as in their different ways had Tyrrell and Maude Petre—a philosophical statement of all the mystical yearnings he had long felt within himself.[62]

So once again, ever so gently, the lines were converging.

IT IS A CERTAINTY that those who gathered privately at the apartment on the Via Tritone or at the house on the Piazza Rondanini never met Rafael Merry del Val there, though it is not unlikely that they frequently invoked his name, albeit through clenched teeth. In 1900 Merry del Val, at thirty-five, was already a titular archbishop and president of the Accademia dei Nobili Ecclesiastici, the prestigious institution that trained papal diplomats. And he already had begun to be seen in these circles as an evil genius. Louis Duchesne, for example, blamed Merry del Val for a campaign of intrigue that led to the

60. Quoted in Tommaso Gallarati-Scotti, *The Life of Antonio Fogazzaro* (New York: n. d. [1922]), 174–81. See also Antonio Piromalli, *Introduzione a Fogazzaro* (Rome: 1990), 29–30.

61. See chapter 5.

62. Gallaratti-Scotti, *Fogazzaro*, 139–42, 198–201.

condemnation of Americanism.[63] The same people also held him responsible—and with more reason—for the refusal of the Vatican to accept the validity of Anglican orders.[64] Indeed, the young archbishop, even at this early date, was well on his way to establishing the mixed reputation that has been his ever since: a reactionary *bête noire* to some, a saintly white knight to others.

His paternal antecedents had moved from Ireland to Spain during the eighteenth century, and his wealthy grandfather had married an Aragonese noblewoman, whose family name he had joined to his own: hence, Merry del Val. Raphael's father was a career officer in the Spanish diplomatic corps, serving with distinction in England, Belgium, Austria, and, for many years, as ambassador to the Holy See. His mother, Sophia Josephine de Zulueta, belonged to a branch of the noble Basque house of Torre Diaz that had settled in England and reaped a fortune in shipping and banking; her mother was Scottish.[65]

This rich cosmopolitan background, so similar to that of Friedrich von Hügel,[66] gave shape to Merry del Val's career. Born in London and largely educated in England—he did the college course at Ushaw a few years after Wilfrid Ward had left there[67]—he thought of himself as an Englishman, to the degree that he entertained any concept of nationality. "I dream in English," he once said half jokingly.[68] But he was fluent in four other languages and had studied also with French and Belgian Jesuits, who taught him, besides the ordinary classical curriculum, the importance of the style and polish proper to a continental aristocrat. By his twentieth birthday he was a crack shot, a daring rider, a proficient fencer and swimmer, and played a mean game of chess. He did not practice these skills later—except perhaps the last—but they helped forge a personality at once disciplined and competitive. Tall and slender, he never put on flesh, and, except for a receding hairline, he kept his darkly Latin good looks till the end of his life. His courtly manners charmed not a few, including von Hügel's daughters and mother-in-law who saw a good deal of him in Rome. Josephine Ward, on the other hand, thought him rather pompous.[69]

From his childhood Rafael had aspired to the priesthood, much to the delight of his exceedingly pious parents. He always claimed that his real ambition was to serve as a simple pastor in a poor parish and that the high offices he held had been thrust upon him more or less against his will. This fairly common clerical posturing—Duchesne had protested much the same in his own case[70]—need not be taken very seriously. Nevertheless, it is undeniable

---

63. Duchesne to Von Hügel, 18 August, 1898, in Neveu (ed.), "Lettres . . . de Duchesne," *Melanges*, 84:586.

64. See chapter 6.

65. Vigilio Dalpiaz, *Cardinal Merry del Val* (London: 1937), 1–5, and Pio Cenci, *Il Cardinale Raffaele Merry del Val* (Rome: 1933), 4–12.

66. See chapter 3.   67. See chapter 6.

68. Marie Cecilia Buehrle, *Rafael Cardinal Merry del Val* (London: 1957), 276.

69. Ward, *The Wilfrid Wards*, 1:229.

70. See chapter 4.

that Merry del Val was a genuinely prayerful man and that, even in the midst
of immense official labors, his works of pastoral mercy abounded: if he did not
manage to keep himself entirely unspotted from this world, yet many Roman
widows and orphans in their tribulation received care from him.[71]

But his true gifts lay in another direction. From the moment in 1885 when,
at the personal insistence of Leo XIII, he was enrolled in the Accademia dei
Nobili Ecclesiastici rather than in an ordinary seminary, his clerical career
passed uninterruptedly from triumph to triumph. He grasped seemingly by
instinct the workings of the ecclesiastical bureaucracy, and the smile of the old
pope's favor beamed down unremittingly upon him: he was appointed a papal
chamberlain, with the title of *monsignore*, even before he was ordained in
1888.[72] His early promotions were no doubt attributable in part to his rank,
his linguistic attainments, his social graces, his willingness to please his superiors. But he also worked hard, even relentlessly, and he displayed the adroit-
ness and the mastery of detail required of an effective administrator. These
qualities did not prevent him, however, from taking a definite stand on a given
issue: when he served as secretary to the pontifical commission inquiring into
the validity of Anglican orders, he lobbied hard for the negative decision the
commission ultimately reached.[73] In 1897 he scored a particularly brilliant
success on a delicate mission to Canada, where Catholics were embroiled in a
dispute with the government over education. The pope paid his young delegate a singular compliment by explicitly praising him in the encyclical he later
wrote on the subject.[74]

There has hardly ever been as attractive a representative as Rafael Merry del
Val of that phenomenon—elusive of definition and yet powerful in its implications—called *romanità*. The Roman ideal, a captivating mixture of myth and
reality, gave form and substance to the life of this handsome, cultivated, single-minded man. No one appreciated better than he the grandeur of papal
Rome, the magnitude of its spiritual and cultural achievement. New centuries
came and went; new sciences appeared and then vanished; but Rome was forever. There could be no higher vocation than upholding, at whatever cost, her
prerogatives. The very survival of Catholic truth depended upon it. If this
conviction brought him enemies, so be it. Wilfrid Ward may have thought
Catholicism's time of siege was over;[75] not so Merry del Val, who from the
battlements of the Vatican saw hordes of new Vandals and Visigoths pressing
toward the gates.

71. Epistle of James, 1:27.

72. Cenci, *Merry del Val*, 34.

73. Dalpiaz, *Merry del Val*, 31–41, Barmann, *Hügel*, 60–61, and, for relevant correspondence,
Hughes, *Absolutely Null*, 295–307

74. *Affari Vos*, 8 December, 1897. English text in Carlen (ed.), *Encyclicals . . . 1878–1903*, 429–
32. "Charged to make a careful survey of the situation and to report upon it to Us, [our Delegate
Apostolic] has with fidelity and ability fulfilled the task we imposed upon him" (430).

75. See chapter 8.

CHAPTER 12

The Perils of Moderation

There are two societies all the more unresponsive and unintelligible one to the other, because their antagonism is an antagonism rooted in ideas. . . . Such indeed is the nature of the conflict between the society of tradition and the new society. . . . We are two civilizations in the same fatherland, inseparable and yet irreconcilable. Where shall we find the calming voices that will establish if not unity, then at least harmony?

—*Pierre Batiffol* (1899)[1]

LOUIS DUCHESNE'S intense dislike of Archbishop Merry del Val was mitigated at least on one occasion by an uncharacteristic sentiment: "I hope that God will forgive him," the historian wrote piously.[2] He had no such prayers to say for Pierre Batiffol. "This gentleman," he told Alfred Loisy, is "an evil beast, absolutely destitute of sincerity in his noisy orthodoxy." He is "a Pharisee," intent upon "wounding you and me."[3] The bitterness of this indictment was perhaps traceable to the fact that Batiffol, as a student at the Institut Catholique of Paris, had been a favorite of Duchesne, and the older man took credit for having launched the younger one on his scholarly career.[4] There had indeed been a time when Duchesne hosted an annual luncheon for his two prize pupils, Batiffol and Loisy. But these two, natural rivals, had never gotten along; their temperaments and their ambitions were too much out of joint. And now that Batiffol had achieved a certain prominence—not unlike his own—Duchesne detected in him traitorous leanings.

For he was now Monseigneur Batiffol, having been appointed in 1898, when he was thirty-seven, rector of the Institut Catholique of Toulouse. He

1. Quoted in Poulat, *Histoire, dogme*, 370.
2. Duchesne to von Hügel, 18 August, 1898, in Neveu (ed.), "Lettres . . . de Duchesne," *Mélanges*, 84:586.
3. Duchesne to Loisy, 25 February, 1898, in Neveu (ed.), "Lettres . . . de Duchesne," *Mélanges*, 84:292–93.
4. See chapter 7.

came to this post with the reputation of a progressive, as might have been expected of one who had been trained by Duchesne, and hard-line conservatives understandably regarded his appointment with some distaste. It was Batiffol's fate not to be wholly trusted by either set of opponents—"la société de tradition" or "la societé nouvelle," to use his own words. He was not a Scholastic, but a historian of liturgy and dogma with an already impressive publication record.[5] He was moreover a man given to frank speech, often sarcastically expressed, which earned him enmities he could ill afford. But it was not this trait that aroused the ire of the similarly acerbic Duchesne, or that of the much milder Friedrich von Hügel, who scolded Batiffol for his hostility toward Loisy.[6]

The fact was that with his rectorship and prelacy Batiffol had attained an ecclesiastical status that automatically—in an institution so respectful of the prerogatives of office—lent weight to everything he did and said. And his prestige increased with the obvious success of his administration at Toulouse: the *institut* there thrived under his forceful leadership and rapidly became the dynamic center of Catholic intellectual life across southern France. He also had at his disposal the journal published by the *institut*—the *Bulletin de littérature ecclésiastique*—thanks to which even his lightest comments were guaranteed an audience.

As to Loisy, what von Hügel considered hostility might better have been described as professional ambivalence. At least Batiffol was willing to recognize in his former schoolfellow

an uncommon scientific talent resulting from a highly developed understanding and penetrating critique, as much in the field of Semitic philology as in that of contemporary religious thought; a remarkable ability also for subtle expression which now and then exhibits an unaffected interior beauty; the sincerity, finally, of a religious spirit that has never evaded the problems its scientific work has inevitably given rise to: these are the reasons that explain the dominance Father Loisy has attained over the minds of many people, and it would be churlish to deny that they are well founded.[7]

Yet, at the same time, the rector of Toulouse was anxious to stake out ground different from that of the recluse of Neuilly and Bellevue—a position that Duchesne, ever ready to rebuke in private, labeled Batiffol's "noisy orthodoxy." A personal epithet of this sort served little purpose perhaps, but the divergence of view that it suggested was of crucial importance in understanding the struggles that were about to begin in earnest. Loisy and those who agreed with him insisted that a sharp distinction existed between critical history and dogmatic theology. The former possessed as much integrity as the latter, and its methodological independence—based upon knowledge of lan-

5. See the list in Rivière, "Batiffol," *Dictionnaire de théologie catholique*, 3:1329.

6. Barmann, *Hügel*, 87–88.

7. Quoted in Rivière, *Modernisme*, 97–98.

guages and of comparative religions—determined that its conclusions were no less valid. It was wrong to contend that the higher critic had to submit his findings to the judgment of the theologian, whose deductive reasonings might or might not be in conformity with what history has revealed. Far from realizing a warrant for his conclusions from the approval of dogmatic teaching, the critic relied for legitimacy solely upon the canons of his science. Thus, as early as 1886, Loisy was convinced that "he suffered under Pontius Pilate" was the sole article of the Catholic creed he could accept as fact, because only Christ's death had been confirmed by the testimony of near-contemporary witnesses.[8]

Pierre Batiffol accepted the distinction up to a point. There was, he agreed, a separation between critique and theology, but neither of these two ought to be considered an "airtight compartment" (the expression was Renan's), so that "the facts that history discovers would be entirely detached from the interpretations and deductions to which said facts give birth and which belong properly to the theologian. This dichotomy I believe is false." What is needed is a critique at once "progessive and theological." Researchers, to be sure, must confront the evidence of history on its own terms, must "study the [biblical] text in itself, without placing in quarantine the rule of faith, but also without considering the conclusions that can be logically deduced from it as the first and authentic meaning of the text." Nevertheless, the status of such criticism, Batiffol argued, is provisional, "a phase," because in the end its findings must be ratified by the dogmatic teaching "to which it is ordered if not subordinated."

In the fevered atmosphere of the time Batiffol's fairly subtle attempt to find a median position was not calculated to please partisans to his right or to his left. Yet he did not hesitate to predict dire consequences for religion if the realm of discoverable fact were to be cut off from conventional theology and institutional structures:

Catholicism is not only a life, an interior and a social life, which is what the Americanists want to reduce it to. Catholicism is also revealed thought that a living authority, aided by the Holy Ghost, upholds and develops. What is one to say of those very imprudent priests who, to preserve the life of the spirit in themselves, of set purpose cultivate only secular and non-Catholic sources, who have only contempt for theology and theologians, who entertain more or less consciously the radical design of transforming defined and objective thought into a totally subjective symbolism? . . . For us the inspiration of Scripture and the authority of the church are of the essence of our religion. For Protestants, on the other hand, such essence consists uniquely in a faith . . . which is not of the intellectual order. Consequently it is independent of facts and . . . addresses only the heart . . . and subjective experience. By abdicating the

8. See John Ratté, *Three Modernists* (New York: 1967), 45, and Ward, *The Wilfrid Wards*, 2:504.

intellectual character of faith, [Protestantism] creates a contradiction between the Christian life and scientific theology.[9]

In these formal statements Batiffol named no names. But in a letter of June 1900 he was less circumspect: "We shall have to be very much on our guard. Loisy's articles on revelation have made quite a stir here, and the Jesuits are going to go after him. I sympathize with them on this point, because this philosophy of religion will end only with the ruin of the little progress our realism has been able to produce." The articles to which he referred were those of "A. Firmin," a "synthesis," to his mind, "of pure Protestantism."[10]

THE FRIEND TO WHOM BATIFFOL addressed this warning was Marie-Joseph Lagrange, the Dominican, now forty-five, who still filled the double role of editor of the *Revue biblique* and director of the École Biblique in Jerusalem, where he usually resided. Since 1892 Batiffol had been secretary of the *Revue* and its agent in Paris.[11] Once installed in his rectorship he offered to establish an academic chair for Lagrange and urged that together they publish an expanded *Revue* out of Toulouse. Lagrange was tempted, though he admitted candidly that if he were to teach regularly he should do so in Paris, where his influence would have more effect. In the end, however, the Dominican authorities vetoed the idea, pointing out the need to concentrate slender resources of men and money.[12] So in 1898 the formal collaboration between Lagrange and Batiffol came to an amicable end. Their intellectual solidarity—"their syndicate," as Loisy called it[13]—did not.

To steer a middle course was particularly hazardous for a Scripture scholar, and Lagrange focused as much as possible his own research and that of the contributors to his journal upon noncontroversial areas. Even so, complaints were heard: one French Dominican forbade his penitents to read the *Revue biblique*. When Lagrange contemplated an article on the tortured question of the origins of the Pentateuch, his advisers, including Batiffol—who "was intimidated for the moment"—tried to dissuade him. The piece appeared in due course,[14] and its author took much heavier fire from the conservative right than from the progressive left. Loisy's sarcastic jibes[15] were mild compared to the harsh accusations leveled by, among others, a Jesuit writing in *Etudes*: We are

9. Quoted in Poulat, *Histoire, dogme*, 366–70.

10. Batiffol to Lagrange, 2 June, 1900, quoted in Pierre Fernessole, *Témoins de la pensée catholique en France sous la IIIe république* (Paris: 1940), 225. For "A. Firmin," see chapter 10.

11. See chapter 7.

12. M.-J. Lagrange, "L'École biblique des Dominicains de Jéruslaem. Souvenirs personnels, 1889–1913," in Pierre Benoit (ed.), *Le père Lagrange: au service de la bible* (Paris: 1967), 89.

13. Loisy, *Mémoires*, 1:486.

14. M.-J. Lagrange, "Les sources du Pentateuch," *Revue biblique* 7 (January 1898): 10–32.

15. See note 70, chapter 10.

afflicted today by "brothers in the faith" who seek out "the enemy encampment," these "turncoats (*transfuges*)," most notably "the eminent editor of the *Revue biblique*," whose passage "to the camp of our adversaries has inflicted grief upon good people."[16] When the Latin patriarch of Jerusalem, an ordinarily jovial Italian Franciscan, paid a ceremonial visit to the École Biblique, he did not bother to tell its director that he had sent to Rome two days before a secret denunciation of him and his article.[17]

All these rumblings made Lagrange's superiors extremely nervous. In the winter of 1899 the Dominican master general laid down new and severe guidelines: "I believe it most necessary, and this I impose as a matter of obedience, that the manuscripts of all pieces you intend to print in the *Revue biblique* be sent to Rome beforehand, and I reserve to myself the choice of censors and to myself as well the definitive decision as to their publication." He also strongly suggested that another priest be put temporarily in charge of the École.[18] "Counsel and command were all one to me," Lagrange said, and a new regime was promptly installed in Jerusalem. This loss of authority—which indeed did prove temporary—and even the censorship of his own writings he resented less than the subsequent reorganization of the *Revue biblique*. Assigned to the journal as secretary was a Parisian Dominican and a Thomist moral philosopher of no mean talent, who, however, knew nothing about biblical studies. Lagrange vainly protested the appointment of one whose clear function as watchdog could only harm the reputation of the *Revue*.[19] Meanwhile, the censors recommended delay in publishing articles he had written on Tobias and Noah. "What somber forebodings I had," Lagrange remembered. And as though his professional difficulties were not enough, he learned in the early summer of 1899 that his widowed mother was seriously ill. But when he proposed a journey to Europe, an aide to the master general replied, "Despite the unhappy situation Madame your Mother finds herself in, your presence in France or in Rome would not be opportune at this moment."[20]

Lagrange suspected that these troubles had befallen him primarily because of the complaint registered by the Latin patriarch. Such at any rate was the rumor current in Rome. "At this moment," Duchesne told Loisy, "it is the *Revue biblique* and the École at Jerusalem that are raising questions here. I have heard that the Holy Office, alerted by the Patriarch of Jerusalem, has taken the matter up. If so, the outcome is uncertain."[21] And it remained so, at least

---

16. Quoted in Lagrange, *Loisy et modernisme*, 102–3.
17. Lagrange, "L'École biblique," 85–86.
18. Frühwirth to Lagrange, 29 January, 1899, in Lagrange, "L'École biblique," 328.
19. The unwelcome secretary was Antonin-Dalmace Sertillanges (1863–1948), author of, among other prestigious works, *La philosophie de Saint Thomas d'Aquin*, 2 vols. (Paris: 1940). In 1907, however, in the wake of *Pascendi*, he fell under official suspicion and was forced to resign his chair at the Institut Catholique of Paris.
20. Lagrange, "L'École biblique," 98–102.
21. Quoted in Loisy, *Mémoires*, 1:515.

until March 26, 1900, when Cardinal Mazzella died. Lagrange thought it no coincidence that only three days later the Dominican master general passed along an invitation to a scholarly conference to be held in Rome and authorized him to accept it. "Rightly or wrongly, it was widely believed that [Mazzella] instigated whatever rigorous measures Leo XIII adopted."[22]

But in a larger sense Lagrange, as he reconstructed the events, came to blame Loisy himself, or rather "the reentry of Monsieur Loisy on the scene" by way of the pseudonymous articles in the *Revue du clergé français* and elsewhere. "There came then a gushing out of the critical spirit, a veritable swarm of criticism. We appeared to be, my collaborators and I, a part of this vast movement (*levée en masse*)." The whole scholarly community knew that Loisy had publicly submitted to the teaching of *Providentissimus Deus*. "If he had since fallen into error, was my fidelity any more assured than his?"

It was a reasonable question to which Lagrange had an answer: "There were always differences between us. First of all, it has to be evident that out of good faith I looked for solutions that the theologians could accept." Such an attitude—disparaged as "a failure of logic or of honesty"—had won him no admirers among non-Catholics who dismissed it as "fatal prejudice." Loisy, by contrast, was lauded by such people for having no care except discovery of the truth, but the praise was misplaced for one "who has the Catholic faith [and therefore] defers to the church in the domain of revealed truth, inaccessible to reason." Other divergences, however, loomed larger.

Clearly Monsieur Loisy did not admit the inerrancy of the Scriptures. He freely employed the term "relative truth," one that I have always avoided, and he never troubled himself to provide a theological explanation which authorized his historical criticism. I have always remained faithful to the tradition asserted anew by Leo XIII . . . that Scripture affirms [*affirme*] nothing erroneous. But the pope admitted that in scientific matters the sacred writer spoke in accord with appearances, in such a way that his wording [*énonciation*] must not be confused with his formal and solemn teaching [*affirmation*]. I have never advanced the foolishness that biblical history is only an appearance, nor have I ineptly confounded history and the sciences. . . . I recognize in primitive history certain manners of popular speech, in more recent texts a rather broader and more systematic mode of expression, in the historical writings themselves certain details . . . that lack full value as history strictly defined. Inspiration does not alter the nature of the literary genres which are linked to the history, nor does it augment the number of solemn teachings [*affirmations*]. But when the solemn teachings exist within their own historical scope, they communicate divine authority to it.

As for the Pentateuch, Lagrange believed "no more than Monsieur Loisy that it issued full-blown from Moses under the form it has now." But he repudiated the religious evolutionism Loisy had allegedly learned from the German critics, and he did apply to those five books "a certain substantial [Mosaic] authen-

22. Lagrange, "L'École biblique," 106.

ticity which however," he admitted ruefully, "I have never been permitted to explain."[23]

Perhaps the turbulent times unhappily made all explanations difficult. One thing in any event seems clear: the strict regimen at Salamanca, where the *Summa* of Aquinas was analyzed article by article, had engendered immeasurably more respect for the traditional theological enterprise than had the casual inquiries carried on in the *grand séminaire* at Chalons-sur-Marne.[24] It may also have engendered more prudence than courage. So concluded one contemporary wag whom Lagrange good-naturedly quoted: "You ask the difference between these two biblical critics? One smelled the burning faggot, and the other did not."[25] But then prudence too is a virtue.

NOT THAT THE SECOND of this duo of biblical critics overlooked the value of prudence, a prudence indeed of a highly self-serving variety. In the wake of Cardinal Richard's censure of the last of his "Firmin" articles,[26] Alfred Loisy received from a consultor of the Holy Office a communication suggesting that he henceforth submit his biblical writings to that Roman congregation for analysis. Though bitter out of the conviction that Richard had delated him to Rome, Loisy prudently complied and sent a copy of "La religion d'Israel" to the functionary with a covering letter in which he said: "I have tried to show how a regenerated history results in testimony favorable to the supernatural reality of revelation . . . I believe the Bible to be inspired whole and entire and inspired for the sake of truth. . . . Permit me to say to you finally, my Very Reverend Father, that I do not believe I have within myself, whatever others may say, the stuff of a heresiarch or even of a heretic."[27]

By the time he offered these assurances Loisy had embarked upon a new undertaking. His disavowal of the archdiocesan pension[28] had removed Fr 800 from his income. Thanks to the intervention of a friend, he was presented with an opportunity to replace that sum and even increase it. The friend was Paul Desjardins,[29] a forty-year-old teacher and administrator in the *université*, who had cemented his position in the educational establishment by marrying the stepdaughter of the president of the Collège de France. Desjardins was intensely interested in religion, about which he held highly eccentric views. He

23. Lagrange, "L'École biblique," 95–97. *Affirmer* and *affirmation* in French suggest a legally binding statement.

24. See chapters 7 and 1.

25. Lagrange, "L'École biblique," 96.

26. See chapter 10.

27. Loisy to Lepidi, 12 May, 1901, quoted partially in Loisy, *Choses passées*, 228–29, and completely in *Mémoires*, 2:37–39, to which is attached an explanatory note, saying that by revelation he meant "the birth of reason" and "human liberty." Besides his consultorship Alberto Lepidi (1838–1925), a Dominican, was at the time master of the Sacred Palace, which meant he was officially the pope's personal theologian.

28. See chapter 10.

29. See Houtin, *Modernisme*, 18–19.

described himself as a "spiritual freethinker" and esteemed the various Christian sects impartially, declaring them to be helpful "introductions" to "true religion"—a term he had difficulty defining. He cultivated clergymen of all denominations, and when he once had an audience with Leo XIII his mother supposedly explained, "Paul has gone to ask the pope's permission to become a Protestant minister."

Desjardins was hardly equipped to understand the technicalities in Loisy's work, or even less its subtly expressed subcurrents. But over the seven or eight years of their acquaintance he had acquired a genuine regard for the exegete, in whose behalf now, in 1900, he used his university connections. The upshot of the negotiations was an offer to Loisy to teach a course in the prestigious École Pratique des Hautes Études[30] with a stipend of Fr 1,000. In addition, he received a guarantee of a further Fr 2,400, to be paid during 1902 and 1903, when he joined a team of scholars preparing collections of sources of ancient Semitic history for publication. On December 12, 1900, "le petit Loisy," neatly garbed in his black soutane, walked up the gentle slope of the rue Saint-Jacques to the Sorbonne to deliver his first lecture; the subject he chose was Babylonian myths and the first chapters of Genesis.[31]

Financial considerations, however, took second place in Loisy's mind as he began this phase of his career. "My joining the staff of the École," he said later, "was a response, indirect but clear, to the censure that had been directed at 'Firmin.' I entered into battle with the archbishop of Paris. Nobody in the ecclesiastical world was under any illusion in this regard."[32] Certainly, Cardinal Richard himself was not. Two weeks after that first lecture he sent word to Loisy that he would be "very happy" to see him. The interview, held the next morning, was stormy but inconclusive. The cardinal regretted that the exegete had chosen to associate himself with Protestants and nonbelievers hostile to the church. The exegete protested that "in civilized countries people were no longer condemned without giving them a hearing." The cardinal brushed aside this reference to "Firmin" and grieved that the exegete had fallen under "German influences." He wondered how attributing the Gospels to the thought processes of the Evangelists left any room for the action of the Holy Ghost. "It would have been very difficult to make the venerable prelate understand that the action of the Holy Ghost, outside the thought of the author, had every chance of losing itself in the void."[33] So they parted, with both of them aware that if Richard had no direct power over Loisy himself, he could interfere with what was published, and to a degree with what was said by a priest within the confines of the archdiocese of Paris.

30. See chapter 1. The École was originally structured into four "sections"—mathematics, physics and chemistry, life sciences, and history and philology. In 1886, when the state faculty of Catholic theology was suppressed, a fifth section, *sciences religieuses*, was added.
31. Houtin and Sartiaux, *Loisy*, 97–101.
32. Loisy, *Mémoires*, 2:9.
33. Loisy, *Choses passées*, 222–24.

That may explain why Loisy's lectures at the École received such mixed reviews. Some said they manifested undiluted rationalism, while others vehemently denied the allegation. His new colleagues tended to find them obscure and fragmentary, as though he were unwilling to reveal his whole mind, and they concluded that, despite his quarrel with Richard, Loisy, as a priest, could not exercise full independence of thought. They may also have been put off by his prickly disposition. In any event, in April 1901 the faculty formally refused to endorse his candidacy for a chair in the École that had just fallen vacant. Loisy's bitter resentment at this slight lasted all his life. "My first contact with lay science convinced me that a certain narrowness of spirit must not be thought of as the monopoly of Catholic theologians. . . . An anticlerical fanatic has exactly the same mean, intransigent, inquisitorial mentality as a clerical fanatic."[34] So he remained an untenured instructor, working under a contract renewable year by year. Nor could he be dissuaded that he would have been awarded a professorship had he been willing to take off the soutane.

ALFRED LOISY CONTINUED to reside in Bellevue, safe from the canonical clutches of Cardinal Richard. Among his neighbors was Abbé Félix Klein, still a professor in the Institut Catholique and still smarting from the wounds inflicted by *l'affaire américaniste*.[35] The two of them were never close friends, but they did often take their daily constitutionals together in the woods of Meudon. At about this time—the summer of 1901—a much more important relationship began for Loisy.

Albert-Jules-Henri Houtin came from Anjou, in the west of France. His father was a baker-turned dry-goods merchant in a succession of small towns, and his mother a prosperous farmer's daughter. Their marriage was not altogether typical of their time and place in that the husband was a nonbeliever—a "deist," according to his son—and the wife very devout. The Angevin villages Albert knew in his boyhood "were still Catholic. On Sunday everybody went to mass in the morning, and it was not rare even for the men of the parish to assist at vespers." So the tension produced in the Houtin household by religious differences was something the lad remembered, as he did his father's reluctance to accept his own desire to be a priest. In 1880, at thirteen, Albert entered the *petit séminaire* at Angers, moved on six years later to the *grand séminiare*, where he was taught by the Sulpicians, and then, in 1888, announced that he wanted to become a Benedictine monk. "My father, who had already made a great sacrifice in allowing me to go to the seminary, fell into a deep depression and at first refused his consent. But he was so good, so respectful of the consciences of others, that he soon relented." Monsieur Houtin need not have worried: his son lasted less than a year in the abbey at nearby Solemnes—

---

34. Loisy, *Mémoires*, 2:32–33.
35. See chapter 11.

celebrated particularly for its revival of Gregorian plainsong—and when his son was ordained in 1891 for the diocese of Angers, he no doubt accepted it as the lesser of two evils.[36]

Though the Benedictine ideal, and with it a hankering after mystical experience, continued to fire the imagination of young Abbé Houtin, his assignment to teach in the same *petit séminaire* he had himself attended opened up other areas of endeavor. He was prodigiously hardworking and serious, and impatient—as most young priests were (and are)—at what seemed to him the stodginess and intellectual sloth of the official church leadership. "The species of liberalism to which I was insensibly drawn proceeded, not only from the generosity of my youth, but also from a reaction against certain exaggerations in the environment in which I lived and which included types of that spiteful credulity often called 'clerical.' " Less attractive than Houtin's youthful idealism were a sharp censoriousness, an intolerance of the human weaknesses he discerned in others, a tendency to see himself as a moral and intellectual arbiter. He liked to recall a holiday in Spain and a conversation there with a couple of senior ecclesiastics, who said on parting: "This young priest has more ideas than the whole Spanish clergy together."[37]

Houtin fed his liberalism on Louis Duchesne's *Bulletin critique* and the various biblical journals edited by Loisy. He proved to be within his small circle almost as productive as they were. He nurtured a newfound passion for the ecclesiastical history of his own region, and, as he probed into its sources, he stumbled over the same issue that had first gotten Duchesne into trouble,[38] only with a local twist. Houtin turned a critical eye upon the venerable traditions that the diocese of Angers had been founded in the first century and that one of its early bishops had been a certain Saint René, "a personage whose very existence is impossible to prove." The earnest researcher presented his documented findings at a meeting of a learned society in Angers, at which "Monseigneur the bishop deigned to be present." There was an ugly scene as the bishop, describing himself explicitly as "the guardian of doctrine," rushed to the rostrum to denounce the paper just read by one of his priests. An acrimonious correspondence followed, and, when Houtin insisted on publishing *La légende de saint René* despite the bishop's objections, he was dismissed from the seminary faculty and not given another assignment.[39]

He retired for a few months to his parental home, and then, in April 1901 he went to Paris. There, thanks to a former seminary professor, now pastor of the parish of Saint-Sulpice, he served as a *prêtre habitué*—a priest, that is, allowed to function outside his own diocese, but with no canonical rights and

---

36. Houtin, *Mon expérience*, 1:9–13.

37. Houtin, *Mon expérience*, 1:142, 126.

38. See chapter 4.

39. A. Houtin, *Mes difficultés avec mon évêque* (Paris: 1905), 2–6, 16–23. Houtin published this pamphlet himself.

at the sufferance of others, including, in Houtin's case, the hostile bishop back in Angers. This tenuous existence, with its indignities and financial uncertainties, went a long way toward permanently embittering Houtin. But not even these misadventures slowed down his pen. By the end of 1902 he had published several learned articles and three long books.

Among the latter was a wider study than Duchesne's of the alleged apostolic origins of French dioceses.[40] This had appeared first in pamphlet form, a copy of which Houtin sent Loisy by way of introduction. And, as a "very humble and very devoted servant," he sought the exegete's opinion: "At this moment, when a great struggle about the Bible is about to begin, I believe that it would be very instructive to sketch the history of the [biblical] controversy in France during the century that has just ended. My intention would be to prepare on this subject a study of the same type as that which I take the liberty of submitting to you herewith." Loisy replied cordially but with a monitum: "I need to tell you that the biblical question is much more grave than the one about apostolicity, . . . and there is much more risk in talking about it freely." Nevertheless, "if you have the courage to take it on, and if you think I can furnish you with any helpful references, I am at your disposal." And he concluded with an invitation to Bellevue.[41]

When this strange love–hate association began, no doubt existed as to who was the dominant partner.[42]

Over the preceding six years [Houtin remembered], I followed his journal attentively; I had read almost all his books; I knew all about the vexations he had been subjected to. He appeared to me wearing the halo of science and of persecution. His gravity and certain devout manners lent him also the halo of sanctity. . . . Monsieur Loisy seemed to me a confessor for the Gospel, persecuted because of his sincerity. I was seduced. His soft voice, which he knew how to use so insinuatingly, would have conquered me had I not been already.[43]

From then on Houtin—at thirty-three plump, balding, his eyes behind rimless spectacles large and riveting—visited the apartment on the Boulevard Verd-de-Saint-Julien almost every week. Occasionally he met Félix Klein there, and also another worshipper at Loisy's shrine, Marcel Hébert, who at that moment had fallen into deep depression: the circulation of his *Souvenirs d'Assise*, with its symbolist implications, had just prompted the officials of the archdiocese of Paris to demand his dismissal from the École Fénelon.[44] Houtin

40. See note 26, chapter 4.

41. Houtin to Loisy, n. d., and Loisy to Houtin, 27 July, 1901, quoted in Houtin, *Mon expérience,* 1:236–37.

42. See Émile Poulat, "Les 'Mémoires' en filigrane. Loisy sous le regard de Houtin," in *Critique et mystique* (Paris: 1984), 44–56.

43. Houtin and Sartiaux, *Loisy*, 93–94.

44. See chapter 10, and Hébert to Laberthonnière, 14 July, 1901, in Perrin (ed.), *Laberthonnière et ses amis,* 31–32. Houtin later wrote a biography of Hébert: *Un prêtre symboliste. Marcel Hébert* (Paris: 1925).

mourned for his new friend whose sweetness of temper entirely won his heart, fretted at the injustice of it all, and, with Loisy's encouragement, worked furiously on a book about biblical controversies in France during the nineteenth century.

THE SECOND SERIES of lectures Loisy delivered at the École des Hautes Études, during the autumn of 1901, was devoted to the Gospel parables. Among his auditors was Père Henri Bremond. "I have been following Loisy's course on the parables," he told Maurice Blondel. "It is very, very good."[45] He did not elaborate, aware perhaps that the philosopher had begun to have some reservations about the exegete. To von Hügel he could speak with more open enthusiasm: "I must tell you that, having followed Loisy's course with passionate attention, I am convinced that for the men of our time he poses no true danger. I emerged from these conferences much more filled with faith than when I entered them, and all the young people there shared that impression."[46]

But even before he heard him lecture Bremond had established contact with Loisy. The preceding January had seen the publication of a volume of his essays that had originally appeared in *Études*. Bremond called it *Inquiétude religieuse*. His childhood friend, Charles Maurras,[47] already well launched on his right-wing movement destined for fame as the Action française, thought the title appropriate. "What singular preoccupation you seem to have," he wrote, tongue in cheek, "with the objective life of the human Christ. You might escape from that to Protestantism, it seems to me; you might even be accused of being as much an idolator as I am." Loisy, to whom Bremond also sent a copy of the book, acknowledged it with guarded cordiality, and Bremond replied that he hoped soon to pay a visit to Bellevue. But for some reason—shyness hardly seems likely—he did not, and even as late as the following November he told von Hügel, "One of these days I shall try to say hello to him and speak to him in the flesh."[48]

During the summer Bremond had learned that *Inquiétude religieuse* was to be awarded a prize of Fr 1,000 by the Académie française.[49] This was a consolation he sorely needed. None of the doubts about his Jesuit vocation had been resolved by the final vows he had taken eighteen months earlier,[50] and so severe was his dejection that friends—von Hügel among them—worried about his physical health. Complicating his situation was a kind of spiritual ménage à

45. Bremond to Blondel, 14 November, 1901, quoted in Virgoulay, *Blondel*, 110.

46. Bremond to von Hügel, n. d. [but before 7 December, 1901], quoted in Blanchet, *Bremond*, 164.

47. See chapter 5.

48. Quoted in Blanchet, *Bremond*, 143, 165.

49. Blanchet, *Bremond*, 215.

50. See chapter 10.

trois into which he had been drawn. The previous October Maude Petre had come to Paris and, at George Tyrrell's suggestion, had sought out Bremond in order to solicit his advice about her feelings for their mutual friend. Those feelings were extremely intense, and they were mixed together with considerations of Tyrrell's work and anxieties about his and her future. "The so-called 'orthodox,' " Petre confided to her diary, "are bent on driving the new thinkers from the Church. God help us all! . . . My lot is cast with theirs, not please God simply because I love them, but because their cause is true." That cause, for her, was incarnated in the Tyrrell whom she longed to embrace: "And I do believe it would be good if I did. But such things can only be done under overmastering impulse, and I, alas, for some reason have learned to overcome impulse." At any rate, "in caring for him I love God and work also for the great cause of faith." She did not want to be a "temptation" to him, yet she remained convinced that "my love [is] intended to save him." "I know I would give him up at once if it were for his good. But he does so need some one to love him just now—to love him through thick and thin."[51]

Petre had plenty of evidence to support this last assertion. On one level, Tyrrell's banishment to Richmond had served as a tonic for him. He had no parochial duties to perform, and his time was his own. He rejoiced in the lovely Yorkshire countryside. The presbytery in which he lived, presided over by its affable rector, was a relaxed and friendly place, a "holiday house" almost, in which assembled an assortment of Jesuits needing temporary rest and recreation. Here, far from the tensions of Farm Street, the enchantingly playful side of Tyrrell's nature could display itself.[52] But down deep he grew increasingly unhappy. He lived to write, and now whatever he wrote had to pass muster with two boards of censorship, one Jesuit and the other diocesan. Wretched migraine headaches continued to sap his mental and physical strength. As he tried to reassure Bremond, his own doubts about the Society of Jesus—"the most 'liberalizing' Order ever conceived has become the one block in the way of the Church's expansion"[53]—seemed to multiply. And even in his Yorkshire "hermitage" he received notices aplenty from troubled Catholics who had heard him preach or read his essays, and who, as one of them put it, "stagger like a drunkard under the theological difficulties that weigh upon my mind."[54]

Into this bleak milieu came Maude Petre's awkward expressions of concern and affection. Tyrrell's reaction was ambivalent.[55] "I doubt that I am any longer capable of a very ardent or absorbing attachment," he wrote to her early

51. Quoted in Leonard, *Transformation*, 26–32.
52. Petre, *Autobiography of Tyrrell*, 2:131–34.
53. Tyrrell to Petre, ? November, 1900, quoted in Petre, *Autobiography of Tyrrell*, 2:78.
54. See the material quoted in Schultenover, *Tyrrell*, 139–43.
55. For a more than adequate refutation of the allegation that Tyrrell's relationship to Petre was determined by his homosexuality, see Schultenover, *Tyrrell*, 174–77 and 394–95.

in their relationship.[56] Yet, as the months passed, he became more comfortable with her, indeed more dependent upon her, more eager for her understanding and approval. At her urging, for example, he began to write his autobiography which he sent to her, section by section. But on other occasions he would express resentment at her cloying attentions, and her brief visits to Richmond were marked by uneasiness and strain. "My very belief in my friend," she wrote, "and my conviction that he was called to do a great work for the Church was a source of frequent irritation to him. I saw him in priestly garments, and he liked mufti."[57]

Enter Henri Bremond. With him Tyrrell shared the irritation he felt, and to him he suggested that the source of irritation go for counsel. Petre stayed at the mother-house of her order in Paris for nearly two months during the autumn of 1900, during which time she met with Bremond often and exchanged many written confidences with him. His first advice was shrewd and helpful, that she should above all cling to her independence, and not only because "independence means dependence upon God." She soon discovered that he possessed, along with "his whimsicality" and his "mocking spirit, . . . the marvelous gift of sympathy, of drawing out of one . . . something one had never known to be there." When later he sensed that his ministrations had come to be of little use to her, he consulted for her that director of directors, Abbé Huvelin, who responded with his customary Delphic solemnity: "Tell her that it is God who has sent this soul to her, and that she will have to suffer much." The soul in question, Tyrrell, was not impressed: he had a "horror of professional soul-readers" like Huvelin.[58]

Before she quite realized it, Petre found that she was giving advice as much as receiving it, that Bremond was more miserable and more unsure in his vocation than the man she loved back in England:

I cannot tell you how wretched I am [he wrote her]. My whole nature is in revolt. . . . Pray [God] to give me a little rest, and the means of giving Him other souls and hearts in order to compensate for my own miserable heart. . . . Your terrible analytic faculty will always find good along with this almost total ugliness. That helps me to hope more in the still more terrible analysis of God. . . . Forgive my utter *unsettlement*. Nothing is of any use to me so long as I drag this chain. . . . I have been through a crisis of disgust, profound disgust for this burden of convention, craving for liberty.[59]

At the beginning of the summer of 1901 Tyrrell invited Bremond to Richmond. "I feel sure your nerves are in a state of high tension. . . . Here . . . you will forget you are in a Jesuit house. . . . We are all mad, the superior included. Come, and be happy. You and I will make a *petite église* of our own—

---

56. Tyrrell to Petre, 3 September, 1900, quoted in Leonard, *Transformation*, 27.
57. Quoted in Leonard, *Transformation*, 30–31.
58. See Leonard, *Transformation*, 28, 33, and Petre, *My Way*, 261, 281.
59. Quoted in Blanchet, *Bremond*, 207–13, and Petre, *My Way*, 261–63.

very fallible and with no religious orders."[60] So the two of them met for the first time, in a little Yorkshire railroad station, and Bremond told Petre in mid-July how splendidly they got on together over the next ten days of incessant conversation. They decided in the end "to attach themselves to what was essential in the church" and "all might still be saved," though they agreed that only sentimental nostalgia kept them in the Society of Jesus. Afterward, his spirits clearly lifted, Bremond reported exultantly to two of his mentors. "I have left my *heretic* of Richmond in a very good condition," he informed Blondel. And he assured von Hügel that nothing scandalous had occurred during "ten days of complete sympathy in ideas and sentiments."[61]

Back in Paris, Bremond was involved willy-nilly in a crisis of a different kind. The French government, after having suppressed the pesky Assumptionists,[62] moved on to bigger game among the "unauthorized" religious orders. The turn of the Jesuits came while Bremond was on his holiday in England. The big house at 15 rue Monsieur was closed, and the staff of the *Études* dispersed. Bremond and one of his confreres moved a few sticks of furniture to a flat not far away, on the avenue de Villars. From here he went to listen to Loisy lecture, and here he worked diligently at a make-shift desk every day. The discontent with the Society of Jesus that had been building within him for so long left him with mixed feelings about the suppression. "This measure is not altogether bad," he told von Hügel, if it teaches our superiors not to depend upon "petty rules and details of religious discipline." Predictably, he laid the ultimate blame for what had happened at the door of the ecclesiastical establishment. And yet he could not but be moved by the unhappy fate of thousands of good men and women, especially that "of the poor nuns." In their sufferings "I find myself more a Jesuit than I would have expected."

The new year of 1902 brought waves of despondency with it. "I am lower than ever—sour, sullen—and I do not smile any more except at small children." Word that his superior at the *Études* had sent a negative fitness report about him to Jesuit headquarters in Rome depressed him still more. "I am reproached for the *eccentricity* of my articles," Bremond complained, "for the absence of a religious sense, etc., etc. It is the first gong of the warning bell." The psychic effect upon him, he protested, was "not bitterness but an immense lassitude." In March he visited Blondel, always a source of calm and soothing reassurance.[63]

Later that spring Maude Petre, at a time when she was looking after her sister's two small sons, went into lodgings with her nephews, their governess, and a female companion at 24 Newbiggen, Richmond, Yorkshire. "I stayed

60. Quoted in Petre, *Autobiography of Tyrrell*, 2:134–35.
61. Quoted in Blanchet, *Bremond*, 214–15.
62. See chapter 11.
63. Blanchet, *Bremond*, 214–17.

for a year. During that time I saw Tyrrell continually, and we formed the habit of reading together most evenings. "[64]

BEFORE HE WENT to Richmond to meet George Tyrrell, Henri Bremond spent a few weeks in London. Duty-bound, he called upon Tyrrell's former colleagues at Farm Street, but he was more interested in contacting those to whom Friedrich von Hügel—who was in Italy—had given him letters of introduction.[65] Among these Catholic "new thinkers," as Maude Petre called them, Bremond discerned a mood of almost unrelieved gloom. The primary reason was the issuance, at the beginning of 1901, of a "Joint Pastoral Letter," signed by all the bishops of England and Wales, on the evils of "liberal Catholicism."[66] The document asserted the most stringent and unnuanced point of view with regard to the relationship between the *ecclesia docens*—which "needs no dictation from without as to the course [it] should pursue in the guardianship of truth and the condemnation of error"—and the *ecclesia discens*—made up "simply [of] disciples" who "as disciples . . . have no right to legislate, to command or to teach in the Church, be they ever so learned."

Bremond heard much discussion as to what had driven their lordships, under the usually bland leadership of Cardinal Vaughan—bosom friend of the Wards and the von Hügels—to assume such a hard line. Tyrrell blamed the machinations of Rome, and, though his own recent bruises may have prompted the accusation, some persons saw a confirmation of his theory when the pope shortly after its publication condoned the pastoral.[67] Undoubtedly a more direct cause was the notorious case of St. George Jackson Mivart, a distinguished scientist and convert to Catholicism, who had gradually drifted into conflict with the *ecclesia docens* over a variety of doctrinal questions. "I [have] come to the conclusion," Mivart wrote early in 1900, "that the Roman Catholic Church must tolerate a transforming process of evolution, with respect to many of its dogmas, or sink, by degrees, into an effete and insignificant body, composed of ignorant persons, a mass of women and children and a number of mentally effeminate men." He died, excommunicated by Vaughan, a few months later, still asserting that among the dogmas necessitating this "transforming process" were the Resurrection and the divinity of Christ.[68] Tyrrell predicted wider trouble as a result: "How horrid all this about

64. Petre, *My Way*, 283, and Leonard, *Transformation*, 32.

65. Blanchet, *Bremond*, 194.

66. Text printed in Weaver (ed.), *Letters of a Modernist*, 131–57. For a useful summary, see William James Schoenl, "The Intellectual Crisis in English Catholicism, 1890–1907. Liberals, Modernists and the Vatican" (doctoral dissertaion, Columbia University, 1968), 143–52.

67. For the part played in the "pastoral" by the Roman Jesuits, see the important and original analysis in Schultenover, *View from Rome*, 131–51.

68. See Jacob W. Gruber, *A Conscience in Conflict: The Life of St. George Jackson Mivart* (New York: 1960), 197–213, and Snead-Cox, *Life of Vaughan*, 2:300–303.

Mivart. It will throw everything back a decade and leave the Ark of God in the hands of the Philistines."[69]

Mivart, his scientific accomplishments aside, had been a prolific writer in popular journals through which his increasingly idiosyncratic views had attained wide currency. This circumstance points to another source of the English bishops' anxiety, specifically to their worry about the equivocal status of the Catholic press. Some periodicals fell under direct episcopal control, and thus arguably could be employed as an organ of the *ecclesia docens*, as the bishops strictly defined it. But others were not, notably the *Weekly Register*, in which "A Perverted Devotion"[70] and other articles by Tyrrell had originally appeared. Tyrrell himself was aroused to fury by the pastoral:

I cannot see that a bishop's *gratia status*[71] means more than that his use of natural means will be blessed. . . . But if he spurns natural means and falls back on miraculous guidance he is but tempting God. If the Bishops themselves had read all that is to be read on modern difficulties; if they had felt and overcome the temptations to which the faithful, educated and uneducated, are exposed, one would feel bound to listen to their warnings; but when they . . . say equivalently "Don't look, don't read, don't think; listen to us; we know *a priori* there are no difficulties; still, don't look or you might see something"—well, nobody will mind them, except those who need no physician. What angers me are . . . the absolute incompetence of our clergy to meet the incoming flood of agnosticism [and] the deep somnolence of the bishops. All they care for is to fetch a few proselytes from [Anglican] ritualism.[72]

Other "new thinkers" reacted just as negatively, if not as eloquently, to the pastoral. Edmund Bishop, a crusty recluse whose expertise in the history of liturgy had won Louis Duchesne's favorable notice,[73] was so disgusted by it that he resolved to sell his books and cancel his subscriptions to professional journals. "Willie" Williams took aim at the bishops' basic contention in a speech he titled "Differences between Private Judgment and the Freedom of the Scientific Spirit." Non-Catholic spokesmen—and especially High Church Anglicans still stung by Leo XIII's refusal to recognize their ordinations—were understandably gleeful at what they chose to see as one more proof of Roman perfidy.

When Wilfrid and Josephine Ward read the joint pastoral, they were just settling into their new home, "Lotus House," near Dorking. They and the five children—the youngest was four years old—exchanged the seascapes of

69. Quoted in Ward, *The Wilfrid Wards*, 1:323.

70. See chapter 10.

71. "Grace of state," that is, the aid of God appropriate to one's office.

72. Tyrrell to Ley, 5 January, 1901, quoted in Petre, *Autobiography of Tyrrell*, 2:152–53.

73. Duchesne to von Hügel, 21 May, 1897, in Neveu (ed.) "Lettres . . . de Duchesne," *Mélanges*, 84:583–84. See also Nigel Abercrombie, *The Life and Work of Edmund Bishop* (London: 1959), 300–301.

Eastbourne for the rolling Surrey hills, "a situation . . . singularly lovely, the grounds slop[ing] steeply in a series of terraces . . . planted with great clumps of azaleas, bamboos and roses." The literary life was pursued as before: Josephine's second novel, *A Light Behind*, was published in 1901, and Wilfrid's collection of essays, *Problems and Persons*, a year later. The household was no less boisterous and lively than at Eastbourne, with the same domestic unpredictability and with guests perpetually coming and going. A new nanny joined the family, and Wilfrid hired a private secretary, a nephew of Lewis Carroll who "had a great deal of his uncle's power of talking delightful nonsense."[74]

The adult Wards did not find the joint pastoral in the least delightful, though its appearance did spark some rueful humor around Lotus House. Wilfrid's brother Bernard, a frequent guest, observed that the attitude of their lordships toward the laity was much like that of the mother in the *Punch* cartoon who says to her little girl: "Go and see what baby's doing and tell him he mustn't." Monsignor Ward—soon to be a bishop himself—also repeated the joke making the rounds that the document had verbally declined step-by-step from "the joint" to "the cold joint" to "the hash."[75]

But Wilfrid upon reflection could not categorize the pastoral as nonsense either, though he deeply regretted its negative tone. In his copy he heavily underscored two words in a passage that had gone virtually unnoticed: "The best antidote to all such poisonous opinions is to be found in a *clear* and *intelligent* belief in the abiding presence within the Church of the Divine Teacher." It seemed that the English bishops, including dear Cardinal Vaughan, valued mute submissiveness far above clarity and intelligence from their people, "be they ever so learned." Here again was the assertion of that siege mentality Ward was so anxious to modify. Yet he appreciated the vulnerability of the little English Catholic minority, largely so very unlearned, so amply endowed with the "pious ears" George Tyrrell was contemptuous of. Newman was Ward's hero, and Newman had consistently practiced candor, to be sure, but also caution, patience, and the need to adapt the message to the status of the hearer.[76] Ward had been sharply critical of Mivart and was growing suspicious of Loisy, and even a little, of von Hügel,[77] so when, after several months, he made his views about the joint pastoral public he could not have expected a chorus of approval rising from either end of the spectrum:

[The] most extreme interpretations of the teaching of the Pastoral [advanced by a prominent Anglican] have long since been universally rejected, and no theologically instructed Catholic would think of accepting them. An average Catholic would regard

74. Ward, *The Wilfrid Wards*, 2:105–13.
75. Ward, *The Wilfrid Wards*, 2:135, 142.
76. See, for example, Newman to Bowles, 5 January, 1882, in *Letters and Diaries*, 30:48.
77. See chapter 8.

the Pastoral as an emphatic protest against a form of "Liberal" Catholicism which required to be denounced, as an insistence on truths known to theologians, but which "Liberal" Catholics have in practice forgotten. On the other hand, he would not approach the Pastoral as though it were an exhaustive theological treatise, but rather as a document which presupposed, for its interpretation, the authorised theology of the Church. . . . The faith and morals of the many are protected by the Episcopate. But Catholic thought has been elaborated through successive ages by the individual Catholic thinkers of genius or learning. . . . When "il buon fra Tommaso [Aquinas]" was depicted by Dante as leading him into the circle of great theologians, he was no canonised saint, but only the holy and learned friar, dead some thirty years, who had elaborated Christian theology in the form called for by the "new learning," with such extraordinary skill, that he, simple friar though he was, was already the acknowledged ruler in the domain of Catholic thought.[78]

Wilfrid Ward, like Pierre Batiffol, was discovering that sometimes the journey proves most difficult when it proceeds along the middle of the road.

Ward was preoccupied much of the rest of that year, 1901, by the work of a royal commission investigating the state of university education in Ireland. His appointment to that body resulted from his intimacy, through the Synthetic, with Arthur Balfour and other leaders of the Conservative party.[79] It was a task he assumed with the utmost seriousness, not only for political reasons—he was a strong Unionist—and not only because it provided an opportunity to serve his Irish coreligionists in an area he regarded as supremely important. He also saw his service on the commission as a way of taking up again the concerns Newman had had in his ill-starred attempts to found a Catholic University in Dublin nearly half a century before.[80]

At Christmas all the Wards went to Arundel Castle to celebrate the holidays with Josephine's kinsman, the duke of Norfolk. It was an especially happy occasion, because completing the family circle was the eldest son, Wilfrid, a sunny child of eleven, now a pupil in a boarding school near Eastbourne. His father met Wilfrid—known familiarly as Boy or Boy-Boy—in London and told his wife: "I enjoyed taking Boy-Boy about. It is well, as I am dissatisfied with self, that I am satisfied with my son." Six weeks later Boy-Boy was dead, a victim of influenza and meningitis.[81] Committed as they may have been to action in the public arena, this crushing private loss devastated the young parents more than anything that would happen to them in the coming years of conflict. Among the messages of condolence they received was an exquisitely

---

78. Quoted in Ward, *The Wilfrid Wards*, 2:137–41. The prominent Anglican Ward's article—which appeared in the *Pilot*—purported to answer was Lord Halifax, chief advocate of the validity of Anglican orders. Ward did not know that most of Halifax's article in the *Nineteenth Century* was written by Tyrrell. See Schultenover, *Tyrrell*, 152–56.

79. See note 47, chapter 9.

80. Ward, *The Wilfrid Wards*, 2:50–79.

81. Ward, *The Wilfrid Wards*, 2:127–33.

tactful note, written by one from whom those years would separate them. It was postmarked Richmond, Yorkshire. "My dear Ward, I will not intrude words upon you except to say that I have heard of your sorrow and will say Mass tomorrow for your boy and for you and Mrs. Ward the next day. Ever yours faithfully, G. Tyrrell." [82]

82. Tyrrell to Ward, 7 February, 1902, in Weaver (ed.), *Letters of a "Modernist,"* 74.

CHAPTER 13

The Little Red Book

I remain . . . convinced that there must be a way to reconcile all these apparent
contrarieties. . . . I have pressed my nose into the books of biblical criticism, and
I have called down blessings again upon the good Loisy. He is truly a Noah, and
the church will be very happy to have his ark once this deluge will have passed.

—*Henri Bremond (1904)*[1]

"I AM INDEED DEEPLY, truly grieved for you and for your wife and
for your other children," wrote Friedrich von Hügel from Rome when
he learned of Boy-Boy Ward's death. "I have many a time wondered, with
affectionate interest, as to what 'Ideal' Ward's grandson and Wilfrid Ward's
son, and eldest grandson and son, would turn into."[2] No doubt these condolences came straight from the baron's large heart, a sympathy the more deeply
felt since he had been no stranger himself to grief and loss during this time:
his beloved sister Pauline had died early in 1901 after a long illness, and his
daughter Gertrud's religious crisis continued to ebb and flow.[3] But, private
sorrow apart, the baron was growing exasperated at Wilfrid Ward's cautious
public positions, particularly on the biblical question. Ward can be "very irritating," he confided to Padre Semeria. And though he "continues to be open
philosophically, I sense a little sadly that he has already given us the best that
is in him."[4]

In the spring von Hügel had left England for a long, restless trip to the
Continent. Alone at the outset—the family was to catch up with him later—
he went first to Paris to visit Alfred Loisy, then to Genoa for ten days of research on the mystical experiences of Saint Catherine, a subject that continued

1. Quoted in Blanchet, *Bremond*, 184.
2. Quoted in Ward, *The Wilfrid Wards*, 2:128–29.
3. See chapter 9.
4. Von Hügel to Semeria, 25 August, 1901, in Zorzi (ed.), *Briefe . . . von Hügels an . . . Semeria*,
2:438.

234

to fascinate him.[5] Before departing Hampstead he had pondered the Joint Pastoral of the English bishops, and, though he subscribed to the Anglican strictures on that document, he remained surprisingly untroubled by it himself.[6] Yet he was quickly apprised of the violent reaction of some of his intimates. "The bishops have mounted on metaphors as witches on broomsticks," Tyrrell wrote him feverishly, "and have ridden to the devil. It is the 'sheep and shepherd' metaphor that does the trick. The sheep are brainless, passive; their part is to be led, fed, fleeced and slain for the profit of the shepherd for whose benefit solely they exist."[7]

From Genoa the baron went to Milan where he spent the latter part of May and all of June, most of it reading assiduously in mystical theology at the great Ambrosiana library, a member of whose staff, Padre Achille Ratti—later Pope Pius XI—proved helpful to him. During this sojourn he also made his first contact with Count Tommaso Gallarati-Scotti and other young Italian Catholic progressives who were themselves in touch with the likes of Murri and Fogazzaro.[8] By the high summer, however, Milan had become unbearably hot, and so the baron, his wife and daughters now with him, repaired to a tourist hotel in southern Switzerland, near the Saint Gothard Pass. Lady Mary thrived more than her husband did in the thin mountain air, but he found some diversion from his relentless intellectual routine in butterfly hunting. As though to confirm his developing Italian connections he was pleased to publish a short piece defending Loisy in Salvatore Minocchi's *Studi Religiosi*.[9]

But he was not prepared to defend the symbolist meanderings of Marcel Hébert, and when that recently suspended Parisian priest[10] proposed to visit the von Hügels in Switzerland, the baron declined to receive him on the grounds of Gertrud's "painful" and "obscure" religious crisis: "I must spare her any new complication of spirit or emotion." Hébert, he told Semeria, has in his rejection of a genuine personality in God "taken a step he thinks is avantgarde, but is really old-fashioned. . . . I regret very much what has happened, for a I love and esteem H[ébert]; but in his philosophy he is neither a Blondel . . . nor a Laberthonnière."[11]

In October the family moved to Rome for the winter. By then the rumors were rife that Cardinal Richard intended to request that Loisy's exegetical work be placed on the Index of forbidden books or be solemnly censured by the Vatican in some other way. From his residence on the Via Veneto von

5. See note 57, chapter 8, and chapter 19.

6. See De la Bedoyere, *Hügel*, 128–30, and von Hügel to Semeria, 25 August, 1901, in Zorzi (ed.), *Briefe . . . von Hügels an . . . Semeria*, 2:437.

7. Tyrrell to von Hügel, 20 February, 1901, quoted in Schultenover, *Tyrrell*, 155.

8. See chapter 11.

9. See Barmann, *Hügel*, 255. For Minocchi, see chapter 11.

10. See chapter 12.

11. Von Hügel to Hébert, 17 July, 1901, in Holland (ed.), *Letters*, 102, and von Hügel to Semeria, 25 August, 1901, in Zorzi (ed.), *Briefe . . . von Hügels an . . . Semeria*, 2:436.

Hügel mounted a campaign to head off any such eventuality. He received little encouragement from Louis Duchesne, whose habitual cynicism had deteriorated into a skeptical indifference: "He could do so much," the baron mourned, "but he does nothing on the pretext that there is nothing to be done." Several unpleasant conversations with Pierre Batiffol, also visiting the Eternal City, heightened the baron's sense of gloom. Batiffol, he told Tyrrell, "*is a man not to be trusted*; pray take my word for it, and look out."[12]

More heartening was the presence of Archbishop Mignot, who had traveled to Rome from Albi prepared to do battle in behalf of modern Scripture studies, and, as the winter of 1902 began, he and the baron joined forces, in concert indeed with the defense Loisy had already initiated himself.[13] The archbishop wrote directly to Leo XIII, a tactic of questionable effectiveness given the pope's great age, and consequently the pervasive feeling that the papacy had already entered an interregnum. Von Hügel meanwhile resumed his role as lobbyist with Cardinal Rampolla and other officials, arguing that any condemnation of Loisy would put the church at odds with the whole European intellectual community and would, more specifically, undermine the favorable reputation Leo XIII enjoyed by and large among English academics. His pleas were listened to, as always, with courteous attention, but his argument, dubious at best, did not prove particularly persuasive. "Touch the Scripture," the pope's personal theologian observed during one conversation, "and you touch the faith, *la foi*." He went on to tell the baron that Leo XIII had decided to form a special panel of cardinals, aided by an international body of scholarly experts, to deal with the tangle of scriptural problems raised by contemporary research. Von Hügel, ever ready to find a silver lining in the darkest sky, took this promise of a biblical commission as a favorable omen, at least to the extent that it signaled the willingness of the authorities to refrain for the time being from any inhibiting measures.[14]

IN BELLEVUE THE NEW YEAR, 1902, commenced quietly and characteristically for Alfred Loisy. His life appeared to move along in its now familiar grooves. He continued to live simply and austerely, careful to fulfill all his priestly duties. Passing most of each day at his desk, he prepared the lectures to be delivered at the École Pratique des Hautes Études and vetted the articles scheduled to appear in his little journal. He was also hard at work at a commentary on the Synoptic Gospels, a companion-piece to a similar study of the Gospel of Saint John which was finished but as yet unpublished. For recreation he walked daily, weather permitting, in the woods of Meudon, often accompanied by Abbé Félix Klein.[15] Then suddenly began a bizarre series of events that would make this year the most fateful of his life.

---

12. See Barmann, *Hügel*, 86–88.

14. De la Bedoyere, *Hügel*, 133–37.

13. See note 27, chapter 12.

15. See chapter 12.

On January 22, a Wednesday, Loisy received a note from Jules Cornély, a well-known journalist and, it was said around Paris, a confidant of Premier Waldeck-Rousseau.[16] Cornély, whom Loisy had never met, merely identified himself as a friend of Monseigneur Lacroix, bishop of Tarentaise, and invited Loisy to come to his apartment at five o'clock the following Friday afternoon to discuss a matter of interest. Loisy had known the forty-eight-year-old Lucien Lacroix casually for some years, and he knew that this Dominican-turned-secular priest, founder of the liberal *Revue du clergé français*, had been made bishop of the little diocese in southeastern France at the insistence of Waldeck-Rousseau and over the strenuous objections of the Holy See.

When, at the designated hour, Loisy presented himself at the fashionable rue de Clichy address, Cornély greeted him warmly and said that the prince of Monaco intended to nominate him, along with Félix Klein and a priest of the diocese of Limoges named Chéri-Louis Pichot, to the vacant bishopric that was coterminous with his principality. The journalist explained that under the terms of the concordat establishing the diocese the prince had the right to present the pope a list of three candidates from which the pope might choose one. If all three were rejected, the prince would then submit another list. The names would be arranged alphabetically—Klein, Loisy, Pichot—but Cornély assured Loisy that if he agreed to have his name included he would be the principal candidate.[17] Loisy accepted the proposal on the spot. When Cornély excused himself to telephone the prince, Loisy mused wryly about the reception the Vatican would accord to this "trinité de suspects": Klein, "compromised by the Americanist affair"; Pichot, "compromised also, but by involvement in the Dreyfus case";[18] and himself, recently denounced to the Holy Office. Cornély returned and said the prince would give audience to Loisy the following Sunday, January 26, at five o'clock.

Klein had received a similar invitation and had arrived at the prince's townhouse on the avenue de Trocadero before Loisy, whose interview nevertheless took place first. Cornély, continuing in his role as intermediary, introduced the exegete to the prince and then withdrew to wait with Klein in an anteroom. Prince Albert, at fifty-three, was a short, wiry, bearded man with the rolling gait of a veteran sailor. Loisy found him courteous, grave, and "without affectation." He said frankly that he was himself an unbeliever but that he recognized "the social importance of religion and of the ecclesiastical ministry." Therefore, the appointment of a bishop to his tiny diocese—four parishes

16. For what follows, see the detailed study in O'Connell, "The Bishopric of Monaco, 1902," 26–51, and the references cited there.

17. The list of candidates in this instance was slightly different from the ordinary "terna," since the prince did not have the right to nominate in order of preference.

18. Pichot (1864–1920), who had published two provocative pamphlets about Dreyfus, had left his diocese, with permission, and was now pastor of one of the four parishes in Monaco.

in a principality whose total population was scarcely fifteen thousand[19]—was of utmost concern to him. He explained the procedure involved, much as Cornély had explained it the Friday before, and added that he was determined to have as bishop a man of broad intellectual views. He then formally asked whether Loisy would agree to have his name placed before the officials of the Holy See. Loisy replied that so long as the continuation in Monaco of his scholarly work were not judged an impediment—and the prince solemnly shook his head—he would be pleased to consent.

Klein's audience followed roughly the same pattern. Loisy waited for him, and together they rode the train from the Montparnasse station back to Bellevue. Their impressions of what had just happened to them were much alike; they marveled at the "unforeseen, singular, fantastic" offer which the prince had made them, and, though they conceded that the odds against either of them being successful were a thousand to one, each laughingly agreed to appoint the other vicar-general, "if indeed," Loisy said, "there was any reason to have a vicar-general in a place like Monaco."

But however much they may have bantered about it between themselves, both men were intrigued by the possibility Prince Albert had opened up to them, and they determined to pursue the prize. The incorrigibly sentimental Klein was perhaps more sanguine about his chances, but Loisy by no means despised his own. When he consulted Mignot, he received the answer he wanted: he should accept the bishopric if it were offered, unlikely as that eventuality might be. The archbishop shared the news with von Hügel, who urged Loisy to agree to the nomination—as a means of rehabilitating himself—and to reject the appointment if it came, since the administration of any diocese, even little Monaco, would deflect Loisy's time and energy from his research. The exegete's reply revealed how earnestly he desired to take advantage of this startling new opportunity. As bishop of Monaco, he told von Hügel, he would write more rather than less, thanks to the secretarial help that would become available. He would perhaps have to compose more gravely in accord with the episcopal dignity, but that was a mere matter of style and easily done. Besides, his departure from Paris might contribute significantly to the general peace of the church. His lectures at the Sorbonne, attended by so many young clergy, deeply troubled Cardinal Richard, who would not be sorry to see Loisy go. Perhaps the see of Monaco provided an honorable solution for all concerned.

Loisy, during these early anxious weeks of his candidacy, made his actions match his aspirations. Never an unorthodox nuance slipped from his lips when he lectured to those bright young priests. The contributors to his journal suddenly discovered in him a grimly ardent censor. By the time, in March, Albert

19. Ironically, Loisy's opponent Pierre Batiffol was considered in later years for the bishopric of Monaco. In an obituary notice of his friend, Marie-Joseph Lagrange described the position as a genuine sinecure, a "poste éminent qui passe pour agréable and peu absorbant", see *La vie intellectuelle* 2 (January 1929): 421.

Houtin published his highly controversial *La question biblique chez les catholiques de France au XIXe siècle*, Loisy had already taken the greatest pains to separate himself from his disciple's suspect opinions, even to the point of insisting that Houtin's book be bound in a color different from that of his own collection of essays, *Études bibliques*, which had appeared in 1901 in its second edition. Even so, he wondered to von Hügel whether Houtin's extravagances "would help or hinder my Monacan candidacy."

But that candidacy depended really upon the initiative of Prince Albert who, despite his overtures of January, did nothing about it the rest of the winter and early spring. No list was sent to Rome, and by April Loisy was convinced the matter was closed. Then, on May 9, the first of several reports appeared in the Parisian press stating that Félix Klein was about to be named bishop of Monaco. An arresting feature of this publicity was, that of the prince's three candidates, it mentioned only Klein, who, when Loisy asked him about it on one of their afternoon walks, denied knowing anything. Whatever the source of the leak to the press—and it was probably Klein himself—Loisy concluded that Rome had not yet decided what to do about the nomination of Klein but had surely eliminated him, Loisy, from consideration. "It matters little," he told Mignot on May 16, not quite convincingly.

In fact the prince's list arrived in the curia on June 14, the eve of the summer holidays, and formal action on it was not taken before late September. In the interval the papal nuncio in Paris bombarded Cardinal Rampolla with negative reports about the three candidates.[20] Klein, "il famoso *Americanista*," was an imprudent trifler, and Pichot so much "a *humanitarian* and a laicist" and "a *dreyfusard*" and "shaped by a modern spirit" that he had been a source of universal scandal. But Loisy was the worst of all. "Though much more talented than Klein, [he] is . . . a man *consumed with resentment*" since his dismissal from the Institut Catholique, "and he does enormous harm to those priests who go to hear him lecture at the Sorbonne." He is given over entirely "to *rationalist biblical criticism*, although he tries to evade the consequences of this by drawing a distinction between the human and critical sense of the Scriptures and the divine and dogmatic sense. This candidate," added the nuncio, who was fond of underlining for emphasis, "falls short even more than Klein in the *sound doctrine* and *tempered language* recommended by Saint Paul, and the promotion of either of them would be most scandalous." Indeed, all three were "deplorable."

Whatever they may have suspected, none of the candidates knew of these denunciations which, during July, were delivered to Rome by diplomatic pouch. Then, abruptly, the plot thickened. On August 13, at a luncheon ar-

---

20. Strictly speaking, the nuncio, Archbishop Benedetto Lorenzelli (1853–1915), had nothing directly to do with negotiations between sovereign Monaco and the Vatican as he did between France and the Vatican. His informal reports nevertheless were incorporated into the file.

ranged by a mutual friend, Loisy met a minor bureaucrat named Alexandre Béard, who described himself as charged to speak in behalf of Charles Dumay, permanent secretary of the ministry of cults, and to inquire if Loisy would allow the Combes government to nominate him to a French diocese. This offer clearly reflected the change at the top of the administration. In June the urbane Waldeck-Rousseau, unwilling to press anticlerical legislation hard enough to suit the Chamber of Deputies, had been replaced as prime minister by Émile Combes, a former seminarian whose single-minded hostility toward Catholicism signaled the beginning of a harsh new phase in the church–state struggle.

Nothing was said about Monaco by either man at the August 13 luncheon, and Béard's proposition was couched in general terms. But Loisy took it seriously, seriously enough to distance himself from another old friend and intellectual comrade, much as he had from Houtin the preceding March. On August 28, in a sharply worded letter intended for publication, he told Marcel Hébert that the symbolist theories as manifested in Hébert's latest publication[21] were "conjectural, overhasty, incomplete," and "corrosive of genuine truth. . . . Despite your apparent reservations, you have reduced religion in general and Christianity in particular to a chimera." When the mild, self-effacing Hébert responded by complimenting "the wise and courageous Father Loisy" in a journal which appeared in mid-September, Loisy labeled it "a malevolent act," and promptly wrote to Cardinal Richard to repudiate any presumed connection between Hébert and himself.

Within days of this prudential act Loisy was summoned to an audience with Prince Albert. The Roman curia, the prince told him angrily on October 5, had rejected all three candidates. He had decided, he continued, to resubmit the same names, but, with what Loisy called "perfect delicacy," he wanted first to secure their consent. Loisy, confronted with this unanticipated embarrassment of riches, asked for a few days to consider the matter. The prince agreed. A hasty appeal to Albi brought Archbishop Mignot's counsel that Loisy should once more accept Prince Albert's offer, because, while the opposition of Cardinal Richard made an appointment to a bishopric under government sponsorship surely unattainable, the advantage of the Monacan negotiation was that at least formally the nuncio could be kept out of the game.[22] There was a glimmer of optimism in Mignot's words, and so Loisy informed the prince he was willing to be renominated.

On October 15 he lunched with Béard again and learned that Dumay was still well disposed toward him and wanted to see him. However, Béard reported, the permanent secretary had laughingly observed in Béard's hearing that "as far as Rome is concerned we might as well nominate Robespierre as

21. "La dernière Idole, étude sur la personnalité divine" appeared in the July 1902 issue of *Revue de métaphysique et de morale*.

22. See note 19, above.

Loisy." That night the exegete wrote to von Hügel that he would probably be nominated to a French see.

His interview with Dumay, six days later, confirmed this impression. To Loisy's relief the permanent secretary waved away any difficulty about the Monacan candidacy, which, he said, should be allowed to proceed. In the meantime the government intended to nominate him to the diocese of Saint-Jean-de-Maurienne, which, along with several other vacant sees, had been the subject of long and so far fruitless negotiations with the papal nuncio. The government's rights of appointment under the concordat had been eroded by the papacy,[23] and Premier Combes, Dumay said, had decided to terminate discussions and present the pope with an official list of names, of which Loisy's would be one. "In the end, Rome always gives in to those who are strong." So the bargain was struck. "If," Dumay said, "the pope accepts your nomination by Prince Albert, we shall in a few years negotiate your transfer to a French see; if the pope refuses to appoint you to Monaco, we shall put you at Saint-Jean-de-Maurienne."

Saint-Jean-de-Maurienne was a poor little diocese tucked away in the mountains of the southeast, not far from Lacroix's Tarentaise.[24] Dumay apologized for its size and insignificance, but Loisy replied that given his frail health, his inexperience, and his studious habits, the place sounded idyllic. Perhaps for the first time he began to think that the long odds had swung in his favor. Houtin even heard him refer to Lacroix as "mon voisin de Tarentaise." But the prospective neighbor was not sure of a happy outcome. Loisy would be wise to press on to Monaco, Lacroix told Mignot, because the clergy of Saint-Jean-de-Maurienne were so uncompromisingly conservative that they would likely murder him.

IT IS A MARK OF Alfred Loisy's immense mental discipline and capacity for concentration that in the midst of these intrigues, these distractions—what could have been more remote from his ordinary experience than negotiating with princes and government ministers?—he composed the most important work of his life. On November 10, 1902, the Parisian publisher Alphonse Picard put on sale at his shop at 82 rue Bonaparte—across the square from the church of Saint-Sulpice—1,500 copies of a book, 235 pages long, bound in orangeish red. There had been an additional run of 100 complimentary copies, a deluxe edition bound in a dusky rose color. "Very few books," Félix Klein observed, "have produced in the religious world, and among those interested in that world, so much uproar and anxiety."[25] The book, titled *L'Évangile et*

23. See chapter 8.

24. When Waldeck-Rousseau forced Lacroix's promotion upon the curia, the nuncio in Paris tried to console Rampolla by describing Tarentaise, accurately enough, as "la più piccola e la meno significante di tutte Diocesi di Francia." Both Tarentaise and Saint-Jean-de-Maurienne have long since disappeared, absorbed into the archdiocese of Chambéry.

25. Félix Klein, *La Route du petit Morvandiau*, 6 vols. (Paris: 1950), 6:9.

l'Église, the first of the celebrated *petits livres rouges*, sold out its first printing in six weeks' time.[26]

Actually Picard offered for sale two of Loisy's books that day. The other was *Études évangéliques*, the published version of the lectures on the Gospel parables Henri Bremond had listened to during the autumn of 1901 and had approved of so heartily.[27] But this sort of publication was the scholar's stock-in-trade, aimed at a specialized audience, a way of gaining for himself a modest reputation outside the classroom. Loisy never prepared a lecture he did not intend ultimately to publish in one forum or another, and in this he was typical of the professional academicians of his generation. *The Gospel and the Church*, on the other hand, fit into an entirely different category. It was a work that aimed its message at a broadly educated public. It addressed contemporary questions in which that public was deeply interested. Far from displaying the tedious trappings of the lecture hall, it sparkled with the literary brilliance of a fine stylist. And—not the least important reason for its immediate notoriety—it challenged the authority of one of the most famous savants of the time.

Adolf Harnack, at fifty-one, was a product, indeed a luminary, of that German university system which so dominated Western intellectual life at the end of the nineteenth century. Having taught theology and church history at Leipzig, Giessen, and Marburg, he was awarded a professorship at Berlin in 1889, despite fierce resistance to the appointment by conservatives. No one could deny his enormous erudition, best displayed perhaps in his *Lehrbuch der Dogmengeschichte* (which was translated into seven English volumes, with the title *History of Dogma*). Opposition to him stemmed rather from his rejection of any doctrinal system whatever, on the grounds that such dogmatism represented an unwarranted intrusion into the primitive Christian texts. Harnack, in short, with all his intimidating learning, was the quintessential higher critic and liberal Protestant.

In the winter term of 1899–1900 he delivered a series of sixteen lectures which were open to members of all the faculties of the University of Berlin. Six hundred students—or perhaps as many as a thousand[28]—regularly jammed into a large hall and listened to his fascinating exposition of what he presented as the essence, the heart, the core meaning of Christianity. Nor did Harnack's words fade away when these crowds of young hearers had returned to their ordinary studies. The lectures were published under the title *Das Wesen des Christentums*, which in its first year sold 50,000 copies. Ultimately the book went into seventy German editions and was translated into fifteen languages. This success was attributable to more than its author's scholarly reputation. Harnack's lectures, as spoken or as written, gave witness to the lively if undog-

26. See Poulat, *Histoire, dogme*, 43, 60.

27. See chapter 12.

28. Léonce de Grandmaison, "Le Christ de M. Harnack," *Études* 90 (March 1902): 738.

matic convictions of a true believer. And he brought to them a sense of mission. "This I know: . . . theologians . . . only half discharge their duties if they think it enough to treat of the Gospel in the recondite language of learning and bury it in scholarly folios."[29]

Indeed, for Harnack the critical scholarship of the nineteenth century had proved to be the precise instrument whereby the primitive simplicity of authentic Christianity, open to everybody, had been rediscovered. "There exists in the Gospel no 'theoretical religion,' nor is there any directive . . . to accept a ready-made theory. Faith and creed . . . develop out of the all-important act of conversion from the world to God, and creed is simply faith reduced to practice." The ruthless analysis of the texts by the rigorous methodology of the higher critics has stripped away the incrustations of eighteen centuries and revealed the essentially ethical message of Jesus for all to see. The Gospels provide no "biography" of Jesus, and they have absorbed into themselves legends and later interpretations. But, critically read, they do supply evidence of a human life of incomparable grandeur based simply upon a recognition of the fatherhood of God and the consequent moral imperative of love of neighbor. This is the essence of Christianity, and all the rest is elaboration, most of it bad. "Jesus . . . said clearly why and with what significance he called himself [Son of God.]: . . . 'No one knows the Son except the Father, just as no one knows the Father except the Son and those to whom the Son chooses to reveal him.' "[30] The dogmatists, said Harnack, preach nonsense when they employ their fanciful metaphysics to distort this verse into a proof of a trinitarian deity. What it really means is that Jesus came to a "consciousness" that "God who rules heaven and earth [was his] father. . . . Rightly understood, 'Son' means nothing but the knowledge of God," a knowledge Jesus invites his followers to share.

Instead the three great branches of Christianity, each in its own way, have larded over and entangled the simple teaching of the Gospel. The Greek Orthodox church "is nothing more than a continuation of the history of the Greek religion under the alien influence of Christianity" or perhaps "the result of a union between an already decadent oriental Hellenism and Christian teaching." As for the Roman claims, "the entire external and visible institution of a church claiming divine dignity has not the slightest foundation in the Gospel. It is a case of total perversion rather than mere distortion. . . . As eastern Orthodoxy may be better regarded as part of the history of Greek religion than of the Gospel, so Roman Catholicism must be viewed as a continuation of the Roman world empire." Even Protestantism, though immeasurably superior to Orthodox and Catholic in its devotion to spirit and truth, has failed to build upon the original genius of its founders. And that genius was itself flawed:

29. Author's preface to the English translation, titled *What Is Christianity?* (London: 1902), iii.
30. Matthew, 11:27.

"[Luther] not only adopted the old dogmas of the Trinity and the two natures [in Christ] as part of the Gospel—he could not examine them historically—and even made up new ones, but he was also completely incapable of distinguishing between 'doctrine' and Gospel. . . . The inevitable result was that intellectualism still held sway [and] that Scholastic doctrine remained a test for salvation."

"Gentlemen," Harnack concluded his final lecture, "it is religion, the love of God and neighbor, that gives life meaning." But bear in mind that the genuine religion of the Gospel has spurned all systems:

It has outlived all the changing philosophies of the world. It has cast aside . . . forms and ideas once held sacred. . . . It has become spiritualized, and in the course of history it has learned to apply more confidently its ethical principles. In its original earnestness and in the solace it offers, it has appealed to thousands in all ages; and in all ages it has thrown off its encumbrances and broken through its barriers.[31]

Given the vast circulation it eventually attained, Harnack's book received at first surprisingly little attention in French intellectual circles.[32] From Jerusalem Marie-Joseph Lagrange gave it a lengthy review, paying tribute to the author's "noble words"—"M. Harnack recognizes that science has not kept its promises, that the soul is empty without religion"—but also reproaching him for, among other things, a typically German Lutheran ignorance of Catholicism.[33] In *Études* a clever young Jesuit named Léonce de Grandmaison also spiced his disagreement with a little faint praise and reached a conclusion similar to Lagrange's: "The first impression of a Catholic reading these pages is that of a complete withdrawal from the real world. . . . What in truth separates us from the liberal Protestant theologians resides much less in the critical divergences in exegesis or history than in the philosophical principles which interpret them." Like all the higher critics, Harnack, tangled in his Kantian web, would, if he could, sweep away every element of religious mystery.[34]

IN THE MIDDLE OF MAY, 1902, a French translation of Harnack's book appeared, titled *L'Essence du Christianisme*. Alfred Loisy read it and was intrigued by it, and he thought he discerned a critical weakness in its lynchpin argument. Harnack had made much of the text from Saint Matthew in which Jesus "defined" his sonship to God.[35] Loisy, hard at work on his own study of the Synoptic Gospels, believed that verse to have been a late interpolation into the Gospel. If so, Harnack's insistence that Jesus's understanding of divine

31. Adolf Harnack, *Das Wesen des Christentums* (Leipzig, 1908 ed.), 93–94, 81, 137–38, 163–64, 182–83, 187–88.

32. Rivière, *Modernisme*, 159.

33. *Revue biblique* 10 (January 1901), 110–11, 122–23.

34. Grandmaison, "Christ de Harnack," 750, 761–62.

35. See note 30, above.

paternity was the "essence of Christianity" opened itself to serious rebuttal. There was at that moment a lull in the affair of the Monacan bishopric; indeed, it seemed likely that Loisy's chances for that dignity had disappeared. After some hesitation, and a canvass of the materials he had ready to hand, he decided that a short, popular book could be written quickly and with little trouble. Six weeks later—at about the time Béard first contacted him—it was finished. He had told no one about the project except Baron von Hügel and Archbishop Mignot, and only the latter read the manuscript prior to publication. It was returned to Bellevue from Albi on September 17, the archbishop professing himself to be "very satisfied." Loisy threw out hints, to be sure, to a few others. A half century later Félix Klein recalled how he talked casually about Harnack's errors and the reasons they should be refuted. "I can still hear the tone of his voice, half-serious, half-playful, but very affirmative, in which he said to me: This time, at least, they are going to be satisfied."[36] Houtin learned of the book's existence only days before it went on sale. Louis Duchesne was told nothing at all.[37]

Presuming Klein's memory to have been reliable, the "they" to whom Loisy referred must have been the ecclesiastical authorities. He realized that such potentates would be reluctant to give him a miter, but since he was seriously engaged in efforts to attain one at the very time he was writing and proofreading *L'Évangile et l'Église*, he could not have thought publication of the book would damage his prospects. Indeed, Loisy heard later that one highly placed prelate confessed himself charmed by the book because it had not bored him as most theological works did; but, even if the rumor were true, Giuseppe Sarto, patriarch of Venice, was far away and had nothing to do, as yet, with the appointment of bishops in France.[38] Perhaps *L'Évangile et l'Église*, a popular statement of the apologetic project Loisy had dreamed of devising since the days he had listened to Renan at the Collège de France,[39] provided also a measure of its author's own preternatural self-confidence.

It was at any rate a stunning performance. Within a few pages of prose hard and brilliant as a diamond Harnack's emotional and overly simple argument lay in tatters. "The aim of this study," Loisy began, "is to deal with history. . . . And since the learned professor proclaims his work to be historical, it will be discussed solely in accord with historical data." Harnack has maintained "that the essence of the Gospel consists solely in faith in God the Father, as revealed by Christ," and in so doing he has forsaken—unintentionally no doubt—the very science he claims to espouse.

36. Klein, *La route*, 6:11.

37. Poulat, *Histoire, dogme*, 59–60.

38. Loisy, *Mémoires*, 2:259. Less than a year after the appearance of *L'Évangile et l'Église*, Sarto was elected Pope Pius X.

39. See chapter 4.

On the validity or insufficiency of this principle depends the value of the judgments given on the development of the church, of its dogma and worship, and of all the different creeds which refer to Jesus and his Gospel from the beginning until now. One should not be surprised, therefore, to feel a certain disquietude at seeing a movement as far-reaching as Christianity described as reducible to a single idea or solitary sentiment. Is this really the definition of a historical reality, or merely a systematic method of inquiry? Can a religion that has filled so large a place in history, and renewed . . . the consciousness of humanity really be said to take its origin and its whole substance from a single thought? How can this great force consist in one element? Can such a reality be other than complex? Is the definition of Christianity according to M. Harnack that of a historian or merely that of a theologian who takes from history as much as suits his theology?

Here, by this last rhetorical question, Loisy ascribed to Adolf Harnack the same fatal flaw as he did to the Scholastics for whom he had such contempt. He could have said nothing worse.

And the relentless pursuit continued through the five chapters of *L'Évangile et l'Église*, demonstrating that wherever Loisy stood it was not on the ground of the liberal Protestants.

The historian cannot but refuse to regard as the essence of living Christianity a germ that multiplies without growing. Rather he should invoke the Parable of the Mustard Seed. . . . This grain . . . enclosed the germ of the tree that we now see. Charity was its sap. The power of its life lay in its hope for the coming of the kingdom. Its energy for expansion expressed itself in the apostolate. Its promise of success depended upon sacrifice. . . . All this was in the little seed, and all this was the real essence of the Christian religion. And all this asked only to grow, and it still lives even after having grown so much.

Thus, in contrast to Harnack's static image of an unsullied seed or core to which sinister barnacles of dogma and cult and institutional structures had fastened themselves, Loisy offered a picture of a vibrant organism which bloomed and blossomed, to be sure, but also shucked off dead skin and useless limbs as occasion demanded, all in accord with the evolutionary laws that determined the fate of living things. This, Loisy maintained, was the proper metaphor to capture the genuine essence of Christianity. This was the Catholicism he presented with exhilarating, if disconcerting, ingenuity.

At a most sacred moment, "at the last supper, when Jesus gave his disciples the symbolic cup . . . and bade them look forward to the festival of the kingdom of God," he offered also the key to his teaching, far removed from Harnack's simplistic understanding of it. "The idea of a heavenly kingdom is nothing but a great hope, and it is in this hope or nowhere that the historian should locate the essence of the Gospel, since no other idea holds so prominent a place in the teaching of Jesus." The kingdom has vast social implications, binding all believers together, and "it implies all the conditions of a happy life, both physical and moral, both external and internal, so that the coming of the kingdom can be described as the completion of history." Harnack, Loisy argued, committed a signal error in trying to divorce Jesus from his own milieu: "Because the eschatological idea of the kingdom belongs to Jewish tradition, M. Harnack considers it merely the husk of the Gospel, while faith in the eternal God is the kernel, the essence. Such a conception . . . is acceptable neither to the philosopher nor the historian, whose duty is only to examine what importance Jesus himself attached to the different . . . aspects of his doctrine."

Of course, Jesus thought "the kingdom was close at hand," and so did his disciples. Since the end was near, there was no need to "organize the little band of disciples into a monastic order, with a code of laws and definite spiritual exercises." Thus Harnack and conventional Catholic theologians repeat the same mistake: they try "to modernize the conception of the kingdom." "If [they] feel the need to supply an interpretation for the needs of the present day, no one will contest [their] right so long as [they] do not confuse [their] commentary with the primitive meaning of the Gospel texts." "The Gospel has not come into this world as an unconditioned and absolute doctrine, a unique and constant truth," subject to such trivialization, "but as a living faith, concrete and complex, whose evolution, to be sure, proceeds . . . from its internal force. . . . But it also has been influenced, in everything and from the beginning, by the surroundings in which the faith had its birth and has since developed."

Harnack's emphasis upon Jesus' sonship amounts to the "expression of a permanent relationship between Father and Son [and is] . . . a deduction of a theologian, not the statement of a doctrine or a sentiment Jesus himself expressed." Rather "it is clear that the title, Son of God, was for the Jews, the disciples, and the Savior himself the equivalent of Messiah." And this latter concept places Jesus squarely in the evolutionary process Loisy had sketched out in the last of his "Firmin" articles, "La religion d'Israel."[40] "Since the kingdom is essentially a phenomenon of the future, the office of Messiah is essentially eschatological." Therefore, "in one sense Jesus was the Messiah, but in another sense he was shortly to become the Messiah." For all humanity is in a perpetual state of flux and becoming, into which condition Jesus is thrust just like every other human being. Yet, in the midst of this whirling vortex, Jesus recognized his mission. When the priest Caiaphas asked him if he were indeed the Messiah, he admitted it was so, and then immediately shifted to the future tense: "And you will see the son of man sitting on the right hand of power and coming in the clouds of heaven."[41] Loisy was no more ready than Harnack to concede Christ's "divinity" or his bodily Resurrection in the conventional sense, but he was more persuasive than his German counterpart because of the

40. See chapter 10.
41. Mark 14:62.

breadth of his textual induction, the supple use he made of symbols, and the very daring of his conclusions. "The Christ of the Gospel did not divide his teaching into one part of absolute value, . . . the other of relative. Jesus spoke in order to say what he thought to be true, without the least regard for our categories of absolute or relative."

It is a worthless philosophy which tries to fix the absolute in any scrap of human activity, intellectual or moral. The full life of the Gospel is not in a single doctrine . . . but in the totality of its manifestation, which begins with the personal ministry of Christ and develops in the history of Christianity. All that has entered into the Gospel of Jesus has entered into Christian tradition. The genuinely evangelical part of Christianity today is not that which has never changed—for, in a sense, everything has changed and has never ceased to change—but that which in spite of all external changes proceeds from the impulse given by Christ . . . and serves the same ideal and the same hope.

That hope has been realized, and continues to be realized in all its richness and complexity, through the progressive unfolding of the Catholic church. "Jesus preached the kingdom, and, behold, it is the church that has come." Harnack adopts the classical Lutheran conceit that the church is the invisible gathering of the elect. But history knows no such phenomenon. "The organization of the body of elders, the preeminence of the bishop . . . [and then] of the bishop of Rome, . . . these changes are only defined and established in the course of time, according to the needs of the evangelical mission." "Needs": here is the term, whether as a verb or a noun or an adjective, that dominates the rest of Loisy's argument. Christianity, driven by its inner dynamism and subject to a mechanism analogous to natural selection, responds to perceived needs in order to survive. Why did it produce a hierarchical structure? "Christian communities . . . needed the preservative element of all societies: authority." More generally, "it would be absurd to desire that Christ determine beforehand the . . . adaptations that time would demand, since they did not exist prior to the hour that rendered them necessary. It was neither possible nor useful for Jesus to foretell . . . the future of the church." "The Pauline theory of salvation was indispensable in its time," as later the "theory of the incarnate Logos was . . . necessary when the Gospel was presented to . . . the pagan world." But those times have passed, and it is only theological fancy that attaches permanence and immutablility to such theories. The same could be said of the "divinity of Christ, [which] was the only possible way of making Greeks understand the [Hebrew] idea of Messiah."

If Jesus "did not lay down the constitution or the dogmas of the church," neither did he "prescribe or practice any external rite . . . which would have characterized the Gospel as religion." Yet Christianity "as a religion needed a ritual" and obtained one "of the kind its origin permitted or compelled. . . . The speed with which it was established demonstrates clearly that it was responding to an intimate and inevitable necessity." But cult like everything else in the Christian dispensation reflects the iron laws of evolution: "As the church did not attain all at once the ordinary development she continues to pursue, so also her ritual has developed, and continues to develop, under the permanent influence which gave it birth." Moreover, "the same necessity that presided at the birth of Christian ritual led to its increase." So, for example, "because Christianity . . . has become a form of worship, it has needed ministers. No assemblies made up of many people can meet often and regularly without chiefs, presidents, superintendents, and lesser officers to impose order." Indeed, the whole "sacramental system is . . . the most remarkable creation [*sic*] that has ever arisen spontaneously out of a living religion." Similarly, on the level of personal piety, "it was very natural that men should pray to God through Jesus, . . . and soon come to pray to Jesus himself. . . . The same spirituality . . . continues to flourish today in the numberless devotions that have become linked to the worship of Jesus, particularly the worship of the Eucharist and of the Sacred Heart." As time passed veneration, intuitively inspired, was extended to those considered close to Jesus—first the martyrs, then the ascetics, and finally and most appropriately the Virgin Mary, whose designation as Mother of God exhibited "a highly vivid sentiment of Christian consciousness." In short, "worship of the saints, like that of the Virgin and of Christ himself, became what it might and ought to have become under the circumstances and at the times when it has developed."

And what, finally, did Alfred Loisy see as the overall lesson of his joust with Harnack, as expressed in "this little volume"?

Certainly the political, intellectual, and economic evolution of the modern world has produced a great and . . . virtually universal religious crisis. The best means of confronting it does not seem to be the suppression of all ecclesiastical organization, all orthodoxy, and all traditional worship . . . but to take advantage of what is, with a view to what ought to be, to repudiate nothing of [our] heritage, . . . to recognize how necessary and useful is the immense development achieved in the church, to gather its fruits and continue it, because the adaptation of the Gospel to the changing conditions of humanity is as pressing a need today as it ever was or ever will be.[42]

SECRETARY DUMAY had advised Loisy to enlist the support of Cardinal Mathieu in his efforts to secure a bishopric, either in Monaco or in France. In Rome, Dumay explained, Mathieu "gets whatever he wants. The problem is to determine what he wants." François-Désiré Mathieu, formerly archbishop of Toulouse, had become a cardinal-in-curia in 1899, and as such he was considered a kind of informal agent for French interests there. Accordingly on

42. Alfred Loisy, *L'Évangile et l'Église* (Paris: 1902), vii-ix, xxvii-viii, 7–8, 12, 22–23, 37–38, 41–42, 53–54, 61, 67–68, 111, 93–95, 113, 136–37, 140, 180–81, 191, 202–3, 206–8, 210–11, 226, 233–34.

October 27, 1902, a few weeks before they were put on sale, Loisy sent Mathieu complimentary copies of *Études évangéliques* and *L'Évangile et l'Église*, together with a long and eloquent letter in which he told the cardinal of his double candidacy and of his conviction that his appointment to a bishopric would serve the best interests of the church. "I confide these things to your Eminence's discretion to make what use of them that seems good to you. I do not ask you to speak for me in high places, . . . but if you would speak I would be very grateful."

Mignot had warned Loisy to expect nothing from Mathieu, and nothing was what he got. The first chilling hint arrived at Bellevue on November 13 in the form of a letter from Louis Duchesne. Cardinal Mathieu had lent him his copy of *L'Évangile et l'Église*; "luckily" the pages of the first two chapters had been uncut, which meant the cardinal had not yet read the material contained therein, "which is so much in advance of the rest of us" that Loisy had better look sharp if he wanted to avoid the fate of Giordano Bruno, "mon voisin de bronze."[43] A week later Loisy received Mathieu's answer. The cardinal thanked him for "the beautiful books" which he found "interesting yet disconcerting. . . . I frankly do not see how to reconcile your views with the traditional teaching. . . . I remain perplexed and somewhat uneasy, perhaps because I am not particularly competent in these matters." At any rate, with regard to the candidacies "I am powerless to help you." Loisy was not, he added, a "reassuring" candidate for a bishopric, and on that word the exegete was left to brood.

Prince Albert had reached the same conclusion as Mathieu, and, though he had resubmitted his original list to the Roman curia, he was concentrating his efforts on securing the appointment of Félix Klein to Monaco. By the end of the year these had clearly come to nothing, and the weary and frustrated prince began to look elsewhere. Eventually he was persuaded to nominate, as Albert Houtin bitterly recalled, "an ignorant priest" who, since he was "rich and titled, was of course immediately approved" by the Vatican. Just before Christmas Loisy learned that the French government had deserted him and had nominated some one else to the see of Saint-Jean-de-Maurienne, this despite prior assurances that Combes and Dumay regarded the Monacan candidacy as "only a trial balloon." "Of course," Loisy confided to his diary, "that did not guarantee that the real balloon would go anywhere." He took what consolation he could when he learned that Rome adamantly refused to accept the government's nominee.

This small triumph did not succor him for long. On January 17, 1903, Cardinal Richard issued a statement condemning *L'Évangile et l'Église* because it had been published in Paris without the archbishop's imprimatur and be-

43. Duchesne's headquarters as director of the École de Rome were in the Palazzo Farnese, only a stone's throw from the Campo dei Fiori where a bronze statue of Bruno stood (and stands) on the spot where he was burned for heresy in 1600.

cause the book was "of a character to disturb gravely the faith of the Catholic people about the fundamental dogmas and teachings of the church." Within days seven more bishops had given public adherence to this sentence.[44]

44. Loisy, *Choses passées*, 249. For a detailed account of Cardinal Richard's action, see Roger Aubert, "Aux origines de la rédaction antimoderniste: deux documents inédits," *Ephemerides Theologicae Lovanienses*, 28 (May–September, 1961): 557–78.

Heart Speaks to Heart

One should not neglect to observe that Father Loisy's book is a sad sign of the times. But a single savant, however lofty a personage he may be, does not constitute the times all by himself. The really sad sign of the times is the reception the book has had and the disarray it has revealed.

—*Marie-Joseph Lagrange (1903)*[1]

NEITHER SIMPLE COURTESY nor the norms of professional confidentiality could prevent Cardinal Mathieu, a gossipy prelate, from sharing the news that Alfred Loisy had sought his intercession in hopes of securing appointment to a bishopric. Among others to whom he confided this information was Pierre Batiffol, who promptly spread it farther abroad, adding the pious observation that a priest who actively solicited promotion to the episcopate automatically disqualified himself.[2] Batiffol of course knew perfectly well that thousands of cathedral thrones would have suddenly become vacant had his absurd dictum been seriously applied.

As for the object of this chatter, it was not in his character to show any disappointment over the failure of his ecclesiastical ambition. Nor did he evince any surprise over the early reactions to *L'Évangile et l'Église*. Reviews in the conservative Catholic press were predictably harsh, and many believed that they led directly to Cardinal Richard's condemnation of the book. Loisy's own later opinion on that matter reflected a growing obsession: Richard had acted out of obedience to the malevolent forces in the Vatican.[3] But there were in any event consolations for the exegete to enjoy as well. "It is all simply superb," Friedrich von Hügel wrote him. "Never have you done anything more powerful, more beautiful, more appropriate to be incorporated, sooner or later, more or less, into the modification in the manner of presenting, of con-

---

1. M.-J. Lagrange, "L'Évangile et l'Église," *Revue biblique* 12 (April 1903): 298.
2. Houtin and Sartiaux, *Loisy*, 111.
3. Loisy, *Choses passées*, 241.

ceiving Catholicism by the official church itself."[4] The baron, as was his wont, began circulating copies of the book to friends and potential reviewers. George Tyrrell, who had read Harnack "with feelings of great contempt and disgust," responded to the refutation of Harnack by writing for the first time to its author: "Your book may, I trust, escape the envious attacks of those who keep the key of knowledge and will neither enter themselves nor suffer others to enter."[5] A particularly comforting notice came from Germany: "Harnack himself wrote a penetrating yet friendly review of [*L'Evangile et l'Église*]."[6] And Henri Bremond, traveling in Italy, assured Loisy that "here you are read, you are followed." Among those thoughtful Italians "entirely captivated by *L'Évangile et l'Église*" was Antonio Fogazzaro, senator and novelist.[7]

Bremond added that "you remain our theologian, and the *Bulletin de Toulouse* will change neither our ideas nor our sentiments." He was referring to Batiffol's critique of Loisy's book that had just been published in Toulouse. But however bad the blood was between the reviewer and the author, Batiffol could not be brushed aside as though he were a hysterical reactionary. His analysis was sober and direct: what Loisy had done, he maintained, was to distort Newman's notion of development by inventing an eschatology—Jesus' "mistaken" preaching of the imminent appearance of the kingdom—and then positing the living experience of the church over time as an adaptation and correction of that original error. What is such a theory, Batiffol asked, but Harnack writ large, whereby revealed religion will inevitably lurch into agnostic symbolism? "I stop short, I have not the courage to style this a philosophy of religion. It is certainly not critical history."[8] Loisy's reaction to this judgment by his old rival was savage. "Batiffol's article has appeared, a masterpiece of hatred and perfidy."[9]

Grandmaison[10] adopted a less strident tone than Batiffol—"a tone very dignified," as Loisy himself conceded, in "an article very sensible, very moderate"[11]—but his conclusion was not materially different: "We doubt that M. Loisy has finished his task."

It is difficult to summarize . . . the general impression that this powerful essay creates. *L'Évangile et l'Église* is the book of a man who knows the New Testament thoroughly and the immense literature—especially that written by Protestants—inspired by the

4. Quoted in Loisy, *Mémoires*, 2:157.

5. Quoted in Nicholas Sagovsky, *"On God's Side": A Life of George Tyrrell* (Oxford: 1990), 155. See also Loisy, *Mémoires*, 2:170.

6. See Loisy, *Mémoires*, 2:270.

7. Bremond to Loisy, 17 January, 1903, quoted in Blanchet, *Bremond*, 169–70. Also see chapter 11.

8. Pierre Batiffol, "L'Évangile et l'Église," *Bulletin de littérature ecclésiastique* 4 (January 1903): 13–15.

9. Loisy to von Hügel, 5 February, 1903, quoted in *Mémoires*, 2:214.

10. See chapter 13.

11. Loisy, *Choses passées*, 249.

Gospels. But the author's philosophical ideas call for sharp reserve, and still more does his manner of presenting and circumscribing the doctrine dealing with the person of the Savior. The Christ that is presented to us here, I am afraid, is neither that of theology nor (and for a Catholic the first conclusion anticipates the second) that of history.[12]

Loisy himself continued his daily round at Bellevue as before, and continued to receive those who, at this difficult time, chose to pay court to him. "Yes, I have gone to Bellevue," Joannès Wehrlé reported to Maurice Blondel in mid-December 1902. Wehrlé, a Parisian parish priest much devoted to Blondel's person and philosophy, was "profoundly impressed" by Loisy, "this modest man, upright, master of himself and indulgent toward others, a truly evangelical priest marked by the genuine imprint of Jesus Christ, that of the cross." Before he left the neighborhood Wehrlé called on the local curé, "who confirmed my impression. He told me that he considered [Loisy] 'as much a saint as a savant without peer,' and that 'his latest book reveals him to be a Father of the church.' "[13]

Blondel was glad to receive this "precious" report about Loisy's person. "It is good to soothe him, to tend his wounds, to console him." But the philosopher of Aix was not so sure that the author of *L'Évangile et l'Église* deserved to rank with Athanasius and Augustine. Loisy had sent him a copy of the book, and the opening chapters of it had alarmed him, much as they had Louis Duchesne.[14] On a quick perusal, he told Lucien Laberthonnière, "it appears to my tired head a little confusing, altogether too subtle, searching for and displaying only the external becoming (*fieri*) of Christ, the human psychology, the historical evolution. But this impression of the first two chapters may be unjust and may be corrected by what follows, though perhaps it is not wrong to say that *our* apologetic is the only guarantee of *their* critique."[15] In acknowledging receipt of the book to Loisy, Blondel offered him congratulations for having successfully navigated "between Ultramontane caesarism and idealist anarchy," but he also added, "timidly," a tentative note of reserve.[16]

Laberthonnière for his part was rather more favorably impressed. "I admire [Loisy's] chapter on the church and particularly the one on dogma. . . . There is in the book a profound grasp of reality. Never has Catholicism been better disengaged from Protestant anarchy and Ultramontane authoritarianism." Yet he agreed with Blondel about the opening section of *L'Évangile et l'Église*:

12. Léonce de Grandmaison, "L'Évangile et l'Église," *Études* 94 (January 1903): 174–75.

13. Wehrlé to Blondel, 12 December, 1902, in Marlé (ed.), *Au coeur*, 50. It should be noted that the editing of the crucial correspondence printed here (see following notes) has been severely criticized by both Poulat, *Histoire, dogme*, 40–41, 514–23, and Virgoulay, *Blondel*, 99–100.

14. See chapter 13.

15. Blondel to Laberthonnière, 17 November, 1902, in Tresmontant (ed.), *Correspondance*, 154–55.

16. Blondel to Loisy, 25 November, 1902, quoted in Virgoulay, *Blondel*, 96, and Blondel to Wehrlé, 10 December, 1902, in Marlé (ed.), *Au coeur*, 49. Loisy later claimed (*Mémoires*, 2:170) that Blondel first responded with "enthusaistic thanks."

"There is there a theology or, more precisely, an underlying Christology which the author leaves confused and which he does not express, not even doubtless to himself. He claims to be only a historian, but willy-nilly he is more than that." A month after offering this judgment, Laberthonnière made his own pilgrimage to Bellevue. "[Loisy] understands the reservations we have about his first chapters. In the next edition, he says, he will clarify matters. But Christology is a very difficult question, and in thinking about it I find that those who deal with it often do so in a puerile manner. They imagine a Christ who is a man only in appearance and only on the outside, who, with a kind of trickery, speaks like a man and thinks like God."[17]

This winter of 1903 was a season of great unsettlement for Laberthonnière. The government's assault upon the French religious orders, intensified by the personal rancor of Premier Combes,[18] continued apace, and, though strictly speaking they did not comprise a congregation, the Oratorians too fell victim to it. Their superior-general and his staff set up a headquarters-in-exile in Switzerland, while the ordinary members were dispersed. In February direction of the Oratorian *collège* at Juilly[19] was turned over to the local diocesan clergy, and Laberthonnière moved himself and his modest belongings to Paris. He took up residence in the fashionable seventh arrondissement, in an apartment at 23 rue Las Cases provided by a group of pious Catholic ladies who acted as a kind of auxiliary to the Oratorians. Across the street stood the massive neogothic church of Sainte-Clotilde whose bells reassuringly tolled the quarter hour. Catty-corner from the front door of number 23 was a little park, its shrubs and flowers and benches fenced in around a stone bas-relief of the recently deceased composer César Franck. As places of banishment go, this was an extremely pleasant one. Here Laberthonnière said mass in his own chapel and acted as spiritual director to these devoted and generous benefactors. In order to augment his small income, he also taught courses at the fashionable Collège Stanislas, where his mentor Blondel had served a decade earlier and where his outspokenness on a variety of issues delighted the pupils and, more often than not, annoyed their parents.[20] But Laberthonnière found that such activites, however worthy, could absorb only a fraction of his restless energy. Somewhat at loose ends, he considered the possibility of editing a learned journal or perhaps of organizing an association of progressive Catholic intellectuals. But for the moment such prospects did not appear likely to be realized.

One happy consequence of his time at the Stanislas was his acquaintance with Édouard Le Roy, who was also on the staff there in 1903. Le Roy, a thirty-three-year-old native Parisian, had studied science and mathematics at

---

17. Laberthonnière to Blondel, 20 November and 21 December, 1902, in Tresmontant (ed.), *Correspondance*, 155–56.
18. See chapter 13.
19. See chapter 9.
20. Beillevert (ed.), *Laberthonnière*, 21–23.

the École Normale Supérieure—Blondel's alma mater[21]—and had been awarded his doctorate in 1898. After that he taught mathematics for some years at several *lycées* and *collèges* in and near Paris. In his deep personal piety and attachment to the church, he was a layman cut in the mold of Blondel and von Hügel, and like them he had committed himself to the intellectual renewal of Catholicism. Thanks perhaps to his association with Laberthonnière, his scientific interests merged early on into philosophical and moral ones.[22] Le Roy for his part offered the uprooted Oratorian the consolation of a sensitive and enduring friendship. When he left the Stanislas for an appointment at another *collège* he wrote: "My dear Father, I hope to have the pleasure of seeing you again very soon. I shall definitely be here in Paris. . . . I rejoice in thinking that we shall be able to resume our former get-togethers. I certainly regret the reason why you have so much free time, but this very freedom is a blessing, because it will be at the service of the work we have undertaken."[23] That work would lead both of them shortly into painful conflict.

CONFLICT WAS ONCE AGAIN the lot of Alfred Loisy, now that Cardinal Richard had condemned *L'Évangile et l'Église*. Two weeks after that sentence the exegete, abiding by the advice of Archbishop Mignot, wrote directly to the cardinal. "Monseigneur, in response to the decision your Eminence has taken with regard to my book,. . . . I have suspended the publication of its second edition. I bow before the judgment your Eminence has given in accord with your episcopal rights." Then, carefully choosing his words, he added, "I condemn . . . all the errors that one can deduce from my book, when one situtates oneself, in order to interpret it, at a viewpoint entirely different from that in which I had placed myself." Richard replied in a friendly tone and invited Loisy to come to see him. But "the oily mawkishness of the good cardinal in similar circumstances never failed to exasperate" Loisy, and so he contented himself by dispatching (on February 5, 1903) another note which "reduced to its appropriate value the [earlier] submission, that is to say, to nothing."[24]

At this impasse the matter, for the moment, rested. Rome remained silent, and indeed late in the spring the rumor reached Bellevue that Leo XIII had refused to sign a censure of *Études évangéliques* as proposed by the Congregation of the Index. The significance of this restraint, however, was difficult to gauge: the pope, in his ninety-fourth year, had only weeks to live and one could legitimately wonder whther he was in full possession of his faculties. Loisy meanwhile mended fences with some of those he had shunned during the recent

21. See chapter 5.

22. See Jean Lacroix, "Édouard Le Roy, philosophe de l'invention," *Les études philosophiques* 10 (1955): 189–209.

23. Le Roy to Laberthonnière, ? September, 1903, in Perrin (ed.), *Laberthonnière et ses amis*, 39.

24. Loisy, *Choses passées*, 251–54.

months when he had hoped for promotion to the episcopate. The editor of the *Revue du clergé français* was one, and Albert Houtin was another. Several French bishops had combined Houtin's *Question biblique*[25] with *L'Évangile et l'Église* in a single denunciation, a circumstance that helped renew the bond between master and disciple. Houtin became once more a regular visitor at the flat on the Boulevard Verd-de-Saint-Julien. But one old friend Loisy continued to hold at arm's length. Marcel Hébert had retired to Brussels and from there informed his former associates that, instead of trying to prop up a disintegrating Catholicism, he would henceforth devote himself to constructing what he called "the House of the People." Loisy dismissed this pretension as "absurde" and its author as afflicted with an "esprit malade."[26]

Houtin noticed that during this late winter and spring of 1903 Loisy himself suffered, if not from an "ailing spirit," then at least from extended periods of ill-humor. One reason was doubtless the resistance to his views that now arose from a particularly significant source. He could brush aside, easily and indeed contemptuously, the disapproval of a mawkish Richard, or of a Batiffol: "Batiffol's [review of *L'Évangile et l'Église*] disgusts me," he told Houtin. "This individual's insolence and false-heartedness are truly inspired!"[27] But adverse criticism from Maurice Blondel was another matter altogether.

The philosopher and the exegete had never met. They were not in regular correspondence. Von Hügel and, to a much lesser extent, Bremond had forged whatever personal link there existed between them. If mutual respect did not necessarily guarantee that they fully understood one another's work, they nevertheless considered themselves comrades-in-arms, both dedicated to the process of intellectual and religious renewal. Loisy had even granted equal stature in this ill-defined movement—an extraordinary gesture for him—to Blondel.[28] Yet the latter had never been entirely at ease with the former's bold and unequivocal commitment to the higher criticism,[29] and a preliminary reading of *L'Évangile et l'Église* did nothing to reassure him.

Not that Blondel sympathized with the conventional attacks upon Loisy's book, shocking attacks, he thought, launched by those whom Laberthonnière dismissed trenchantly as "adventurers."[30] That one of them, in criticizing Loisy, should have "declared that *our faith is a matter of historical fact*, meaning that the supernatural is demonstrated in the same way as the shining of the sun," Blondel found simply "monstrous." Nor did he put much stock in the competence of the Holy Office or the Index to deal effectively with the prob-

25. See chapters 12 and 13.

26. Houtin and Sartiaux, *Loisy*, 114–15.

27. Quoted in Poulat, *Histoire, dogme*, 373.

28. See chapter 9.

29. See, for example, von Hügel to Blondel, 5 August, 1901, and Blondel to von Hügel, 31 December, 1901, quoted partially in Marlé (ed.), *Au coeur*, 42–44.

30. Marlé (ed.), *Au coeur*, 69.

lems of biblical exegesis. But saying so did not suggest to Blondel that he had put himself out of harmony with "the affirmations of the councils, the popes, or Leo XIII himself" that "the Bible cannot legitimately or with impunity be treated solely by exegetical methods." And here precisely was what troubled him about *L'Évangile et l'Église*: Loisy appeared to assume that "the Bible had become the object of a separate science, fixing itself upon its own exclusive terrain, upon a terrain closed totally to the penetration of the inspired Magisterium [of the church]."[31]

Blondel shared his early apprehension privately with several friends, but, as he continued to pore over Loisy's text, it was chiefly to Abbé Wehrlé that he elaborated on his misgivings and worked them out in his mind. That worthy curé, so devoted to him, was an easy convert. Wehrlé also had a sharp ear for ecclesiastical gossip, and his original enthusiasm for Loisy and Loisy's book was further undermined by the persistent rumors, circulated by reliable sources, that the exegete did not in fact believe in the divinity of Christ. Nevertheless, Wehrlé urged Blondel to contact Loisy "in this cruel hour" and to present to him candidly whatever objections he had. But Blondel's native reserve gave him pause. "I am a little reluctant to address Father Loisy directly, as though I had to teach him a lesson, or to reprimand him, or to explain methodology and metaphysics to him." So, in order to get round this fastidious scruple, it was decided that Blondel should write to Wehrlé who would in turn deliver the missive to Bellevue.[32]

The letter was written on February 6, and it initiated a literary dialogue that lasted for a month: Blondel wrote four times, Loisy three.[33] Blondel's contributions were of such enormous length that Loisy was moved to observe, ironically, "You must have been born to write encyclicals, and, if I am admitted to the approaching conclave, I shall propose your candidacy [for the papacy]." Though, predictably, Loisy's prose was the more pungent, courtesy was meticulously maintained by both sides and expressions of regard exchanged. Yet to a considerable extent it was a dialogue of the deaf. Neither man really spoke the other's language, and when Loisy, clearly out of patience—"[Blondel] prescribed the special conception of blondelianism as a means of surmounting all the problems of exegesis"[34]—stopped the correspondence at the beginning of March, Blondel reacted with a sigh of relief.

Blondel, for all his diffidence, assumed the offensive. Loisy certainly has dispatched Harnack, but his "scientific attitude seems to me disconcerting and enigmatic, because it rests upon a threefold equivocation." In the first place, "when one studies the Gospel and tries to show that the church legitimately

31. Blondel to Wherlé, 6 January, 1903, in Marlé (ed.), *Au coeur*, 57.
32. Wehrlé to Blondel, January 26 and 3 February, 1903, and Blondel to Wehrlé, 4 February, 1903, in Marlé (ed.) *Au coeur*, 66–72.
33. See Marlé (ed.), *Au coeur*, 72–113. See also the analysis of Poulat, *Histoire, dogme*, 520—33.
34. Loisy, *Mémoires*, 2:228–31.

issues from that source, should one take as a starting point . . . (a) the consciousness that the authors of the New Testament had of the Christian reality [or] (b) the consciousness that Christ had of himself and of his work . . . and mission?" So much of Loisy's argument depended upon Jesus's preaching of the kingdom, and certainly "the first Christian generation lived in the expectation of an . . . imminent Parousia," to which fact the Synoptic Gospels testify. But does this mean that Jesus himself thought the end was near? After all— and here, in this dictum of Blondel, can be discerned the stark difference of personal religiosity in the two men—"for each of us the end of the world is very close."[35] Loisy, therefore, by muddling this distinction, has failed to describe the "authentic development of the Gospel in the Church and by the Church."

Second, "Father Loisy declares modestly that he is merely a poor decipherer of texts," with no theological or metaphysical pretentions. But, countered Blondel, echoing Batiffol and Grandmaison, how far can this "methodical doubt," this "systematic neutrality" be carried? The assumptions of metaphysics and theology are inevitably interwoven into any analysis of the kind Loisy had undertaken. No one can present an estimation of the relation of the Gospel to the church as a pure historian, no one can come to the literary evidence innocent of presuppositions and points of view. Indeed, the notion of "pure historian" is precisely that, a notion. What has Loisy done but adopted the Thomistic epistemology he pretends to despise, by attempting to divide the sciences one from another on the basis of their supposed objects? The author of *L'action*, the teacher of the method of immanence, could hardly be expected to suffer gladly the manifestation of such scraps of rationalist Scholasticism.

Finally, in its worst display of ambiguity, *L'Évangile et l'Église* had attempted to distinguish between the historical Jesus and Christ, the God-man, between "the psychological person and the metaphysical personality." So once again Scholasticism has reared its ugly head. Loisy had assured Laberthonnière, among others, that in the first two chapters of his book[36]—which had startled everybody who read them, even Louis Duchesne—only historical facts were at issue. There was in them no attempt to frame a Christology, a teaching on the nature and person of the Savior. If so, how can the development of the church's Christology, defended in Loisy's later chapters, be an "authentic" development of the Gospel? Such a non sequitur, said Blondel, can be justified only by invoking the logic-chopping favored by the Scholastic manuals. Loisy's tragic misunderstanding has been to deny to the historical Jesus a consciousness of his own divinity, to lock Jesus into the iron chain of evolution, specifically to ascribe to Jesus the monumental error of proclaiming the imminent end of the world. "Jesus preached the kingdom, and, behold, it is the church that has

35. Blondel to Wehrlé, 6 January, 1903, in Marlé (ed.) *Au coeur*, 59.
36. "Le royaume du Cieux" and "Le Fils de Dieu."

come." And if the kingdom Jesus preached is different from the church of Christ that has actually unfolded, then the whole process of Catholic development that Loisy so brilliantly described in his refutation of Harnack has been stunted and defective at its roots. For the prophet of *action*, for whom only the totality of experience—cognitive and affective, social and moral—could provide the ground of being, this distinction was radically intolerable. "To suppose that the Christ intellectualized by faith *(le Christ nouménal)* is God while Jesus is circumscribed by the ordinary limitations of an ordinary man, this is to return to that Scholasticism which slices reality into essences and existences, as though they were realities, and to indulge in verbal abstractions." Every man, whatever his intellectual limitations, knows that he is a man. Can less be ascribed to the Messiah? "To deny Jesus the consciousness that he was divine is to deny the divinity of Christ."

Here was the sticking point. Whether one read *L'Évangile et l'Église* with the hard eye of a Scholastic or with the relatively sympathetic one of an immanentist like Blondel, this central doctrine of orthodox Catholicism appeared to have been jettisoned in the name of critical history. Loisy had foreseen the difficulty and had written in the introduction to his book: "There is no intention on my part to offer a defense of Catholicism or of traditional dogma. If such had been my purpose, this work would be highly defective, particularly with regard to the divinity of Christ and the authority of the church." He proposed, he said, simply to examine the bonds "that unite the Gospel and Catholic Christianity in history, and the reader of good faith will not be misled."[37] Despite this disclaimer, the exegete realized that Blondel's challenge was too crucial to be avoided. Thus he met most of Blondel's labored objections with a direct denial—"I know perfectly well that the distinction between the metaphysical personality and the psychological person [of Christ] does not bear upon the actual Christological problem"—or with an enigmatic maxim—"I have not placed Christ at the summit of history in order to deny that he was within it"—or, most often, with a reassertion of the critic's autonomy—"[The official] theology makes it necessary for the historian to barricade himself against it and so, alas, to seclude himself where he can hide from its tyrannical surveillance." But on the issue of Christ's knowledge of himself, and hence of his divinity, Loisy answered Blondel straightforwardly and with the full courage of his convictions.

The idea that Christ had a consciousness of being personally God from the moment of his conception . . . is for the historian pure fiction. . . . No doubt you will admit that the divine consciousness of Jesus would develop in him in accord with the law of development of human consciousness. Historically, the personal, messianic, and divine consciousnesses of Christ are mixed up together in their development. I do not see, and I certainly cannot prove, that this process attained during the earthly life of

37. Loisy, *L'Évangile et l'Église*, vi-vii.

Jesus the consciousness of his absolute identity with God. . . . I leave you perfectly free to think that you have found extrahistorical means of defining historically the consciousness of Jesus. As for me, a historian, I know nothing of such means, and even if I understood them I would hesitate to use them, because they are not the method of history.[38]

So, out of a cascade of words, the fundamental disagreement emerged clearly, and Blondel pondered how he might resolve it. He received little consolation from his and Loisy's mutual friend, Friedrich von Hügel, to whom, even before his correspondence with the exegete began, Blondel had confided his reservations. The baron, while willing to grant that historians as a group—and Loisy was no exception—took too little account of metaphysical considerations, remained nevertheless firmly in support of the contentions advanced in *L'Évangile et l'Église.* Blondel, "my very dear friend and comrade in struggle and in hope," had to bear in mind that history had now achieved a maturity which the oldfashioned apologetic had to respect on its own grounds. As for the substantive, "the most formidable," issue, von Hügel could not agree that Loisy had exceeded legitimate limits in the explanation he gave of Christ's attitude to the Parousia or of his self-consciousness. Indeed, the baron was astonished that Blondel did not distinguish between the terrestrial and the glorified Christ. "When I pray to him and adore him here in my room, or before the Tabernacle [in church], it is without doubt *the same Christ* who preached on the shore of the Sea of Galilee, *but the same Christ in a different condition.*" Very much in character, von Hügel asked Blondel to concede that Loisy's treatment would result in a greater devotion to the person of Jesus, and, as well, to take into account the exegete's own spiritual temperament: "The God of all gifts has endowed [Loisy] admirably, with peerless veracity and discernment, with moral courage, with insuppressible perseverance."

But Blondel remained unconvinced, even though von Hügel wrote to him at a length matching his own.[39] Loisy's historicity, Blondel insisted to his "precious friend," had degenerated into historicism. He has "substituted the idea of evolution for that of development." "If the idea of the kingdom has been the principal vehicle [of Catholic development] at the beginning, I do not believe it has ever possessed this entirely Scholastic precision that [Loisy] has been inclined to attribute to it." "In order to find Christ, if he is the Incarnate Word, we cannot simply . . . depend on historical determinism, dictated by a regressive and analytical procedure. To define [Christ] only by his earliest interpreters [i. e., the synoptics] is to cut off *a priori* and without discussion the consideration of his supernatural character." On the contrary, "I believe in the identity and deep-seated unity of all the Christs of tradition, that of Mark,

38. Marlé (ed.), *Au coeur,* 96, 72–74, 75–76, 77–79, 84, 103, 81, 83–84, 103.
39. See Marlé (ed.), *Au coeur,* 114–50.

that of John, that of Athanasius and Augustine and Thomas [Aquinas] and Teresa [of Avila] and Margaret Mary.[40] . . . One can see Jesus only in his total work and by way of his immanence in the church as well as in the Gospel."

Early in April 1903 von Hügel wrote plaintively to Aix: "I tell myself, very dear Friend, that the time has come when it would be well if we, very calmly, returned to our respective studies. At least I have the feeling . . . that I ought not *actually* attempt to see any further or better. God will help us, I believe, both of us, if we try to desire only him and the reign of his Christ." The pain was felt mutually. "The [recent] letter of Baron von Hügel," Blondel had reported to Wehrlé as early as February—"I venerate him as one of the richest spirits, the most vital, the holiest that one could meet in this world, and of an erudition so prodigious that his vitality remains fresh and new—his letter cost me hours, long nights of disquiet, of torments even, as though a tempest had uprooted something deep inside me."[41] The pain was felt mutually, and more was to come.

"THIS BOOK IS A GAMBLE." So began a review of *L'Évangile et l'Église*, which appeared during that same sad April when Friedrich von Hügel was, to a degree at least, separating himself from Maurice Blondel. "To have accepted debate with a great Protestant theologian on the ground the latter had chosen," Marie-Joseph Lagrange continued, for "a Catholic priest, condemned by his archbishop," to have crumpled "the edifice of . . . a master in Germany . . . like a house of cards," this is "a gamble" and also "an interesting paradox, . . . and many have thought the game won." But in fact "it is Christianity whole and entire that has been put to the wager, and gravely compromised thereby, however pure may have been the author's intention." Like so many other commentators on the little red book, Lagrange rejected Loisy's claim that he spoke only as a historian. "One might have smiled at this conceit addressed to theologians when it was a question merely of Babylonian mythology. But the shorter the jests the better. One needs to have read only two lines of Father Loisy to realize the invincible attraction theological problems have for him." Indeed, "it is one of the seductions of his marvelous talent, this instinct that draws him to the consideration of divine things." There followed a lengthy textual analysis, citation by citation, of the historical evidence put forth by Loisy, leading Lagrange—no mean exegete himself—to assert: "If [Loisy] really thinks that [the primitive] faith has been transformed, we ask [him] at least for some convincing proof. We doubt very strongly that [he] will be able to furnish it."[42]

40. Margaret Mary Alacoque (1647–90) was a visionary largely responsible for the spread of the cultus of the Sacred Heart of Jesus, a devotion particularly popular in France. She was beatified in 1864 and canonized in 1920.

41. See Marlé (ed.), *Au coeur*, 140, 126, 132, 129–31, 146, 148.

42. Lagrange, "L'Évangile et l'Église," *Revue biblique* 12 (1903): 292, 300–301.

Lagrange wrote these comments in Rome. His arrival there a month or so earlier marked the climax of a period of incessant work, travel, and anxiety. Keeping afloat the École at Jerusalem and the *Revue biblique* in Paris took its toll on his energies as well as on his highly strung personality. He seemed to be constantly on the road or on the sea. In the autumn of 1901 he had gone to Rome to receive the degree of *Magister* in theology—a politic gesture arranged by the Dominican master general as a means of neutralizing the mounting conservative criticism of the École and its director. From there he traveled to France and visited his mother for the last time (she died the following May). Back in Palestine he worked with his accustomed doggedness at various research projects—mostly related to the Old Testament and to Semitic religions generally[43]—and worried all the while about money and personnel. Attacks upon him and his work continued from the "intransigent conservatives" and no less from *les loisystes*, who accused him of "affecting prudence in order to distance himself" from their mentor.[44]

Lagrange returned to Europe in the autumn of 1902. "Scarcely arrived in Paris, I was called to the deathbed of my sister. I experienced the profound consolation but also the sorrow of assisting as a priest during her last agony." October he spent at the Dominican friary in Toulouse, preparing the six lectures his friend Monseigneur Batiffol had invited him to deliver at the Institut Catholique. The rector, fearful of hostile demonstrations, had carefully restricted the audience to two hundred. Apparently he expected females to be particularly troublesome at hearing discourses on such subjects as "Primitive History" and "The Historical Character of Hebrew Civil Legislation," because only a dozen women were admitted to the hall, and they "by special ticket in advance, in order to avoid any irritability (*pour éviter les susceptibilités*)." Complaints were registered with the local archbishop about Lagrange's "novelties," but that prelate's supportive appearance on the fifth evening tended "to calm the malcontents."[45]

Immediately after the sixth lecture, Lagrange caught the night train to Marseilles and next day, November 12, boarded a packet bound for Palestine. But a cholera epidemic was raging in Haifa, and so the ship was diverted to Beirut. With heavy rains making overland travel for the time being impossible, the Latin bishop of Beirut offered Lagrange temporary hospitality and lent him a copy of a document just received from the Vatican. The papal letter, titled *Vigilantiae*, announced the formation of that biblical commission von Hügel had heard about the year before.[46] "I was struck," Lagrange remembered, "by

43. See Braun (ed.), *L'oeuvre du . . . Lagrange*, 207–15, for Lagrange's publications during this time.

44. Lagrange, "L'École biblique," 117, 112. See also chapter 12.

45. Lagrange, "L'École biblique," 115–16. The lectures were published under the title *La methode historique* (Paris: 1903).

46. See chapter 13.

the new tone in the pope's words." The pontiff by no means surrendered any of the principles enunciated consistently through his long pontificate, but he did show himself open to "another aspect of the scriptural question." For Leo XIII stated explicitly that he intended the new commission to take into account, indeed to rely upon, the research of the modern critics. So much, exulted Lagrange, for his reactionary antagonists who insisted that nothing new could be learned about the Bible. "The Holy Father had opened a royal road. . . . Those sciences that generally attack the Sacred Scriptures must supply the arms with which such attacks can be successfully combated." Not that the pope failed "to warn against what politicians might have called the peril from the left." Particularly dangerous were those scholars—and Lagrange must have thought of Loisy—"who habitually and frequently indulge their taste for rash judgment." Some days later, the rains having abated, Père Lagrange with a lighter heart than before took the road to Jerusalem.

"After a long absence and so difficult a return, I thought I should have the whole winter for tranquil study." But on February 1, 1903, he received a message from the master general calling him back to Rome. Only days before a copy of *L'Évangile et l'Église* had arrived in Jerusalem. "I put the little book in my bag and read it during the five days we were quarantined before taking ship out of Alexandria." Though Lagrange pondered Loisy's argument and considered his response to it on the brief voyage to Italy, other musings also occupied his mind. Once in Rome he inquired, "not without some anxiety," the reason for the summons. "Go and ask Cardinal Rampolla," the master general replied. "It is he who wants to see you."

The secretary of state received Lagrange graciously and, going straight to the point, said that the pope wished to associate the *Revue biblique* with the new biblical commission. Leo XIII could of course command this to be done, but he preferred to allow the Dominicans of Jerusalem to weigh the matter and then to make a decision "in perfect liberty." "I asked the cardinal if I could speak freely, and when he smiled in assent, I dared to suggest that [because of so many attacks on us] the real intention . . . was to bring us to Rome in order to keep us under surveillance and to hold us on a short rein." "You have badly misunderstood Leo XIII's thinking," Rampolla replied sharply. "His intent is the opposite. He wants to show that one can write in Rome, under his very eyes, with complete scientific freedom, without attempting to undermine any dogma well understood!" And there was more. The original list of expert consultors to the commission had not included Lagrange's name. That oversight, the cardinal said, had been corrected. Finally, the pontiff intended to found an institute of biblical studies in Rome in which Lagrange would have a place while he continued to edit the *Revue*.

During the weeks that followed this remarkable interview, Lagrange was filled with what he called "hésitations et perplexité." What had happened since the denunciation of four years earlier to bring down this shower of official favoritism? One of the secretaries of the biblical commission, an English Franciscan named David Fleming, told him it marked the victory of "moderate progressivism" in the biblical field or, as an Italian cleric put it, "del progresso senza rottura."[47] Lagrange naturally welcomed this improved climate, but he recognized that it posed as many questions as it answered. For example, if the *Revue biblique* became the organ of the commission, might not its standards be lowered, might it not have to accept "collaborators more illustrious than competent?" And what would happen to Saint-Étienne de Jerusalem if a center for biblical studies were set up in Rome? Would the Dominicans have to move their operation *en bloc*? If so, what would happen to the structures so painfully put together in Palestine? And who would pay for such an institutional transfer? Roman authorities over the centuries were notorious for initiating grandiose projects and leaving others to find the money to support them.

Most important of all, "what would be the character of the commission itself?" That body, despite the general outlines of it sketched in *Vigilantiae*, was still in a state of flux. Lagrange was confident he could work out a modus vivendi with Fleming, but what about the other permanent secretary, Fulcran Vigouroux—Loisy's old rival at the Institut Catholique of Paris—whose "conservative apprehensions" about Lagrange were matched by Lagrange's own reservations about Vigouroux's competence.[48] But beyond any problem that might arise between persons was the graver need to define what status the commission would enjoy within the Roman curia. Even at this moment the Index and the Holy Office were examining Loisy's writings. Would these entrenched bureaucratic watchdogs of orthodoxy cheerfully cede their traditional authority at the behest of an upstart collection of international "experts"? In his heart Lagrange doubted the proposed system could work, because it purported to combine two irreconcilable functions, scholarly evaluation and authoritative decision. This was to attempt to square the circle. "I must admit," said Lagrange wryly, "I shared M. Loisy's aversion for administrative science."

For the moment, however, the only pressing requirement was to settle the relationship of the commission to the *Revue biblique*. After weeks of negotiation between Lagrange and Fleming, a formal agreement was drawn up and, on March 28, approved by the pope. It specified that from January 1, 1904, the journal would be considered an organ of the commission and would be known as the *Revue biblique internationale*. The Dominican fathers of Saint-Étienne would continue to administer it and its language (except for Latin documents) would continue to be French. Its headquarters would be located in Rome, though, due to contractual arrangements still in force, it would still be printed in Paris. Consultors of the biblical commission, although not Dominicans, would be encouraged to publish articles in it. General supervision of its ortho-

47. "Progress without rupture."
48. See note 39, chapter 4.

doxy would be exercised by the master of the Sacred Palace, that is, by the pope's personal theologian, traditionally a Dominican. "Otherwise [the *Revue*] will be considered the official organ of the commission in that it will publish that body's public rulings; the rest of [the journal's] content will be of a purely scientific character, for which the commission will assume no responsibility. . . . Writers in the *Revue* will enjoy complete liberty in their scientific work, so long as they abide by the limits of Catholic doctrine, as explained in the encyclical *Providentissimus* and in the apostolic letter *Vigilantiae.*"

Despite his misgivings, Lagrange put the best face he could upon these developments. Yet he could not but wonder whether the Vatican establishment really accepted the shift in emphasis with regard to biblical studies that the pope had decreed. One day an Italian Jesuit, a professor at the Gregorian University, remarked to him: "Father Lagrange, are you acquainted with what the physical scientists call emdosmosis?"[49] Lagrange had to confess that he was not. The professor described the phenomenon and then said, "It is the same with biblical criticism. Only after the whole world has been saturated with it will it begin to infiltrate into Rome." Reflecting upon this sober prophecy Lagrange, at a farewell audience, stressed to the pope his desire to return to Jerusalem. But the aged pontiff ignored the hint. "Yes, by all means," he said kindly, "go to Jerusalem for Easter. Then you will come back here. I want you working close by me." As it turned out, however, Lagrange fell ill at Brindisi and did not reach Saint-Étienne de Jerusalem until May 2. Ten weeks later, on July 20, 1903, Leo XIII died.[50]

THE NEW POPE who emerged from the dramatic conclave that followed was sixty-eight-year-old Giuseppe Sarto, formerly patriarch of Venice. He assumed the name Pius X. The drama, however, had not been of his making. It had stemmed rather from the veto leveled against Rampolla by one of his fellow cardinals in the name of the emperor of Austria. The employment of this absurd anachronism—as though Franz-Josef spoke with the voice of Charlemagne—probably did not affect the outcome of the election; the chances of Leo XIII's able and strong-willed secretary of state were slim to begin with.[51] Indeed, if the powers of the Triple Alliance—Austria, Germany, and Italy— had been displeased by Rampolla's vigorous pro-French policy, many of the cardinal-electors were disillusioned by the failure of the strictly ecclesiastical aspect of that policy, the so-called *ralliement*.[52]

Pius X[53] was a rarity among popes in that his entire priestly career had been

---

49. Osmosis toward the interior of a cell or cavity.

50. Lagrange, "L'École biblique," 122–33, 338–42.

51. Aubert, "Trois pontificats," 23–24.

52. See chapter 8.

53. See, among other works, Ernesto Vercesi, *Il Pontificato di Pio X* (Milan: 1935), Charles Ledré, *Pie X* (Paris: 1952), and Pierre Fernessole, *Pie X: Sa vie et son oeuvre*, 2 vols. (Paris: 1952).

spent in the parochial ministry. Born into a family of modest means in Venetia, he had served as pastor of a rural parish and then of an urban one. Bishop first of Treviso and, from 1884, of Mantua, he had established a record of administrative efficiency in dioceses notably lacking in that quality before. But his reputation did not rest upon his sure-handed boldness, his attention to detail, or his other formidable skills as a manager. He was seen rather as a zealous and fervent priest, for whom the religious and moral well-being of his flock was the be-all and end-all. Nor did he doubt for a moment his capacity to define what that well-being consisted of. The personal piety he practiced in his daily life was the ultimate arbiter of all his decisions, and if he imposed high spiritual standards upon the people in his charge, and higher still upon his priests and nuns, he reserved the highest standard of all for himself.

These attributes led Leo XIII to promote Sarto to the great see of Venice in 1893. Yet the contrast between the two men could hardly have been more striking (unless it was that between Cardinal Pecci and *his* predecessor[54]): the sophisticated, remote, austerely slender nobleman gave way to the ruddy, somewhat corpulent, affable man of the people. A more-or-less conventional degree of spirituality was replaced by a devotional life of extreme intensity. The cosmopolitan Leo XIII, who gloried in the intellectual challenge of diplomacy and politics, stepped aside, so to speak, in favor of the highly parochial Pius X, who on principle distrusted compromise. The new pontiff believed that his sublime office committed him to deal in absolutes; he had little taste for the art of the possible. If, in adopting as his motto "To Restore all Things in Christ" he intended no rebuke to his predecessor, there were some who found one there.

Pius X, in short, adopted a set of working assumptions more reminiscent of his namesake, Pius IX, than of Leo XIII. This fact was reflected in the administration he formed, the key members of which shared his own admirable if narrow dedication to evangelization, clerical discipline, and unquestioning adherence to doctrinal teaching. Since the pope recognized fully his own inexperience in the world outside his beloved homeland—indeed, his single diplomatic inititative led ultimately to much reduced tensions with the kingdom of Italy—he attached particular importance to the appointment of a cardinal secretary of state. Rampolla he shunted off to the presidency of the biblical commission. To replace him in the secretariat—the powers of which were considerably expanded—the pope chose the young Anglo-Spanish aristocrat, Rafael Merry del Val.[55]

"TIMES HAVE CHANGED since the month of July," Louis Duchesne told Alfred Loisy shortly after the election of Pius X. "The hand that held back the

54. See chapter 2.
55. See chapter 11.

[inquisitors'] fires is no longer there." Vatican rumor was rife that Loisy would shortly be condemned. "Father Vigouroux anathemizes you, and the good cardinal [Richard] thinks of nothing but your extermination. . . . Now they are reinforced by Monseigneur Merry del Val, who would rather be persuaded to believe that Jonah swallowed the whale than to allow anyone to doubt the contrary." Scarcely less bad were the scribblings of Lagrange: "I need hardly tell you that the abominable style of that author and the wicked manner in which he speaks of you nauseates me." What if "these so orthodox people" demand next that we accept the historicity of the Book of Judith? "We are far from that, thanks in large measure to your courage."[56]

Loisy had long since learned to take in stride Duchesne's blend of clever cynicism and flattery. But, in the light of his extraordinary self-confidence, the news of an approaching Vatican condemnation of his work may have startled him. That work had proceeded at a furious pace during "the period of truce"[57] that had extended from the censure of Cardinal Richard in January through the last days of Leo XIII and the election of the new pope. In the early days of October Picard put on sale three new books by Loisy: a thousand-page commentary on the Gospel of John, a collection of previously published essays on the Sermon on the Mount, and a spirited apologia for *L'Évangile et l'Église*, titled *Autour d'un petit livre*. The author, convinced that for readers of good will a second little red book would suffice to explain and elaborate on the first, took nothing back.

The little book has resounded like a funeral bell in the ears of people who cannot, or will not, picture to themselves the present or the future of Catholicism except under the static and banal form of a past which in fact never existed. They have imagined that [*L'Évangile et l'Église*] has celebrated the death of the old exegesis and that it has proposed to conduct to the tomb Christ himself and his Gospel, the church and its authority, dogma and its truth, theology whole and entire, along with the sacraments and traditional Catholic worship. But far from being a work of skepticism and death, the little red book was a work of hope and of life. . . . The little book was, despite its faults and its didactic dryness, a homage to Christ-God and to the church, the living body of the immortal Christ.[58]

In form *Autour d'un petit livre* was composed of seven letters addressed to various friends and acquaintances of Loisy—among them Father Ludot, his philosophy professor at Chalons-sur-Marne,[59] Archbishop Mignot, and Félix Klein. Each of the "letters" treated a specific topic, like "la question biblique" or "la critique des Évangiles." In the light of the reaction to *L'Évangile et l'Église*, perhaps the most crucial of them, that addressed to Mignot, dealt with

---

56. Duchesne to Loisy, 17 October and 26 November, 1903, in Neveu (ed.), *Mélanges*, 84: 298–99.

57. Houtin and Sartiaux, *Loisy*, 116.

58. Alfred Loisy, *Autour d'un petit livre* (Paris: 1903), 20–22.

59. See chapter 1.

the divinity of Christ. About this central Catholic mystery Loisy argued as eloquently as before and, on the basis of his autonomy as a historian, reached the same conclusion as before: "[Jesus'] discourses, his conduct, the attitude of his disciples and his enemies alike, all these demonstrate that he was a man among men, 'like them in all things save sin,' and save also, one must add, in the intimate and indefinable mystery of his relationship with God."[60] The seventh "letter," directed to his confessor, the Sulpician Frédéric Monier, discussed "the institution of the sacraments." "It was the least original," Loisy recalled, but "it irritated the orthodox theologians most, because they understood it better than the others."[61] Original or not, the content was no surprise. And it seemed that at least in its polemic intent the exegete's argument here, as frequently elsewhere, amounted to reducing discussion to a single and simplistic choice, that between his position and the position of the most extreme conservatives. "The systematic conception of a program of ritual set up by Jesus before he died, in which the seven sacraments have their determined place, with an indication of what the Scholastic theologians like to call their matter and form, will not bear critical examination."[62]

Autour d'un petit livre circulated if anything even more widely than its red-bound predecessor, but it aroused the same negative reaction from the same chorus of conservatives and moderates.[63] More troubling to Loisy was the unenthusiastic reception given it by the archbishop of Albi, who had advised against writing it in the first place. Mignot suggested to Loisy that he had perhaps overemphasized rational development in his argument at the cost of God's omnipotent will to reveal.[64] If the rumor Blondel heard was true, the archbishop now believed the Vatican had little choice but to censure Loisy.[65] In any event Mignot, as a conscientious shepherd of souls, could not blithely ignore the danger of "offense to pious ears." Loisy, he told von Hügel at the end of October, "in writing only for intellectuals, has been wrong in not having sufficient compassion for those who are not intellectuals, and their number is very large."[66] But this opinion did not mean that Mignot was prepared to desert the exegete; in November he went off to Rome yet again in hopes of warding off a condemnation.

As for the baron, he was bending every effort in the same cause. He bombarded friends and acquaintances, both in England and abroad, with calls for solidarity and appeals to them to stand fast with Loisy. He submitted pieces of his own to the secular and the Catholic press and arranged for others to do

60. Loisy, *Autour*, 121.
61. Loisy, *Choses passées*, 267.
62. Loisy, *Autour*, 254. See the summary and analysis in Poulat, *Histoire, dogme*, 162–89.
63. For a summary, see Poulat, *Histoire, dogme*, 190–243.
64. Loisy, *Mémoires*, 2:261–62.
65. Wehrlé to Blondel, 17 and 21 December, 1903, in Marlé (ed.), *Au coeur*, 167.
66. Quoted in Poulat, *Histoire, dogme*, 476.

the same.[67] When David Fleming of the biblical commission—whom von Hügel up till then had considered an ally—published a letter unfriendly to Loisy in the *Times* of London, the baron hastened to reply to it. When he had read *Autour d'un petit livre*—a project that he, like Mignot, had originally discouraged—he assured Loisy of his support if not of his complete agreement: "You know that I am wholly with you; that these are *our* affairs, *our* hopes, *our* sweats, *our* crowns."[68] In mid-November, as he told Padre Semeria, he even sent a plea to Merry del Val, whom he did not much like or trust: "I tried to underscore for him the indubitable fact, and I know it very well, that a condemnation [of Loisy] will discredit Rome in the intellectual world, where all these questions will continue to be debated but where the Catholic solution to them will be wanting."[69]

The secretary of state's reply was a bare acknowledgment, which von Hügel took as a "snub." But in fact a decision had probably already been made. On December 16 a decree of the Holy Office was signed, directing that five of Loisy's books, including *L'Évangile et l'Église* and *Autour d'un petit livre*, be placed on the Index.[70] A week later, thanks to a leak to the press, the news reached the exegete even before it was communicated to him officially by Cardinal Richard. "From the beginning I was resolved to make a respectful submission, with explicit reservations that would vouch for my sincerity." Once more spurning the advice of his closest associates, he determined to address the Roman authorities directly rather than through Richard, for whom he had such contempt. Accordingly, on January 12, 1904, and again on January 25, he sent Merry del Val statements of compliance, but these, because of their "explicit reservations"—"I reserve the right of my conscience;" "I condemn . . . whatever from the point of view of faith may be reprehensible"— were deemed insufficient. Nothing short of a total and unequivocal recantation would do, Richard told him. With the threat of imminent excommunication hanging over him, Loisy played out the most poignant act in what he would call later "this odious comedy." "Very Holy Father," he wrote on February 28, echoing the motto Cardinal Newman had chosen for his coat of arms, *cor ad cor loquitur*,

I know the kindness of Your Holiness, and it is to your heart that I address myself today. I want to live and die in communion with the Catholic church. I do not want to contribute to the ruin of the faith in my homeland. It is not in my power to destroy in myself the result of my works. Insofar as it is in me, I submit to the judgment taken against my writings by the Holy Office. In testimony of my good will, and in hopes

67. See Barmann, *Hügel*, 105–9.

68. Quoted in De la Bedoyere, *Hügel*, 154.

69. Von Hügel to Semeria, 16 November, 1903, in Zorzi (ed.), *Briefe . . . von Hügels an . . . Semeria*, 2:487.

70. The others were *La religion d'Israel* (1901), *Études évangéliques* (1902), and *Le quatrième Évangile* (1903).

of pacifying troubled souls, I am ready to abandon my teaching in Paris, and I will suspend the scientific publications I have presently in preparation. I remain, very Holy Father, yours with the most profound respect.

But Pius X was no more persuaded than his various underlings had been. This "appeal to my heart," the pontiff proclaimed sternly in a letter to Richard, "does not come from his heart."

All these declarations are rendered null by [Loisy's] explicit protestation that he cannot renounce the result of his works. . . . I wish your Eminence [Richard] to make known to him in my name that in order to accept as sincere all his protestations, it is absolutely necessary that, confessing his own errors, he submit himself, fully and without reservation, to the judgment pronounced against his works by the Holy Office.[71]

On March 12 Loisy confronted Richard for the last time. When he departed the cardinal's office he called at the home of friends, who urged him to submit without condition. He agreed and placed in their hands a signed statement one sentence long, which was delivered to Richard later that day: "Monseigneur: I declare to your Eminence that, in a spirit of obedience to the Holy See, I condemn the errors that the Congregation of the Holy Office has condemned in my writings."[72]

71. Quoted in Loisy, *Mémoires*, 2:360–61.
72. Loisy, *Choses passées*, 272–99, and Houtin and Sartiaux, *Loisy*, 118–27.

CHAPTER 15

Histoire et Dogme

If Hügel . . . says that my thought is in agreement with that of Loisy, he is mistaken, and he gravely injures me without doing any service to his friend. . . . In fact, neither in method nor in doctrinal conclusions do we converge. Loisy maintains that there is a terrain upon which the historian is absolutely and definitively his own master; I deny this. Loisy does not believe that there is a formally miraculous revelation; I believe that there is one and that it is completely wrong to content oneself with some vague and infinitesimal religious spirit. Loisy does not radically distinguish a specific supernatural order; I consider it, on the contrary, beyond any naturalization. Loisy will not admit that Christ was conscious of his own divinity; I judge this a decisive point of difference. Loisy thinks the Eucharist is a symbol; I see it as the reality of realities.

—*Maurice Blondel* (1904)[1]

HERBERT CARDINAL VAUGHAN died a month and a day before Leo XIII. The friend of the von Hügels and of two generations of the Wards—the bluff country gentleman who had found himself thrust into an intellectual maelstrom he scarcely understood—Vaughan endured a harsh final rite of passage. A chronic heart condition had gradually reduced the big, handsome, silver-haired prelate to a feeble shadow. By the spring of 1903 he was clearly dying. Racked by sleeplessness and depression, his "poor heart labored and the breath came slowly, but the soul seemed to pant in a deeper agony within. It was not an attack delivered against any one revealed doctrine in particular; . . . the horror, the cruelty of the temptation lay in its whisper that 'nothing was true, all beliefs were false together, there was no God, no hereafter.' "[2]

Among the last visitors the cardinal received was Wilfrid Ward. "[He] talked of his love for my father and mother, and said he could wish nothing

1. Blondel to Bremond, 15 March, 1904, quoted in Blanchet, *Bremond*, 180–81.
2. Snead-Cox, *Vaughan*, 2:483–85.

better than that I should walk in my father's footsteps. He embraced me as I left and gave me his blessing and asked me to pray for him."[3] Ward knew nothing then of the mental trials to which Vaughan's simple faith was being subjected, and so he could only rejoice when he learned later that, just before the end, "a great calm came over the dying man, and his soul at last knew a perfect peace. . . . 'Don't let my thoughts get entangled tonight by stimulants and drugs,' [Vaughan] said earnestly and repeatedly. 'I want only to be with Jesus and the Holy family.' "[4]

The funeral mass, on June 25, 1903, served as the official opening of the great cathedral in Westminster which Manning had planned and Vaughan had brought to fruition. Friedrich von Hügel did not attend, though Lady Mary and Gertrud did. In September the bishop of Southwark, Francis Bourne, was promoted to the see of Westminster. "I have never exchanged one word with the new Archbishop," von Hügel told Ward, "and have only seen him once. But I thought it right to write him a carefully thought-out letter of congratulation, and his answer was somehow touching in its simplicity and humility. May he turn out either to already have all the essential qualities or to be able to acquire and develop them." Bourne proved to be the temperamental opposite of the impulsive Vaughan. Reserved, chilly even, he seemed to Ward "a sphinx" for whom it was hard to feel any affection. Yet he displayed far more than his predecessor did the kind of prudence proper to a ruler for which in due time Ward had reason to be grateful.[5]

In far-off Yorkshire, the changing of the ecclesiastical guard at Rome and Westminster had no bearing upon George Tyrrell's routine. Every day, in his plain little room in the Richmond presbytery, he pored over large tomes filled with the dense prose of philosophers and critics. Loisy's articles he read, and *L'Évangile et l'Église*, and Houtin's tract on French biblical criticism.[6] He rooted time and again through Blondel's obscurities and Laberthonnière's pungent manifestos, seeking, always seeking. After years of nagging by von Hügel he set himself to learn German. "But oh! what a language! Hebrew seems a simple task in comparison."[7] The delighted baron responded by dispatching to Richmond stacks of books by his favorite post-Kantian savants, which Tyrrell struggled to read in tandem with the daring speculations of a Frenchman named Henri Bergson. Some days the migraine and the nausea he suffered from left him spent and sluggish and yet sleepless on his bed. But never for long. Soon he was back at his table again, and his pen raced across the paper in front of him with a fury and a relentlessness that affirmed as much a seething unhappiness as it did a sense of mission.

3. Ward, *The Wilfrid Wards*, 2:147.
4. Snead-Cox, *Vaughan*, 2:489.
5. Ward, *The Wilfrid Wards*, 2:150.
6. See chapters 12 and 13.
7. Quoted in Schultenover, *Tyrrell*, 201.

Visitors, except for Henri Bremond, were received with reluctance. The Wards came the summer Vaughan died, and Josephine recorded that "the visit was not a success. I realised . . . that Wilfrid . . . got upon Father Tyrrell's nerves, and that the last thing he wanted was his advice."[8] Von Hügel stayed in Richmond for three summer weeks during each of the five years of Tyrrell's residence there, and at least once he brought Gertrud with him. The baron's Italian disciple, Giovanni Semeria, came and enthralled Tyrrell with provocative conversation about biblical criticism: "How wonderfully buoyant [he is]," Tyrrell confided to Bremond, "in the midst of the ruins he is creating!"[9] But on another occasion the number and persistence of the outlanders left him feeling "sick and silent."

Even the hovering and ever-solicitous Maude Petre grated on him. "Yes, I am a little tired of Vescovina—full of goodness and virtue, to be sure, but certainly full also of childishness; and, as you have observed, she fails regularly in reserve and discretion."[10] Whatever precisely these prudential shortcomings of hers may have been, the presence of Petre in Richmond inevitably gave rise to gossip, and finally Tyrrell told her she must leave: "I have never felt so sad as I did in telling her this, and, even more, in insisting on my decision in the teeth of her own conviction about what is just and prudent. . . . I am afraid the separation may kill her."[11] Though Tyrrell's overly dramatic fear did not materialize, Petre's return to London did cause her searing pain. "How I love him! and how I long to be with him!" she wrote in her diary. And yet a later visit to Richmond brought her no solace. "[I] can't understand why being near him always causes nervousness and depression. Perhaps it is the inevitable barrier which nearness makes visible."[12]

The barriers rose up all around him. The sense of isolation deepened. Increasingly, he felt trapped in a life he could not live and yet could not leave. Most of the English Jesuits he knew were sympathetic to Tyrrell, most of his superiors tried to accommodate him; but they could not understand the demons that drove him. He prowled the countryside on long walks with his terrier, Jack, returned to the presbytery unrefreshed and unappeased, and went back to his room to write letters of bitter complaint to Bremond or to ruminate on paper for Maude Petre about his youth. After a while he could no longer endure to pen the autobiographical essays she had induced him to send her. He could not find himself any more. "Our whole and entire life," he told Bremond, "in the pulpit, in the confessional, in counselling, or in presiding

8. Quoted in Ward, *The Wilfrid Wards*, 2:165.

9. Tyrrell to Bremond, 3 November, 1901, quoted in Schultenover, *Tyrrell*, 253.

10. Tyrrell to Bremond, 2 (?) January and 19 August, 1904, in Louis-David (ed.), *Lettres de Tyrrell*, 159, 170. "Vescovina," feminine diminutive of the Italian *vescovo*, meant "the little lady bishop." The unkind nickname may have referred to Petre's general demeanor as well as to her position as English provincial of her religious order. See chapter 10.

11. Tyrrell to Bremond, 18 September, 1904, in Louis-David (ed.), *Lettres de Tyrrell*, 172–73.

12. Quoted in Leonard, *Transformation*, 35–36.

at a meeting obliges us to play a role; we speak in the name of the Church or of the Society or of a system and a tradition which is *ours* the way our clothing is ours. But it is not *we*. All we are doing is defending a thesis that has been proposed to us by somebody else. I am beginning to think that the only sin is suicide or the failure to be one's self."[13] And inevitably there accompanied these dark thoughts even darker judgments of his brethren who, unlike himself, gave "docile submission" to "the Jesuit system" and so became "dreary, tiresome, self-centered, emasculated."[14] Nor had he, for a long time, hesitated to draw invidious comparisons between his own virtues and the inadequacies of others similarly situated: "There is not a single priest at Farm Street or, I fancy, in all London to whom I could recommend an *educated* agnostic to go with any hope, I do not say of being satisfied but even, of being understood." He grew to despise "the superficiality" of London, epitomized for him by his former colleagues: "I could not live on so little thought and reflection as suffices those good priests at [Farm Street] who never open a book from year's end to year's end, and who by posing as oracles to crowds of uncritical admirers lose their sense of proportion."[15]

Despite the clash he had had with Cardinal Vaughan in 1902 over the collection of essays called *Oil and Wine*—which dispute resulted, Tyrrell charged bitterly, in "a double censorship" being imposed upon him, one by the Jesuits and another by the cardinal—yet the two men had maintained a wary regard for each other.[16] Bourne, while still at Southwark, had granted an imprimatur to a new book of Tyrrell's—*Lex Orandi*, it was called—but aside from that he was as unknown a quantity to Tyrrell as he was to von Hügel and Ward. Then, at the end of 1903, Bourne, now archbishop of Westminster, actually read the book for the first time, and objected strenuously to the Jesuit provincial about the treatment in it of the virgin birth—a doctrine that Tyrrell did not bother to deny but to which he gave an emphasis indicative of the stage his thinking had now arrived at: "If we would find the religious and spiritual value of the doctrine we must seek it in the influence it has in fact exercised upon the heart [*sic*] of Christians and Saints. We must see in the Virgin Mother the highest expression and embodiment of Christian sanctity which the Holy Spirit has brought forth in the hearts of the faithful."[17] When informed of the new archbishop's complaints, Tyrrell offered to provide for the second edition an "amendment" consistent with "sincerity." But privately he expressed his "profound distrust of that gentleman who is a dangerous gossip and a trimmer"[18]—

---

13. Tyrrell to Bremond, 19 September, 1901, in Louis-David (ed.), *Lettres de Tyrrell*, 96.

14. Tyrrell to Bremond, 7 March, 1902, in Louis-David (ed.), *Lettres de Tyrrell*, 114.

15. Tyrrell to Gerard, 17 November, 1900, and Tyrrell to Raffalovich, 16 June, 1903, quoted in Sagovshy, *Tyrrell*, 120, 164.

16. See Schultenover, *Tyrrell*, 177–83.

17. George Tyrrell, *Lex Orandi or Prayer and Creed* (London: 1903), 174–75.

18. Tyrrell to von Hügel, 6 February, 1904, quoted in Schultenover, *Tyrrell*, 242.

an instance of the personal invective that seemed increasingly to pepper his speech when he appraised anyone of whatever rank who disagreed with him. Driven at any rate by his raging inner discontents, Tyrrell had reached a point past caring who the archbishop was or what he stood for.

Bourne preferred for the moment to let sleeping dogs lie, and so *Lex Orandi* went unchanged into a second printing. It was sandwiched between two other short books, both of which were published under pseudonyms and circulated privately. This trilogy testified to the distance Tyrrell had come from "mediating liberalism" and the degree that he had shaken loose from the influence of Newman. The author, perhaps too modestly, disclaimed "all pretence to being more than a weaver of materials gathered from many quarters which in the present fabric may acquire a very different significance from that which was theirs in the original texture from which they have been torn."[19] And to von Hügel he wrote: "My theory is an amalgam of Loisy, Blondel, . . . Eucken, etc.—nothing being my own but the amalgamation; some day you shall read it—for your sins."[20] Certainly, it was true that Tyrrell had drawn his argument from a great variety of unacknowledged sources—from Loisy, as he said, and from the baron's German philosophers and psychologists, from Blondel and Laberthonnière, most of all perhaps from Bergson[21]—and that not all of them had he been able fully to digest. But there is more than one kind of originality; Tyrrell, with his wonderful gift for clear and sparkling English prose, put together a synthesis of those authors he had been obsessively studying, a synthesis which, if incomplete and extremely difficult to follow, nevertheless possessed authenticity and a rough coherence.

The first of the pseudonymous works—"This synthesis is absolutely unpublishable [because of censorship] during the present century!"[22]—was a long pamphlet called *Religion as a Factor of Life*, written by "Dr. Ernest Engels." Throughout the essay's composition Tyrrell submitted it, piece by piece, to the scrutiny of Maude Petre, whose frank and informed comments demonstrated that the ill-starred relationship between the two was based as much on mutual respect as it was on emotion. She praised his initial efforts as "*pioneer* work," but, while encouraging him to press on with it, she did not hesitate to dispute this assertion or that, and to insist that he refine and clarify his positions. And, when it was finished, she provided the money to have the little book printed. Tyrrell then approached an Anglican friend with "Dr. Engels's" finished product, and persuaded him to see it through to publication. This initiative was to cause considerable trouble later on.[23]

19. Tyrrell, *Lex Orandi*, xxxii.

20. Tyrrell to von Hügel, 12 April, 1902, in Petre, *Autobiography of Tyrrell*, 2:176. On Tyrrell's eclecticism, see Ellen Leonard, *George Tyrrell and the Catholic Tradition* (New York: 1982), 68–69.

21. So maintains Schultenover in his perceptive analysis, *Tyrrell*, 208, 216–36.

22. Tyrrell to Bremond, 17 February, 1902, in Louis-David (ed.), *Lettres de Tyrrell*, 108.

23. See chapter 17.

There is something almost eerie in the fact that Tyrrell, in 1902, should have used the word "synthesis" in characterizing *Religion as a Factor of Life* (and implicitly using it of *Lex Orandi*, which was an elaboration, often verbatim, of it). In 1907, when he condemned what he called "Modernism," Pius X described it as "the synthesis of all heresies." This verbal repetition was no more than a coincidence, but it remains the case that Tyrrell's philosophy of religion already at this stage of his thinking did attempt to bring together and harmonize—sometimes in a muddled form, to be sure—a variety of elements to which the pope would later object so strenuously.

At the heart of Tyrrell's argument lay the conviction that institutional Catholicism—with which, it should be remembered, he was desperately unhappy for all sorts of personal and professional reasons—had become irrelevant to men and women of the new twentieth century, because it refused to come to terms with the findings of modern science, philosophy, and criticism. The chief villain here was that Thomism or neo-Scholasticism that Tyrrell himself had once championed. The church committed itself to an anachronistic intellectualism which put it at odds with the physicist and the biologist who, following in the track of Copernicus, had further unlocked the secrets of the universe. Moreover, it had ignored the insights into the human condition provided, in somewhat different ways, by Blondel and by the intuitional psychologists. Modern people rightly rejected a religious system based upon philosophical realism and Aristotle's discredited dictum—"Nothing is in the mind which is not first in the senses"—because they recognized, with Descartes and Kant, a ground of being the intellect cannot catch with its puny powers. Christianity could withstand the assault of scientific data only if it reached beyond science and discovered the genuine life force that propelled human beings to their destined end. Blondel called this *action*, Bergson called it (or would call it) *élan vital*.

"We are nothing else but wills," said Tyrrell, quoting Saint Augustine (but also echoing the German post-Kantians he had been reading). In a world of wills the divine will forms the center and binds the others together. "Affection" and "sentiment" therefore precede thought, not the other way around. To seek identity with the divine will "is the foundation of the religious sentiment or affection, which is inclusive and regulative of the sentiments of particular and collective love founded on the other relationships. Religion is the principal element in the life of the affections, and therefore in the whole organism of human life." Genuine religion must penetrate to this deepest level of reality, concerning itself with what people *do* and only derivatively with what they *think*. What they think is not, to be sure, insignificant, so long as thought provides a guide and a stimulus to action. The function of thought is always practical, never speculative. The goal is always love, never understanding, or rather a love that encompasses understanding. The instruction offered by religion "is not in the interest of intellectualism, but of life and action. . . . Its chief aim is the shaping of the affections and sentiments."

In this "modern" scheme of things, the "objective" character of knowledge, so prized by the Thomists, shows itself to be a mere chimera, as do abstractions like "immutable truth" or "deposit of faith." Everything human save this convergence of wills is in a state of flux. And since Christianity, with all its divine implications, remains a human enterprise, even the "architectural" theory of dogmatic development advanced by Newman—the reflective mind builds, so to speak, stone by stone upon the original and objective edifice of revelation—must give way to modern science's discernment of a perpetual "organic" evolution, by reason of which all claims of permanence are dreams and delusions. The only "truth of a religion" lies in "its utility for eternal life, i. e., for the life of correspondence with the Absolute [Will]." Creeds and dogmas, therefore, as well as institutional forms, must be judged by their utility, and their usefulness in promoting proper affections and sentiments for one generation does not guarantee a usefulness for the next. That doctrinal forumlaries should alter—indeed, constantly alter—merely reflects the ordinary course of human affairs. But official Catholicism has clung stubbornly to an outmoded manner of understanding man and his universe, and as a consequence has either quarreled with or fled from the certainties that modern research has provided. The church's obsessive insistence upon a static rather than a genuinely dynamic view of life, and so of religion itself, has led it into a blind alley where thoughtful persons will no longer follow. "Precisely as a work of understanding, i. e., as a theology, a religion is as purely a human effort as ethics or logic; but the world with which it deals is given to it, not all at once, but progressively, by what may be called 'revelation,' and from such revelation springs by natural consequence a desire of and effort at new utterance, that may be called 'inspiration.' "[24]

Tyrrell's objective was not substantially different from Alfred Loisy's in *L'Évangile et l'Église.*[25] If modern science and history had rendered unacceptable, and indeed unintelligible, the intellectual assumptions upon which traditional Catholic doctrine had been based, the solution lay not in insisting upon those assumptions in the teeth of contrary evidence, but in recognizing their transient character. Such an admission by no means invalidates Catholicism, but it does demand that modern Catholicism be understood in a manner consistent with the stage to which evolution has brought modern human beings. The accounts of legends in the Old Testament and of miracles in the New—like the virgin birth of Jesus—were "true" in the sense that they possessed "utility" for promoting the "affections" and "sentiments" which led unsophisticated people to "the life of correspondence with the Absolute." But

24. "Ernest Engels," *Religion as a Factor of Life* (Exeter: 1902), 2–4, 7, 13–14.
25. See chapter 13.

the advanced state of scientific culture now requires that such legends and mir-acles be understood in a way consonant with that state, if the one fixed human purpose—"the life of correspondence with the Absolute"—is to be achieved. This is not to say that older versions of Catholic teaching have to be rejected; evolution or development, after all, is the antithesis of creation/destruction theories. Accommodation, not rejection, is the crying need of the hour. In fact, traditional doctrines, practices, and institutions have been absorbed into the ever-changing human condition, so that Loisy could argue plausibly for the contemporary "utility" of veneration of the Virgin and the saints.

To the degree that he understood Blondel's "method of immanence,"[26] Tyr-rell employed it to fashion a philosophy for the modern Catholic that at once accepted and still eluded the consequences of modern science. It mattered not that with the repudiation of philosophical realism the old apologetics were invalidated, that the individual believer, his mind locked into itself with a Cartesian key, was deprived of those comforting "facts" that had previously undergirded his religion. The age-old struggle to harmonize faith and reason had foundered because it had attempted to posit the two as existing on the same plane, at opposite ends, so to speak, of the same spectrum. What did matter—and what left scientific challenges to Christian teaching radically ir-relevant—was that immanence whereby the chasm between the natural and the supernatural, between faith and reason, was bridged, whereby the will of each human person could come into direct contact with the Absolute Will. And in this process Catholic Christianity plays a vital role.

As a school of dogmatic teaching in faith and morals the Christian Church gives us . . . the highest mental expression of the will-world that the collective understanding of believers has elaborated by the spiritual labour of centuries—the joint work of the old-world prophets, completed by Christ and developed by the Church. Therein she gives us an external and authoritative standard by which our personal religious under-standing is to be rectified. The right aim and justification of such social and public standards is not to cramp and restrain, but to stimulate and provoke private initiative. If the Church's teaching hampers us, it is because we misuse it or misconstrue it; be-cause we forget its practical origin and aim, its reference to the will-world.[27]

Tyrrell's spirits were buoyed by the reception his friends gave the privately circulated copies of *Religion as a Factor of Life* and by the survival through two levels of censorship of its complement, *Lex Orandi*—"a cousin of Dr. Engels," Tyrrell called the second book. He was disappointed, however, that the latter made so little an impression on the public at large—"owing," he lamented, "to the need of obscurities and circumlocutions in order to evade the snares of the Philistines."[28] So he resolved to take the pseudonymous route once more:

26. See chapter 5.
27. Tyrrell, *Lex Orandi*, 46.
28. Tyrrell to Halifax, 19 November, 1903, quoted in Schultenover, *Tyrrell*, 241, 239.

imitating Loisy who gave to the world the writings of "Firmin" and "Després,"[29] Tyrrell followed "Ernest Engels" with "Hilaire Bourdon," who forswore any shade of circumlocution. *The Church and the Future*, the last of this decisive trilogy, appeared at the end of 1903. Tyrrell began it by defining

> this controversy [as] one between what I shall call "official" and "liberal" Catholicism: between the theology of those who are at present in the seat of Moses, and who can impose their interpretation of Catholicism upon others as the solely orthodox; and the theology of those who are at present a feeble minority, but who claim to be no less, if not more, orthodox in holding to a wider interpretation than the "official"—meaning by "wider," more in harmony with newer acquisitions of knowledge and newer modes of thought.

Tyrrell hoped that this small book would offer to his coterie an introduction to the work on the Bible done by Loisy and the other higher critics. He only half-succeeded in this ambition, largely because he had only half-learned a discipline for which he lacked both the training and the temperament. But *The Church and the Future*, in its candor and eloquence, represented an appropriate conclusion to the argument of its two predecessors and, moreover, the climax to the long and harrowing mental process through which its author had been passing.

> The "official" view of the Church's doctrinal vice-regency . . . assumes that Christ's mission was as directly dogmatic as it was prophetic; that he attached the same kind of importance to theological orthodoxy as the Catholic Church has done for centuries, and does today not less but more than ever; that by Faith he meant orthodoxy, correctness of theological position; that he meant believing things intellectually perplexing because they were proved by miracle to have been revealed by God. If he fell foul of Jewish theologians, it was, we are to believe, by setting up a counter-theology and not by disdaining theology in its too arrogant pretensions. Faith was a humble sense of one's own theological incompetence. . . . And so he taught the whole Catholic creed in substance, leaving merely the "explication" and application of it to the Church of after times.
> This seems . . . [a] grotesque . . . travesty of the whole spirit and meaning of Christ's work as shown us in the Gospels. . . . [But] in the measure that we live in the light of these doctrines [of the Christian creed] . . . we shall be brought into closer spiritual harmony with the Absolute which reveals itself to us in these forms through and in the mind of the Christian Church stimulated and guided in its selection of beliefs by the spirit of Christ. . . . If in any point of philosophy, history or science, the traditional Christian belief should prove, as it so often has proved, mistaken, it matters as little as the discovery that Dives and Lazarus never existed. . . . It only means that the revelation has been recorded in blue ink rather than in red or black.[30]

29. See chapter 10.
30. "Hilaire Bourdon," *The Church and the Future* (n. p.: 1903). I use here the posthumous reprint (London: 1910), 1, 39–40, 96–97.

George Tyrrell had still much to write, but little more to say. Recapitulation, refinement, restatement of these basic arguments would engage him for the rest of his career. An indication of this circumstance came almost immediately. At the end of 1903 "Anon," following in the footsteps of "Engels" and "Bourdon," circulated privately a short tract called "A Letter to a University Professor." In it Tyrrell proposed to address not so much an individual academic experiencing doubts of faith as the "multitude of those who had got to know me and trust me through my writings, . . . whose mentality is specifically modern, whose minds are well-knit together and unified by the categories and methods of current thought, who will necessarily realize the difficulty of assimilating a theology fabricated to suit the mentality of an earlier day." To such persons, "so many of them . . . referred to me in their perplexities," Tyrrell offered no new message but rather a lively analogy drawn from the political arena and the market place:

The truth is that our official representatives, . . . being but mortals, are dominated by a sort of corporate or class interest, and are prone to exaggerate their own importance and to identify themselves with "the Church" much as social and political theorists and agitators are prone to identify themselves with the people. . . . We are apt to be passively receptive under the self-assertion and self-advertisement of a class whose interest it is to prove its own services to the community to be as indispensable as possible, to show that there is no hope for us unless we accept their views, follow their directions, and buy their wares.

So much for "our official representatives, . . . Popes, Councils, Bishops, theologians."[31]

DESPITE TYRRELL'S PRECAUTIONS a copy of *Religion as a Factor of Life* turned up in Toulouse, where a colleague of Pierre Batiffol at the Institut Catholique reviewed it in tones of horror. The unique character of the Christian Gospel, the objectivity of divine revelation, the legitimacy of the church's constitution, even God's transcendance over nature—all these and much more have been forfeited in this "inestimable compendium of agnostic and symbolist theology." The reviewer, who did not know "Engels's" identity, made the reasonable point that the book's argument depended upon the validity of the psychology and metaphysics upon which it rested. "Engels" reduced the human condition to a bizarre type of voluntarism, and then spun out from that subjectivist fancy a set of eccentric and dangerously naturalistic theories. And, asked the reviewer, where was his proof? "All he proves is the possibility of founding on experience a religion from which nothing follows."[32]

31. George Tyrrell, *A Much Abused Letter* (London: 1906), 16, 30, 38, 58, 57. This publication included the original anonymous "Letter," together with an introduction, selected correspondence, and a brief "Epilogue." See chapter 17.
32. Quoted in Schultenover, *Tyrrell*, 236–37.

This criticism indicated not only how the battle lines were forming but also how fundamental were the differences between the two sides. Tyrrell's friends meanwhile reacted in various ways to his bold new orientation. Maude Petre bitterly regretted what she judged in retrospect to have been a disastrous shift in the career of the man she loved: "Had he been left in his own place, and at his own job, he might have worked towards a revolution in the understanding of religious truth without any rebellion." Tyrrell was "nervous and passionate, uncalculating and impetuous," and once "drawn out of the circle of those who looked to him for spiritual guidance into the company of those whose character was militant rather than apostolic, . . . he fought for the ideas of others [and] lost the opportunity of developing his own." And the blame for this "great mistake" she laid at the door of Friedrich von Hügel.[33]

Blame is one thing, guilt is another. If in fact the baron had led his friend into waters too deep for him, the cause was lack of judgment, not malice. Von Hügel's enthusiasms for this intellectual fashion or that were oustripped only by his good intentions and his loyalty both to persons and to the cause of Catholic intellectual reform. But he may have overestimated Tyrrell's spiritual stamina, much as he had earlier that of his daughter Gertrud.[34] Shortly after the appearance of *Religion as a Factor of Life* an exchange with von Hügel led Tyrrell to remark, only half-jokingly, that the "Ernest Engels" he had thought was an ultraliberal von Hügel considered an Ultramontane. "The baron has just come and gone," he once observed, "and, as usual, he has left me more to think about than I can digest. I wish he'd draw up a list, not of what he doesn't believe but of what he does."[35] Yet there could be little doubt of the baron's genuine if somewhat naive sincerity when he addressed Tyrrell "with my heart prayerfully and affectionately full of you, my intensely alive, immensely impulsive and hence astonishingly, most meritoriously and fruitfully balanced Friend."[36]

As he alternated between encouraging and fretting over his embattled friends, von Hügel at this time was much preoccupied with domestic matters. In September 1903, after twenty-six years in Hampstead, the family moved into 13 Vicarage Gate, a "large and delightfully situated house" in Kensington. Located in a quiet and elegant cul-de-sac only a block or two from busy Kensington Church Street and securely within the fashionable district south of Hyde Park, the handsome four-storied residence, fronted by pillars of white stucco, testified to the baron's continued prosperity. Gertrud, still physically delicate but emotionally more settled, had left home and was being courted, very decorously, by an Italian count whom ultimately she would marry. The convenient new location allowed the other two girls to enjoy a bit more of the social whirl in London than before, while the baron could take his daily

33. Petre, *My Way*, 290–92. But see also Barmann, *Hügel*, 166–67.
34. See chapter 9.
35. Tyrrell to Bremond, 19 September, 1902, in Louis-David (ed.), *Lettres de Tyrrell*, 134.
36. Von Hügel to Tyrrell, 4 December, 1902, quoted in Schultenover, *Tyrrell*, 239.

constitutional now within the mellow confines of the Kensington Gardens instead of the unkempt and windswept Hampstead Heath. Other diversions were more readily available to him as well; never a snob when it came to recreation, he frequented the music halls no less than the galleries and museums. Aside from abstruse letters to editors in defense of Loisy, he continued to publish very little himself—during 1904 a single article, though a very important one[37]—but the book on the mysticism of Saint Catherine of Genoa proceeded steadily, if with pedantic slowness. He and Lady Mary entertained more than they had in Hampstead, though the visitors who most often passed through their drawing room were still those bent upon discussing serious religious subjects seriously.

Particularly agreeable to the baron were the ten days in July 1904 when the archbishop of Albi was his guest. Mignot, who came on this holiday much depressed by the general ecclesiastical situation, was treated to a whirlwind tour of intellectual London, Oxford, and Cambridge, and no doubt returned to the south of France more fatigued if not more cheerful. Tyrrell, invited to come south and meet the archbishop, refused to budge from Richmond.[38]

A predictable result of the new direction George Tyrrell's thought had taken was the alienation of Wilfrid Ward. Ward and Tyrrell had never been intimate, but they had been on cordial terms for some years, had corresponded regularly, and had shared membership in the Synthetic Society.[39] Each of them assumed in the other, with reason, an agreed commitment to the intellectual life and especially to the harmonization of Catholicism with modern culture. Both were skillful professional writers whose prose, however, suggested the deep temperamental disparities that divided them: Ward's style was somewhat ponderous, phlegmatic, extremely cautious, reflecting the born historian always anxious about the integrity of his sources; and Tyrrell's style was soaring, intuitional, affective in its purpose, manifesting the born spiritual director (as Maude Petre might have said) who appeared more adept at influencing a reader's heart than at persuading his head. Ward was a layman of independent means who moved easily through the high society of late Victorian and Edwardian England; Tyrrell was a displaced Irish priest who harbored resentments, many of them unconscious, against establishments of whatever variety. But the closest intellectual bond between them—a devotion to Newman—had been for a while enough to surmount all the natural and social contrasts.

Josephine Ward liked Tyrrell's *Lex Orandi* better than her husband did. Wilfrid, though a first reading of *L'Évangile et l'Église* had impressed him favorably, had already grown fidgety over the speculations of Loisy. Now he began to harbor serious doubts about Tyrrell who, in his latest work, clearly seemed

---

37. See the list in Barmann, *Hügel*, 255, and also see chapter 16.
38. De la Bedoyere, *Hügel*, 167–71, and Sagovsky, *Tyrrell*, 184.
39. See chapter 10.

about to jettison his loyalty to the teaching of Newman. For Ward this was a shock and a disappointment, and Tyrrell, trying to elucidate his view, managed only to heighten those feelings. " 'Newmanianan' insofar as it implies 'mania' I never was," he told Wilfrid. "Many of us go through a Newman phase or fever which is a purgative and constructive state in our mental history, but it is not the end. It is when the fever passes and the power of criticism revives that we begin to reap the benefits of the innoculation." This imagery must have disturbed Ward for whom "Newman fever" was a permanent and prized affliction. But Tyrrell remained adamant: "Newman will be an everlasting source of light if he is studied critically in relation to his own past, present and future, if his necessary limitations are carefully defined and recognized. . . . You say his 'principles' will never die; I say his 'spirit.' . . . While I agree . . . that Newman's prophetic insight foresaw *in the vague* the intellectual revolution that is now upon us and with which e. g. Loisy is, I think vainly, trying to cope, he did not and could not have anticipated and prepared for the precise problem which is now presented to us."[40]

Just at the moment this serious breach between the two men was developing, a separate imbroglio, trivial in itself, served to hasten the process. In the issue of the *Month* for January 1904 appeared an article by Tyrrell—his last in that journal—called "Semper Eadem" (Always the same). It purported to be a review of a collection of Ward's essays, published under the title *Problems and Persons*. In his discussion of the book and related matters Tyrrell stressed the confrontation between "liberal" and "Scholastic" theology, and seemed to assume a rigidly conservative stance in order to criticize Ward for his liberalism. There followed a tedious and confusing three-cornered correspondence among Ward, Tyrrell, and the Jesuit editor of the *Month*, a correspndence Tyrrell labeled "most annoying, most disingenuous, most characteristic of [the] Jesuit *menage*." It may have been that Tyrrell in "Semper Eadem" was indulging in some dark humor at the expense of the censors—he chuckled later over receiving congratulations from many right-wing "Philistines." Ward confessed puzzlement to his wife: "Tyrrell's article is too odd. It is impossible to believe it's ironical. He appears to be in a very odd state possessed alternately by two spirits. I *can't* make him out. The article is largely true though too conservative. I prefer him in that state of mind to him in the state of mind of his letters to me." In one of those letters, even while his review of *Problems and Persons* was in press, Tyrrell had written, "I cannot but think that if the church is to live it will be through the very converse of what occurred as to Aristotelianism, i. e., through its absorption of our theology into the contemporary philosophical synthesis."[41]

40. Tyrrell to Ward, 3 December and 11 December, 1903, in Weaver (ed.), *Letters*, 84–87. Also see note 59, in chapter 9.
41. Ward, *The Wilfrid Wards*, 2:165–68, and Tyrrell to Ward, 11 December, 1903 and 19 January, 1904, in Weaver (ed.), *Letters*, 90, 96.

As time went on it became increasingly clear to the Wards that this last was the real spirit moving Tyrrell. By the end of the year the correspondence between them had virtually ceased, with this sad parting shot from Tyrrell:

I don't pay much heed to gossip; but I think there is now a . . . consensus . . . to the effect that . . . you consider you have a grievance against me in regard to . . . "Semper Eadem." . . . Of course I feel that our paths have long since bifurcated and are bound to diverge more and more; that my faith in the *bona fides* of our officialdom is as weak as yours is strong; still, while recognizing your unwillingness to be identified with me as quite reasonable under all the difficult circumstances, I should be most sorry to leave you with the idea that I had in any intentional way been unfair or unfriendly towards you.

Handsome and no doubt heartfelt as it was, this expression of personal regret left the essentials of the story untold. The misunderstanding over "Semper Eadem," whatever the mysterious causes of that minor incident, could have been easily resolved. The fact was that Tyrrell and Ward no longer agreed on fundamentals, that Ward still clung to Newman while Tyrrell—asserting that "it is not a question of Newman but of truth"—had shifted into a "conviction that a compromise between static and dynamic conceptions, between the philosophy of mental development and the patristic conception of the deposit is impossible and even dangerous."[42]

IF WARD WAS DISCOMFITED by Tyrrell's rejection of Newmanite principles, he was exasperated on similar grounds by another troubled Jesuit, Tyrrell's friend Henri Bremond. Beginning in 1904 Bremond, long fascinated by English Catholicism in general and by Newman in particular,[43] published in three years three separate studies of Newman's thought and person. The centerpiece of this trilogy—and the most important of the books—indicated by its title Bremond's major preoccupation: *Newman: Essai de biographie psychologique.* He followed this attempt to scrutinize the mind and emotions of his subject with a tract on Newman's spirituality, and preceded it with an examination of the by-now much-battered theory of development. Ward rendered a bleak judgment of this project from its inception. He maintained that Bremond, with his indelicate psychological probings, consistently misunderstood and misrepresented Newman, not least because of a Frenchman's inability to grasp the nuances of the English idiom. Bremond understandably took umbrage at this challenge to his credentials, and so was ushered in another little controversy destined to drag on for several years. "I shall try to bear myself as an honorable opponent," huffed Bremond, "and shall not accuse you of not

42. Tyrrell to Ward, 1 December, 1904, in Weaver (ed.), *Letters*, 100–101. See the perceptive comments in Mary Jo Weaver, "Wilfrid Ward, George Tyrrell and the Meanings of Modernism," *Downside Review* 96 (January 1978): 32–34.

43. See chapter 10.

knowing French." And later Tyrrell broke his silence in order to upbraid Ward: "Your worst sin . . . is that you seem to claim a monopoly of the understanding of Newman and to warn others off the field by representing it as a task of superhuman difficulty to which you alone are equal. . . . As an interpreter of [Newman's] thought you are [merely] one of many." Von Hügel, pained at this evidence of the unraveling of the progressive coalition, wrung his hands and hoped for the best. But he did not disguise his sympathies, and—half-warning, half-pleading—he said to Ward: "[Bremond] and Tyrrell are especially my friends."[44]

Henri Bremond stood in need of friends just then. The agonizing decision of February 1900 to take final vows as a member of the Society of Jesus[45] had brought no lasting solace. Four years later he had become, in his own words, "a vagabond," "a wandering Jew." If his temperament differed markedly from that of Tyrrell—who nevertheless now routinely addressed him as "Carissime"—his vocational predicament was stirkingly similar. Technically he was still on the staff of *Études*, as Tyrrell was of the *Month*, but he was perceived, like Tyrrell, as troublesome by his local superiors and suspect at Jesuit headquarters in Rome. And, like Tyrrell, Bremond had come to despise the Jesuit life-style, and yet he could not face the prospect of giving up the vocation that he and his two brothers had embraced in their youth.

At the end of 1902, with the permission and indeed the encouragement of his superiors, he had gone on an extended trip to Italy. They hoped that an absence from Paris might temper his liberal opinions as well as deliver him from the growing influence of Alfred Loisy. But, since he went south armed with introductions from Baron von Hügel to the latter's progressive Italian friends, Bremond's tour produced the opposite effect. He delighted in the outspokenness of Giovanni Semeria and Salvatore Minocchi,[46] who if anything seemed more aggressively Loisyist than the exegete's adherents back home. He was charmed by Gallarati-Scotti and his aristocratic circle at Milan—young, lively, upper-class Catholics dedicated to reform and flatteringly attentive to the right kind of French intellectual. He spent some happy days in Venice with Antonio Fogazzaro and his family. It was not surprising that these two men, bound by their common literary sympathies no less than by their dreams of promoting a modern Catholicism, should have immediately hit it off, but Bremond was particularly captivated by the way Fogazzaro patiently included his fourteen-year-old daughter in their erudite conversations. This domestic scene unsettled Bremond still more. "It is so evident that I was made for that life and not for mine. . . . I look back at the expression of Fogazzaro's little girl . . . as I was speaking to her father, and nothing can surpass that plea-

44. Ward, *The Wilfrid Wards*, 2:172–76, and Tyrrell to Ward, 17 August, 1906, in Weaver (ed.), *Letters*, 111.
45. See chapter 10.
46. See chapter 11.

sure."[47] "I beleive," he reported more circumspectly to the baron, "we are well understood [here] and loved."[48]

When he returned home in mid-March 1903 Bremond was informed that he could take up residence in any Jesuit house he chose except in Paris. "They [his superiors] imagine I see Loisy every day," he observed bitterly. They may have imagined other things as well, because Bremond—in Italy or France or wherever he was—stubbornly refused to abide by the norms of Jesuit decorum. He had acquired in their view the tastes and habits of a secular priest, or perhaps of an ordinary bachelor. In Richmond both George Tyrrell and Maude Petre grew alarmed that their friend's reputation might be compromised by his own carelessness. Tyrrell sent him a stern warning: "I suspect that out of a variety of gossip and denunciations and consultations they have determined to bring you to heel—one of their habitual stupidities—and they want to get you away from Paris because of piecemeal allegations of womanizing (histoire de femme). The very angels of God are not pure in their eyes; all the more so a being like you, so fanciful and so little submissive to established conventions." Petre for her part despaired of Bremond surviving in the Society of Jesus; she hoped that he would consent to serving as a diocesan priest in England or Italy, but in the final analysis she even preferred that he repudiate the priesthood altogether and marry rather than to persist in a pointless rebellion against his self-imposed "slavery."[49] Perhaps she put greater stock than Tyrrell did in the wicked eventuality of a concocted histoire de femme; the mother-general of her order had warned her about gossip concerning her relations with Bremond.[50]

In the end Bremond chose to be exiled to London and found himself assigned to, of all places, Farm Street. But before he could take up residence there he had to undergo treatment in Paris for nervous exhaustion. And scarcely had he landed in England when he petitioned to go on holiday to a Jesuit house in Bavaria, out in the countryside, where the rural peace enveloped him in its calming embrace. He decided he would remain in the Society of Jesus forever! Tyrrell dismissed out of hand this "mending" of the spirit: "It is impossible for me to think that what you call 'mending' (raccomandage) is more than temporary. . . . Between you and the S. J. the incompatibility is of nature; it is fire and water."[51] He might have been describing his own situation; at any rate he knew whereof he spoke.

It is a tribute to Bremond's professional dedication that throughout this period of painful indecision and illness and restless travel he never ceased working. Besides initiating the studies of Newman to which Ward would object so strongly, he published several learned articles[52] and a short biography of

47. Bremond to Petre, 10 January, 1903, quoted in Petre, My Way, 265.
48. Bremond to von Hügel, 8 January, 1903, quoted in Blanchet, Bremond, 236.
49. Tyrrell to Bremond, 28 March, 1903, in Louis-David (ed.), Lettres de Tyrrell, 147–48.
50. See the entry from Petre's diary, quoted in Blanchet, Bremond, 256.
51. Tyrrell to Bremond, 20 August, 1903, in Louis-David (ed.), Lettres, 154.
52. For a list, see Blanchet, Bremond, 251.

Thomas More. But during a gloomy autumn spent in London, increasingly in the company of Friedrich von Hügel, Bremond's mood grew ever more dark and tense. When, in December, the authorities directed that he should leave Farm Street for the novitiate in Canterbury, he refused to go. "They want to banish me from here for being a *liberal*. . . . They want to bury me in Canterbury. . . . I have appealed to our Caesar in Rome. I await his sentence." The sentence was rendered on Februay 6, 1904, when Henri Bremond, by mutual agreement, resigned from the Society of Jesus and was dispensed from his vows. He was never canonically irregular, because he was immediately and cordially incardinated as a secular priest into the archdiocese of Aix. But even this formal association with his beloved native town did not relieve him of soreness and uncertainty: "The archbishop of Aix has taken me under his mantle, but I fear I am no longer enough of an *aixois* to install myself there definitively."[53] Nor did he ever do so.

HAD BREMOND EVER SERVED as a parish priest in Aix-en-Provence he would have been thrown into the company of his first beloved master. But in fact he did not, and he had anyway put himself at the behest of other masters now, so that his association with Maurice Blondel had become inevitably diminished. Bremond's letters came less frequently, and the personal crisis he was enduring was described much more obliquely in Aix than it was in Richmond or in Kensington. As was his wont, and consistent with his deep, undeviating piety, Blondel responded to Bremond's troubles much as he did to his own, with reminders of Christ's Passion and of the need every believer has to take up the cross as the Master did. "I wish very much," he commented to a mutual friend, "that [Bremond] would willingly bend to what after all is only the common circumstance of the religious life, that he would smile at the petty literary vexations, that he would accept joyfully the misunderstandings, the disagreements, all the external foolery (*spectacles*) by which 'the saints have always made the saints suffer.' "[54]

But Bremond had become less susceptible than before to Blondel's godly counsel. The comradeship with Tyrrell and the womanly compassion of Maude Petre sustained him now. Intellectually, he had found a new mentor in von Hügel and then, through him, in Loisy, with whom the baron was in constant correspondence. Blondel had argued with them both before,[55] and, as 1903 drew to an end—as the threat of a Roman condemnation first loomed over Loisy and his little red books and then became a reality—word reached London that he was about to renew the argument. "I shall read very avidly your anti-Loisy," Bremond wrote wistfully on December 27, "and I shall be very un-

---

53. See Blanchet, *Bremond*, 252–61.
54. Blondel to Mourret, 5 April, 1903, in Maurice Blondel and Auguste Valensin, *Correspondance, 1899–1912*, 2 vols., ed. by Anon. (Paris: 1957), 1:117.
55. See chapter 14.

happy, caught between my heart which will follow your reasonings, and a corner of my head which will cling fast to this philosophy produced by two heads, Loisy and Hügel. I cannot say that the book [L'Évangile et l'Église or Autour d'un petit livre] satisfies me entirely, but it does confirm me in a little parallel pathway which I've found for myself and which is, I believe, Tyrrell's pathway too. We shall conduct you down it one day."[56]

Blondel was indeed preparing a tract on the biblical question, though he winced at it being described simply as "anti-Loisy." He had contemplated for many years preparing a summa of modern apologetics that would demonstrate the utility of his method of immanence. In such a study a treatment of the Bible and criticism would have had its due place. But, thanks to the developments of the 1890s, the controversies over Catholic attitudes toward scriptural research had become so hot and all-absorbing—after the Roman condemnation the popular press began to couple l'affaire Dreyfus with la question Loisy—that Blondel was moved to wonder whether he should not stake out his position on that matter independent of a later, more elaborate treatise, whether he should not say in public what he had already said to Loisy and von Hügel privately. Blondel subscribed to the principles of the philosophy of action with a religious fervor, not simply because he had originated that philosophy—pride of that sort would have been culpable in Blondel's eyes—but because of a disinterested conviction that such principles alone would enable the church to confront the intellectual challenges of the modern world. But what if the authorities were to lump together his own speculations with the exaggerations and distortions—as he judged them—of Loisy?

Throughout the summer and autumn of 1903 Blondel's closest confidants and disciples bombarded him with this question or variants of it. Abbé Wehrlé, once so fervent a Loisyist,[57] was seized with "an inexpressible sadness" once he had read Autour d'un petit livre. "I am terribly disturbed," he told Blondel, "lest people will try to attach your influence, however remote," to certain specific passages in that book. Blondel, he said, must issue a contrary "manifesto" before "any doctrinal condemnation can intervene." "You are almost rendered indictable," wrote another friend, "by certain of Father Loisy's expressions. I was talking this very morning to a thoughtful priest who thinks it right to interpret the doctrine of L'action according to the norms of L'Évangile et l'Église."[58] This sort of information tended to be more persuasive than did hints that a failure to distance himself from Loisy might lead to his own condemnation; it never occurred to his luminously chaste conscience that self-service was in any way at issue.

As the pressure on him mounted, Blondel fidgeted and fell ill and all the

56. Bremond to Blondel, 27 December, 1903, quoted in Blanchet, Bremond, 173–74.
57. See chapter 14.
58. Wehrlé to Blondel, 22 October, 1903, and Mourret to Blondel, 7 November, 1903, quoted in Virgoulay, Blondel, 111–12.

while worried about "the opportuneness of my intervention," about "the degree to which it is proper for me to break my ties (*désolidariser*) with [Loisy's] experiment, very beautiful and very fruitful from certain aspects, very ruinous and very perturbing from others." By late autumn he had decided and had contracted to furnish the editors of *La quinzaine* with three articles to appear in successive issues. The impending reality startled Blondel's friends into shifitng ground and, together with Madame Blondel, into advising against publication: they were afraid, with reason, that if Blondel chastised Loisy with whips, he would also chastise the Scholastics with scorpions. They were not mistaken on that score. Blondel went to work "rereading most closely Father Loisy's texts, in order not to risk any false interpretations or orientations; everything in such a subject is important." But that analysis did not tempt him to give aid and comfort to Loisy's conservative opponents: "It is true that these new ideas seem disastrous, but it is not less true that the conventional methods [of apologetics] are destitute and have themselves become perilous." And, as Advent arrived and then Christmas and as he scratched pen across paper, Blondel remained all too aware of his greatest liability, of the literary cross he had to carry: "The necessity to be brief and clear paralyzes me."[59]

Brevity and clarity are relative terms. *Histoire et dogme*, which appeared serially from mid-January to mid-February, 1904, ran to about eighty pages of print, and, like most Blondelian prose, its argument ranged between the intricate and the obscure. The pressing contemporary problem, he began, is "that there are now two entirely incompatible 'Catholic mentalities,' particularly in France. Clearly this is an abnormal situation, for there cannot be two Catholicisms." Both sides in this dispute "maintain that they recognize practically and justify theoretically the divinity of Christianity and the legitimacy of the claims of the Catholic church." Both cannot be right; indeed, said Blondel, both are wrong on the fundamental issue of the relation between the Gospel and the church.

Or rather each offers an incomplete solution to the problem. "I shall use a couple of barbarous neologisms in order to fix the attention and to throw into proper relief the exclusive character of each thesis." "Extrinsicism"—a barbrous invention to be sure—is the method adopted by the Scholastics, for whom the historical facts recorded in the Scriptures have only an "extrinsic" value. According to this view, dogma expresses revealed truth by an exclusively deductive procedure, which has only an accidental or "extrinsic" relation to the world of fact. Thus, New Testament miracles "prove" the divinity of the Christian message; but that proof is merely "a sign, a label, which has been detached from the facts and placarded over the entrance of the dogmatic fortress" whose battlements have alrady been secured. "The Bible is guaranteed

59. Blondel to Leger, 6 December, 1903, and Blondel to Mourret, 3 December, 1903, in Marlé (ed.), *Au coeur*, 164–65.

as a whole, not by its content but by an external seal of the divine. Why bother to verify its details? It is replete with absolute science, fixed in its eternal truth. Why search out its human conditions and its relative senses?" Perhaps such an attitude was defensible in earlier, simpler times. "But now the day has come when, thanks to the discoveries of archaeology and philology, the past has been resurrected, . . . and has confronted hide-bound deductions with facts that give the lie to them, not just on matters of detail but on a whole section of teaching extracted from the Bible. A dangerous crisis has become inevitable."

Nor did the solution lie in "historicism"—Blondel's second "incomplete" solution. Here, though he does not name him, the object of Blondel's criticism was Alfred Loisy. "Can one pretend that [history] is self-sufficient? Obviously not; it depends upon a number of other sciences." The historian's claim to autonomy is a delusion. Moreover, "no one should think that history by itself can know a fact which would be no more than a fact or which would be the whole fact." History deals with human life, and "human life is metaphysics in act. To claim that the science of history is innocent of any speculative preoccupation, or even to imagine that the smallest details of history could be, strictly speaking, a simple matter of observation, is to fall victim to prejudice under the pretext of an unattainable neutrality." What Loisy has offered in his exegetical works—his explanation, for example, of the imminence of the kingdom or of Christ's self-knowledge as understood by his first disciples—is an "historical positivism" which "seems to provide a means or even *the* means of attaining the reality of history." But this too is a delusion, a kind of disguised Scholasticism: "Historicism tends to take the external act, the expressive trait, the concrete image for the [real] object itself, to substitute surreptitiously the fact for the actor, the testimony for the witness, the portrait for the real person." And so a historicist like Loisy only "registers the effects of phenomena" and situates them in an evolutionary pattern from which they receive an artificial intelligibility.

Neither of these soi-disant solutions to the contemporary religious crisis, Blondel concluded, could really answer the fundamental question: "How does it happen that legitimately the Bible supports and guarantees the church, and the church supports and interprets the Bible?" Neither dogmatic formularies nor scientific history—though both have their uses—can avoid in this matter falling victim to a vicious circle. "Therefore it follows that a principle distinct [from both] must align, harmonize, and organize them." To fill this role Blondel trotted out that hoary old nostrum, "ecclesiastical tradition." He did not, however, mean tradition as it was ordinarily understood, "a transmission, usually by word of mouth, of historical facts, received truths, accepted teachings, hallowed practices and ancient customs." Instead, he explained the term through a bold application of his *philosophie d'action* and the method of immanence:

Tradition anticipates the future and is disposed to clarify that future by the effort it makes to remain faithful to the past. Guardian of the initial gift [of revelation]—but to the degree that this has not been entirely formulated or even fully understood, although it is always fully possessed and used—tradition frees us from the Scriptures themselves on which it never ceases to rely with devout respect. Tradition, without relying exclusively on texts, helps us to reach the real Christ whom no literary description could exhaust or replace. Thus the Gospel itself appears as part of the deposit [of faith], not as the whole deposit; for even if the text is divine we cannot safely rest all dogma and all faith on that alone.

Just as that mysterious but ever-vital force called *action* provides the link between the natural and the supernatural,[60] so does it also impart to tradition a richness and fullness that gives us "after more than nineteen centuries of Christianity . . . a method . . . of attaining Christ, of determining what he wanted, . . . of explaining the significance of the supernatural gifts that he brought to us." Let "the historian . . . ridicule the 'extra-historical' method of penetrating the consciousness of Jesus." The illuminating and liberating truth remains that "the active principle of the synthesis resides neither in the facts by themselves, nor in the ideas alone, but in the tradition which includes within itself the data of history, the effort of reason and the accumulated experiences of the faithful."

This last category was especially important to the devout Blondel. Tradition to him revealed the "collective experience of a holy society." "Let us talk no more of a purely individual, a purely intellectual criterion for linking facts with beliefs," something both Scholastics and historicists tend to do. "The infallible Magisterium is the higher and really supernatural guarantee of a function which is naturally rooted in the concert of all the powers of each Christian and of all Chrstianity." Tradition "is not a simple substitute for written teaching. It has a different purpose. . . . It preserves not the intellectual aspect of the past but the living reality of the past." As for the person of Jesus, tradition, rightly understood, delivers us from slavish, positivist adherence to "texts [which] give an insufficient account of feelings and of actions. The personal if unexpressed influence of Christ began a tradition of devotion and adoration that Christian literature neither exhausts nor fully represents, even when closest to its source."

To separate the speculations of Maurice Blondel from the intensely spiritual, almost mystical, life he lived every day would be ipso facto to misunderstand him. After all, this man had not forsaken the fervor of his youth when he had said: "My God, I wish I were the good bread of the altar, over which you would pronounce the words of transubstantiation!"[61] And though the expression "Practice makes perfect" may be in most settings a banality, yet for him it remained the all-encompassing truth:

60. See chapter 5.
61. Blondel, *Carnets intimes*, 1:19.

One realizes . . . by the practice of Christianity that its dogmas are rooted in reality. One therefore has no right to set facts on one side and theological data on the other without returning to the sources of life and of action where the indivisible synthesis is to be found. Facts and formularies are merely a twofold and faithful translation of it into different languages. The link between facts and beliefs will never be justified by erudition or dialectic. . . . To achieve such justification one must consider the effort of every human being and, what is more, take account of the consensus of all the human beings who participate in the same life and share the same love.[62]

62. Maurice Blondel, *Histoire et dogme. Les lacunes philosophiques de l'exégèse moderne*, in *Premiers écrits*, 149–50, 155, 158–60, 164, 168, 171–73, 205–7, 215–16, 204, 180, 227.

CHAPTER 16

Disarray

I followed with the keenest interest the debates in the Chamber [of Deputies] relative to the separation of the churches and the state. . . . The attitude imposed
upon our unhappy clergy by the pope sickened me. When I saw all the efforts of
Roman policy aimed toward creating among us an upheaval that could lead to civil
war, . . . all for the sake of promoting the miserable prestige of the Roman pontiff, then did I despair, I confess, of the future of Catholicism in our country, and I
felt happy at no longer being Roman and being, therefore, even more entirely
French.

—*Alfred Loisy (1913)*[1]

IF, IN *Histoire et dogme*, Maurice Blondel devoted most of the space to a
rebuttal of "historicism," he reserved his harshest language for the other
theory he disapproved of, the oldfashioned and outmoded "extrinsicism." The
practitioners of this "intransigent absolutism," he said, reveal themselves to be
"obstinate people who think they know everything without having examined
anything, mystical ideologues who want to impose their systems upon the concrete truth of history and who on principle close their eyes so that they need
not even acknowledge too crudely within themselves the embarrassing liter-
alness they continue to teach the simple."[2] Those thus indicted were not slow
in responding through the various journals at their disposal. "God prevent me
from thinking," one of them observed sarcastically, "that Monsieur Blondel
has taken aim at the apologetic sanctioned by the Vatican Council; but certainly it is unfortunate that the erroneous method to which he gives the ridiculous name *extrinsicism* is hard to distinguish at first glance, even for a Scholastic
theologian, from that of the council." "Monsieur Blondel," said another, "has
simply dismissed all Catholic theology as extrinsicism."[3] Still another de-

1. Loisy, *Choses passées*, 323–24.
2. Blondel, *Histoire et dogme*, 159.
3. For the quotations and a general summary, see Poulat, *Histoire, dogme*, 567–73.

294

scribed *Histoire et dogme* as "the most notable attempt which has been made to rehabilitate for Catholic opinion the ideas of Abbé Loisy."[4]

But fear of this reaction—which Blondel had expected and could therefore take in stride—had not been the reason that he had hesitated to write and publish his articles. He dreaded rather the prospect of grieving his close associates and damaging the common cause. Once he had in hand the articles in pamphlet form, he sent a copy to Alfred Loisy with a covering letter. "Dear Father," he wrote on February 28, 1904, "allow me to say a word about all this to you, first of all. . . . If, despite a long hesitation, I have taken up the pen, . . . I have not done so without compunction. Seeing what I think I see, it seemed to me a duty to speak out. There is a line which cannot be expunged from the Gospel because, under an equivalent form, it has been graven on the heart: He who loves his kindred or friends better than me is not worthy of me." Blondel realized full well that the timing of the publication of *Histoire et dogme* coincided with Loisy's struggle with Pius X, Richard, and Merry del Val.[5] "How I would have wished not to pain you, not to add but rather even to alleviate something of the sadness of your present ordeal." That was why, he explained, he had carefully "put the discussion upon terrain where personalities were not directly involved and where passions could give way to calm discussion." Indeed, he added, not very convincingly, he had intended only "to trace two caricatures" of positions whose "tendencies I consider illegitimate." He concluded with a plea: "Though I live in a place isolated and distant from you, I have suffered exceedingly with you. For your own peace, for the good of your work which can only bear fruit within the church, for all those who are attached to you by the strongest intellectual and spiritual bonds, it is imperative that you should accept your humiliation heroically."[6]

Loisy, not much given to pious platitudes, responded to Blondel's apologia with a *carte postale* expressing his "thanks." Many years later he commented with a rhetorical shrug: "Blondel was a philosopher; he was in no sense an exegete. Nothing obliged him to intervene in the biblical or historical question, except a desire to plant his flag, the standard of the philosophy of *action*, the unique and sufficient means of salvation for the church and for science."[7] But at the time the terseness of Loisy's bare acknowledgment contrasted with the lengthy missives that crammed Blondel's postbox. His friends rallied to him. "Admirable, admirable," wrote one of them. "Till now no one has examined this subject with the thoroughness that you have, and with a sensitivity so Christian and Catholic."[8] "It is important that you should realize," said another, "the *immense* scope of your work. I have read your articles four times.

4. Quoted in Virgoulay, *Blondel*, 124.
5. See chapter 14.
6. Blondel to Loisy, 28 February, 1904, in Marlé (ed.), *Au coeur*, 199–200.
7. Loisy, *Mémoires*, 2:392.
8. Mourret to Blondel, 4 February, 1904, in Marlé (ed.), *Au coeur*, 183.

. . . What illumination I have found in them!"[9] Not all the communications he received, however, were so favorable. One priest couched his objections courteously, yet firmly: "If the texts will not permit us to affirm the Resurrection [of Christ] as a fact *historically* certain, we can accept it as believers for very serious reasons, reasons perhaps more decisive than the texts themselves, but *as historians* we have to affirm that it is not a demonstrated fact. . . . It seems to me that in your [articles] you have been too severe in separating methodologies and in dividing the means of inquiry. This at any rate will be the conclusion of the middling intellects who make up the great majority of your readers."[10]

Blondel scrupulously replied to all the correspondence he received, both positive and negative. To be sure, not everybody was moved to write him: Louis Duchesne in Rome expressed his displeasure at the articles only in the salons he frequented, and Marie-Joseph Lagrange in Jerusalem remained silent, though one of his Dominican confreres at the École Biblique wrote to convey "a genuine sympathy" for what Blondel was trying to accomplish.[11] In Toulouse, Lagrange's friend, Pierre Batiffol, protesting that he was no philosopher, assigned a colleague to write an unsigned review of *Histoire et dogme* in the Institut Catholique's *Bulletin*; the result was an ambiguous article that seemed, in Wehrlé's rather outlandish judgment, "to have been cooked up among Batiffol, Loisy and the prudently anonymous author" in order "to reconcile differences and blur nuances."[12]

But all the while Blondel was looking uneasily toward London. Even before the articles were available there he received a troubling note from Bremond: "Our poor baron is overwhelmed with cares and controversies; he is bending every effort to defend his friend [Loisy]."[13] That defense had been composed largely of a series of letters sent to newspapers in England, France, and Italy. But then, when Gertrud von Hügel, who was in Paris, alerted her father that Blondel's articles were about to appear in *La quinzaine*, he determined to answer them. "Nothing is more desirable or useful for us all," he wrote Blondel, "than a discussion carried on in a high and broad and dignified tone which in these matters is so often lacking and of which you possess so fully the mastery." In his heart the baron was convinced that, given Loisy's current troubles, Blondel should have refrained from writing against him. Yet, now that it had been done, it could prove "a great service to Father Loisy" by instilling into the debate "the proper respect every man, every Christian, owes to another." He asked Blondel to send him "as soon as possible" the proofs of *Histoire et*

9. Combes to Blondel, 7 March, 1904, in Blondel and Valensin, *Correspondance*, 1:126.
10. Anon. to Blondel, 17 February, 1904, in Marlé (ed.), *Au coeur*, 192.
11. See Marlé (ed.), *Au coeur*, 182, 203.
12. Quoted in Virgoulay, *Blondel*, 132
13. Bremond to von Hügel, 9 February, 1904, quoted in Blanchet, *Bremond*, 174.

dogme to which he would prepare a response, and asked him also to remember "that no friend of Father Loisy loves you more or as much as I do."[14]

Over the next month Blondel complied with the baron's request, sending each installment as it appeared and then the whole pamphlet. In an affectionate but defensive letter he tried to justify for von Hügel the timing of *Histoire et dogme*. "At first, during the pending [Roman] procedure [against Loisy], I did not want to publish anything, lest I should provide ammunition to our adversaries. I decided to proceed with publication only after the condemnation and [Loisy's] first submission,[15] at a moment when it was important to provide a precise object for discussion, to permit proper distinctions, to show the depth and complexity of the issues involved." The baron had to understand the "agony" that "my poor articles" had cost their author. "For three months I have endured frightful pain of heart and spirit, and I remain broken even now." But the baron also had to understand the damage Loisy was doing: "Perhaps . . . you should know that a young priest (we have mutual friends) has submitted his resignation to the archbishop of Paris, saying that Father Loisy's books do not permit him any longer to believe what it is necessary to believe in order to carry on the sacred ministry."[16]

Von Hügel set to work on his response, driven by his conviction that "Loisy has had to suffer more [than anyone], and his martyrdom is far from finished." Meanwhile the ever-restless Henri Bremond—in the midst of his traumatic separation from the Society of Jesus—went off on a holiday to the lake country of northern Italy. From there he tried to play the mediator, but his new allegiance made this a difficult task. "The baron," he told Blondel, "has read your articles and is ruminating about them. I feel sorry for him. You know his German and neurasthenique temperament. . . . As for me, Loisy has helped me preserve my faith in the divinity of Our Lord, and I owe him a debt of gratitude." When Blondel expressed mock surpirse that Loisy had served Bremond as a source of "edification," the latter replied, in the same ironic coin, that "the point of your letter, for me, is that I ought not to interfere in things I know nothing about. . . . But it does seem to me that your L[oisy] is not ours."[17] Von Hügel in essence took the same line: "I believe that you understand Loisy very little. A person only understands that for which he has some more or less instinctive sympathy. You do not possess such sympathy . . . for [a historian's] study of the contingent and relative. . . . This is by no means a sin, but in the end you do reveal all too clearly this deficiency."

The baron's final salutation—"Your very cordially devoted old friend"— startled Blondel, who had to be reassured that "old" in the English idiom did

14. Von Hügel to Blondel, 9 February, 1904, in Marlé (ed.), *Au coeur*, 211–12.

15. See chapter 14.

16. Blondel to von Hügel, 11 February, 1904, in Marlé (ed.), *Au coeur*, 213–14.

17. Bremond to Blondel, 27 February and n.d. [mid-March 1904], quoted in Blanchet, *Bremond*, 179–81.

not mean "former."[18] Von Hügel's own grasp of that idiom, however, re-mained in many respects as perverse as ever. He commissioned Bremond to translate his rebuttal of Blondel into French, and Bremond, back from Italy and staying with Tyrrell in Richmond, found the job awesomely difficult. "You cannot imagine the pain this translation has given me. This German thought, here I encounter it for the first time, and I am obliged to be faithful to it. Three or four times I have decided to give up the struggle against this utter unintelligibility (*grimoire*), these concentrations of ten phrases into one."[19] But he finished it at last—"the result is depolorable," he said—and the article appeared in *La quinzaine* for June 1. The argument of von Hügel's "Du Christ éternel et de nos christologies successives"[20] was the by-now famil-iar one based upon the distinction between what an historian qua historian can know about the person of Jesus and what the person of faith can know.[21] It occasioned a rejoinder in the same journal by Blondel's disciple, Joannès Wehrlé,[22] the harsh tone of which led the baron to a bitter conclusion: "I have . . . recognized in . . . [the] most implacably heresy-hunting paragraphs, not only the inspiration but the actual writing of my close friend Maurice Blondel." What made such conduct all the more lamentable was the unworthy cause of it: "Though [Blondel] is sincere in his opinions, his present distinctly feverish and over-emphatic insistence upon them, cannot be altogether disso-ciated from the storm-clouds visible on the ecclesiastical heavens."[23] Perhaps "old" friend meant "former" after all.

WHETHER OR NOT von Hügel's dark suspicions were justified, it was true that Blondel, and Lucien Laberthonnière too, had become the center of a swir. of rumors coming out of Rome and reported in various French and Italian newspapers. A curious alliance of theological conservatives and social liberal: was allegedly lobbying officials in the Congregation of the Index to censure the philosophers of *action*. "After the exegetes," Blondel commented, "the seek the heads of the philosophers. Just as I had foreseen, my articles have enraged the Right as well as the Left."[24] Nothing came of these threats sav heartache for Blondel and especially for his wife, and it may have been that h overestimated the danger despite reassurances to the contrary. A friend, writ ing from Rome, quoted the secretary of the Index: " 'Tell [Blondel] once mor that he should put his mind at ease.' " Nevertheless, with the policy of Piu X and Merry del Val clearly aimed at a greater measure of Roman control ove

18. Von Hügel to Blondel, 19 February, 1904, in Marlé (ed.), *Au coeur*, 218–20.
19. Bremond to Blondel, 23 May, 1904, in Marlé (ed.), *Au coeur*, 221.
20. *La quinzaine* 58 (1 June, 1904): 285–312.
21. A good description of the article and its context is in Barmann, *Hügel*, 122–23.
22. Joannès Wehrlé "Le Christ et la conscience catholique," *La quinzaine* 59 (16 August, 1904 421–47.
23. Von Hügel to Bishop, 16 September, 1904, quoted in *Dublin Review* 227 (April 1953): 18:
24. Blondel to Loisy, 28 February, 1904, in Marlé (ed.), *Au coeur*, 201.

the speculations of Catholic savants, the gossip persisted. For example, it was said that the pope, in a private audience, had observed that "he was anxious to push forward a program of social action, but that this had to be strictly distinguished from controversial movements in philosophy and apologetics. . . . He added that two or three others [besides Loisy] would be condemned."[25]

This last bit of news was relayed from Paris to Aix by Laberthonnière who, given his feisty temperament, was perhaps more exhilarated than depressed by potential danger. He was at any rate predictably hearty in his support for *Histoire et dogme*—"a major work of Christian thought," he called it[26]—though he believed Lagrange and Batiffol fell under its strictures more than Loisy did.[27] As for "our dear baron's" response to Blondel, "I ask myself whether we are not separated from him by misunderstandings rather than by truly different ideas. At bottom what he wants to insist upon is a Christ truly and fully human. But we hold this as much as he does. The problem is to know what are the conditions required for this."[28] It is doubtful such a judgment comforted Blondel, who had already decided to be offended by the manner in which the baron had foisted his views upon a French readership: "What pains me most is to think that dear Henri Bremond has placed his pen and his ingenuity at the service of Baron von Hügel in order to give his complaints against me the fullest possible clarity and precision. . . . And Hügel knew perfectly well how grieved I would be."[29]

However that may have been, rumors of disapproval in high ecclesiastical circles did not discourage Laberthonnière from publishing his most blistering attack so far upon the theological establishment. *Le réalisme chrétien et l'idéalisme grec* appeared in May 1904, its hundred printed pages describing "the encounter between Christianity and Greek philosophy" which began when the apostles departed Jerusalem to preach the Gospel and which "has given way to what is called the conflict between faith and reason, between science and religion." The root problem has been, through all these centuries, the Greeks' obsession with nature and with the human person's sensual knowledge of it. "The beauty of form and of color seduced them. Like children, they were insatiable in their desire to see." Socrates may have introduced a moral element into their thought with his "Know thyself," but "we cannot fail to recognize that in place of searching, as we Christians do, to resolve the problem of the world by resolving the problem of life, Greek speculation did just the reverse. The Greeks

---

25. Beaudoin to Blondel, 5 March, 1904, and Laberthonnière to Blondel, 11 March, 1904, quoted in Blondel and Valensin, *Correspondance*, 137–38. See also Lecanuet to Laberthonnière, 31 July, 1904, in Perrin (ed.), *Laberthonnière et ses amis*, 45.

26. Laberthonnière to Blondel, 3 February, 1904, in Tresmontant (ed.), *Correspondance*, 172.

27. Laberthonnière to von Hügel, 29 May, 1904, quoted in Poulat, *Histoire, dogme*, 563.

28. Laberthonnière to Blondel, 31 May, 1904, in Tresmontant (ed.), *Correspondance*, 175–76.

29. Blondel to Laberthonnière, 16 May, 1904, quoted in Blanchet, *Bremond*, 184.

always sought to find out directly how and of what things are made." This inquiry, essentially pagan, has been perpetuated to this day by the intellectual descendants of the Greeks, the Scholastics, who have built their theory of abstract knowledge upon it. They call it realism, but it is idealism of the worst kind.

Of course for Laberthonnière the method of immanence[30] put the lie to this Scholastic epistemology and all its baleful theological consequences. Reasoning from the "extrinsic" is no less wrong in the supernatural than in the physical order. One who knows oneself reaches out inevitably for the supernatural, and so revelation cannot be merely the introduction into us from the outside of a series of abstract propositions, entirely foreign to what we are, and then laid, so to speak, on top of our natural understanding. Revelation consists rather in an illumination of what already is now and always has been and always will be. Properly speaking, there is no conflict between faith and reason or between science and religion, because faith swallows up reason into a larger reality, and because science, with all due regard to the enlightenment it affords, cannot speak to religious reality. "Religion is essentially an affair of the soul. Nor does this mean an affair of vague sentimentality or aspirations badly defined. Rather it means an affair of supreme importance, in which is engaged our very being in its totality. This is what people forget when, under the pretext of understanding religious truth scientifically, they try to square it with historical truth." With a clarity that eluded Blondel—and perhaps went beyond Blondel's purposes—Laberthonnière brushed aside the conventional formulations and went to the heart of the Christian mystery:

God is no longer the idea of ideas or an essence from which other essences proceed by logical participation. God is the being of beings and the life of their life. He is the one who is and who lives in himself and by whom other beings live and are. He is not a supreme concept but a supreme action and an immanent action. God is not an unmoved prime mover, completely at rest above all movement and life. He is the very movement of life as principle and as end. He is in the process of becoming, at the very point where the Greeks saw only blind fate. He is in the very chaos of reality, properly conferring upon it his own character of infinity and presenting himself to it from within by means of an immediate encounter, in order to discover, organize, and establish itself in him.[31]

THE EVER-ENERGETIC PÈRE LABERTHONNIÈRE was not content merely to compose literary tracts. Ever since he had settled in the rue Las Cases he had looked round restlessly for some organizational structure in which to fix his intellectual work. Finding none, he formed one of his own: the Société d'Études Religieuses took shape at the time he was writing *Le réalisme chrétien.*

30. See chapter 5.
31. Lucien Laberthonnière, *Le Réalisme chrétien, précédé de essais de philosophie religieuse* (Paris: 1966 ed.), 243, 247, 304, 278.

It was made up of a dozen or so individuals "dedicated," as Laberthonnière told Blondel, "to the intellectual apostolate." He intended the association to be similar to the Oratory, "but altogether secular, so secular that it would be well if laymen formed a part of it."[32]

One layman who participated in the society and to a degree dominated it was Laberthonnière's friend, the mathematician Édouard Le Roy.[33] No one was more active than he in setting the society's progressive agenda, in pressing forward its claims, in recruiting appropriate new members for it. In the regular meetings of the society, at which high-toned discussion was often geared to later publication, Le Roy readily assumed the lead. Laberthonnière was justly seen as a bold and fearless controversialist, but even he could not match thirty-four-year-old Le Roy's brash self-confidence which seemed, at times, to merge into self-righteousness.

A telling example of this characteristic appeared in an article Le Roy wrote during the autumn of 1904. He titled it, "What Is a Dogma?"[34] That he could "claim no particular knowledge about the subject," indeed that he "freely admitted [his] incompetence," did not inhibit him, because, he maintained, "I am situated to appreciate correctly the point of view of contemporary philosophers opposed to the understanding of Christian truth." So, as a preamble to answering the question he had posed, Le Roy cited the reasons why "contemporary philosophers" refused even to consider the possibility of dogmatic propositions. Dogmas are unproved and unprovable, according to the Cartesian and Kantian norms now accepted by all responsible thinkers, Christian and non-Christian alike; dogma "is radically opposed to the very life of the spirit, to its need of autonomy and sincerity, to its generative . . . principle of immanence"; all truth is immanent revelation, and so dogmas couched in Aristotelian or Neoplatonic terms cannot be successfully thrust into the mind from the outside; and, finally, religious dogmas as commonly understood display a static character: "Being unalterable they appear foreign to progress, which is the very essence of thought. Being transcendent they exist without relation to effective intellectual life. They bring no increase of light to any of the riddles that occupy science and philosophy."

There was a charming ingenuousness to these assertions, delivered by Le Roy with such panache. He considered it necessary only to state them, not to prove their validity. And the way he stated them demonstrated perhaps better than any other single piece of writing how central the epistemological problem continued to be in the controversies now dramatically unfolding. What does one know, and how does one know it, undergirded the question, "What is a dogma?" Le Roy did not doubt for a moment that knowledge stems from posi-

---

32. Laberthonnière to Blondel, November 1903, in Perrin (ed.), *Laberthonnière et ses amis*, 49.
33. See chapter 14.
34. Édouard Le Roy, "Qu'est-ce qu'un dogme?," *La quinzaine* 73 (16 April, 1905): 495–526, reprinted with other essays in *Dogme et critique* (Paris: 1907), 1–34.

tivist science and immanent self-revelation. For him, therefore, the intellectualist claims of Scholastic theology and the oldfashioned apologetic—based upon abstraction from sense data and upon the proclamation of an extrinsic revelation—fall to the ground. Dogmatic statements based on such erroneous methodology are not only not true: they are meaningless.

Where does such a conclusion leave the dogmatic teaching of the church? What happens, in such a dispensation, to the articles of the creed? Le Roy, the intensely pious Catholic layman, offered a twofold reply. First, dogmas have a negative use. For example, "God is a person" means that "God is not impersonal," that is to say, "not simply a law, a formal category, an ideal principle, an abstract entity, . . . or some unknown cosmic force" which might suggest a form of pantheism. Similarly, the dogma of the Resurrection of Jesus "does not communicate a concept to me" about this unique and therefore unknowable fact, but it does "exclude certain ideas I might be tempted to adopt. . . . Death has not been for him, as it is for ordinary mortals, the cessation of practical activity." As for the real presence of Christ in the Eucharist, that dogma "does not tell me in what the presence consists" but only that "the consecrated host must not be treated solely as a symbol."

But dogma as affirmation is even more important than dogma as negation, because "the value of a truth is measured above all by the services it renders. . . . A dogma above all has a *practical* meaning. It is . . . the formula of a rule of practical conduct." Dogma worthy of the name, in other words, must display moral utility. So " 'God is a person' means that you should conduct your relations with God as you would with a person." " 'Jesus is risen' means that you should relate yourself to him as if he had not died, as if he were a contemporary." And the presence of Christ in the Eucharist means that "one should have the same attitude toward the consecrated host as one would have toward Jesus were he visible." Such is the only iron law of dogma, and the Catholic who strictly observes it—who complies with "the practical edicts prescribed by the dogma"—then "retains full liberty to forge for himself any dogmatic theory . . . that suits him. . . . His position in this regard is the same as that toward any scientific or philosophical speculation."[35]

Le Roy's article, which seemed to many critics the extreme restatement of a nominalist voluntarism, sparked the usual uproar in the learned Catholic press.[36] The author, however, remained undaunted. "More numerous and more menacing signs are abroad," he told Laberthonnière, "of a campaign against us. Monseigneur Batiffol is alarmed; he has the impudence to spread the rumor that he *declined* to join our Société [d'Études Religieuses]. The Jesuits are decidedly and violently against us. And the bishops talk about seeking a sentence from Rome against this monstrous distortion, this latest invention

35. La Roy, "Qu'est-ce qu'un dogme?," 495–96, 501–9, 511–12, 509, 517–18, 524.
36. See Rivière, *Modernisme*, 252–54.

of hell which they call immanentism, pragmatism, moral dogmatism, and I know not what else."[37] Le Roy busied himself through the summer and autumn of 1905 answering the criticism of his views that had appeared in the various journals like *Études* and the *Revue du clergé français*.

But no attack to which Le Roy felt obliged to respond was so ominous as that which had been published in the *Revue biblique*, a piece written by Joannès Wehrlé.[38] Its very appearance pointed to dissent from Le Roy's provocative views by Maurice Blondel and his close associates. Though he had not mentioned Blondel's name in "What Is a Dogma?"—and Le Roy may very well, like Tyrrell, have been more influenced by Bergson[39]—hostile reviewers had discerned in his argument the specter of the method of immanence. Blondel, who had known Le Roy casually since 1900, was annoyed and alarmed by this suggested connection. "[Le Roy] is a little too sure of himself," he confided to Wehrlé:

In pretending to raise a question he instead lays down an ultimatum and excludes in advance any rejoinders with which he does not agree. In so doing he sets aside the possibility of appeal [from his opinions] and hurls a kind of defiance at authority, which strikes me as an immediate and formidable danger. I don't say this out of any sense of rivalry with him; but it does seem to me that he has come to hunt in my forest, and, whereas I have for some years advanced my ideas with prudence, folly of this sort puts such efforts at risk.

Blondel, who was uneasy at Le Roy's influence over Laberthonnière, also wrote to the Oratorian: "[Le Roy] has energetically justified the manner in which you and I have posed the [epistemological] problem. But does he not exaggerate his anti-intellectualism? Dogma, like thought in general, does not express adequately the whole mystery of reality. But certainly it stands for more than a symbol of proper practice."[40] Wehrlé assumed a sharper tone. "I am surprised," he told Laberthonnière, who had protested the article in the *Revue biblique*, "that you should consider that this is simply a quarrel between Monsieur Le Roy and me. . . . I am further surprised that anyone today would not take into account the dreadful responsibility one incurs who controverts in the public forum with eloquence, to be sure, but also with frivolity. [Others] have challenged Le Roy's scientific theories. Why do I not have the right to question his religious philosophy, which is essentially the same?"[41]

As in the case of Loisy's alleged "historicism," a whiff of schism was blowing in from Aix-en-Provence.

37. Le Roy to Laberthonnière, 15 August, 1905, in Perrin (ed.), *Laberthonnière et ses amis*, 51–52.

38. Joannès Wehrlé, "De la nature de dogme," *Revue biblique* 14 (July 1905): 323–49. See also Lagrange, "L'École biblique," 152.

39. So at any rate Aubert, *L'acte de foi*, 366. For Tyrrell, see note 21, in chapter 15.

40. Blondel to Wehrlé, 14 May, 1905, and Blondel to Laberthonnière, 22 April, 1905, quoted in Virgoulay, *Blondel*, 138.

41. Wehrlé to Laberthonnière, 7 July, 1905, in Perrin (ed.), *Laberthonnière et ses amis*, 62.

LABERTHONNIÈRE sent a copy of *Le réalisme chrétien et l'idéalisme grec* to Alfred Loisy, who, having paged through it, wrote down his first impressions in his journal. He was pleased that Laberthonnière had properly distinguished faith from science, though he could not agree, "as the author would wish, . . . that faith would authorize one to conclude—despite history—the physical and material reality of notions such as the virgin birth."

Otherwise Laberthonnière's system, which is Maurice Blondel translated into French and without the latter's learned pretentions, is simply a renewal of Protestant illuminism. It is the essential denial of theological dogma transmitted by tradition and by the authority of the church, which is its sovereign guarantee. These people believe all the dogmas of the church, but they do not believe them in the way that is necessary, in accord, that is, with an objective revelation and on the testimony of the church. They have for their only warrant their internal experience, just like the Protestants. They are subjectivists. They are not orthodox. But then nobody is orthodox. Orthodoxy is a fantasy of people who do not think.[42]

Two months after making this entry, in July 1904, Loisy left Bellevue and took up residence in a cottage near the village of Garnay, forty miles or so west of Paris, where he was to spend the next three years. He owed this welcome change once more to the kindness of François Thureau-Dangin, his former student at the Institut Catholique and, though still young, already a renowned Assyrioligist. This was the second time that Loisy had received solace from the same family. François, the son of Paul Thureau-Dangin,[43] in addition to his credentials as an accomplished professional scholar, was also a well-fixed man of property whose large and splendid chateau cast a long shadow over the whole district around Garnay. His local influence was extended in his guest's behalf almost immediately. Together they rode in Thureau-Dangin's automobile to Chartres and called at the diocesan chancery to which the parish in Garnay was subject. The bishop's secretary greeted them warmly and readily registered Loisy's indult to celebrate mass privately.

Loisy's little peasant house and its adjoining garden lay between the edge of the chateau's park and the village. Not far away was the forest of Dreux, a pleasant locale for the exegete to take his walks in. The place was, all in all, an agreeable retreat for one who, like Loisy, had just passed through a period of excruciating emotional tension. But it was a lonely place as well, with hardly anyone to talk to: Thureau-Dangin and his wife were seldom in residence and the curé stationed in the village remained suspicious of this strange confrere who said mass at home and spoke in sardonic riddles. The priests at Dreux, to which Loisy had to go, on foot, twice a week to shop for his food and other staples, were even more hostile. So the notorious savant, whose books, it was widely known, were forbidden by the Holy Father himself, bided his time

42. Loisy, *Choses passées*, 307–8.
43. See note 43, in chapter 9.

and tended his garden, in which he raised turnips and other vegetables. He also kept a small flock of chickens, to each of which he wryly assigned the name of an ancient Assyrian king."I went to see him at the beginning of the winter after his move to Garnay," Albert Houtin recalled. "He had the air of a man enduring the tortures of being buried alive."[44]

None of his friends besides Monsieur and Madame Thureau-Dangin—particularly outspoken on the point had been Archbishop Mignot and Baron von Hügel—had approved of his withdrawal into rural solitude. But Loisy was a man who was selective in the advice he took to heart. Much of his lonely day was devoted to the kind of work he had been doing for years. By March 1905 he finished his commentary on the Synoptic Gospels, but, in accord with the commitment he had made to Cardinal Richard and Merry del Val, he refrained, for the time being, from publishing it. This scruple did not prevent him from sharing his views with those who approached him privately and asked his opinion, as did Von Hügel's friend, Giovanni Semeria. The metaphysical arguments for the existence of God, he advised the Italian Barnabite, seem to rest upon "an immensity of forces, an ocean of life which we grasp but which does not appear as though it were governed by a will external to itself." He went on, "It appears evident to me that the notion of God has never been more than a sort of ideal projection, a splitting off [*dedoublement*] of the human personality, and that theology has never been, nor could it ever be, more than a mythology that becomes with time more and more sanitized."[45]

Several essays, already in press, Loisy allowed to become public, as well as a collection of other short pieces, on the grounds that their composition antedated the unhappy negotiations of the spring of 1904. He also wrote a couple of anonymous articles on the impending church–state crisis in France.

IT MAY BE RECALLED that in his appeal for forebearance to Pius X Loisy had protested that he did not "want to contribute to the ruin of the faith in my homeland."[46] There had been in this assertion as much a veiled threat as a plea—a warning to the pope that Catholicism in France stood in mortal peril if it did not adapt itself to modern realities, of which the specific area of biblical scholarship was only one. The church's predicament moved along a lengthy spectrum of issues and trials. And there was a sense in which the challenges to orthodoxy posed by the new physical and social sciences merely provided a different arena for the struggle that had been raging among Frenchmen since the Revolution. It was by now a commonplace that two cultures were in conflict, that two mutually hostile nations had come to occupy the same sacred soil: the one liberal, positivist, statist, and republican; and the other tradition-

44. Houtin and Sartiaux, *Loisy*, 130–32.
45. Loisy to Semeria, 22 April, 1906, quoted in *Mémoires*, 2:469–70.
46. See chapter 14.

alist, conservative, Catholic, and nostalgically royalist. The signs of the times seemed to confirm Loisy's admonition. Out of the affair of Captain Dreyfus and the consequent wreckage of the *ralliement* had emerged the latest stage in the confrontation, and, as far as its political manifestation was concerned, the final stage.

Now the specific issue was the Napoleonic concordat itself. Ever since the founding of the Third Republic the call to rescind that agreement between church and state had been standard rhetoric for the various anticlerical factions. But the immense practical difficulties involved had given them pause, as had their own deep divisions. Thus the bourgeois parties of the center believed they needed the votes of the clerical right to fend off the progressive income tax, which they feared and despised even more than they did the priests; while the socialists, gaining electoral strength year by year, tended to suspect that conventional anticlerical fulminations were largely the diversionary tactics adopted by a middle class resistant to needed social change. Other related considerations led successive governments to put off the fatal day. One was simply the internal weakness of coalition ministries, many of them racked by financial and sexual scandals. Another was the widespread conviction, even among the harshest anticlericals, that the concordat was a useful tool—in the prerevolutionary Gallican sense—whereby the state could control the only other institution in the nation capable of competing with it. But the Dreyfus case, having left the church's putative ally, the army, in disgrace, had altered the political landscape, and three factors combined to lead to the unilateral repudiation of the concordat.

The first was the general election of 1902. The popular vote was very close, but in the runoff the *bloc de gauche* secured a majority of 130 in the Chamber of Deputies. The second was the conversion to the cause of the socialist leader, Jean Jaurès—the same Jaurès who, as a student at the École Normale Supérieure, had rallied support for the rights of the Catholic professor, Ollé-Laprune.[47] Jaurès committed not only his party but also his immense personal prestige when he proclaimed in the summer of 1904, "It is time for this great but obsessive problem of the relations of church and state to be finally settled, so that democracy can devote all its attention to the . . . difficult task of social reform . . . which the proletariat is demanding." And the third factor was Premier Émile Combes.[48]

The Combes ministry lasted thirty-one months (June 1902–January 1905). Though, like Moses on the borders of the promised land, he did not survive in office quite long enough to secure his final purpose, "the little father," as his colleagues called Combes behind his back, made the definitive break between church and state inevitable. This diminutive, goateed, frock-coated provincial

47. See chapter 5.
48. See chapter 13.

politician in his late sixties earned the ironic nickname—half-admiring, half-contemputous—because of his unbending clerical demeanor. As a seminarian he had written a dissertation in which he hinted that Thomas Aquinas had been a dangerous liberal. But when the diocesan authorities had denied him ordination to the priesthood—due, they said, to his "pride"—the intellectual ground beneath him had shifted dramatically. He became a medical doctor, then a devoted Freemason, and finally, when elected to the Senate at the age of fifty, the most virulent foe of the ecclesiastical system that had rejected him. Unlike many of the pragmatists who surrounded him, Combes pursued Catholicism, and all its works and pomps, with the fervor of a red-hot fanatic. "You cannot confine the policy of a great country to a mere struggle against the religious orders," protested one veteran politician. "I took office solely for that purpose," replied the prime minister.

This in fact was an understatement: Combes's target was much broader and deeper. He agreed whole-heartedly with a socialist colleague who described Catholicism as "a scourge whose ravages on the human mind can only be compared to those of alcoholism." His predecessor, the *politique* Waldeck-Rousseau, had begun the assault on the religious orders, but, in accord with his own austere sense of practicality, he had done so selectively and with a weather eye carefully cocked on public opinion.[49] Combes felt bound by no such constraints. Confident by reason of his huge majority in the Chamber of Deputies, he swept the board clean and even suppressed the most popular of the religious, the teaching nuns, thousands of whose schools were closed across the country. His ministry survived the riots that followed in Brittany and elsewhere to go after the biggest game of all.

Through a variety of initiatives it formally challenged the papacy over the most sensitive and contentious article of the concordat, that which regulated the appointment of bishops. No longer would the government accede to the cozy arrangement whereby French dioceses would be filled by prior negotiations between the papal nuncio to Paris and the minister of cults.[50] Under the concordat, Combes maintained, bishops were salaried officers of the state, and therefore no one would be appointed a bishop who was not a reliable republican. So it was that sees remained unfilled and that even the likes of Alfred Loisy could aspire to a bishopric.[51] A test case of another kind arose when two bishops were summoned to Rome to answer charges, one that he cavorted with Freemasons and the other that he cavorted with a mother-superior. Combes forbade them to go. The prime minister had clearly jettisoned the time-tested procedure followed by moderate anticlericals such as Waldeck-Rousseau of attacking the orders while conciliating the laity and the secular clergy. In doing

49. See chapter 11.
50. See chapters 8 and 13.
51. See chapter 12.

so he left the Vatican with litle room to maneuver, if indeed it had desired to do so.

At the beginning of his pontificate Pius X had indicated a willingness for accommodation with the French Republic, but, considering the pope's temperament and pastoral intentions, this aspiration was exceedingly fragile. "To restore all things in Christ"—the papal motto—did not leave much room for pragmatic stratagem, and the undisguised hostility of the regime in Paris inevitably sparked a reaction in Rome. At the head of each administration now stood an uncompromising intransigent. As the truculent and deliberately provocative Combes had succeeded the adaptable Waldeck-Rousseau, so had the straightforward peasant, Sarto, followed the wily and diplomatic aristocrat, Pecci. The new pontiff had little patience with politics. The undeniable spiritual warmth and zeal and courage that contributed to Pius X's canonization as a saint forty years after his death were not calculated to deal successfully with the tangled problems presented by at least a century of French history and by the conundrums raised by contemporary scientific research. Nor did the appointment of his chief aide give him the supple administrator who might have tempered his own single-mindedness. Rafael Merry del Val,[52] now a cardinal and secretary of state, gifted as he may have been, was no Rampolla; he was too young and inexperienced, too brash, too cocksure of himself to deal with the complex issues presented him from Paris and indeed, given the Vatican's interests, from around the world.

It was in fact a diplomatic blunder by Merry del Val that brought the crisis to a head. The beguiling fiction that the pope was still de jure a civil ruler led the secretary of state to dispatch a formal note, dated April 28, 1904, to the European foreign offices. In a stiff and haughty tone, the cardinal protested the recent ceremonial visit of the president of the French Republic to the king of Italy, on the grounds that the latter was a usurper and held court in the Quirinal in defiance of international law. This exercise in futility and bad manners—it had been France, after all, that had shored up the remnant of the pope's temporal power in its last years—was leaked by Loisy's erstwhile patron, the prince of Monaco, to Jaurès, who had it printed verbatim in the socialist press. Gleeful anticlericals dubbed Merry del Val's note an unwarranted intrusion into the conduct of French foreign policy, and embarrassed Catholics had to endure Combes's proclamation in the Chamber of Deputies that he intended "to put an end to this antiquated fable of a temporal sovereignty that disappeared thirty-four years ago." At the end of July the French ambassador to the Holy See asked for his passports.

Within the Chamber there already existed a committee charged with investigating and overseeing church–state relations. This body now moved forward, expeditiously but carefully, to frame legislation that would annul the

52. See chapter 11.

concordat. If Combes had had his way the result would have been drastically Erastian—"un règne concordataire sans le Concordat"—whereby the state would have entirely controlled the church as a prelude to destroying it. But in January 1905 Combes's ministry collapsed thanks to another tawdry scandal—this one, ironically enough, stemming from the revelation of the enormous influence wielded by the Freemasons in government appointments. "An inverted form of Jesuitism," observed one anticlerical enemy of Combes in disgust. The following July the new premier carried a more moderate bill through the Chamber of Deputies by a vote of 314 to 233, and for the first time since Clovis, king of the Franks, had embraced Christianity, church and state in France were divorced.

There followed a period of messy and awkward adjustment to the new ecclesiastical order. "A free church in a free state" may appear eminently sensible after the fact, but to accomplish it in the teeth of thirteen centuries of contrary practice was more easily said than done. Painful quarrels arose over the disposal of the church's material fabric, since 1801 supported by state funds. It went without saying that clerics would no longer receive salaries from the government. But what about seminaries, presbyteries, episcopal palaces, and even the church buildings themselves, all of which technically belonged to the state. At one point the government attempted to draw up inventories of liturgical vessels; a few inspectors had the temerity to demand the right to peer and poke inside tabernacles, which, for Catholics, was the ultimate profanity. Such officious clumsiness prompted disorder in many places, including the Parisian parish-church of Sainte-Clothilde; Lucien Laberthonnière could look out his window and watch the mob clashing with the police all along the rue Las Cases.[53] The process reached something of a symbolic culmination in December 1906, when the seminarians were expelled from Saint-Sulpice, and, a few blocks from Sainte-Clotilde, when Cardinal Richard, aged eighty-seven, was evicted from his chancery and residence at 127 rue de Grenelle.[54] Thousands of people were waiting for him in the street outside and singing the hymn "Sauvez, sauvez la France." When the old man, leaning on the arm of his coadjutor, emerged from the colonnaded doorway and stepped into his carriage, twenty men picked up its traces and pulled it themselves across the *arrondissement septième* to the temporary lodgings arranged for the cardinal on the rue de Babylone.

It is highly significant that events like these should have served as the backdrop to the intellectual crisis within Catholicism now approaching a climax of its own. French Catholics stood almost as one in opposing the end of the concordatory regime. This resistance predictably included extreme royalists, who claimed that state support had been merely inadequate compensation for

53. See chapter 14.
54. Adjacent to Les Invalides and now home to the Ministry of Labor.

the spoliation of the church during the Revolution, but it proved persuasive also to those of a more liberal bent, who feared that an unsubsidized Catholicism would become captive to rural magnates and the rich bourgeoisie. Nine out of ten of them could have understood little of Loisy's writings (and perhaps ninety-nine out of hundred of Blondel's). But it was easy for them to assume that Catholic savants who were in conflict with the embattled church authority were somehow allies of Combes, that such thinkers were of a piece with the gendarmes who shut down the religious school and threw the nuns into the street, or with the village atheist who mocked the Corpus Christi procession.

Little wonder, then, that complaints about Loisy and Blondel should have been registered at the Vatican chiefly by their fellow countrymen. And little wonder as well that there the aberrations shortly to be termed "Modernist" by Pius X appeared to be—despite English and Italian outriders and German sympathizers—an overwhelmingly French phenomenon. For the Roman mind to have linked hostile French politicians and apparently hostile French intellectuals into a single enemy was not particularly outlandish. The papacy, itself a traditional institution, has always been above all a defender of Tradition, a commitment unavoidably and often extended to lesser traditions which the wisdom of hindsight alone can dismiss as merely reflecting the status quo. Certainly in this instance Merry del Val was right to object on legal grounds to the unilateral repudiation of an international treaty; but he was guilty of an absurd exaggeration when he asserted that the separation law of 1905 was a worse blow to the church in France than had been the civil constitution of 1790. Yet for him and for the French Catholics the concordat had been more than a scrap of paper defining certain financial and administrative arrangements. It had been a sacred sign—a sacrament almost—that France was still the eldest daughter of the church, still, despite Robespierre and Combes and their ilk, the France of Saint Louis IX and of Bossuet.

For people who held such sentiments the relative moderation of the law of 1905 was no consolation. But one need only refer to the preamble of the concordat to realize that they were desperately grasping at an illusion: "The government of the Republic recognizes that the Catholic, Apostolic, and Roman religion is the religion of the great majority of French citizens." This statement of 1801 was a kind of legal stipulation, and, except for rites of passage like a christening or a marriage or a burial—which could be interpreted as social functions as much as religious—a century of relentless secularization had invalidated it: Catholicism no longer played a serious role in the lives of most French citizens, and probably had not for a long time. The results of the general election of May 1906 strongly confirmed this conclusion: the parties supporting the concordat, already a minority, lost sixty seats in the Chamber of Deputies. The fact was—and not only in France—that institutional Christianity could no longer claim to be an integral part of the *res publica* of Western nations. What had begun with Constantine had finally passed away, and religion, if it were to survive at all, would have to survive as a private concern. In later years French Catholics would come to see that freedom from the state had its advantages. But at the moment it was so crudely and callously pressed upon them that their new status was a bitter pill for them to swallow, and it did not dispose them to look kindly upon coreligionists who rhapsodized over the glories of things modern.[55]

DURING THE COURSE of 1906, and into early 1907, the pope issued a series of documents instructing the French bishops and their flocks to resist the law of separation, and specifically its provisions defining the status of ecclesiastical property, by any means short of violence. They complied with virtual unanimity, though not always with enthusiasm. The only bishop to break ranks was Lucien Lacroix of Tarentaise—Loisy's patron in the Monaco affair[56]—who resigned his see rather than abide by the papal directives. At the oppposite end of the ideological spectrum Henri Bremond's boyhood chum, Charles Maurras,[57] found among outraged Catholics a fertile ground of recruitment for his aggressive nationalist movement, the Action française. The enigmatic Maurras purported to be a conventional royalist, but he was in fact driven mostly by a pseudo mystical faith in France as the repository of the values of classical Greek and Roman civilization. Himself an atheist, he regarded the church as a treasured national institution and a bulwark against bourgeois republicans and Jews. "A patriotic Frenchman," he said, "knows no other religious interest than that of Catholicism."[58] Desperate for allies, many Catholics in France and in Rome were to listen to Maurras's siren song—even though it was often accompanied by the clatter of riot in the streets—for many years to come.

A few other persons in high places tried to find a softer solution. In Albi Eudoxe-Irénée Mignot invited a few like-minded bishops to confer with him as to the best practical means of dealing with the crisis and of finding a modus vivendi with the state. At the end of their deliberations, in January 1906, Mignot sent his vicar general and confidant, Louis Birot, to Rome with a letter for Merry del Val, in which it was suggested that patient negotiation with the government might still produce an acceptable settlement. Abbé Birot, a close friend of Laberthonnière and known to be as much a Gallican as his archbishop, received a courteous if somewhat chilly reception. The secretary of state feigned surprise that any French prelate could discern a silver lining in such a mass of dark political clouds, while Pius X in a private audience explained

55. See Dansette, *Histoire religieuse*, 586–624; McManners, *Church and State*, 129–57; Hausser, *Paris au jour*, 132–249; and Brogan, *Development*, 361–87.

56. See chapter 13.

57. See chapter 5.

58. Eugen Weber, *Action Française: Royalism and Reaction in Twentieth-Century France* (Stanford, Calif.: 1962), 33–36.

patiently and, Birot reluctantly admitted, persuasively why the Vatican could not agree to compromise.[59] But neither the pope nor the cardinal expressed aloud what was surely in their minds, that the Mignot who now recommended indulgence to the pagan politicians was the same Mignot who had proved himself the stoutest defender of Alfred Loisy.

Meanwhile the exegete himself had arrived at a critical moment in his career. While the debate on the law of separation was going on in the Chamber of Deputies, he held his peace, not wishing, he said, "to increase the disarry" in which French Catholicism found itself. But once the legislation had passed, and the resistance to it was manifest, Loisy strongly defended the government's position, at least in private correspondence and anonymous publications. As for his own situation, he had no doubt that a rupture between himself and the church was inevitable, but he was determined to be expelled rather than to secede and thus appear to declare himself a rationalist or an agnostic, putting at risk all his work. In the same spirit he brushed aside the suggestion of an acquaintance that he join the antipapal Old Catholics;[60] he had to remain in the church, he said, until he was formally condemned and deprived of the right to say mass privately.

That right depended on the papal indult granted at the request of Archbishop Mignot in 1899.[61] In October 1906 the seven-year term of the indult was due to expire. Loisy accordingly on September 23 wrote from Garnay to the bishop of Chartres and requested a renewal. There followed an inconclusive correspondence involving the chanceries of Chartres, Paris, and Chalons-sur-Marne—the last-named being still canonically Loisy's home diocese—none of which would assume responsibility for forwarding the petition to Rome. On October 19 the exegete told Albert Houtin: "This indult, I always thought that it would not be given me. *I hope for it.* . . . Yet I find it repugnant to initiate a secession. Perhaps this business of the indult will open a door for me." On November 1, the Feast of All Saints, Alfred Loisy celebrated mass for what proved to be the last time. The next day and for several days thereafter he was ill, and, once recovered, he did not approach the altar again. "It was not that [the mass] had lost for me all spiritual significance. But it had become recently a burden for me, because it seemed to imply a profession of official Catholicism. In renouncing it I took a long step toward the secularization of my life."[62]

---

59. See Dansette, *Histoire religieuse*, 613, and McManners, *Church and State*, 160–61.
60. See note 10, in chapter 6.
61. See chapter 10.
62. Houtin and Sartiaux, *Loisy*, 135–37, and Loisy, *Choses passées*, 317–23.

CHAPTER 17

The Practice of Dying

I recommend myself to your prayers and sacrifices, I, a poor priest practically de-
frocked, but suffering much from a nostalgia for the altar.

—*George Tyrrell* (1906)[1]

ON WEDNESDAY, February 14, 1906, a little less than eight months
before Alfred Loisy had done so, George Tyrrell celebrated his last mass.
The setting was the Catholic church in Eastbourne on the East Sussex coast,
where the Wards had once lived and where Tyrrell was staying briefly at the
home of his friend "Willie" Williams.[2] He had departed his beloved Richmond on New Year's Day—"One must practise dying," he wrote Maude Petre—and, thanks to her arrangements, had been able to seek a respite from his
troubles at a seaside resort at Tintagel, in Cornwall. But January can be a cruel
month along the Saint George's Channel, and it seemed a kind of symbol to
Tyrrell that upon his arrival the skies had opened and left him soaked and
shivering with cold. After four weeks of solitude—undergoing which, he concluded, "was *not* wise: it mean[t] obsession by . . . worry; no work by day, no
sleep at night"—he moved on from there to Clapham where friends received
him for a few days, and then to Eastbourne.[3] Two days before he approached
the altar for the last time he informed Petre of his intention: "Wednesday is
positively the last Mass till the reign of Pope Angelus. It shall be for you."[4]

So it had come to pass that by the end of 1906 both Loisy and Tyrrell had
ceased to perform that function which is central to the Catholic priesthood and
which indeed defines it. But the paths that had led these remarkable men to
the same critical juncture in their lives were as different as their temperaments.
The Frenchman, always a model of propriety, consistency, and rigid self-con-

1. Tyrrell to Laberthonnière, 22 March, 1906, in Perrin (ed.), *Laberthonnière et ses amis*, 69.
2. See chapters 8 and 10.
3. Tyrrell to Petre, 30 December, 1905 and 3 and 8 January, 1906, quoted in Petre, *Autobiography of Tyrrell*, 2:258–60.
4. Tyrrell to Petre, 12 February, 1906, quoted in Sagovsky, *Tyrrell*, 202.

trol, had simply let events unfold inexorably until a relatively trivial formality—the expiration of his indult—allowed him to take "a long step in the secularization of [his] life."[5] He accepted the situation as logical and foreseeable. The displaced Irishman, by contrast, whose clashing emotions were ever at war within himself, stumbled through a labyrinth of contradiction and confusion, loving and at the same time hating the church he had embraced in the fervor of his youth, searching for a Catholicism with which he could live, and reviling the only Catholicism that actually existed.

Tyrrell's instincts were the same as Loisy's in that he was resolved to await expulsion from the institutional church rather than to secede from it. Yet he vacillated. He daydreamed about placing an advertisement in the press: "A Roman Catholic priest, retiring from the exercise of his ministry for reasons of conscience, desires temporary occupation, literary, secretarial, or even tutorial. . . . And then something says: No, wait till you are driven. Initiate nothing." But the difficulty in exercising this "frail prudence" lay in the revulsion that was gradually mastering his ambivalent feelings. "I have the horrors on me, and feel tangled in the arms of some marine polypus or giant octopus. The Church sits on my soul like a nightmare, and the oppression is maddening. . . . I do not wonder that to Savonarola and the medieval mystics Rome seemed anti-Christ. The misery is that she is both Christ and anti-Christ; wheat and tares; a double-faced Janus looking heavenwards and hellwards."[6]

The more specific object of Tyrrell's bile continued to be a "Jesuitism" still "intoxicated with its first successes" in the far-off days of Saint Ignatius, but now sunk in "fundamental corruption," obsessed by the "childish absurdities" of its discipline, "stiffen[ed] with the rigidity of its spiritual pride," given over to an "appalling . . . corporate self-complacency." He set down these and countless similar accusations in an interminable screed to the Jesuit general in Rome—when printed it ran to forty pages[7]—in which he castigated "your Society" for "crippling the mind and character. . . . If there is any manhood left in [a Jesuit] it is in spite and not because of your methods." But once having given verbal expression to his loathing, he drifted back into indecision and did not post the letter.

This detailed indictment of the Society of Jesus lay in a drawer for more than a year while the writer of it toiled with his own doubts and misgivings. Today he decided to go, and tomorrow he changed his mind. Meantime most of those who loved and admired Tyrrell—including many English Jesuits—remained unaware of the depths of his unhappiness and unaware too of just

5. See chapter 16.
6. Tyrrell to Petre, 5 November, 1904, in M. D. Petre (ed.), *George Tyrrell's Letters* (London: 1920), 109.
7. Tyrrell to Martin, 26 June, 1904, in Petre, *Autobiography of Tyrrell*, 2:458–99. The quotations in the text are from 481–83, 487.

how far he had departed in his private thoughts from what they understood to be Catholic orthodoxy. Besides genuine and heartfelt uncertainty there was a measure of calculation in his public conduct: if he took care not to scandalize persons of good will unnecessarily, he was also disinclined to burn all his boats.

But to his intimates he revealed a bleak and almost frightening melancholy. We must reckon, he wrote to one of them, with "the Cat-theory of the universe. . . . The mixture of good and evil, kindness and cruelty in the world . . . is [best] explained by an all-governing Cat. . . . [P]uss allows the mouse little runs and counterfeit liberties and escapes, and smiles at his gambols and dandles him lovingly in velvet paws, but all with a view to a final grab and crunch. . . . [T]he argument from design makes for the Cat-theory. . . . Give me the faith of the mouse who dies squeaking out: 'O lovely Pussy! O Pussy, my love! What a lovely Pussy you are, you are!' "[8] "The parochialism of Christianity gets very oppressive," he wrote another. "Its ridiculous little world-scheme and its fussy little god [*sic*] and above all its deplorable history. I suppose it is better than that of the [primitives], but it is only a question of more or less." What he longed for, he said, was "the religion of Jesus" rather than "that *about* Jesus."[9] The distinction, to the degree that it was operative, imparted no more peace to his mind than the chronic migraine allowed comfort to his body.

Central to Tyrrell's predicament was the nagging problem posed by Maude Petre. The more he came to depend upon her, the more he resented that dependence. Her possessiveness and jealousy of Tyrrell's other female friends drove him to fury. And yet he found he could not do without her support and sympathy. When it became clear that he would eventually leave or be driven from the Society of Jesus, and thus be without means of support, he even accepted from her an annuity of £100. For her part, Petre grew increasingly despondent. "I want to give so much more than he wants to take," she wrote. "If he should settle his life in some way irrespective of me I should have to bury myself in a convent—or in some country place among the poor."[10] In her desperation she proposed that she and Tyrrell settle in the prayerful tranquility of Assisi. It would be Richmond again, where they had spent all those happy evenings together,[11] only this time under the patronage of Saint Francis, *il poverello*.

At first Tyrrell dismissed the idea as bizarre and as productive of "all the scandal of an elopement without the pleasures."[12] But Petre persisted. " 'There is . . . in this Italian project,' " Tyrrell quoted her, " 'a perspective literally

8. Tyrrell to Dora Williams, 12 January and 6 March, 1905, in Petre (ed.), *Tyrrell's Letters*, 285–86, 289. Dora was Willie Williams's sister and housemate.

9. Tyrrell to Petre, 1 January, 1905, in Petre (ed.), *Tyrrell's Letters*, 25.

10. Quoted in Leonard, *Transformation*, 36.

11. See chapter 12.

12. Tyrrell to Bremond, 2 August, 1905, in Louis-David (ed.), *Lettres de Tyrrell*, 188.

. . . of life as opposed to the state of exhaustion to which the uncertainties and continual disappointments have reduced me. For a considerable time I have felt my life simply slipping away from me, and the constant effort to hide my weariness and depression go beyond anything you could imagine. I tell you all this because I want you to know how important this is to me; it will save me even more than it will save you.' " Tyrrell, though he expressed himself in a jocular fashion, was genuinely touched: "No matter what *man*, to say nothing of an impulsive Irishman: could he do less than put an immediate end to her agony?" Assisi remained out of the question: "I can see myself there being confined to a constant intimacy with her in a little Umbrian village, far from all my friends and from my whole life, in a perfectly ridiculous, uncomfortable and scandalous position. She thinks pious reminiscences of St. Francis would sanctify everything." Perhaps Genoa, he reflected more or less idly, and pious reminiscences of Baron von Hügel's Saint Catherine, would provide a safe haven. As for London, where he and Petre could live close together without arousing comment, "O, how I *detest* the place. . . . Besides which, if I were alone there, I would no doubt contract syphilis within a week."[13] None of these musings—the last one clearly an instance of dark Celtic humor—came to anything, but Maude Petre's appeal did have one decisive result: Tyrrell formally applied to the general in Rome for release from the Society of Jesus. When that worthy informed him of the need to submit reasons for his request, Tyrrell, on September 2, 1905, sent him the long and bitter letter he had composed more than a year before.[14]

That document was hardly calculated to gain the petitioner a friendly hearing, even had the officials in Rome been otherwise disposed to grant him one. There dragged on through the autumn a tedious and increasingly acrimonious correspondence between Tyrrell and the father general, Luis Martín,[15] each of them intent to place the blame for the rupture upon the other. Dispensation from solemn vows necessarily involved the Congregation of Bishops and Regulars, and the mills of that venerable bureaucracy ground slowly. The canonical process of "secularization" turned in the final instance upon finding a bishop willing to "incardinate" the petitioner into his diocese. For Tyrrell was not only a solemnly committed religious, he was also an ordained priest, and release from his vows as a Jesuit did not include canceling out his sacramental ordination. Church law sensibly forbade an individual to perform priestly min-

13. Tyrrell to Bremond, 22 August, 1905, in Louis-David (ed.), *Lettres de Tyrrell*, 190–91.
14. See note 6, above.
15. For Martín (1846–1906), see Schultenover, *View from Rome*, 188–216, which uses Martín's diary to provide evidence of the general's "troubled sexuality," among other private matters. The relevance of this material is not altogether clear. Father Schultenover fits it into what he calls his "anthropological brief" on the "Mediterranean mind" (168). The official reaction to Modernism, he argues—at considerable length and with his usual perspicacity but, to me, not very persuasively—involved "the peculiar pathology of Mediterranean culture" (215).

istrations unless he were responsible either to a religious superior or to a bishop. Therefore, if he were to carry out any sacerdotal functions—like saying mass—the former religious had to do so as a "secular" priest, subject to a diocesan bishop. Tyrrell's friend Henri Bremond, under similar circumstances a few years earlier, had found such an *episcopus benevolus* in the person of the archbishop of Aix.[16]

The burden of finding a bishop to take him in, so to speak, rested upon Tyrrell, though he had reason to expect Martín and the Jesuit officialdom to aid him in this respect. Such help was not forthcoming. He applied to the archbishops of Westminster and Dublin, both of whom replied that it was against their policy to incardinate former religious. He then considered seeking a place abroad, at Aix, like Bremond, or at San Francisco. "If things get bad enough," he told Bremond bitterly, "there is always the Archbishop of Canterbury."[17] Meanwhile Tyrrell grew ever angrier, ever more convinced that the Roman delays were attributable to simple vindictiveness. He contemplated approaching the congregation without an *episcopus benevolus* as a way of forcing its hand. Von Hügel and Petre and others of his friends dreaded this prospect, because it could result in a sentence that would in effect deprive Tyrrell of the legal right to exercise his Catholic priesthood in any way. The baron, relying on his social connections, even attempted a clumsy intervention of his own in Rome, which succeeded only in a recommendation of Tyrrell's case to the largess of Cardinal Merry del Val. Tyrrell received this news with "gusts of laughter": Merry del Val and Martín were, he said, "as identical as any two persons of the Trinity."[18]

In the midst of these tortuous negotiations Tyrrell found himself embarrassed by earlier indiscretions and by the equivocation he employed in explaining them. He had already had to fend off complaints about "Ernest Engels's" *Religion as a Factor of Life* once its true authorship came to be known in Rome. He did so by declaring that that book, a "lengthy correspondence with an agnostic," had been printed and distributed without his permission; it had fallen, he said disingenuously, "into mischievous hands."[19] This falsehood did not spare him, at the end of 1905, when excerpts from another of his heretofore unacknowledged works surfaced in the Milanese daily *Corriere della Sera*. Martín passed on to Tyrrell the protest of the archbishop of Milan, who demanded to know the identity of the unnamed "English Jesuit" responsible for "A Letter to a University Professor."[20] Tyrrell responded haughtily that it was

16. See chapter 15.

17. Tyrrell to Bremond, 10 November, 1905, in Louis-David (ed.), *Lettres de Tyrrell*, 200.

18. Tyrrell to von Hügel, 19 November, 1905, quoted in Barmann, *Hügel*, 172. For a clear and succinct summary of these negotiations, see Sagovsky, *Tyrrell*, 194–202.

19. See chapter 15, and Sagovsky, *Tyrrell*, 144, 182.

20. See chapter 15.

not his policy to comment upon pseudonymous or anonymous publications, but, aside from a few inconsequential errors of the translation into Italian, he conceded that the views expressed in the article in the *Corriere* were indeed his own. "What I want to know *at once*," he added peremptorily, "and with a view to external arrangements, is whether you will now, on your own initiative, send me out of the Society."

Three days later he regretted this ultimatum, sent off from amid the depressing cold and rain on the coast of Cornwall, and on January 13, 1906, he wrote to Martín admitting the authorship of the original "Letter" and complaining about the freedom of the translation in the *Corriere*. But this second thought did him no good. Martín now believed he possessed enough evidence to send Tyrrell "out of the Society." The pope himself had been apprised of the offensive article and had declared that, unless its author unequivocally repudiated the doctrine contained in the "Letter," he had to be expelled from the Society of Jesus. The provincial of the English Jesuits was so informed, and shortly before noon on February 19, 1906, five days after his last mass in Eastbourne, George Tyrrell, with the tearful provincial looking on, signed the formal documents that placed him in an ecclesiatical limbo.

The Rubicon had been crossed, and so had the English Channel. A week later Tyrrell was in Paris for the first time, the guest of Henri Bremond. The two of them stayed there long enough for Tyrrell to meet Lucien Laberthonnière, with whom acquaintance proved to be primarily a matter of nods and smiles, since neither spoke the other's language. Nor did they, despite their intellectual pretensions, speak Latin with enough facility to bridge the linguistic gap. Yet they recognized each other as friends and allies in a common cause. Tyrrell was not so ready to embrace Loisy's disciple, Albert Houtin, whom he found even more bitter and hostile toward the established order than he was himself.

From Paris, Tyrrell and Bremond repaired to Freiburg-im-Breisgau, on the edge of the Black Forest. During the month they stayed there together they followed a regular routine. Tyrrell attended the mass Bremond said every morning at seven, but "I don't communicate lest the faithful should be scandalized." Then each of them settled down to literary work, interrupted only by walks along "the wooded hills-upon-hills, soft and beautiful," and by visits to local German Catholic savants. The whole atmosphere was eerily surreal, with Bremond planning "12 book[s] and 20 articles and 50 changes of residence every day. . . . Yes, we are quite opposites," Tyrrell told Maude Petre. "His interest in religion is artistic, mine is puritanical and Miltonian; he saves me from ponderosity and I him from frivolity."[21] He continued to recite the breviary.

21. Tyrrell to Petre, 9 March, 1906, quoted in Petre, *Autobiography of Tyrrell*, 2:265, and in Sagavosky, *Tyrrell*, 204.

Then, early in April, they returned to Paris to consult with and perhaps to console Laberthonnière whose *Essais de philosophie religieuse* and *Le réalisme chrétien et l'idéalisme grec*[22] had just been placed on the Roman Index. The same condemnation had fallen upon Antonio Fogazzaro's latest novel, *Il Santo*.[23]

REFLECTING ON EVENTS in later years, Marie-Joseph Lagrange testified to more than the traditional rivalry between Dominicans and Jesuits when he observed that "his confreres had treated [Father Tyrrell] with a strange indulgence." Jesuit controversialists had not treated Lagrange indulgently, or so he thought:[24] ever since the appearance of *La methode historique*[25] they had regularly accused him of an "impiety which aimed at the same objective as [David] Strauss, the overthrow of revealed religion."[26] Lagrange pleaded naïveté:

I was still, in 1905, so little au courant with the real situation that I prepared an article for the *Revue biblique* about the Patriarchs, how they belonged to history. I intended this to be a kind of preparation for my commentary on the Book of Genesis. I argued in the article against the view that the Patriarchs were merely mythical figures, while conceding that the description of them in Genesis was popular rather than learnedly historical. . . . This essay, with which I was very happy, was not approved by the censors "because of certain unspecified circumstances," and it remained unpublished.

The commentary on Genesis also languished—restricted to sixty copies, each marked *pro manuscripto*—for lack of a Dominican censor brave enough to award it a *nihil obstat*.[27] Early in 1906 one of Lagrange's colleagues at the École Biblique, at an audience with Pius X, pointedly asked that the work be given approval for publication. "It is a difficult moment," the pope replied evasively. "Better to wait for the official documents and decisions now under preparation." On June 27 an official document was issued, the decision of the biblical commission[28] that endorsed the Mosaic authorship of the Pentateuch.[29]

Or, more precisely, the commission decreed that modern criticism had not adduced evidence sufficient to impugn that authorship. The decision—ludicrous to Loisy, a tragedy to von Hügel[30]—satisfied Lagrange, because it did not "rule out either the theory of many sources or of the partial adaptation of

22. See chapter 16.

23. The decree of 4 April, 1906 also listed an unrelated work, *L'infaillibilité pontificale et le Syllabus* by Paul Viollet (1840–1914).

24. See especially Alphonse Delattre, *Autour de la question biblique* (Liège, France: 1904), and M.-J. Lagrange, *Éclaircissement sur la méthode historique, à propos d'un livre du R. P. Delattré, S.J.* (Paris: 1905).

25. See note 41, in chapter 14.

26. David Friedrich Strauss (1808–74), whose *Leben Jesu* (1836) denied all supernatural elements in the Gospels.

27. Literally "nothing stands in the way," the censor's printed notation that, whatever the opinions expressed in it, nothing in the book at hand is contrary to Catholic doctrine.

28. See chapter 14.

29. Lagrange, "L'École biblique," 174, 153–59.

30. See Barmann, *Hügel*, 132.

the primitive work to new social and historical circumstances."[31] The details involved in the composition of the first five books of the Bible therefore remained open. Nevertheless, this intervention in one of the most hotly disputed exegetical questions of the time was the strongest indication so far to Lagrange of the "very conservative sentiment that now prevailed in Rome," a sentiment not naturally sympathetic to admitting a distinction "between the criticism of Loisy and that of legitimate methods." "We are witnessing a kind of terrorism," the Dominican master general wrote from Rome to Jerusalem. "I neither understand it, nor support it, nor exercise it myself." But he also reminded Lagrange that the apprehensions which tempted officials to "terrorize" savants like him were genuinely grounded: "Fears for young ecclesiastics, weak in knowledge and virtue, who appeal to *exegesis* in order to exalt their independence of spirit and to mock at tradition, just as they appeal to *democracy* with a secret longing to see it used as a way to overturn ecclesiastical discipline. Fears also for those who possess more talent and priestly virtue but who are threatened—without willing it, without suspecting it even, perhaps denying it in all good faith—with losing or at least having diminished their proper sense of divine things."[32]

LAGRANGE took the general's point, but, though he lived in Jerusalem and was in many respects a citizen of the world, he also shared ordinary French prejudices, and so he readily attributed the stirring up of official intransigence and "terrorism" to the perversity of his Ultramontane brethren. The Roman curia—understandably, given the makeup of its personnel—always paid most attention to matters Italian. And, consistent with an intellectual culture that was, in Lagrange's opinion, disruptive rather than creative, "only after the condemnation of Monsieur Loisy did his opinions win widespread acceptance in Italy. His partisans maintained that it was one thing to put his works on the Index, and quite another to extract from them propositions truly subversive of Christianity. Callow youths and ladies of fashion [*femmes du monde*] bragged about the merits of biblical criticism." The collapse of discipline in several seminaries reflected this malaise, and Lagrange heard rumors of one Italian diocese in which twenty *grands séminaristes* stalked out of the chapel rather than make the profession of faith asked of them by their bishop.[33]

At Christmas 1905 the archbishops of Turin and Vercelli, in a joint pastoral, gave expression to the alarm increasingly felt by conservative Italian ecclesiastics at the spread of dangerous new ideas, and in doing so they gave currency, if not precision, to a term shortly to become renowned. They and their suffragans, they said, particularly deplored the appearance of "modernismo nel

31. See F.-M. Braun, *L'oeuvre du père Lagrange* (Fribourg, Switzerland: 1943), 111.
32. Quoted in Lagrange, "L'École biblique," 154–61.
33. Lagrange, "L'École biblique," 157.

clero." Their consternation was echoed soon after by a similar statement signed by twenty-eight bishops from central Italy, who denounced "this morbid fancy of introducing . . . into the whole of Christianity a rebirth, which, because of its intention to modernize everything, has received the name modernism."

Before that, in January 1904, another Italian voice had been raised, one which spoke, at this date at least, with less authority, but, as time would prove, far more ominously.[34] Umberto Benigni was a forty-two-year-old domestic prelate who taught in a Roman seminary, and at the same time edited an obscure religious periodical. He was a man of a singularly powerful personality whose disdain for all the works and pomps of the contemporary world amounted to a fanatical hatred. A native of Perugia, he had drifted restlessly from his home diocese first to Genoa and then, in 1895, to Rome. He was a sociable man, and he moved for a while in Giovanni Genocchi's sophisticated circle, where he regularly met Murri, Fogazzaro, and Semeria.[35] He was by no means unintelligent, demonstrating enough skill as an ecclesiastical historian to have attracted the favorable attention of Louis Duchesne, among others. But the intellectual life, as such, held small interest for him. Politics broadly defined was his all-consuming passion. If he was driven by the ravenous ambition with which his host of enemies ultimately came to charge him,[36] his aim was never merely to accumulate titles and perquisites. And, a born intriguer, his was never the intrigue of a careerist. The exercise of power was his goal, and the Rome of Pius X, increasingly obsessed by conspiracy theories, provided an ideal locale for Benigni to employ his peculiar combination of gifts, aspirations, and animosities. Banal as his denunciation may have sounded, it had the ring of elemental conviction coming as it did from one who was more a counterrevolutionary than a conservative: "Modernism is the specific error of the Revolution—that is to say, the condemnation and suppression en masse of everything old because it is old, the approval and adoption of everything new because it is new."[37]

The cast of progressive Italian Catholics had not changed much from before,[38] but their influence, at least among the leisured classes, did appear to have increased markedly. Padre Gennochi still hobnobbed among ecclesiastical notables even as he hovered along the margins of the group of suspect savants.[39] Padre Semeria, von Hügel's friend and disciple, remained the most celebrated pulpit orator in Italy. But these individuals and their exploits mattered less than those who were a more-or-less permanent literary presence. Sal-

34. See chapter 19.

35. See Houtin, *Modernisme*, 109, and chapter 11.

36. See Houtin, *Modernisme*, 162–63.

37. See Rivière, *Modernisme*, 26, 21, and esp. Émile Poulat (ed.) *Intégrisme et catholicisme intégral* (Paris: 1969), 61–65.

38. See chapter 11.

39. See, for example, Genocchi to Fracassini, 11 November and 18 December, 1903, in Scoppola, *Crisi Modernista*, 120.

vatore Minocchi—"a bull-necked man, with a big, wrinkled face, . . . a Danton tempered by ecclesiastical prudence and Italian subtlety"—continued to edit *Studi Religiosi* and in its pages bring to his readers studies of Loisy, Houtin, and Lagrange. Closely associated with him was Ernesto Buonaiuti, who had become an enthusiast for the *philosophie d'action* of Blondel and Laberthonnière;[40] then, in 1905, Buonaiuti founded a journal of his own, the *Revista Storico-critica delle Scienze Teologiche*. Finally in January, 1907, appeared the first number of *Il Rinnovamento*, paid for and edited by some of the young Milanese silk-stockings Bremond had cultivated during his Italian excursions.[41] "For us," they proclaimed in their prospectus, "Christianity is life. It is vain for anyone to try to wall it up in certain intellectual systems, as though they could be definitive expressions of its development. Christianity is, by its very nature, in a continual evolution, ever breaking old formulas in order to construct new ones."[42]

But more worrisome by far than these others to the Vatican was tumultuous young Don Romolo Murri. Eloquent, charismatic, a tireless organizer and propagandist, he too had his own journal, the *Cultura Sociale*, and then, when that closed down, another called *Rivista di Cultura*, which continued the policy of publishing articles by or about Loisy, Bremond, Tyrrell, and Archbishop Mignot. More than that, Murri had at his disposal the Lega Demoratica Nazionale—his "partito non cattolico, ma di cattolici"[43]—with its cells in every corner of the country. His preoccupations continued to be principally social and political, but he did not fail to see the relevance to his concerns of more speculative matters: "Christian democracy," in the words of his colleague, Semeria, "has to be a movement of both facts and ideas, a conciliation between action and science, . . . a fertile marriage between new social aspirations and a vigorous movement of intellectual renewal."[44] The restraint that Murri had displayed during the days of Leo XIII's *non expedit*[45] had passed away, and the veneration he had felt for the old pope had given place to a hostility toward the rigid and clericalist regime, as he judged it, of Pius X. A striking indication of the direction in which his thinking had gone was the publication, in 1905, of his translation of George Tyrrell's *Religion as a Factor of Life*.[46] He increasingly echoed the moral dogmatism associated with Laberthonnière and, like Édouard Le Roy, he had come to assume that the truth of religious dogma depended upon its ethical utility. He longed for a Christianity "more pure, more intense, more practical," one that did away with "semipagan customs, legalism rooted

40. Houtin, *Modernisme*, 431–32.
41. See chapter 15.
42. Quoted in Rivière, *Modernisme*, 276–79.
43. See Cappelli, *Murri*, 66–68.
44. Quoted in Scoppola, *Crisi Modernista*, 146.
45. See chapter 11.
46. Claudio Giovanni, *Romolo Murri: Dal Radicalismo al Fascismo* (Bologna, Italy: 1981), 12–13. See also chapter 15.

in Roman law, Scholasticism, monastic institutions decayed by time and incapable of renewal."[47]

It was not Murri, however, who first felt the sting of ecclesiastical censure. *Il Santo*, by Antonio Fogazzaro,[48] went on sale in November 1905. It was the third novel in a tetralogy its eminent author had begun ten years earlier. During that interval he had continued to publish short stories, poetry, even an unsuccessful play or two, as well as the lectures that gained for him new and appreciative audiences. During that time too he grew ever more intimate with the Milanese progressives who were shortly to found *Il Rinnovamento*. He corresponded frequently with von Hügel, and read approvingly Albert Houtin's books as they appeared. He was particularly charmed by Laberthonnière's strong advocacy of a holistic approach to moral action.[49] When Loisy fell afoul of the Index, Fogazzaro addressed him directly: "Some Italian Catholics who admire and love you desire to say to you, through me, that it is their firm conviction that the day will come whereon, by the power of facts, your theses will be accepted by that Catholicism of the future, *at once positive and mystical*, which we are laboring to prepare, each in his own field."[50]

Il Santo is not exactly a roman à clef—the aged and ailing pope, for example, is certainly not a portrayal of the robust Pius X—but it is a commentary, only thinly disguised as fiction, on contemporary Italian Catholic life. Its protagonist, Fra Benedetto—drawn, it is said, from Fogazzaro's perception of the characters of Murri and Tyrrell[51]—is a Benedictine lay brother of surpassing intelligence and sensitivity who comes into contact with all shades of society, clerical and lay. Semipagan peasants regard him with superstitious awe, while fashionable Romans view his preaching of an austere and self-effacing Gospel as a kind of fad. He proves in the end, by means of a sacrificial death, to be an instrument of conversion and reconciliation. But the climax of the book occurs before that, when Benedetto has an interview with the pope. "Holy Father," he informs the pontiff, "the church is grievously sick. Four evil spirits have entered her body, to wage war against the Holy Spirit."

One is the spirit of falsehood. . . . Holy Father, today few Christians know that religion does not consist chiefly in intellectual adhesion to formulas of truth, but rather in action. . . . [Good] men . . . are branded as heretics and reduced to silence all through the spirit of falsehood, which for centuries has been weaving, in the church, a web of traditional deceit. The second evil spirit which infests the church . . . is the spirit of domination of the clergy. Those priests who have [this] spirit . . . are ill-pleased when souls communicate directly and in the natural way with God, going to Him for counsel and direction. [This spirit] has suppressed the ancient, sacred Catholic liberty. It desires

47. Quoted in Rivière, *Modernisme*, 281–82.
48. See chapter 11.
49. See chapter 9.
50. Fogazzaro to Loisy, 26 December, 1903, quoted in Gallarati-Scotti, *Fogazzaro*, 220.
51. See Donatella Piccioni and Leone Piccioni, *Antonio Fogazzaro* (Turin, Italy: 1970), 382–83.

to impose submission, . . . retractions where the individual conscience does not approve. The third evil spirit which is corrupting the church is avarice. The Vicar of Christ dwells in this royal palace . . . with the pure heart of poverty. But the spirit of poverty is not preached sufficiently, not preached as Christ preached it. . . . Let us prepare for the day when the priests . . . shall set the example of true poverty.

The fourth spirit of evil . . . is the evil of immovability. . . . Catholics who are dominated by [this] spirit . . . believe they are pleasing God, as did those zealous Jews who caused Christ to be crucified. . . . [A]ll the religious men, . . . who today oppose progressive Catholicism, would, in all good faith, have caused Christ to be crucified in the name of Moses. They are worshippers of the past; they wish everything to remain immovable in the church. . . . It is the spirit of immovability which, by straining to preserve what it is impossible to preserve, exposes us to the derision of unbelievers; and this is a great sin in the sight of God.[52]

Whether Fogazzaro would have spoken so bluntly to Pius X, had he had a chance to do so, remains moot: on the one occasion the novelist requested an audience, the pope—who was known to dislike both him and his books[53]—declined to see him. Fogazzaro's purpose in any case had been that *Il Santo* should "place the crown" on his literary endeavors," should be his "last and fiercest battle, waged in the cause of that orthodox religious renewal which is not only of supreme necessity but is already in the course of accomplishment."[54] Nevertheless, he was shocked when *Il Santo* was placed on the Index in April 1906, for many of his friends, high ecclesiastics included, had assured him that he had no fears on that score. His immediate concern—consistent with his status as a pious Catholic layman—was whether he would be allowed to receive the Eucharist at Easter. He found a confessor at Milan who put such anxieties to rest. Shortly afterward he expressed, sadly, his resolution for the future: "From the very beginning it has been my intention to render obedience to the decree which my duty as a Catholic imposes upon me. . . . I shall refrain from discussing it, and also from any other act that is contrary to its dictates, such as the authorization of translations and editions other than those for which I had signed agreements previous to the decree and which it would be impossible to cancel."[55]

But Senator Fogazzaro found this pledge easier to make than to keep. He possessed no less vanity than any other author, and he could hardly be expected to ignore the statistics. Once the condemnation of the Index was promulgated, *Il Santo* became a best-seller: 30,000 copies were sold in Italy in a single month and for a while, when an English translation appeared, 1,000 copies a day were sold in Britain and the United States.[56]

52. Antonio Fogazzaro, *The Saint*, trans. by M. Prichard-Agnetti (London: n. d.), 281–87.
53. Robert Hall, *Antonio Fogazzaro* (New York: 1978), 83.
54. Quoted in Gallarati-Scotti, *Fogazzaro*, 230.
55. Fogazzaro to Crispolti, 18 April, 1906, quoted in Gallarati-Scotti, *Fogazzaro*, 256.
56. See De la Bedoyere, *Hügel*, 182.

Such commercial success, however, could not obscure another harbinger of trouble to come. In July 1906 Pius X issued a stern rebuke to the clergy of Italy "for the spirit of *insubordination* and *independence*. . . . This unfortunate spirit is doing . . . damage especially among young priests, spreading among them new and reprehensible theories." One reason for the problem, maintained the pontiff—he seldom failed to be candid—was that too many aspirants were being ordained. "Venerable Brethren," he said to the Italian bishops, "what reason is there for imposing hands so frequently? . . . Let the seminaries be jealously guarded. . . . Let philosophy, theology, and . . . especially Sacred Scripture be studied along the lines of pontifical directives. . . . Let [the bishops] recall to their duty those [professors] who run after certain dangerous novelties. If they do not profit from these warnings, let them be removed—cost what it may—from their teaching position."[57]

"I GRIEVED OVER THE CONDEMNATION of Fogazzaro and Laberthonnière, but I gather that putting a book on the Index means in these days very little indeed." So observed Wilfrid Ward in the late summer of 1906. "I think," he continued, citing Louis Duchesne, who had recently visited him, "there is a strong anti-intellectual temper just now in Rome among the authorities," not unlike that which had prevailed during the time of Pius IX. "The cause in both cases was somewhat similar—a Pope who, though almost saintly, was himself unintellectual, and a panic caused by political aggressions on the Church. . . . This to me is a most grievous state of things, . . . [but] we must submit to it." While "I [have no] sympathy whatever with the policy of intellectual repression in itself, . . . the true remedy is not to be found in a policy which should lead . . . Catholics . . . devoted to the interests of thought and learning to go over to the extreme left wing and agitate, but rather in the formation of a strong centre party which will by degrees convince the authorities that there is no essential antagonism between devotion to thought and loyalty to the Church."[58]

The diffident Ward was not in the habit of issuing manifestos, but neither did he lack the courage of his convictions. "The formation of a strong centre party" had long been his goal, and now it seemed to him more imperative than ever. In choosing, as had Lagrange, to tread the hazardous middle of the road, it was not irrelevant that Ward had now begun writing his monumental biography of Newman, who in his day had eschewed both liberals and Ultramontanes. But, as in Newman's case, doing so involved the risk of taking fire from both flanks. In the present heated state of things, convincing authorities would be far from easy, and convincing them "by degrees" was not the style of George

57. Pius X, *Pieni l'animo* (28 July, 1906), in *Acta Sanctae Sedis*, 39: 321–30; English translation in Claudia Carlen (ed.), *The Papal Encyclicals, 1903–1939* (Raleigh, N.C.: 1981), 57–61.

58. Ward to Sabatier, August 1906, quoted in Ward, *The Wilfrid Wards*, 2:255.

Tyrrell or Friedrich von Hügel, from whom Ward had inevitably become alienated. Indeed Tyrrell at least now assumed that an "essential antagonism" existed between true religion and Catholic orthodoxy, while von Hügel—who had not interrupted personal relations with Ward—grieved that "the whole entourage of the Pope is so oppressively black and narrow." If the baron took some small pleasure in thinking that Ward, "poor fellow," had been made "very nervous" over the Fogazzaro affair,[59] he could not have been comforted by a statement of Ward's published a few months later: "[I do not] deny that criticism leads to partially true results. But [I do say] that the constitution of the *human mind* is such, and the nature of our hold on supernatural truth such, that the mutilation of the traditional form in which our Christian faith has been assimilated, may destroy for some their hold on Christianity and lead to its abandonment."[60]

This assertion appeared as a leader in the pages of the *Dublin Review*, the editorship of which Ward had just assumed. There was a measure of nostalgia involved, since William George Ward had edited the same journal thirty years earlier. But, for all the affection in which Wilfrid held his father's memory,[61] he was determined that his *Dublin Review* would be a very different kind of venture. Times had changed since the days when W. G. Ward had been the Ultramontane hammer, for whom, as Newman had said acidly, "controversy [was] meat and drink—and he seems to consider it his mission to pick as many holes in others as he can, and to destroy to the uttermost the adhesive qualities of Catholic brotherhood."[62] Wilfrid, by contrast, intended to provide a platform upon which all parties could meet, to publish a review that catered to a wide range of Catholic interests—political, literary, and scientific, as well as theological and philosophical—without, however, avoiding the controversial issues of the day.

Most disinterested observers appear to have agreed that he succeeded. Like Fogazzaro and *Il Santo*, Ward could point with satisfaction to statistics: the readership of the heretofore drab *Dublin Review* quadrupled during his stewardship. Nevertheless, Josephine Ward was less than enthusiastic about her husband's new enterprise. She believed that absorption in an exclusively Catholic journal diluted the influence he had exercised by his contributions to secular organs like the *Nineteenth Century* and the *Edinburgh Review*. Nor did the passage of time change her mind: "This undertaking," she said after he died, "was more ephemeral than the rest of Wilfrid's literary work and relatively not so important." Perhaps her judgment was influenced by the memory of the buffeting Wilfrid had to endure as he tried to conduct his review through the

59. Von Hügel to Petre, 17 April, 1906, quoted in De la Bedoyere, *Hügel*, 183.
60. [Wilfrid Ward], "For Truth or for Life," *Dublin Review* 139 (October 1906): 235–36.
61. See chapter 6.
62. Newman to Mivart, 22 April, 1877, Dessain et al. (eds.), *Letters and Diaries*, 28: 195.

controversial minefield. Conservative complaints flooded the chancery at Westminster, and more than once Ward was delated to Rome by English Catholics for articles described as "scandalous and offensive" and containing "dangerous errors." But the laconic Archbishop Bourne consistently gave the *Dublin Review* sturdy support, and even Merry del Val responded to protests that reached him with a lightness of touch not always associated with that prelate: "Personally I should describe [Ward's] theology as 'acrobatic'—he attempts the feat of sitting between two stools—and occasionally comes down with a bump—[but] he quickly regains his balance and is able to assure everybody that he is all right again."[63]

BY THIS TIME Lucien Laberthonnière was an editor too. Filling such a position had long been an ambition of his,[64] and it had become a reality through the direct intervention of Maurice Blondel. Early in the summer of 1905, upon the death of the director of the *Annales de philosophie chrétienne*, Blondel purchased the journal, though he took pains not to allow that fact to become publicly known: "With my financial support, which must remain absolutely secret, F[ather] L[aberthonnière] has taken charge of the *Annales*."[65] Édouard Le Roy, delighted at the prospect of this "Trojan horse," shared the new editor's euphoria,[66] but Blondel was more circumspect. "Wisely conducted," he told Joannès Wehrlé, "this review can render very great service. . . . I think it important that F. L. be sustained in as intelligent and supportive a fashion as possible. His journal . . . can be an incomparable instrument of peaceful progress."[67] It may have been because Blondel was surer of Laberthonnière's pluck and determination than of his resolve to progress peacefully that he kept his own hand in the governance of the *Annales* while cautiously keeping his name out of the limelight. Even the articles he wrote appeared under pseudonyms.[68]

But spicing Laberthonnière's and Le Roy's enthusiasms with a pinch of prudence proved no easy task for Blondel or others now associated with the *Annales*. When Wehrlé tried to urge discretion upon him, Laberthonnière, resentful of such "Torquemadism," talked about resigning a post he had scarcely begun to serve in. "I have put [Laberthonnière] on guard as much as I can against his weakness for questionable initiatives," said Blondel. "I have done my best to warn him off from a certain militant optimism. . . . We must

63. Quotations in Ward, *The Wilfrid Wards*, 2:203, 217, 231–33.
64. See chapter 14.
65. Blondel to Mourret, 21 June, 1905, quoted in Blondel and Valensin, *Correspondance*, 223.
66. Laberthonnière to Portal, 11 September, 1905, in Perrin (ed.), *Laberthonnière et ses amis*, 59.
67. Blondel to Wehrlé, 26 June and 9 July, 1905, quoted in Blondel and Valensin, *Correspondance*, 223.
68. Virgoulay, *Blondel*, 84, speaks of Blondel buying the journal "discrètement." For the pseudonyms, see Perrin (ed.), *Laberthonnière et ses amis*, 59.

remain irenic and positive. I constantly exhort [Laberthonnière] to avoid polemic, to leave aside any discourteous or irritating assertions . . . or spiteful insinuations," even when provoked by the right-wing Catholic press.[69] So the enterprise began in double harness, not without the emergence of small signs of tension between master and disciple that would, in later years, end in bitter estrangement.

It could not be denied, however, that Laberthonnière enhanced the quality and relevance of the *Annales*, just as Wilfrid Ward had done in editing the *Dublin Review*. This success, such as it was, was swiftly followed by a new and heavy trial. "My very dear friend," Laberthonnière wrote Henri Bremond on April 15, 1906, "your good letter and that of Father Tyrrell . . . went straight to my heart. . . . I am resigned to this and to anything else that proves necessary. I suffered much at the first moment, but, thanks be to God, I have recovered myself. And it was with a good heart that I sang the Easter Alleluia."[70] The "first moment" had occurred ten days before—a Saturday noon—when a seminarian from the Institut Catholique called on Laberthonnière in his flat on the rue Las Cases. The young man offered condolences in his own name and in that of his fellow students. "Condolences?," Laberthonnière inquired. "For what reason?" Had not Father Laberthonnière heard, stammered the seminarian, that two of his books had been placed on the Index? He had not: a leak to the Italian press had preceded any formal notice. A few moments later friends of the priest arrived, bent upon the same consoling mission. They found him sadly tranquil.[71]

Other friends rallied to him. Von Hügel confessed that in his "admiration [for] and adhesion" to the teaching in the condemned *Essais philosophiques* he had not realized till now that they had been also "exercises in courage." "Rest assured," Louis Birot wrote from Albi, "that the archbishop [Mignot] and I grieve from the bottom of our hearts. Both of us hope that this ordeal will prove short-lived and that you will come out of it stronger than ever. What should you do? Your priestly conscience will dictate your proper attitude." This last was Birot's delicate way of advising Laberthonnière to submit to the sentence and await a better day, which proved to be the burden of most of the counsel he received. "You will not lack the consolations of religion," another wrote in the same vein, "and, knowing that, despite all, you have done good work, you will continue to do it, however desolating it is to feel this wind of mediocrity, of meanness, of spite blowing over us."[72] Even the alienated Bremond and Tyrrell did not contradict the general drift of these recommendations,

69. Blondel to Wehrlé, 3 July, 1905, and Blondel to Mourret, 5 July and 24 August, 1905, quoted in Blondel and Valensin, *Correspondance*, 224–25.

70. In Perrin (ed.), *Laberthonnière et ses amis*, 74.

71. Diary of Geroges Goyau, quoted in Blondel and Valensin, *Correspondance*, 253.

72. Birot to Laberthonnière, 9 April, 1906; von Hügel to Laberthonnière, 10 April, 1906; and Sertillanges to Laberthonnière, n. d., in Perrin (ed.), *Laberthonnière et ses amis*, 76–81.

though they were probably at pains to point out that the cardinal-prefect of the Index was a German Jesuit.[73]

In Dijon, where Maurice Blondel had been called to assist at his father's deathbed, "there arrived during this agony the news of the blow struck F[ather] L[aberthonnière], which strikes me too, to the depths of my soul."[74] The elder Blondel died—"having endured extreme suffering in the midst of continuous prayer"—several hours afterward, at ten minutes before six on the morning of April 9. Later in the day Maurice sent off a message to Paris: "Let us adore together the always loving will of God. . . . From the depth of our sorrows I raise my heart to yours, I offer my pain to assuage yours, I suffer from not being with you now, [but] I have faith that this hour of mourning and extreme disappointment includes a promise of the future fruitfulness of your work."[75] There was no question in Blondel's mind as to what Laberthonnière's deportment ought to be at this moment of crisis: "It seems to me that he should speak a word of submission—very simple, very dignified, very brief— and then should withdraw the books in question from the market."[76] After the two men had met in Dijon for the funeral, Laberthonnière, back in Paris, followed this advice to the letter.[77]

THE APPARENTLY easy manner in which Laberthonnière accepted this severe setback did not surprise Blondel. "What I admire about F. L.," he observed to Bremond, "is his absolute detachment from what he considers contingencies. This is part of his total integrity."[78] The case proved different for George Tyrrell, who, having offered what solace he could to his new friend, had returned to England in the middle of April. The ambiguity of his canonical position—he was embarrassed at wearing clerical garb while being prohibited from saying mass—left him fidgety and anxious. He went first to his friends in Clapham from which he wrote to Bremond who had remained in Paris: "Now I really feel for the first time that I am alone, without attachments, one of those pebbles, torn from the crag, that roll across the shore of time. One never intends to leave the Church. But what happens if the Church leaves us—like boats abandoned on the beach when the tide goes out."[79]

His return coincided with the appearance of his latest book, called *Lex Credendi*, the proofs of which he had read while in Germany with Bremond. Contrary to what was said in the Catholic press,[80] Tyrrell did not consider it

73. Andrea Steinhüber (1825–1907), rector of the German College in Rome from 1867, created cardinal 1893.

74. Blondel to Bremond, 9 April, 1905, quoted in Blondel and Valensin, *Correspondance*, 252.

75. Blondel to Laberthonnière, 9 April, 1906, in Tresmontant (ed.), *Correspondance*, 195.

76. Blondel to Mourret, 8 April, 1906, quoted in Blondel and Valensin, *Correspondance*, 252.

77. Laberthonnière to the Vicar General (Paris), 1 May, 1906, in Perrin (ed.), *Laberthonnière et ses amis*, 85–86.

78. Blondel to Bremond, 18 April, 1906, quoted in Blondel and Valensin, *Correspondance*, 252.

79. Tyrrell to Bremond, 25 April, 1906, in Louis-David (ed.), *Lettres de Tyrrell*, 219.

80. For example, W[ilfrid] W[ard], "Lex Credendi," in *Dublin Review* 139 (July 1906): 182–87.

a response to criticisms of the intentionally pugnacious *Lex Orandi* of 1903.[81] Indeed, *Lex Credendi* was much more reminiscent of its author's earlier work which had focused on the devotional rather than the controversial. Its hauntingly beautiful and meditative prose—"Prayer . . . must be . . . the utterance of vision and feeling, proceeding from the spirit and the heart, from the secret chamber where the soul meets God as the stem meets its root in the bosom of the earth"—exhibited yet again Tyrrell's uncanny ability to express the longings and to engage the sympathies of many a troubled modern Christian. "In its form, its modes of thought and language, the Gospel necessarily belongs to a certain time and place; but in its substance it belongs to eternity. It gives us the very essence of religion: human and divine, external and internal, the one thing needful."[82]

The one thing needful for Tyrrell just then was to find a place to live. In the middle of May he left Clapham and went to stay in the Premonstratensian priory in Storrington, Sussex, forty miles or so southwest of central London. He had been attracted to this lovely little market town, set in the gently rolling greenery on the edge of the South Downs, by the circumstance that several close friends and relatives had already settled there. Storrington lies near Arundel, the seat of the duke of Norfolk, where the duke's niece, Josephine Ward, had spent her early childhood;[83] thanks to his largess, the White Canons of Premontré, expelled from their monastery in France in 1880, had found a refuge in the locality and built their modest priory. By 1906 there were only three of them left, and they were more than happy to provide two pleasant rooms and board for thirty shillings a week. Tyrrell found them delightfully "anti-Jesuit." He "explained to the Prior all the ecclesiastical perils he would be exposed to" in renting space to one under official suspicion, but the prior "merely treated the warning with scorn and said that he would receive the devil if he wanted to and no bishop could gainsay him." The cooking and overall ambience were Provençal—the monks had come originally from the valley of the Rhône, not far from Aix-en-Provence—and Tyrrell extended in their name an open invitation to Bremond, a fellow countryman. "In one sense they are pagans, and yet, because they are unconscious of this, they are genuinely human and Christian."[84]

Tyrrell's spirits rose during this initial stay in Storrington, so much so that Maude Petre thought she discerned the possibility of resurrecting there the happy days at Richmond. By June she was looking round for some property, and before the end of the year she had bought an eighteenth-century house on the central square of the village, "Mulberry House," which she planned to convert into a convalescent home for needy women. Adjacent to the main

81. See chapter 15.
82. George Tyrrell, *Lex Credendi: A Sequel to Lex Orandi* (London: 1906), 92, 250.
83. See chapter 6.
84. Tyrrell to Bremond, 15 May, 1906, in Louis-David (ed.), *Lettres de Tyrrell*, 221.

building was a hay-store and garden-room—"Malt Cottage," as it came to be called—which she outfitted as a study for Tyrrell.[85] What neither she nor he could have foreseen, she was setting the scene for his death less than three years later.

Meanwhile the unequal battle raged on. A Belgian bishop[86] offered to incardinate Tyrrell and the Roman authorities agreed, with the proviso that both his publications and his private correspondence be submitted to episcopal censorship. This latter stipulation drove Tyrrell to a new pitch of anger and disdain. "Neither Abbé Loisy," he wrote furiously, "nor any other priest whose books are on the Index [as Tyrrell's were not] has been . . . subjected to such monstrous conditions."[87] But in fact Tyrrell had been hoisted with his own petard: what he conveniently overlooked was that neither Loisy nor anyone else had tried to avoid censure, as Tyrrell had, by falsely claiming that an objectionable publication had really been private correspondence leaked without the writer's approval.[88]

By the time he learned of Rome's conditioned response to the Belgian proposal, Tyrrell had rejoined Bremond in France. They spent July and part of August in a fishing village in Brittany, and then moved to the Bremond country house in Provence. Tyrrell had agreed to edit Friedrich von Hügel's study of Genoese mysticism, now at last completed, and the massive typescript—2,000 pages long—reached him during this French sojourn. He worked at it diligently for as much as six hours a day, trying to make it readable. And trying too to respect von Hügel's stated convictions that the institutional church, for all its faults, had to be maintained—convictions Tyrrell had long since given up. Bremond, who himself had once wrestled with the baron's impenetrable prose,[89] sympathized with his friend, but it remained a trying time. He hoped Laberthonnière would visit them and share some of the strain: "Dear Father, come, do come; but, on second thought, maybe not for a while." Tyrrell was "still feeling the first blow of this iniquity"—the requirement to submit his correspondence to censorship—"and he has a great need of silence. . . . Irishman that he is, he closes himself in himself. I am there to ring the bell for meals or to go for walks with him on the beach and to make silly remarks. But I do not intrude into his thoughts."[90]

Those thoughts were increasingly dark, and, when he shipped von Hügel's typescript back at the beginning of October, Tyrrell appended a note. "I am

---

85. Florence M. Greenfield, *Round about Old Storrington* (Storrington, England: 1972), 53.

86. Désiré Joseph Mercier (1851–1926), prolific Thomist, ecumenist, archbishop of Malines (1906), cardinal (1907), and hero of resistance to the German occupation of Belgium during World War I. Tyrrell's *Medievalism* (see chapter 19) was written in response to Mercier's anti-Modernist pastoral of 1908.

87. Tyrrell to Lilley, 30 June, 1906, quoted in Sagovsky, *Tyrrell*, 208.

88. See note 18.

89. See chapter 16.

90. Bremond to Laberthonnière, n.d., in Perrin (ed.), *Laberthonnière et ses amis*, 96.

sure it would not be prudent for you to entertain me in my present dismantled state. Indeed I am going to ask you to erase my name when it occurs in two or three places of [your] . . . MS. I never felt less inclined to be 'good,' and so we had better confine our meetings to the neutral territory of K[ensington] Gardens."[91] However, upon his return to England a month later he and the baron did meet regularly in the Kensington Gardens and elsewhere, and compared notes, and discussed forthcoming publications, but, try as they might, they could not recapture the heady camaraderie of earlier days. The sense of impending doom was too thick around them. In November Tyrrell saw through the press *A Much Abused Letter*, which incorporated the text of his orginal "Letter to a Professor" with a selection of his correspondence with the Roman authorities. One result of this effort to discomfit his enemies was a loss of friends who had heretofore stood by him. "The English Jesuits have been 'converted' against me since . . . the revelations about [the pseudonymous writings]. They are furious at the impression made by *A Much Abused Letter.* . . . They are great imbeciles."[92] In December he went back to Storrington where the gloom was not relieved. "I go on living, but my heart is dead."[93]

91. Tyrrell to von Hügel, 6 October, 1906, quoted in Barmann, *Hügel*, 181.
92. Tyrrell to Bremond, 6 December, 1906, in Louis-David (ed.), *Lettres de Tyrrell*, 231.
93. Tyrrell to Bremond, 27 December [1906], in Louis-David (ed.), *Lettres de Tyrrell*, 233.

CHAPTER 18

"Feeding the Flock of the Lord"

Can anybody who takes a survey of the whole system be surprised that We should define Modernism as the synthesis of all heresies?

—*Pius X (1907)*[1]

EARLY IN THE NEW YEAR of 1907 Antonio Fogazzaro came to Paris to deliver a lecture at the École Pratique des Hautes Études. The distinguished Italian novelist already had several acquaintances in the French capital, including Félix Klein and Henri Bremond. These and several others urged Lucien Laberthonnière to invite Fogazzaro to a meeting of his study group, the Société d'Études Religieuses,[2] and Laberthonnière readily complied. The gathering on January 20 had for its subject "Authority in the Church." The discussion was diffuse, a not uncommon characteristic when intellectuals sit down together, but a certain consistent theme did emerge.

"When it comes to discipline," Fogazzaro observed, "I think one can refer oneself, even in spiritual matters, to the analogy of military law. This has to do with externals; it can never usurp the conscience. Legitimate authority can demand that I conform my acts to its directives, but it can never force my interior adhesion."

"But it is necessary also to form our conscience within the larger society," mused Édouard Le Roy.

Fogazzaro did not find this remark particularly relevant, but he replied: "I will say one other thing. It is necessary to respect authority and not to raise oneself against it."

Laberthonnière caught the temper of the dozen or so participants and of the

---

1. Pius X, *Pascendi Dominici Gregis*, 8 September, 1907, in *Acta Sanctae Sedis* (Rome: 1907): 40:593–650 (33). English version in Thomas E. Judge (ed.), *Doctrines of the Modernists* (Chicago: n. d. [1908]), 49–102 (85).
2. See chapter 16.

evening when he said, somberly, "There is no progress of thought without many bruises."[3]

The same dark mood, combined with the same determination to insist upon the rights of conscience, was felt at the same moment in Kensington. Yet it was not always easy, there or elsewhere, to discern precisely what those rights might be. "The Church, i.e. ecclesiastical officials," Friedrich von Hügel told George Tyrrell, "has a right to many, even great sacrifices on our part, but not simply to anything and everything. . . . And we will even try . . . to give the benefit of the doubt to these authorities. . . . [But] the Church is more and other than just these Churchmen, and religion is more, and largely other, than even the best theology." The most distressful happenstance in the present juncture was the decision that Alfred Loisy and Albert Houtin had clearly arrived at and, the baron feared, Tyrrell had too: to give up the battle for the church, to leave the field to the Scholastic and Ultramontane enemy, so that it would appear to all the world as though "Cardinal Merry [del Val is] . . . the true, sincere type of Catholic and . . . none of our group are . . . Catholics at all."[4] But the note of desperation was wasted on Tyrrell, who had sacrificed enough, he thought, and had given the benefit of the doubt to his superiors in the church more than enough. Moving restlessly that winter and spring between Clapham and Storrington, he declined Laberthonnière's invitation. Von Hügel also stayed away, though, as ever courteous, he did so "with lively regret" and sent a wire expressing "sentiments of respect and of fraternal sympathy to the distinguished company."[5]

Maurice Blondel, who seldom left his academic nest in Aix-en-Provence, saw no compelling reason to do so on this occasion. His growing disenchantment with the speculations of Le Roy may have been an added factor contributing to his disinclination to join the little caucus.[6] Archbishop Mignot, who had come to Paris on episcopal business shortly before the soirée in honor of Fogazzaro, had left again by the time it was held. As for Loisy, Laberthonnière's "petit concile"—as the exegete called it—had no interest for him, and he discouraged a suggestion that Fogazzaro come and visit him.[7] He remained in seclusion at Garnay, where the villagers, few of whom practiced their religion, noted that this curious ecclesiastic no longer practiced his either, even in private. Meanwhile, Mignot and others of his friends worried about Loisy's health, as he did himself. A physical examination in March revealed no organic disorder, but the doctor recommended that he give up his isolation and settle in more congenial surroundings. Loisy accordingly bought property in his home country, at Ceffonds, near where his sister, Marie-Louise,

3. Quoted in Perrin (ed.), *Laberthonnière et ses amis*, 118–21.
4. Von Hügel to Tyrrell, 18 December, 1906, in Holland (ed.), *Letters*, 136–37.
5. Quoted in De la Bedoyere, *Hügel*, 189.
6. See Blondel and Valensin, *Correspondance*, 293–94, 296.
7. Loisy, *Mémoires*, 2:501–2.

and her family lived and only twenty miles or so from Ambrières. "It is just," he told Houtin, "that my heirs should look after me"—a gratuitously cynical remark, since he had never made a secret of his affection for Marie-Louise and her children.[8]

On April 11 von Hügel paid a visit to Garnay—a highly emotional one, as Loisy remembered it[9]—and then went off to Paris to confer with Laberthonnière and Le Roy. The single fruit of these discussions was Le Roy's plea that Loisy delay for two years the publication of his commentary on the Synoptic Gospels, then in press, so that the Catholic public could be prepared for it. The baron also took the occasion to make his pilgrimage to Saint–Augustin, where he found Father Huvelin, though bedridden with gout, as "good and generous and high-minded" as ever. Back in England von Hügel transmitted by post Le Roy's request, along with Huvelin's "sympathetic" greetings.[10] By that time the exegete had moved to Ceffonds. There he followed the routine that had now become invariable. He worked at his desk for much of the day, walked in the coolness of the late afternoon, and puttered about in the vegetable garden and poultry yard that abutted his little house. He serenely put the finishing touches on an article for his *Revue d'histoire et de littérature religieuses*, an article which, by debunking the accounts of Christ's Transfiguration in the Synoptic Gospels, was in effect a reply to Le Roy's appeal.[11]

ALL THROUGH THE SPRING of 1907 rumors multiplied that the Vatican was bent upon a decisive intervention in the intellectual crisis that had now been building within the Catholic church for fifteen years. Loisy was reminded that the threat of a new "Syllabus of Errors" had been in the air since the condemnation of his own books, in December 1903.[12] Now events seemed to be rushing toward that eventuality. On April 17 Pius X, in a speech to a consistory at which he had created several new cardinals, denounced the "rebels who profess and in cunning ways spread monstrous errors on the evolution of dogma. . . . We must with all our strength defend what has been handed down to us . . . in the face of this attack, which is not a heresy but the poisonous sum-total of all heresies."[13] At about the same time Don Romolo Murri was suspended *a divinis*, that is, he was formally forbidden to exercise any offices of his priesthood. The source of this harsh sentence was Murri's public stance not on doctrine but on politics—his endorsement of socialism—and yet, given Murri's own principles,[14] this distinction was a hazy one at best.

8. See Houtin and Sartiaux, *Loisy*, 43, 138–39 and chapter 4.

9. Loisy, *Mémoires*, 2:516–17.

10. See Portier, *Huvelin*, 79–80.

11. Alfred Loisy, "La transfiguration," *Revue d'histoire et littérature religieuses* 12 (September–December, 1907): 464–82.

12. See Loisy, *Choses passées*, 347, and chapter 14.

13. Quoted in Michele Ranchetti, *The Catholic Modernists* (New York: 1969), 218.

14. See chapter 17.

"It was a matter," said Murri's friend, Ernesto Buonaiuti, "of the competence of the ecclesiastical authorities in political and social matters, . . . not, as in Loisy's case, a matter of the relationship between criticism and theology, nor as [with] . . . Tyrrell, . . . a case of the native and inalienable rights of a human individual in the face of authority." As for Murri himself, he offered a sad but phlegmatic testament: "I am a priest, and a priest I remain, respecting the authorities, faithful to all my duties. . . . [But] the standards behind my criticism and action will give religious society new vigor and will make it more fruitful and efficacious in civil life. I plead for the tacit sympathy of all free believers."[15]

Two weeks later the prefect of the Index, Cardinal Steinhuber, published a protest, addressed to the archbishop of Milan, in which he deplored the publication in that Italian city "by so-called Catholics of a journal notoriously opposed to Catholic teaching and spirit." This was *Il Rinnovamento*, the first number of which had appeared only a few months earlier,[16] and which, according to Steinhuber "want[ed] to arrogate to itself a magisterium in the church and to teach lessons even to the pope," thus exhibiting "the same spirit as Fogazzaro, Tyrrell, von Hügel, Murri, and the like." This outburst, which by no means elicited unanimous support among the Italian hierarchy, von Hügel shrewdly characterized as "a piece of administrative rhetoric, something intended not to define a reality but to affect a situation."[17]

Nevertheless, that situation was growing ever more tense. On May 10 the rector of the Institut Catholique of Paris informed Paul Le Jay that, unless he severed his association with the *Revue d'histoire et de littérature religieuses*, he would be dismissed from his professorship.[18] A week later the cardinal-vicar of Rome, who a year before had banned from the pope's own diocese the latest installment of Houtin's hostile analysis of Catholic biblical scholarship in France,[19] celebrated that anniversary by meting out the same proscription to a book just published, Édouard Le Roy's *Dogme et critique*, in which the author offered an elaborate defense of his controversial article of two years earlier, "Qu'est-ce qu'un dogme?"[20] Having declared in advance that he would adhere to the judgment of the church, even if it were "contrary to our personal opin-

15. Quoted in Ranchetti, *Catholic Modernists*, 204–5.

16. See chapter 17.

17. Steinhuber's text is in Houtin, *Modernisme*, 156–57. The reply (the text in Ranchetti, *Catholic Modernists*, 198) offered by the editors of *Il Rinnovemento*, which the incurably sarcastic Houtin described as "long and unctuous," Baron von Hügel characterized otherwise: "These young fellows in Milan are acting *admirably*, like the chivalrous, high-minded gentlemen, and strong-souled, tough-willed Christians and Catholics that they are—their answer to Rome is the very model of what such things should be." See von Hügel to Petre, 23 May, 1907, in Holland (ed.), *Letters*, 140, and von Hügel to Tyrrell, 8 May, 1907, quoted in De la Bedoyere, *Hügel*, 192.

18. Loisy, *Mémoires*, 2:522. For Le Jay, see note 43, in chapter 9.

19. Albert Houtin, *La question biblique au XXe siècle* (Paris: 1906). For the genesis of this project, see chapter 12.

20. See chapter 16.

ions,"[21] Le Roy forfeited Loisy's support as well as that of the cardinal-vicar and Cardinal Richard (who also censured *Dogme et critique*), but for very different reasons:

I will not conceal from you [Loisy wrote on May 9] that the critical part of your work satisfies me more than the positive. Theological symbolism has its raison d'être only for those who, intellectually accustomed to the old dogmas, neverthless cannot accommodate themselves to their literal sense. But the moral significance of most of the Christian dogmas, that which has value for us and our contemporaries, is so far removed from their original meaning and theological tenor, I ask whether it is very useful to sketch in [*ebaucher*] a metaphysical connection between the old symbols and the actual rules of ethical conduct. . . . Your doctrine of the Resurrection is a beautiful poem;[22] but is it anything more than a poem? Your general philosophy of knowledge is of great interest, but is it anything more than a brilliant essay, upon which it would hardly be necessary to make moral beliefs rest?[23]

Maurice Blondel also took exception to Le Roy's work, but once again for reasons of his own: "I am very distressed. . . . The intellectual difficulties, the doctrinal struggles, are becoming more and more grave. And there is, I believe, a real danger that authority wants to set in opposition, all in a bloc, 'modernists' versus 'traditonalists.' It is imperative to understand that books like that of Le Roy are of a nature to justify all [authority's] fears and all the severity."[24] When he made his "total disavowal" public, in a letter printed in the *Revue du clergé français*, this latest sign of a once hopeful movement's internal disintegration afforded Loisy a certain malicious pleasure. "I see," he told Le Roy, "that such a great Catholic philosopher finds this moment opportune to declare haughtily that he does not agree with you. He did the same to me three years ago.[25] I do not know whether many people are inclined to confuse his opinions with ours [*sic*]. Perhaps there is also at work some vanity . . . in believing oneself to be the providential organ of a philosophical revelation so pure and so delicate."[26]

Meanwhile the straws continued to swirl in the wind. On May 29 the Dominican master general informed Marie-Joseph Lagrange that Merry del Val, expressing the explicit wish of the pope, forbade publication in any form of Lagrange's commentary on Genesis.[27] A few days later the biblical commission confirmed John, the Beloved Disciple, as author of the Fourth Gospel, this in the teeth of contrary conclusions expressed in print by both Loisy and von Hügel.[28] Judicial sentences like these were merely preludes to such works finding

---

21. Édouard Le Roy, *Dogme et critique* (Paris: 1907), xvii.
22. Le Roy treated the Resurrection at great length; see *Dogme et critique*, 155–257.
23. Quoted in Loisy, *Mémoires*, 2:521–22.
24. Blondel to Valensin, 24 May, 1907, in Blondel and Valensin, *Correspondance*, 319–20.
25. See chapter 16.
26. Loisy to Le Roy, 1 June, 1907, quoted in *Mémoires*, 2:529–30.
27. Lagrange, "L'École biblique," 168–89.
28. See De la Bedoyere, *Hügel*, 190–91.

a place on the Index of forbidden books, which indeed—except for Loisy's treatise on Saint John's Gospel, which was already there—occurred in Houtin's and Le Roy's cases within a matter of a few months.

IMMEDIATE PRELUDES also to the release of what came to be popularly called the "new Syllabus," issued by the Holy Office on July 3, 1907. The decree *Lamentabili Sane Exitu* contained a brief preface—"With truly lamentable results, our age, casting aside all restraint in its search for the ultimate causes of things, frequently pursues novelties so ardently that it rejects the legacy of the human race"—followed by sixty-five propositions, all declared worthy of "condemnation and proscription." The list displayed a rough sort of order: the first twenty-four propositions dealt with scriptural matters; twenty-five and twenty-six with the nature of faith; twenty-seven through thirty-eight treated the person of Christ; thirty-nine through fifty-two the sacraments, in general and in particular; and the rest focused on the character and constitution of the church.

A sampling indicates the thrust of the Vatican's attack. "Even by dogmatic definitions the church's magisterium cannot determine the genuine sense of the Sacred Scriptures" (4). "If he wishes to apply himself usefully to biblical studies, the exegete must first put aside all preconceived opinions about the supernatural origin of Sacred Scripture and interpret it the same as any other merely human document" (12). "The narrations of John are not properly history, but a mystical contemplation of the Gospel" (16). "The dogmas of the church . . . are an interpretation of religious facts which the human mind has acquired by laborious effort" (22). "The dogmas of the Faith are to be held only according to their practical sense; that is to say, as preceptive norms of conduct and not as norms of believing" (26). "The Resurrection of the Savior is not properly a fact of the historical order. It is a fact of merely the supernatural order (neither demonstrated nor demonstrable) which the Christian consciousness gradually derived from other facts" (36). "It was far from the mind of Christ to found a church as a society that would continue on earth. . . . [Rather] in the mind of Christ the Kingdom of Heaven together with the end of the world was about to come immediately" (52). "Dogma, sacraments, and hierarchy, both their notion and reality, are only interpretations and evolutions of the Christian intelligence which have increased and perfected by an external series of additions the little germ latent in the Gospel" (54). "Truth is no more immutable than man himself, since it evolved with him, in him, and through him" (58).[29]

There was in fact only a superficial resemblance between *Lamentabili* and Pius IX's celebrated *Syllabus Errorum* (1864). The eighty statements in the latter document had been expressed in affirmative terms and then dubbed as erro-

---

29. *Acta Sanctae Sedis* (Rome: 1907), 40:470–78.

neous, but the doctrines involved had all been drawn from earlier papal pronouncements—reaffirmations, so to speak, of specific elements of Pius IX's teaching[30]—while *Lamentabili* based its list of condemnations upon the formal assessment of *L'Evangile et l'Église* and *Autour d'un petit livre* prepared by Parisian theologians under the directive of Cardinal Richard three years earlier.[31] Though it was hardly a laughing matter, Loisy later made fun of the decree by a mock analysis in which he mimicked the procedure employed in the original *Syllabus* by simply inserting or removing a negative particle from each condemned proposition.[32] When, in a more serious vein, he inquired privately of Minocchi and Buonaiuti about the Italian sources of *Lamentabili*, they replied—predictably—that the Holy Office had "voluntarily deformed [Loisy's views] or altered them out of ignorance."[33] Nor was the exegete amused when, on August 3, the "fanatical" curé of the parish adjoining Ceffonds read out from the pulpit the text of *Lamentabili* to the "bewildered congregation" attending Sunday mass.[34]

That text, signed by Cardinals Rampolla and Steinhuber and apparently redacted by the English Franciscan scripturist David Fleming,[35] had become available in various translations by the middle of July. The mainstream Catholic press received it much as did George Tyrrell's former associates at the *Month*, which described it as "a fair and singularly moderate statement."[36] Archbishop Mignot, on the other hand, discerned reference to a recent published speech of his in the sixth proposition,[37] while Wilfrid Ward worried lest the twenty-fifth might be interpreted as a censure of Newman.[38] There was by contrast a measure of rejoicing in Aix-en-Provence. "As far as this decree itself is concerned," Maurice Blondel observed, "we have won a great victory, in that our views are not even touched upon." Laberthonnière saw a bright side too, as he scanned the commentary in the theological journals and found that the *philosophie de l'action* was judged to have emerged unscathed from the proscriptions of *Lamentabili*.[39]

For someone like Albert Houtin, now almost totally alienated from the church, the lesson of the decree was eminently clear: "Loisy is an utter heretic; one would have to be blind not to see that. What he proposed was a structure

---

30. See chapter 2, and O'Connell, "Ultramontanism and Dupanloup," 211–17.
31. See the chart in Marcel Clément, *Vie du cardinal Richard* (Paris: 1924), 408.
32. Alfred Loisy, *Simples réflexions sur le décret du saint-office, "Lamentabili sane exitu," et sur l'encyclique "Pascendi dominici gregis"* (Paris: 1908), 117–38.
33. Loisy, *Mémoires*, 2:555.
34. Loisy, *Mémoires*, 2:546.
35. See Rivière, *Modernisme*, 334–41. For Fleming, see chapter 14.
36. Leader in the *Month*, 110 (August 1907), 113–14.
37. "The 'Church learning' and the 'Church teaching' collaborate in such a way in defining truths that it only remains for the 'Church teaching' to sanction the opinions of the 'Church learning.' "
38. "The assent of faith ultimately rests on a mass of probabilities."
39. Blondel to Mourret, 21 July, and Laberthonnière to Blondel, 23 August, 1907, quoted in Blondel and Valensin, *Correspondance*, 342–43.

in which the church could have survived at least for a while. . . . That structure has been repudiated [by *Lamentabili*]. Too bad."[40] This judgment was not out of tune with the reaction of the secular and anticlerical world, expressed succinctly by Jaurès, the French socialist leader, in his newspaper *L'humanité*: "The pope is perfectly consistent. By his rejection [of the abrogation of the concordat[41]] he has decidedly separated himself from democracy. By his syllabus he has isolated himself from science."

For his part Friedrich von Hügel determined to maintain silence with regard to *Lamentabili* unless he were asked formally to subscribe to it, in which case he would refuse to do so. He persuaded Tyrrell to follow the same course and urged Loisy to do likewise, at least until a response being drawn up by Le Roy was ready. The baron took curious consolation in the circumstance that *Lamentabili* had been issued on a Wednesday; really serious condemnations by the Holy Office, he explained, always appeared on Thursdays.[42] In this mood—half fearful, half fanciful—he left England for Italy early in August. At Molveno, a resort town in the Tyrol, he met for three days with the embattled editors of *Il Rinnovamento*. Buonaiuti, Murri, and several other likeminded persons were also in attendance.[43] The baron urged upon the participants in the conference the moderate stance which he claimed to have detected in recent correspondence with Loisy. "The baron's commentary must have been more edifying than what I actually wrote him," commented the exegete years later. However that may have been, the ranks at Molveno suffered at least one casualty. Romolo Murri, von Hügel reported, "has been with us only by accident. [He is] a close-minded and unconvertible scholastic, a spirit with no critical historical sense and even less commitment to research and to mysticism." This latter failing Loisy could sympathize with: like Murri, he admitted, he had "no sense of the immutable."[44]

THOUGH THE COMPARISON is faulty for the reasons already suggested, it was nevertheless noted at the time that, as the original *Syllabus Errorum* had been accompanied by an expository encyclical,[45] so, forty-three years later, the "new Syllabus" shortly had an elaborate papal document for a companion piece. "The office committed to us of feeding the flock of the Lord has especially this duty assigned to it by Christ, to guard with the greatest vigilance the deposit of the faith delivered to the saints, rejecting the profane novelties of words and the oppositions proposed by knowledge falsely so-called." Thus

---

40. Houtin to Baudrillart, 31 July, 1907, quoted in Loisy, *Mémoires*, 2:552.

41. See chapter 16.

42. Loisy, *Mémoires*, 2:547. *Lamentabili* was indeed dated on a Wednesday, 3 July, but it received sanction from the pope the next day.

43. See Houtin, *Modernisme*, 177, and Barmann, *Hügel*, 194–95.

44. Loisy, *Mémoires*, 2:556–61.

45. This was *Quanta Cura*, issued the same day as the *Syllabus*, 8 December, 1864.

begins *Pascendi Dominici Gregis*, promulgated by Pius X on September 8, 1907. It was lengthy as encyclicals go, taking up not quite twice the printed space of Leo XIII's celebrated *Rerum Novarum*. Most interested parties concluded that the principal authors of *Pascendi*'s doctrinal section were the French Jesuit Louis Billot[46] and the Italian *monsignore* Umberto Benigni, who had swiftly risen from obscurity to high rank within the Roman curia,[47] while the disciplinary section had been virtually dictated by the pope himself. These suppositions have been much debated since 1907,[48] but, as Loisy said, the same spirit imbued both parts of the document. "Pius X was responsible for all of it, whatever may have been the number, the competence, and the character of the persons who collaborated in writing the encyclical."[49]

A striking feature of *Pascendi* is its harsh rhetoric, its tone of personal denunciation, its exercise of apparently rash judgment. The narrative, even when treating of highly abstruse matters, is often interrrupted to give vent to what seem to be vindictive outbursts. Those whom it indicts "are striving, by arts entirely new and full of subtlety, to destroy the vital energy of the Church and . . . to overthrow utterly Christ's kingdom itself." "They seize upon chairs in the seminaries and universities, and gradually make of them chairs of pestilence." "Lost to all sense of modesty, [they] vaunt themselves as reformers of the Church," when in fact they are "the most pernicious . . . adversaries of the Church." "Blind that they are, and leaders of the blind, inflated with a boastful science, . . . they pervert the eternal concept of truth and the true nature of religious sentiment . . . [because of their] blind and unchecked passion for novelty." "They go their way, reprimands and condemnations notwithstanding, masking an incredible audacity under a mock semblance of humility." They exhibit "a boundless effrontery. . . . Let one of them but open his mouth and the others applaud him in chorus, proclaiming that science has made another step forward." "Under their own names and under pseudonyms they publish numbers of books, newspapers, reviews, and sometimes one and the same writer adopts a variety of pseudonyms to trap the incautious reader into believing there is a whole multitude of . . . writers." "It is pride which fills [them] with that confidence in themselves and leads them to hold themselves

---

46. Louis Billot (1846–1931), was ordained for Angers, then entered the Society of Jesus, was created cardinal in 1911, and was dismissed from the sacred college in 1927, after the publication of "revealing documents" linking him to the recently condemned Action française. See *Dictionnaire de biographie française* (Paris: 1954), 6:481.

47. See chapter 17 and chapter 19. As under secretary of the Congregation of Extraordinary Ecclesiastical Affairs, Benigni was in effect fifth in rank within the secretariat of state. See Poulat, *Modernistica*, 52.

48. Most illuminatingly in Gabriel Daly, *Transcendance and Immanence: A Study in Catholic Modernism and Integralism* (Oxford: 1980), 232–34, which assigns as chief doctrinal author Joseph Lemius (1860–1923), then procurator general of the Oblates of Mary Immaculate. See also Poulat, *Histoire, dogme*, 627–28.

49. Loisy, *Mémoires*, 2:566.

up as the rule for all; pride which puffs them up with . . . vain glory . . . and makes them say, inflated with presumption, We are not as the rest of men."

Pascendi does, to be sure, offer grudging admission once or twice that such persons are not altogether moral reprobates. Yet this concession amounts to hardly more than damning with faint praise. Thus it may be that "they lead a life of the greatest activity, of assiduous and ardent application to every branch of learning, and that they possess, as a rule, a reputation for the strictest morality." But their probity, such as it is, "is well calculated to deceive" the unwary and impressionable. Even if personally they "are perhaps not devoid of a certain merit," yet "none is more skillful, none more astute than they in the employment of a thousand noxious arts." Though the pope occasionally acknowledges that there might be distinctions among them—that some might be more moderate than others—this nuance appears in context as an inconsequential afterthought or a quibble. He much prefers to lump them all together in their desire "to embrace all kinds of the most absurd novelties" and in their craving to be "reformers of others, while they forget to reform themselves." These are "the Modernists, as they are commonly and rightly called," and their ideology is Modernism.[50]

"Commonly called Modernists" was a strange expression when in fact the term was new and, as Loisy cogently observed, equivocal.[51] The use of it stemmed perhaps from the conviction of the pope and his advisers that at issue was a conscious conspiracy, hatched by contemporary intellectuals in the name of modern research and aimed at subverting the church across the broad spectrum of its teaching and polity. "[T]heir system does not consist in scattered and unconnected theories, but in a perfectly organized body, all the parts of which are solidly joined, so that it is not possible to admit one without admitting all."[52] This assertion no doubt caricatured the Modernist reality, by lending it a coherence it did not possess and by failing to take account of the deep differences between, say, Blondel and Le Roy, or between Loisy and Lagrange. "[The pope] defines the system," commented Loisy, not without justice, "and, at the same time, he invents the system such as he represents it, since it never has been taught by anybody. . . . [His is] an arbitrary perspective." And yet even Loisy—who, however ruefully, accepted and used the term "Modernist"—had to grant that *Pascendi* had based its indictment upon the essential sources. Out of "Blondel's and Laberthonnière's philosophy of *immanence*; out of intimate religious experience and moral dogmatism, into which had penetrated a certain Kantian element; out of Tyrrell's mystical theology, which

50. Judge (ed.), *Pascendi*, 49, 91, 50, 58, 74, 80, 88, 65, 84, 51. The context (81) makes it clear that by "moderate Modernists" the encyclical meant Blondel and the other philosophers of *action*. Ironically, in the light of the terminology developed after 1907 (see chapter 19), nonmodedrate Modernists are here called "integralists."

51. Loisy, *Mémoires*, 2:565.

52. Judge (ed.), *Pascendi*, 85.

exhibited a certain Protestant individualism and illuminism; . . . out of my books wherein there was above all critical history and an evolutionary conception of the Hebrew religion and Christianity, of Catholic dogma, cult and constitution"—out of all this "the theologians of His Holiness constructed a sort of encyclopedic doctrine of which the most radical agnosticism is the foundation."[53]

Immanuel Kant's name does not figure in the pages of *Pascendi*, nor does René Descartes's.[54] But these two philosophical giants, these makers of the modern mind, provide the frame of reference against which the encyclical hurls its anathemas. "The philosopher leads the way," the pope insists over and over again:

Some Modernists, devoted to historical studies, seem to be greatly afraid of being taken for philosophers. About philosophy, they will tell you, they know nothing whatever—and in this they display remarkable astuteness, for they are particularly anxious not to be suspected of being prejudiced in favor of philosophical theories which would lay them open to the charge of not being objective, to use the word in vogue. And yet the truth is that their history and their criticism are saturated with their philosophy, and that their historico-critical conclusions are the natural fruit of their philosophical principles.[55]

And what is the philosophical root of all these aberrations? Agnosticism, the pope replies. "According to this teaching human reason is confined entirely within the field of phenomena, that is to say, to things that are perceptible to the senses and in the manner in which they are perceptible. . . . Hence it is incapable of lifting itself up to God and of recognizing his existence . . . by means of visible things." The word "agnosticism," with its popular connotation of religious indifference, seems excessively harsh when applied, as it was here, to persons for whom religion was of dominant, even of obsessive, interest. Certainly, as Loisy might have said, it is by itself an equivocal term. But the pope left no doubt as to his meaning, for he promptly quotes the solemn and unequivocal proclamation of the First Vatican Council: "If anyone says that the one true God, our Creator and Lord, cannot be known with certainty by the natural light of reason by means of the things that are made, let him be anathema."[56] Whatever their virtues—from the brilliance of Loisy to the courage of Laberthonnière to the personal piety of Blondel and von Hügel—those who subscribed to Cartesian and particularly to Kantian epistemology could not but find this a hard saying.

"When the encyclical tries to show the modernist that he is no Catholic, it

53. Loisy, *Mémoires*, 2:565.

54. Nor indeed any specific person or work.

55. Judge (ed.), *Pascendi*, 80, 75.

56. Judge (ed.), *Pascendi*, 52. The reference is to one of the canons attached to the dogmatic constitution "De Fide et Ecclessia." See Denzinger, Bannwart, et al. (eds.), *Enchiridion Symbolorum*, 492–93, 498–99.

mostly succeeds only in showing him that he is no scholastic—which he knew."[57] This, George Tyrrell's bitter rejoinder to *Pascendi*, did indeed put the basic quarrel into focus. Scholasticism for Tyrrell meant "a science-theory and psychology that are as strange as astrology to the modern mind." But Scholasticism for Pius X meant a commitment to a metaphysical realism that had been interwoven for centuries into the church's intellectual fabric. And intimately related to this was the Pauline dictum, "Fides ex auditu."[58] If indeed faith comes from hearing, then was the Scholastic assertion that, through the grasp of the mind upon the evidence provided by the senses, the human being could discern the existence of God and some of his attributes as fatuous as Tyrrell and his colleagues insisted?

More specifically, the pope reiterated a commitment to a realist epistemology. What can one know, and how can one know it? Here, it seems, in clashing theories of knowledge, lay the central quarrel of the Modernist crisis. Certainly those whom *Pascendi* labeled Modernists had much to complain about in conventional Scholasticism, which—to paraphrase Abbé Huvelin—ruthlessly cut down the trees in order to see the forest more clearly.[59] But it is no less certain that the same people were unable or unwilling to distinguish between good Scholasticism and bad, between the monumental achievement of Aquinas and the frequently trivial applications of it in the manuals written by his overly self-satisfied disciples. Yet such considerations were in the final analysis beside the point. The skeptical cast of establishment thought since Descartes, and especially since Kant, was what the pope called "agnosticism." Whether warranted or not in doing so, he could hardly have spoken otherwise, unless he was prepared to jettison the whole of Catholic tradition. And in any case he was surely correct in insisting that no scholar, in whatever field, comes to his research without epistemological assumptions. Not even the exceptionally persuasive Loisy could tempt Lagrange or Blondel into agreeing that the critic approached his material with no mental presuppositions, no frame of reference.[60] It therefore seems not too much to say that whatever exaggerations or misstatements are to be found in *Pascendi*, "the philosopher leads the way" was not one of them.

Having posited "agnosticism" as its root principle, the encyclical proceeds relentlessly to describe the Modernist "system." "When natural theology has

57. The *Times* (London), 1 October, 1907. Tyrrell's friend Edmund Bishop, also a convert to Catholicism, offered the same distinction, put somewhat differently: "All the papal artillery of the *Pascendi gregis* . . . is to me so much *bruum fulmen* [dull thunderclaps]. Catholicity is a great *religion*; it is the *only one* (sad as such a case may be) to which I own and can feel allegiance. But the 'Catholic intellectual system of the universe'—the great intellectual system elaborated by the theologians—that is a different matter. *I* never became a Catholic . . . . as *a solution to intellectual difficulties*." Quoted in Thomas Michael Loome, *Liberal Catholicism, Reform Catholicism, Modernism* (Mainz, 1979), 64.

58. Romans, 10:17.

59. See chapter 3.

60. See chapter 14.

been destroyed, the road to revelation closed through the rejection of the arguments of credibility, and all external revelation absolutely denied," religion, "a form of life," can be explained only by "religious immanence." And "since God is the object of religion, we must conclude that faith . . . consists in a sentiment [*sensus*] which originates from a need of the divine." This "religious sentiment, which through the agency of vital immanence emerges from the lurking-places of the subconscious, is the germ of all religion." Immanence thus puts the believer into direct contact with the Unknowable, a circumstance that determines the relation of faith to science: "Science is entirely concerned with the reality of phenomena [in the Kantian sense], into which faith does not enter at all; faith on the contrary concerns itself with the divine reality which is entirely unknown to science." But what if "there are some things in the visible world that appertain to faith, such as the human life of Christ?" The Modernist historian, as scientist, sees no difficulty. "For though such things come within the category of phenomena, still insofar as they are lived by faith . . . and transfigured by faith, . . . they have been removed from the world of sense and translated to become material for the divine." Did Christ really perform miracles? Did he really utter prophecies? Did he really rise from the dead? "The answer of agnostic science will be in the negative and the answer of faith in the affirmative—yet there will not be . . . any conflict between them." Christ in his historical reality was bound by the iron laws of evolutionary development like every other man. But, thanks to vital immanence, his life can be captured by the believer and "lived again by the faith and in the faith."[61] *Pascendi* at this point appears to have laid bare the nerve center of the "system" it aimed to discredit: if critical history has revealed the Bible to be a collection of venerable and edifying myths, and Catholic tradition a morally utilitarian response to the evolutionary process, the believer need not be distressed or disconcerted, since his faith, thanks to vital immanence, depends ultimately upon the heart, the "sentiment," the yearning which God has rooted in his subconscious.

But Pius X discerned other specific consequences to abominate. The Modernists—in whichever of their self-appointed roles as philosopher, believer, theologian, historian, critic, or reformer—have thus staked out their essential ground. And upon it they build their intellectual edifice. "[All] representations of the divine reality are [only] symbolical." When the intellect encounters "the [inner] sentiment, directs itself upon it, and produces in it a work resembling that of a painter who restores and gives new life to a picture that has perished with age," formal dogma takes shape. But immanent sentiment, like everything else human, is constantly evolving, and so dogma, the reflection upon that sentiment, is ever changing. Moreover, "the Church and the sacraments . . . are not to be regarded as having been instituted by Christ

61. Judge (ed.), *Pascendi*, 53–54, 61–62.

Himself. . . . Christ [is] nothing more than a man whose religious consciousness has been, like that of all men, formed only by degrees." How, then, can
the church and its cult claim divine foundation? Only in accord with the iron
law of evolution whereby "the consciousness of all Christians was . . . virtually
included in the consciousness of Christ, as the plant is included in the seed.
. . . And since this life produced in the course of ages both the Church and
the sacraments, it is quite right to say that their origin is from Christ and is
divine." Of course, it almost goes without saying that the sacramental system
is, in the Modernists' view, the result of a felt need, "since everything in [their]
system is explained by inner impulses and necessities." So it follows that the
efficacy of the sacraments rests upon the need to give "some sensible manifestation to religion" and to provide "the vehicle[s] of certain great ideas that strike
the public mind."

As for the Scriptures, they, say the Modernists, "may be rightly described
as a collection of experiences. . . . God does indeed speak in these books . . .
by vital immanence. . . . Inspiration . . . is distinguished only by its vehe-
mence, . . . something like that which happens in poetical inspiration. . . .
The Bible . . . [is in any case] a human work, made by men for men." Similarly, the church "is the product of the collective consciousness" of believers,
and, as such, it must alter its constitution in accord with the advancement of
society. The authority the church claims "is a vital emanation of the collectiv-
ity," and therefore, "in an age when the sense of liberty has reached its fullest
development," such authority must "shape itself to democratic forms. . . .
The penalty of refusal is disaster, for it is madness to think that the sentiment
of liberty . . . can surrender." This is but one instance, argue the Modernists,
of a universal law.

[I]n a living religion everything is subject to change, and must in fact change. . . .
To the laws of evolution everything is subject—dogma, Church, worship, the Books
we revere as sacred, even faith itself. . . . The primitive form of faith, [the Modernists]
tell us, was rudimentary and common to all men alike, for it had its origin in human
nature. . . . Vital evolution brought with it progress, not by the accretion of new . . .
forms from without, but by an increasing penetration of the religious sentiment in the
consciousness. . . . Thus . . . has it happened in the case of Christ. In Him that divine
something [*divinum illud qualecumque*] which faith admitted in Him expanded in such
a way that He was at last held to be God.[62]

No names were named in *Pascendi*, no specific literary works alluded to. The
text did, however, contain explicit statements that left no doubt as to whom
they referred. Thus a distinction put forward by Blondel and the other philosophers of *action* received direct attention: "We cannot but deplore, . . . and
grievously, that there are Catholics who, while rejecting immanence as a doc-

62. Judge (ed.), *Pascendi*, 64–72.

trine, employ it as a method of apologetics, and who do this so imprudently that they seem to admit that there is in human nature a true and rigorous necessity with regard to the supernatural order—and not merely a capacity and suitability for the supernatural, such as has at all times been emphasized by Catholic apologists." And similarly the central tenet of Loisy's *L'Evangile et l'Église* drew special notice: "[The Modernists] proclaim that Christ Himself manifestly erred in determining the time when the coming of the Kingdom of God was to take place, and they tell us that we must not be surprised at this since even Christ was subject to the laws of life!"

The disciplinary regime laid down in the final section of *Pascendi*—nearly 20 percent of the whole text—was extremely detailed and rigorous. It included the purging of seminary faculties, rigid new norms of censorship, and the formation in every diocese of a "council of vigilance," whose members— secular and religious priests—"shall meet every two months under the presidency of the Bishop. . . . They shall watch most carefully for every sign and trace of Modernism both in publications and in teaching, and, to preserve the clergy and the young from [Modernism], they shall take all prudent, prompt and efficacious measures." Nor was Pius X content to leave implementation of his directives to the discretion of local authorities. "We will and ordain that the Bishops of all dioceses, a year after the publication of this letter and every three years thereafter, furnish the Holy See with a diligent and sworn report on all the prescriptions contained here, and on the doctrines that find currency among the clergy, and especially in the seminaries and other Catholic institutions."[63]

The justification for this repressive apparatus was clear enough, at least in Pius X's mind:

We have to lament at the sight of many young men, once full of promise and capable of rendering great services to the Church, now gone astray. And there is another sight that saddens Us too: that of so many other Catholics who . . . have . . . grown into the habit as though they had been breathing a poisoned atmosphere, of thinking and speaking and writing with a liberty that ill-becomes Catholics. . . . They are possessed by the empty desire of being talked about, and they know they would never succeed in this were they to say only what has always been said. . . . They offend . . . less perhaps by their works . . . than by the spirit in which they write and by the encouragement they are giving to the extravagances of the Modernists.[64]

PASCENDI, according to Alfred Loisy, was "the most important doctrinal act of the reign of Pius X."[65] Perhaps so, but it was not an act that aroused the interest of the masses of the Catholic people. Addressed as all encyclicals are to the pope's fellow bishops—presumably theologians of a sort—*Pascendi* dealt

63. Judge (ed.), *Pascendi*, 99–101.
64. Judge (ed.), *Pascendi*, 91–92.
65. Loisy, *Mémoires*, 2:565.

with issues of such complexity that it could hardly have had much impact among the men and women in the pews. Modernism, despite *Pascendi*'s sometimes hysterical language, was an elitist movement, confined to a very small number of people. That is not to say that elitist movements never develop into popular ones, a possibility which perhaps an alarmed Pius X kept at the front of his mind. The large-hearted Baron von Hügel at any rate, elitist though he doubtless was, appeared to sense something of the kind: "I must admit, even now and in spite of everything, I have a feeling as to the pathetic position of the Pope, holding that most difficult of posts not through his own choosing, a peasant of simple seminary training and speaking to some 200 million souls, of whom doubtless a good nine-tenths, at least, are even less cultured than himself, and whom he is sincerely trying to defend against what he conceives to be deadly error. We can afford to be magnanimous."[66]

Magnanimity, however, was not the common response of those presumably targeted to one degree or another by *Pascendi*. "*Nothing* is sadder," said Édouard Le Roy in a fury, "than to listen to the apostolic authority speaking the language of a pamphleteer. The pontifical document oozes hatred and scorn. It is heartbreaking. Never, never would I have thought the Roman theologians capable of such sentiments."[67] The archbishop of Albi was more sardonic than passionate. The encyclical, he said to Loisy, is praised by those who have "neither read it nor understood it, that is, by journalists and many curés." There is no definition of Modernism; "there is instead block condemnation without definition." Is it necessary to believe "that the stars were created on the fourth day of the world?" Must we "become again *geocentrists?*" But the fire seemed to have gone out of Mignot, replaced by a dull acknowledgment of the inevitable. The pope "says too much and not enough. . . . Far from bringing about peace, as Pius X hopes, the encyclical will only feed the divisions."[68]

In Aix-en Provence, Maurice Blondel, numb with grief, wrote to a friend, "I am suffering deeply. It almost makes one cry out, Happy are those who are dead in the Lord!" And to another friend a few days earlier: "I have read the encyclical, and I am in a stupor. Is it possible? What attitude should one take? Internal attitude, I mean, as well as external. And, above all, how does one prevent so many souls from just giving up, just doubting the *goodness* of the church?"[69] But for all his sensitivity and his dedication to abstract thought, Blondel was not without a pragmatic streak. He moved quickly to insulate the *Annales de philosophie chrétienne* and its collaborators from suspicion by inserting into the October number a repudiation of "the doctrines censured by the encyc-

---

66. Von Hügel to Tyrrell, 1 October, 1907, in Holland (ed.), *Letters*, 141.

67. Le Roy to Laberthonnière, 20 September, 1907, in Perrin (ed.), *Laberthonnière et ses amis*, 148.

68. Mignot to Loisy, 3 October, 1907, quoted in Loisy, *Mémoires*, 2:575. Loisy noted parenthetically that Umberto Benigni was a journalist.

69. Blondel to Valensin, 20 September and to Mourret, 17 September, 1907, quoted in Virgoulay, *Blondel*, 230.

lical. . . . We reject them in the same sense as they are rejected there."
Though Laberthonnière, the journal's editor, at first resisted this hasty submission, Blondel, its owner, prevailed. Henri Bremond, with whom Blondel
shared "the little manifesto" prior to publication, judged it "absurd of course
in itself but necessary under the circumstances. Absurd, because nothing
obliges us to repeat that we are children of the church."[70]

Bremond was more worried about George Tyrrell's reaction to *Pascendi*, and
with reason. Tyrrell was staying with Friedrich von Hügel in Kensington on
September 19 when the latter received a copy of the encyclical, sent from Italy
by his future son-in-law. The two of them studied the document and discussed
it for several days, with the baron contending that the pope "personally neither
wrote nor thought" the doctrinal section which, he opined, Benigni had put
together with "a certain lawyer's cleverness."[71] By the time Tyrrell departed,
muttering ominously, he had been invited by the *Giornale d'Italia* and by the
Times to express his views on the encyclical. He complied with both requests,
which appeared on September 25 and September 30–October 1, respectively.
He did not offer and did not ask for quarter:

Neither the engineered enthusiasm of *la bonne presse*, nor the extorted acquiescence and
unanimity of a helplessly subjugated episcopate, nor the passive submission of uncomprehending sheeplike lay multitudes will deceive [the Modernist] into thinking that
this Encyclical comes from, or speaks to, the living heart of the Church—the intelligent, religious-minded, truth-loving minority.[72]

"I deplore Tyrrell's outbursts," commented Bremond sadly. "It is his Irish
frenzy. The deceit of this world enraged him and he lashed out at it."[73] Three
years later—after Tyrrell was dead—von Hügel tried to recapture his friend's
mood at that calamitous moment.

As to *Pascendi*, [Tyrrell's] anger rose from its apparent contempt for mysticism and
all the dim inchoate gropings after God; its wholesale imputation of bad motives to
respectable, hard-working scholars and thinkers, and its disciplinary enactments. . . .
I must admit that I could not discover how to defend these peculiarities; especially,
did I find that the more one attempted to palliate the disciplinary enactments, the
more sure one was, at least, amongst free peoples and amongst men of liberal education, to arouse prompt anger and contempt for church officials.[74]

La bonne presse to which Tyrrell had contemptuously referred included those
Catholic papers, represented by *L'Univers* in France and the *Tablet* in England,
which suggested that neither the denunciatory language nor the sheer technical intricacy of the encyclical should have presented any serious problem to the

70. See Perrin (ed.), *Laberthonnière et ses amis*, 163–66. See also chapter 17.
71. Von Hügel to Loisy, 27 September, 1907, quoted in Loisy, *Mémoires*, 2:569.
72. George Tyrrell, "The Pope and Modernism," *Times* (London), 1 October, 1907.
73. Bremond to Laberthonnière, 5 October, 1907, in Perrin (ed.), *Laberthonnière et ses amis*, 167.
74. Quoted in De la Bedoyere, *Hügel*, 201.

reader.[75] More sophisticated support was given to *Pascendi* by Tyrrell's former colleagues at the *Month*, who, in a measured commentary, concentrated their fire on the Modernist assumption of Kantian epistemology and psychology. The task of theology, they argued, was to reflect "upon truths which faith certifies as data," and not, as the Modernists would have it, "to reconcile faith with science, that is to say, the demands of the religious sentiment with the demands made by contemporary science on those religious formulas by which . . . the intellect assists the believer to give an account of his faith."[76] A similar, if somewhat less specialized and more personal, appraisal appeared in the review Bremond had once written for, the *Études* of Paris.[77]

The editor of another journal found the autumn of 1907 a time of special trial. Wilfrid Ward thought *Pascendi* "ill-drawn," "a muddle," filled with "difficulties." "Explain and interpret the difficult passages; don't pretend they have no existence [as the *Tablet* did]." And yet, even as he called for candor, he could not ignore the suspicions that had been growing within him for years about the speculations of Tyrrell, von Hügel, and especially Loisy. And so profoundly entwined with his ideal of Catholicism was a respect for authority—"A Catholic's final duty is to obey authority in its rightful sphere"—it never crossed Ward's mind to disavow the encyclical. But such loyalty did not commit him to accepting the doctrine of *Pascendi* outside its appropriate context. Every document, he insisted, even that issuing from the highest ecclesiastical authority, needs to be sifted and analyzed, needs mature interpretation so that it can take its proper place within the whole corpus of Catholic teaching. So Newmanesque an attitude was of course characteristic of Ward, but never more so than now, when he was deep into preparing his great biography of Newman. Indeed, his greatest fear in the wake of *Pascendi* was that one of Tyrrell's assertions—that the encyclical condemned Newman as much as anyone else[78]—might become widely accepted. Ward lobbied friends in Rome to secure an official statement to the contrary, but in vain. Meanwhile, as he pondered what to say in the leader he would have to write for the *Dublin Review*, he was bombarded from the Right as a trimmer and from the Left as a neanderthal.[79]

In Jerusalem, Marie-Joseph Lagrange, already under a cloud, maintained a prudent silence. Louis Duchesne was on holiday in Brittany when *Pascendi* appeared, and, though he too carefully held his peace in public, he privately indulged his taste for sarcasm when describing the pontifical mass at which the archbishop of Rennes promulgated "the encyclical *Bilem commovent* [they

75. See Ward, *The Wilfrid Wards*, 2:266.
76. Sydney Smith, "The Encyclical 'Pascendi,' " *Month* 110 (November 1907): 450–51, 458.
77. Maurice de la Taille, "Sur l'encyclique 'Pascendi,' " *Études* 113 (November 1907): 645–69.
78. "The encyclical clearly condemns Newman as much as it does T[yrrell]", von Hügel to Semeria, 19 October, 1907, in Zorzi (ed.), *Briefe . . . von Hügels an . . . Semeria*, 2:510.
79. Ward, *The Wilfrid Wards*, 2:260–82.

violently shake out their bile]. Thanks be to heaven, that excellent prelate was able to congratulate himself on not having a single Modernist in his diocese. . . . But *quod abundat non vitiat* [one cannot have too much of a good thing], so he ordered us to sing the creed in salutation to the Blessed Sacrament. I assisted in this exercise and sang along with the rest."[80] At another festive mass, this one celebrated at Toulouse in early November to mark the opening of the academic year of the Institut Catholique, Pierre Batiffol addressed his colleagues and students in these terms: "Let us cultivate, gentlemen, sentiments of filial respect. . . . The Vicar of Jesus Christ . . . does not ask that we desert our times, but rather to be of them and to act upon them, and that our scientific action, like our social action, be exercised in modes wisely and opportunely modern. . . . Let us cultivate a docility rooted in charity." Docility had never been a virtue that came easily for Batiffol, and less so now that his book on the history of the Eucharist had been placed on the Index.[81]

In Italy Romolo Murri cheerfully and publicly gave his adherence to *Pascendi*, which moved von Hügel to repeat his earlier judgment: "[Murri] has been a Scholastic all along. We leave him at his point of arrival."[82] The status of another Italian cleric, Giovanni Semeria, caused the baron graver concern, not only because of his affection for the eloquent Barnabite but also for immediate family reasons. The previous April the youngest von Hügel daughter, Thekla, had been professed a Carmelite nun, thus embracing the kind of mystical vocation her father so prized. Now, in the autumn, her older sister, Gertrud, was about to marry the papal count, Francesco Salmei. Semeria, an old friend of the Salmei family, was scheduled to preside at the wedding in Genoa, but Pius X, exercising his rights as Salmei's feudal lord, pettily forbade him to do so. The nuptials were celebrated in front of the shrine of the baron's favorite mystic, Saint Catherine of Genoa, with Padre Semeria sitting with the groom's relatives.[83]

Before he left Italy von Hügel met again briefly with the editors of *Il Rinnovamento*, urging them to persevere. This they agreed to do, but just before Christmas the archbishop of Milan threatened major excommunication to all associated with the journal if publication did not cease immediately. That prelate acted under authority of a *motu proprio*, issued November 18, 1907, in which the pope directed that such a penalty be applied to anyone defending the doctrine condemned in *Lamentabili* and *Pascendi*.[84]

80. Duchesne to von Hügel, 30 September, 1907, in Neveu (ed.), "Lettres . . . de Duchesne," *Mélanges*, 84:595.

81. *La Croix* (Paris), 7 November, 1907. The censure of *L'Euchariste* (Paris: 1905) was issued on 26 July, 1907, but not made public until 1911. A new, approved edition appeared in 1913. See Rivière, "Batiffol," *Dictionnaire de théologie catholique* (Paris: 1929): 3:1327–30.

82. Von Hügel to Loisy, 27 September, 1907, quoted in Loisy, *Mémoires*, 2:570.

83. See De la Bedoyere, *Hügel*, 205–7, and Loisy, *Mémoires*, 2:592–5.

84. See Houtin, *Modernisme*, 199–200. A "motu proprio" (by his own impulse) is letter written at the personal initiative of the pope and signed by him.

THE BISHOP OF SOUTHWARK did not wait for the pope's *motu proprio* to excommunicate George Tyrrell. Peter Amigo, the forty-three-year-old successor of Francis Bourne as head of the diocese to which the Catholic parishes in Clapham and Storrington were subject,[85] issued the decree on October 22. Drawing upon a nice distinction in the canon law, the bishop smoothly explained that Father Tyrrell fell under the penalty of a "minor," not a "major," excommunication—that is, Catholics need not cease associating with him, though he himself was deprived of receiving the sacraments, unless he were in danger of death. What the bishop did not say was that he had leveled this sentence against Tyrrell at the direct instruction of Cardinal Merry del Val.[86] The Vatican secretary of state, an accomplished linguist who needed to keep abreast of contemporary commentary, had no doubt read Tyrrell's violent denunciations of *Pascendi* in both the *Times* and in the *Giornale d'Italia*.

Tyrrell replied in the spirit of confrontation that had now become his habitual mode: "Your Lordship, . . . if . . . my offence lies in having protested publicly, in the name of Catholicism, against a document destructive of the only possible defence of Catholicism and of every reason for submitting, within due limits, to ecclesiastical authority, . . . I am absolutely and finally impenitent." There was a further brief exchange of correspondence, which Tyrrell challenged the bishop to make public. When Amigo declined, Tyrrell did so himself. The bishop meanwhile notified his deans that Father Tyrrell, should he present himself at the communion rail of any church in the diocese of Southwark, was to be denied the Eucharist.[87]

Friedrich von Hügel, who had deprecated the tone if not the substance of Tyrrell's journalistic outbursts against *Pascendi*—an extreme instance, he feared, of his friend's propensity to "throw bombs"—urged him now "not to 'submit' unconditionally, but to send in an expression of regret, of retraction and of non-repetition, of such expressions, such a tone or temper, such directly anti-Pope's person passages as, especially in the *Giornale d'Italia* article, have pained or scandalized souls. . . . [Thus] you would have undone whatever temporary obscuration or pain you may have aroused in some really well-disposed but ill-prepared minds by that tone, temper, etc."[88] He sought to firm up this appeal by several trips to Storrington, but he found little solace there. "The baron came here yesterday," Tyrrell reported to Bremond. "He was in tears, because he feared I had embarked upon some new line of thought and was going to abandon him. He is as sensitive as a woman. I told him I would

---

85. See chapter 15. Peter Emmanuel Amigo (1864–1949), born in the crown colony of Gibraltar and educated entirely in England, was a parish priest before being appointed bishop and later (1937) archbishop of Southwark. "[Tyrrell] delivered the fleet over to the enemy" was Amigo's nautical (and private) metaphor. See Schultenover, *Tyrrell*, 182–83.

86. See the authority cited in Sagovsky, *Tyrrell*, 228, 248.

87. Tyrrell to Amigo, 27 October and 1 November, 1907, in Petre, *Autobiography of Tyrrell*, 2:341–34.

88. Von Hügel to Tyrrell, 24 October, 1907, in Holland (ed.), *Letters*, 143–44.

play the game as long as there was still one man on the field with me; that it was only faithfulness to my fellow-players that has kept me where I am; and that when they have all kissed the pope's toe and have disowned me, I shall return without a fuss to the Church of my baptism and shall die a country parson."

But in this self-righteous and self-pitying mood, von Hügel was not the only "fellow-player" Tyrrell found wanting, found all too ready to "kiss the pope's toe." Wilfrid Ward as a teammate he had dismissed years before,[89] yet he could not resist a passing shot in that direction: "The *Dublin {Review}* did not comment on *[Pascendi]* in October. . . . I suppose it will do so in January if Ward has not gone to Canossa by that time." More ominous in Tyrrell's judgment was the submission to the encyclical of the *Annales de philosophie chrétienne*. "We should stand for death before dishonor," he insisted. "We are much more dangerous [to the papacy] in dying than in living." Affection prevented him from assuming that as editor "Laberthonnière had failed in courage," and yet the public endorsement of *Pascendi* together with "the unpardonable attack upon Le Roy" made him fear that those directing the *Annales* had simply lost their nerve.[90] Or perhaps, Tyrrell speculated, the problem was of a different character:

Blondel and Lab[erthonnière] are as wedded to their philosophy as the scholastics are to theirs, and we shall in either case have little liberty left to us. Our whole position has been that philosophy is of little importance to us, that the error [of orthodoxy] has been to link philosophy to Catholicism. And in the last analysis, who in the whole world really understands the philosophy of *action*? The baron certainly doesn't; you don't, nor do I. Not even Blondel does. Whereas Le Roy is at least *clear* and so far as I can see profoundly correct.[91]

Another visitor to Storrington at about this time—and a not particularly welcome one[92]—was Albert Houtin, who afterward spent a few days with Loisy at Ceffonds. "He [Houtin] appears very calm," Loisy observed, "and in some respects he is more amused than saddened by what has taken place. I must admit that I am not too much afflicted. What has happened is in accord with the logic of things."[93] Although Houtin's "hatred" for the church was a passion Loisy considered beneath himself, he neverthless agreed that to seek a compromise with *Pascendi*—to attempt to find a mode of modernity acceptable

89. See chapter 15.

90. The "attack" refers to two articles in the *Annales* critical of Le Roy (154 [July 1907]: 561–601, and 155 [October 1907]: 10–65). Blondel rejoiced in them: "I found [them] marvelously strong. . . . This is a great service which has been rendered us and for which we must be grateful to F[ather] L[aberthonnière] who has found the courage to change his mind and to face the inevitable accusations that he is an opportunist and a time-server." See Blondel to Mourret, 14 October, 1907, quoted in Blondel and Valensin, *Correspondance*, 355.

91. Tyrrell to Bremond, 6 November [1907], in Louis-David (ed.), *Lettres de Tyrrell*, 271–73.

92. See chapter 17, and Albert Houtin, *Mon expérience*, 1:411.

93. Loisy to von Hügel, 27 October, 1907, quoted in Loisy, *Mémoires*, 2:585.

to Pius X and his minions—would be, as Houtin put it, to preach "a bitter-sweet homily, . . . going back again to that noble procedure, used commonly by the so-called liberal Catholics, to lecture an authority whose divinity they have already conceded."[94]

So Loisy took up his pen and wrote a scalding missive to Merry del Val, accusing the encylical of defamation and misrepresentation.[95] Then, character-istically, he began gathering materials for a published reply. Like Tyrrell he looked round for allies, and, like Tyrrell, he found very few. Unlike Tyrrell, however, Loisy felt small need for allies. Even so, the Italians Semeria, Minoc-chi, and Buonaiuti, with whom he was in fitful correspondence, appeared stal-wart: the last named indeed was just finishing a powerful rebuttal to *Pascendi*.[96] But when Loisy inquired of Laberthonnière whether "in the encyclical there is anything specifically yours or perhaps Monsieur Blondel's," the answer must have sounded to him like "a bitter-sweet homily":

> You ask me a question [Laberthonnière replied] difficult to answer. Modernism? it is the whole world. . . . Since my name and that of Blondel are associated with the word "immanence," one could say we are alluded to throughout the encyclical. But what is there called "immanentism," in all sincerity I see the exact contrary of what I myself hold. . . . Difficulties arise when people use the method of immanence with such a lack of moderation that they end up saying the supernatural is necessarily demanded by the natural. I have always—and Blondel has too—protested against this under-standing of the method of immanence.[97]

Le Roy evaded a similar request addressed to him, which led Loisy to confide to von Hügel, "These brave *immanentists* have a critical sense worth about two farthings." Later he wondered why he had not likewise chided the baron, who refused to believe that his views were just as much censured in the pages of *Pascendi* as those of his friends and associates. But at the time he refrained and instead contented himself with a laconic observation: "I think Tyrrell and I have furnished the major part of the condemned opinons."[98]

94. Loisy, *Mémoires*, 2:571. Houtin formally left the priesthood in 1912. By that time he had lost faith in Christianity and indeed in theism, but his scholarly interests remained focused on the contemporary religious situation in France. He became bitterly disillusioned with Loisy years before his death in 1926 (see Poulat, *Critique et mystique*, 44–56).

95. Text in Loisy, *Mémoires*, 2:587–91.

96. [Ernesto Buonaiuti], *Il Programma dei Modernisti* (Rome: 1907). See chapter 19.

97. Loisy to Laberthonnière, 1 October, and Laberthonnière to Loisy, 11 October, 1907, in Perrin (ed.), *Laberthonnière et ses amis*, 158–60

98. Loisy to von Hügel, 13 and 14 October, 1907, quoted in Loisy, *Mémoires*, 2:577–80.

Amiable Sentiments and Untenable Persuasions

The Modernist starts with the orthodox but untenable persuasion that Catholicism comprehends all that is good; he adds the heterodox though amiable sentiment that any well-meaning ambition of the mind, any hope, any illumination, any science must be good and therefore compatible with Catholicism. [Then he] bathes himself in idealistic philosophy, he dabbles in liberal politics, he accepts and emulates rationalist exegesis and anti-clerical church history.

—George Santayana (1912)[1]

THERE IS LITTLE DOUBT that *Lamentabili Sane Exitu* and *Pascendi Dominici Gregis*, along with the disciplinary measures Pius X introduced—heightened censorship, diocesan vigilance committees, tighter control over seminary education—accomplished the goals the pope had in mind. The Catholic Modernist movement—to the degree that it had ever been a movement—collapsed into a gaggle of individual voices more or less muted. As long as he lived George Tyrrell attempted to organize an opposition, but Tyrrell did not live long and, as the always realistic Alfred Loisy observed, with his death "Modernism as a party of open resistance to Roman absolutism [ended]."[2]

There is little doubt either that the pope intended his strictures to apply primarily to the church in Italy and France, the places where he discerned the greatest peril. Other Catholic countries appeared to have been relatively immune from the contagion, and England—mostly because of Tyrrell and Friedrich von Hügel—was a special case. In the United States, where theological and biblical studies were carried on at a very rudimentary level, the Modernist crisis caused hardly more than a ripple. A few seminary teachers—one of whom had studied under Loisy at the Institut Catholique of Paris—fell under

1. George Santayana, *Winds of Doctrine* (New York: 1912), 50–51.
2. Loisy, *Mémoires*, 3:127.

suspicion and lost their positions. An eccentric Paulist priest, who later became a Unitarian minister, published a tract and a novel, both with Modernist themes, and these achieved a limited notoriety.[3] Another American, a wealthy man who had left the priesthood some years before *Pascendi*, maintained a close relationship with Albert Houtin.[4] The most celebrated case was probably that of a Dutch-born professor of Scripture at The Catholic University of America who found himself at odds with the biblical commission and who, after a bitter confrontation with Cardinal Merry del Val, was dismissed from the faculty of that institution.[5] The bishops of the United States, still smarting at the rebuff they had received from Leo XIII's *Testem Benevolentiae*,[6] were now more anxious than ever to display their Ultramontane credentials. They noted that *Pascendi* had in passing raised again the specter of "Americanism,"[7] and they kept a close eye upon that rare individual who might have had the interest or the capacity to engage in questionable research. The leading Americanist among them, the aging John Ireland, was indeed acquainted with Louis Duchesne, and he had corresponded occasionally with Loisy and with Marie-Joseph Lagrange.[8] But the archbishop of Saint Paul would have had not the slightest sympathy for the tenets of Modernism, even if he had understood them.[9]

Germany, like England, also was a special case, but for a very different reason. Its intellectual class was a mixture of Catholics and Protestants organized into a unique university culture understood by few in Rome. The pope and the curia looked in that direction with intense misgivings, not only because of the German roots of Kantianism and the higher criticism, but also because there still lingered among German Catholic savants a vein of hostility to Ultramontanism that dated back at least to the days of Döllinger and the Munich Brief of 1863.[10]

Yet hardly anything like the phenomenon *Pascendi* called Modernism was to be found among German Catholics. They had developed, as Newman had, a non-Scholastic approach to apologetics that was perfectly orthodox and that avoided the extreme subjectivism that seemed to beguile those Frenchmen

3. See Ratté, *Three Modernists*, 259–329. William L. Sullivan (1872–1935) was the author of *Letters to His Holiness Pope Pius X, by a Modernist* (Chicago: 1910) and *The Priest: A Tale of Modernism in New England* (Boston: 1914).

4. Houtin, *Mon expérience*, 1:403, 2:18–19.

5. See Ellis, *Gibbons*, 2:170–82, and Gerald Fogarty, *American Catholic Biblical Scholarship* (San Francisco: 1989), 108–16. For the professor's rebuttal, see Henry A. Poels, *A Vindication of My Honor* (Washington, D.C.: 1910).

6. See chapter 11.

7. "With regard to morals, [the Modernists] adopt the principle of the Americanists, that the active virtues are more important than the passive, both in the estimation in which they must be held and in the exercise of them"; see Judge (ed.), *Pascendi*, 85.

8. See, for example, Lagrange, "L'École biblique," 161, and Houtin and Sartiaux, *Loisy*, 64–65.

9. For some details, see R. Scott Appleby, *"Church and Age Unite!" The Modernist Impulse in American Catholicism* (Notre Dame Ind.: 1992). See also Schultenover, *View from Rome*, 39–54. But see also O'Connell, *John Ireland*, 588, note 15.

10. See chapter 2.

who subscribed to Cartesian or Kantian presuppositions. The very proximity of the best higher critics and most learned liberal Protestants, like Harnack, left their Catholic fellow countrymen wary of too much exuberance in biblical research. German Catholicism, moreover, flourishing as it did in a mixed society and a sometimes hostile political climate, possessed an internal cohesion and discipline which, in marked contrast to conditions in Italy or France, automatically discouraged maverick speculation. This is not to say that all was sweetness and light between the Vatican and the church in Germany. But even those thinkers who had recently been sharp thorns in the Roman curia's side— Franz Xaver Kraus and Herman Schell, who had died in 1901 and 1906, respectively—could not have been reasonably associated with the mind-set the encyclical condemned. To be sure, two or three Catholic academics of lesser fame and accomplishment broke with the church over *Pascendi*, but the German bishops stood on solid ground when they assured Pius X that Modernism had made virtually no inroads in their country.[11]

All the more reason, then, for the resentment in Germany at the rigid controls over intellectual life proposed by the encyclical. From university common rooms and episcopal chanceries a chorus of protest arose against the formation of vigilance committees and the insistence on the primacy of neo-Scholasticism. Pius X nevertheless held firm, buoyed up perhaps by the report that Kaiser Wilhelm II was pleased at this papal resolution to uphold traditional Christian principles and by a letter—allegedly inspired within the imperial court—that congratulated the pope for his strong stand and which was signed, curiously enough, by Adolph Harnack, among other non-Catholic scholars. But when, in 1910, the Vatican instituted its most radical measure, designed to "expose" what it maintained was a host of conspiratorial Modernists, German Catholic resistance scored a modest success. The oath against Modernism—to be solemnly sworn by all the clergy at their reception of major orders and to be renewed at each significant professional appointment—committed those who took it to accept the basic pronouncements of the First Vatican Council as well as to submit explicitly to the teaching of *Lamentabili* and *Pascendi*. Of the tens of thousands of clerics worldwide to whom the oath was tendered, only a handful refused it. But in Germany the pope had to exempt professors in the state faculties of theology, the very Germans, one might assume, he was most anxious to have swear.[12]

TAKING INTO ACCOUNT his relatively unsophisticated and parochial antecedents, it may well have been that Pius X worried most about the affect of

---

11. See the excellent summary in Thomas Franklin O'Meara, *Church and Culture: German Catholic Theology, 1860–1914* (Notre Dame, Ind.: 1991), 165–174. See also Rivière, *Modernisme,* 72–82, 287–96, 416–21; Houtin, *Modernisme,* 213–30; and Poulat, *Histoire, dogme,* 17–20. For a different view, see Loome, *Liberal Catholicism,* 103–8.

12. The oath was incorporated into the pontifical letter of 1 September, 1910, *Sacrorum Antistitum,* in *Acta Apostolicae Sedis* (Rome: 1910), 2:655–80 (the oath itself is on pp. 669–72).

Modernism upon those closest at hand, upon Italians, and especially upon Italian priests and seminarians under baleful French influence. If so, the strong measures taken against Tyrrell might be explained on the same grounds, that is, more by reason of his Italian than his English connections. Tyrrell's offensive articles, at any rate, had appeared in the *Corriere della Sera*[13] as well as in the *Giornale d'Italia* and *Il Rinnovamento,* and he had been instrumental earlier in 1907 in the dissemination of a pamphlet published by a group of unnamed Italian priests and considered pernicious and impudent by the Vatican.[14]

As the tumultuous days of 1907 were running out, another instance of this collaboration became public, when Tyrrell translated and published a version of *Il Programma dei Modernisti.* This short treatise, written virtually before the ink on *Pascendi* was dry, also appeared anonymously, though its author was almost certainly Ernesto Buonaiuti.[15] It purported to be a rebuttal to the encyclical—"We present ourselves . . . with a profound sense of the rights of our religious personality before the tribunal of the community to which we belong to answer the accusations alleged against us"—and, whatever its polemical value at the time, it remains perhaps the most succinct and coherent statement of the Modernist position[16] ever attempted. *Il Programma* did not mince words or hide behind equivocation: "The Church and Society can never meet on the basis of those ideas which prevailed at the Council of Trent. . . . The Church cannot, and ought not to, pretend that the *Summa* of Aquinas answers to the exigencies of religious thought in the twentieth century." Only the admission of "evolution [can justify] the notion of the permanence of something divine in the life of the Church."

Consciously reversing the order found in *Pascendi,* Buonaiuti presented first and at considerable length his analysis of the results of the higher criticism applied to the Bible and to the history of the primitive Christian church. His argument was as confident as it was undocumented, and not seldom it descended into glibness: "Often the very same saying of Christ is reported in a different sense in different Gospels. . . . Had God formed the ideas and then transmitted them to the Evangelists, we should have to say that, being dissatisfied with His first attempt, He had repeatedly revised, corrected and rearranged it like any human author." Only toward the end of his tract did Buonaiuti address the agnostic and immanentist roots of Modernism so stressed by *Pascendi,* and here again he offered no compromise. "Philosophical knowledge," he said in his best post-Kantian mode, "is the interpretation of the

13. See chapter 17.

14. *Quello che Vogliamo* (Milan, Italy: 1907), translated by Tyrrell and his Anglican friend, Alfred Lilley, as *What We Want* (London: 1908).

15. See Scoppola, *Crisi Modernista,* 269.

16. "Let us say, once and for all," wrote Buonaiuti, "that we use this term [Modernist] only that we may be understood by those who have learnt it from the encyclical, and that we do not need a new name to describe an attitude which we consider to be simply that of Christians and Catholics who live in harmony with the spirit of their day."

universe according to certain inborn categories of the human mind; . . . religious knowledge . . . is our actual experience of the divine which works in ourselves and in the whole world." As for immanentism, he espoused a position which Laberthonnière, for one, claimed had never been that of the philosophers of *action*:[17] "Religion is shown to be the spontaneous result of irrepressible needs of man's spirit, which find satisfaction in the inward and emotional experience of the presence of God within us."[18]

This forthright if contentious manifesto Tyrrell, displaying once again his remarkable literary gift, put into a lucid and crackling English. "This very beautiful work," he told Bremond, proposes "a religion altogether acceptable and will be received with open arms by a large majority of Anglicans and Protestants; and once the papacy has been thoroughly confounded and discredited, we shall march into the Vatican and install the Baron [von Hügel] upon the throne of Peter as the first layman-pope."[19]

Neither the serious nor the jocular parts of this prophecy were fulfilled. Buonaiuti himself, after publishing another, more personal testament,[20] was suspended in 1910. The year before Romolo Murri, already suspended, was excommunicated *nominatim*, because in defiance of canonical restrictions he had campaigned for (and been elected to) a seat in the Chamber of Deputies. He married in 1912. Salvatore Minocchi left the priesthood in 1909 and married in 1911, the year Antonio Fogazzaro died. The unreconstructed liberal, Bishop Bonomelli of Cremona, was among the mourners at the deathbed of Fogazzaro, "the last Catholic of the romantic school," who received the sacraments of the dying from the hands of a Franciscan friar.[21] Giovanni Genocchi, ever the politique, survived severe attacks upon him as a crypto-Modernist and returned to service in the Vatican diplomatic corps in which he had made his reputation originally. Giovanni Semeria, the eloquent Barnabite, though protected for a time by Pius X's personal affection—the pope even allowed Semeria to swear the oath against Modernism with reservations—was nevertheless suspended from priestly functions in 1912. Cardinal Mercier[22] provided refuge for him in Belgium, and then in 1915, when Italy entered the war, he returned home to become a popular military chaplain. After the war he devoted the rest of his life to caring for Italian children orphaned by the carnage of 1915–18.[23]

17. See chapter 18.

18. [Ernesto Buonaiuti], *The Programme of Modernism* (London: 1908), 1, 5–6, 21, 60, 96, 100.

19. Tyrrell to Bremond, November 6 [1907], and n. d. [1907], in Louis-David (ed.), *Lettres de Tyrrell*, 272, 280.

20. [Ernesto Buonaiuti], *Lettere di un Prete Modernisti* (Rome: 1908).

21. Gallarati-Scotti, *Fogazzaro*, 305–9.

22. See note 84, in chapter 17.

23. See chapter 11. Semeria died in 1931, Genocchi in 1926, Minocchi in 1943. Buonaiuti lingered formally within the church until 1926, when he was excommunicated. He died in 1946. Murri died in 1944, but not before he was reconciled to the church by his old schoolfellow, Eugenio Pacelli (Pius XII).

The papal wrath, however, was not reserved for individuals such as these, who, whatever their deserts in the matter, enjoyed no particular standing within clerical officialdom. That could hardly be said of the cardinal-arch-bishop of Milan, head of the greatest see in the Catholic world. Andrea Ferrari had held that post since 1894. During his tenure he had shown himself learned, pious, and alert to the spiritual needs of the people in his vast jurisdic-tion. He had steered clear of politics for the most part, though he publicly rebuked his suffragan, Bonomelli—with whom otherwise he was on friendly terms—when the latter published a pamphlet praising the separation of church and state in France.[24] In the spring of 1911 a Catholic newspaper in Venice charged that the major seminary in Milan was rife with Modernist tendencies. The cardinal retorted bitterly in the press to what he maintained were groundless and irresponsible accusations. He repeated his rebuttal in a speech to the seminarians, one of whom sent a stenographic copy of his remarks to Rome. The pope reacted by dispatching a letter of reprimand to Ferrari, in which he described the Milanese situation as "the gravest sorrow of my pon-tificate." The cardinal was further informed that if he came to Rome Pius X would decline to see him. Shortly afterward administration of the seminary was removed from Ferrari's control and placed in the hands of apostolic visi-tors, appointed directly by the Vatican.[25]

L'AFFAIRE FERRARI, however painful and embarrassing it may have been for the cardinal, had no long-lasting effects. But it proved symptomatic of the atmosphere of suspicion and even panic that pervaded the Vatican bureaucracy for the remainder of Pius X's pontificate and beyond. Here was an instance of the green wood and the dry: if the archbishop of Milan was not beyond the reach of casual denunciation, what were the prospects of lesser ecclesiastical mortals?[26] The strong men in the papal entourage—Merry del Val, Gaetano de Lai (a cardinal in 1907), Louis Billot (a cardinal in 1911)[27]—were all con-vinced that Modernism posed an imminent and mortal threat to the church. They also believed that the danger was not restricted to a few highly visible intellectuals expounding complex scientific and philosophical theories. Far more worrisome in their judgment—because far more numerous—were the fellow travelers, so to speak, the sympathizers, the closet Modernists who hid

---

24. Giuseppe Gallina, *Il Problema religioso nel Risorgimento e il Pensiero di Geremia Bonomelli* (Rome: 1974), 397–400

25. See P. Zerbi, "Ferarri (Andrea)," *Dictionnaire d'histoire et de géographie ecclesiatiques* (Paris: 1967) 6:1203–10, and Carlo Snider, *L'Episcopato del Cardinale Andrea Ferrari*, 2 vols. (Venice, Italy: 1982), 2:264–65, 312–15. Ironcially enough the process of Ferrari's canonization began in 1951, the year Pius X was beatified.

26. For Ferrari's treatment of the alleged Modernists of *Il Rinnovamento*, see chapter 18.

27. For Billot, see note 46, in chapter 18. De Lai (1853–1928), a lifelong curial official, became secretary (the pope himself was prefect) of the powerful Consistorial Congregation in 1908. See Lorenzo Bedeschi, *La Curia Romana durante la Crisi Modernista* (Parma, Italy: 1968), 87–94.

their radical infidelity beneath an outward show of compliance. What in fact was the difference between a Catholic Modernist and a Catholic modernizer, between, say, a disciple of Loisy and a member of Marc Sangnier's Le Sillon, which had evolved from its simple beginnings[28] into a more specifically political movement? Was it not inevitable that an alliance should have been formed between the external enemies of the church—Freemasons, anticlerical politicians, and liberals generally—and those sons of the church who secretly lusted after compromise with modern culture at whatever cost?

Such rhetorical questions raised by curial functionaries would have mattered little had the pope himself not asked them, and had he not already answered them to his own satisfaction. Pius X's relentless pursuit, not so much of acknowledged Modernists as of the Modernists' putative allies, appears startlingly inconsistent with the ordinary and much romanticized image of the saintly Giuseppe Sarto who, as pope, brought the Eucharistic Christ to little children and who concerned himself with enhancing the beauty and significance of liturgical worship. It was indeed his anti-Modernist crusade—the mean-spirited witch-hunt he consciously unleashed—which stood forty years later as the single greatest barrier to Pius X's canonization.[29] An explanation for this seeming aberration remains elusive. Perhaps it is somehow related to the pope's understanding of the infinitive in the motto he had chosen for his pontificate, "To Restore All Things in Christ."

However that may be, the figure who now strode to center stage was the sinister Umberto Benigni.[30] His physical characteristics—grossly fat, awkward and shambling, his small, cunning eyes veiled by gold-rimmed spectacles—made him look almost like the caricature of what he now became, the spy-master of a ragtag crew of informers and fanatics.[31] As early as 1904 Benigni had described the collusion he saw undergirding the internal plot against the church: "Nothing is easier than to recognize a Modernist philosopher of *action*, because he will always sympathize with Loisy, though he has never read a word of Loisy's. Similarly, a Loisyist always applauds the social theory of Christian democracy, though he knows nothing about it. All one need do is to mingle a little in our Catholic world, and to read the lines, and between the lines, of certain journals to get at the heart of this business."[32] And six years later he elaborated the point:

The danger of Modernist propaganda is always present, and it is all the more to be feared because it is often in a fluid state, inconsistent, so as to be overlooked by those

---

28. See chapter 9.

29. For an analysis of the documentation, see Poulat (ed.), *Intégrisme*, 45–55. As an instance, see the printed (but unpublished) "Novissima Positio super Virtutibus" (Rome: 1950), in which Pius X's actions in this regard are defended, not altogether persuasively. I owe my possession of this document to my former colleague, the late Niels Krogh Rasmussen, O.P.

30. See chapter 17.

31. See Rivière, *Modernisme*, 469.

32. Quoted in Houtin, *Modernisme*, 99.

who are unprepared for it, who do not pay close attention, who are seduced by their own optimism to see everything in a rosy light. It is a tactic employed by the most cunning [Modernists] to speak of the "failure" of Modernism. Quite frankly, they want us to go to sleep. . . . So one sees excellent Catholics allowing themselves to be [favorably] impressed by the articles of our adversaries which "admit" the failure of Modernism . . . [and which then] furiously and scornfully accuse Rome and those faithful to her of seeing Modernists "everywhere," of suspecting good people because their opinions are a little venturesome. . . . Good Catholics must beware of falling into this trap. Modernism spreads and organizes by means of the malice of some and by the naïveté and carelessness of others. . . . More than ever it is necessary to struggle against the enemy who hides himself, masks himself, who tries clandestinely [*sous main*] to achieve a work of destruction.[33]

This is the doctrine Pope Pius X made his own.

At the time of *Pascendi* Benigni was still formally attached to the secretariat of state. But now his gifts and experience as a journalist came to the fore. He put together within the Vatican what might be called a bureau of propaganda that served the double purpose of providing information about Modernists or alleged Modernists to interested periodicals and of receiving such information from sympathetic correspondents all over Europe. Out of this initiative a conglomerate of anti-Modernist publications quickly developed, one of which, *La Riscossa* of Venice, launched the attack upon Cardinal Ferrari. The flagship of this journalistic flotilla was Benigni's own *Corrispondenza Romana*, founded in May 1907. By the end of 1909 this weekly collection of articles and bulletins had been converted into a French-language journal, the *Correspondance de Rome*. The linguistic shift was indicative of Benigni's judgment as to where the really lethal danger lay: "The Modernism that has been finally vanquished by Pius X," he wrote, "is doctrinal and organized Modernism. What remains is the state of the Modernist spirit, the modernizers, of whom we shall not be rid except by the force of a more serious theological instruction and by ceaselessly recalling Catholics to those objective truths that are the very foundations of the church."[34]

Benigni's voyage was not all smooth sailing. The secretary of state, his nominal superior, disliked him and his methods intensely, and the leadership of the Society of Jesus, many of whose fathers were being entangled in his web, was gradually alienated from him.[35] At the end of 1912, the *Correspondance* was suppressed, and twenty months before that, due to German pressure—the anti-Modernist campaign had even been attacked on the floor of the Reichstag[36]—Benigni himself was forced to give up his post in the secretariat of state. Nobody believed the official explanation that he had resigned because of ill-

33. Quoted in *La Croix*, 12 August, 1910.
34. Quoted in Poulat, *Intégrisme*, 184.
35. See Aubert, "La crise moderniste," *Nouvelle histoire*, 5:215–17.
36. See Poulat, *Modernistica*, 52.

health, and everybody noted that Pius X promptly awarded him the honorary
title of protonotary apostolic. And though his review was gone after 1912, the
international news service he had instituted circulated the desired notices and
commentary even more widely than before. Visitors from abroad, moreover,
continued to attest to the power he obviously wielded within the curia,[37] while
the disapproval of Cardinal Merry del Val appeared to have been nicely check-
mated by the powerful support of Cardinal De Lai.

The only support that mattered in the last analysis was the pope's, and that
Benigni could count upon as he inaugurated the most malevolent of his anti-
Modernist enterprises. In 1909 or perhaps a little later—the exact date is disputed—he established the Sodality of Saint Pius V—the Sodalitium Pianum—an organization designed to expose crypto-Modernists and to denounce
them and their activities to the Roman authorities. This secret society, with
its pseudo-Masonic trappings—it even devised a fantastic cover-name, La Sa-
pinière, "the piney wood"—seems almost comic in retrospect, but it was far
from funny at the time. Grown out of the network of stringers Benigni had
established to supply material for his journalistic ventures, the sodality provided an opportunity for all those who cared to to label as Modernists their
bishops, parish priests, professors, local editors, or indeed anyone with whom
they disagreed.

No one was safe. The cardinal of Vienna was accused of "sadly" loose morals
as well as doctrinal transgressions. The cardinal of Paris, Richard's successor,
was delated for being soft on Modernism. So was Cardinal Mercier. So were the
Jesuits who staffed the *Études*. The Dominican theologians at the University of
Fribourg in Switzerland constituted a veritable "soup of Modernist culture."[38]
The files of the sodality eventually bulged with the names of such alleged male-
factors,[39] whose guilt was maintained simply by the fact that they had been
denounced. There was something pathological about this campaign or maybe
something simply wicked; in either case, it forcibly reminds one of Stanley
Baldwin's famous remark about the reckless extravagances of a partisan press:
"Power without responsibility [is] the prerogative of the harlot throughout the
ages." But the otherwise saintly and simple man who was responsible never
grasped the reality that employing such scattergun tactics served merely to
dishearten his natural allies, who were as anxious as he to protect the church's
traditional teaching. "I have presented to the Holy Father," De Lai wrote Benigni as late as 1913, "the program of the *Sodalitium Pianum*. . . . The Pope

37. See Houtin, *Modernisme*, 211, 261.

38. See the list reproduced in Nicolas Fontaine, *Saint-Siège, "Action française" et "Catholiques intégraux"* (Paris: 1928), 143–44. "Fontaine" was the nome de plume of Louis Canet (1883–1958), career
government bureaucrat, friend of Laberthonnière (whose posthumous works he edited), and also friend
of Loisy (whose executor he was—see Prologue).

39. These began their passage into the public forum when German soldiers—part of the occupation
garrison in Belgium—inadvertently stumbled upon them in the spring of 1915. See Poulat (ed.),
Intégrisme, 11–15.

has approved and blessed this initiative, and he assures you and your associates his prayers that your work may redound to the glory of God and the well-being of souls."[40]

In France, it was inevitable that a kind of unholy alliance should have been formed between Benigni's "integrists"—so-called because they described themselves as defenders of the "integral" Catholic faith—and the activist cadres of Charles Maurras's Action française. Benigni had never made a secret of his contempt, indeed his hatred, for all the manifestations of political liberalism—"the white international" of Christian democracy, he used to say, merely set the table for "the red international" of socialism[41]—while Maurras, despite his personal atheism, never flagged in his conviction that the Catholic church in its Gallican form remained as one of the essential buttresses of French culture and civilization: "Une loi, un roi, une foi."[42]

This association occasioned more than a little consternation within the Vatican, where Maurras's blatantly pagan published works fell routinely under the examination of the Congregation of the Index. When Pius X was confronted with incontrovertible evidence that Maurras's consistently proclaimed ideas, no less than the violence perpetrated by the thugs under his orders, stood in direct contradiction to Catholic teaching and therefore deserved explicit censure—"The pitcher that goes too often to the well at last gets broken," was Merry del Val's homely image—the pope could not but agree. Nevertheless, beguiled perhaps by the evangelical assurance that "anyone who is not against you is for you,"[43] he reserved to himself the precise moment at which the condemnation of Maurras and his movement should be made public, a moment that never arrived during the pontiff's lifetime.[44] Meanwhile, in 1910, a cabal of integrists and Maurrasians engineered the condemnation of Le Sillon, the only organization capable of competing with Action française for allegiance of French Catholic youth. Marc Sangnier immediately submitted. "Since I am, and intend to remain, above all a Roman Catholic," he said in a public interview, "the question does not even arise whether I shall or shall not submit to the discipline of the church."[45]

IT WAS WHAT LOISY CALLED, with justice, "the black terror."[46] The ever-candid Archbishop Mignot, who dubbed it the "white terror," protested to Rome against this "combisme ecclésiastique," this "irresponsible and occult

40. Quoted in Poulat (ed.), *Intégrisme*, 114.
41. See Poulat, *Modernistica*, 53.
42. See chapter 16.
43. Luke 9:50.
44. See Weber, *Action Française*, 221–22. Action française was condemned by Pius XI in 1926.
45. See Alec R. Vidler, *A Variety of Catholic Modernists* (Cambridge: 1970), 214–18. See also Lester R. Kurtz, *The Politics of Heresy. The Modernist Crisis in Roman Catholicism* (Berkeley, Calif.: 1986), 79–82.
46. Loisy, *Mémoires*, 3:194.

power installed next to the legitimate authority in the church and even to a degree supplanting it. . . . The most innocent words and deeds, odiously parodied, have been presented as though they were acts of treason to the faith or to the hierarchy. The victim can do nothing but yield, because it is impossible to establish his innocence against a secret and anonymous calumniator."[47] Only in 1921, the year the Sodalitium Pianum was exposed and then suppressed by Pius X's successor, did Maurice Blondel become fully aware of the scope of Benigni's operation; he then expressed himself in characteristically pietistic and personal terms:

Christ truly will be in agony till the end of the world. If there is any solace for us in learning how and by whom the anti-Modernist campaign has been too often conducted, what sorrow remains in seeing the kind of methods employed and the kind of people authority allowed to manipulate it, indeed, to dominate it! I suffer truly at the intellectual and moral baseness of these buffoons [*comparses*] become quasi-officials, and at the mentality of our leaders who did not realize the vileness of those they listened to and employed. It seems doubtful to me that anyone operating such an agency of delation with so much *false* zeal could have himself believed *sincerely* in its principles and jurisdiction.[48]

Sangnier, Mignot, and Blondel who, each in his own way, persisted in discerning through the gloom of the moment a brighter vision of the church, appeared to suffer more from "the black terror" than the phlegmatic Loisy did. And there were others. Early in 1908 Pierre Batiffol was dismissed from the rectorship of the Institut Catholique of Toulouse. For some years, by reason of his prickly temperament, he had had bad relations with many of his professors, and his reputation as a liberal had alienated other influential persons, including some who were intimates of the local archbishop. But, asserted Mignot, "it is Rome that has done it, though not in a brutal fashion—the curia weighs its words in order to be able to say it was misunderstood if its initiative turns out badly—but in a fashion that leaves no room for error."[49] It did not matter, Batiffol's friend Lagrange commented bitterly, that the rector of Toulouse had been among the first to write energetically against the errors of Loisy and Tyrrell or that he had enthusiastically accepted *Lamentabili* and *Pascendi*. "He had been at first much more optimistic than I," Lagrange recalled, "about the dangers we might encounter if a reaction were unloosed."[50] Batiffol returned to Paris and resumed his former position as chaplain at the Collège Sainte-Barbe. Highly influential works of historical scholarship flowed from his pen in suc-

47. Mignot to Ferrata, 4 October, 1914, in Fontaine, *Saint-Siège*, 126–27. " 'Combisme ecclesiastique,' so-called in memory of the hypocritical persecution carried on against Catholics by Prime Minister Combes."

48. Blondel to Mourret, 26 April, 1921, quoted in Poulat (ed.), *Intégrisme*, 41.

49. Mignot to Loisy, 5 January, 1908, in Loisy, *Mémoires*, 2:602–3.

50. Lagrange, "L'École biblique," 174–75.

ceeding years; the first of them, published in 1909, he dedicated to Mother Church, *Matri Ecclesiae*.[51]

Lagrange, over whom the birds of prey had long been hovering,[52] soon had a crisis of his own to face. As in Batiffol's case, the assault issued from the Modernist scare coupled with an academic turf war: in this instance, the age-old rivalry between Jesuits and Dominicans. Early in the summer of 1912, "l'année terrible," Lagrange was not reappointed prior of Saint-Étienne in Jerusalem—"the father general found me too weak" to be an effective religious superior, "too impressionable, too volatile." Rumors quickly spread that he had been discharged from that post. Substantiation of these reports appeared to come at the end of July when the Consistorial Congregation—Cardinal De Lai's department—issued a decree which, on grounds of their relativist tendencies, banned from use in seminary curricula books by two eminent Protestant biblical scholars and "several writings of Père Lagrange."[53] The vagueness of this designation made specific rebuttal impossible, but Lagrange, intent upon saving what he could of the school and the journal into which he had poured his lifeblood, immediately dispatched his submission to Rome. He also proposed that the *Revue biblique* be converted into a *Revue palestinienne et orientale* and that he himself step down, at least for a time, from the directorship of the École in Jerusalem.

Pius X was immensely pleased by Lagrange's "beautiful letter," which he directed to be published. Meanwhile, on September 5, Lagrange departed Jerusalem for Paris, where he settled with several other Dominicans in a small apartment on the rue de Bac. There he had much restless leisure to contemplate his predicament, brought on, he believed, by the intrigues of the Jesuits whose ambitions included establishing a hegemony over Catholic biblical studies. To be sure, not all Dominicans supported Lagrange—the French provincial was particularly hostile—nor did all Jesuits reproach him: Père Grandmaison,[54] who was himself being harassed by the integrists, went out of his way to call at the rue de Bac and assure Lagrange of his good opinion of him and his work. In the end, however, it was Lagrange's patience and docility—together with the timely intervention at Rome by influential elements of the French hierarchy—that won him reprieve. In June 1913 he returned to Jerusalem and resumed his work with his students and his beloved brethren; he did so with the personal blessing of Pius X, who nevertheless suggested that out of prudence he might consider concentrating his future researches on the New Testament. That advice Père Lagrange abided by, and, as his École and *Revue* flourished again, he produced over the next quarter of a century those monumental studies of the Four Gospels upon which rests his scholarly fame. But

---

51. Batiffol died in 1929. See Lagrange's obituary, *La vie intellectuelle* (March 1929).
52. See chapters 12 and 17.
53. The text is printed in the English translation of Braun, *Lagrange* (Milwaukee: 1962), 303.
54. See chapters 13 and 14.

all the while there lay gathering dust in his files a reminder of harsh times past: his commentary on Genesis, which was never published.[55]

Less supple a personality than Lagrange, or perhaps more committed as a philosopher to views apparently proscribed by Pius X, Lucien Laberthonnière found it impossible to fit himself smoothly into a post-*Pascendi* world. Nor was he a man, like Lagrange, who could reasonably expect champions to intercede for him in high Vatican places. He swore the anti-Modernist oath when it was tendered to him, and he was never personally censured. But two more of his books were placed on the Index in 1913, the same year that witnessed the disappearance—because of official displeasure inspired, it was commonly said, by Charles Maurras—of the journal he had edited since 1905, the *Annales de philosophie chrétienne*.[56] The heaviest blow fell in 1916 when, after a process initiated by his fellow Oratorians, Laberthonnière was in effect forbidden to publish. He obeyed the prohibition, though his posthumous publications demonstrate that his commitment to the intellectual wars had not diminished.[57] He even became during the 1920s a ghostwriter for preachers at Notre Dame. An implacable foe of Action française, he lived long enough to rejoice at the condemnation of that movement by the Vatican. But he lived long enough too to endure the sorrow of personal and professional alienation from Maurice Blondel, who, he came to believe, had betrayed their *philosophie d'action* to the hated Scholastics. Étienne Gilson remembered when, as a student at the Sorbonne, he occasionally rode a trolley with Père Laberthonnière who invariably harangued the younger man about the evils inflicted upon the church and upon mankind by Thomas Aquinas.[58]

The estrangement of the two comrades-in-arms was, if anything, more painful for the intensely sensitive Blondel than for Laberthonnière, who was always contentious if not quarrelsome. Blondel did indeed modify his epistemology in later years, at least to the extent that he admitted much more than he had in *L'action* and its companion pieces the force of abstract reasoning. But this hardly made of him a full-blown Thomist or an Aristotelian, and according to his own lights he remained faithful to a Platonic and Cartesian orientation. Even after failing eyesight forced his retirement from teaching in 1927, he continued to work relentlessly, turning out tome after tome of speculation which, however dense and difficult, created a small but dedicated band of disciples. He also continued to practice his Catholicism at a level of personal fervor that smacked almost of the mystical. "O Jesus," he prayed shortly before

55. See Lagrange, "L'École biblique," 200–215, Braun, *Lagrange*, 125–27, and Guitton, *Lagrange*, 83–93. Lagrange died in Jeruslaem on 10 March, 1938, forty-eight years to the day after he had first arrived in the Holy City.

56. See chapter 17.

57. See note 38, above.

58. See Étienne Gilson, *Le philosophe et la théologie* (Paris: 1962), 60–61, and, for a summary, see Beillevert (ed.), *Laberthonnière*, 25–42. Laberthonnière died in 1932.

he died, "you have experienced upon Calvary a sorrowful and bloody death. You have willed that you should be immolated throughout time upon the altars erected all over the world, in order to be with dying humanity and to accompany us through our brutally difficult journey. Death is hard only for those who have something to atone for and who have not detached themselves from this world. That is only just."[59]

No one ever accused Louis Duchesne of following a mystical vocation. The wily historian, in the wake of *Pascendi*, carefully guarded his reputation for orthodoxy and kept his peace, at least in public. He could not but reflect upon the ruined careers of his two favorite students, Batiffol and Loisy, but, even so, he was not one to cry over spilt milk. In 1910 he attained the highest honor his native country could bestow upon an intellectual, election to the Académie française. But he had scarcely had a chance to savor his status as an "Immortal" when, two years later, his magnum opus, the three-volume *L'histoire ancienne de l'église chrétienne*, was placed upon the Index of forbidden books. It was as though the birds of thirty years before had come home to roost.

Shortly after this bitter sentence Duchesne went on holiday to Egypt. One morning he met by chance on a Cairo street an acquaintance from Paris.

"Monseigneur," the man said, "what brings you to Egypt?"

"My dear fellow," replied Duchesne, "I am waiting for the death of King Herod."[60]

ALFRED LOISY remained of the opinion that Duchesne, whatever his public protestations, was in fact an unbeliever, that the historian never took seriously, among other things, "the reality of the Virgin Birth and the Resurrection of Christ."[61] It is not likely, however, that at the beginning of 1908 Duchesne was much on the exegete's mind. At home in Ceffonds, he had been absorbed during the preceding weeks in examining the proofs of his formal reply to *Lamentabili* and *Pascendi*[62] and of his long-delayed critique of the Synoptic Gospels. Both books went on sale at the end of January. "I was very tranquil," he remembered.[63] He was also quite delighted at the news of the fall of Pierre Batiffol:

Such was the reward of [Batiffol's] magnificent orthodoxy which he had manifested by an immediate adherence to *Pascendi*. The testimonies of this orthodoxy were particu-

---

59. Blondel, *Carnets intimes*, 2:387. Blondel died in 1949. He was never interfered with by the ecclesiastical authorites.

60. This anecdote was told to me in 1956 by my mentor, Philip Hughes. Duchesne died in 1922. See chapter 4.

61. Loisy, *Mémoires*, 3:423, This opinion was voiced in rebuttal to von Hügel's obituary notice for Duchesne, which had praised the historian's deep faith.

62. See note 31, in chapter 18.

63. Loisy, *Mémoires*, 2:592.

larly exuberant. . . . Monseigneur Batiffol, after his disgrace, did not cease to be as magnificently orthodox as before. Rome, however, never pardoned him for the crime of Modernism which he did not commit. Perhaps it had been suggested to the authorities that the orthodoxy of Monseigneur Batiffol, although always magnificent and professionally virginal, was not altogether certain.[64]

Loisy greeted the passing of another nemesis of his with similar sarcasm. "Full of days and merits," he wrote, François de la Vergne Cardinal Richard, archbishop of Paris, died in his ninetieth year on January 27. The vast crowds of Parisians who jammed the funeral mass at Notre Dame five days later did not include any government officials, but many people entertained the hope that Léon-Adolphe Amette, who as coadjutor automatically succeeded to the see, might prove more willing than Richard had been to seek improved relations with the state.[65] Even Loisy admitted that Amette, who had been a friend of Marcel Hébert[66] since their student days together at Saint-Sulpice, was relatively liberal, "a pious and moderate priest," but nevertheless he considered the new archbishop at heart a chancery hack who would do whatever Rome told him to do.

This judgment was not really fair to Amette, who, in the light of the course of action Loisy himself had chosen, had little choice in what followed. The publication of *Simples réflexions* was sufficient cause to invoke the penalties of the *motu proprio* of the preceding November,[67] and anyway there is no reason to assume that the archbishop, however "moderate" he may have been, harbored any doubts about the appropriateness of imposing them in this case. The canonical machinery in any event began to grind on February 14 when Amette formally forbade the reading of Loisy's books "under the pain not only of grave sin but of excommunication reserved to the Sovereign Pontiff."[68] On February 22 Merry del Val wrote the bishop of Langres—Ceffonds was in his diocese—that "the Holy Father, wishing to give proof of his magnanimity and, if possible, . . . to save a soul," asked the bishop to direct "a final, formal, and peremptory admonition" to Loisy that unless he submitted within ten days he would be excommunicated *nominatim*. The bishop did so, and Loisy replied with cold courtesy: "Monseigneur, the formal threat of excommunication changes nothing. . . . It is impossible for me in all honesty to offer the retraction and submission demanded by the Sovereign Pontiff." On March 7, 1908—the eighteenth anniversary of his reception of the doctorate from the hands of Maurice d'Hulst[69]—the Holy Office issued a decree excommunicat-

---

64. Loisy, *Mémoires*, 2:602–4.
65. Hausser, *Paris au jour le jour*, 288–89.
66. See chapter 10. Hébert died in 1916. At his direction the stone over his grave bore only the words *In Spe* (In Hope).
67. See chapter 18.
68. Text in Loisy, *Choses passées*, 395–97.
69. See chapter 4.

ing "the priest Alfred Loisy" personally and by name and declaring him *vitandus*.[70]

"My first reaction, which is still very much with me," Loisy said five years afterward, "was that of infinite relief."[71] He immediately exchanged the soutane for sober secular garb, and within two months he began to negotiate for a position at the prestigious Collège de France.[72] The competition was keen and the process of selection complicated and prolonged, and not until Easter week of 1909 was Loisy named professor of the History of Religions. On April 24 he delivered his inaugural lecture on the nature of sacrifice in the various religious traditions. Thus he became a colleague of giants like Durkheim and Bergson and, later, of Édouard Le Roy, with whom he maintained friendly relations despite the latter's continued fervent dedication to Catholicism.[73]

Ceffonds remained Loisy's primary place of residence, but during academic terms he lived in a modest second-floor flat at number 4, rue des Écoles.[74] He needed only to walk a few blocks up that gently rising street, lined with small shops, until he reached the corner of the rue Jean de Beauvais. There, inside a fence of iron spokes, stood a statue of Ronsard, and behind the statue the squat, grey, three-storied building that housed the Collège de France. He needed only to climb the incongruously pompous stone stairway and enter the courtyard to feel the comforting presence of the ghost of Renan, whose sublime self-assurance Alfred Loisy had brought to life again. "The Catholicism of the pope being neither reformable nor acceptable, another Catholicism will have to come into being, a humane Catholicism, in no way conditioned by the pontifical institution or the traditional forms of Roman Catholicism."[75]

THAT SAME SELF-ASSURANCE made Loisy impatient and censorious toward Friedrich von Hügel and other erstwhile associates—except perhaps Archbishop Mignot[76]—who were not prepared to join him in seeking out "another Catholicism." If the baron held the same views as Loisy—"he remained a Modernist till the end," the exegete maintained[77]—why did he not display the courage of his convictions? Tyrrell was not so much put off by von Hügel's posture as puzzled and slightly shocked by it:

---

70. Texts in Houtin and Sartiaux, *Loisy*, 151. *Vitandus* means "he must be avoided," that is, the faithful must have no relations with the excommunicated person. This was "major" excommunication as distinguished from "minor," which was imposed on Tyrrell in October 1907. See chapter 18.

71. Loisy, *Choses passées*, 367.

72. See chapter 1.

73. In 1921 Le Roy succeeded to the chair in the Collège de France up till then held by Bergson. He was elected to the Académie Française in 1945 and died nine years later.

74. See Prologue.

75. Loisy, *Mémoires*, 2:585.

76. Though much preoccupied after 1914 by the war, and much consoled by the policies of Pius X's successor, Benedict XV, Mignot remained in friendly contact with Loisy till his death in 1918.

77. Loisy, *Mémoires*, 2:650. See also 3:12–20.

Wonderful man! Nothing is true; but the sum total of nothings is sublime! Christ was not merely ignorant but a *tête brulé* [*sic*]; Mary was not merely not a virgin, but an unbeliever and a rather unnatural mother; the Eucharist was a Pauline invention—yet [von Hügel] makes his daily visit to the Blessed Sacrament and for all I know tells his beads devoutly. Bremond's French logic finds it all very perplexing.[78]

The baron was disturbed by the excommunication of Loisy but hardly surprised by it. Ever ready to grasp at straws, he rejoiced in the newly reissued *L'Évangile et l'Église*: here was the Loisy he desperately wanted, not the Loisy of *Simples réflexions*. But their author was having none of it: "To tell the truth, I reprinted the first of my little [red] books, because there was a steady demand for it. . . . Ecclesiastical authority itself has ruined the whole apologetic of *L'Évangile et l'Église*."[79] The baron had to content himself by sending to Ceffonds a wire that promised "continuous affection, respect, sympathy, and . . . conviction that we all act with strength of chivalrous moderation."

What von Hügel may have meant by "strength of chivalrous moderation" remains veiled by the overall enigma of his use of the English language. What he surely did not mean was the position taken by Wilfrid Ward, who declared in the leader he wrote for the *Dublin Review*: "When the Supreme Authority has just made a momentous decision, its public discussion is no more compatible with discipline and loyalty than would have been the public discussion of the tactics of Lord Roberts or General Buller during the Boer War." But absolute acceptance of a decision of the "Supreme Authority"—even if reluctantly accepted, even if accepted with all the nuances and safeguards Ward had learned from his beloved Newman—could not satisfy the consistently inconsistent baron: "[A] Catholic will, or ought, to feel such acceptance, or non-criticism, to be *presumptively* due; it is impossible, I think, in view of history, to maintain that there cannot be, that there have not been exceptions."[80]

The difference between the two old friends, however, went deeper than a mere question of tactics. In the same article Ward had briskly dissected Modernism as "a body of thought . . . the root principle [of which] . . . is subjectivism in religion—the identification of religion with sentiment or emotion rather than with belief in objective truth, issuing in the conception of a deity immanent in man and not transcendent, and of dogmatic formulae as no longer the expression of facts—of the dogmatic truths of revelation—but as the mind's reflection on its subjective religious experience." The "most conspicuous offence" engendered by this system, he added, was the denial of Christ's divinity.[81] Ward had to pay a heavy emotional cost for his stance, as the baron did for his. Complete reconciliation between them was no longer thinkable.

---

78. Tyrrell to Lilley, 14 August, 1908, quoted in Sagovsky, *Tyrrell*, 246. See also the imaginary dialogue in De la Bedoyere, *Hügel*, 214–15. *Tête brulée* could mean "hothead."

79. Loisy, *Mémoires*, 2:649.

80. Von Hügel to Ward, 10 February, 1908, quoted in Barmann, *Hügel*, 214.

81. [Wilfrid Ward], "The Encyclical 'Pascendi,' " *Dublin Review* 142 (January 1908): 1–3.

Josephine Ward, for her part, brushed aside her husband's and the baron's painful ruminations and maneuverings. "Modernism," she said, "was a spirit, a tone, a temper of mind. . . . That spirit, tone and temper of mind had become unmistakably mutinous. . . . The Encyclical *Pascendi* was the riot act that was read to the mutineers."[82]

AT THE END of 1908 von Hügel's magnum opus appeared at last. *The Mystical Element of Religion as Studied in Saint Catherine of Genoa and Her Friends*—two thick volumes and nearly a thousand pages of print—was the fruit of years of intense labor, and it clearly demonstrated that the kind of arduous, detailed intellectual inquiry he so freely urged upon others he was capable of accomplishing himself. The book also proved that the baron was not so distracted by the controversies he was intimately involved in that he could not set them aside in order to deal exhaustively with extremely esoteric subject matter. But the Teutonic discipline and thoroughness on display in *The Mystical Element* was not matched by readability, and one wonders if its prose would have been intelligible at all had not that superb stylist George Tyrrell gone over the manuscript word by word.[83]

Tyrrell was much in the baron's thoughts as he riffled the pages of his new book. The year just past had been a time of feverish activity for his Irish friend, who, without the slightest political gifts, was trying to shore up a movement of which he, willy-nilly, was a leader. He traveled incessantly, from Storrington to Clapham, then to France and back again, to stay for a while with friends in London. He wrote public letters to newspapers, private letters to disturbed friends. He counseled priests troubled in their faith, and he fended off well-disposed Anglicans and continental Old Catholics who urged him to find relief by joining their communities. He wondered fretfully when his "minor" excommunication would be converted, like Loisy's, into a "major" one. His world was collapsing around him, and the turmoil in his mind matched that in his heart. But, despite all, he had one more strong arrow in his quiver.

In the spring of 1908 Cardinal Mercier had written a pastoral letter to the Catholics of the archdiocese of Malines, a section of which he had devoted to a criticism of "the English priest Tyrrell" as a crypto-Protestant.[84] The superficiality of the treatment—a pastoral letter is of course not a scholarly document—from a person who had once offered to give him refuge[85] moved Tyrrell to high passion, and it provided him an opportunity to write what was in effect his last testament. *Medievalism* took the form of a long letter to Mercier. It was, in Loisy's judgment, the best book Tyrrell ever wrote.[86] However that

82. Quoted in Ward, *The Wilfrid Wards*, 2:558. Wilfrid Ward's magisterial biography of Newman appeared in 1912. He died four years later. Josephine Hope Ward died in 1932.

83. See chapter 17.

84. Désiré Joseph Mercier, *Le Modernisme* (Paris: 1909), 32–34.

85. See chapter 17.

86. Loisy, *Mémoires*, 3:131.

may be, it was certainly, for all its harsh polemics, an eloquent statement of what its author had come to believe. "Can it be true that the Church," he asked Mercier rhetorically, "is to fall the prey of a selfish and godless bureaucracy? that the gates of hell so long resisted are at last to prevail against her and shut her up into medieval darkness forever?"

Medievalism is an absolute, Modernism a relative term. The former will always stand for the same ideas and institutions; the meaning of the latter slides on with the times. If we must have a sect-name, we might have a worse than one that stands for life and movement as against stagnation and death; for the Catholicism that is of every age as against the sectarianism that is of one. . . . To believe in the living historical Catholic community means to believe that by its corporate life and labour it is slowly realizing the ideas and ends in whose service it was founded. . . . One's belief in the Church as the organ of religion is to some extent one's belief in the laws of collective psychology, which are the laws of nature, which are the laws of God.[87]

Tyrrell wrote much of *Medievalism* while he was staying with Bremond in Provence. When he returned to England he found that, thanks to the fine hand of Bishop Amigo,[88] he was no longer welcome at the priory in Storrington. "The monks here, formerly very kind and civil, have suddenly cut me dead."[89] He then moved reluctantly into Malt Cottage—two dark rooms attached to the rear of Maude Petre's Mulberry House in the center of the village. This circumstance at once underscored and heightened the ambiguity of their relationship. Tyrrell hated the dependence that the arrangement implied, and Petre—who had now separated herself from her religious order and was generally under suspicion as "this Modernist woman"—mourned that "I want what I cannot have. . . . I can do nothing for him now—the life has gone out of me."[90] And as 1908 gave way to 1909, she worried that Tyrrell, frailer and more wasted than ever, appeared to be suffering from more than the usual migraine.

Among the signs of this physical deterioration was not only his impatience with her—"Dear Lord, what we have to put up with because of the devotion of a woman!"[91]—but also the unaccountable outbursts of exasperation and even anger at those with whom he was most closely associated. Von Hügel's fear of excommunication infuriated Tyrrell and moved him at one point to label the baron "a lost man as far as I am concerned. . . . The man who has been a sort of conscience to me never existed!" He similarly lashed out at recently excommunicated Alfred Loisy as an arid spirit without "taste or judgment. He never seems to think of other people, neither his friends, nor the simple."[92]

87. George Tyrrell, *Medievalism. A Reply to Cardinal Mercier* (London: 1909), 183–84, 144–46.
88. See chapter 18.
89. Tyrrell to Dell, 2 September, 1908, quoted in Petre, *Autobiography of Tyrrell*, 2:363.
90. Quoted in Leonard, *Transformation*, 53.
91. Tyrrell to Bremond, 12 May, 1908, in Louis-David (ed.), *Lettres de Tyrrell*, 289.
92. Quoted in Sagovsky, *Tyrrell*, 237, 235.

During the spring of 1909, as the local vigilance committee kept an eye on the Modernist doings at Mulberry House, Tyrrell was hard at work on still another book.[93] He fell severely ill in March, but he seemed to recover quickly and resumed his writing and fulfilled several lecture engagements. His mood, however, was increasingly dark and somber. At meals he scarcely spoke or ate. In June he read a paper at Oxford, but when he came back to Storrington he was visibly drained and weary. On July 6 he was stricken by pain in his head and incessant vomiting. Two days later paralysis struck his left side, his speech grew slurred, and he began to vomit blood. Doctors were called in, and their diagnosis was that Tyrrell was suffering from an advanced case of Bright's disease or chronic nephritis, inflammation of the kidneys.

A priest was called in as well, a secular priest whom Tyrrell had once befriended. The priest heard the sick man's confession, but because Tyrrell's speech was so indistinct only conditional absolution was imparted to him. Von Hügel,[94] summoned by Petre's telegram, hurried to Storrington and saw the patient appear to rally, only to relapse again on July 12. Petre in a panic sent for the Premonstratensian prior, Tyrrell's formerly affable landlord, who administered extreme unction to the unconscious man. Henri Bremond arrived the next morning, July 13, and, garbed in surplice and stole, gave his friend absolution. All that day and the next Tyrrell lingered in a coma, and on the morning of July 15 he died. The poignancy of these events can best be told in the brief, nonconsecutive entries in Maude Petre's diary: "July 6: GT taken ill. July 7 to 8: First kiss! July 15: He died. July 14: Knew me for the last time, threw his arm round me. . . . July 22: Nothing can hurt any more."[95]

Bishop Amigo, declaring that the deceased had not retracted his heretical views, denied him Catholic burial. Accordingly, on July 21, a small group of friends, headed by Bremond, von Hügel, and Petre, gathered at Mulberry House and recited the ordinary Catholic prayers for such an occasion. Then they formed a sad procession and accompanied the body to the Anglican cemetery not far away, where the rector had assured them the remains would be honorably received. At the graveside Bremond, in street clothes, spoke briefly and movingly—Tyrrell, he said, had "clung to the Church of his conversion with the same deep-rooted conviction and the same love with which he clung to the Gospel and to the Divine Person of our Lord"—and then all withdrew.[96]

93. George Tyrrell, *Christianity at the Cross-Roads* (London: 1909), published posthumously.

94. Friedrich von Hügel continued his scholarly endeavors for the rest of his life. He was never interfered with by the ecclesiastical authorities. He died in 1926.

95. Quoted in Leonard, *Transformation*, 57. See Sagovsky, *Tyrrell*, 258–62, for a moving account of the details. Maude Petre remained faithful to her understanding of Modernist Catholicism. After a long life of scholarship and social service, she died in 1942.

96. See Petre, *Autobiography of Tyrrell*, 2:420–46. Bremond was suspended for his participation in Tyrrell's burial (see Bremond to Laberthonnière, 8 August, 1909, in Perrin [ed.], *Laberthonnière et ses amis*, 197), from which sentence, with his usual aplomb, he soon extricated himself. He went on to enjoy a brilliant literary career, for which he was rewarded in 1922 with the clerical appointment to the Académie Française as the successor to Duchesne. He died in 1933.

Tyrrell had written in his last will that "if a stone is put over me, let it state that I was a Catholic priest, and bear the Chalice and Host." Petre carefully followed his instructions, and engaged a promising young stonecarver from London named Eric Gill, whose wonderful skills were only then beginning to manifest themselves. Ironically enough, Gill converted to Catholicism a few years after he had executed this commission. Beneath the representation of the host and chalice Gill carved this epitaph: "Of your charity Pray for the soul of GEORGE TYRRELL, Catholic priest, who died July 15, 1909, Aged 48 years, Fortified by the Rites of the Church. R. I. P."

There he lies still, with Maude Petre beside him, in the green sweep of the cemetery sloping gently down from the fourteenth-century Anglican church that stands on a little hill at the edge of Storrington. The gravestones, many of them dark with moss and age, mark hundreds of years of history in Sussex. Tyrrell's final resting-place is in the center and yet off on the far edge and flanked by shrubs, as though to testify that even in death he remains fitful and apart. The grass is lush, and pines and oaks offer their cool shade on a summer day. Next to Tyrrell's grave stands now a holly tree with its shiny and spiky leaves. Whoever planted it there perhaps remembered the words of the old English carol:

> The holly and the ivy,
> When they are both full-grown,
> Of all the trees that are in the wood
> The holly wears the crown.
>
> The holly bears a berry
> As red as as any blood.
> And Mary bore sweet Jesus Christ
> To do poor sinners good.

Bibliography

The following list includes only those works cited in the text.

Abercrombie, Nigel. *The Life and Work of Edmund Bishop*. London, 1959.

Aigrain, René. *Les universités catholiques*. Paris, 1935.

Alcan, Felix (ed.). *Les premiers écrits de Maurice Blondel*. Paris, 1956.

Anderson, Lavinia. *Windhorst, a Political Biography*. Oxford, 1981.

Anon. *Quello che Vogliamo*. Milan, 1907.

Appleby, R. Scott. *"Church and Age Unite!" The Modernist Impulse in American Catholicism*. Notre Dame Ind., 1992.

Aubert, Roger. *Aspects divers de neo-thomisme sous le pontifacat de Léon XIII*. Rome, 1961.

———. *Le pontificat de Pie IX*. Paris, 1952.

———. *Le problème de l'acte de foi*. Louvain, 1969.

———. "Aux origines de la rédaction antimoderniste: deux documnets inédits." *Ephemerides Theologicae Lovanienses* 28 (1961).

Aubert Roger, et al. (eds.). *Nouvelle histoire de l'église*, 5 vols. Paris, 1975.

Barmann, Lawrence F. *Baron Friedrich von Hügel and the Modernist Crisis in England*. Cambridge, 1972.

———. "Friedrich von Hügel as Modernist and as More than Modernist." *Catholic Historical Review* 75 (1989).

Barry, Colman J. (ed.). *Readings in Church History*, 3 vols. Westminster, Md. 1965.

Barthelemy-Modaule, Madeleine. *Marc Sangnier, 1873–1950*. Paris, 1973.

Bastgen, Hubert. *Die Römische Frage. Dokumente und Stimmen*, 3 vols. Freiburg-im-Breisgau, 1919.

Batiffol Pierre. "L'Évangile et l'Église." *Bulletin de littérature ecclesiastique* 14 (1903).

Baudrillart, Alfred. *L'Institut catholique*. Paris, 1930.

———. *Vie de Mgr d'Hulst*, 2 vols. Paris, 1921.

Bedeschi, Lorenzo. *La Curia Romana durante la Crisi Modernista*. Parma, 1968.

Beillevert, Paul (ed.). *Laberthonnière, l'homme et l'oeuvre*. Paris, 1972.

Benoit, Pierre (ed.). *Le père Lagrange: au service de la bible*. Paris, 1967.

Binchy, D. A. *Church and State in Fascist Italy*. Oxford, 1970.

Blanchet, André. *Henri Bremond, 1865–1904*. Paris, 1975.

———, (ed.). *Henri Bremond, Maurice Blondel: Correspondance*, 3 vols. Paris, 1971.

————. *Histoire d'une mise à l'index. La "sainte Chantal" de l'abbé Bremond d'après documents inédits*. Paris, 1967.

Blondel, Maurice. *L'action. Essai d'un critique de la vie et d'une science de la pratique*. Paris, 1893.

————. *Carnets intimes,* 2 vols. Paris, 1966.

————. *Dialogues avec les philosophes*. Paris, 1966.

————. *Léon Ollé-Laprune. L'achèvement et l'avenir de son oeuvre*. Paris, 1923.

————. "Histoire et dogme. Les lacunes philosophiques de l'exégèse moderne." *La quinzaine* 58 (1903).

Blondel, Maurice, and Valensin, Auguste. *Correspondance, 1899–1912*. 2 vols. Paris, 1957.

Bossy, John. *The English Catholic Community, 1570–1850*. New York, 1976.

Bouillard, Henri. *Blondel and Christianity*. Washington, 1969.

"Bourdon, Hilaire" [George Tyrrell]. *The Church and the Future*. N.p., 1903.

Boyer, John W. *Political Radicalism in Late Imperial Vienna. Origins of the Christian Social Movement*. Chicago, 1981.

Braun, F.-M. *L'oeuvre du père Lagrange*. Fribourg, 1943.

Bredin, Jean-Denis. *The Affair: The Case of Alfred Dreyfus*. New York, 1986.

Bremond, André. "Henri Bremond." *Etudes* 217 (1933).

Bremond, Henri. *Histoire littéraire du sentiment religieux en France*. 11 volumes. Paris, 1932.

————. *Newman: essai de biographie psychologique*. Paris, 1906.

————. *La Provence mystique au XVIIe siècle. Antoine Yvan et Madeleine Martin*. Paris, 1908.

Brogan, Denis. *The Development of Modern France, 1870–1939*. London, 1953.

Buehrle, Marie Cecilia. *Rafael Cardinal Merry del Val*. London, 1957.

[Buonaiuti, Ernesto]. *Lettere di un Prete Modernisti*. Rome, 1908.

————. *Il Programma dei Modernisti*. Rome, 1907.

Burtchaell, James T. *Catholic Theories of Biblical Inspiration since 1810*. Cambridge 1969.

Calvert, J. "Catholic University Education in France." *Catholic University Bulletin* 13 (1907).

Candeloro, Giorgio. *Il Movimento Cattolico in Italia*. Rome, 1974.

Cappelli, Giampiero. *Romolo Murri. Contributo per una Biografia*. Rome, 1965.

Carlen, Claudia (ed.). *The Papal Encyclicals, 1878–1903, 1903–1939*. Raleigh, N.C., 1981.

Caron, Jeanne. *Le Sillon et la démocratie chrétienne, 1894–1910*. Paris, 1967.

Cenci, Pio. *Il Cardinale Raffaele Merry del Val*. Rome, 1933.

Chadwick, Owen. *Catholicism and History: The Opening of the Vatican Archives*. Cambridge, 1978.

Chesterton, G. K. *Saint Thomas Aquinas*. New York, 1956.

Cistellini, Antonio. *San Filippo Neri: l'Oratorio e la Congregazione oratoriana, Storia e Spiritualità*. Brescia, 1989.

Clement, Marcel. *Vie du cardinal Richard*. Paris, 1924.

Crankshaw, Edward. *Bismarck*. New York, 1981.

Cross, F. L. (ed.). *Oxford Dictionary of the Christian Church*. London, 1963.

Dalpiaz, Virgilio. *Cardinal Merry del Val*. London, 1937.

Daly, Gabriel. *Transcendence and Immanence. A Study in Catholic Modernism and Integralism*. Oxford, 1980.

Dansette, Adrien. *Histoire religieuse de la France contemporaine*. Paris, 1965.

de Bertier, Guillaume. *Metternich*. N.p. (Paris), 1986.

de Grandmaison, Léonce. "Le Christ de M. Harnack." *Études* 90 (1902).

————. "L'Évangile et l'Église." *Études* 94 (1903).

De la Bedoyere, Michael. *The Life of Baron von Hügel*. London, 1951.

de la Taille, Maurice. "Sur l'encyclique 'Pascendi,' " *Études* 113 (1907).

Denziger, Henricus, et al. (eds.). *Enchiridion Symbolorum* . . . Freiburg-im-Breisgau, 1952.

"Deprés, Isidore" [Alfred Loisy]. "La lettre de Léon XIII au clergé de France et les études d'écriture sainte." *Revue du clergé français* 23 (1990).

————. "Opinions catholiques sur l'origine du Pentateuque." *Revue du clergé français* 17 (1899).

D'Espezel, P. "Duchesne." *Dictionnaire d'histoire et de géographie ecclésiastiques* 14. Paris, 1960.

Dessain, Stephen, et al. (eds.). *The Letters and Diaries of John Henry Newman*. 31 vols. London and Oxford, 1961–.

Deufel, Konrad. *Kirche und Tradition*. Munich, 1976.

D'Haboville, Claude. *Grands figures de l'église contemporaine*. Paris, 1925.

D'Hulst, Maurice. *Mélanges philosophiques*. Paris, 1892.

École française de Rome (eds.). *Monseigneur Duchesne et son temps*. Rome, 1975.

Edwards, Francis. *The Jesuits in England*. London, 1985.

Ellis, John Tracy. *The Life of James Cardinal Gibbons*. 2 vols. Milwaukee, 1952.

"Engels, Ernest" [George Tyrrell]. *Religion as a Factor of Life*. Exeter, 1902.

Evennett, H. Outram. *The Spirit of the Counter Reformation*. Cambridge, 1968.

Fabregues, Jean de. *Le Sillon de Marc Sangnier*. Paris, 1964.

Falconi, Carlo. *Il Cardinale Antonelli*. Milan, 1983.

Fernessole, Pierre. *Pie IX, pape (1792–1878)*. 2 vols. Paris, 1963.

————. *Pie X. Sa vie et son oeuvre*. 2 vols. Paris, 1952.

————. *Témoins de la pensée catholique en France sous la IIIe république*. Paris, 1940.

Ferrier, F. "Huvelin." *Dictionnaire de biographie française*, 18. Paris, 1989.

Firmin, A. [Alfred Loisy]. "Le developpement chrétien d'après le cardinal Newman." *Revue du clergé français* 17 (1898).

————. "La religion d'Israel, les origines." *Revue du clergé français* 24 (1900).

Fogarty, Gerald P. *American Catholic Biblical Scholarship*. San Francisco, 1989.

————. *The Vatican and the Americanist Crisis: Denis J. O'Connell, American Agent in Rome, 1885–1903*. Rome, 1974.

Fogazzaro, Antonio. *Il Santo*. Rome, 1905.

Folscheid, Dominique (ed.). *Maurice Blondel. Une dramatique de la modernité*. Paris, 1990.

Fontaine, Nicolas [Louis Canet]. *Saint-Siège, "Action française" et "Catholiques intégraux."* Paris, 1928.

Friedrich, J. *Ignaz von Döllinger. Sein Leben auf seines schriftlichen Nachlasses*. 3 vols. Munich, 1901.

Gallarati-Scotti, Tommaso. *The Life of Antonio Fogazzaro*. New York, n.d. [1922].

Gallina, Giuseppe. *Il Problema religioso nel Risorgimento e il Pensiero di Geremia Bonomelli*. Rome, 1974.

Gargan, Edward T. (ed.). *Leo XIII and the Modern World*. New York, 1961.

Geoffroy, A. "La nouvelle École française de Rome." *Revue des deux mondes* 16 (1876).

Gilson, Étienne. *Le philosophe et la théologie*. Paris, 1962.

Giovanni, Claudio. *Romolo Murri: dal Radicalismo al Fascismo*. Bologna, 1981.

Gleason, Philip. *Speaking of Diversity. Language and Ethnicity in Twentieth-Century America*. Baltimore, 1992.

Goldberg, Harvey. *The Life of Jean Jaurès*. Madison, WI, 1968.

Gray, Robert. *Cardinal Manning. A Biography*. New York, 1985.

Greenfield, Florence M. *Round About old Storrington*. Storrington, West Sussex, 1972.

Gruber, Jacob. *A Conscience in Conflict. The Life of St. George Jackson Mivart*. New York, 1960.

Guy, Jean-Claude. "Henri Bremond et son commentaire des Exercises de Saint Ignace." *Revue d'ascétique et de mystique* 45 (1969).

Hall, Robert A., Jr. *Antonio Fogazzaro*. New York, 1978.

Harnack, Adolf. *Das Wesen des Christentums*. Leipzig, 1908.

Harney, Martin R. *The Jesuits in History*. New York, 1941.

Hayes, Carlton J. H. *A Generation of Materialism, 1871–1900*. New York, 1941.

Hogarth, Henry. *Henri Bremond. The Life and Work of a Devout Humanist*. London, 1950.

Holmes, J. Derek. "Some English Reactions to the Publication of *Aeterni Patris*." *Downside Review* 93 (1975).

Holmes, J. Derek, and Robert Murray (eds.). *On the Inspiration of Scripture*. Washington, 1967.

Hopkins, Gerard Manley. *The Journals and Papers*. London, 1959.

Houtin, Albert. *La controverse de la apostolicité des églises de France au XIXe siècle*. Paris, 1903.

———. *Mes difficultés avec mon evêque*. Paris, 1905.

———. *Mon expérience. 1 Une vie de prêtre. 2 Ma vie laique*. Paris, 1928.

———. *Histoire du modernisme catholique*. Paris, 1913.

———. *Un prêtre symboliste. Marcel Hébert*. Paris, 1925.

———. *La question biblique chez les catholiques de France au XIXe siècle*. Paris, 1902.

———. *La question biblique chez les catholiques de France au XXe siècle* Paris, 1906.

Houtin, Albert, and Félix Sartiaux. *Alfred Loisy, sa vie et son oeuvre*. Paris, 1960.

Hügel, Friedrich von. *Essays and Addresses on the Philosophy of Religion*. London, 1921.

———. *Eternal Life: A Study of Its Implications and Applications*. Edinburgh, 1912.

———. *Selected Letters, 1896–1924*. London, 1927.

———. *The Mystical Element of Religion as Studied in Saint Catherine of Genoa and Her Friends*. 2 vols. (London, 1908).

———. *Some Notes on the Petrine Claims*. London, 1930.

———. "Du Christ éternel et de nos christologies successives." *La quinzaine* 58 (1904).

———. "The Church and the Bible: The Two Stages of Their Interrelation." *Dublin Review* 115–17 (1894–95).

———. "Eudoxe-Irénée Mignot." *Contemporary Review* 113 (1918).

————. "The Historical Method and the Documents of the Hexateuch." *Catholic University Bulletin* 4 (1898).

Hughes, John Jay. *Absolutely Null and Utterly Void.* Washington, 1968.

Ireland, John. *The Church and Modern Society. Lectures and Addresses.* 2 vols. New York, 1902.

Johnson, Humphrey. *The Papacy and the Kingdom of Italy.* London, 1926.

Judge, Thomas E. (ed.). *Doctrines of the Modernists.* Chicago, n.d. (1908).

Keane, John J. "The Catholic Universities of France." *Catholic World* 47 (1888).

Kelly, James J. "The Abbé Huvelin's Counsel to Baron Friedrich von Hügel." *Bijdragen Tijdschrift voor Filosofie en Theologie* 39 (1978).

Ker, Ian. *John Henry Newman. A Biography.* Oxford, 1989.

Killen, David, "Americanism Revisited: John Spalding and *Testem Benevolentiae.*" *Harvard Theological Review* 66 (1973).

Kitchen, Paddy. *Gerard Manley Hopkins.* New York, 1979.

Klein, Félix. *La route du petit Morvandiau.* 6 vols. Paris, 1950.

Kleutgen, Josef. *Der Philosophie der Vorzeit.* 2 vols. Rome, 1863.

————. *Die Theologie der Vorzeit.* 5 vols. Rome, 1853–74.

Kselman, Thomas. *Miracles and Prophecies in Nineteenth Century France.* New Brunswick, N.J., 1983.

Kurtz, Lester R. *The Politics of Heresy. The Modernist Crisis in Roman Catholicism.* Berkeley, 1986.

Laberthonnière, Lucien. *Oeuvres.* 8 vols. Paris, 1935–55.

————. "Le dogmatisme morale." *Annales de philosophie chrétienne* 138–39 (1898).

————. "La philosophie est un art." *L'Enseignement chrétien* 10 (1891).

————. "Le problème religieux à propos de la question apologétique." *Annales de philosophie chrétienne* 133 (1896–97).

————. *Le réaliseme chretien, précédé de essais de philosophie religieuse.* Paris, 1966.

Lacroix, Jean. *Maurice Blondel.* New York, 1968.

————. "Édouard Le Roy, philosophe de l'invention." *Les études philosophiques* 10 (1955).

Lagrange, F. *Life of Monseigneur Dupanloup,* 2 vols. London, 1885.

Lagrange. Marie-Joseph. *Éclaircissement sur la Methode Historique.* Paris, 1905.

————. *M. Loisy et le modernisme.* Paris, n.d. [1932].

————. *La methode historique.* Paris, 1903.

————. "L'Évangile et l'Église." *Revue biblique* 12 (1903).

————. "M. Harnack." *Revue biblique* 12 (1903).

————. "Les sources du Pentateuque." *Revue biblique* 7 (1898).

"Leblanc, Sylvain" [Henri Bremond]. *Un clerc qui n'a pas trahi. Alfred Loisy d'après ses Mémoires.* Paris, 1931.

Lecanuet, Edouard. *L'Église de France sous la troisième république. Les dernières années de Pie IX, 1870–1878.* Paris, 1931.

————. *L'Église de France sous la troisième république. Les premières années du pontificat de Leon XIII.* Paris, 1931.

Leclerq, H. "Monsignor Duchesne," *Dictionnaire d'archéologie chretiénne et de liturgie* 6. Paris, 1925.

Leo XIII. "Providentissimus Deus." *Acta Sanctae Sedis* 26 (1893).

Leonard, Ellen. *George Tyrrell and the Catholic Tradition.* New York, 1982.

———. *Unresting Transformation. The Theology and Spirituality of Maude Petre*. Lanham, Md, 1991.

Le Roy, Édouard. *Dogme et critique*. Paris, 1907.

———. "Qu'est ce qu'un dogme?" *La quinzaine* 73 (1905).

Leslie, Shane (ed.). *Letters of Herbert Cardinal Vaughan to Lady Herbert of Lea, 1867–1903*. London, 1942.

Lester-Garland, L. V. *The Religious Philosophy of Baron F. von Hügel*. New York, 1933.

Liberatore, Matteo. *Institutiones Philosophicae. Ethica et Jus Naturae*. Rome, 1847.

Loisy, Alfred. *Autour d'un petit livre*. Paris, 1903.

———. *Choses passées*. Paris, 1913.

———. *L'Évangile et l'Église*. Paris, 1903.

———. *George Tyrrell et Henri Bremond*. Paris, 1935.

———. *Mémoires pour servir à l'histoire religieuse de nôtre temps*. 3 vols. Paris, 1931.

———. *La religion d'Israel*. Paris, 1901.

———. *Simples réflexions sur le décret du saint-office, "Lamentabili sane exitu," et sur l'encyclique "Pascendi dominici gregis."* Paris, 1908.

———. "La confession de Pierre et la promesse de Jésus." *Revue anglo-romaine*, 12 (1895).

———. "La transfiguration." *Revue d'histoire et littérature religieuses* 12 (1907).

Loome, Thomas Michael. *Liberal Catholicism, Reform Catholicism, Modernism*. Mainz, 1979.

Louis-David, Anne (ed.). *Lettres de George Tyrrell à Henri Bremond*. Paris, 1971.

McAvoy, Thomas T. *The Great Crisis in American Catholic History*. Chicago, 1957.

McClelland, Vincent Alan. *Cardinal Manning. His Public Life and Influence*. London, 1962.

McCool, Gerald A. *From Unity to Pluralism. The Internal Evolution of Thomism*. New York, 1989.

———. "The Centenary of *Aeterni Patris*." *Homiletic and Pastoral Review* 79 (1979).

McCormack, Arthur. *Cardinal Vaughan*. London, n.d. (1966).

McManners, John. *Church and State in France, 1870–1914*. New York, 1972.

Magnus, Phililp. *Gladstone, A Biography*. London, 1963.

Malusa, Luciano. *Neotommismo e Intrasigentismo Cattolico*. Milan, 1986.

Marlé, René (ed.). *Au coeur de la crise moderniste*. Paris, 1960.

Maurras, Charles. *Lettres de prison*. Paris, 1958.

Mercier, Désiré Joseph. *Le modernisme*. Paris, 1909.

Mollat, G. *La question romaine de Pie VI à Pie XI*. Paris, 1932.

Montclos, Xavier de (ed.). *Le toast d'Alger. Documents, 1890–1891*. Paris, 1966.

Morley, John. *The Life of William Gladstone*. 3 vols. London, 1903.

Murray, Placid (ed.). *Newman the Oratorian*. Dublin, 1969.

Nédoncelle, Maurice, and Jean Dagens (eds.). *Entretiens sur Henri Bremond*. Paris, 1967.

Newman, J. H. *An Essay in Aid of a Grammar of Assent*. London, 1871.

———. *An Essay on the Development of Christian Doctrine*. London, 1846.

———. "An Essay on the Inspiration of Scripture." *Nineteenth Century* 15 (1884).

Neuveu, Bruno (ed.). "Lettres de . . . Duchesne . . . à. . . . Loisy et à . . . von Hugel." *Mélanges de l'école française de Rome* 84 (1972).

O'Connell, Marvin R. *The Counter Reformation, 1559–1610.* New York, 1974.

———. *John Ireland and the American Catholic Church.* St. Paul, 1988.

———. *The Oxford Conspirators. A History of the Oxford Movement, 1833–1845.* New York, 1969.

———. "The Beginning of the End, the End of the Beginning: Newman and Tract Ninety." *Renascence* 43 (1991).

———. "The Bishopric of Monaco, 1902: A Revision. *Catholic Historical Review* 71 (1985).

———. "Duchesne and Loisy on the Rue de Vaugirard." In Nelson H. Minnich et al. (eds.), *Studies in Catholic History in Honor of John Tracy Ellis.* Wilmington, 1985.

———. "Modernism in Retrospect." *Center Journal* 1 (1982).

———. "Montalembert at Mechlin: A Reprise of 1830." *Journal of Church and State* 26 (1984).

———. "Newman: The Victorian Intellectual as Pastor." *Theological Studies* 46 (1985).

———. "Newman: The Limits of Certitude." *Review of Politics* 35 (1973).

———. "Ultramontanism and Dupanloup." *Church History* 53 (1984).

O'Meara, Thomas Franklin. *Church and Culture. German Catholic Theology, 1860–1914.* Notre Dame, Ind., 1991.

———. *Romantic Idealism and Roman Catholicism. Schelling and the Theologians.* Notre Dame, Ind., 1982.

Osborne, C. E. *The Life of Father Dolling.* London, 1903.

Perrin, Marie-Thérèse. *La jeunesse de Laberthonnière.* Paris, 1980.

———. (ed.). *Laberthonnière et ses amis.* Paris, 1975.

Petre, M. D. *Alfred Loisy. His Religious Influence.* Cambridge, 1944.

———. *Autobiography and Life of George Tyrrell.* 2 vols. London, 1914.

———. *My Way of Faith.* London, 1937.

———. (ed.) *{Tyrrell's} Essays on Faith and Immortality.* London, 1914.

———. (ed.) *George Tyrrell's Letters.* London, 1920.

Piccioni, Donatella, and Leone Piccioni. *Antonio Fogazzaro.* Turin, 1970.

Piromalli, Antonio. *Introduzione a Fogazzaro.* Rome, 1990.

Pius X. "Pascendi Dominici Gregis." *Acta Sanctae Sedis* 40 (1907).

Poels, Henry A. *Vindication of My Honor.* Washington, 1910.

Portier, Lucienne. *Un précurseur: l'abbé Huvelin.* Paris, 1979.

Émile Poulat. *Critique et mystique.* Paris, 1984.

———. *Histoire, dogme et critique dans la crise moderniste.* Paris, 1962.

———. *Modernistica.* Paris, 1980.

———. (ed). *Intégrisme et catholicisme intégral.* Paris, 1969.

Pouthas, Charles. *Le pontificat de Pie IX.* Paris, n.d. (1968).

Purcell, Edmund Sheridan. *Life of Cardinal Manning, Archbishop of Westminster.* 2 vols. London, 1896.

Ranchetti, Michele. *The Catholic Modernists.* New York, 1969.

Ratté, John. *Three Modernists.* New York, 1967.

Reardon, Bernard. *Liberalism and Tradition. Aspects of Catholic Thought in Nineteenth-Century France.* Cambridge, 1975.

Renan, Ernest. *Souvenirs d'enfance et de jeunesse.* Paris, 1883.

Rivière, Jean, *Modernisme dans l'église*. Paris, 1929.

Royce, Josiah. "Pope Leo's Philosophical Movement: Its Relation to Modern Thought." *The Tablet* 102 (15 August 1903).

Ruggles, Eleanor. *Gerard Manley Hopkins, A Life*. New York, 1944.

Sagovsky, Nicholas. "*On God's Side.*" *A Life of George Tyrrell*. Oxford, 1990.

Sánchez, José. *Anticlericalism: A Brief History*. Notre Dame, Ind., 1972.

Santayana, George. *Winds of Doctrine*. New York, 1912.

Schoenl, William James. "The Intellectual Crisis in English Catholicism, 1890–1907. Liberals, Modernists and the Vatican. Doctoral dissertation, Columbia University, 1968.

Schmidlin, Josef. *Papstgeschichte der neuesten Zeit*. 4 vols. Munich, 1939.

Schultenover, David G. *George Tyrrell: In Search of Catholicism*. Shepherdstown, W. Va., 1981.

———. *A View from Rome on the Eve of the Modernist Crisis*. New York, 1992.

Schwalm, M. B. "Les illusions de l'idéalisme et leur dangers pour la foi." *Revue thomiste* 4 (1896).

Scoppola, Pietro. *Crisi Modernista e Rinnovamento cattolico in Italia*. Bologna, 1961.

Sedgwick, Alexander. *The Ralliement in French Politics*. Cambridge, Mass., 1965.

Smith, Sydney. "The Encyclical 'Pascendi.' " *The Month* 105 (1907).

Snead-Cox, J. G. *Life of Herbert Vaughan*. 2 vols. London, 1910.

Snider, Carlo, *L'Episcopato del Cardinale Andrea Ferrari*. 2 vols. Venice, 1982.

Soderini, Eduardo. *Il Pontificato di Leone XIII*. 3 vols. Rome, 1933.

Steinmann, Jean. *Friedrich von Hügel: sa vie, son oeuvre, ses amities*. (Paris, 1962).

Sutton, Michael. *Nationalism, Positivism and Catholicism*. Cambridge, 1982.

Thibault, Pierre. *Savoir et pouvoir*. Quebec. 1972.

Thureau-Dangin, Paul. *La renaissance catholique dans Angleterre*. 3 vols. Paris, 1899.

Tresmontant, Claude (ed.). *Maurice Blondel, Lucien Laberthonnière: correspondance philosophique*. Paris, 1961.

Trevor, Meriol. *Newman: The Pillar of the Cloud*. London, 1962.

Tyrrell, George. *Christianity at the Cross-Roads*. London, 1909.

———. *The Faith of Millions*. 2 vols. London, 1902.

———. *Hard Sayings*. London, 1898.

———. *Lex Orandi, or Prayer and Creed*. London, 1903.

———. *Lex Credendi. A Sequel to Lex Orandi*. London, 1906.

———. *Medievalism. A Reply to Cardinal Mercier*. London, 1909.

———. *A Much Abused Letter*. London, 1906.

———. *Nova et Vetera*. London, 1897.

———. *Through Scylla and Charybdis*. London, 1907.

———. "Aquinas Resuscitatus." *American Catholic Quarterly Review* 16 (1891).

———. "The Church and Scholasticism." *American Catholic Quarterly Review* 23 (1898).

———. "Liberal Catholicism." *The Month* 91 (1908).

Vercesi, Ernesto. *Il Pontificato di Pio X*. Milan, 1935.

Vidler, Alec. *A Variety of Catholic Modernists*. Cambridge, 1970.

Virgoulay, Rene. *Blondel et le modernisme*. Paris, 1980.

Ward, James E. "The Algiers Toast: Lavigerie's Work or Leo XIII's?" *Catholic Historical Review* 51 (1965).

————. "Leo XIII: The Diplomat Pope." *Review of Politics* 28 (1966).

Ward, Josephine. *One Poor Scruple*. London, 1899.

Ward, Maisie. *The Wilfrid Wards and the Transition*. 1. New York, 1934.

————. *The Wilfrid Wards and the Transition*. 2. New York, 1937.

Ward, Wilfrid. *The Life of John Henry Cardinal Newman*. 2 vols. London, 1912.

————. *The Life and Times of Cardinal Wiseman*. London, 1897.

————. *Problems and Persons*. London, 1903.

————. *William George Ward and the Oxford Movement*. London, 1899.

————. *William George Ward and the Catholic Revival*. London, 1893.

————. "The Encyclical 'Pascendi.' " *Dublin Review* 142 (1908).

Ward, W. G. *Essays in Theism*. 2 vols. London, 1884.

Weaver, Mary Jo (ed.). *Letters from a "Modernist."* London, 1981.

————. "Wilfrid Ward, George Tyrrell and the Meaning of Modernism." *Downside Review* 96 (1978).

Weber, Eugen. *Action Française. Royalism and Reaction in Twentieth-Century France*. Stanford, 1962.

Webster, Richard. *Christian Democracy in Italy*. London, 1961.

Wehrlé, Joannès. "Le Christ et la conscience catholique." *La quinzaine* 59 (1904).

————. "De la nature de dogme." *Revue biblique* 14 (1905).

Williams, Peter. "Abbé Huvelin, Mediator of a Tradition." *Bijdragen Tijdschrift voor Filosofie en Theologie* 41 (1981).

Williams, William J. *Newman, Pascal, Loisy and the Catholic Church*. London, 1906.

Woodham-Smith, Cecil. *Florence Nightingale*. New York, 1983.

Zeldin, Theodore. "Higher Education in France." *Journal of Contemporary History* 2 (1967).

Zorzi, Giuseppe (ed.). *Auf der Suche nach der verlorenen Katholizität. Die Briefe Friedrich von Hügels an Giovanni Semeria*. 2 vols. Mainz, 1991.

Index

Critics on Trial: An Introduction to the Catholic Modernist Crisis was composed in 10.5/12 Garamond #3 by World Composition Services, Inc., Sterling, Virginia; printed on 60-pound Glatfelter Supple Opaque Recycled paper and bound by Thomson-Shore, Inc., Dexter, Michigan; and designed and produced by Kachergis Book Design, Pittsboro, North Carolina.